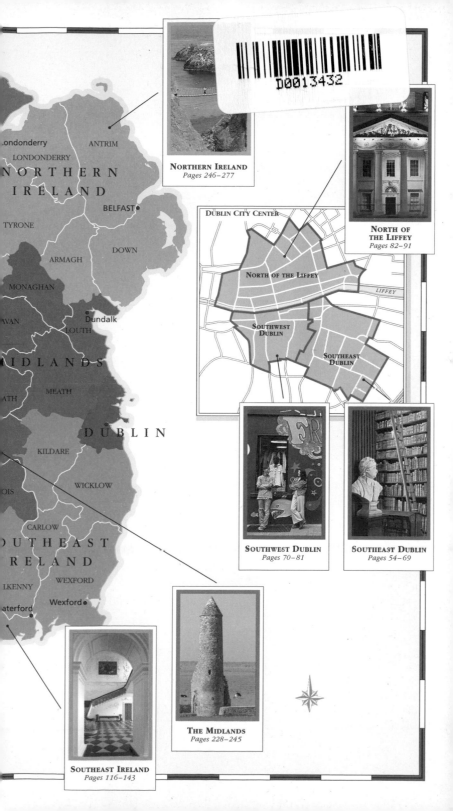

Londonderry

LONDONDERRY

ANTRIM

**NORTHERN IRELAND**
*Pages 246–277*

NORTHERN
IRELAND

BELFAST

TYRONE

DOWN

ARMAGH

MONAGHAN

AVAN

Dundalk

LOUTH

MIDLANDS

MEATH

ATH

DUBLIN

KILDARE

WICKLOW

OIS

CARLOW

SOUTHEAST
IRELAND

LKENNY

WEXFORD

Wexford

aterford

DUBLIN CITY CENTER

NORTH OF THE LIFFEY

LIFFEY

SOUTHWEST
DUBLIN

SOUTHEAST
DUBLIN

**NORTH OF THE LIFFEY**
*Pages 82–91*

**SOUTHWEST DUBLIN**
*Pages 70–81*

**SOUTHEAST DUBLIN**
*Pages 54–69*

**THE MIDLANDS**
*Pages 228–245*

**SOUTHEAST IRELAND**
*Pages 116–143*

D0013432

EYEWITNESS *TRAVEL GUIDES*

# IRELAND

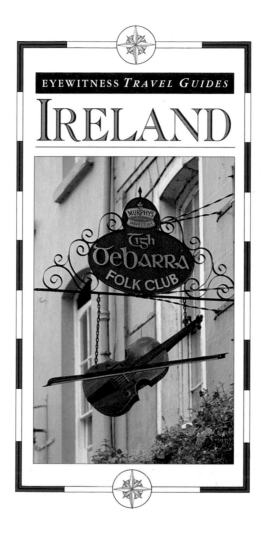

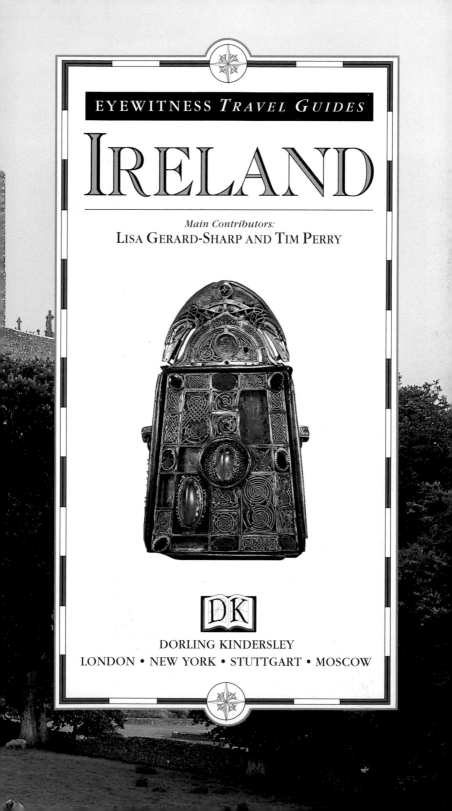

# EYEWITNESS *TRAVEL GUIDES*

# IRELAND

*Main Contributors:*
LISA GERARD-SHARP AND TIM PERRY

**DK**

**DORLING KINDERSLEY**

LONDON • NEW YORK • STUTTGART • MOSCOW

# A DORLING KINDERSLEY BOOK

PROJECT EDITOR Ferdie McDonald
ART EDITOR Lisa Kosky
EDITORS Maggie Crowley, Simon Farbrother, Emily Hatchwell,
Seán O'Connell, Jane Simmonds
US EDITOR Mary Sutherland
DESIGNERS Joy FitzSimmons, Jaki Grosvenor,
Katie Peacock, Jan Richter
MAP COORDINATORS Michael Ellis, David Pugh
RESEARCHERS John Breslin, Andrea Holmes

MANAGING EDITORS Vivien Crump, Helen Partington
MANAGING ART EDITOR Steve Knowlden
DEPUTY EDITORIAL DIRECTOR Douglas Amrine
DEPUTY ART DIRECTOR Gaye Allen

PRODUCTION David Proffit, Hilary Stephens
PICTURE RESEARCH Sue Mennell, Christine Rista
DTP DESIGNER Adam Moore

CONTRIBUTORS
Una Carlin, Polly Phillimore, Susan Poole, Martin Walters

MAPS
Gary Bowes, Margaret Slowey, Richard Toomey
(ERA-Maptec, Dublin, Ireland)

PHOTOGRAPHERS
Joe Cornish, Tim Daly, Alan Williams

ILLUSTRATORS
Draughtsman Maps, Maltings Partnership, Robbie Polley
•
Film outputting bureau Cooling Brown (London)
Reproduced by Colourscan (Singapore)
Printed and bound by G. Canale & C. (Italy)

First American edition 1995
2 4 6 8 10 9 7 5 3 1
Published in the United States by
Dorling Kindersley Publishing, Inc.,
95 Madison Avenue, New York, NY 10016

Distributed by Houghton Mifflin Company, Boston.

Library of Congress Cataloging-in-Publication Data
Ireland. – – 1st American ed.
p.      cm. – –  (Eyewitness travel guides)
ISBN 0-7894-0188-6
1. Ireland – – Guidebooks.
I. Series.
DA980.I52  1995                               95–7605
914.1504'824– – dc20                           CIP

Every effort has been made to ensure that the information in this book is as
up-to-date as possible at the time of going to press. However, details such
as telephone numbers, opening hours, prices, gallery hanging arrangements
and travel information are liable to change. The publishers cannot accept
responsibility for any consequences arising from the use of this book.

We would be delighted to receive any corrections and suggestions for
incorporation in the next edition. Please write to:
Deputy Editorial Director, Eyewitness Travel Guides
Dorling Kindersley, 9 Henrietta Street, London WC2E 8PS, UK.

THROUGHOUT THIS BOOK, FLOORS ARE REFERRED TO IN ACCORDANCE WITH EUROPEAN
USAGE, I.E., THE "FIRST FLOOR" IS ONE FLIGHT UP.

# CONTENTS

HOW TO USE
THIS GUIDE 6

An evangelical symbol from the
Book of Kells (see p62)

## INTRODUCING
## IRELAND

PUTTING IRELAND
ON THE MAP 10

A PORTRAIT OF
IRELAND 12

THE HISTORY OF
IRELAND 28

IRELAND THROUGH
THE YEAR 46

## DUBLIN AREA
## BY AREA

DUBLIN
AT A GLANCE 52

Georgian doorway in Fitzwilliam
Square, Dublin (see p67)

SOUTHEAST DUBLIN *54*

SOUTHWEST DUBLIN *70*

NORTH OF THE LIFFEY *82*

FARTHER AFIELD *92*

ENTERTAINMENT IN DUBLIN *102*

DUBLIN STREET FINDER *108*

**IRELAND REGION BY REGION**

Lighthouse at Spanish Point near Mizen Head *(see p159)*

**TRAVELERS' NEEDS**

WHERE TO STAY *280*

RESTAURANTS, CAFÉS AND PUBS *302*

SHOPPING IN IRELAND *322*

ENTERTAINMENT IN IRELAND *328*

**SURVIVAL GUIDE**

PRACTICAL INFORMATION *338*

TRAVEL INFORMATION *350*

GENERAL INDEX *362*

ROAD MAP *Inside back cover*

Detail of the Chorus Gate at Powerscourt *(see pp126–7)*

IRELAND AT A GLANCE *114*

SOUTHEAST IRELAND *116*

CORK AND KERRY *144*

THE LOWER SHANNON *172*

THE WEST OF IRELAND *192*

NORTHWEST IRELAND *212*

THE MIDLANDS *228*

NORTHERN IRELAND *246*

Façade of a pub in Dingle *(see p149)*

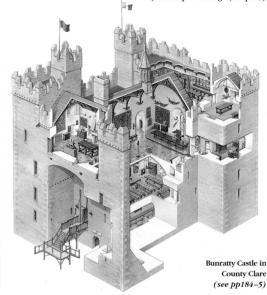

Bunratty Castle in County Clare *(see pp184–5)*

# HOW TO USE THIS GUIDE

THIS GUIDE helps you to get the most from your visit to Ireland. It provides both expert recommendations and detailed practical information. *Introducing Ireland* maps the country and sets it in its historical and cultural context. The seven regional chapters, plus *Dublin Area by Area*, contain descriptions of all the important sights, with maps, pictures and illustrations. Restaurant and hotel recommendations can be found in *Travelers' Needs*. The *Survival Guide* has tips on everything from the telephone system to transportation both in the Republic and in Northern Ireland.

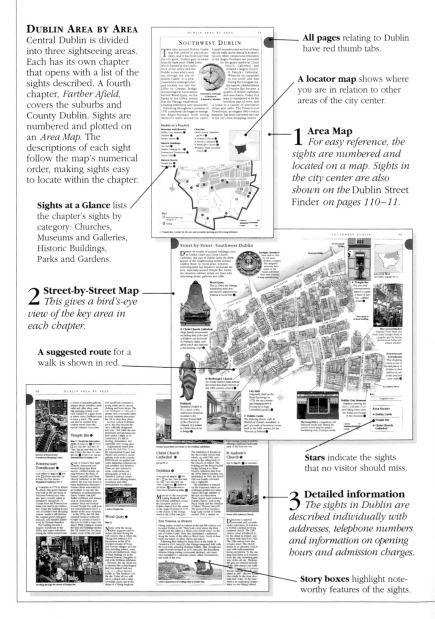

## DUBLIN AREA BY AREA

Central Dublin is divided into three sightseeing areas. Each has its own chapter that opens with a list of the sights described. A fourth chapter, *Farther Afield*, covers the suburbs and County Dublin. Sights are numbered and plotted on an *Area Map*. The descriptions of each sight follow the map's numerical order, making sights easy to locate within the chapter.

**Sights at a Glance** lists the chapter's sights by category: Churches, Museums and Galleries, Historic Buildings, Parks and Gardens.

**2 Street-by-Street Map**
*This gives a bird's-eye view of the key area in each chapter.*

A **suggested route** for a walk is shown in red.

**All pages** relating to Dublin have red thumb tabs.

**A locator map** shows where you are in relation to other areas of the city center.

**1 Area Map**
*For easy reference, the sights are numbered and located on a map. Sights in the city center are also shown on the* Dublin Street Finder *on pages 110–11.*

**Stars** indicate the sights that no visitor should miss.

**3 Detailed information**
*The sights in Dublin are described individually with addresses, telephone numbers and information on opening hours and admission charges.*

**Story boxes** highlight noteworthy features of the sights.

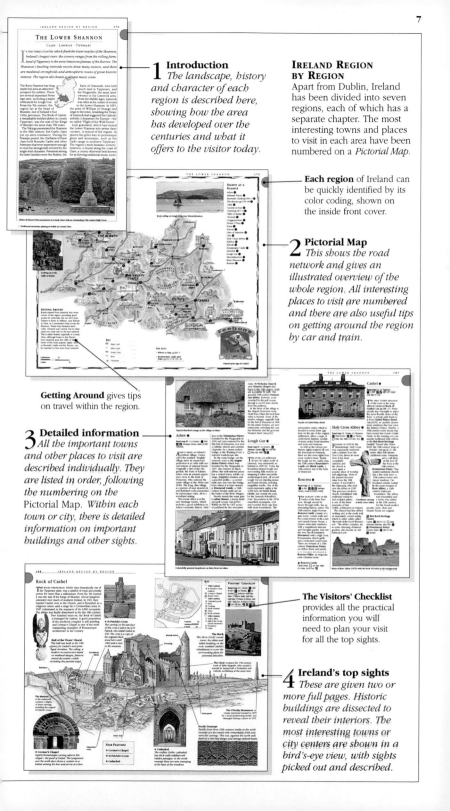

**1 Introduction**
The landscape, history and character of each region is described here, showing how the area has developed over the centuries and what it offers to the visitor today.

**IRELAND REGION BY REGION**
Apart from Dublin, Ireland has been divided into seven regions, each of which has a separate chapter. The most interesting towns and places to visit in each area have been numbered on a *Pictorial Map*.

**Each region** of Ireland can be quickly identified by its color coding, shown on the inside front cover.

**2 Pictorial Map**
This shows the road network and gives an illustrated overview of the whole region. All interesting places to visit are numbered and there are also useful tips on getting around the region by car and train.

**Getting Around** gives tips on travel within the region.

**3 Detailed information**
All the important towns and other places to visit are described individually. They are listed in order, following the numbering on the Pictorial Map. Within each town or city, there is detailed information on important buildings and other sights.

**The Visitors' Checklist** provides all the practical information you will need to plan your visit for all the top sights.

**4 Ireland's top sights**
These are given two or more full pages. Historic buildings are dissected to reveal their interiors. The most interesting towns or city centers are shown in a bird's-eye view, with sights picked out and described.

# INTRODUCING IRELAND

PUTTING IRELAND ON THE MAP 10-11

A PORTRAIT OF IRELAND 12-27

THE HISTORY OF IRELAND 28-45

IRELAND THROUGH THE YEAR 46-49

# Putting Ireland on the Map

T HE ISLAND OF IRELAND covers an area of 84,175 sq km (32,500 sq miles). Lying in the Atlantic Ocean to the northwest of mainland Europe, it is separated from Great Britain by the Irish Sea. The Republic of Ireland takes up 85 percent of the island with a population of 3.5 milllion. Northern Ireland, part of the United Kingdom, has 1.5 million people. Dublin is the capital of the Republic and has good international communications.

**EUROPE**

NORWAY

SWEDEN

NORTHERN
IRELAND

DENMARK

REPUBLIC OF
IRELAND

UNITED
KINGDOM

NETHERLANDS

GERMANY

BELGIUM

LUXEMBOURG

CZECH
REPUBLIC

FRANCE

SWITZERLAND

AUSTRIA

SPAIN

ITALY

### Europe

*Most visitors to Ireland come through Dublin, either on the ferry to Dun Laoghaire or by air. The main ferry routes are from Wales, Scotland and France. There are international flights to Shannon, Belfast and Cork airports as well as Dublin. Many European flights are routed via Great Britain, although flight times are generally only around an hour from British airports.*

| 0 kilometers | | 100 |
| 0 miles | 50 | |

### KEY

✈ Airport

⛴ Ferry port

═ Highway

▬ Major road

— Railroad line

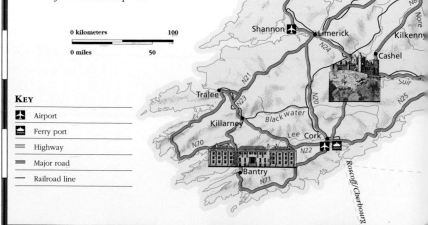

*Atlantic Ocean*

Londonderry
(Derry)

Donegal

N O R
I R E

Lower Lough
Erne

Enniskillen

N15 N16

Upper Lough
Erne

Sligo

N4

N59

Lough
Allen

Knock ✈ R E P U B L I C

N5

I R E L A N

Lough
Mask

N17

Lough
Ree

N4

Lough
Corrib

Athlone

N6

N59

Galway

*Shannon*

Lough
Derg

N7

N18

N8

Shannon ✈ Limerick

Kilkenny

N24

Cashel

N21

*Suir*

Tralee

N20

N23

N25

*Blackwater*

Killarney

*Lee* Cork ✈⛴

N70

N22

Bantry

N71

*Roscoff/Cherbourg*

## GREATER DUBLIN

Swords

N1

Malahide

N3

N2    Dublin
Airport

Finglas

M50

Glasnevin

Royal Canal

Liffey

N4

Marino

Howth

Lucan

Grand Canal

Kilmainham

Dublin

Clondalkin

Ballsbridge

Dublin Bay

Rathmines

N7

N81

Dundrum

N11

Dun
Laoghaire

0 Km        5

M50

0 miles

5

### Greater Dublin

*Nearly one third of the Republic's population lives in Dublin. Nevertheless the city is relatively uncongested and access to the center from the ports and airport is easy.*

Islay

SCOTLAND

Glasgow

Arran

A83

A83

North Channel

Coleraine

Cairnryan

A37

A2

A26

A75

A77

A36

Larne

Stranraer

THERN

Lough Neagh

Belfast

LAND

M1

M2

ENGLAND

A595

rmagh

A4

M1

A1

A2

A6

A65

Newry

N2

Isle of Man

Dundalk

Douglas

OF

M6

Irish  Sea

Boyne

Manchester

M62

DUBLIN

Liverpool

N1

N4

M62

Dun Laoghaire

Holyhead

M56

N7

M50

A5

M6

Liffey

N11

A55

A5

M7

Carlow

N9

A487

M54

A470

M6

N11

Slaney

Severn

N25

WALES

M50

Wexford

Waterford

Rosslare

Fishguard

A487

St   George's   Channel

A40

M4

Le Havre/Cherbourg

A40    A477

M4

M5

Pembroke

Swansea

CARDIFF

Bristol

Bristol   Channel

M5

# A Portrait of Ireland

*M*ANY VISITORS *see Ireland as a lush green island, full of thatched cottages, pubs, music, wit and poetry. Like all stereotypes, this image of the country has a basis in truth and the tourist industry helps sustain it. The political and economic reality is, of course, rather less ideal, but the relaxed good humor of the people still makes Ireland a most welcoming place to visit.*

Ireland, at least for the time being, is a divided island. History and religion have created two hostile communities, with the Protestant majority in the North implacably opposed to the idea of a united Ireland. In recent years the focus of the world's attention has been the Troubles, the campaigns of bombings and shootings in Northern Ireland, but the cease-fire of 1994 has brought a new climate of hope.

Ireland has had more than its fair share of wars and disasters, culminating in the Great Famine of 1845–8. Since then, poverty and emigration have been part of the Irish way of life. More people of Irish descent live in the US than in Ireland itself. Suffering and martyrdom in the cause of independence also play an important part in the Irish consciousness. The heroine of WB Yeats's play *Cathleen ni Houlihan* inspires young men to lay down their lives for Ireland. Her image appeared on the first bank note issued by the newly created Irish Free State in 1922.

**Cathleen ni Houlihan, personification of Ireland**

Yet, in spite of the past, the Irish retain their usual easy-going attitude to life. Both parts of the island have a young, highly educated population and are working hard to make their way in today's European Union. In the Republic, 50 percent of the population is under age 25.

Façade of Trinity College, Dublin, the Republic's most prestigious university

◁ **Thatching a traditional cottage in Adare, County Limerick**

Young first communicant in County Kerry

Despite its high birth rate, rural Ireland is sparsely populated. The Industrial Revolution of the 19th century barely touched the South and the Republic seems an old-fashioned place, poorer than almost all its fellow members of the European Union. With large families and high unemployment, the ratio of dependants to wage-earners is the highest in Europe.

### ECONOMIC DEVELOPMENT

Traditionally, Northern Ireland had far more industry than the South, but during the 25 years of the Troubles, old heavy industries, such as shipbuilding, have declined and new investors have been scared away. For both parts of Ireland, geography is a serious barrier to prosperity. Located on the periphery of Europe, the island is isolated from its main markets and thus saddled with high transportation costs. Subsidies from the European Union have helped improve the transportation infrastructure in the Republic, especially the roads and ports.

Traditional Irish dancing

Tax breaks and low inflation have attracted foreign investment to the Republic and many multinationals, especially computing and chemical companies, have subsidiaries in Ireland. Even so, the economy still depends heavily on agriculture and there are more cattle than people on the island. Another important industry is tourism. The Republic receives over 3 million visitors a year and the North is well prepared for an influx of tourists, now the Troubles appear to be at an end.

### RELIGION AND POLITICS

The influence of Catholicism is strong. In the Republic, the Church runs most schools, along with some hospitals and social services. Irish Catholicism runs the gamut from missionary zeal to simple piety. According to some estimates, over 90 percent of the

Pavement artist on O'Connell Street, Dublin

population goes to Mass. Religion plays an important role in the politics of the Republic and moral conservatism is evident in attitudes to issues such as divorce, contraception, abortion and homosexuality.

The election of liberal lawyer Mary Robinson as President in 1990, the first woman to hold the post, was seen as a sign of more enlightened times by many people, not only women. A new political climate has favored the quiet spread of feminism and challenged the old paternalism of Irish politics, not only in social issues but

Traditional farming: a field of haystacks overlooking Clew Bay, County Mayo

also in helping break down the clannish cronyism of the traditional parties Fianna Fáil and Fine Gael.

### LANGUAGE AND CULTURE

Ireland was a Gaelic-speaking nation until the 16th century, since when the language has declined. Today, however, the Republic is officially bilingual and knowledge of Irish is a requirement for university entrance and a career in the public sector. While 11 percent of the population speak Gaelic fluently, only three percent use it regularly in daily life.

Connemara pony show

Irish culture, on the other hand, is in no danger of being eroded. The people have a genuine love of old folk legends, epic poetry and songs; festivals play an important part in community life. Festivals may be dedicated to St. Patrick or James Joyce, pubs or oysters, salmon or sailing, music or matchmaking. Music is a national passion – from the rock of U2 and the Cranberries to the folk music of Clannad, the Chieftains and Mary Black.

Another national passion is horse racing. Ireland's breeders and trainers are masters of their trade and enjoy astonishing international success for such a small country. Other sports are followed with equal intensity, as witnessed during the 1994 soccer World Cup. Drinking also plays an important part in Irish culture: social life centers on the pub and the "crack" (convivial chat) to be enjoyed there. When the Republic introduced stricter drunk driving laws in 1994, many rural publicans said traditional Irish society would collapse. Given the attachment to Guinness, gossip and music, this is extremely unlikely.

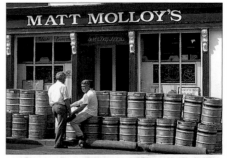

Matt Molloy's pub in Westport, County Mayo

# The Landscape and Wildlife of Ireland

**Corncrake**

THE LANDSCAPE is one of the Ireland's greatest attractions. It varies from bogs and lakes in the central lowlands to mountains and rocky islands in the west. Between these two extremes, the island has abundant lush, green pastureland, the result of plentiful rainfall, but little natural woodland. Parts of the far west, where the land is farmed by traditional methods, are havens for threatened wildlife, including the corncrake, which needs undisturbed hay fields in which to nest.

## THE FAUNA OF IRELAND

**Natterjack toad**

Many animals (including snakes) did not make it to Ireland before the Irish Sea rose after the Ice Age. Other surprising absentees are the mole, weasel and common toad (the natterjack, however, can be seen at a few sites). Red squirrels are more widespread than gray, while the wood mouse is the only small native rodent.

## ROCKY COASTS

## LAKES, RIVERS AND WETLANDS

**Chough**

The Dingle Peninsula (see pp150–51) is part of a series of rocky promontories and inlets created when sea levels rose at the end of the Ice Age. Cliffs and islands offer many sites for sea birds, with some enormous colonies, such as the gannets of Little Skellig (pp156–7). The chough still breeds on cliffs in the extreme west. Elsewhere in Europe, this rare species of crow is declining in numbers.

**Great crested grebe**

This watery landscape around Lough Oughter is typical of the lakelands of the River Erne (pp262–3). Rainfall is high throughout the year, which results in many wetlands, especially along the Shannon (pp176–7) and the Erne. The elegant great crested grebe breeds mainly on the larger lakes in the north.

***Thrift*** *grows in cushionlike clumps, producing its papery pink flower heads from spring right through to autumn.*

***Water lobelia*** *grows in the shallows of stony lakes. Its leaves remain below the water, while the pale lilac flowers are borne on leafless stems above the surface.*

***Sea campion*** *is a low-growing plant. Its large white flowers brighten many clifftops and seaside shingle banks.*

***Fleabane***, *once used to repel fleas, thrives in wet meadows and marshes. It has yellow flowers like dandelions.*

**Gray seals** *are a common sight in the waters off the Atlantic coast, feeding on fish and occasionally on sea birds.*

**Red deer** *have been introduced into many areas, notably the hills of Connemara.*

**Pine martens***, though mainly nocturnal, may be spotted in daytime during the summer.*

**Otters** *are more likely to be seen in the shallow seas off rocky coasts than in rivers and lakes, though they live in both habitats.*

## MOUNTAIN AND BLANKET BOG

## PASTURELAND

**Wheatear**

As well as the raised bogs of the central lowlands *(p244)*, much of Ireland's mountainous ground, particularly in the west, is covered by blanket bog such as that seen here in Connemara *(pp198–201)*. On drier upland sites this grades into heather moor and poor grassland. The wheatear, which inhabits rocky scree and heathland, is a restless bird with an unmistakable white rump. It flits about, dipping and bobbing in pursuit of flies.

**Rook**

Rolling pastureland with grazing livestock, as seen here in the foothills of the Wicklow Mountains *(pp130–31)*, is a very common sight throughout Ireland. The traditional farming methods employed in many parts of the island (particularly in the west) are of great benefit to wildlife. Rooks, for example, which feed on worms and insect larvae found in pastures, are very common.

**Bog myrtle** *is an aromatic shrub, locally common in Ireland's bogs. Its leaves can be used to flavor drinks.*

**Meadow vetchling** *uses its tendrils to climb up grasses and other plants. It has clusters of pretty pale yellow flowers.*

**Common butterwort** *is a carnivorous plant, trapping small insects on its sticky leaves. Its flowers are held up on long stalks from a rosette of leaves.*

**Marsh thistle** *is a common flower of wet meadows and damp woodland. It is a tall species with small, purple flower heads.*

# Architecture in Ireland

**Window of an Irish cottage**

IRELAND'S TURBULENT HISTORY has done incalculable damage to its architectural heritage. Cromwell's forces, in particular, destroyed scores of castles, monasteries and towns in their three-year campaign against the Irish in the mid-17th century. However, many fascinating buildings and sites remain, with Iron Age forts being the earliest surviving settlements. Christianity in Ireland gave rise to monasteries, churches and round towers; conflict between Anglo-Norman barons and Irish chieftains created castles and tower houses. The later landlord class built luxurious country mansions, while their laborers had to make do with basic, one-room cottages.

**LOCATOR MAP**

|  |  |
|---|---|
| ☐ | Iron Age forts |
| ☐ | Round towers |
| ☐ | Tower houses |
| ☐ | Georgian country houses |

## IRON AGE FORT

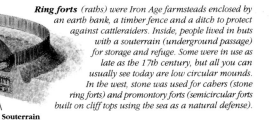

***Ring forts*** *(raths) were Iron Age farmsteads enclosed by an earth bank, a timber fence and a ditch to protect against cattleraiders. Inside, people lived in huts with a souterrain (underground passage) for storage and refuge. Some were in use as late as the 17th century, but all you can usually see today are low circular mounds. In the west, stone was used for cahers (stone ring forts) and promontory forts (semicircular forts built on cliff tops using the sea as a natural defense).*

**Thatched hut**          **Entrance**     **Souterrain**

## ROUND TOWER

**Lookout window**   **Conical roof**

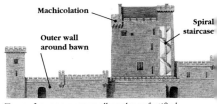

***Round towers***, *often over 30m (100 ft) tall, were built between the 10th and 12th centuries on monastic sites. They were bell towers, used as places of refuge and to store valuable manuscripts. The entrance, which could be as high as 4 m (13 ft) above ground, was reached by a ladder that was hauled up from the inside. Other movable ladders connected the tower's wooden floors.*

**Wooden floor**

**Movable ladder**

## TOWER HOUSE

**Machicolation**

**Outer wall around bawn**

**Spiral staircase**

***Tower houses*** *were small castles or fortified residences built between the 15th and 17th centuries. The tall square house was often surrounded by a stone wall forming a bawn (enclosure), used for defense and as a cattle pen. Machicolations (projecting parapets from which to drop missiles) were located at the top of the house.*

## COTTAGE

***One-room cottages***, *thatched or slate-roofed, are still a common feature of the Irish landscape. Built of local stone with small windows to retain heat, the cottages were inhabited by farm workers or smallholders.*

**Bog-oak timbers**       **Thatched, clay-lined chimney**

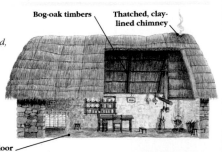

**Clay floor**

## Iron Age Forts

① Staigue Fort *p156*
② Dún Aonghasa *p206*
③ Craggaunowen *p182*
④ Grianán of Aileach *pp218–19*
⑤ Hill of Tara *p240*

## Round Towers

⑥ Kilmacduagh *p204*
⑦ Ardmore *p137*
⑧ Clonmacnoise *pp242–3*
⑨ Devenish Island *p263*
⑩ Kilkenny *pp136*
⑪ Glendalough *pp132–3*

## Tower Houses

⑫ Aughnanure Castle *p201*
⑬ Thoor Ballylee *pp204–5*
⑭ Knappogue Castle *p181*
⑮ Blarney Castle *p163*
⑯ Donegal Castle *p222*

## Georgian Country Houses

⑰ Strokestown Park House *pp210–11*
⑱ Castle Coole *p264*
⑲ Emo Court *p245*
⑳ Russborough House *pp124–5*
㉑ Castletown House *pp122–3*

**The well-preserved round tower at Ardmore**

## Georgian Country House

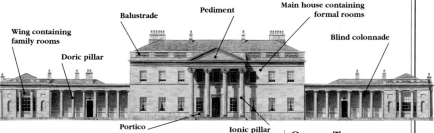

Wing containing family rooms
Doric pillar
Balustrade
Pediment
Main house containing formal rooms
Blind colonnade
Portico
Ionic pillar

*Between the 1720s and 1800, prosperous landlords commissioned palatial country mansions in the Palladian and Neo-Classical styles popular in England over that period. Castle Coole (above) has a Palladian layout, with the main house in the center and a colonnade on either side leading to a small pavilion. The Neo-Classical influence can be seen in the unadorned façade and the Doric columns of the colonnades. Noted architects of Irish country houses include Richard Castle (1690–1751) and James Wyatt (1746–1813).*

## Stucco

Stucco (decorative relief plasterwork), popular in the 18th century, is found in many Georgian country houses as well as town houses and public buildings. The Italian Francini brothers were particularly sought after for their intricate stuccowork (notably at Castletown and Russborough) as was Irish craftsman Michael Stapleton (Trinity College, Dublin and Dublin Writers Museum).

**Trompe l'oeil detail at Emo Court**

**Ceiling at Dublin Writers Museum**

**Stucco portrait at Castletown House**

**Stuccowork at Russborough House**

## Other Terms used in this Guide

**Beehive hut**: Circular stone building with a domed roof created by corbeling (laying a series of stones so that each projects beyond the one below).

**Cashel**: Stone ring fort.

**Crannog**: Defensive, partly artificial island on a lake. Huts were often built on crannogs *(see p31)*.

**Curtain wall**: Outer wall of a castle, usually incorporating towers at intervals.

**Hiberno-Romanesque**: Style of church architecture with rounded arches highly decorated with geometric designs and human and animal forms. Also called Irish-Romanesque.

**Motte and bailey**: Raised mound (motte) topped with a wooden tower, surrounded by a heavily fenced space (bailey). Built by the Normans in the 12th century, they were quickly erected in time of battle.

**Tympanum**: Decorated space over a door or window.

# Literary Ireland

FOR A LAND the size of Ireland to have produced three Nobel prizewinners in Shaw, Yeats and Beckett is a considerable feat. Yet it is not easy to speak of an "Irish literary tradition" since the concept needs to embrace rural and urban experiences, Protestant and Catholic traditions and the Gaelic and English languages. Irish fiction today, as in the past, is characterized by a sense of community and history, a love of storytelling and a zest for language.

**A first edition of *Ulysses***

WB Yeats – Ireland's most famous poet

The Blasket Islands, which provided inspiration for several writers

## GAELIC LITERATURE

IRISH LITERATURE proclaims itself the oldest vernacular literature in Western Europe, dating back to early monastic times when Celtic folklore and sagas such as the epics of Cuchulainn *(see p24)* were written down for the first time. The disappearance of Gaelic literature followed the demise, in the 17th century, of the Irish aristocracy for whom it was written. Gaelic literature has had several revivals. Peig Sayers is famous for her accounts of the harsh life on the Blasket Islands *(see p150)* in the early 20th century.

**Novelist Maria Edgeworth**

## ANGLO-IRISH LITERATURE

THE COLLAPSE of Gaelic culture and the Protestant Ascendancy led to English being the dominant language. Most literature was based around the privileged classes.

An early Anglo-Irish writer was satirist Jonathan Swift *(see p80)*, author of *Gulliver's Travels*, who was born in Dublin in 1667 of English parents. Anglo-Irish literature was strong in drama, the entertainment of the cultured classes, and owed little to Irish settings or sensibilities. By the 1700s, Ireland was producing an inordinate number of leading playwrights, many of whom were more at home in London. These included Oliver Goldsmith, remembered for his comedy *She Stoops to Conquer*, and Richard Brinsley Sheridan, whose plays include *The School for Scandal*. Near the end of the century, Maria Edgeworth set a precedent with novels such as *Castle Rackrent*, based on class differences in Irish society.

The 19th century saw an exodus to England of Irish playwrights, including Oscar Wilde, who entered Oxford University in 1874 and later became the darling of London society, with plays such as *The Importance of Being Earnest*. George Bernard Shaw *(see p98)*, writer of *St. Joan* and *Pygmalion*, also made London his home. This dramatist, critic, socialist and pacifist continued to write until well into the 20th century.

Playwright George Bernard Shaw

## 20TH-CENTURY WRITERS

IN 1898, WB Yeats and Lady Gregory founded Dublin's Abbey Theatre *(see p86)*. Its opening, in 1904, heralded the Irish Revival, which focused on national and local themes. Playwright John Millington Synge drew inspiration from a love of the Aran Islands and Irish folklore, but the "immoral language" of his *Playboy of the Western World* caused a riot when first performed at the Abbey Theatre. Along with contemporaries, like Sean O'Casey and WB Yeats, Synge influenced subsequent generations of Irish writers, including novelist Seán O'Faolain, humorous writer and columnist Flann O'Brien, and hard-drinking, quarrelsome playwright Brendan Behan. The literary revival also produced many notable poets in the mid-20th century such as the gifted Patrick Kavanagh and Belfast-born Louis MacNeice, often considered to be one of the finest poets of his generation.

The writer Brendan Behan enjoying the company in a Dublin pub

Caricature of protesters at Dublin's Abbey Theatre in 1907

## THREE LITERARY GIANTS

FROM the mass of talent to emerge in Irish literature, three figures stand out as visionaries in their fields. WB Yeats *(see p225)* spent half his life outside Ireland but is forever linked to its rural west. A writer of wistful, melancholic poetry, he was at the forefront of the Irish Revival, helping forge a new national cultural identity. James Joyce *(see p88)* was another trailblazer of Irish literature – his complex narrative and stream of consciousness techniques influenced the development of the modern novel. *Ulysses* describes a day in the life of Joyce's beloved Dublin and shaped the work of generations of writers. Bloomsday, which is named after one of the novel's characters, Leopold Bloom, is still celebrated annually in the city. The last of the three literary giants, novelist and playwright Samuel Beckett *(see p60)*, was another of Dublin's sons, although he later emigrated to France. His themes of alienation, despair, and the futility of human existence pervade his best-known plays, *Waiting for Godot* and *Endgame*.

**The poet Patrick Kavanagh celebrating Bloomsday**

## CONTEMPORARY WRITERS

IRELAND'S proud literary tradition is today upheld by a stream of talented writers from both North and South. Among the finest are Cork-born William Trevor, regarded as a master of the short story, and Brian Moore, whose stories of personal and political disillusionment are often based in his native Belfast. Similarly, Dubliner Roddy Doyle mines his working-class origins in novels such as *The Snapper* and *Paddy Clarke Ha Ha Ha*. Other established Irish writers are Brian Friel and Edna O'Brien. Out of Ireland's contemporary poets, the Ulster-born writers Seamus Heaney and Derek Mahon are considered among the most outstanding.

---

## IRELAND IN THE MOVIES

Ireland has long been fertile ground for the world's filmmakers. Hollywood invaded it as early as 1951 with *The Quiet Man*, starring John Wayne and set in the picturesque village of Cong. In recent years, Ireland and its people have been the subjects of several major films, notably *My Left Foot* (1989), *The Field* (1990) and *In the Name of the Father* (1994). Another popular film was *The Commitments* (1991). Filmed on location in and around Dublin with an all-Irish cast, it was based on a novel by Roddy Doyle.

**Cast of *The Commitments*, written by Roddy Doyle**

# The Music of Ireland

IRELAND IS THE ONLY COUNTRY in the world to have a musical instrument – the harp – as its national emblem. In this land, famous for its love of music, modern forms such as country-and-western and rock flourish, but it is traditional music that captures the essence of the country. Whether you are listening to Gaelic love songs that date back to medieval times or 17th- and 18th-century folk songs with their English and Scottish

**An Irish jig** influences, the music is unmistakably Irish. Dance is an equally important aspect of Irish traditional music, and some of the most popular airs are derived from centuries-old reels, jigs and hornpipes. Nowadays these are mainly performed at *fleadhs* (festivals) and *ceilidhs* (dances).

***Turlough O'Carolan** (1670–1738) is the most famous Irish harper. The blind musician traveled the country playing his songs to both the rich and poor. Many of O'Carolan's melodies, such as* The Lamentation of Owen O'Neill, *still survive.*

**Piano accordion**

The ***bodhrán*** is a handheld goatskin drum that is usually played with a small stick. It is particularly effective when accompanying the flute.

**Flute**

***John F McCormack** (1884–1945) was an Irish tenor who toured America to great acclaim during the early part of this century. His best-loved recordings were arias by Mozart. Another popular tenor was Derry-born Josef Locke. A singer of popular ballads in the 1940s and '50s, he was the subject of the 1992 film,* Hear My Song.

**Two-row button accordion**

## THE CURRENT MUSIC SCENE

**Mary Black**

Ireland today is a melting pot of musical styles. The resurgence of Irish traditional music has produced many highly respected musicians, such as the pipe-players Liam Ó Floin and Paddy Keenan from Dublin. Groups like the Chieftains and the Fureys have gained world-wide fame by melding old with new. Ireland is also firmly placed on the rock'n'roll map, thanks to bands such as Them in the 1960s and Thin Lizzy a decade later. But the most famous rock band to come out of Ireland is Dublin's U2 who, in the 1980s, became one of the world's most popular groups. More recently, the series of albums entitled *A Woman's Heart* has been a showcase for the talents of Mary Black, Eleanor McEvoy, Sinéad O'Connor and other Irish female musicians.

**Bono of U2**

**Traditional Irish dancing** *is currently enjoying renewed popularity. Since the 17th century, the social focus in rural areas was the village dance held every Sunday. From these gatherings, Irish dancing became popular.*

### LIVE TRADITIONAL MUSIC

Wherever you go in Ireland, you won't be far from a pub with live music. For the Irish traditional musician, there are few set rules – the improvisational nature of the music means that no two performances of any piece are ever likely to be the same.

**Violins,** or fiddles, can either be tucked under the chin or held against the upper arm, shoulder or chest.

*Irish folk songs, such as this one about the 1916 Easter Rising, tend to have a patriotic theme. But some of the most powerful songs have been written not just about the national struggle, but also on hardship, emigration and the longing for the homeland.*

## TRADITIONAL INSTRUMENTS

There is no set line-up in traditional Irish bands but the fiddle is probably the most common instrument used. Like the music, some instruments have Celtic origins – the uillean pipes are related to the bagpipes played in Scotland and Brittany today.

**The melodeon** *is a basic version of the button accordion. Both these instruments are better suited to Irish music than the piano accordion.*

**The uillean pipes** *are similar to bagpipes and are generally considered to be one of the main instruments in Irish traditional music.*

**The harp** *has been played in Ireland since the 10th century. In recent years, there has been a keen revival of harp playing in Irish traditional music.*

**The banjo** *comes from the Deep South in the US and adds a new dimension to the sound of traditional bands.*

**Tin whistle**

**Flute**

**The flute and tin whistle** *are among the most common instruments used in traditional Irish music. The latter is often called the penny whistle.*

**The violin** *is called a fiddle by Irish musicians. The style of playing and sound produced varies from region to region.*

# Ireland's Celtic Heritage

Stone carving on Boa Island

IRELAND'S RICH TRADITION of storytelling embraces a folk heritage that abounds with myths and superstitions. Some stories have been in written form since the 8th century, but most originated over 2,000 years ago when druids passed on stories orally from one generation to the next. Like the Gaelic language itself, many of Ireland's legends have links with those of ancient Celtic races throughout Europe. As well as the heroic deeds and fearless warriors of mythology, Irish folklore is also rich in tales of fairies, leprechauns, banshees and other supernatural beings.

The formidable Queen Maeve of Connaught

Part of the 2,300-year-old Gundestrup Cauldron unearthed in Denmark, which depicts Cuchulainn's triumph in the Cattle Raid of Cooley

## CUCHULAINN

THE MOST FAMOUS warrior in Irish mythology is Cuchulainn. At the age of seven, going by the name of Setanta, he killed the savage hound of Culainn the Smith by slaying it with a hurling stick (one of the first times the sport of hurling is mentioned in folklore). Culainn was upset at the loss so Setanta volunteered to guard the house, earning himself the new name of Cuchulainn, meaning the hound of Culainn.

Before he went into battle, Cuchulainn swelled to magnificent proportions, turned different colors and one of his eyes grew huge. His greatest victory was in the "Cattle Raid of Cooley," when Queen Maeve of Connaught sent her troops to capture the coveted prize bull of Ulster. Cuchulainn learned of the plot and defeated them single-handedly. However, Queen Maeve took revenge on Cuchulainn by using sorcerers to lure him to his death. Today, in Dublin's GPO (see p87), a statue of Cuchulainn commemorates the heroes of the 1916 Easter Rising.

## FINN MACCOOL

THE WARRIOR Finn MacCool is the most famous leader of the Fianna, an elite band of troops chosen for their strength and valor and who defended Ireland from foreign forces. Finn was not only strong and bold but also possessed the powers of a seer, and could obtain great wisdom by putting his thumb in his mouth and sucking on it. When they were not at war, the Fianna spent their time hunting. Finn had a hound called Bran which stood almost as high as himself and is said to be the original ancestor of the breed known today as the Irish wolfhound. Many of the

## FAIRIES, LEPRECHAUNS AND BANSHEES

The diminutive figure of the leprechaun

The existence of spirits, and in particular the "little people," plays a large part in Irish folklore. Centuries ago, it was believed that fairies lived under mounds of earth, or "fairy raths," and that touching one of these tiny figures brought bad luck. The most famous of the "little people" is the leprechaun. Legend tells that if you caught one of these, he would lead you to a crock of gold, but take your eyes off him and he would vanish into thin air. The banshee was a female spirit whose wailing presence outside a house was said to signal the imminent death of someone within.

A banshee with long flowing hair

Fianna possessed supernatural powers and often ventured into the life beyond, known as the Otherworld. Among these was Finn's son Ossian who was not only a formidable warrior, like his father, but was also renowned as a wise and knowledgeable poet. Through time, Finn has come to be commonly portrayed as a giant. Legend says it that he constructed the Giant's Causeway in County Antrim *(see pp254–5)*.

**The children of King Lir being turned into white swans**

**A 19th-century engraving of Finn MacCool dressed for battle**

## The Children of Lir

O NE OF the saddest tales in Irish folklore involves King Lir, who so adored his four children that their stepmother was driven wild with jealousy. One day she took the children to a lake and cast a spell on them, turning them into white swans confined to the waters of Ireland for 900 years. However, as soon as she had done the deed, she became racked with guilt and bestowed upon them the gift of exquisite song. The

end of the children's 900-year ordeal coincided with the coming of Christianity. The four children regained human form but were wizened and weak. They died soon afterward, but not before being baptized. King Lir then decreed that no swan in Ireland should be killed – an act which is still illegal today.

## Saint Brendan

B RENDAN THE NAVIGATOR, like many other 6th-century monks, traveled widely. It is known that although he lived in western Ireland, he visited Wales, Scotland and France. It is likely, though, that his most famous journey is fictitious. This story tells of a shipload of monks who, after seven years of all kinds of strange encounters designed to test their faith, found the Land of Promise. It is essentially a Christian retelling of the common tales of the Celtic Otherworld. The Feast of St. Brendan on May 16 is celebrated in Kerry by the climbing of Mount Brandon.

**Engraving showing St. Brendan and his monks encountering a siren**

## Origins of Irish Place Names

The names of many of Ireland's cities, towns and villages today are largely based on ancient Gaelic terms for prominent local landmarks, some of which no longer exist. Here are just a few elements of the place names the traveler may come across.

**The fort on the Rock of Cashel that gives the town its name**

**Ar, ard** – *high, height*
**Ass, ess** – *waterfall*
**A, ah, ath** – *ford*
**Bal, bally** – *town*
**Beg** – *small*
**Ben** – *peak, mountain*
**Carrick, carrig** – *rock*
**Cashel** – *stone fort*
**Crock, knock** – *hill*
**Curra, curragh** – *marsh*
**Darry, derry** – *oak tree*
**Dun** – *castle*
**Eden** – *hill brow*
**Innis, inch** – *island*
**Inver** – *river mouth*
**Isk, iska** – *water*
**Glas, glass** – *green*
**Glen, glyn** – *valley*
**Kil, kill** – *church*
**Lough** – *lake, sea inlet*
**Mona, mone** – *peat bog*
**Mor** – *great, large*
**Mullen, mullin** – *mill*
**Rath, raha** – *ring fort*
**Slieve** – *mountain*
**Toom** – *burial ground*
**Tul, tulagh** – *small hill*

**St. Canice's Cathedral in Kilkenny (the town's name means "church of Canice")**

# The Year in Sports

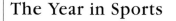

ALL MAJOR INTERNATIONAL team sports are played in Ireland, but the most popular games are the two uniquely native ones of Gaelic football and hurling. Most of the big games, plus soccer and rugby internationals, are sold out well in advance. However, if you can't get a ticket you'll find plenty of company watching the event in pubs. Horse racing, with over 240 days of racing a year, attracts fanatical support. For those who want participatory sports, there are also Ireland's famous fishing waters and golf courses *(see pp332–3).*

***The North West 200*** *is the fastest motorcycle race in the world over public roads – held near Portstewart* (see p252).

**Football Association of Ireland Cup – the Republic's soccer final**

**Irish Gold Cup: steeplechase at Punchestown**

**Around-Ireland Yacht Race – held every two years**

***The Irish Grand National*** *is a grueling steeplechase run at Fairyhouse in County Meath.*

| January | February | March | April | May | June |
|---|---|---|---|---|---|

**Irish Champion Hurdle, run at Leopardstown, County Wicklow**

**The International Rally of the Lakes** is a prestigious car rally around the Lakes of Killarney *(see pp154–5).*

**Start of the salmon fishing season**

***The Five Nations Rugby Tournament****, between Ireland, Scotland, Wales, England and France, runs until April. Ireland play its home games at Lansdowne Road, Dublin.*

**Irish Football League Cup – Northern Ireland's final**

## KEY TO SEASONS

- Hurling
- Gaelic football
- Flat racing
- National Hunt racing
- Rugby
- Soccer
- Salmon fishing
- Horseback riding

***The Irish Derby****, Ireland's premier flat race, attracts many of Europe's best three-year-olds to the Curragh (see p121).*

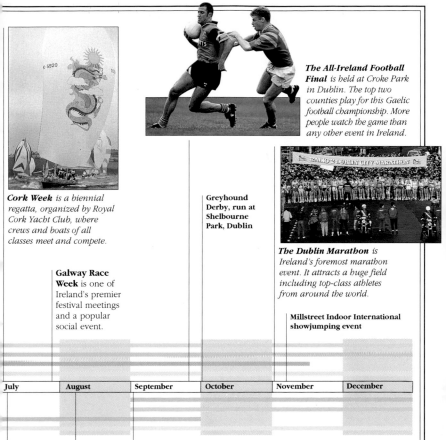

**The All-Ireland Football Final** is held at Croke Park in Dublin. The top two counties play for this Gaelic football championship. More people watch the game than any other event in Ireland.

**Cork Week** is a biennial regatta, organized by Royal Cork Yacht Club, where crews and boats of all classes meet and compete.

Greyhound Derby, run at Shelbourne Park, Dublin

**The Dublin Marathon** is Ireland's foremost marathon event. It attracts a huge field including top-class athletes from around the world.

**Galway Race Week** is one of Ireland's premier festival meetings and a popular social event.

Millstreet Indoor International showjumping event

| July | August | September | October | November | December |
|------|--------|-----------|---------|----------|----------|

**The Dublin Horse Show** is Ireland's premier horse show and a major event in the social calendar.

All-Ireland Hurling Final at Croke Park, Dublin

**The Irish Open Golf Championship** is held at a different course each year and attracts a world-class field to courses such as Ballybunion in County Kerry.

## THE GAELIC ATHLETIC ASSOCIATION

The GAA was founded in 1884 to promote indigenous Irish sport and discourage British influences – members were once forbidden from playing foreign games such as cricket. Today, despite heavy competition from soccer, the most popular sport in Ireland remains Gaelic football. However, the more intriguing GAA game is hurling – a fast and physical field sport played with sticks – which is said to have originated in ancient Celtic times. Both Gaelic football and hurling are played at parish and county level on a wholly amateur basis. The season ends with the All-Ireland finals, which draw large and passionate crowds to Dublin.

**Camogie, a version of hurling played by women**

# THE HISTORY OF IRELAND

IRELAND'S RELATIVE ISOLATION has cut it off from several of the major events of European history. Roman legions, for example, never invaded and the country's early history is shrouded in myths of warring Gods and heroic High Kings. Nevertheless, the bellicose Celtic tribes were quick to embrace Christianity after the arrival of St. Patrick on the island in AD 432.

Until the Viking invasions of the 9th century, Ireland enjoyed an era of relative peace. Huge monasteries like Clonmacnoise and Glendalough were founded, where scholarship and art flourished. The Vikings never succeeded in gaining control of the island but in 1169 the Anglo-Normans arrived with greater ambitions. Many Irish chiefs submitted to Henry II of England, who declared himself Lord of Ireland. He left in 1172, and his knights divided large baronies between themselves.

Matters changed when Henry VIII broke with the Catholic church in 1532. Ireland became a battleground between native Irish Catholics and the forces of the English Crown. Where the Irish were defeated, their lands were confiscated and granted to Protestants from England and Scotland. England's conquest was completed with the victory of William of Orange over James II at the Battle of the Boyne in 1690. The new order was backed up by repressive Penal Laws that denied the Irish the most basic freedoms, but opposition to English rule was never totally quashed.

The Famine of 1845 to 1848 was the bleakest period of Irish history. Over two million either died or were forced to emigrate. Many who stayed were evicted by absentee English landlords. A campaign for Home Rule gathered strength, but it took decades of parliamentary infighting and bloody battles before the Government of Ireland Act of 1920 divided the island, The South became the Irish Free State, gaining full independence in 1937. Northern Ireland, where Protestants have a majority, has remained, despite bombing campaigns, part of the United Kingdom.

**South Cross, Clonmacnoise**

Map of Ireland, printed in 1592, showing the four traditional provinces

◁ *The Feast of St. Kevin amid the Ruins of Glendalough* by Joseph Peacock (1813)

# Prehistoric Ireland

UNTIL ABOUT 9,500 YEARS ago Ireland was uninhabited. The first people, who may have crossed by a land bridge from Scotland, were hunter-gatherers and left few traces of permanent settlement. The 4th millennium BC saw the arrival of Neolithic farmers and herdsmen who built stone field walls and

**Early Bronze Age stone axe-head**

monumental tombs such as Newgrange. Metalworking was brought from Europe around 2000 BC by the Bronze Age Beaker people, who also introduced new pottery skills. The Iron Age reached Ireland in the 3rd century BC along with the Celts, who migrated from Central Europe, via France and Britain, and soon established themselves as the dominant culture.

**IRELAND C. 8000 BC**

☐ *Former coastline*

☐ *Present-day coastline*

**The terminal disks** were worn on the shoulders.

## GLENINSHEEN GORGET

Many remarkable pieces of gold jewelry were created in the late Bronze Age. This gold collar dates from about 700 BC. The Iron Age Celts produced similarly fine metalwork and ornaments.

**Dolmens or Portal Tombs**
*These striking megalithic tombs date from around 2000 BC. Legananny Dolmen in the Mountains of Mourne (see p276) is a fine example.*

**Three strands of ropework**

**Wooden Idol**
*This Iron Age fetish would have played a role in pagan fertility rites.*

**Celtic Stone Idol**
*This mysterious three-faced head was found in County Cavan. In Celtic religion the number three has always had a special significance.*

**Bronze Bridle Bit**
*Celtic chiefs rode into battle on two-horse chariots with beautifully decorated harnesses.*

## TIMELINE

| 8000 BC | 6000 | 4000 | 2000 | 1000 |
|---|---|---|---|---|
| **c. 7500 BC** First inhabitants of Ireland<br>*Extinct giant deer or "Irish Elk"* | | **5000–3000** Ireland covered by dense woodland dominated by oak and elm | **2500** Building of Newgrange passage tomb *(see pp238–9)* | **1500** Major advances in metalworking, especially gold |
| | **6000** Date of huts excavated at Mount Sandel, Co Londonderry; oldest known dwellings in Europe | **3700** Neolithic farmers reach Ireland; they clear woods to plant grains | **2050** Beaker people (so-called for their delicate pottery vessels) reach Ireland at the beginning of Bronze Age | |

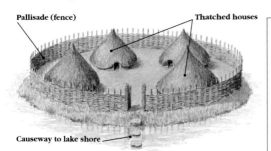

**Pallisade (fence)** **Thatched houses**

**Causeway to lake shore**

### Reconstruction of a Crannog
*Originating in the Bronze Age, crannogs were artificial islands built in lakes. At first used for fishing, they soon developed into well-protected homesteads. Some remained in use up to the 17th century.*

**The raised bands** on the collar were created by *repoussé* work, pushed through from the back. The delicate rope motifs were added from the front with a knife.

### Bone Slip
*(c. AD 50)*
*This may have been used for divination or for gambling.*

**Gold Boat**
*Part of a hoard of gold objects found at Broighter, County London-derry, the boat (1st century AD) was made as a votive offering.*

## WHERE TO SEE PREHISTORIC IRELAND

Prehistoric sites range from individual tombs such as Newgrange, Browne's Hill Dolmen *(see p133)* or Ossian's Grave to whole settlements, as at Céide Fields *(p196)* and Lough Gur *(p186)*. The largest Stone Age cemetery is at Carrowmore *(p226)*. Good reconstructions of prehistoric structures can be seen at Craggaunowen *(p182)* and the Ulster History Park *(p261)*. The National Museum in Dublin *(pp64–5)* houses the finest collection of artifacts, including wonderful gold objects from the Bronze Age.

**Newgrange** (pp238–9) *is Ireland's finest restored Neolithic tomb. At the entrance lie huge spiral-patterned boulders.*

**Ossian's Grave** *is a court grave, the earliest kind of Neolithic tomb (p259). An open court stood before the burial mound.*

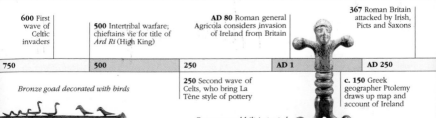

**600** First wave of Celtic invaders

**500** Intertribal warfare; chieftains vie for title of *Ard Ri* (High King)

**AD 80** Roman general Agricola considers invasion of Ireland from Britain

**367** Roman Britain attacked by Irish, Picts and Saxons

750 | 500 | 250 | AD 1 | AD 250

*Bronze goad decorated with birds*

**250** Second wave of Celts, who bring La Tène style of pottery

**c. 150** Greek geographer Ptolemy draws up map and account of Ireland

*Bronze sword hilt imported from southern France*

# Celtic Christianity

**Monk illuminating a manuscript**

CELTIC IRELAND was divided into as many as 100 chiefdoms, though these often owed allegiance to kings of larger provinces such as Munster or Connaught. At times, there was also a titular High King based at Tara (*see p240*). Ireland became Christian in the 5th century AD, heralding a golden age of scholarship centered on the new monasteries, while missionaries such as St. Columba traveled abroad. At the end of the 8th century, Celtic Ireland was shattered by the arrival of the Vikings.

**IRELAND IN 1000**

&#9632; Viking settlements

&#9633; Traditional Irish provinces

**Ogham Stone**
*The earliest Irish script, Ogham, dates from about AD 300. The notches correspond to Roman letters, like a form of Morse code.*

## CELTIC MONASTERY

Monasteries were large centers of population. This reconstruction shows Glendalough (*see pp132–3*) in about 1100. The tall round tower served as a lookout for Viking raiders.

**Craftmen's dwellings**

**Refectory and kitchen**

**Round tower**

**Abbot's house**

**St. Mary's Church**

**The watermill** was used for grinding wheat and barley.

**The Magnus Domus** was a large communal building used by the abbot and the monks.

**St. Kevin's Church**

**Drystone bridge**

**A High Cross** marks the monastery boundary.

**Battle of Clontarf**
*After their defeat by the Irish High King, Brian Boru, in 1014, the Vikings began to integrate more fully with the native population. Brian Boru himself was killed in the battle.*

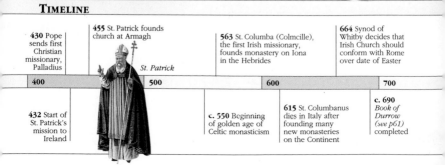

## TIMELINE

**430** Pope sends first Christian missionary, Palladius

**455** St. Patrick founds church at Armagh

*St. Patrick*

**563** St. Columba (Colmcille), the first Irish missionary, founds monastery on Iona in the Hebrides

**664** Synod of Whitby decides that Irish Church should conform with Rome over date of Easter

| 400 | 500 | 600 | 700 |
|---|---|---|---|

**432** Start of St. Patrick's mission to Ireland

**c. 550** Beginning of golden age of Celtic monasticism

**615** St. Columbanus dies in Italy after founding many new monasteries on the Continent

**c. 690** *Book of Durrow* (*see p61*) completed

## Viking Raids and Settlements

*The first longships reached Ireland in 795. Although notorious for pillaging monasteries, the Vikings introduced new farming methods and coinage. They also founded walled cities such as Dublin, Waterford and Limerick.*

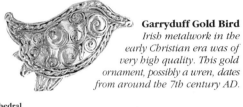

### Garryduff Gold Bird

*Irish metalwork in the early Christian era was of very high quality. This gold ornament, possibly a wren, dates from around the 7th century AD.*

Cathedral

Gatehouse

Guesthouse and stables

Monks' dwellings and barns

St. Kieran's Church and other important churches were built of stone, but most buildings were wood.

### Clonmacnoise Crozier

*This 11th-century bishop's staff is decorated with an ornate silver casing. The style of the incised patterns shows Viking influence.*

## WHERE TO SEE EARLY CHRISTIAN IRELAND

Important early monastic sites besides Glendalough include Clonmacnoise and Devenish Island. Churches from this period can also be seen at Gallarus *(see p149)*, Clonfert *(p205)* and the Rock of Cashel *(pp188–9)*, while High Crosses *(p235)* and round towers *(p18)* survive all over Ireland. Dublin's National Museum *(pp64–5)* has the best collection of ecclesiastical (and Viking) artifacts and Trinity College *(pp60–62)* houses the finest illuminated manuscripts.

*Devenish Island has a fine 12th-century round tower and enjoys a peaceful setting on Lower Lough Erne (p263).*

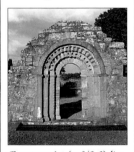

*Clonmacnoise (pp242–3) lies on the east bank of the Shannon. This Romanesque doorway is part of the ruined Nuns' Church.*

*Viking silver brooch*

**795** First Viking invasion of coastal monasteries

**807** Work starts on Kells monastery *(see p233)*

**841** A large Viking fleet spends the winter at Dublin

**967** Irish warriors sack Limerick and begin military campaign against Viking overlords

**999** Sitric Silkenbeard, the Viking king of Dublin, surrenders to Brian Boru

**1014** High King Brian Boru of Munster defeats joint army of Vikings and the King of Leinster at Clontarf

*Viking coin*

**1166** Dermot McMurrough, King of Leinster, flees overseas

**1134** Cormac's Chapel is built at Cashel *(see pp188–9)*

**1142** Ireland's first Cistercian house founded at Mellifont *(see p237)*

| 800 | 900 | 1000 | 1100 |

# Anglo-Norman Ireland

**13th-century gold brooch**

Anglo-Norman nobles, led by Richard de Clare (nicknamed Strongbow), were invited to Ireland by the King of Leinster in 1169. They took control of the major towns and Henry II of England proclaimed himself overlord of Ireland. In succeeding centuries, however, English power declined and the Crown controlled just a small area around Dublin known as the Pale *(see p124)*. Many of the Anglo-Norman barons living outside the Pale opposed English rule just as strongly as did the native Irish clans.

**IRELAND IN 1488**

▨ *Extent of the Pale*

## CARRICKFERGUS CASTLE

The first Anglo-Norman forts were wooden structures, but they soon started to build massive stone castles. Carrickfergus *(see p267)* was begun in the 1180s and by 1250 had acquired a keep and a gatehouse.

**The keep** contained a hall on the first floor and, above that, the lord's private apartments.

**Guardroom**

**Storeroom**

**Stables**

**Bakery**

**Marriage of Strongbow**
*The King of Leinster gave his daughter to Strongbow for helping him regain his lands. Daniel Maclise's painting (1854) emphasizes Anglo-Norman power over the Irish.*

**Norman Weapons**
*These bows and arrows, unearthed at Waterford, may be relics of Strongbow's assault on the city in 1170.*

## TIMELINE

**1172** Pope affirms King Henry II of England's lordship over Ireland

**1177** John de Courcy's forces invade Ulster

*Dermot McMurrough, King of Leinster, who invited Strongbow to come to his aid*

**1318** Bruce killed in battle

**1315** Scots invade Ireland; Edward Bruce crowned king

| 1200 | 1250 | 1300 |

**1169** Strongbow's Anglo-Normans arrive at invitation of exiled King of Leinster, Dermot McMurrough

**1224** Dominican order enters Ireland and constructs friaries

**1260** Powerful Irish chieftain Brian O'Neill killed at the Battle of Down

**1297** First Irish Parliament meets in Dublin

**Richard II's Fleet Returning to England in 1399**
*Richard made two trips to Ireland – in 1394 and 1399.*
*On the first he defeated Art McMurrough, King of Leinster,*
*and other Irish chiefs, but the second was inconclusive.*

Kitchen

**The gatehouse** was the last addition made in the 13th century. The two towers have arrow loops for longbowmen.

**Drawbridge**

Chapel

**The Hall** was where the lord of the castle held public court and decided cases brought before him.

**Éamonn Burke**
*The 14th-century Lord of Mayo was a typically independent chieftain of Anglo-Norman descent.*

## WHERE TO SEE ANGLO-NORMAN IRELAND

The strength of Norman fortifications is best seen in the castles at Carrickfergus, Limerick *(see p183)* and Trim *(p240)* and in Waterford's city walls. Gothic cathedrals that survive include Dublin's Christ Church *(pp78–9)* and St. Patrick's *(pp80–81)* and St. Canice's *(p136)* in Kilkenny. There are impressive ruins of medieval Cistercian abbeys at Jerpoint and Boyle *(p211)*.

**Jerpoint Abbey** (p137) *has a well-preserved 15th-century cloister decorated with carvings of curiously elongated figures.*

**Waterford's** *Anglo-Norman city walls include this sturdy watchtower (pp138–9).*

*Great Charter Roll of Waterford (1372) showing portraits of the mayors of four medieval cities*

**1394** King Richard II lands with army to reassert control; returns five years later but with inconclusive results

**1471** 8th Earl of Kildare made Lord Deputy of Ireland

**1496** Kildare regains Lord Deputy position

**1491** Kildare supports Perkin Warbeck, pretender to the English throne

| 1350 | 1400 | 1450 |
|------|------|------|

**1366** Statutes of Kilkenny forbid marriage between Anglo-Normans and Irish

**1348** The Black Death: one third of population killed in three years

*English forces* (left) *confront Irish horsemen on Richard II's return expedition*

**1487** Kildare crowns Lambert Simnel, Edward VI in Dublin

**1494** Lord Deputy Edward Poynings forbids Irish Parliament to meet without royal consent

# Protestant Conquest

**Hugh O'Neill, Earl of Tyrone**

Eengland's break with the Catholic Church, the dissolution of the monasteries and Henry VIII's assumption of the title King of Ireland incensed the Anglo-Norman dynasties and Irish clans such as the O'Neills. Resistance to foreign rule was fierce and it took 150 years of war to establish the English Protestant ascendancy. Tudor and Stuart monarchs adopted a policy of military persuasion, then instituted Plantation. Oliver Cromwell was even more forceful. Irish hopes were raised when the Catholic James II ascended to the English throne, but he was deposed and fled to Ireland, where he was defeated by William of Orange (William III) in 1690.

**IRELAND IN 1625**

Main areas of Plantation in the reign of James I

**The first relief ship** to reach Londonderry was the *Phoenix*. For three months English ships had been prevented from sailing up the Foyle by a wooden barricade across the river.

**James II's army** on the east bank of the Foyle attack the ship.

**Battle of the Boyne**
*This tapestry, from the Bank of Ireland (see p58), shows William of Orange leading his troops against the army of James II in 1690. His victory is still celebrated by Orangemen in Northern Ireland.*

**Silken Thomas Fitzgerald**
*Silken Thomas, head of the powerful Kildares, renounced his allegiance to Henry VIII in 1534. He was hanged along with his five uncles in 1537.*

**The artist's depiction** of 17th-century weapons and uniforms is far from accurate.

## TIMELINE

*Henry VIII*

**1541** Henry VIII declared King of Ireland by Irish Parliament

*Sir Thomas Lee, an officer in Elizabeth I's army, dressed in Irish fashion*

**1585** Ireland is mapped and divided into 32 counties

**1592** Trinity College, Dublin founded

| 1500 | 1525 | 1550 | 1575 | 16 |

**1534** Silken Thomas rebels against Henry VIII

**1504** 8th Earl of Kildare becomes master of Ireland after victory at Knocktoe

**1539** Henry VIII dissolves monasteries

**1557** Mary I orders first plantations in Offaly and Laois

**1582** Desmond rebellion in Munster

**1588** Spanish Armada wrecked off west coast

**The Siege of Drogheda**
*Between 1649 and 1652 Cromwell's army avenged attacks on Protestant settlers with ruthless efficiency. Here Cromwell himself directs the gunners bombarding Drogheda.*

## PLANTATION IRELAND

James I realized that force alone could not stabilize Ireland. The Plantation program uprooted the native Irish and gave their land to Protestant settlers from England and Scotland. London livery companies organized many of the new settlements. The policy created loyal garrisons who supported the Crown.

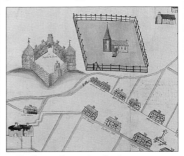

***Bellaghy*** *in County Londonderry was settled by the Vintners Company. This map of the neatly planned town dates from 1622.*

**The Walls of Derry** have never been breached by any attacker and many of the original 17th-century gates and bastions that withstood the siege of 1689 are still in place *(see pp250–51).*

St. George's flag

Ship Quay

**Protestants** emerge from the besieged city to greet the English relieving force and to engage the enemy.

**Loftus Cup**
*Adam Loftus, Chancellor of Ireland, used his position to enrich his family. In 1593 he had the Great Seal of Ireland melted down and made into this silver-gilt cup.*

## THE RELIEF OF DERRY *(1689)*

Some 20,000 Protestants were besieged for 105 days in Londonderry by James II's forces. Thousands died from starvation, until relief finally came from English warships. This 18th-century painting by William Sadler II gives a rather fanciful picture of the ending of the siege.

| | | | | |
|---|---|---|---|---|
| **1607** Flight of the Earls: old Irish leaders flee to the Continent; Plantation of Ulster | **1632** Important Irish history book, *The Annals of the Four Masters*, written by four Franciscan friars from Donegal | *Protestant apprentice boys closing the gates of Derry before the siege of 1689* | | **1690** William of Orange defeats James II at Battle of the Boyne; James's army surrenders the following year in Limerick |
| **1625** | | **1650** | **1675** | **1700** |
| **1603** Earl of Tyrone ends eight years of war by signing the Treaty of Mellifont | | | **1688** James II, deposed Catholic king of England, flees to Ireland and raises army | **1695** Penal code severely reduces rights of Roman Catholics |
| **1641** Armed rebellion in Ulster opposes Plantation | | **1649** Cromwell lands in Dublin; razes Drogheda and Wexford; Catholic landowners transplanted to far west | | **1689** Siege of Derry |

# Georgian Ireland

**Lacquer cabinet in Castletown House**

The PROTESTANT ASCENDANCY was a period of great prosperity for the landed gentry, who built grand country houses and furnished them luxuriously. Catholics, meanwhile, were denied even the right to buy land. Toward the end of the century, radicals, influenced by events in America and France, started to demand independence from the English Crown. Prime Minister Henry Grattan tried a parliamentary route; Wolfe Tone and the United Irishmen opted for armed insurrection. Both approaches ultimately failed.

**IRELAND IN 1703**

▨ *Counties where Protestants owned over 75 percent of land*

**The Irish House of Commons**
*This painting shows Irish leader Henry Grattan addressing the house (see p58). The "Grattan Parliament" lasted from 1782 to 1800, but was then abolished by the Act of Union.*

**State Bedroom**

**The parlor**, the Casino's main room, was used for formal entertaining. It has a magnificent parquet floor.

**Stone lions by Edward Smyth (1749–1812)**

**The basement** contains the servants' hall, the kitchen, pantry and wine cellar.

**Surveyors**
*The 18th century saw work begin on ambitious projects such as the Grand Canal, new roads and Dublin's network of wide streets and squares.*

## TIMELINE

*Jonathan Swift (1667–1745)*

**1724** Swift attacks Ireland's penal code in *A Modest Proposal*

**1731** Royal Dublin Society founded to encourage agriculture, art and crafts

**1738** Death of Ireland's most famous harper, Turlough O'Carolan *(see p22)*

| 1710 | 1720 | 1730 | 1740 | 1750 |
|---|---|---|---|---|

**1713** Jonathan Swift appointed Dean of St. Patrick's Cathedral *(see p80)*

**1731** First issue of the *Belfast Newsletter*, the world's oldest continually running newspaper

**1742** First performance of Handel's *Messiah* given in Dublin

**1751** Dublin's Rotunda Lying-In Hospital is first maternity hospital in the British Isles

## Linen Bleaching

*Ulster's linen industry flourished thanks to the expertise of Huguenot weavers from France. The woven cloth was spread out in fields or on river banks to bleach it (see p260).*

**The Classical urns** on the roof conceal chimneys.

**The china closet** was originally designed as a bedroom.

### Irish Painting

*Aristocratic patronage encouraged the development of an Irish school of painting. This picture, by an unknown artist, shows Leixlip Castle in an idealized rural setting.*

**The hall** ends in a semicircular apse leading to the saloon.

**Entrance**

## MARINO CASINO

This frivolous summer house was built in the 1760s for the first Earl of Charlemont on his estate just north of Dublin *(see p98)*. Palladian architecture of this kind was popular among the Irish aristocracy, who followed 18th-century English fashions.

## WHERE TO SEE GEORGIAN IRELAND

Dublin preserves many fine Georgian terraces and public buildings such as the Custom House *(see p86)* and the Four Courts *(p91)*. Around Dublin, the grand houses at Castletown *(pp122–3)*, Russborough and Powerscourt *(pp126–7)* are fascinating reminders of the lifestyle of the gentry. Other 18th-century country seats open to the public include Emo Court, Westport House *(pp196–7)* and Castle Coole *(p264)*.

***Emo Court's*** *façade, with its plain Ionic portico, is by James Gandon, architect of many of Dublin's public buildings* (p245).

***Russborough House*** *(p124) was built in 1741 by Richard Castle. Elegant niches with Classical busts flank the grand fireplace in the entrance hall.*

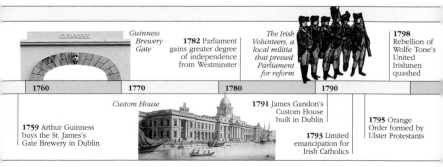

Guinness Brewery Gate

**1782** Parliament gains greater degree of independence from Westminster

*The Irish Volunteers, a local militia that pressed Parliament for reform*

**1798** Rebellion of Wolfe Tone's United Irishmen quashed

| 1760 | 1770 | 1780 | 1790 |
|------|------|------|------|

*Custom House*

**1791** James Gandon's Custom House built in Dublin

**1795** Orange Order formed by Ulster Protestants

**1759** Arthur Guinness buys the St. James's Gate Brewery in Dublin

**1793** Limited emancipation for Irish Catholics

# Famine and Emigration

Ration card from Famine period

T HE HISTORY of 19th-century Ireland is dominated by the Great Famine of 1845–8, which was caused by the total failure of the potato crop. Although Irish grain was still being exported to England, around one million people died from hunger or disease, with even more fleeing to North America. By 1900, the prefamine population of eight million had fallen by half. Rural hardship fueled a campaign for tenants' rights, which evolved into demands for independence from Britain. Great strides towards "Home Rule" were made in Parliament by the charismatic politician, Charles Stuart Parnell.

IRELAND IN **1851**

☐ *Areas where population fell by over 25% during the Famine*

**The ships** that brought the Irish to America were overcrowded and fever-ridden, and known as "coffin ships."

**Daniel O'Connell**
*Known as "The Liberator," O'Connell organized peaceful "monster rallies" of up to a million people in pursuit of Catholic emancipation. He was elected MP for Clare in 1828.*

**Castle Clinton** was used for processing new arrivals to New York prior to the construction of the huge depot on Ellis Island.

**The Boycotting of Landlords**
*In 1880, troops guarded the crops of Captain Boycott, the first notable victim of a campaign to ostracize landlords guilty of evicting tenants. His name later passed into the English language.*

## TIMELINE

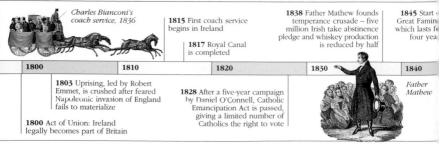

*Charles Bianconi's coach service, 1836*

**1815** First coach service begins in Ireland

**1817** Royal Canal is completed

**1838** Father Mathew founds temperance crusade – five million Irish take abstinence pledge and whiskey production is reduced by half

**1845** Start Great Famin which lasts fo four yea

| 1800 | 1810 | 1820 | 1830 | 1840 |
|------|------|------|------|------|

**1803** Uprising, led by Robert Emmet, is crushed after feared Napoleonic invasion of England fails to materialize

**1800** Act of Union: Ireland legally becomes part of Britain

**1828** After a five-year campaign by Daniel O'Connell, Catholic Emancipation Act is passed, giving a limited number of Catholics the right to vote

*Father Mathew*

**Eviction of Irish Farmers**
*In the late 1870s, agricultural prices plummeted. Starving tenant farmers fell into arrears and were mercilessly evicted. Their plight spawned the Land League, which lobbied successfully for reform.*

## THE IRISH ABROAD

One result of the Famine was the growth of a strong Irish community in the US. From the lowest rung of American society, the immigrants rose up the social scale and became rich by Irish Catholic standards. They sent money to causes back home, and as a well-organized lobby group put pressure on the American government to influence British policies in Ireland. A more militant group, Clan na Gael, sent veterans of the American Civil War to fight in the Fenian risings of 1865 and 1867.

***New Yorkers*** *stage a huge St. Patrick's Day parade, March 17, 1870.*

**The Irish** were widely perceived as illiterate peasants and were often given a hostile reception.

## IMMIGRANTS ARRIVE IN NEW YORK
The Irish who survived the journey to America landed at Castle Garden in New York, seen here in a painting by Samuel Waugh (1855). Although mainly country people, most new arrivals settled in Manhattan, often enduring horrific living conditions.

**Charles Stuart Parnell**
*A campaigner for the Land League and Home Rule, Parnell saw his political career ruined in 1890, when he was cited as co-respondent in a divorce case.*

---

*Dublin Exhibition*

**1853** Dublin Exhibition is opened by Queen Victoria

**1877** Charles Stuart Parnell becomes leader of the new Home Rule Party

**1884** Founding of Gaelic Athletic Association, first group to promote Irish traditions

**1892** Second Home Rule Bill is defeated

| 1850 | 1860 | 1870 | 1880 | 1890 |
|---|---|---|---|---|

**1867** Irish-Americans return home to fight in a rising led by the Irish Republican Brotherhood, also known as the Fenians

**1881** Parnell is jailed in Kilmainham, Dublin

**1886** British PM Gladstone sponsors first Home Rule Bill but is defeated by Parliament

**1848** Failure of the Young Ireland Uprising – a spontaneous response to insurrections elsewhere in Europe

**1879–82** Land War, led by Michael Davitt's Land League, campaigns for the reform of tenancy laws

# War and Independence

**P**LANS FOR IRISH HOME RULE were shelved because of World War I; however, the abortive Easter Rising of 1916 inspired new support for the Republican cause. In 1919 an unofficial Irish Parliament was established and a war began against the "occupying" British forces. The Anglo-

**Irish Free State stamp of 1922** Irish Treaty of 1921 divided the island in two, granting independence to the Irish Free State, while Northern Ireland remained in the United Kingdom. There followed a civil war between pro-Treaty and anti-Treaty factions in the South.

**IRELAND IN 1922**
- ▨ *Northern Ireland*
- ☐ *Irish Free State*

**The Unionist Party**
*Leader of the campaign against Home Rule was Dublin lawyer Edward Carson. In 1913 the Ulster Volunteer Force was formed to demand that six counties in Ulster remain part of the UK.*

**Sean J Heuston**

**Thomas McDonough**

**Major John McBride**

**The 1916 Service Medal**, issued to all who fought in the Easter Rising, depicts, on one side, the mythical Irish warrior Cuchulainn.

**William Pearse**

**Patrick Pearse**, a poet, read the Proclamation of the Republic from the steps of the GPO on Easter Monday.

**The Black and Tans**
*Named for their makeshift uniforms, these British troops – mostly demobbed World War I soldiers – carried out savage reprisals against the Irish in 1920–21.*

## TIMELINE

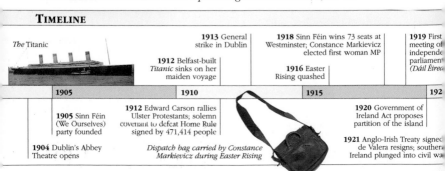

*The* Titanic

**1913** General strike in Dublin

**1912** Belfast-built *Titanic* sinks on her maiden voyage

**1916** Easter Rising quashed

**1918** Sinn Féin wins 73 seats at Westminster; Constance Markievicz elected first woman MP

**1919** First meeting of independe parliament (*Dáil Éirea*

| 1905 | 1910 | 1915 | 192 |
|---|---|---|---|

**1905** Sinn Féin (We Ourselves) party founded

**1904** Dublin's Abbey Theatre opens

**1912** Edward Carson rallies Ulster Protestants; solemn covenant to defeat Home Rule signed by 471,414 people

*Dispatch bag carried by Constance Markievicz during Easter Rising*

**1920** Government of Ireland Act proposes partition of the island

**1921** Anglo-Irish Treaty signed de Valera resigns; southern Ireland plunged into civil wa

### The General Post Office, Easter 1916
*What was supposed to be a national uprising
is confined to 2,500 armed insurgents in
Dublin. They managed to hold the GPO and
other public buildings for five days.*

**This Mauser rifle**, smuggled
in from Germany in 1914, was
used by rebels in the Rising.

Tom Clarke

James Connolly

Joseph Plunkett

**Mementoes**
of the Rising
at Dublin's
Kilmainham
Gaol (*see
p95*) include
this crucifix made
by a British soldier
from rifle bullets.

## EAMON DE VALERA (1882–1975)

After escaping execution for his part in
the Easter Rising, American-born de
Valera went on to dominate Irish politics
for almost 60 years. The opposition of
his party, Sinn Fein, to the Anglo-Irish
Treaty of 1921 plunged the new Irish
Free State into civil war. After forming
a new party, Fianna
Fáil, he became
Prime Minister
(*Taoiseach*) in
1932. De Valera
remained in
office until
1948, with
further terms
in the 1950s.
Between 1959
and 1973 he was
President of Ireland.

**THE SHADOW
OF THE GUNMAN**

KEEP
IT
FROM
YOUR HOME

VOTE
FOR

**CUMANN
NA nGAEDHEAL**

**Election Poster**
*Cumann na nGaedheal, the
pro-Treaty party in the Civil
War, won the Free State's
first general election in 1923.
It merged with other parties
in 1933 to form Fine Gael.*

## LEADERS OF THE 1916 RISING
This collage portrait shows 14 leaders of the Easter
Rising, who were all court-martialed and shot at
Kilmainham Gaol. The brutality of their executions
(the badly injured James Connolly was tied to a
chair before being shot) changed public opinion of
the Rising and guaranteed their status as martyrs.

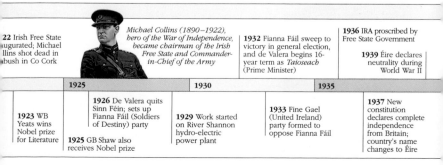

**22** Irish Free State
inaugurated; Michael
Collins shot dead in
ambush in Co Cork

*Michael Collins (1890–1922),
hero of the War of Independence,
became chairman of the Irish
Free State and Commander-
in-Chief of the Army*

**1932** Fianna Fáil sweep to
victory in general election,
and de Valera begins 16-
year term as *Taoiseach*
(Prime Minister)

**1936** IRA proscribed by
Free State Government

**1939** Éire declares
neutrality during
World War II

|  | 1925 | | 1930 | | 1935 | |
|---|---|---|---|---|---|---|

**1923** WB
Yeats wins
Nobel prize
for Literature

**1926** De Valera quits
Sinn Féin; sets up
Fianna Fáil (Soldiers
of Destiny) party

**1925** GB Shaw also
receives Nobel prize

**1929** Work started
on River Shannon
hydro-electric
power plant

**1933** Fine Gael
(United Ireland)
party formed to
oppose Fianna Fáil

**1937** New
constitution
declares complete
independence
from Britain;
country's name
changes to Éire

# Modern Ireland

Mary Robinson, Ireland's first woman President

Since joining the European Economic Community (now called the European Union) in 1973, the Irish Republic has done much to modernize its traditional rural-based economy. There have been social changes too, and laws prohibiting abortion and divorce have slowly been relaxed. Meanwhile, Northern Ireland has lived through more than 25 years of bombings and shootings, with British soldiers permanently on the streets. Industry declined during the Troubles, however the 1994 cease-fire has brought new hope to the province.

**1972** Bloody Sunday – British soldiers shoot dead 13 demonstrators in Derry. Northern Ireland Parliament is suspended and direct rule from Westminster imposed

**1970** Reverend Ian Paisley, a radical Protestant Unionist, wins the Bannside special election

**1969** Violent clashes between the police and demonstrators in Belfast and Derry. British troops sent to restore order

**1956** IRA launches a terrorism campaign along the border with Northern Ireland which lasts until 1962

**1967** Northern Ireland Civil Rights Association is set up to fight discrimination against Catholics

| NORTHERN IRELAND | | |
|---|---|---|
| 1945 | 1955 | 1965 |
| **REPUBLIC OF IRELAND** | | |

**1949** New government under John A Costello. Country changes name from Éire to Republic of Ireland and leaves British Commonwealth

**1959** Eamon de Valera resigns as *Taoiseach* (Prime Minister) and is later elected President

**1955** Republic of Ireland joins United Nations. Irish troops have played an important role in UN peace-keeping missions around the world ever since

**1969** Samuel Beckett, seen here rehearsing one of his own plays, is awarded the Nobel prize for literature, but does not go to Oslo to receive the honor

**1963** John F Kennedy, the first American President of Irish Catholic descent, visits Ireland. He is pictured here with President Eamon de Valera

**1947** Statue of Queen Victoria is removed from the courtyard in front of the Irish Parliament in Dublin

**1973** Republic of Ireland joins the European Economic Community at same time as the UK. Membership has given the country access to much-needed development grants

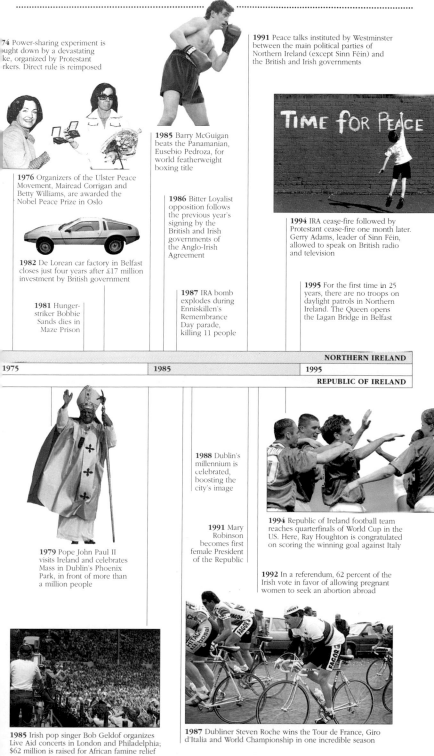

**74** Power-sharing experiment is ~~b~~ught down by a devastating ~~stri~~ke, organized by Protestant ~~wo~~rkers. Direct rule is reimposed

**1976** Organizers of the Ulster Peace Movement, Mairead Corrigan and Betty Williams, are awarded the Nobel Peace Prize in Oslo

**1982** De Lorean car factory in Belfast closes just four years after £17 million investment by British government

**1981** Hunger-striker Bobbie Sands dies in Maze Prison

**1985** Barry McGuigan beats the Panamanian, Eusebio Pedroza, for world featherweight boxing title

**1986** Bitter Loyalist opposition follows the previous year's signing by the British and Irish governments of the Anglo-Irish Agreement

**1987** IRA bomb explodes during Enniskillen's Remembrance Day parade, killing 11 people

**1991** Peace talks instituted by Westminster between the main political parties of Northern Ireland (except Sinn Féin) and the British and Irish governments

**1994** IRA cease-fire followed by Protestant cease-fire one month later. Gerry Adams, leader of Sinn Féin, allowed to speak on British radio and television

**1995** For the first time in 25 years, there are no troops on daylight patrols in Northern Ireland. The Queen opens the Lagan Bridge in Belfast

**NORTHERN IRELAND**

1975    1985    1995

**REPUBLIC OF IRELAND**

**1988** Dublin's millennium is celebrated, boosting the city's image

**1991** Mary Robinson becomes first female President of the Republic

**1979** Pope John Paul II visits Ireland and celebrates Mass in Dublin's Phoenix Park, in front of more than a million people

**1994** Republic of Ireland football team reaches quarterfinals of World Cup in the US. Here, Ray Houghton is congratulated on scoring the winning goal against Italy

**1992** In a referendum, 62 percent of the Irish vote in favor of allowing pregnant women to seek an abortion abroad

**1985** Irish pop singer Bob Geldof organizes Live Aid concerts in London and Philadelphia; $62 million is raised for African famine relief

**1987** Dubliner Steven Roche wins the Tour de France, Giro d'Italia and World Championship in one incredible season

# IRELAND THROUGH THE YEAR

POPULAR MONTHS for visiting Ireland are July and August, though whatever the season it's rarely crowded. June and September can be pleasant but never count on the weather, because Ireland's lush beauty is the product of a wet climate. Be aware that most tourist sights are open from Easter to September but have restricted opening hours or close in the off season. During spring and summer, festivals are

Ladies' Day at Dublin Horse Show

held in honor of everything from food to religion. A common thread is music, and few festivities are complete without it. Ireland is at its best when it has something to celebrate, so it's an inspired choice for Christmas or New Year. Watch for the word *fleadh* (festival) on your travels but remember that the Irish are a spontaneous people: festivities can spring from the air, or from a tune on a fiddle.

Dublin's annual parade to celebrate St. Patrick's Day (March 17)

## SPRING

ST. PATRICK'S DAY is often said to mark the beginning of the tourist season. The spring bank holiday weekend in May, when accommodations are in short supply, is celebrated with music in most places. After the quiet winter months, festivals and events start to become more common.

## MARCH

**Adare Jazz Festival** *(mid-Mar, see p186).* Staged in pubs and hotels throughout the town over five days.
**St. Patrick's Day** *(Mar 17).* Parades and pilgrimages held at Downpatrick, Armagh, Dublin, Cork, Limerick and many other places.
**Horse Ploughing Match and Heavy Horse Show**, Bally-castle *(Mar 17, see p258).* The annual competition is more than 100 years old.

A St. Patrick's Day float advertising Guinness

## APRIL

**Feis Ceoil**, Dublin *(early Apr).* A classical music festival held at many different places throughout the city.
**Pan Celtic Festival**, Tralee *(mid-Apr, see p148).* A lively celebration of Celtic culture, with music, dance and song.
**Cork Choral Festival** *(late Apr–May, see pp166–7).*

## MAY

**Belfast Civic Festival and Lord Mayor's Show** *(mid-May, see pp268–71).* Street parade with bands and floats.
**Royal Ulster Agriculture Society Show**, Belfast *(mid-May).* A three-day show with diverse events ranging from sheep-shearing competitions to fashion shows.
**"A Taste of Baltimore" Shellfish Festival** *(end May, see p162).*
**Fleadh Nua**, Ennis, *end May, see p181).* Four days of traditional Irish music, songs and dance.

## SUMMER

FOR THE VISITOR, summer represents the height of the festive calendar. This is the busiest time of year for organized events, from music and arts festivals to lively local race meetings, summer schools and matchmaking festivals. Book accommodations ahead if your plans include a popular festival.

Beach races at Laytown (August)

## JUNE

**County Wicklow Garden Festival** *(all month).* Held at private and public gardens around the county, including Powerscourt *(see pp126–7).*
**An Tostal**, Drumshanbo, Co Leitrim *(mid-Jun).* A pageant of Irish music and dance.
**Maracycle**, Belfast and Dublin *(mid-Jun).* Many thousands of people cycle each way between the two cities.
**Bloomsday**, Dublin *(Jun 16).* Lectures, pub talks and walks to celebrate James Joyce's greatest novel, *Ulysses.*
**Scurlogstown Olympiad Celtic Festival**, Trim *(mid-Jun, see p240).* Traditional Irish music, dance, fair and

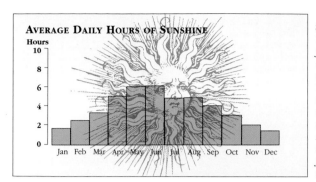

**AVERAGE DAILY HOURS OF SUNSHINE**

**Sunshine Chart**
*The chart gives figures for Dublin, though conditions are similar around the country. The Southeast enjoys more sunshine hours than any other part of Ireland, while Northern Ireland receives marginally fewer hours of sun than the Republic.*

selection of a festival queen.
**Music in Great Irish Houses** *(second and third weeks).* Classical music recitals in grand settings at various places.
**Castle Ward Opera**, Strangford *(end Jun, see p276).* Opera festival in the grounds of 18th-century stately home.
**County Wexford Strawberry Fair**, Enniscorthy *(end Jun–early Jul, see p141).* Includes a craft fair, music, street theater and, of course, strawberries.

## JULY

**Battle of the Boyne Day** *(12 Jul, see p236).* Members of the Orange Order march in towns across Northern Ireland to celebrate the Protestants' landmark victory over King James II's Catholic army in 1690.
**Cork Regatta Week**, Crosshaven, Co Cork *(mid-Jul).*
**Galway Arts Festival** *(third & fourth weeks, see pp202–3).* Processions, concerts, street theater, children's shows and other events in the medieval city center. Followed immediately by Galway's popular five-day race meeting.

Traditional sailing craft in the Cruinniu na mBad at Kinvarra (August)

**Mary from Dungloe International Festival**, Dungloe *(last week, see p220).* Dancing, music and selection of "Mary," the beauty queen.
**Ballyshannon International Folk Festival** *(end Jul, see p223).* Three days of traditional Irish music.
**Lughnasa Fair**, Carrickfergus Castle *(end Jul, see p267).* A popular medieval-style fair.
**O'Carolan Harp and Traditional Music Festival**, Keadue, Co Roscommon *(end Jul–early Aug).* Music recitals and traditional dance.

Orangemen parading on Battle of the Boyne Day

## AUGUST

**Letterkenny Folk Festival** *(early Aug, see p219).* A week-long celebration.
**Stradbally Steam-engine Rally**, Co Laois *(early Aug).* Many types of steam-engine join this rally.

**Dublin Horse Show** *(second week).* A premier showjumping competition and important social event.
**Puck Fair**, Killorglin, Co Kerry *(mid-Aug, see p157).* A wild goat is crowned "king" at this traditional festival.
**Laytown Beach Races**, Co Meath *(mid-Aug).* Horse races on the sand.
**Blessing of the Sea** *(second or third Sunday).* Held in seaside towns all over Ireland.
**Oul' Lammas Fair**, Ballycastle *(mid-Aug, see p258).* A popular fair that is particularly famous for its edible seaweed.
**Kilkenny Arts Week** *(fourth week, see pp134–6).* A major arts festival including poetry, film, crafts and classical music.
**Rose of Tralee Festival**, *(end Aug, see p148).* Bands, processions, dancing and selection of the "Rose."
**Cruinniú na mBad**, Kinvarra *(end Aug, see pp203–4).* Various types of traditional sailing craft take part in this "gathering of the boats."

Steam engine at Stradbally Rally (August)

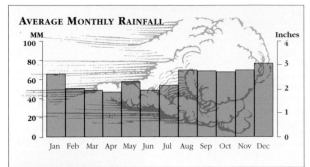

AVERAGE MONTHLY RAINFALL

**Rainfall Chart**
*Ireland is one of the wettest countries in Europe, with rainfall distributed evenly throughout the year. The figures displayed here are for Dublin. The West has the heaviest annual rainfall, while the Southeast is usually the driest region.*

**Galway Oyster Festival (September)**

## AUTUMN

OYSTERS AND OPERA are the two big events in autumn. There are also festivals devoted to jazz, film and music. The October bank holiday weekend is celebrated with music in many towns; though it is off season, it can be difficult to find accommodations.

## SEPTEMBER

**All-Ireland Hurling Final**, Croke Park, Dublin *(first Sunday, see p27)*.
**Lisdoonvarna Matchmaking Festival** *(all month and first*

week of Oct, see p180). Single people gather together for traditional music and dance.
**Waterford International Festival of Light Opera** *(mid-Sep–early Oct, see p329)*. Musicals and operettas at the Theatre Royal.
**All-Ireland Football Final**, Croke Park, Dublin *(3rd Sunday, see p27)*. Gaelic football final.
**Sligo Arts Festival** *(last week, see p226)*. Street entertainment, jazz, Irish music and dance.
**Galway Oyster Festival** *(end Sep, see pp202–3)*. Oyster tastings at different places.

## OCTOBER

**Octoberfest**, Londonderry *(all month, see pp250–51)*. Dance, poetry, film, comedy, theater and music.
**Cork Film Festival** *(early Oct, see pp166–7)*. Irish and international films.
**Kinsale Gourmet Festival** *(early Oct, see pp164–5)*. Superb food is served in the

**Horse and trap at Lisdoonvarna fair**

**All-Ireland Hurling at Croke Park, Dublin**

hotels, restaurants and pubs of Ireland's "Gourmet Capital."
**Ballinasloe Fair**, Co Galway *(first week)*. One of Europe's oldest horse fairs, staged amid lively street entertainment.
**Dublin Theatre Festival** *(first and second week)*. Features works by both Irish and foreign playwrights.
**Wexford Opera Festival** *(last week Oct–first week Nov, see p329)*. A festival of lesser known operas.
**Hallowe'en (Shamhana)** *(Oct 31)*. An occasion celebrated all over the country.
**Cork Jazz Festival** *(end Oct, see pp166–7)*. An extremely popular festival, with music all over the city.

## NOVEMBER

**Sligo International Choral Festival** *(early Nov, see p226)*. Choirs from around the world in concert and competition.
**Carrick Theatre Festival**, Carrick-on-Shannon, Co Leitrim *(mid-Nov, see p227)*. One-act plays in qualifying festival for the All-Ireland Drama Festival.
**Belfast Festival at Queen's**, Queen's University *(last three weeks, see pp268–71)*. Arts festival featuring drama, ballet, film and all types of music from classical to jazz.

**Traditional horse fair at Ballinasloe in County Galway (October)**

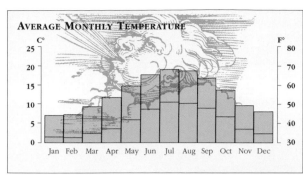

**Temperature Chart**
*This chart gives the average minimum and maximum temperatures for the city of Dublin. Winter is mild throughout Ireland, except in the high mountain ranges, while the warmest summer temperatures are in the Southeast.*

## WINTER

**A**LTHOUGH a quiet time for festivals, there's a range of entertainment including musical and theatrical events. Christmas is the busiest social period and there are plenty of informal celebrations. There is also a wide choice of National Hunt race meetings *(see p26)*.

## DECEMBER

**Pantomime Season** *(Dec–Jan)*. Traditional pantomime performed at many theaters throughout Ireland.
**Leopardstown Races** *(Dec 26, see p121)*. The biggest meeting held on this traditional day for racing. There are other fixtures at Limerick and Down Royal.
**St. Stephen's Day** *(Dec 26)*. Catholic boys traditionally dress up as Wren boys (chimney sweeps with blackened faces) and sing hymns to raise money for charitable causes.

Young boys dressed up as Wren boys on St. Stephen's Day

## JANUARY

**Salmon and Sea Trout Season** *(Jan 1–end Sep)*. Start of the season for one of the most popular pastimes in Ireland.

## FEBRUARY

**Dublin Film Festival** *(end Feb–early Mar)*. International films at various spots.
**Belfast Music Festival** *(end Feb–mid-Mar)*. Young people take part in music (and speech and drama) competitions.
**Five Nations Rugby Tournament**, Lansdowne Road, Dublin *(varying Saturdays Feb–Apr, see p26)*.

---

### PUBLIC HOLIDAYS

**New Year's Day** (Jan 1)
**St. Patrick's Day** (Mar 17)
**Good Friday**
**Easter Monday**
**May Day** (May 1)
**Spring Bank Holiday** (Northern Ireland: last Mon in May)
**June Bank Holiday** (Republic: first Mon in Jun)
**Battle of the Boyne Day** (Northern Ireland: Jul 12)
**August Bank Holiday** (first Mon in Aug)
**Summer Bank Holiday** (Northern Ireland: last Mon in Aug)
**October Bank Holiday** (last Mon in Oct)
**Christmas Day** (Dec 25)
**St. Stephen's Day** (Republic: Dec 26)
**Boxing Day** (Northern Ireland: Dec 26)

---

Glendalough *(see pp132–3)* in the snow

# DUBLIN AREA BY AREA

DUBLIN AT A GLANCE 52-53
SOUTHEAST DUBLIN 54-69
SOUTHWEST DUBLIN 70-81
NORTH OF THE LIFFEY 82-91
FARTHER AFIELD 92-101
ENTERTAINMENT IN DUBLIN 102-107
DUBLIN STREET FINDER 108-111

# Dublin at a Glance

IRELAND'S CAPITAL has a wealth of attractions, most within walking distance of each other. For the purpose of this guide, central Dublin has been divided into three sections: *Southeast Dublin*, heart of the modern city and home to the prestigious Trinity College; *Southwest Dublin*, site of the old city around Dublin Castle; and *North of the Liffey*, the area around the imposing O'Connell Street. The map references given for sights in the city refer to the *Dublin Street Finder* on pages 110–111.

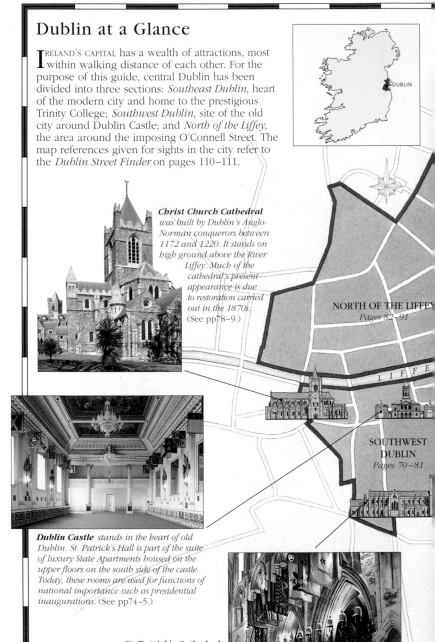

***Christ Church Cathedral***
*was built by Dublin's Anglo-Norman conquerors between 1172 and 1220. It stands on high ground above the River Liffey. Much of the cathedral's present appearance is due to restoration carried out in the 1870s. (See pp78–9.)*

**NORTH OF THE LIFFEY**
*Pages 82–91*

LIFFE

**SOUTHWEST DUBLIN**
*Pages 70–81*

***Dublin Castle*** *stands in the heart of old Dublin. St. Patrick's Hall is part of the suite of luxury State Apartments housed on the upper floors on the south side of the castle. Today, these rooms are used for functions of national importance such as presidential inaugurations. (See pp74–5.)*

***St. Patrick's Cathedral***
*has a spectacular choir displaying banners and stalls decorated with the insignia of the Knights of St. Patrick. The cathedral also holds Ireland's largest and most beautiful organ, as well as memorials to Dean Jonathan Swift and prominent Anglo-Irish families. (See pp80–81.)*

**O'Connell Street**, *Dublin's main and busiest thoroughfare, has a fine mix of architectural styles and a grand central mall punctuated with statues of famous Irish citizens. Just off O'Connell Street, on Moore Street, is a colorful and lively market. (See pp86–7.)*

**The Custom House**, *a classic Georgian public building by James Gandon, was built between 1781 and 1791. The sculpted heads on the keystones are personifications of the rivers of Ireland; the one shown above represents the River Foyle. (See p86.)*

**Trinity College** *is home to the Old Library which contains priceless, illuminated manuscripts. These include the* Book of Durrow, *which dates from the middle of the 7th century. (See pp60–62.)*

**SOUTHEAST DUBLIN**
*Pages 54–69*

| 0 meters | 400 |
| 0 yards | 400 |

**The National Gallery** *was opened in 1864. Housed on two floors, the well-organized gallery holds an eclectic collection, particularly strong on Irish and Italian paintings. The gallery's most prized painting is its recent acquisition,* The Taking of Christ, *by Caravaggio. (See pp68–9.)*

**The National Museum** *has an impressive collection of artifacts dating from the Stone Age to the 20th century. The Ardagh Chalice (c. 800 AD) is one of the many Celtic Christian treasures on display. (See pp64–5.)*

# SOUTHEAST DUBLIN

**D**ESPITE ITS location close to the old walled city, this part of Dublin remained virtually undeveloped until the founding of Trinity College in 1592. Even then, it was almost a hundred years before the ancient common land farther south was enclosed to create St. Stephen's Green, a spacious city park.

The mid-18th century saw the beginning of a construction boom in the area. During this time, magnificent public buildings such as the Old Library at Trinity College, Leinster House and the Bank of Ireland were built. However, the most conspicuous reminders of Georgian Dublin are the beautiful squares and terraces around

*Georgian doorknocker in Merrion Square*

Merrion Square. Many of these buildings still have their original features, including doorknockers, fanlights and wrought-iron balconies.

Today, Southeast Dublin is very much the tourist heart of the city: few visitors can resist the lively atmosphere and attractive stores of Grafton Street. The area is also home to much of Ireland's cultural heritage. The National Gallery has a good collection of Irish and European paintings while the National Museum has superb displays of Irish Bronze Age gold and early Christian treasures. Nearby, the fascinating Natural History Museum has preserved its wonderful Victorian interior.

## SIGHTS AT A GLANCE

**Museums, Libraries and Galleries**
*National Gallery pp68–9* ⓫
National Library ❽
*National Museum pp64–5* ❼
Natural History Museum ❿
Royal Hibernian Academy ⓭

**Historic Buildings**
Bank of Ireland ❶
Leinster House ❾
Mansion House ❺
*Trinity College pp60–61* ❷

**Historic Streets**
Fitzwilliam Square ⓮
Grafton Street ❸
Merrion Square ⓬

**Churches**
St. Ann's Church ❻

**Parks and Gardens**
St. Stephen's Green ❹

### KEY

| | |
|---|---|
| ▨ | Street-by-Street map *See pp56–7* |
| 🚇 | Railroad station |
| 🚉 | DART station |
| P | Parking |
| ℹ | Tourist information |

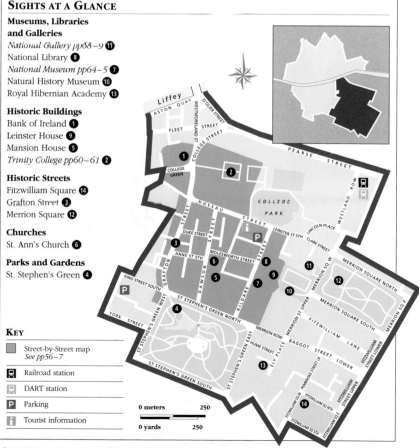

◁ **Marble bust of Jonathan Swift in the Old Library, Trinity College**

# Street-by-Street: Southeast Dublin

T HE AREA AROUND COLLEGE GREEN, dominated by the
façades of the Bank of Ireland and Trinity College, is
very much the heart of Dublin. The alleys and malls
cutting across busy pedestrianized Grafton Street boast
many of Dublin's better stores, hotels and restaurants. Just
off Kildare Street are the Irish Parliament, the National
Library and the National Museum. To escape the city bustle
many head for sanctuary in St. Stephen's Green, which is
overlooked by fine Georgian buildings.

**To Dublin Castle**

**COLLEGE GREEN**

**Bank of Ireland**
*This grand Georgian
building was origi-
nally built as the
Irish Parliament* ❶

**Statue of Molly
Malone (1988)**

**Grafton Street**
*Bewley's Oriental Café is the social hub of
this busy pedestrian street, alive with
talented street performers* ❸

**GRAFTON STREET**

**DUKE ST**

**St. Ann's Church**
*The striking façade of
the 18th-century
church was
added in 1868.
The interior
features lovely
stained-glass
windows* ❻

**ANNE ST STH**

**Mansion House**
*This has been the official
residence of Dublin's Lord
Mayor since 1715* ❺

**DAWSON STREET**

**Fusiliers' Arch (1907)**

**ST. STEPHEN'S GREEN NORTH**

★ **St. Stephen's Green**
*The relaxing city park is surrounded by many
fine buildings. In summer, lunchtime
concerts attract tourists and workers alike* ❹

**To O'Connell Bridge**

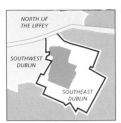

★ **Trinity College**
*Pomodoro's sculpture,*
Sphere within Sphere
*(1982), adds a modern
dimension to the
grand buildings
of the campus* ➋

**National Library**
*Saintly cherubs appear on the frieze
around the library's magnificent old
reading room, once a hangout of
novelist James Joyce* ➑

**Leinster House**
*This grand
house has been
the home of the
Irish Parliament
since 1922* ➒

★ **National Museum**
*The museum's
collection of Irish
antiquities includes a
mysterious bronze
object known as the
Petrie Crown (2nd
century AD)* ➐

NASSAU STREET

FREDERICK STREET

MOLESWORTH STREET

KILDARE STREET

**The Shelbourne Hotel**,
built in 1867, dominates the
north side of St. Stephen's Green.
It is a popular spot with tourists
and locals for afternoon tea.

**STAR SIGHTS**

★ **Trinity College**

★ **National Museum**

★ **St. Stephen's Green**

| 0 meters | 50 |
| 0 yards | 50 |

**KEY**

– – – Suggested route

Original chamber of the Irish House of Lords at the Bank of Ireland

# Bank of Ireland ❶

2 College Green. **Map** D3. 🚇 *661 5933 ext 2265.* 🕐 *10am–4pm Mon– Wed & Fri, 10am–5pm Thu.* 🔒 *public hols.* **House of Lords** 🕐 *10:30am, 11:30am & 1:45pm Tue or by appt.*

THE PRESTIGIOUS offices of Ireland's national bank began life as the first specially built parliament house in Europe. The original central section was started by Irish architect Edward Lovett Pearce and completed in 1739 after his death. Sadly, Pearce's masterpiece, the great octagonal chamber of the House of Commons *(see p38)*, was destroyed by fire in 1792. The House of Lords, however, remains gloriously intact. Attendants lead tours that point out the coffered ceiling and oak paneling. There are also huge tapestries of the *Battle of the Boyne* and the *Siege of Londonderry*, and a splendid 1,233-piece crystal chandelier dating from 1788.

The east portico was added by architect James Gandon in 1785. Further additions to the building were made around 1797.

After the dissolution of the Irish Parliament in 1800, the Bank of Ireland bought the building. The present structure was then completed in 1808 with the transformation of the former lobby of the House of Commons into a magnificent cash office and the addition of a curving screen wall and the Foster Place annex.

At the front of the bank on College Green – common grazing land in the 17th century – is a statue (1879) by John Foley of Henry Grattan *(see p38)*, the most formidable leader of the old parliament.

# Trinity College ❷

*See pp60–61.*

# Grafton Street ❸

**Map** D4.

THE SPINE OF DUBLIN'S most popular and stylish shopping district runs south from Trinity College to the glass St. Stephen's Green Shopping Center. At the junction with Nassau Street is a statue by Jean Rynhart of *Molly Malone* (1988), the celebrated street trader from the traditional song "Molly Malone." This pedestrianized strip, characterized by energetic street musicians and theater artists,

Bronze statue of *Molly Malone* on Grafton Street

boasts Brown Thomas, one of Dublin's finest department stores *(see p325)*. However, the street's most famous landmark is Bewley's Oriental Café at No. 78 *(see p306)*. Although not the oldest branch of this 150-year-old Dublin institution, this is Bewley's most popular location. It stands on the site of Samuel Whyte's school, whose illustrious roll included Robert Emmet *(see p75)*, leader of the 1803 Rebellion, and the Duke of Wellington.

Despite the removal of the old wooden pews, the café retains its Victorian ambience, especially in the James Joyce Room on the first floor.

# St. Stephen's Green ❹

**Map** D5. 🕐 *daylight hours.* **Newman House** 85–86 St. Stephen's Green. 🚇 *706 7422.* 🕐 *Jun–Sep: 10am–4:30pm Tue–Fri, 2–4:30pm Sat, 11am–2pm Sun (Oct–May: group tours only).* 🔒 *public hols.* 🏛 🎥

Royal College of Surgeons, which overlooks St. Stephen's Green

ORIGINALLY one of three ancient commons in the old city, St. Stephen's Green was enclosed in 1664. The 9-ha (22-acre) green was laid out in its present form in 1880, using a grant given by Lord Ardilaun, a member of the Guinness family. Landscaped with flowerbeds, trees, a fountain and a lake, the green is dotted with memorials to eminent Dubliners, including Ardilaun himself. There is a bust of James Joyce *(see p88)*, and a memorial by Henry Moore (1967) dedicated to WB Yeats *(see pp224–5)*. At

**Dubliners relaxing by the lake in St. Stephen's Green**

the Merrion Row corner stands a massive monument (1967) by Edward Delaney to 18th-century nationalist leader Wolfe Tone – it is known locally as "Tonehenge." The 1887 bandstand is still the focal point for free daytime concerts in summer.

The imposing Royal College of Surgeons stands on the west side. Built in 1806, it was commandeered by rebel troops under Countess Constance Markievicz in the 1916 Rising (see pp42–3) and its columns still bear the marks of bullets from the fighting.

The busiest side of the Green is the north, known during the 19th century as the Beaux' Walk and still home to several gentlemen's clubs. The most prominent building is the venerable Shelbourne Hotel (see p287). Dating back to 1867, its entrance is adorned by statues of Nubian princesses and attendant slaves. It is well worth going in for a look at the chandeliered foyer, or to stop for afternoon tea in the Lord Mayor's Lounge.

Situated on the south side is Newman House, home of the Catholic University of Ireland (now part of University College). Opened in 1854, its first rector was English theologian John Henry Newman. Famous past pupils include Patrick Pearse, a leader of the 1916 Rising, former Taoiseach Eamon de Valera (see p43) and author James Joyce.

Tours reveal some of the best Georgian interior decor to survive in the city. The walls and ceilings of the Apollo Room and Parlor at No. 85 are festooned with intricate Baroque stuccowork (1739) by the Swiss brothers Paolo and Filippo Francini. The Bishops' Room at No. 86 is decorated with heavy 19th-century furniture.

The small University Church (1856) next door has a colorful, richly marbled Byzantine interior. Also on the south side of St. Stephen's Green is Iveagh House, a town house once owned by the Guinness family and now the Department of Foreign Affairs.

## Mansion House ❺

Dawson St. **Map** E4. ⬤ to the public.

SET BACK from Dawson Street by a neat cobbled forecourt, the Mansion House is an attractive Queen Anne-style building. It was built in 1710 for the aristocrat Joshua Dawson, after whom the street is named. The Dublin Corporation bought it from him five years later as the official residence of the city's Lord Mayor. A gray stucco façade was added in Victorian times.

The Dáil Éireann (see p63), which adopted the Declaration of Independence, first met here on January 21, 1919. The building is now used mostly for civic functions and receptions.

## St. Ann's Church ❻

Dawson St. **Map** E4. ⬤ 676 7727. ◷ 10am–4pm Mon–Fri.

FOUNDED IN 1707, St. Ann's striking Romanesque façade was added in 1868. Inside is a series of colorful stained glass windows, dating from the mid-19th century. The church has a long tradition of charity work: in 1723 Lord Newton left a bequest to the church to buy bread for the poor. The original shelf for the bread still stands next to the altar.

Famous past parishioners include Wolfe Tone (see p39), who was married here in 1785, Douglas Hyde (see p43) and Bram Stoker (1847–1912), author of Dracula.

**Detail of window depicting Faith, Hope and Charity, St. Ann's Church**

# Trinity College ❷

**Trinity College coat of arms**

T RINITY COLLEGE was founded in 1592 by Queen Elizabeth I on the site of an Augustinian monastery. Originally a Protestant college, it was not until the 1970s that Catholics started attending the university. Among its many famous students were playwrights Oliver Goldsmith and Samuel Beckett, and political writer Edmund Burke. Trinity's lawns and cobbled quads provide a pleasant haven in the heart of the city. The major attractions are the Old Library and the *Book of Kells*, housed in the Treasury with other illuminated manuscripts.

**★ Campanile**
*The 30-m (98-ft) bell tower was built in 1853 by Sir Charles Lanyon, architect of Queen's University, Belfast (see p270).*

**Reclining Connected Forms (1969) by Henry Moore**

**Dining Hall (1761)**

**Chapel** *(1798)*
*This is the only chapel in the Republic to be shared by all denominations. The painted window above the altar dates from 1867.*

**Parliament Square**

**Statue of Edmund Burke (1868) by John Foley**

**Main entrance**

## SAMUEL BECKETT (1906–89)

Nobel prizewinner Samuel Beckett was born at Foxrock, south of Dublin. In 1923 he entered Trinity, where he was placed first in his modern literature class. He was also an avid member of the college cricket team. Forsaking Ireland, Beckett moved to France in the early 1930s. Many of his major works such as *Waiting for Godot* (1951) were written first in French, and later translated, by Beckett, into English.

**Statue of Oliver Goldsmith (1864) by John Foley**

**Provost's House (c. 1760)**

**Examination Hall**
*Completed in 1791 to a design by Sir William Chambers, the hall features a gilded oak chandelier and ornate ceilings by Michael Stapleton.*

**Library Square**
*The redbrick building (known as the Rubrics) on the east side of Library Square was built around 1700 and is the oldest surviving part of the college.*

**VISITORS' CHECKLIST**

College Green. **Map** D3. 677
2941. DART to Tara Street.
14, 15, 46 & many other
routes. **Old Library and Treasury**
9:30am– 5:30pm Mon–Sat
(last adm: 5pm), noon–5pm Sun
& some public hols (last adm:
4:30pm). 10 days at
Christmas. by
arrangement. **Chapel** 9am–
6pm Mon–Fri. **Douglas Hyde
Gallery** for exhibitions only.

**Shop and entrance to
Old Library**

**The Museum Building**, completed in
1857, is noted for its Venetian exterior,
and its magnificent multicolored hall
and double-domed roof.

**New Square**

***Sphere within Sphere***
(1982) was given to the
college by its sculptor
Arnaldo Pomodoro.

**Berkeley Library
Building by Paul
Koralek (1967)**

**Fellows' Square**

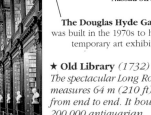

**★ Treasury**
*This detail is from
the* Book of Durrow,
*one of the other
magnificent illuminated
manuscripts housed in
the Treasury along with
the celebrated* Book of
Kells *(see p62).*

**Entrance from
Nassau Street**

**The Douglas Hyde Gallery**
was built in the 1970s to house
temporary art exhibitions.

**★ Old Library** *(1732)*
*The spectacular Long Room
measures 64 m (210 ft)
from end to end. It houses
200,000 antiquarian
texts, marble busts of
scholars and the oldest
surviving harp in Ireland.*

**STAR FEATURES**

★ **Old Library**

★ **Treasury**

★ **Campanile**

# The Book of Kells

THE MOST RICHLY decorated of Ireland's medieval illuminated manuscripts, the *Book of Kells* may have been the work of monks from Iona, who fled to Kells *(see p233)* in AD 806 after a Viking raid. The book, which was moved to Trinity College *(see p60–61)* in the 17th century, contains the four gospels in Latin. The scribes who copied the texts also embellished their calligraphy with intricate interlacing spirals as well as human figures and animals. Some of the dyes used were imported from as far as the Middle East.

**Pair of moths**

**Stylized angel**

**The Greek letter "X"**

***The symbols** of the four evangelists are used as decoration throughout the book. The figure of the man symbolizes St. Matthew.*

**The letter** that looks like a "P" is a Greek "R."

**The letter "I"**

**Interlacing motifs**

btzheptoo

**Cat watching rats**

**Rats eating** bread could be a reference to sinners taking Holy Communion. The symbolism of the animals and people decorating the manuscript is often hard to interpret.

## MONOGRAM PAGE

This, the most elaborate page of the book, contains the first three words of St. Matthew's account of the birth of Christ. The first word "XRI" is an abbreviation of "Christi."

***A full-page portrait** of St. Matthew, shown standing barefoot in front of a throne, precedes the opening words of his gospel.*

***The text** is in a beautifully rounded Celtic script with brightly ornamented initial letters. Animal and human forms are often used to decorate the end of a line.*

**The magnificent domed Reading Room on the first floor of the National Library**

## National Museum ❼

See pp64–5.

## National Library ❽

Kildare St. **Map** E4. **⒞** 661 8811. ☐ Jan–Nov: 10am–9pm Mon, 2–9pm Tue & Wed, 10am–5pm Thu & Fri, 10am–1pm Sat. ● public hols.

Dᴇsɪɢɴᴇᴅ ʙʏ Sir Thomas Deane, the National Library was opened in 1890. It was built to house the collection of the Royal Dublin Society, which was formed in 1731 to promote the arts and sciences and improve conditions for the poor. On display in the entrance hall are temporary exhibitions of treasures from the library's archive. This includes manuscripts by playwright George Bernard Shaw, and politician and liberator, Daniel O'Connell (see p40). The 13th-century manuscript of Giraldus Cambrensis's *Topographia Hiberniae* is a prized acquisition, as is the huge collection of photographs of Victorian Ireland.

The first-floor Reading Room (where Joyce sited the literary debate in *Ulysses*) has well-worn desks and green-shaded lamps. Just ask an attendant for a visitor's pass. There is also a small genealogy exhibit; a more extensive display,

along with details on how to trace family trees, can be found at the Heraldic Museum in the Genealogical Office a few doors down at Nos. 2 and 3 Kildare Street.

## Leinster House ❾

Kildare St. **Map** E4. **⒞** 678 9911. ● to the public. ⒢ by arrangement, ask at Kildare St. entrance or phone for details.

Tʜɪs sᴛᴀᴛᴇʟʏ ᴍᴀɴsɪᴏɴ houses the *Dáil* and the *Seanad* – the two chambers of the Irish Parliament. It was originally

built for the Duke of Leinster in 1745. Designed by German-born architect Richard Castle, the Kildare Street façade resembles that of a large town house. However, the rear, looking on to Merrion Square, has the air of a country estate complete with sweeping lawns. The Royal Dublin Society bought the building in 1815. The government obtained a part of it in 1922 for parliamentary use and bought the entire building two years later.

Visitors can arrange to tour the main rooms, including the *Seanad* chamber with its heavily ornamented ceiling.

---

### Tʜᴇ Iʀɪsʜ Pᴀʀʟɪᴀᴍᴇɴᴛ

The Irish Free State, forerunner of the Republic of Ireland, was inaugurated in 1922 (see p42), although an unofficial Irish parliament, the *Dáil*, had already been in existence since 1919. Today, parliament is made up of two houses: the *Dáil* (House of Representatives) and the *Seanad Éireann* (Senate). The Prime Minister is the *Taoiseach* and the deputy, the *Tánaiste*. The *Dáil's* 166 representatives – *Teachta Dala*, known as TDs – are elected by proportional representation. The 60-strong *Seanad* is appointed by various individuals and authorities, including the *Taoiseach* and the University of Dublin.

**Opening of the first parliament of the Irish Free State in 1922**

# National Museum

THE NATIONAL MUSEUM OF IRELAND was built in the 1880s to the design of Sir Thomas Deane. Its splendid domed rotunda features marble pillars and a zodiac mosaic floor. The Treasury houses priceless items such as the Broighter gold boat *(see p31)*, while *Ór – Ireland's Gold*, an exhibition focusing on Ireland's Bronze Age gold, contains beautiful jewelry such as the Gleninsheen Gorget *(see pp30–31)*. Other permanent displays include Irish silver and glassware.

**Irish Silver**
*This silver-gilt bowl by Thomas Bolton dates from 1703. Also known as a monteith, it was used for cooling wineglasses.*

**★ Ór – Ireland's Gold**
*This is one of the most extensive collections of Bronze Age gold in Western Europe. This gold lunula (c. 1800 BC) is one of many pieces of fine jewelry in the exhibition.*

**The ceramics** display includes pieces from Europe and the Far East.

**Flag from 1916 Rising**
The Road to Independence *exhibition covers historical events between 1900 and 1921. This flag flew over Dublin's GPO during the Easter Rising* (see p87).

## GALLERY GUIDE
*The ground floor holds The Treasury,* Ór – Ireland's Gold *exhibition,* The Road to Independence *and the* Prehistoric Ireland *display. The first floor houses Viking artifacts and displays of silver, glass and ceramics. There may be other new displays, while some rooms may be closed to the public – this is due to the continuing reorganization of the musuem.*

## KEY TO FLOORPLAN

| | |
|---|---|
| ☐ | The Road to Independence |
| ☐ | Ór – Ireland's Gold |
| ☐ | The Treasury |
| ☐ | Prehistoric Ireland |
| ☐ | Ceramics |
| ☐ | Irish glass |
| ☐ | Irish silver |
| ☐ | Scientific instruments |
| ☐ | Viking exhibition |
| ☐ | Nonexhibition space |

**The domed rotunda**, based on the design of the Altes Museum in Berlin, makes an impressive entrance hall.

**Main entrance**

**The Treasury** houses masterpieces of Irish crafts such as the Ardagh Chalice *(see p53)*.

**First floor**

### Scientific Instruments

*A fascinating display of surveying
and navigation aids includes this
astrolabe (c. 1580–90) made in
Prague by Erasmus Habermel.*

**The Viking exhibition** houses
many items, including coins,
pottery and swords uncovered in
the 1970s from the Viking
settlement, discovered beside the
Liffey at Wood Quay *(see p76).*

**Ground
floor**

### ★ Cross of Cong

*Some 75 cm (30
inches) in height,
this processional
cross shows a high
level of craftsman-
ship. Dating
from 1123, its gilt-
bronze plating is
adorned with silver
wire, crystals and
enameled studs.*

### Crucifixion Plaque

*This plaque is one of the
earliest depictions of the
crucifixion found in
Ireland. Dating from the
late 7th century, it may
have been decoration for a
manuscript cover.*

**St. Patrick's
Bell**, made of
bronze-coated
iron, is housed in a
beautiful 12th-century
shrine *(see inset p3).*

### ★ Tara Brooch

*Found at Bettystown, County Meath, this ornate
brooch dates from the 8th century AD. It is decorated
on the front and back with a filigree of gold wire
entwined around settings of amber and enamel.*

### STAR EXHIBITS

★ **Ór – Ireland's Gold**

★ **Cross of Cong**

★ **Tara Brooch**

## Natural History Museum ⑩

Merrion St. **Map** E4. 〖 661 8811.
○ 10am–5pm Tue–Sat, 2–5pm Sun.
● public hols. 🚶 ground floor only.
📷 May–Sep.

K NOWN AFFECTIONATELY as the "Dead Zoo," this museum is crammed with antique glass cabinets containing stuffed animals from around the world. The museum was opened to the public in 1857 with an inaugural lecture by Dr. David Livingstone on African fauna. It remains virtually unchanged from Victorian times and is now a museum piece itself.

The Irish room on the ground floor holds exhibits on Irish wildlife. Inside the front door are three huge skeletons of the extinct giant deer, better known as the "Irish elk." Also on this floor are shelves stacked with jars of bizarre creatures such as octopuses, leeches and worms preserved in embalming fluid.

The upper gallery houses the noted Blaschka Collection of glass models of marine life, and a display of buffalo and deer trophies. Suspended from the ceiling are the skeletons of a fin whale, found at Bantry Bay (see p159) in 1862, and a humpback whale, which was found stranded at Inishcrone in County Sligo in 1893.

**Lawn and front entrance of the Natural History Museum**

## National Gallery ⑪

See pp68–9.

**Georgian town houses overlooking Merrion Square gardens**

## Merrion Square ⑫

**Map** F4.

M ERRION SQUARE is one of Dublin's largest and grandest Georgian squares. Covering about 5 ha (12 acres), the square was laid out by John Ensor around 1762.

On the west side are the impressive façades of the Natural History Museum, the National Gallery and the front garden of Leinster House (see p63). However, this august triumvirate does not compare with the lovely Georgian town houses on the other three sides of the square. Many have brightly painted doors with original features such as wrought-iron balconies, ornate doorknockers and fanlights. The oldest and finest houses are on the north side.

Many of the houses – now predominantly used as office space – have plaques detailing the rich and famous who once lived in them. These include Catholic emancipation leader Daniel O'Connell (see p40), who lived at No. 58 and poet WB Yeats (see pp224–5), who lived at No. 82. The playwright Oscar Wilde (see p20) spent his childhood at No. 1.

The attractive central park features colorful flower and shrub beds. In the 1840s it served a grim function as an emergency soup kitchen, feeding the hungry during the Great Famine (see p211). On the northwest side of the park stands the restored Rutland Fountain. It was originally erected in 1791 for the sole use of Dublin's poor.

Just off the square, at No. 24 Merrion Street Upper, is the birthplace of the Duke of Wellington, who, when teased about his Irish background, said, "Being born in a stable does not make one a horse."

## Royal Hibernian Academy ⑬

15 Ely Place. **Map** E5. 〖 661 2558.
○ 11am–5pm Mon–Wed, Fri & Sat,
11am–9pm Thu, 2–5pm Sun.
● public hols.

T HE ACADEMY is one of the largest exhibition spaces in the city. It puts on touring exhibitions and mounts shows of painting, sculpture and other work by Ireland's best young art and design students. This modern brick-and-plate-glass building does, however, look out of place at the end of Ely Place, an attractive Georgian cul-de-sac.

## Fitzwilliam Square ⑭

**Map** E5. **No. 29 Fitzwilliam St Lower**
〖 702 6165. ○ 10am–5pm Tue–Sat, 2–5pm Sun & public hols. ● 3 weeks at Christmas. 📷

D ATING FROM 1825, this was one of the last Georgian squares to be laid out in central Dublin. Much smaller than Merrion Square, it is a popular location for doctors' offices.

In the 1960s, more than 20 town houses on Fitzwilliam Street Lower, a continuation of the east side of the square, were destroyed to make way for the headquarters of the Electricity Supply Board. The company has since tried to appease public indignation by renovating No. 29 as a Georgian showpiece home.

# Dublin's Georgian Terraces

THE 18TH CENTURY was Dublin's Age of Elegance, a time of relative prosperity when the Irish gentry, eager not to appear as the poor relations of Britain, set about remodeling Dublin into one of the most elegant cities in Europe. Terraced town houses were built, forming handsome new streets and squares. During the 19th century the city's wealth declined,

**Doorknocker, Merrion Square**

forcing some middle-class families to divide their homes into tenements. Many of Dublin's once grand streets slowly deteriorated. A century later the property boom of the 1960s threatened to rip out what was left of Georgian Dublin. Fortunately, much has survived and some of the city's finest architecture can be seen in Merrion Square and Fitzwilliam Square.

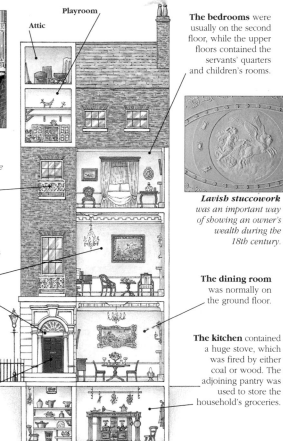

**Playroom**

**Attic**

**The bedrooms** were usually on the second floor, while the upper floors contained the servants' quarters and children's rooms.

*Lavish stuccowork* *was an important way* *of showing an owner's* *wealth during the* *18th century.*

**The drawing room** was always on the first floor. The high ceiling was decorated with the finest plasterwork.

**Architrave**

**The dining room** was normally on the ground floor.

**The kitchen** contained a huge stove, which was fired by either coal or wood. The adjoining pantry was used to store the household's groceries.

*Wrought-iron* *balconies gave added* *prestige to the Georgian* *house. Those still in place* *today are mostly later* *Victorian additions.*

*The doorway was* *usually crowned with a* *segmented fanlight. The* *principal decoration on* *the door itself was a* *heavy brass knocker.*

### GEORGIAN TERRACED HOUSE

While Georgian streetscapes may appear uniform, closer inspection reveals a diversity of styles in terms of details such as fanlights, architraves and balconies. The hallways usually had stone floors and, facing the hall door, a staircase rising to the upper floors. Many of the town houses did not have gardens since the fenced-off parks in the center of the squares were reserved for residents only.

# National Gallery ⑪

THIS SPECIALLY DESIGNED gallery was opened to the public in 1864. It houses many excellent exhibits, largely due to generous bequests, such as the Milltown collection of works of art from Russborough House *(see p124)*. Playwright George Bernard Shaw was also a benefactor, leaving a third of his estate to the gallery. More than 2,000 works are on display in the gallery and, although there is much emphasis on Irish landscape art and portraits, every major school of European painting is well represented.

*The Houseless Wanderer by John Foley*

**Pierrot**
*This Cubist-style work, by Spanish-born artist Juan Gris, is one of many variations he painted on the theme of Pierrot and Harlequin. This particular one dates from 1921.*

First floor

**★ For the Road**
*A whole room is dedicated to the works of Jack Yeats (1871–1957). This mysterious late painting reflects the artist's obsession with the Sligo countryside.*

**The Shaw Fund Gallery** is an elegant hall, lined with full-length portraits, dating from the 17th century onward, and lit by magnificent Waterford Crystal chandeliers.

## GALLERY GUIDE
*The collection is housed on two floors. On the ground floor are the Irish and British rooms: Room 32 has portraits by artists from all schools. The mazelike first floor features works hung in broadly chronological order according to nation. The Italian, French, Dutch and Flemish collections account for most of the space.*

9

22

3

1A

3

2

1

32

Main entrance

19th-century façade

Lecture theater

---

### STAR PAINTINGS

**★ The Taking of Christ by Caravaggio**

**★ Castle of Bentheim by Ruisdael**

**★ For the Road by Jack Yeats**

**The French Rooms** hold works by artists such as Poussin, Monet and Degas, as well as a few Impressionist paintings.

**The Spanish Room** houses a small collection, including works by Goya and Zurbarán.

23

**Stairway**

**The Dutch, Flemish and German rooms** feature works by Rubens, Rembrandt and Hobbema.

**Ground floor**

**Judith with the Head of Holofernes**
Renaissance artist Andrea Mantegna (c. 1431–1506) used a monochrome scheme to depict this image of the decapitation of an Assyrian chief, in the style of a Classical Roman stone carving.

## VISITORS' CHECKLIST

Merrion Square West. **Map** E4.
661 5133. DART to Pearse Station. 5, 7, 8, 44, 45, 47 & 48. Mon–Wed, Fri & Sat 10am–5.30pm, Thu 10am–8:30pm, Sun 2–5pm. Good Fri & Dec 24–26. for special exhibitions only.

★ **The Taking of Christ**
Rediscovered in the Dublin Jesuit House of Study in 1990, this 1602 composition by Caravaggio has enhanced the gallery's reputation.

★ **Castle of Bentheim**
This 17th-century Dutch landscape was painted by Jacob van Ruisdael when he was only 24 years old.

**The Sick Call**
Painted in a Pre-Raphaelite style by Matthew James Lawless, this 1863 canvas evokes the suffering and poverty of the Irish population in the years following the Famine.

## KEY TO FLOORPLAN

- Irish
- British
- Baroque
- French
- Italian
- Spanish
- Dutch, Flemish and German
- Nonexhibition space

# SOUTHWEST DUBLIN

THE AREA around Dublin Castle was first settled in prehistoric times, and it was from here that the city grew. Dublin gets its name from the dark pool *(Dubh Linn)* which formed at the confluence of the Liffey and the Poddle, a river that once ran through the site of Dublin Castle. It is now channeled underground and trickles out into the Liffey by Grattan Bridge. Archaeological excavations behind Wood Quay, on the banks of the Liffey, reveal that the Vikings established a trading settlement here around 841.

Following Strongbow's invasion of 1170, a medieval city began to emerge; the Anglo-Normans built strong defensive walls around the castle.

**Memorial to Turlough O'Carolan in St. Patrick's Cathedral**

A small reconstructed section of these old city walls can be seen at St. Audoen's Church. More conspicuous reminders of the Anglo-Normans are provided by the grand medieval Christ Church Cathedral and Ireland's largest church, St. Patrick's Cathedral. When the city expanded to the north and east during the Georgian era, the narrow cobbled streets of Temple Bar became a quarter of skilled craftsmen and merchants. Today this area is considered to be the trendiest part of town, and is home to a variety of alternative stores and cafés. The Powerscourt Townhouse, an elegant 18th-century mansion, has been converted into one of the city's best shopping centers.

## SIGHTS AT A GLANCE

### Museums and Libraries
Dublin Civic Museum **4**
Dublinia **9**
Marsh's Library **13**

### Historic Buildings
City Hall **2**
*Dublin Castle pp74–5* **1**
Powerscourt Townhouse **5**
Tailors' Hall **11**

### Historic Streets
Temple Bar **6**
Wood Quay **7**

### Churches
*Christ Church Cathedral
pp78–9* **8**
St. Audoen's Church **10**
St. Patrick's Cathedral **12**
St. Werburgh's Church **3**
Whitefriar Street Carmelite
Church **14**

### KEY

Street-by-Street map
*See pp72–3*

**P** Parking

0 meters 250

0 yards 250

◁ **Temple Bar, a center for the arts and a popular meeting spot for young Dubliners**

# Street-by-Street: Southwest Dublin

**D**ESPITE ITS WEALTH of ancient buildings, such as Dublin Castle and Christ Church Cathedral, this part of Dublin lacks the sleek appeal of the neighboring streets around Grafton Street. In recent years, however, redevelopment has helped to rejuvenate the area, especially around Temple Bar, where the attractive cobbled streets are lined with interesting stores, galleries and cafés.

**Sunlight Chambers**
were built in 1900 for the Lever Brothers company. The delightful terra-cotta decoration on the façade advertises their main business of soap manufacturing.

**Wood Quay**
*This is where the Vikings established their first permanent settlement in Ireland around 841* **7**

WELLINGTO

ESSEX QUAY

ESSEX ST EAS

PARLIAMENT STREET

CRANE LANE

FISHAMBLE ST

ESSEX ST WEST

EXCHANGE ST

DAME STRE

**★ Christ Church Cathedral**
*Huge family monuments, including that of the 19th Earl of Kildare, can be found in Ireland's oldest cathedral, which also has a fascinating crypt* **8**

LORD EDWARD ST

CHRISTCHURCH PL

CASTLE ST

**St. Werburgh's Church**
*An ornate interior hides behind the somewhat drab exterior of this 18th-century church* **3**

**Dublinia**
*Medieval Dublin is the subject of this interactive museum, located in the former Synod Hall of the Church of Ireland. It is linked to Christ Church by a bridge* **9**

**City Hall**
*Originally built as the Royal Exchange in 1779, the city's municipal headquarters is fronted by a huge Corinthian portico* **2**

**★ Dublin Castle**
*The Drawing Room, with its Waterford crystal chandelier, is part of a suite of luxurious rooms built in the 18th century for the Viceroys of Ireland* **1**

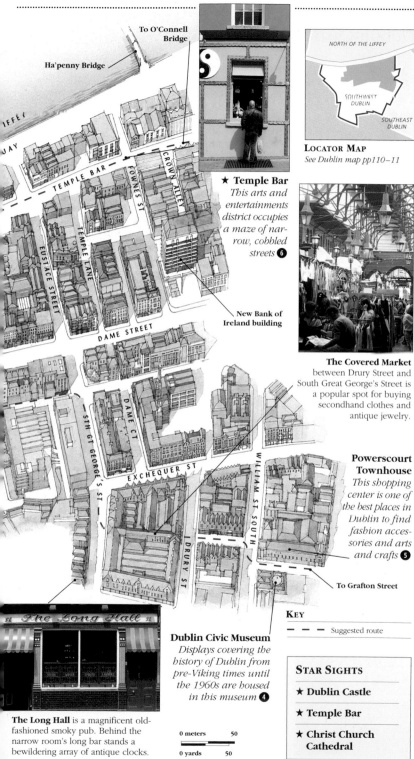

★ **Temple Bar**
*This arts and entertainments district occupies a maze of narrow, cobbled streets* ❻

**New Bank of Ireland building**

**To O'Connell Bridge**

**Ha'penny Bridge**

**LOCATOR MAP**
*See Dublin map pp110–11*

**The Covered Market** between Drury Street and South Great George's Street is a popular spot for buying secondhand clothes and antique jewelry.

**Powerscourt Townhouse**
*This shopping center is one of the best places in Dublin to find fashion accessories and arts and crafts* ❺

**To Grafton Street**

**Dublin Civic Museum**
*Displays covering the history of Dublin from pre-Viking times until the 1960s are housed in this museum* ❹

**The Long Hall** is a magnificent old-fashioned smoky pub. Behind the narrow room's long bar stands a bewildering array of antique clocks.

**KEY**

– – – Suggested route

**STAR SIGHTS**

★ **Dublin Castle**

★ **Temple Bar**

★ **Christ Church Cathedral**

0 meters    50

0 yards    50

# Dublin Castle ●

**St. Patrick by Edward Smyth**

F OR SEVEN CENTURIES Dublin Castle was a symbol of English rule, ever since the Anglo-Normans built a fortress here in the 13th century. Nothing remains of the original structure except the much modified Record Tower. Following a fire in 1684, the Surveyor-General, Sir William Robinson, laid down the plans for the Upper and Lower Castle Yards in their present form. On the first floor of the south side of the Upper Yard are the luxury State Apartments, including St. Patrick's Hall. These rooms, with Killybegs carpets and chandeliers of Waterford glass, served as home to the British-appointed Viceroys of Ireland.

**Figure of Justice**
*Facing the Upper Yard above the main entrance from Cork Hill, this statue aroused much cynicism among Dubliners, who felt she was turning her back on the city.*

**★ Throne Room**
*Built in 1740, this room contains a throne said to have been presented by William of Orange after his victory at the Battle of the Boyne (see p236).*

**Bedford Tower (1760)**

**Entrance from Cork Hill**

**Wedgwood Room**

**Picture Gallery**

**Entrance to State Apartments**

**Upper Yard**

**Bermingham Tower** dates from the 14th century. It was turned into an elegant supper room about 1740.

**Entrance to Upper Yard**

**Octagonal Tower (c. 1812)**

**Record Tower (1258)**

**★ St. Patrick's Hall**
*This hall, with its banners of the now-defunct Knights of St. Patrick, has ceiling paintings by Vincenzo Valdré (1778), symbolizing the relationship between Britain and Ireland.*

**The Church of the Most Holy Trinity** was completed in 1814 by Francis Johnston. The 100 heads on the exterior of this Neo-Gothic church were carved by Edward Smyth.

## ROBERT EMMET

Robert Emmet (1778–1803),
leader of the abortive 1803
rebellion, is remembered
as a heroic champion of
Irish liberty. His plan was
to capture Dublin Castle
as a signal for the country
to revolt against the Act of
Union (see p40). Emmet
was caught and publicly
hanged, but the defiant,
patriotic speech he made
from the dock helped to
inspire future generations
of Irish freedom fighters.

Government
offices

...er Yard

Dame Street

Oval stairwell at City Hall

# City Hall ❷

Lord Edward St. **Map** C3. ● to the
public.

**D**ESIGNED BY Thomas Cooley,
this imposing Corinthian-
style building was built
between 1769 and 1779 as the
Royal Exchange. It was taken
over by Dublin Corporation
in 1852 as a meeting place for
the city council – a role it
keeps to this day.

Beyond the ornate balustrade
and columned façade which
is particularly impressive when
viewed from Parliament Street,
is the striking entrance rotunda
with its softly illuminated
dome supported by six pairs
of fluted columns. The city's
coat of arms with the motto
*Obedientia Civium Urbis
Felicitas* (Happy the city where
citizens obey) is depicted in
mosaic form on the floor of
the rotunda. A pair of magnificent oval staircases lead to
the Council Chamber.

# St. Werburgh's Church ❸

Entrance through 7–8 Castle St.
**Map** C4. ☎ 478 3710. ◻ 10am–
4pm Mon–Fri, ring bell if doors locked.

**B**UILT ON late 12th-century
foundations, St. Werburgh's
was designed by Thomas
Burgh in 1715, and then rebuilt
after a fire in 1754. It served
as the parish church of Dublin
Castle hosting many state cere-
monies, including the swearing
in of Viceroys. However, this
role was later taken over by

the Church of the Most Holy
Trinity within the castle walls.

Beyond the shabby pallor
of its exterior walls lies some
fine decorative work. There
are massive memorials to
members of the Guinness
family, and a finely carved
Gothic pulpit by Richard
Stewart. Also worth viewing
are the 1767 organ case and
the stuccowork in the chancel.

Beneath the church lie 27
vaults including that of Lord
Edward Fitzgerald, who died
during the 1798 Rebellion
(see p39). The body of his
captor, Major Henry Sirr, is in
the church's graveyard. John
Field, a composer and creator
of the nocturne, was baptized
here in 1782.

# Dublin Civic Museum ❹

58 South William St. **Map** D4.
☎ 679 4260. ◻ 10am–6pm Tue–
Sat, 11am–2pm Sun. ● 10 days at
Christmas & public hols.

**T**HIS SMALL MUSEUM, set in the
former City Assembly
House, depicts Dublin from
Viking times to the 20th
century through paintings,
photographs, old newspaper
cuttings and an assortment of
objects, including the head
from a 40-m (134-ft) high
Nelson Pillar. This massive
monument was erected in
1808, predating Nelson's
Column in London's Trafalgar
Square by several decades. It
loomed over O'Connell Street
until anti-British protestors
blew it up on March 8, 1966.

Nave of St. Werburgh's Church,
showing gallery and organ case

**Interior of Powerscourt
Townhouse Shopping Centre**

## Powerscourt Townhouse **❺**

South William St. **Map** D4. **📞** 679
4144. **◷** 8:30am–6pm Mon–Sat
(8:30am–7pm Thu). See also
*Shopping in Ireland* pp322–5.

COMPLETED IN 1774 by Robert
Mack, this grand mansion
was built as the city home of
Viscount Powerscourt, who
also had a country estate at
Enniskerry *(see pp126–7)*.
Granite from the Powerscourt
estate was used in its construction. Today the building houses
one of Dublin's best shopping
centers. Inside it still features
the original grand mahogany
staircase, and detailed plasterwork by Michael Stapleton.
    The building became a
drapery warehouse in the
1830s, and major restoration
during the 1960s turned it into

a center of specialty galleries,
antique shops, jewelry stalls,
cafés and other shop units.
The enclosed central courtyard, topped by a glass dome,
is where many Dubliners stop
to have a snack. The center
can also be reached from
Grafton Street down the
narrow Johnson Court alley.

## Temple Bar **❻**

**Map** C3. **Temple Bar Information
Centre** 18 Eustace St. **📞** 671 5717.
**◷** Jun–Aug: 9am–7pm Mon–Fri,
11am–7pm Sat, noon–6pm Sun; Sep–
May: 9:30am–6pm Mon–Fri, noon–
6pm Sat. **●** Dec 23–Jan 3. See also
*Entertainment in Dublin* p106.

SOME OF DUBLIN'S best night
spots, restaurants and
unusual shops line these
narrow, cobbled streets running between the Bank of
Ireland *(see p58)* and Christ
Church Cathedral. In the 18th
century the area was home to
many insalubrious characters –
Fownes Street was noted for
its brothels. It was also the
birthplace of parliamentarian
Henry Grattan *(see p38)*.
Skilled craftsmen and artisans,
such as clockmakers and
printers, lived and worked
around Temple Bar until post-
war industrialization led to a
decline in the area's fortunes.
    In the 1970s, the CIE (the
national transit authority)
bought up parcels of land in
this area to build a major bus
depot. While waiting to acquire
the land and buildings needed,
the CIE rented out, on cheap
leases, some of the old retail

and warehouse premises to
young artists and to record,
clothing and bookshops. The
area developed an "alternative"
identity and a successful lobby
by local residents persuaded
the CIE to drop their plans.
    As more cynical Dubliners
put it, the area became the
city's "officially designated
arts zone." But while the new
investment and planning may
have added a slight air of
contrivance, it's still an
exciting, atmospheric and
essentially very young place.
    Organizations based here
include the Irish Film Centre,
the experimental Project Arts
Centre and about a dozen
galleries such as the popular
DESIGNyard, an applied arts
center displaying contemporary
Irish jewelry and furniture.
There are also centers for
music, multimedia and photography as well as a Children's
Cultural Centre – an arts
center that offers theater,
workshops and other entertainment for children.

**A pub in Temple Bar**

## Wood Quay **❼**

**Map** B3.

NAMED AFTER the strong
timber supports used to
reclaim the land during the
13th century, this is where the
Vikings first settled in 841.
Excavations in the 1970s
revealed remains of Norse
and Norman villages, and artifacts including pottery, coins,
swords and leatherwork. Many
of these findings are at the
National Museum *(see pp64–5)*
and at the Dublinia exhibition.
    However, the city chose not
to develop this archaeological
find, but instead built two
large civic offices (known
locally as "The Bunkers") on
the site. Today all you will
see is a plaque and a rather
surrealistic picnic site in the
shape of a Viking longboat.

**Strolling through the streets of Temple Bar**

Former Synod Hall, now home to the Dublinia exhibition

## Christt Church Cathedral ❽

*See pp78–9.*

## Dublinia ❾

St. Michael's Hill. **Map** B3. ☎ 679 4611. ◯ Apr–Sep: 10am–5pm daily; Oct–Mar: 11am–4pm Mon–Sat, 10am–4.30pm Sun. ● Good Iri & Dec 24–26. 🎟 includes entry to Christ Church Cathedral via bridge. ♿

Managed by the nonprofit-making Medieval Trust, the Dublinia exhibition covers the formative period of Dublin's history from the arrival of the Anglo-Normans in 1170 to the closure of the monasteries in the 1540s *(see p36)*.

The exhibition is housed in the Neo-Gothic Synod Hall, which, up until 1983, was home to the ruling body of the Church of Ireland. The building and the humpbacked bridge linking it to Christ Church Cathedral date from the 1870s. Before Dublinia was established in 1993, the Synod Hall was briefly converted into a nightclub.

The exhibition is entered via the basement where an audiotape-guided tour takes visitors through exhibits of life-size reconstructions. These depict major events in Dublin's history, such as the Black Death and the rebellion of Silken Thomas *(see p36)*. The ground floor houses a large scale model of Dublin around 1500, a display of

artifacts from the Wood Quay excavation, and reconstructions including the inside of a late medieval merchant's kitchen. There are also information panels on the themes of trade, merchants and religion. On the first floor is the dark-wood panelled Great Hall, where there is a multiscreen presentation on Dublin's medieval history.

The 60-m (200-ft) high St. Michael's Tower is one of the best vantage points in Dublin, offering a splendid bird's-eye view of the low-rise city.

## St. Audoen's Church ❿

High St. **Map** B3. ● for restoration.

Tower of St. Audoen's Church

Designated a national monument and currently under restoration, St. Audoen's is Dublin's earliest surviving medieval church. The 12th-century tower is believed to be the oldest in Ireland, and its three bells date from 1423. The 15th-century nave also remains intact. The church stands in an attractive churchyard with well-maintained lawns and shrubs. To the rear, steps lead down to St. Audoen's Arch, the only remaining gateway of the old city. Flanking the gate are restored sections of the 13th-century city walls.

Next door stands St. Audoen's Roman Catholic Church, completed in 1847. The two Pacific clam shells by the front door hold holy water. In the basement is an audiovisual presentation on pre-Viking Ireland.

### The Vikings in Dublin

Viking raiders arrived in Ireland in the late 8th century and founded Dublin in 841. They built a fort where the River Poddle met the Liffey at a black pool *(Dubh Linn)*, on the site of Dublin Castle. They also established a settlement along the banks of the Liffey at Wood Quay. Much of their trade was based on silver, slaves and piracy.

Following their defeat by Brian Boru at the Battle of Clontarf in 1014 *(see p32)*, the Vikings integrated fully with the local Irish, adopting Christian beliefs. After Strongbow's Anglo-Norman invasion in 1170 *(see p34)*, the flourishing Hiberno-Viking trading community declined, and many were banished to a separate colony called Oxmanstown, just north of the river.

Artist's impression of a Viking ship in Dublin Bay

# Christ Church Cathedral ●8

CHRIST CHURCH CATHEDRAL was commissioned in 1172 by Strongbow, Anglo-Norman conqueror of Dublin *(see p34)*, and Archbishop Laurence O'Toole. It replaced an earlier wooden church built by the Vikings in 1038. At the time of the Reformation *(see p36)*, the cathedral passed to the Protestant Church of Ireland. By the 19th century it was in a bad state of repair, but was completely remodeled by architect George Street in the 1870s. In the crypt are monuments removed from the cathedral during its restoration.

**Arms on Lord Mayor's pew**

### ★ Medieval Lectern
*This beautiful brass lectern was hand-wrought during the Middle Ages. It stands on the left-hand side of the nave, in front of the pulpit. The matching lectern on the right-hand side is a copy, dating from the 19th century.*

**The Lord Mayor's pew** is usually kept in the north aisle, but is moved to the front of the nave when used by Dublin's civic dignitaries. It features a stand for the civic mace and a carving of the City Arms.

### Great Nave
*The 25-m (68-ft) high nave has some fine early Gothic arches. On the north side, the original 13th-century wall leans out by as much as 50 cm (18 in) due to settling.*

**Entrance**

**The bridge** to the Synod Hall was added when the cathedral was being rebuilt in the 1870s.

### ★ Strongbow Monument
*The large effigy in chain armor is probably not Strongbow. However, his remains are buried in the cathedral and the curious half-figure may be part of his original tomb.*

### STAR FEATURES
- ★ **Strongbow Monument**
- ★ **Crypt**
- ★ **Medieval Lectern**

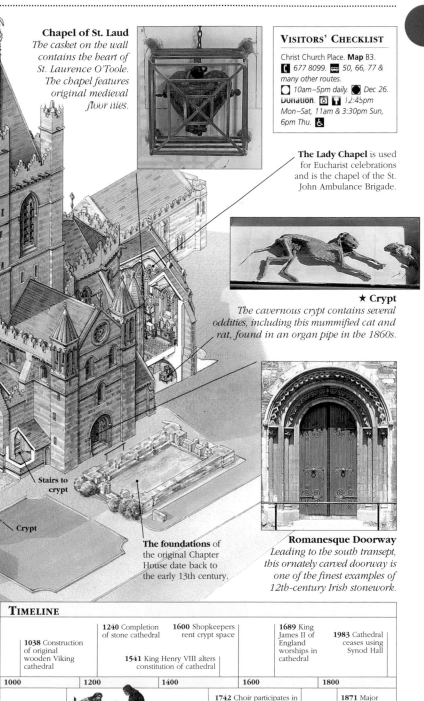

**Chapel of St. Laud**
*The casket on the wall contains the heart of St. Laurence O'Toole. The chapel features original medieval floor tiles.*

**The Lady Chapel** is used for Eucharist celebrations and is the chapel of the St. John Ambulance Brigade.

**★ Crypt**
*The cavernous crypt contains several oddities, including this mummified cat and rat, found in an organ pipe in the 1860s.*

**Stairs to crypt**

**Crypt**

**The foundations** of the original Chapter House date back to the early 13th century.

**Romanesque Doorway**
*Leading to the south transept, this ornately carved doorway is one of the finest examples of 12th-century Irish stonework.*

**TIMELINE**

**1038** Construction of original wooden Viking cathedral

**1240** Completion of stone cathedral

**1600** Shopkeepers rent crypt space

**1541** King Henry VIII alters constitution of cathedral

**1689** King James II of England worships in cathedral

**1983** Cathedral ceases using Synod Hall

| 1000 | 1200 | 1400 | 1600 | 1800 |
|------|------|------|------|------|

**1172** St. Laurence O'Toole and Strongbow commission the new stone cathedral

*Meeting between Lambert Simnel and the Earl of Kildare (see p35)*

**1742** Choir participates in first performance of Handel's *Messiah*

**1487** Coronation of 10-year-old Lambert Simnel as King of England

**1871** Major rebuilding of the cathedral begins, including Synod Hall and bridge

## Tailors' Hall ⓫

Back Lane. **Map** B4. ◑ *to the public.*

DUBLIN'S only surviving guildhall preserves a delightful corner of old Dublin in an otherwise busy redevelopment zone. Built in 1706, it stands behind a limestone arch in a quiet cobbled yard. The building is the oldest guildhall in Ireland and was used by various trade groups including hosiers, saddlers and barber-surgeons as well as tailors. It also hosted many political meetings – Wolfe Tone addressed a public United Irishmen rally here before the 1798 rebellion *(see p39)*. The building closed in the early 1960s due to neglect, but a successful appeal by Desmond Guinness saw the hall completely refurbished. It is now the home of *An Taisce* (the Irish National Trust).

**Façade of Tailors' Hall, home of the Irish National Trust**

**St. Patrick's Cathedral with Minot's Tower and spire**

## St. Patrick's Cathedral ⓬

St. Patrick's Close. **Map** B4.
◖ 475 4817. ◗ *May–Oct: 9am–6pm Mon–Fri, 9am–5pm Sat, 10–11am & 12:45–3pm Sun; Nov–Apr: 9am–6pm Mon–Fri, 9am–4pm Sat, 10:30am–11am & 12:45–3pm Sun.* 📷

IRELAND'S LARGEST CHURCH was founded beside a sacred well where St. Patrick is said to have baptized converts around AD 450. A stone slab bearing a Celtic cross and covering the well was unearthed at the turn of the 20th century. It is now preserved in the west end of the cathedral's nave. The original building was just a wooden chapel and remained so until 1192 when Archbishop John Comyn rebuilt the cathedral in stone.

Over the centuries, St. Patrick's came to be seen as the people's church, while the older Christ Church Cathedral *(see pp78–9)* nearby was more associated with the British establishment. In the mid-17th century, Huguenot refugees from France arrived in Dublin, and were given the Lady Chapel by the Dean and Chapter as their place of worship. The chapel was separated from the rest of the cathedral and used by the Huguenots until the late 18th century. Today St. Patrick's Cathedral is the Protestant Church of Ireland's national cathedral.

Much of the present building dates back to work completed between 1254 and 1270. The cathedral suffered over the centuries from desecration, fire and neglect but, thanks to the generosity of Sir Benjamin Guinness, it underwent extensive restoration during the 1860s. The building is 91 m (300 ft) long; at the western end is a 43-m (141-ft) tower, restored by Archbishop Minot in 1370 and now known as Minot's Tower. The spire was added in the 18th century.

The interior is dotted with memorial busts, brasses and monuments. A leaflet available at the front desk helps identify and locate them. The largest, most colorful and elaborate tomb was dedicated to the Boyle family in the 17th century. Erected by Richard Boyle, Earl of Cork, in memory of his second wife Katherine, it is decorated with painted figures of his family,

### JONATHAN SWIFT (1667–1745)

Jonathan Swift was born in Dublin and educated at Trinity College *(see pp60–61)*. He left for England in 1689, but returned in 1694 when his political career failed. Back in Ireland he began a life in the church, becoming Dean of St. Patrick's in 1713. In addition to his clerical duties, Swift was a prolific political commentator – his best-known work, *Gulliver's Travels*, contains a bitter satire on Anglo-Irish relations. Swift's personal life, particularly his friendship with two younger women, Ester Johnson, better known as Stella, and Hester Vanhomrigh, attracted criticism. In his final years, Swift suffered from Menière's disease – an illness of the ear that led many to believe him insane.

including his wife's parents. Other famous citizens remembered in the church include the harpist Turlough O'Carolan (1670–1738) and Douglas Hyde (1860–1949), the first President of Ireland.

Many visitors come to see the memorials associated with Jonathan Swift, the satirical writer and Dean of St. Patrick's. In the north transept is "Swift's Corner," containing various memorabilia such as an altar table and a bookcase holding his death mask and various pamphlets. A self-penned epitaph can be found on the wall on the southwest side of the nave. A few steps away, two brass plates mark his grave and that of his beloved Stella, who died in 1728.

At the west end of the nave is an old door with a hole in it – a relic from a feud which took place between the Lords Kildare and Ormonde in 1492. The latter took refuge in the Chapter House, but a truce was soon made and a hole was cut in the door by Lord Kildare so that the two could shake hands in friendship.

## Marsh's Library ⑬

St. Patrick's Close. **Map** B4.
454 3511. ☐ 10am–12:45pm & 2–5pm Mon & Wed–Fri, 10:30am–12:45pm Sat. ● 10 days at Christmas a public hol.

THE OLDEST public library in Ireland was built in 1701 for Archbishop Narcissus Marsh, a Dean of St. Patrick's Cathedral. It was designed by Sir William Robinson, architect of much of Dublin Castle *(see pp74–5)* and the Royal Hospital Kilmainham *(see p95)*.

Inside, the bookcases are topped by a miter and feature carved gables with lettering in gold leaf. To the rear of the library are wired alcoves (or "cages") where readers were locked in with rare books. The collection of books from the 16th, 17th and early 18th centuries includes irreplaceable volumes, such as Bishop Bedell's 1685 translation of the Old Testament into Irish. There is also a volume of Clarendon's *History of the Rebellion*, with anti-Scottish margin notes by Jonathan Swift.

**Statue of Virgin and Child in Whitefriar Street Carmelite Church**

## Whitefriar Street Carmelite Church ⑭

56 Aungier St. **Map** C4. 475 8821. ☐ 8am–6:30pm Mon & Wed–Fri, 8am–9:30pm Tue, 8am–7pm Sat, 8am–7:30pm Sun.

DESIGNED by George Papworth, this Catholic church was built in 1827. It stands on the site of a 16th-century Carmelite priory of which nothing remains.

In contrast to the two Church of Ireland cathedrals, St. Patrick's and Christ Church, which are usually full of tourists, this church is frequented by local worshipers. Every day they come to light candles to various saints, including St. Valentine – the patron saint of lovers. His remains, previously buried in the cemetery of St. Hippolytus in Rome, were offered to the church as a gift from Pope Gregory XVI in 1836. Today they rest beneath the commemorative statue of St. Valentine, which stands in the northeast corner of the church beside the high altar.

Nearby is a Flemish oak statue of the Virgin and Child, dating from the late 15th or early 16th century. It may have belonged to St. Mary's Abbey *(see p91)* and is believed to be the only wooden statue of its kind to escape destruction when Ireland's monasteries were sacked at the time of the Reformation *(see p36)*.

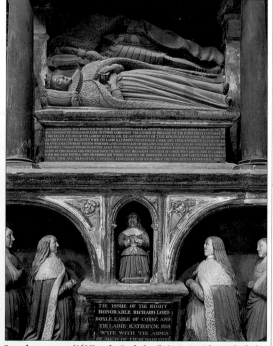

**Carved monument (1632) to the Boyle family in St. Patrick's Cathedral**

# NORTH OF THE LIFFEY

**D**UBLIN'S NORTHSIDE was the last part of the city to be developed during the 18th century. The city authorities envisioned an area of wide, leafy avenues, but the reality of today's heavy traffic has rather spoiled their original plans. Nevertheless, O'Connell Street, lined with fine statues and monuments, is an impressive thoroughfare. This is where Dubliners come to shop and some of the adjacent streets, particularly Moore Street, have a colorful parade of stalls and street vendors offering discount tobacco.

**Statue of James Joyce on Earl Street North**

Some public buildings, such as James Gandon's glorious Custom House and majestic Four Courts, together with the historic General Post Office (see p87), add grace to the area. The Rotunda Hospital, Europe's first specially designed maternity hospital, is another fine building. Dublin's two most celebrated theaters, the Abbey and the Gate, act as cultural magnets, as do the Dublin Writers Museum and the James Joyce Cultural Centre, two museums dedicated to writers who lived in the city.

Some of the city's finest Georgian streetscapes are found in the north of the city. Many have been neglected for decades, but thankfully some areas, most notably North Great George's Street, are undergoing restoration.

## SIGHTS AT A GLANCE

### Museums and Galleries
Dublin Writers Museum **9**
Hugh Lane Municipal Gallery
  of Modern Art **10**
Irish Whiskey Corner **13**
James Joyce Cultural Centre **5**

### Historic Buildings
Custom House **1**
Four Courts **15**
King's Inns **11**
Rotunda Hospital **7**

### Historic Streets and Bridges
Ha'penny Bridge **17**
O'Connell Street **3**
Smithfield **12**

### Theaters
Abbey Theatre **2**
Gate Theatre **6**

### Churches
St. Mary's Abbey **16**
St. Mary's Pro-Cathedral **4**
St. Michan's Church **14**

### Parks and Gardens
Garden of Remembrance **8**

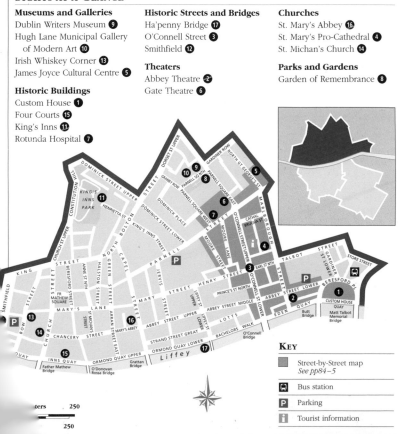

### KEY

| | |
|---|---|
| ▨ | Street-by-Street map See pp84–5 |
| 🚌 | Bus station |
| P | Parking |
| ℹ | Tourist information |

250 meters
250

# Street-by-Street: Around O'Connell Street

Throughout the Georgian era, O'Connell Street was very much the fashionable part of Dublin to live. However, the 1916 Easter Rising destroyed many of the fine buildings along the street, including much of the General Post Office – only its original façade still stands. Today, this main thoroughfare is lined with stores and businesses. Other attractions nearby include St. Mary's Pro-Cathedral and James Gandon's Custom House, overlooking the Liffey.

**Detail of pavement mosaic, Moore Street**

**James Joyce Cultural Centre**
*This well-restored Georgian town house contains a small Joyce museum* **5**

**Parnell Monument (1911)**

**Gate Theatre**
*Founded in 1928, the Gate is renowned for its productions of contemporary drama* **6**

**Rotunda Hospital**
*Housed in the Rotunda Hospital is a chapel built in the 1750s to the design of Richard Castle. It features lovely stained-glass windows, fluted columns, paneling and intricate iron balustrades* **7**

**Moore Street Market**
is the busiest of the streets off O'Connell. Be prepared for the shrill cries of the stall holders offering an enormous variety of fresh fruit, vegetables and cut flowers.

**Anna Livia Fountain (1988)**

**The General Post Office,**
the grandest building on O'Connell Street, was the center of the 1916 Rising.

**James Larkin Statue (198**

**KEY**

– – –  Suggested route

0 meters    50
0 yards     50

**STAR SIGHTS**

★ **Custom House**

★ **O'Connell Stre**

**St. Mary's Pro-Cathedral**
*Built around 1825, this is Dublin's main place of worship for Catholics. The plaster relief above the altar in the sanctuary depicts* The Ascension ❹

**LOCATOR MAP**
*See Dublin map pp110–11*

**The statue of James Joyce** (1990), by Marjorie Fitzgibbon, commemorates one of Ireland's most famous novelists. Born in Dublin in 1882, he cataloged the people and streets of Dublin in *Dubliners* and in his most celebrated work, *Ulysses*.

**Abbey Theatre**
*Ireland's national theater is known throughout the world for its productions by Irish playwrights, such as Sean O'Casey and JM Synge* ❷

**★ O'Connell Street**
*This monument to Daniel O'Connell by John Foley took 19 years to complete from the laying of its foundation stone in 1864* ❸

**Butt Bridge**

O'Connell
Bridge

To Trinity College

**★ Custom House**
*This grotesque head, by Edward Smyth, symbolizes the River Liffey. It is one of 14 carved keystones that adorn the building* ❶

**Illuminated façade of the Custom House reflected in the Liffey**

# Custom House ●

Custom House Quay. **Map** E2. ● *to the public.*

THIS MAJESTIC BUILDING was designed as the Custom House by the English architect James Gandon. However, just nine years after its completion, the 1800 Act of Union *(see p40)* transferred the custom and excise business to London, rendering the building practically obsolete. In 1921, supporters of Sinn Fein celebrated their election victory by setting light to what they saw as a symbol of British imperialism. The fire blazed for five days causing extensive damage. Reconstruction began in 1926, but further deterioration meant that the building was not completely restored until 1991, when it re-opened as government offices.

The main façade is made up of pavilions at each end with a Doric portico in its center. The arms of Ireland crown the two pavilions and a series of 14 allegorical heads, by Dublin sculptor Edward Smyth, form the keystones of arches and entrances. These heads depict Ireland's main rivers and the Atlantic Ocean. Topping the central copper dome is a statue of Commerce, while the north façade is decorated with figures representing Europe, Africa, America and Asia.

The best view of the building is from the south of the Liffey beyond Matt Talbot Bridge, especially at night when it is illuminated. Sadly, the Loop Line railway bridge spoils the view from O'Connell Bridge.

# Abbey Theatre ●

Lower Abbey St. **Map** E2. ● *878 7222.* ● *for performances only.* **Box office** ● *10:30am–7pm Mon–Sat. See also* **Entertainment in Dublin** *p107.*

**Logo of the Abbey Theatre**

FOUNDED in 1898 with WB Yeats and Lady Gregory as co-directors, the Abbey staged its first play in 1904. The early years of this much lauded national theater witnessed works by WB Yeats, JM Synge and Sean O'Casey. Many were controversial: nationalist sensitivities were severely tested in 1926 during the premiere of O'Casey's *The Plough and the Stars* when the flag of the Irish Free State appeared on stage in a scene that featured a pub frequented by prostitutes.

The Abbey remains best known for its productions of early 20th-century Irish work, though in recent years it has done much to encourage new writing talent, particularly in the small Peacock Theatre downstairs. One of the most acclaimed performances staged in the main theater was Brian Friel's *Dancing At Lughnasa* (1990). The walls of the foyer and bar are lined with portraits of famous names linked with the theater.

# O'Connell Street ●

**Map** D1–D2.

O'CONNELL STREET is very different from the original plans of Irish aristocrat Luke Gardiner. When he bought the land in the mid-18th century, Gardiner envisioned a grand residential parade with an elegant mall running along its center. Such plans were short-lived. The construction of Carlisle (now O'Connell) Bridge in 1790 transformed the street into the city's main north-south route. Also, several buildings were destroyed during the 1916 Easter Rising and the Irish Civil War. Since the 1960s many of the old buildings have been replaced by the plate glass and neon of fast food joints, amusement arcades and chain stores.

A few venerable buildings remain, such as the General Post Office (1818), Gresham Hotel (1017), Clery's department store (1822) and the Royal Dublin Hotel, part of which occupies the street's only original town house.

A walk down the central mall is the most enjoyable way to see the street's mix of architectural styles and take a close look at the series of monuments lining the route. At the south end stands a massive monument to Daniel O'Connell (see p40), unveiled in 1882. The street, which throughout the 19th century had been called Sackville Street, was renamed after O'Connell in 1922. Higher up, almost facing the General Post Office, is an animated statue of James Larkin (1867–1943), leader of the Dublin general strike in 1913. The next statue is of Father Theobald Mathew (1790–1856), founder of the Pioneer Total Abstinence

**South end of O'Connell Street with monument to Daniel O'Connell**

Movement. At the north end of the street is the obelisk-shaped monument to Charles Stewart Parnell (1846–91), who was leader of the Home Rule Party and known as the "uncrowned King of Ireland" (see p41). Also on O'Connell Street, at the junction of Cathedral Street, is the ridiculous Anna Livia Millennium Fountain, which was unveiled during the city's millennium celebrations in 1988. It is supposed to represent the River Liffey but most Dubliners dismiss it as the "Floozie in the Jacuzzi."

**Statue of James Larkin (1981) in O'Connell Street**

## St. Mary's Pro-Cathedral ❹

Marlborough St. **Map** D2. 【 874 5441. ◯ 8am–7pm daily.

DEDICATED in 1825 before Catholic emancipation was fully effected (see p40), St. Mary's is Dublin's Catholic cathedral. Its backstreet site was the best the city's Anglo-Irish leaders would allow.

The façade will be based on the Temple of Theseus in Athens. Its six Doric columns support a pediment with statues of St. Laurence O'Toole, 12th-century Archbishop of Dublin and patron saint of the city, St. Mary and St. Patrick. The most striking feature of the interior is the intricately carved high altar.

St. Mary's is home to the famous Palestrina Choir, started in 1902. In 1904 the great tenor, John McCormack (see p22), began his career with the choir, which can be heard every Sunday at 11am.

**Austere Neo-Classical interior of St. Mary's Pro-Cathedral**

---

### THE GENERAL POST OFFICE (GPO)

Built in 1818 halfway along O'Connell Street, the GPO became a symbol of the 1916 Irish Rising. Members of the Irish Volunteers and Irish Citizen Army seized the building on Easter Monday, and Patrick Pearse (see p42) read out the Proclamation of the Irish Republic from its steps. The rebels remained inside for a week, but shelling from the British eventually forced them out. At first, many Irish people viewed the Rising unfavourably. However, as WB Yeats wrote, matters "changed utterly" and a "terrible beauty was born" when, during the following weeks, 14 of the leaders were caught and shot at Kilmainham Gaol (see p95). Inside the building is a sculpture of the mythical Irish warrior Cuchulainn (see p24), dedicated to those who died for their part in the Easter Rising.

**Irish Life magazine cover showing the 1916 Easter Rising**

## James Joyce Cultural Centre ❺

35 North Great George's St. **Map** D1.
🎫 *873 1984*. ⏰ *10am–4:30pm
Mon–Sat, 12:30–4:30pm Sun.*
⬤ *Good Fri & Dec 25.* 🈳

THIS AGREEABLE STOP on the literary tourist trail is primarily a meeting place for Joyce enthusiasts, but is also worth visiting for its remarkable Georgian interior. The center is located in a 1784 town house, which was built for the Earl of Kenmare. Michael Stapleton, one of the greatest stuccodores of his time, contributed to the plasterwork, of which the friezes are particularly noteworthy.

The main literary display is an absorbing set of biographies of around 50 characters from Joyce's novel *Ulysses*, who were based on real Dublin people. Professor Dennis J Maginni, a peripheral character in *Ulysses*, ran a dancing school from this town house. Leopold and Molly Bloom, the central characters of *Ulysses*, lived a short walk away at No. 7 Eccles Street. The center also organizes literary events throughout the year, and walking tours of Joyce's Dublin.

At the head of the road, on Great Denmark Street, is the Jesuit-run Belvedere College attended by Joyce between 1893 and 1898. He recalls his unhappy schooldays there in *A Portrait of the Artist as a Young Man*. The college's interior contains some of Stapleton's best and most colorful plasterwork (1785).

### JAMES JOYCE (1882–1941)

Born in Dublin, Joyce spent most of his adult life in Europe. He used the city of Dublin as the setting for all his major works including *Dubliners, A Portrait of the Artist as a Young Man* and *Ulysses*. Joyce claimed that if the city was ever destroyed it could be re-created through the pages of *Ulysses*. However, the Irish branded the book pornographic and banned it until the 1960s.

## Gate Theatre ❻

Parnell Square East. **Map** D1.
🎫 *874 4368*. ⏰ *for performances
only.* **Box office** 🎫 *874 4045 or
874 6042*. ⏰ *10am–7pm Mon–Sat.*
*See also **Entertainment in Dublin**
pp102–7.*

**Entrance to the Gate Theatre**

RENOWNED FOR its staging of contemporary international drama in Dublin, the Gate Theatre was founded in 1928 by Hilton Edwards and Mícheál Mac Liammóir. The latter is now best remembered for *The*

*Importance of Being Oscar*, his long-running one-man show about the writer Oscar Wilde *(see p20)*. An early success was Denis Johnston's *The Old Lady Says No*, so called because of the margin notes made on one of his scripts by Lady Gregory, founding director of the Abbey Theatre *(see p86)*. Although still noted for staging new plays, the Gate's current output often includes classic Irish plays. Among the young talent to get their first break here were James Mason and a teenaged Orson Welles.

## Rotunda Hospital ❼

Parnell Square West. **Map** D1.
🎫 *873 0700*.

STANDING in the middle of Parnell Square is Europe's first specially designed maternity hospital. Founded in 1745 by Dr. Bartholomew Mosse, the hospital's design is similar to that of Leinster House *(see p63)*. German-born architect, Richard Castle, designed both.

At the east end of the hospital is the Rotunda, after which the hospital is named. It was built in 1764 by John Ensor as Assembly Rooms to host fundraising functions and concerts. Franz Liszt gave a concert here in 1843.

On the first floor is a chapel featuring striking stained-glass windows and exuberant Rococo plasterwork and ceiling (1755) by the stuccodore Bartholomew Cramillion.

Across the road from the hospital is Conway's Pub. Opened in 1745, it is a popular retreat for expectant fathers.

**Stained-glass Venetian window (c. 1863) in Rotunda Hospital's chapel**

## Garden of Remembrance ⑧

Parnell Square. **Map** C1.
○ *dawn–dusk daily.*

A<small>T THE NORTHERN END</small> of Parnell Square is a small, peaceful park, dedicated to the men and women who have died in the pursuit of Irish freedom. The Garden of Remembrance marks the spot where several leaders of the 1916 Easter Rising were held overnight before being taken to Kilmainham Gaol *(see p95)*, and was also where the Irish Volunteers movement was formed in 1913.

Designed by Daithí Hanly, the garden was opened by President Eamon de Valera *(see p43)* in 1966, to mark the 50th anniversary of the Easter Rising. In the center of the garden's well-kept lawns is a cruciform pool. A mosaic on the floor of the pool depicts abandoned, broken swords, spears and shields, symbolizing peace. The focal point at one end of the garden is a large bronze sculpture by Oisín Kelly (1971) of the legendary *Children of Lir*, who were changed into swans by their stepmother *(see p25)*.

*Children of Lir* **in the Garden of Remembrance**

**Gallery of Writers at Dublin Writers Museum**

## Dublin Writers Museum ⑨

18 Parnell Square North. **Map** C1.
⬚ *872 2077.* ○ *10am–5pm Mon–Sat, 11:30am–6pm Sun & public hols.*
● *Dec 25–27.* 🗗

O<small>PENED IN 1991</small>, the museum occupies a tasteful 18th-century town house. There are displays relating to Irish literature in all its forms from around the 10th century to the present day. The exhibits include paintings, manuscripts, letters, rare editions and mementos of many of Ireland's finest authors. There are a number of temporary exhibits and a sumptuously decorated Gallery of Writers upstairs. The museum also hosts frequent poetry readings and lectures. An excellent restaurant, the Chapter One *(see p307)*, and a specialty bookstore, providing an out-of-print search service, add to the relaxed, friendly ambience.

## Hugh Lane Municipal Gallery of Modern Art ⑩

Charlemont House, Parnell Square North. **Map** C1. ⬚ *874 1903.*
○ *9:30am–6pm Tue–Fri, 9:30am–5pm Sat, 11am–5pm Sun.* ● *Dec 24–26 & public hols.*

N<small>OTED ART COLLECTOR</small> Sir Hugh Lane donated his valuable collection of Impressionist paintings to Dublin Corporation in 1905. However, the failure to find a suitable location for them prompted Lane to consider transferring his gift to the National Gallery in London. The Corporation then proposed Charlemont House and Lane relented. However, in 1915, before Lane's revised will could be witnessed, he died on board the torpedoed liner *Lusitania (see p170)*. This led to a 50-year dispute, which has been resolved by Dublin Corporation and the National Gallery swapping the collection every five years.

Besides the Lane bequest, which includes paintings by Degas, Courbet and Monet, the gallery also has a sculpture hall with work by Rodin and others. There is also an extensive collection of modern Irish canvasses, including Michael Farrell's *Madonna Irlanda* (1977) and Patrick Graham's disturbing *Ire/land III* (1982).

***Beach Scene*** **(c. 1876) by Edgar Degas, Hugh Lane Municipal Gallery**

Detail of wood carving (c. 1724) at St. Michan's Church

## King's Inns ⓫

Henrietta St/Constitution Hill.
**Map** B1. 🔴 *to the public.*

THIS CLASSICALLY PROPORTIONED
public building was
founded in 1795 as a place of
residence and study for
lawyers. To build it, James
Gandon chose to seal off the
end of Henrietta Street, which
at the time was one of Dublin's
most famous addresses.
Francis Johnston added the
graceful cupola in 1816, and
the building was finally completed in 1817. Inside is a fine
Dining Hall and the
Registry of Deeds
(formerly the
Prerogative
Court). The
west façade has
two doorways
flanked by
Classical
caryatids carved
by Edward
Smyth. The male
figure, with book
and quill, repre-
sents the law.
Sadly, much of
the area around
Constitution Hill
is less attractive
than it was in
Georgian times. However, the
gardens, which are open to
the public, are still pleasing.

**Caryatid,
King's Inns**

## Smithfield ⓬

**Map** A2.

LAID OUT in the mid-17th
century as a marketplace,
this vast cobbled expanse is a
welcome respite from Dublin's
traffic-laden streets. Most of
the time Smithfield is a relatively tranquil place, although
it springs to life on the first

Sunday of each month when
it hosts a horse and pony
sale. However, don't expect
to see any thoroughbreds
here; none of the animals on
sale are ever likely to run in
the Irish Derby. Nevertheless,
the occasion is a delightful
cameo of Dublin life.

## Irish Whiskey Corner ⓭

Bow St. **Map** A2. 📞 872 5566.
🕙 9am–5pm Mon–Sat by appt.
🔴 10 days at Christmas & Good Fri.
📷 🎥 obligatory.

YOU WILL KNOW you are
nearing Irish Whiskey
Corner by the cavalcade of
tourist buses blocking the
narrow Bow Street. This small
museum is located in part of
Jameson's disused Bow Street
distillery. Tours, which you
can book in advance, start with
a video called *Uisce Beatha*
(the Water of Life). This traces
the history of Irish whiskey
distillation from its beginnings
in 6th-century monasteries to
the current production plant
in Midleton (*see p171*).
Next comes a visit to the
Ball o' Malt Bar for a tasting
of some brands of Irish whiskey. Visitors can then wander
around the exhibition detailing
how whiskey is made.

**Sampling different brands at
Irish Whiskey Corner**

## St. Michan's Church ⓮

Church St. **Map** B3. 📞 872 4154.
🕙 mid-Mar–Oct: 10am–12:45pm &
2–4:45pm Mon–Fri, 10am–12:45pm
Sat; Nov–mid-Mar: 12:30–3:30pm
Mon–Fri, 10am–12:45pm Sat. 📷 🎥

LARGELY REBUILT in 1686 on
the site of an 11th-century
Hiberno-Viking church, the
dull façade of St. Michan's
hides a more exciting interior.
Deep in its vaults lie a number
of bodies that have barely
decomposed because of the
dry atmosphere created by the
church's magnesian limestone
walls. Their wooden caskets,
however, have cracked open,
revealing the preserved
bodies, complete with skin
and strands of hair. Among
those thought to have been
mummified in this way are
the brothers Henry and John
Sheares, leaders of the 1798
rebellion (*see p39*), who were
executed that year.
Other less gory attractions
include the magnificent wood
carving of fruits and violins
and other instruments above
the choir. There is also an
organ (1724) on which Handel
is said to have played. It is
thought that the churchyard
contains the unmarked grave
of United Irishman Robert
Emmet (*see p75*), leader of
the abortive 1803 Rising.

## Four Courts ⓯

Inns Quay. **Map** B3. 📞 872 5555.
🕙 10am–1pm, 2–4:30pm Mon–Fri
(when courts in session).

COMPLETED IN 1802 by James
Gandon, this majestic
public building overlooks the
River Liffey. It was virtually

gutted 120 years later during the Irish Civil War *(see pp42–3)* when government forces bombarded anti-Treaty rebels into submission. The adjacent Public Records Office, with its irreplaceable collection of historical and legal documents dating back to the 12th century, was destroyed by fire.

By 1932, the main buildings were sympathetically restored using Gandon's original design. An imposing copper-covered lantern dome rises above the six-columned Corinthian portico, which is crowned with the figures of Moses, Justice and Mercy. This central section is flanked by two wings containing the four original courts: Common Pleas, Chancery, Exchequer and King's Bench. It is possible to walk into the central waiting hall under the grand dome; an information panel to the right of the entrance gives details of the building's history and functions.

## St. Mary's Abbey ⑯

Meetinghouse Lane. **Map** C2.
📞 872 1490. 🕐 *mid-Jun–mid-Sep: 10am–5pm Wed.* 🏛

F OUNDED BY Benedictines in 1139, but transferred to the Cistercian order just eight years later, this was one of the largest and most important monasteries in medieval Ireland. As well as controlling extensive estates, including

The Ha'penny Bridge looking from Temple Bar to Liffey Street

whole villages, mills and fisheries, the abbey acted as state treasury and meeting place for the Council of Ireland. It was during a council meeting in St. Mary's that "Silken Thomas" Fitzgerald *(see p36)* renounced his allegiance to Henry VIII and marched out to raise the short-lived rebellion of 1534. The monastery was dissolved in 1539 and during the 17th century the site served as a quarry. Stone from St. Mary's was used in the construction of Essex Bridge (replaced by Grattan Bridge in 1874), just to the south of the abbey.

All that remains of the abbey today is the vaulted chamber of the Chapter House. This contains a historical display and a model of how the entire complex would have looked 800 years ago.

## Ha'penny Bridge ⑰

**Map** D3.

L INKING the Temple Bar area *(see p76)* and Liffey Street, this high-arched cast-iron foot bridge is used by thousands of people every day. It was built by John Windsor, an ironworker from Shropshire, England. One of Dublin's most photographed sights, it was originally named the Wellington Bridge. It is now officially called the Liffey Bridge, but is also known as the Metal Bridge. Opened in 1816, the bridge got its better known nickname from the halfpenny toll that was levied on it up until 1919. A recent restoration, which included the installation of period lanterns, has made the bridge even more attractive.

James Gandon's Four Courts overlooking the River Liffey

# FARTHER AFIELD

THERE ARE many interesting sights just outside the city center. The best part of a day can be spent exploring the western suburbs taking in the modern art museum housed in the splendid setting of the Royal Kilmainham Hospital and the eerie Kilmainham Gaol. Phoenix Park, Europe's largest city park, offers the opportunity for an afternoon stroll. Farther north are the National Botanic Gardens, home to over 20,000 plant species from around the world. Nearby is Marino Casino, one of the finest examples of Palladian architecture in Ireland.

*Candelabra at Malahide Castle*

The magnificent coastline with its stunning views of Dublin Bay is easily reached by the DART rail network. It encompasses the towering promontory of Howth, while the highlight of the riviera-like southern stretch is around Dalkey village, especially the lovely Killiney Bay. One of many Martello towers built along the coast to defend Ireland against Napoleonic attacks now houses a collection of Joyce memorabilia and is known as the James Joyce Tower. To the northeast, slightly farther from the city center, is Malahide Castle, former home of the Talbot family.

## SIGHTS AT A GLANCE

**Museums and Galleries**
Chester Beatty Library and
  Gallery of Oriental Art **9**
Guinness Hop Store **4**
James Joyce Tower **13**
Kilmainham Gaol **2**

Royal Hospital Kilmainham **3**
Shaw's Birthplace **6**
Waterways Visitors' Centre **8**

**Parks and Gardens**
National Botanic Gardens **5**
Phoenix Park **1**

**Historic Buildings**
Malahide Castle **10**
Marino Casino **7**

**Towns and Villages**
Dalkey **14**
Dun Laoghaire **12**
Howth **11**
Killiney **15**

### CENTRAL DUBLIN

### GREATER DUBLIN AND ENVIRONS

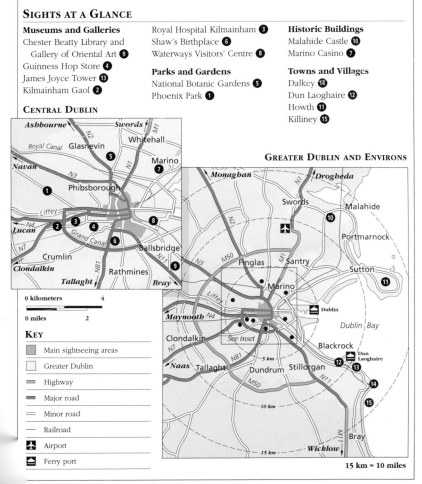

**KEY**

| | |
|---|---|
| ▨ | Main sightseeing areas |
| ▢ | Greater Dublin |
| ▭ | Highway |
| ▭ | Major road |
| ▭ | Minor road |
| — | Railroad |
| ✈ | Airport |
| ⚓ | Ferry port |

0 kilometers 4
0 miles 2

15 km = 10 miles

Martello tower at Howth Head

# Phoenix Park ❶

Park Gate, Conyngham Rd, Dublin 8.
🚌 *10, 25, 26, 37, 38, 39.*
⏰ *6:30am–11pm daily.* **Phoenix Park Visitor Centre** 🕿 *677 0095.*
⏰ *Apr–May: 9:30am–5:30pm daily; Jun–Sep: 9:30am–6:30pm daily; Oct–Nov & Mar: 10am–5pm daily.* 📷
**Zoological Gardens** 🕿 *677 1425.*
⏰ *9:30am–6pm (sunset in winter) Mon–Sat, 10:30am–6pm Sun.* 📷

A LITTLE to the west of the city center, ringed by a wall 11 km (7 miles) long, is Europe's largest enclosed city park. The name "Phoenix" is said to be a corruption of the Gaelic *Fionn Uisce*, meaning "clear water." This refers to a spring that rises near the **Phoenix Column**, which, to add confusion, is crowned by a statue of the mythical bird.

Phoenix Park originated in 1662, when the Duke of Ormonde turned the land into a deer park. In 1745 it was landscaped and opened to the public by Lord Chesterfield.

Near Park Gate is the lakeside **People's Garden** – the only part of the park that has been cultivated. A little farther on are the **Zoological Gardens**, established in 1830, making them the third oldest zoo in the world. The zoo is renowned for the successful breeding of lions, including the one that appears at the beginning of MGM movies.

In addition to the Phoenix Column, the park has two other conspicuous monuments. The **Wellington Testimonial**, a 63-m (204-ft) obelisk, was begun in 1817 and completed in 1861. Its bronze bas-reliefs were made from captured French cannons. The 27-m (90-ft) steel **Papal Cross** marks the spot where the pope celebrated Mass in front of one million people in 1979.

**Pope John Paul II celebrating Mass in Phoenix Park in 1979**

Buildings within the park include two 18th-century houses: **Áras an Uachtaráin**, the Irish President's official residence, and **Deerfield**, home of the US Ambassador. The only building open to the public is **Ashtown Castle**, a restored 17th-century tower house which contains the Phoenix Park Visitor Centre.

Five times the size of Hyde Park in London, Phoenix Park has playing fields for Gaelic football, hurling and polo, and running and cycling trails.

**Jogger in Phoenix Park**

## PHOENIX PARK

Áras An Uachtaráin ⑤
Ashtown Castle ①
Deerfield ②
Papal Cross ③
People's Garden ⑧
Phoenix Column ④
Wellington Testimonial ⑦
Zoological Gardens ⑥

**KEY**

| 🚌 | Bus stop |
| P | Parking |
| ℹ | Tourist information |
| ▦ | Park wall |

0 meters 500
0 yards 500

**Restored central hall at Kilmainham Gaol**

## Kilmainham Gaol ❷

Inchicore Rd, Kilmainham, Dublin 8.
☎ 453 5984. 🚌 23, 51, 51A, 78,
79. ◻ May–Sep: 10am–6pm daily;
Oct–Apr: 1–4pm Mon–Fri, 1–6pm
Sun. ◼ Dec 25 & 26. ♿ 🎦

A LONG, TREE-LINED avenue runs
from the Royal Hospital
Kilmainham to the grim gray
bulk of Kilmainham Gaol.
Built in 1789, the jail was
extensively restored in the
1960s. During its 130 years as
a prison, it housed many of
those involved in the fight for
Irish independence, including
Robert Emmet *(see p75)* and
Charles Stewart Parnell *(p41)*.
The last prisoner to be held at
the jail was Eamon de Valera
*(p43)*, who was released from
here on July 16, 1924.

Tours start in the chapel,
where Joseph Plunkett married
Grace Gifford just a few hours
before he faced the firing
squad for his part in the 1916
Rising *(see pp42–3)*. The tours
end in the prison yard where
Plunkett's badly wounded
colleague James Connolly, unable to stand up, was strapped
into a chair before being shot.

You also pass the dank cells
of those involved in the 1798,
1803, 1848 and 1867 uprisings,
as well as the punishment
cells and hanging room. There
is a video presentation, and
in the central hall are exhibits
depicting various events that
took place in the jail until it
closed in 1924. There are also
personal mementos of some
of the former inmates.

Standing in the courtyard
is the *Asgard*, a ship used to
deliver arms from Germany to
the Nationalists in 1914.

## Royal Hospital Kilmainham ❸

Kilmainham, Dublin 8. ☎ 671 8666.
🚌 24, 78, 90. **Irish Museum of
Modern Art** ◻ 10am–5:30pm
Tue–Sat, noon–5:30pm Sun & public
hols. ◼ Good Fri & Dec 24–25. 🎦

I RELAND'S FINEST surviving
17th-century building was
laid out in 1680, styled on Les
Invalides in Paris. It was built
by Sir William Robinson as a
home for 300 wounded
soldiers – a role it retained
until 1927. When it was
completed, people were so
impressed by its Classical
symmetry that it was sug-
gested it would be better
used as the main campus of
Trinity College. In contrast to
the functional design of the
building, the Baroque chapel
has fine woodcarvings and
intricate heraldic stained
glass. The plaster ceiling is a
replica of the original, which
fell down in 1902.

In 1991, the hospital's
former residential quarters
were converted to house the
Irish Museum of Modern Art.
Corridors were painted white
and floors uniformly covered
in gray to create a stunning
home for the museum. Since
its opening the museum has
established a collection
through purchases, donations
and long-term loans. The
exhibits, which include a
cross-section of Irish and
international art, are shown
on a rotating basis. Theatrical
and musical performances are
also staged at the museum.

**The Royal Hospital Kilmainham**

**Sampling Guinness at the Hop Store**

## Guinness Hop Store ❹

Crane St, Dublin 8. 📞 453 6700
ext 5155. 🚌 78A, 68A, 123.
🕐 10am–4:30pm Mon–Fri.
⬤ public hols. 🎦 📷 ♿

THE WORLD OF GUINNESS exhibition is housed in a 19th-century warehouse, which was used for storing bales of hops until the 1950s.

A self-guided tour takes the visitor through displays that chronicle 200 years of brewing at St. James's Gate. The tour starts at an enormous Victorian kieve (or mash tun), and goes on to examine all other stages of the brewing process. Displays show how production methods have changed over the years from when Arthur Guinness took over the backstreet brewery in 1759, to today's state-of-the-art techniques. There is also a cooperage display with life-size models showing the craftmen's skills involved in making the wooden barrels which used to store the stout. Since the 1950s Guinness has used metal containers.

On the ground floor, in the Transport Gallery, is a narrow-gauge steam locomotive that once ferried materials around the factory site. Other displays include models of the company's fleet of barges that plied the Grand Canal, ocean tankers, and the once familiar dray horses which transported the stout to the ports.

The tour ends with an audio-visual show on the company's development, followed by a visit to the sampling bar where you can enjoy a couple of glasses of draft Guinness.

# The Brewing of Guinness

**Label from a Guinness bottle**

GUINNESS IS A BLACK BEER, known as "stout," renowned for its distinctive malty flavor and smooth creamy head. From its humble beginnings over 200 years ago, the Guinness brewery site at St. James's Gate now sprawls across 26 ha (65 acres). It is the largest brewery in Europe and exports beers to more than 120 countries throughout the world. Other famous brands owned by Guinness include Harp Lager and Smithwick's Ale.

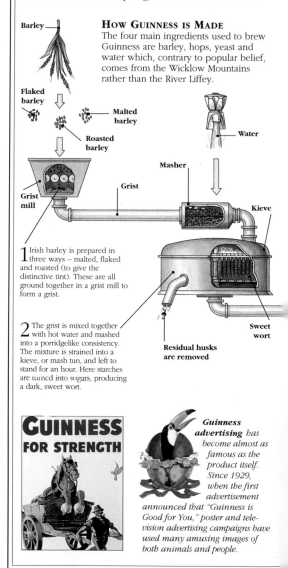

### HOW GUINNESS IS MADE

The four main ingredients used to brew Guinness are barley, hops, yeast and water which, contrary to popular belief, comes from the Wicklow Mountains rather than the River Liffey.

**Barley**

**Flaked barley**

**Malted barley**

**Roasted barley**

**Water**

**Grist mill**

**Grist**

**Masher**

**Kieve**

1 Irish barley is prepared in three ways – malted, flaked and roasted (to give the distinctive tint). These are all ground together in a grist mill to form a grist.

2 The grist is mixed together with hot water and mashed into a porridgelike consistency. The mixture is strained into a kieve, or mash tun, and left to stand for an hour. Here starches are turned into sugars, producing a dark, sweet wort.

**Residual husks are removed**

**Sweet wort**

**GUINNESS FOR STRENGTH**

*Guinness advertising* has become almost as famous as the product itself. Since 1929, when the first advertisement announced that "Guinness is Good for You," poster and television advertising campaigns have used many amusing images of both animals and people.

## ARTHUR GUINNESS

In December 1759, 34-year-old Arthur Guinness signed a 9,000-year lease at an annual rent of £45 to take over St. James's Gate Brewery, which had been vacant for almost ten years. At the time, the brewing industry in Dublin was at a low ebb – the standard of ale was much criticized and in rural Ireland beer was virtually unknown, as whiskey, gin and poteen were the more favored drinks. Furthermore, Irish beer was under threat from imports. Guinness started brewing ale, but was also aware of a black ale called porter, produced in London. This new beer was so called because of its popularity with porters at Billingsgate and Covent Garden markets. Guinness decided to stop making ales and develop his own recipe for porter (the word "stout" was not used until the 1920s). So successful was the switch that he made his first export shipment in 1769.

**Arthur Guinness**

**Engraving (c. 1794) of a satisfied customer**

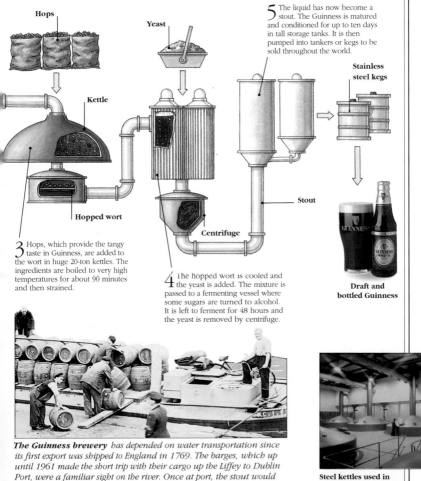

Hops

Yeast

5 The liquid has now become a stout. The Guinness is matured and conditioned for up to ten days in tall storage tanks. It is then pumped into tankers or kegs to be sold throughout the world.

Kettle

Stainless steel kegs

Hopped wort

Stout

Centrifuge

3 Hops, which provide the tangy taste in Guinness, are added to the wort in huge 20-ton kettles. The ingredients are boiled to very high temperatures for about 90 minutes and then strained.

4 The hopped wort is cooled and the yeast is added. The mixture is passed to a fermenting vessel where some sugars are turned to alcohol. It is left to ferment for 48 hours and the yeast is removed by centrifuge.

**Draft and bottled Guinness**

*The Guinness brewery has depended on water transportation since its first export was shipped to England in 1769. The barges, which up until 1961 made the short trip with their cargo up the Liffey to Dublin Port, were a familiar sight on the river. Once at port, the stout would be loaded on to huge tanker ships for worldwide distribution.*

**Steel kettles used in modern-day brewing**

Giant water lilies in the Lily House, National Botanic Gardens

## National Botanic Gardens ❺

Botanic Ave, Glasnevin, Dublin 9.
📞 837 4388. 🚌 13, 19, 19A, 34, 34A. 🕐 Mar–Oct: 9am–6pm Mon–Sat, 11am–6pm Sun; Nov–Feb: 10am–4:30pm Mon–Sat, 11am–4:30pm Sun. ● 25 Dec. **Glasnevin Cemetery** Finglas Rd. 🕐 Apr–Oct: 8am–5pm Mon–Fri, 8am–4pm Sat, 9:30am–5pm (Nov–Mar: 9:30am–4pm) Sun.

O PENED in 1795, the gardens house Ireland's foremost collection of botany and horticulture. They still possess an old-world feel, thanks to the beautiful cast-iron Palm House and other curvilinear greenhouses. These were built between 1843 and 1869 by Richard Turner, who was also responsible for the Palm House at Kew Gardens, London, and the greenhouses at Belfast's Botanic Gardens (see p270).

The 20-ha (49-acre) park contains over 20,000 different plant species. A particularly attractive feature is the display of colorful, old-fashioned Victorian carpet bedding. Other highlights include a celebrated rose garden and rich collections of cacti and orchids. There is also a 30-m (100-ft) high redwood tree.

The gardens back on to the huge Glasnevin or Prospect Cemetery where many of Ireland's political figures are buried, including Charles Stewart Parnell (see p41) and Daniel O'Connell (see p40).

## Shaw's Birthplace ❻

33 Synge St, Dublin 8. 📞 475 0854. 🚌 16, 19, 22. 🕐 May–Oct: 10am–1pm, 2–5pm Mon–Sat & 11:30am–1pm, 2–6pm Sun & public hols. 🈂️

Kitchen at Shaw's Birthplace

P LAYWRIGHT and Nobel prize-winner George Bernard Shaw was born in this house on July 26, 1856. In 1876 he followed his mother to London. She had left four years earlier with her daughters, fed up with her husband's drinking habits. It was in London that Shaw met his wife Charlotte Payne-Townsend. He stayed in England until his death in 1950.

Inside the house visitors can see the young Shaw's bedroom and the kitchen where the author remembered he drank "much tea out of brown delft left to 'draw' on the hob until it was pure tannin." Although there is little on Shaw's productive years, the home gives a fair idea of the lifestyle of a Victorian middle-class family.

## Marino Casino ❼

Fairview Park, off Malahide Rd, Dublin 3. 📞 833 1618. 🚌 20A, 20B, 27, 42, 42B, 43. 🕐 May–Oct: 10am–6:30pm daily; Feb–Apr: noon–4pm Wed & Sun. 🈂️ 🎫 obligatory.

T HIS DELIGHTFUL little villa (see pp38–9), built by Sir William Chambers in the 1760s for Lord Charlemont, now sits rather incongruously next to a busy road and public housing. Originally built as a summer house for the Marino Estate, the villa survives today although the main house was torn down in 1921. The Casino is acknowledged to be one of the finest examples of Palladian architecture in Ireland. Some fascinating innovative features were used in its construction,

**Carved stone lion at Marino Casino**

including chimneys disguised as urns and hollow columns that accommodate drains. Outside, four fine carved stone lions, thought to be by English sculptor Joseph Wilton, stand guard at each of the corners.

The building's squat, compact exterior conceals eight rooms built on three floors around a central staircase. The ground floor comprises a spacious hall and a parlor, with beautiful silk hangings, elaborate parquet flooring and a coffered ceiling. On the first floor is the ostentatious State Room, decorated in green and white.

# Waterways Visitors' Centre ❽

Grand Canal Quay, Dublin 2.
**☎** *677 7510.* **🚌** *3.* **🚪** *Jun–Sep: 9:30am–6:30pm daily; Oct–May: 12:30–5pm Wed–Sun.* **●** *25 Dec.* **📷 🎬** *on request*

Fifteen minutes' walk from Trinity College along Pearse Street, this building overlooks the Grand Canal Basin. Audiovisual displays and models illustrate Ireland's inland waterways. One of the most interesting displays focuses on their construction: in the 18th century, canals were often called "navigations" and the men who built them were "navigators," a term shortened to "navvies." There are also exhibits on the wildlife found on the canals and surrounding marshlands.

**Stretch of the Grand Canal near Waterways Visitors' Centre**

**Manuscript (1874) from the Holy Koran written by calligrapher Ahmad Shaikh in Kashmir, Chester Beatty Library**

# Chester Beatty Library and Gallery of Oriental Art ❾

20 Shrewsbury Road, Dublin 4.
**☎** *269 2386.* **🚆** *DART to Sandymount.* **🚪** *10am–5pm Tue–Fri, 2–5pm Sat.* **●** *public hols & Tue after public hols.* **📷 🎬** *2:30pm Wed & Sat.*

This collection of Oriental manuscripts and art was bequeathed to Ireland by the American mining magnate and art collector Sir Alfred Chester Beatty, who died in 1968. This generous act no doubt led to his selection as Ireland's first honorary citizen in 1957.

During his lifetime Beatty accumulated almost 300 copies of the Koran, representing the works of master calligraphers from Iran, Turkey and the Arab world. Other exhibits include 6,000-year-old Babylonian stone tablets, Greek papyri dating from the 2nd century AD and biblical material written in Coptic, the original language of Egypt.

In the Far Eastern Gallery is a collection of Chinese jade books; each leaf of these unique books is made from thinly cut jade, engraved with Chinese characters, which are then filled with gold. Other displays include hundreds of Chinese snuff bottles, imperial robes and rhinoceros horn cups. Tibetan and Mongolian treasures are also on display. Burmese and Siamese art is represented in the collection of 18th-century *Parabaiks*, books of folk tales illustrated with colorful paintings on mulberry leaf paper. The Japanese collection includes paintings, woodblock prints and books and scrolls from the 16th to 18th centuries, containing popular Japanese stories. The illustrations were painted by Buddhist monks from the city of Nara.

There is also a collection of western European manuscripts. One of the most beautiful is the *Coëtivy Book of Hours,* an illuminated French prayer book, dating from the 15th century. There is also a collection of printed books, many with fine engravings.

## DUBLIN'S CANALS

The affluent Georgian era saw the building of the Grand and Royal Canals linking Dublin with the River Shannon and the west coast. These two canals became the main arteries of trade and public transportation in Ireland from the 1760s until the coming of the railroads, which took much of the passenger business, almost a century later. However, the canals continued to carry freight until after World War II, finally closing to commercial traffic in 1960. Today the canals are well maintained and used mainly for pleasure-boating, cruising and fishing.

**Late 18th-century engraving of passenger ferry passing Harcourt Lock on the Grand Canal, taken from a painting by James Barralet**

**The oak-beamed Great Hall at Malahide Castle**

## Malahide Castle ⑩

Malahide, Co Dublin. 🚌 🚆 *42 from Dublin.* ☎ *846 2184.* ◯ *10am– 12:45pm & 2–5pm Mon–Fri, 11am– 6pm Sat, 11:30am– 6pm Sun & public hols (Nov–Mar: 2–5pm Sat, Sun & public hols).* **Fry Model Railway** ◯ *Jun–Aug: 10am–1pm & 2–6pm Mon–Fri, 11am–6pm Sat, 2–6pm Sun (Sep & Apr–May: Mon–Thu); Oct–Mar: 2–5pm Sat, Sun & public hols.* 🎟 *Combined ticket available.*

Near the seaside dormitory town of Malahide stands a huge castle set in 100 ha (250 acres) of grounds. The castle's core dates from the 14th century but later additions, such as its rounded towers, have given it a classic fairy-tale appearance. Originally a fortress, the building served as a stately home for the Talbot family until 1973. They were staunch supporters of James II: the story goes that on the day of the Battle of the Boyne in 1690 *(see p236)*, 14 members of the family breakfasted here; none came back for supper.

Guided tours take you around the castle's collection of 18th-century Irish furniture. You will also see the oak-beamed Great Hall and the carved paneling of the Oak Room. Part of the Portrait Collection, on loan from the National Gallery *(see pp68–9)*, can be seen at the castle. It includes portraits of the Talbot family, as well as other figures such as Wolfe Tone *(see p39)*.

In the old corn store is the Fry Model Railway, started in the 1920s by Cyril Fry, a local railway engineer. The 240 sq m (2,500 sq ft) exhibit contains models of Irish trains, miniatures of stations, streets and local landmarks such as the River Liffey and Howth Head.

## Howth ⑪

Co Dublin. 🚆 *DART.* **Howth Castle grounds** ◯ *8am–sunset daily.*

The commercial fishing town of Howth marks the northern limit of Dublin Bay. Howth Head, a huge rocky mass, has lovely views of the bay. A footpath runs around the tip of Howth Head, which is known as the "Nose." Nearby is Baily Lighthouse (1814). Sadly, much of this area – some of Ireland's prime real estate – has suffered from building development.

To the west of the town is Howth Castle, which dates back to Norman times. Its grounds are particularly beautiful in May and June when the rhododendrons and azaleas are in full bloom.

A short boat ride out from the harbor is the rocky islet, Ireland's Eye, which is a bird sanctuary where puffins nest. Boat trips from Howth run there throughout the summer.

## Dun Laoghaire ⑫

Co Dublin. 🚆 *DART.* **National Maritime Museum of Ireland** ☎ *280 0969.* ◯ *May–Sep: 2:30– 5:30pm Tue–Sun (Oct: Sat & Sun).* 🎟

Ireland's major passenger ferry port and yachting center, with its brightly painted villas, parks and palm trees, makes a surprising introduction to Ireland. On a

**Baily Lighthouse on the southeastern tip of Howth Head**

**Yachts anchored in Dun Laoghaire harbor**

good day it exudes a decidedly continental feel. Many visitors head straight out of Dun Laoghaire (pronounced Dunleary) from the ferry. However, the town offers some magnificent walks around the harbor and to the lighthouse along the east pier. The villages of Sandycove and Dalkey can be reached via "The Metals" footpath, which runs along an unused railroad.

Located in the 1837 Mariners' Church is the National Maritime Museum. Exhibits tell the story of Robert Halpin, who captained the ship that laid the first transatlantic telegraph cable in 1866. Also on display are a huge clockwork-driven lighthouse lens formerly used at Howth and a longboat used by French officers during Wolfe Tone's unsuccessful invasion at Bantry in 1796 *(see pp160–61)*.

## James Joyce Tower ⑬

Sandycove, Co Dublin. 【 280 9265. 🚆 *DART to Sandycove.* ◯ *Apr–Oct: 10am–1pm & 2–5pm Mon–Sat, 2–6pm Sun & public hols.* 🌐

S TANDING on a rocky promontory above the village of Sandycove is a Martello tower. It is one of 5 defensive towers which ere erected between Dublin d Bray in 1804 to withstand reatened invasion of oleon. One hundred

years later James Joyce *(see p88)* stayed here for a week as the guest of Oliver St. John Gogarty, poet and model for the *Ulysses* character Buck Mulligan. Gogarty rented the tower for a mere £8 (about $12) per year. Inside the squat 12-m (40-ft) tower's granite walls is a small museum with some of Joyce's correspondence, personal belongings, such as his guitar, cigar case and walking stick, and his death mask. There are also photographs and first editions of his works, including a deluxe edition (1935) of *Ulysses* illustrated by Henri Matisse. The roof, originally a gun **Guitar at James** platform but later used **Joyce Tower** as a sunbathing deck by Gogarty, affords marvelous views of Dublin Bay. Directly below the tower is Forty Foot Pool, traditionally an all-male nude swimming pool, but now open to all.

## Dalkey ⑭

Co Dublin. 🚆 *DART.*

D ALKEY was once known as the "Town of Seven Castles," but only two of these now remain. They are both on the main street of this attractive village whose tight, winding roads and charming villas give it a Mediterranean feel.

A little way offshore is tiny Dalkey Island, a rocky bird sanctuary with a Martello tower and a medieval Benedictine church, both now in a poor state of repair. In summer the island can be reached by a boat ride from the town's Coliemore harbor.

## Killiney ⑮

Co Dublin. 🚆 *DART to Dalkey or Killiney.*

S OUTH OF DALKEY, the coastal road climbs uphill before tumbling down into the village of Killiney. The route offers one of the most scenic vistas on this stretch of the east coast, with views often compared to those across the Bay of Naples. Howth Head is clearly visible to the north, with Bray Head *(see p125)* and the foothills of the Wicklow Mountains *(see pp130–31)* to the south. There is another exhilarating view from the top of Killiney Hill Park, off Victoria Road – well worth tackling the short steep trail for. Down below is the popular pebbly beach, Killiney Strand.

**Storefronts on the main street of Dalkey**

# ENTERTAINMENT IN DUBLIN

ALTHOUGH DUBLIN is well served by theaters, movie houses, night-clubs and rock clubs, what sets the city apart from other European capitals is its pubs. Lively banter, impromptu music sessions and great Guinness are the essential ingredients for an enjoyable night in any one of these atmospheric hostelries.

**Olympia Theatre façade**

One of the most popular entertainment districts is the rejuvenated Temple Bar area. Along this narrow network of cobbled streets you can find everything from traditional music in grand old pubs to the latest dance tracks in a postindustrial setting. The many pubs and venues around this area make the city center south of the Liffey the place to be at night. The north side does, however, boast the two most illustrious theaters, the largest movie houses and the 7,000-seater Point Theatre, a converted 19th-century rail terminal beside the docks. It is now the place for all major rock concerts and stage musicals as well as a number of classical music performances.

**Buskers playing near Grafton Street in southeast Dublin**

## ENTERTAINMENT LISTINGS

THE MAIN LISTINGS magazine, *In Dublin*, comes out every two weeks and is readily available from all newsstands. *Hot Press*, a national bimonthly newspaper that covers both rock and traditional music, has comprehensive listings for Dublin. The *Dublin Event Guide* is a free sheet available from pubs, cafés, restaurants and record shops. Also published every two weeks, it is particularly strong on music and nightclubs.

## BOOKING TICKETS

TICKETS FOR MANY EVENTS are available on the night, but it is usually safer to book in advance. All the major venues take credit card payment over the telephone. The **Ticket Shop** accepts phone bookings by credit card for many of the major shows and events in and around Dublin, while the main branches of **HMV** sell tickets over the counter for some of the top theater shows and most major rock gigs.

## THEATER

ALTHOUGH DUBLIN has only a limited number of theaters, there is almost always something worth seeing and the productions are of a very high standard. Most of Dublin's theaters are closed on Sunday.

The most famous venue is Ireland's national theater, the **Abbey** *(see p86)*, which concentrates on major new Irish productions as well as revivals of work by Irish playwrights such as Brendan Behan, Sean O'Casey, JM Synge and WB Yeats. The smaller Peacock Theatre downstairs covers more experimental works. Also on the north side is the **Gate Theatre** *(see p88)* founded in 1929 and noted for its interpretations of well-known international plays.

The main venue south of the Liffey, the **Gaiety Theatre**, stages a mainstream mix of plays, emphasizing the work of Irish playwrights. Some of the best fringe theater and modern dance in Dublin can be seen at the **Project Arts Centre** in Temple Bar and the **City Arts Centre**, which sometimes has midnight performances. **Andrews Lane Theatre** provides a forum for new writers and directors. The **Olympia Theatre** has the feel of a Victorian music hall. It specializes in comedy and popular drama and occasionally stages rock and Irish music concerts.

Every October the **Dublin Theatre Festival** takes over all the venues in the city with mainstream, fringe, Irish and international plays.

**Record shop and ticket office in Crown Alley, Temple Bar**

Crowds enjoying the Temple Bar Blues Festival

## CLASSICAL MUSIC, OPERA AND DANCE

DUBLIN may not have the range of classical concerts of other European capitals, but it has a great venue in the **National Concert Hall**. In the 1980s, this 19th-century exhibition hall was completely redesigned and acoustically adapted, and is where the National Symphony Orchestra plays most Friday evenings. The National Concert Hall's program also includes opera, chamber music, jazz, dance and some traditional music.

The **Hugh Lane Municipal Gallery of Modern Art** (see p89) has regular Sunday lunchtime concerts. Other classical venues include the **Royal Hospital Kilmainham** (see p95) and the **Royal Dublin Society (RDS)** main hall and showground. International opera is staged in the **Point Theatre**. The DGOS (Dublin Grand Opera Society) performs every April and November at the Gaiety Theatre.

## TRADITIONAL MUSIC AND DANCE

TO MANY IRISH PEOPLE the standard of music in a pub is just as important as the quality of the Guinness. Central Dublin has a host of pubs reverberating to the sound of bodhráns, fiddles and uilleann pipes. One of the most famous is **O'Donoghue's**, where the

The listings magazine
*In Dublin*

legendary Dubliners started out in the early 1960s. **An Béal Bocht, Slattery's** and the **Auld Dubliner** are also famous spots. Established acts play venues such as **Mother Redcap's Tavern**, a fun place occupying an old factory. **Jury's Hotel** and the **Castle Inn** stage nightly Irish cabaret featuring dancing, singing and music.

## ROCK, JAZZ, BLUES AND COUNTRY

DUBLIN has had a thriving rock scene ever since local band Thin Lizzy made it big in the early 1970s. U2's international success has acted as a further catalyst for local bands, and each night there's usually an interesting gig somewhere in the city. **Whelan's** and the **Baggot Inn** feature the best up-and-coming Irish bands

nightly. The upstairs room at the likable **International Bar** caters mostly to acoustic acts and singer-songwriters. The **Waterfront Rock Bar** is a late-night music bar and restaurant next to U2's offices and studio. All the big names play at either the Point Theatre or, in summer, local sports stadia. The Olympia Theatre attracts some top performers with its more intimate setting.

Jazz and blues musicians play occasionally in large and small venues; an annual highlight is the **Temple Bar Blues Festival** in July. Country music enjoys a massive following in Ireland, and country acts play regularly at several Dublin pubs. **Bad Bob's Backstage Bar** is a lively country music nightclub where there's usually lots of dancing.

## NIGHTCLUBS

UNTIL A CLUSTER of new dance clubs opened in the early 1990s, Dublin's clublife was fairly unremarkable. Nowadays the **POD** (Place of Dance) attracts visiting stars taking time out from their movie or video shoots in the city. Another extremely trendy place is the **Kitchen** downstairs in the (U2-owned) Clarence Hotel. **Ri-Rá** is a venue at the cutting edge of dance music, while **Lillie's Bordello** caters to a more mainstream dance sound.

Most clubs close at 2am. For more action, head for the stretch of clubs on Leeson Street that stay open until around 5am. Admission is free, but drink prices are high.

A traditional Irish music session in O'Donoghue's

**Traditional façade of Doheny and Nesbitt**

## PUBS AND BARS

DUBLIN'S PUBS are a slice of living history. These are the places where some of the best-known scenes in Irish literature have been set, where rebellious politicians have met and where world-famous music acts have made their debuts. Today, as well as the memorabilia on the walls, it's the singing, dancing, talk and laughter that make a pub tour of Dublin a must.

There are nearly 1,000 pubs inside the city limits. Among the best of the traditional bars are **Neary's**, popular with actors and featuring a gorgeous marble bar, the atmospheric **Long Hall** and the friendly **Stag's Head**, dating from 1770. Cozy snugs – where drinkers could lock themselves away for private conversation – were an important feature of 19th-century bars. A few remain, notably at the tiny journalists' haunt of **Doheny and Nesbitt** and the intimate **Kehoe's**.

The **Brazen Head** claims to be the city's oldest pub, dating back to 1198. The present pub, built in the 1750s, is lined with old photographs and dark wood paneling. Every pub prides itself on the quality of its Guinness, though it's often acknowledged that **Mulligan's**, founded in 1782, serves one of the best pints in the city.

The range extends beyond smoky pubs with nicotine-stained ceilings: the splendid decor of the **Shelbourne Bar**, in the Shelbourne Hotel, attracts a more sophisticated clientele. New bars abound in the Trinity College and Temple Bar areas. **Mr Pussy's Café de Luxe** and the **Garage**, a bar with a Trabant car as the central focus, are two of the most talked about.

## A LITERARY PUB CRAWL

PUBS with strong literary associations abound in Dublin, particularly around Grafton Street. **McDaid's**, an old pub with an Art Deco interior, still retains some of the Bohemian air from the time when famous writer-drinkers such as Patrick Kavanagh and Brendan Behan were regulars. **Davy Byrne's** has much plusher decor than when Leopold Bloom dropped in for a gorgonzola and mustard sandwich in *Ulysses*, but it is still well worth paying a visit.

These and about six other pubs, once frequented by Ireland's most famous authors

**GUINNESS TIME**
A Guinness sign on the outside of a Dublin pub

and playwrights, are featured on the excellent **Dublin Literary Pub Crawl**. This is by far the most entertaining way to get a real feel for the city's booze-fueled literary heritage. The two-and-a-half-hour tours, led by actors, start with a beer in the Duke, Duke Street. Tours take place daily in summer, but are usually only on weekends in winter.

## MOVIES

DUBLIN'S MOVIE HOUSES have had a boost thanks to the success of Dublin-based films such as *My Left Foot* (1989) and *The Commitments* (1991) and a huge growth in the country's movie production industry.

The **Irish Film Centre** opened its doors in 1992 and is a most welcome addition to the city's entertainment scene. Showing mostly independent and foreign films, along with a program of lectures and seminars, it boasts two screens, a bar and a restaurant. Two other theaters whose repertoire is mostly art house are the **Screen**, near Trinity College, and the **Light House**, which is north of the river. The large first-run theaters are all located on the north side. These usually offer tickets at reduced prices for their afternoon screenings and show late-night movies on the weekend. The **Dublin Film Festival**, which is held for ten days between late February and early March, shows international and Irish releases.

**Bustling interior of the Oliver St. John Gogarty pub in Temple Bar**

## DIRECTORY

### BOOKING TICKETS

**HMV**
18 Henry St. **Map** D2.
( 873 2899.
65 Grafton St. **Map** D4.
( 679 5334.

**Ticket Shop**
2nd Floor, Grafton House,
70 Grafton St. **Map** D4.
( 677 5930.

### THEATER

**Abbey Theatre**
Abbey St Lower. **Map** E2.
( 878 7222.

**Andrews Lane Theatre**
9–17 St. Andrew's Lane.
**Map** D3.
( 679 5720.

**City Arts Centre**
23–25 Moss St. **Map** E2.
( 677 0643.

**Dublin Theatre Festival**
47 Nassau St. **Map** D3.
( 677 8439.

**Gaiety Theatre**
King St South. **Map** D4.
( 677 1717.

**Gate Theatre**
Parnell Sq East. **Map** D1.
( 874 4368.

**Olympia Theatre**
Dame St. **Map** C3.
( 677 7744.

**Project Arts Centre**
39 Essex St East, Temple
Bar. **Map** C3.
( 671 2321.

**Riverbank Theatre**
Merchant's Quay. **Map** B3.
( 677 3370.

### CLASSICAL MUSIC, OPERA AND DANCE

**Hugh Lane Municipal Gallery of Modern Art**
Charlemont House, Parnell
Sq North. **Map** C1.
( 874 1903.

**National Concert Hall**
Earlsfort Terrace. **Map** D5.
( 671 1533.

**Point Theatre**
East Link Bridge, North
Wall Quay.
( 836 3633.

**Royal Dublin Society (RDS)**
Ballsbridge.
( 668 0866.

**Royal Hospital Kilmainham**
Kilmainham.
( 671 8666.

### TRADITIONAL MUSIC AND DANCE

**An Béal Bocht**
58 Charlemont St.
( 475 5614.

**Auld Dubliner**
24–25 Temple Bar.
**Map** D3.
( 677 0527.

**Castle Inn**
5–7 Lord Edward St.
**Map** C3.
( 475 1122.

**Jury's Hotel**
Pembroke Rd, Ballsbridge.
( 660 5000.

**Mother Redcap's Tavern**
Back Lane, Christchurch.
**Map** B4.
( 453 8306.

**O'Donoghue's**
15 Merrion Row. **Map** E5.
( 660 7194.

**Slattery's**
129 Capel St. **Map** C2.
( 872 7971.

### ROCK, JAZZ, BLUES AND COUNTRY

**Bad Bob's Backstage Bar**
Essex St East, Temple Bar.
**Map** C3.
( 677 5482.

**Baggot Inn**
143 Baggot St Lower.
**Map** E5.
( 676 1430.

**International Bar**
23 Wicklow St. **Map** D3.
( 677 9250.

**Temple Bar Blues Festival**
Temple Bar Information
Centre, 18 Eustace St.
**Map** C3.
( 671 5717.

**Waterfront Rock Bar**
14 Sir John Rogerson's
Quay.
( 677 8466.

**Whelan's**
25 Wexford St. **Map** C5.
( 478 0766.

### NIGHTCLUBS

**Kitchen**
6–8 Wellington Quay.
**Map** C3.
( 662 3066.

**Lillie's Bordello**
Adam Court, off Grafton St.
**Map** D4.
( 679 9204.

**POD**
Harcourt St. **Map** D5.
( 478 0166.

**Ri-Rá**
11 South Great George's St.
**Map** C3.
( 677 4835.

### PUBS AND BARS

**Brazen Head**
20 Bridge St Lower.
**Map** A3.
( 677 9549.

**Davy Byrne's**
21 Duke St. **Map** D4.
( 677 5217.

**Doheny and Nesbitt**
5 Baggot St Lower.
**Map** E5.
( 676 2945.

**Dublin Literary Pub Crawl**
35 Heytesbury St. **Map** C5.
( 454 0228.

**Garage**
6–8 Wellington Quay.
**Map** C3.
( 662 3066.

**Kehoe's**
9 Anne St South. **Map** D4.
( 677 8312.

**Long Hall**
South Great George's St.
**Map** C4.
( 475 1590.

**McDaid's**
3 Harry St, off Grafton St.
**Map** D4.
( 679 4395.

**Mr. Pussy's Café de Luxe**
21 Suffolk St. **Map** D3.
( 677 4804.

**Mulligan's**
8 Poolbeg St. **Map** E3.
( 677 5582.

**Neary's**
1 Chatham St. **Map** D4.
( 677 8596.

**The Norseman**
29 Essex St East, Temple
Bar. **Map** C3.
( 671 5135.

**Oliver St. John Gogarty**
58–59 Fleet St, Temple Bar.
**Map** D3.
( 671 1822.

**Queen's**
12 Castle St, Dalkey.
( 285 4569.

**Shelbourne Bar**
27 St. Stephen's Green
North. **Map** E4.
( 676 6471.

**Stag's Head**
1 Dame Court, off Dame
Lane. **Map** D3.
( 679 3701.

**Toner's**
139 Baggot St Lower.
**Map** E5.
( 676 3090.

### MOVIE HOUSES

**Dublin Film Festival**
1 Suffolk St. **Map** D3.
( 679 2937.

**Irish Film Centre**
6 Eustace St, Temple Bar.
**Map** C3.
( 679 5744.

**Light House**
106 Abbey St Middle.
**Map** D2.
( 873 0438.

**Screen**
D'Olier St. **Map** D3.
( 671 4988.

# Dublin's Best: Entertainment

IT'S EASY TO PACK a lot into a night out in Dublin. Most of the best nightspots are located close to each other and, in the Temple Bar area alone, there are plenty of exciting hangouts to try. The city offers something to suit every taste and pocket: choose from world-class theater, excellent concert halls, designer café-bars and lively or laid-back clubs hosting nights of traditional, country, jazz or rock music. Even when there is no specific event that appeals, you can simply enjoy Dublin's inexhaustible supply of great traditional pubs.

**Gate Theatre**
*The Gate puts on both foreign plays and Irish classics such as Sean O'Casey's Juno and the Paycock. (See p88.)*

**Stag's Head**
*This gorgeous Victorian pub has a long, mahogany bar and has retained its original mirrors and stained glass. Located down an out-of-the-way alley, this atmospheric pub is well worth seeking out. (See p105.)*

NORTH OF THE LIFFEY

SOUTHWEST DUBLIN

0 meters     500
0 yards     500

## THE TEMPLE BAR AREA

It will take more than a couple of evenings to explore fully all that these narrow streets have to offer. Many of Dublin's best midpriced restaurants are here, while modern bars sit next to traditional pubs hosting fiddle sessions. There are also theaters and the Irish Film Centre. Later, clubs play music ranging from country to the latest dance sounds.

LIFFEY
HA'PENNY BRIDGE
WELLINGTON QUAY
THE GARAGE BAR
PROJECT
ESSEX STREET EAST
THE AULD DUBLINER
TEMPLE BAR
CROWN ALLEY
THE BAD ASS CAFÉ
BAD BOBS
SYCAMORE ST
MEETING HOUSE SQUARE
TEMPLE LANE
FOWNNES STREET
COPE STREET
CROW ST
Irish Film Centre
OLYMPIA
DAME STREET

0 meters     100
0 yards     100

**Lining up for a concert in Temple Bar**

**Street theater events** take place throughout the summer in Temple Bar. This actor is portraying George Bernard Shaw in a typical street performance.

### Abbey Theatre
*Despite recurring financial problems, Ireland's prestigious national theater still manages to stage compelling new drama, such as* Dancing at Lughnasa *by Brian Friel. (See p86.)*

### Point Theatre
*Once a Victorian railroad terminal, this is now the country's top live-music arena. Major acts, including Van Morrison (above) and Luciano Pavarotti, have appeared here. It's also a popular venue for hit musicals. (See p105.)*

LIFFEY

SOUTHEAST DUBLIN

### McDaid's
*Playwright Brendan Behan (see p21) downed many a pint in this pub, which dates from 1779. Although firmly on the tourist trail, McDaid's retains its bohemian charm, and bars upstairs and downstairs provide space for a leisurely drink. (See p105.)*

### National Concert Hall
*The National Symphony Orchestra performs most Friday evenings. A combination of dance, chamber music and other performance arts makes up a full program of events. From May to July, inexpensive Tuesday lunchtime concerts are held. (See p103.)*

# Street Finder Index

## KEY TO THE STREET FINDER

| | | |
|---|---|---|
| ■ Major sight | 🚕 Taxi stand | ⊠ Post office |
| ■ Place of interest | 🅿 Parking | ═ Railroad line |
| ■ Railroad station | 🛈 Tourist information office | → One-way street |
| 🚃 DART station | ✚ Hospital with emergency room | ▬ Pedestrian street |
| 🚌 Main bus stop | 🚓 Police station | 0 meters        200 |
| 🚌 Coach station | ✚ Church | 0 yards         200 |

1:11,500

## KEY TO ABBREVIATIONS USED IN THE STREET FINDER

| **Ave** | Avenue | **E** | East | **Pde** | Parade | **Sth** | South |
|---|---|---|---|---|---|---|---|
| **Br** | Bridge | **La** | Lane | **Pl** | Place | **Tce** | Terrace |
| **Cl** | Close | **Lr** | Lower | **Rd** | Road | **Up** | Upper |
| **Ct** | Court | **Nth** | North | **St** | Street/Saint | **W** | West |

### A

| | |
|---|---|
| Abbey Street Lower | D2 |
| Abbey Street Middle | D2 |
| Abbey Street Old | E2 |
| Abbey Street Upper | C2 |
| Abbey Theatre | D2 |
| Adair Lane | D3 |
| Adelaide Hospital | C4 |
| Amiens Street | F1 |
| Anglesea Row | C2 |
| Anglesea Street | D3 |
| Anne Street North | B2 |
| Anne Street South | D4 |
| Anne's Lane | D4 |
| Ardee Row | A5 |
| Ardee Street | A5 |
| Arran Quay | A3 |
| Arran Street East | B2 |
| Asdill's Row | D3 |
| Ash Street | A4 |
| Aston Place | D3 |
| Aston Quay | D3 |
| Aungier Place | C5 |
| Aungier Street | C5 |

### B

| | |
|---|---|
| Bachelors Walk | D3 |
| Back Lane | B4 |
| Baggot Court | F5 |
| Baggot Rath Place | E5 |
| Baggot Street Lower | F5 |
| Ball's Lane | B2 |
| Bank of Ireland | D3 |
| Bass Place | F4 |
| Beaver Street | F1 |
| Bedford Row | D3 |
| Bella Place | F1 |
| Bella Street | E1 |
| Bell's Lane | E5 |
| Benburb Street | A2 |
| Beresford Lane | E2 |
| Beresford Place | E2 |
| Beresford Street | B2 |
| Bewley's Oriental Café | D4 |
| Bishop Street | C5 |
| Blackhall Parade | A2 |
| Blackhall Place | A2 |
| Blackhall Street | A2 |
| Blackpitts | B5 |
| Bolton Street | C1 |
| Bonham Street | A3 |
| Borris Court | B3 |
| Bow Lane East | C4 |
| Bow Street | A2 |
| Boyne Street | F4 |
| Brabazon Row | A5 |
| Brabazon Street | A4 |
| Bracken's Lane | E3 |
| Braithwaite Street | A4 |
| Bride Road | B4 |
| Bride Street | C4 |

| | |
|---|---|
| Bride Street New | C5 |
| Bridge Street Lower | A3 |
| Bridge Street Upper | A3 |
| Bridgefoot Street | A3 |
| Britain Place | D1 |
| Brown Street North | A2 |
| Brown Street South | A5 |
| Brunswick Street North | A2 |
| Buckingham Street Lower | F1 |
| Bull Alley Street | B4 |
| Burgh Quay | D3 |
| Busáras | E2 |
| Butt Bridge | E2 |
| Byrne's Lane | C2 |

### C

| | |
|---|---|
| Camden Place | C5 |
| Camden Row | C5 |
| Camden Street Lower | C5 |
| Capel Street | C2 |
| Carman's Hall | A4 |
| Castle Market | D4 |
| Castle Steps | C3 |
| Castle Street | C3 |
| Cathal Brugha Street | D1 |
| Cathedral Lane | B5 |
| Cathedral Street | D2 |
| Cathedral View Court | B5 |
| Chamber Street | A5 |
| Chancery Lane | C4 |
| Chancery Place | B3 |
| Chancery Street | B3 |
| Chapel Lane | C2 |
| Charles Street West | B3 |
| Chatham Row | D4 |
| Chatham Street | D4 |
| Christ Church Cathedral | B3 |
| Christchurch Place | B4 |
| Church Avenue West | B2 |
| Church Lane South | C5 |
| Church Street | B3 |
| Church Street New | A2 |
| Church Street Upper | B2 |
| Church Terrace | B2 |
| City Hall | C3 |
| City Quay | F2 |
| Clanbrassil Street Lower | B5 |
| Clare Lane | E4 |
| Clare Street | E4 |
| Clarence Mangan Road | A5 |
| Clarendon Row | D4 |
| Clarendon Street | D4 |
| Clonmel Street | D5 |
| Coke Lane | A3 |
| Coleraine Street | B1 |
| College Green | D3 |
| College Lane | E3 |
| College Street | D3 |
| Commons Street | F2 |
| Connolly Station | F1 |

| | |
|---|---|
| Constitution Hill | B1 |
| Convent Close | F5 |
| Cook Street | B3 |
| Coombe Court | A4 |
| Cope Street | D3 |
| Copper Alley | C3 |
| Cork Hill | C3 |
| Cork Street | A5 |
| Corporation Street | E1 |
| Crane Lane | C3 |
| Creighton Street | F3 |
| Crown Alley | D3 |
| Cuckoo Lane | B2 |
| Cuffe Street | C5 |
| Cumberland Street North | D1 |
| Cumberland Street South | F4 |
| Custom House | E2 |
| Custom House Quay | E2 |

### D

| | |
|---|---|
| D'Olier Street | D3 |
| Dame Lane | C3 |
| Dame Street | C3 |
| Dawson Lane | D4 |
| Dawson Street | D4 |
| Dean Street | B4 |
| Dean Swift Square | B4 |
| Denzille Lane | F4 |
| Diamond Park | E1 |
| Digges Street Upper | C5 |
| Dominick Lane | C1 |
| Dominick Place | C1 |
| Dominick Street Lower | C1 |
| Dominick Street Upper | B1 |
| Donore Road | A5 |
| Dorset Street Upper | C1 |
| Dowlings Court | F3 |
| Drury Street | D4 |
| Dublin Castle | C3 |
| Dublin Civic Museum | D4 |
| Dublin Writers Museum | C1 |
| Dublinia | B4 |
| Duke Lane | D4 |
| Duke Street | D4 |

### E

| | |
|---|---|
| Earl Place | D2 |
| Earl Street North | D2 |
| Earl Street South | A4 |
| Earlsfort Terrace | D5 |
| Ebenezer Terrace | A5 |
| Eden Quay | D2 |
| Ellis Quay | A3 |
| Ely Place | E5 |
| Erne Place Lower | F3 |
| Erne Street Upper | F4 |
| Erne Terrace Front | F3 |
| Essex Quay | C3 |
| Essex Street East | C3 |
| Essex Street West | C3 |

| | |
|---|---|
| Eustace Street | C3 |
| Exchange Street Lower | C3 |
| Exchange Street Upper | C3 |
| Exchequer Street | D3 |

### F

| | |
|---|---|
| Fade Street | C4 |
| Father Mathew Bridge | A3 |
| Father Mathew Square | B2 |
| Fenian Street | F4 |
| Fishamble Street | B3 |
| Fitzwilliam Lane | E5 |
| Fitzwilliam Square North | E5 |
| Fitzwilliam Square West | E5 |
| Fitzwilliam Street Lower | F5 |
| Fitzwilliam Street Upper | F5 |
| Fleet Street | D3 |
| Foley Street | E1 |
| Foster Place | D3 |
| Fountain Place | A2 |
| Four Courts | B3 |
| Fownes Street | D3 |
| Francis Street | B4 |
| Frederick Street South | E4 |
| Frenchman's Lane | E2 |
| Friary Avenue | A2 |
| Fumbally Lane | B5 |

### G

| | |
|---|---|
| Garden Lane | A4 |
| Garden of Remembrance | C1 |
| Gardiner Street Lower | E1 |
| Gardiner Street Middle | D1 |
| Gate Theatre | D1 |
| General Post Office | D2 |
| Geoffrey Keating Road | A5 |
| George's Dock | F2 |
| George's Hill | B2 |
| George's Lane | A2 |
| George's Quay | E2 |
| Gloucester Diamond | E1 |
| Gloucester Place | E1 |
| Gloucester Street South | E3 |
| Glover's Alley | D4 |
| Golden Lane | C4 |
| Grafton Street | D4 |
| Granby Lane | C1 |
| Granby Place | C1 |
| Granby Row | C1 |
| Grangegorman Upper | A1 |
| Grant's Row | F4 |
| Grattan Bridge | C3 |
| Gray Street | A4 |
| Greek Street | B2 |
| Green Street | B2 |

## H

| | |
|---|---|
| Hagan's Court | F5 |
| Halston Street | B2 |
| Hammond Lane | A3 |
| Hammond Street | A5 |
| Hanbury Lane | A4 |
| Hanover Lane | B4 |
| Hanover Street | B4 |
| Hanover Street East | F3 |
| Ha'penny Bridge | D3 |
| Harbour Court | D2 |
| Harcourt Street | D5 |
| Hawkins Street | E3 |
| Haymarket | A2 |
| Hendrick Lane | A2 |
| Hendrick Street | A2 |
| Henrietta Lane | B1 |
| Henrietta Place | B2 |
| Henrietta Street | B1 |
| Henry Place | D2 |
| Henry Street | D2 |
| Herbert Lane | F5 |
| Herbert Street | F5 |
| Heytesbury Street | C5 |
| High Street | B3 |
| Hill Street | D1 |
| Hogan Place | F4 |
| Holles Place | F4 |
| Holles Row | F4 |
| Holles Street | F4 |
| Hugh Lane Municipal Gallery of Modern Art | C1 |
| Hume Street | E5 |

## I

| | |
|---|---|
| Inner Dock | F2 |
| Inns Quay | B3 |
| Irish Whiskey Corner | A2 |
| Island Street | A3 |
| Iveagh Gardens | D5 |

## J

| | |
|---|---|
| James Joyce Cultural Centre | D1 |
| James's Place | F5 |
| James's Place East | F5 |
| Jervis Lane Lower | C2 |
| Jervis Lane Upper | C2 |
| Jervis Street | C2 |
| John Street North | A3 |
| John Street South | A5 |
| John Dillon Street | B4 |
| John's Lane East | B3 |
| John's Lane West | A4 |
| Johnson Court | D4 |

## K

| | |
|---|---|
| Kevin Street Lower | C5 |
| Kevin Street Upper | B5 |
| Kildare Street | E4 |
| Killarney Street | F1 |
| King Street North | A2 |
| King Street South | D4 |
| King's Inns | B1 |
| King's Inns Park | B1 |
| King's Inns Street | C1 |
| Kirwan Street | A1 |

## L

| | |
|---|---|
| Lad Lane | F5 |
| Lamb Alley | B4 |
| Leeson Lane | E5 |
| Leeson Street Lower | E5 |
| Leinster House | E4 |
| Leinster Street South | E4 |
| Lemon Street | D4 |
| Liberty Lane | C5 |
| Liberty Park | E1 |
| Liffey Street Lower | D2 |
| Liffey Street Upper | C2 |
| Lincoln Place | E4 |
| Linenhall Parade | B1 |
| Linenhall Street | B2 |
| Linenhall Terrace | B1 |
| Lisburn Street | B2 |
| Little Britain Street | B2 |
| Little Green Street | B2 |
| Litton Lane | D2 |
| Loftus Lane | C2 |
| Lombard Street East | F3 |

| | |
|---|---|
| Long Lane | B5 |
| Longford Street Great | C4 |
| Longford Street Little | C4 |
| Lord Edward Street | C3 |
| Lotts | D2 |
| Luke Street | E3 |
| Lurgan Street | B2 |

## M

| | |
|---|---|
| Mabbot Lane | E1 |
| Madden Road | A5 |
| Magennis Place | F3 |
| Malpas Street | B5 |
| Mansion House | D4 |
| Mark Street | E3 |
| Mark's Alley West | B4 |
| Mark's Lane | F3 |
| Marlborough Street | D1 |
| Marshall Lane | A3 |
| Marsh's Library | B4 |
| Mary Street | C2 |
| Mary Street Little | B2 |
| Mary's Lane | B2 |
| Matt Talbot Memorial Bridge | E2 |
| May Lane | A2 |
| Mayor Street Lower | F2 |
| Meade's Terrace | F4 |
| Meath Hospital | B5 |
| Meath Place | A4 |
| Meath Street | A4 |
| Meetinghouse Lane | C2 |
| Mellowes Bridge | A3 |
| Memorial Road | E2 |
| Mercer Street Upper | C5 |
| Merchant's Quay | B3 |
| Merrion Row | E5 |
| Merrion Square | F4 |
| Merrion Square East | F5 |
| Merrion Square North | F4 |
| Merrion Square South | E4 |
| Merrion Square West | E4 |
| Merrion Street Lower | F4 |
| Merrion Street Upper | E5 |
| Michael's Terrace | A5 |
| Mill Street | A5 |
| Molesworth Place | D4 |
| Molesworth Street | D4 |
| Montague Place | C5 |
| Montague Street | C5 |
| Moore Lane | D1 |
| Moore Street | D2 |
| Morning Star Avenue | A1 |
| Moss Street | E2 |
| Mount Street Lower | F4 |
| Mount Street Upper | F5 |
| Mountjoy Street | C1 |
| Mountjoy Street Middle | B1 |

## N

| | |
|---|---|
| Nassau Street | D3 |
| National Gallery | E4 |
| Natural History Museum | E4 |
| National Library | E4 |
| National Museum | E4 |
| New Row South | B5 |
| New Street North | B2 |
| New Street South | B5 |
| Newman House | D5 |
| Newmarket | A5 |
| Nicholas Street | B4 |
| North Great George's Street | D1 |
| North Wall Quay | F2 |

## O

| | |
|---|---|
| O'Carolan Road | A5 |
| O'Connell Bridge | D2 |
| O'Connell Street Lower | D2 |
| O'Connell Street Upper | D1 |
| O'Curry Avenue | A5 |
| O'Curry Road | A5 |
| O'Donovan Rossa Bridge | B3 |
| Oliver Bond Street | A3 |
| O'Rahilly Parade | D2 |
| Oriel Street Upper | F1 |
| Ormond Quay Lower | C3 |
| Ormond Quay Upper | B3 |
| Ormond Square | B3 |

| | |
|---|---|
| Ormond Street | A5 |
| Oscar Square | A5 |
| Oxmantown Lane | A2 |

## P

| | |
|---|---|
| Palmerston Place | B1 |
| Parliament Street | C3 |
| Parnell Place | D1 |
| Parnell Square East | D1 |
| Parnell Square West | C1 |
| Parnell Street | C2 |
| Patrick Street | B4 |
| Pearse Station | F3 |
| Pearse Street | E3 |
| Pembroke Lane | E5 |
| Pembroke Row | F5 |
| Pembroke Street Lower | E5 |
| Peter Row | C4 |
| Peter Street | C4 |
| Peterson's Court | F3 |
| Phibsborough Road | B1 |
| Phoenix Street North | A3 |
| Pimlico | A4 |
| Pleasants Street | C5 |
| Poolbeg Street | E3 |
| Poole Street | A4 |
| Powerscourt Townhouse | D4 |
| Prebend Street | B1 |
| Preston Street | F1 |
| Price's Lane | D3 |
| Prince's Street North | D2 |
| Prince's Street South | F3 |

## Q

| | |
|---|---|
| Queen Street | A2 |
| Quinn's Lane | E5 |

## R

| | |
|---|---|
| Railway Street | E1 |
| Rath Row | F3 |
| Redmond's Hill | C5 |
| Reginald Street | A4 |
| River Liffey | A3 |
| Ross Road | B4 |
| Rotunda Hospital | D1 |
| Royal Hibernian Academy | E5 |
| Rutland Place | D1 |
| Rutland Street Lower | E1 |
| Ryder's Row | C2 |

## S

| | |
|---|---|
| Sackville Place | D2 |
| St. Andrew's Street | D3 |
| St. Ann's Church | D4 |
| St. Audoen's Church | B3 |
| St. Augustine Street | A3 |
| St. Cathedral Lane East | A4 |
| St. Kevin's Avenue | B5 |
| St. Mary's Abbey | C2 |
| St. Mary's Pro-Cathedral | D1 |
| St. Mary's Terrace | C1 |
| St. Michael's Close | B3 |
| St. Michael's Hill | B3 |
| St. Michan's Church | A2 |
| St. Michan's Street | B2 |
| St. Paul Street | A2 |
| St. Patrick's Cathedral | B4 |
| St. Patrick's Close | B4 |
| St. Patrick's Park | B4 |
| St. Stephen's Green | D5 |
| St. Stephen's Green East | E5 |
| St. Stephen's Green North | D4 |
| St. Stephen's Green South | D5 |
| St. Stephen's Green West | D5 |
| St. Thomas Road | A5 |
| St. Werburgh's Church | B4 |
| Sampson's Lane | D2 |
| Sandwith Street Upper | F4 |
| Sandwith Street Lower | F3 |
| Schoolhouse Lane | E4 |
| Schoolhouse Lane West | B3 |
| Sean Mac Dermott Street Lower | E1 |
| Sean Mac Dermott Street Upper | D1 |

| | |
|---|---|
| Setanta Place | E4 |
| Seville Place | F1 |
| Seville Terrace | F1 |
| Shaw Street | E3 |
| Shelbourne Hotel | E4 |
| Sheriff Street Lower | F1 |
| Ship Street Great | C4 |
| Ship Street Little | C4 |
| Smithfield | A2 |
| South Great George's Street | C4 |
| Spring Garden Lane | E3 |
| Stable Lane | A3 |
| Stanhope Street | A1 |
| Stephen Street Lower | C4 |
| Stephen Street Upper | C4 |
| Stephen's Lane | F5 |
| Stephen's Place | F5 |
| Stirrup Lane | B2 |
| Stokes Place | D5 |
| Stoneybatter | A2 |
| Store Street | E2 |
| Strand Street Great | C3 |
| Strand Street Little | C3 |
| Strong's Court | D1 |
| Suffolk Street | D3 |
| Summerhill | E1 |
| Susan Terrace | A5 |
| Swift's Alley | A4 |
| Swift's Row | C3 |
| Sycamore Street | C3 |

## T

| | |
|---|---|
| Tailors' Hall | B4 |
| Talbot Place | E2 |
| Talbot Street | D2 |
| Tara Street | E3 |
| Tara Street Station | E3 |
| Temple Bar | C3 |
| Temple Cottages | B1 |
| Temple Lane North | D1 |
| Temple Lane South | C3 |
| The Coombe | A4 |
| Thomas Court | A4 |
| Thomas Court Lane | A4 |
| Thomas Davis Street South | B4 |
| Thomas Street West | A4 |
| Thomas's Lane | D1 |
| Townsend Street | E3 |
| Trinity College | E3 |
| Trinity Street | D3 |

## U

| | |
|---|---|
| Usher Street | A3 |
| Usher's Island | A3 |
| Usher's Quay | A3 |

## V

| | |
|---|---|
| Vicar Street | A4 |

## W

| | |
|---|---|
| Wards Hill | B5 |
| Watkins Buildings | A4 |
| Weaver's Square | A5 |
| Weaver's Street | A4 |
| Wellington Quay | C3 |
| Werburgh Street | C4 |
| Western Way | B1 |
| Westland Row | F4 |
| Westmoreland Street | D3 |
| Wexford Street | C5 |
| Whitefriar Place | C4 |
| Whitefriar Street | C4 |
| Whitefriar Carmelite Church | C4 |
| Wicklow Street | D3 |
| William Street South | D4 |
| William's Place South | B5 |
| William's Row | D2 |
| Windmill Lane | F3 |
| Windsor Place | E5 |
| Winetavern Street | B3 |
| Wolfe Tone Park | C2 |
| Wolfe Tone Street | C2 |
| Wood Quay | B3 |
| Wood Street | C4 |

## Y

| | |
|---|---|
| York Street | C4 |

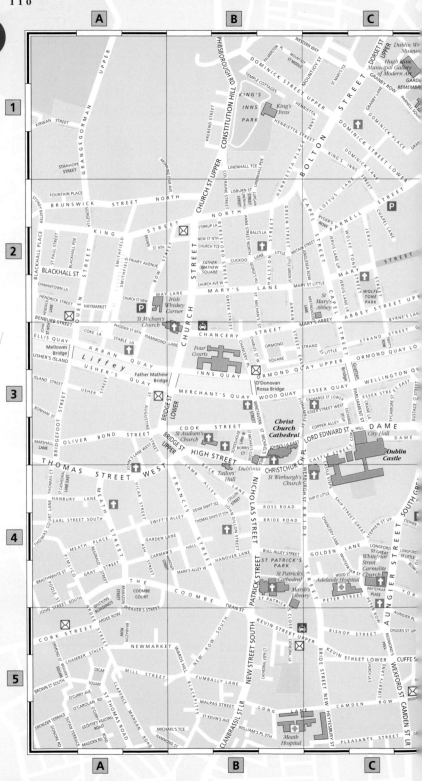

1

2

3

4

5

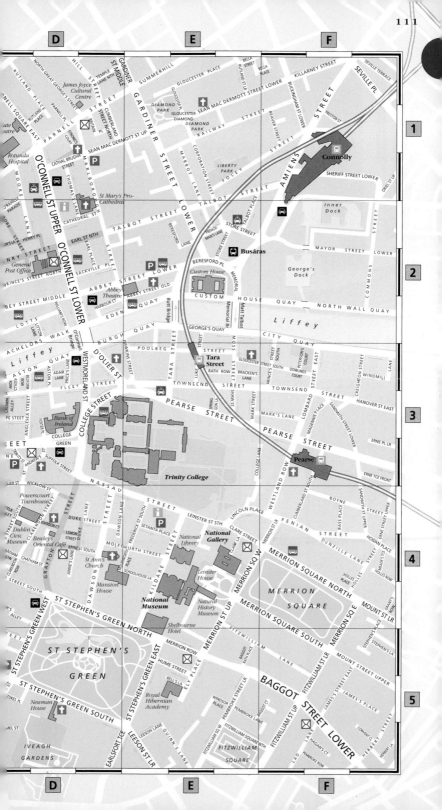

# IRELAND REGION BY REGION

IRELAND AT A GLANCE 114-115
SOUTHEAST IRELAND 116-143
CORK AND KERRY 144-171
THE LOWER SHANNON 172-191
THE WEST OF IRELAND 192-211
NORTHWEST IRELAND 212-227
THE MIDLANDS 228-245
NORTHERN IRELAND 246-277

# Ireland at a Glance

T HE LURE of Ireland's much-vaunted Atlantic
shores, from the wild coastline of Cork and
Kerry to the remote peninsulas of the Northwest,
is strong. However, to neglect the interior would
be to miss out on Ireland's equally characteristic
landscapes of lush valleys, dark peatlands and
unruffled loughs. Most regions are rich in historic
sights: from world-famous Neolithic sites in the
Midlands to imposing Norman castles in the
North and Palladian mansions in the Southeast.

*Yeats Country is a
charming part of County
Sligo closely associated
with WB Yeats. The
poet was born here
and is buried within
sight of Ben Bulben's
ridge. (See pp224–5.)*

NORTHW
IRELANI
(See pp212–

*Connemara National Park in County
Galway boasts stunning landscapes in which
mountains and lakes are combined with a
dramatic Atlantic coastline. The extensive
blanket bogs and moorland are rich in
wildlife and unusual plants. (See p200.)*

**THE WEST
OF IRELAND**
*(See pp192–211)*

**Bunratty Castle
(See pp184–5)**

*The Rock of Cashel, a
fortified medieval abbey,
perches on a limestone
outcrop in the heart of
County Tipperary. It boasts
some of Ireland's finest
Romanesque sculpture.
(See pp188–9.)*

**THE LOWER
SHANNON**
*(See pp172–91)*

**CORK AND KERRY**
*(See pp144–71)*

**Bantry House
(See pp160–61)**

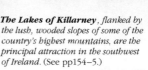

*The Lakes of Killarney, flanked by
the lush, wooded slopes of some of the
country's highest mountains, are the
principal attraction in the southwest
of Ireland. (See pp154–5.)*

**NORTHERN IRELAND**
*(See pp246–77)*

**The Giant's Causeway**, *where ancient lava flows have been eroded to reveal columns of unnatural regularity, is Northern Ireland's most curious sight. According to local mythology, the rocks were placed here by a giant called Finn MacCool to enable him to walk across the sea to Scotland.* (See pp254–5.)

**Newgrange** *(See pp238–9)*

**THE MIDLANDS** *(See pp228–45)*

**Mount Stewart House**, *a 19th-century mansion, is most renowned for its magnificent gardens. These were created as recently as the 1920s, but a colorful array of exotic plants has thrived in the warm microclimate enjoyed in this part of County Down.* (See pp274–5.)

**SOUTHEAST IRELAND** *(See pp116–43)*

**Powerscourt** *is a large estate in superb countryside on the edge of the Wicklow Mountains. Its grounds rank among the last great formal gardens of Europe. Originally planted in the 1730s, they were restored and embellished in the 19th century.* (See pp126–7.)

0 kilometers   50

0 miles   25

**Kilkenny Castle** *was for centuries the stronghold of the Butler dynasty, which controlled much of southeast Ireland in the Middle Ages. The vast Norman fortress was remodeled during the Victorian period and still dominates Kilkenny – one of the country's most historic and pleasant towns.* (See pp134–6.)

# SOUTHEAST IRELAND

## KILDARE · WICKLOW · CARLOW · KILKENNY
## WATERFORD · WEXFORD

**B**LESSED WITH *the warmest climate in Ireland, the Southeast has always presented an attractive prospect for settlers. Landscapes of gently rolling hills have been tamed by centuries of culti-vation, with lush farmland, imposing medieval castles and great houses enhancing the region's atmosphere of prosperity.*

The Southeast's proximity to Britain meant that it was often the first port of call for foreign invaders. Viking raiders arrived here in the 9th century and founded some of Ireland's earliest towns, including Water-ford and Wexford. They were followed in 1169 by the Anglo-Normans *(see pp34–5)*, who shaped the region's subsequent development.

Given its strategic importance, the Southeast was heavily protected, mostly by Anglo-Norman lords loyal to the English Crown. Remains of impressive castles attest to the power of the Fitzgeralds of Kildare and the Butlers of Kilkenny, who between them virtually controlled the Southeast throughout the Middle Ages. English influence was stronger here than in any other part of the island.

From the 18th century, wealthy Anglo-Irish families were drawn to what they saw as a stable zone, and felt confident enough to build fine mansions like the Palladian masterpieces of Russ-borough and Castletown. English rule, however, was not universally accepted. The Wicklow Mountains became a popular refuge for opponents to the Crown, including the rebels who fled the town of Enniscorthy after a bloody battle during the uprising against the English in 1798 *(see p39)*.

This mountainous region is still the only real wilderness in the Southeast, in contrast to the flat grasslands that spread across Kildare to the west. To the east, sandy beaches stretch almost unbroken along the shore between Dublin and Rosslare in Wexford.

**Traditional thatched cottages in Dunmore East, County Waterford**

◁ **Staircase hall with ornate 18th-century stuccowork in Castletown House, County Kildare**

# Exploring Southeast Ireland

THE SOUTHEAST has something for everyone, from busy seaside resorts to quaint canalside villages, Norman abbeys and bird sanctuaries. The Wicklow Mountains, the location of several major sights such as the monastic complex of Glendalough and the magnificent gardens of Powerscourt, provide perfect touring and walking territory. Farther south, the most scenic routes cut through the valleys of the Slaney, Barrow and Nore rivers, flanked by historic ports such as New Ross, from where you can explore local waterways by boat. Along the south coast, which is more varied than the region's eastern shore, beaches are interspersed with rocky headlands, and quiet coastal villages provide good alternative bases to the busy towns of Waterford and Wexford. Farther inland, the best places to stay include Lismore and Kilkenny, which is one of the finest historic towns in Ireland.

**Graiguenamanagh, on the Barrow north of New Ross**

## SIGHTS AT A GLANCE

Ardmore **19**
Avondale House **14**
Bray **8**
Browne's Hill Dolmen **15**
*Castletown House pp122–3* **1**
Dunmore East **21**
Enniscorthy **24**
Glendalough **13**
Hook Peninsula **22**
Irish National Heritage Park **25**
Jerpoint Abbey **17**
Johnstown Castle **27**
Kildare **5**
*Kilkenny pp134–6* **16**
Killruddery House **9**
Lismore **18**
Monasterevin **4**
Mount Usher Gardens **12**
New Ross **23**
Peatland World **3**
*Powerscourt pp126–7* **7**
Robertstown **2**
Rosslare **29**

Russborough House **6**
Saltee Islands **28**
*Waterford pp138–9* **20**
Wexford **26**
Wicklow Mountains **11**

**Tours**
Military Road **10**

PEATLAND WORLD
RATHANG

MONASTEREVIN **4**
Port

Portlaoise
Casbel
KILKENNY **16**
CALLAN
JERPOINT **17**
ABBEY    INIST
Fermoy
Suir
WATERFORD
R666
LISMORE **18**
Mallow
DUNGARVAN
Cork
ARDMORE **19**

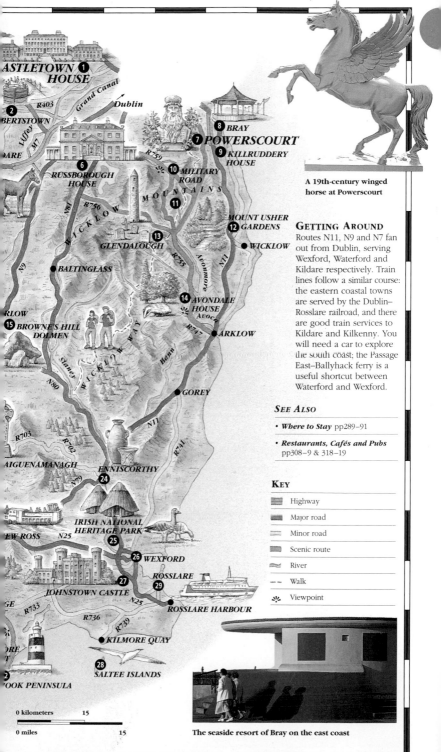

# CASTLETOWN HOUSE ❶

R403

*Dublin*

Grand Canal

❷ ROBERTSTOWN

Liffey

DARE

M7

❻ RUSSBOROUGH HOUSE

R759

❽ BRAY

❼ POWERSCOURT

❾ KILLRUDDERY HOUSE

❿ MILITARY ROAD

WICKLOW MOUNTAINS

⓫

N81

R756

**A 19th-century winged horse at Powerscourt**

⓬ MOUNT USHER GARDENS

● WICKLOW

N9

⓭ GLENDALOUGH

R755

● BALTINGLASS

Avonmore

⓮ AVONDALE HOUSE

Avoca

N11

❿RLOW

WICKLOW WAY

⓯ BROWNE'S HILL DOLMEN

R747

● ARKLOW

Slaney

Benn

N80

● GOREY

R703

N11

R702

AIGUENAMANAGH

N79

⓸ ENNISCORTHY

R741

EW ROSS

N25

IRISH NATIONAL HERITAGE PARK

⓸ 25

⓸ 26 ● WEXFORD

ROSSLARE

GE

⓸ 27

⓸ 29

JOHNSTOWN CASTLE

N25

R733

● ROSSLARE HARBOUR

R736

R739

ORE
T

● KILMORE QUAY

⓸ 28 SALTEE ISLANDS

OOK PENINSULA

## GETTING AROUND

Routes N11, N9 and N7 fan out from Dublin, serving Wexford, Waterford and Kildare respectively. Train lines follow a similar course: the eastern coastal towns are served by the Dublin–Rosslare railroad, and there are good train services to Kildare and Kilkenny. You will need a car to explore the south coast; the Passage East–Ballyhack ferry is a useful shortcut between Waterford and Wexford.

## SEE ALSO

• *Where to Stay* pp289–91

• *Restaurants, Cafés and Pubs* pp308–9 & 318–19

## KEY

| | |
|---|---|
| | Highway |
| | Major road |
| | Minor road |
| | Scenic route |
| | River |
| | Walk |
| ☼ | Viewpoint |

0 kilometers 15

0 miles 15

**The seaside resort of Bray on the east coast**

# Castletown House ❶

*See pp122–3.*

# Robertstown ❷

**Road map** D4. Co Kildare. 🏃 240. 🚌

TEN LOCKS WEST along the Grand Canal from Dublin, Robertstown is a characteristic 19th-century canalside village, with warehouses and cottages flanking the waterfront. Freight barges plied the route until about 1960, but pleasure boats have since replaced them. Visitors can take barge cruises from the quay and the Grand Canal Company's Hotel, built in 1801 for canal passengers, is now used for banquets.

Near Sallins, about 8 km (5 miles) east of Robertstown, the canal is carried over the River Liffey along the **Leinster Aqueduct**, an impressive structure built in 1783.

# Peatland World ❸

**Road map** D4. Lullymore, Co Kildare. 📞 045 60133. 🚌 🚌 to Newbridge. ⬤ daily. ⬤ 10 days at Christmas. 🅿 ♿ limited.

ANYONE INTERESTED in the natural history of Irish bogs should visit Peatland World, an exhibition housed in an old farm at Lullymore, 9 km (6 miles) northeast of Rathangan. It lies right at the heart of the Bog of Allen, a huge expanse of raised bog *(see p244)* that extends across the counties of Offaly, Laois and Kildare.

The Grand Canal Company's Hotel in Robertstown

There is an exhibition devoted to the history and ecology of the bog, with displays of flora and fauna and archaeological finds from the surrounding area. Guided walks across the peatlands are also organized to introduce visitors to the bog's delicate ecosystem.

**Stacking peat for use as fuel**

# Monasterevin ❹

**Road map** D4. Co Kildare. 🏃 2,200. 🚌

THIS GEORGIAN market town lies west of Kildare, where the Grand Canal crosses the River Barrow. Waterborne trade brought prosperity to Monasterevin in the 18th century, but the locks now see little traffic. However, you can still admire the aqueduct, which is a superb example of canal engineering.

**Moore Abbey**, next to the church, was built in the 18th century on the site of a monastic foundation, but the grand Gothic mansion owes much to Victorian remodeling. Once the ancestral seat of the Earls of Drogheda, in the 1920s Moore Abbey became the home of the celebrated tenor, John McCormack *(see p24)*. It is now a hospital.

# Kildare ❺

**Road map** D4. Co Kildare. 🏃 4,200. 🚌 🚌 🛈 *Market House (045 22696)*. ⬤ Thu.

THE CHARMING and tidy town of Kildare is dominated by **St. Brigid's Cathedral**, which commemorates the saint who founded a religious community on this site in 490. Unusually, monks and nuns lived there under the same roof, but this was not the only unorthodox practice associated with the community. Curious pagan rituals, including the burning of a perpetual fire, continued until the 16th century. The fire pit is visible in the grounds today. So too is a round tower with a Romanesque doorway, probably

**St. Brigid's Cathedral and roofless round tower in Kildare town**

**Japanese Gardens at Tully near Kildare**

built in the 12th century. The cathedral was rebuilt in the Victorian era, but the restorers largely adhered to the original 13th-century design.

**⌂ St. Brigid's Cathedral**
Market Square. **[** 045 21229.
**○** May–Oct: daily. **Donation.** **⌖**

**ENVIRONS:** Kildare lies at the heart of racing country: the Curragh racecourse is nearby, stables are scattered all around and thoroughbred sales take place at Kill, northeast of town.

The **National Stud** is a state-run thoroughbred farm at Tully, just south of Kildare. It was founded in 1900 by an eccentric Anglo-Irish colonel called William Walker. He sold his foals on the basis of their astrological charts, and put skylights in the stables to allow the horses to be "touched" by sunlight or moonbeams. Walker received the title Lord Wavertree in reward for bequeathing the farm to the British Crown in 1915.

Visitors can explore the 400-ha (1,000-acre) grounds and watch the horses being exercised. Mares are normally kept in a separate paddock from the stallions, though a "teaser" stallion is introduced to discover when the mares come into season. Breeding

stallions wait in the covering shed: each one is expected to cover 50 mares per season. There is a special foaling unit where the mare and foal can remain undisturbed for a few days after the birth.

The farm has its own forge and saddlery, and also a Horse Museum. Housed in an old

stable block, this illustrates the importance of horses in Irish life. Exhibits include the frail skeleton of Arkle, the champion steeplechaser who shot to fame in the 1960s.

Sharing the same estate as the National Stud are the **Japanese Gardens**, created by Lord Wavertree at the height of the Edwardian penchant for Orientalism. The gardens were laid out in 1906–10 by a Japanese landscape gardener called Tassa Eida, with the help of his son Minoru and 40 assistants. The impressive array of trees and shrubs includes maples, mulberries, bonsai, magnolias, sacred bamboos and cherry trees.

The gardens take the form of an allegorical journey from the cradle to the grave, beginning with life emerging from the Gate of Oblivion (a dark cave) and leading to the Gateway of Eternity, a contemplative Zen rock garden. The route incorporates a variety of elaborate rockeries, symbolic stone lanterns and miniature bridges.

**♣ National Stud and Japanese Gardens**
Tully. **[** 045 21617. **○** Mar–Oct: daily. **⌘** **⌖**

---

## HORSE RACING IN IRELAND

Ireland has a strong racing culture and, thanks to its non-elitist image, the sport is enjoyed by all. Much of the thoroughbred industry centers around the Curragh, a grassy plain in County Kildare stretching unfenced for more than 2,000 ha (5,000 acres). This area is home to many of the country's studs and training yards, and every morning horses are put through their paces on the "gallops." Most of the major flat races, including the Irish Derby, take place at the Curragh racecourse just east of Kildare. Other popular fixtures are held at nearby Punchestown – most famously the steeplechase festival in April – and at Leopardstown, which also hosts major National Hunt races (see pp26–7).

**The homestretch at the Curragh racecourse**

# Castletown House ●

**B**UILT IN 1722–32 for William Conolly, Speaker of the Irish Parliament, Castletown was the stateliest house in the country at the time. The work of Florentine architect, Alessandro Galilei, the building gave Ireland its first taste of Palladianism. The magnificent interiors date from the second half of the 18th century. They were commissioned by Lady Louisa Lennox, wife of William Conolly's great-nephew, Tom, who took up residence here in 1758. Castletown remained in the family until 1965, when it was taken over by the Irish Georgian Society. The house now belongs to the state and is open to the public.

**Conolly crest on an armchair**

★ **Long Gallery**
*Pompeiian-style friezes adorn the cobalt-blue walls of this magnificent room. The niches frame statues of figures from Classical mythology.*

**Green Drawing Room**

**Red Drawing Room**
*The room takes its name from the red damask on the walls, which is probably French and dates from the 1820s. This exquisite mahogany bureau was made for Lady Louisa in the 1760s.*

**West wing with kitchen**

**Boudoir Wall Paintings**
*The boudoir's decorative panels, moved here from the Long Gallery, were inspired by the Raphael Loggia in the Vatican.*

**The Dining Room** was designed by William Chambers, architect of the Marino Casino (*see pp38–9*). The mantelpiece and door cases show his strong Neo-Classical inspiration.

### ★ Print Room
*In this, the last surviving print room in Ireland, Lady Louisa indulged her taste for Italian engravings. In the 18th century, it was fashionable for ladies to paste prints directly onto the wall and frame them with elaborate festoons.*

**The Boar Hunt,** painted by
Paul de Vos (1596–1678)

### ★ Staircase Hall
*This portrait of Lady Louisa is part of the superb Rococo stuccowork by the Francini brothers which decorates the staircase.*

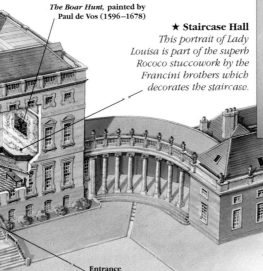

**The east wing** originally
housed the stables.

**Entrance**

**The Entrance Hall** is an
austere Neo-Classical room.
Its most decorative feature is
the delicate carving on the
pilasters of the upper gallery.

## STAR FEATURES

★ Long Gallery

★ Print Room

★ Staircase Hall

## CONOLLY'S FOLLY

This whimsical structure, which lies just beyond the grounds of Castletown House, can be seen from the Long Gallery. Speaker Conolly's widow, Katherine, commissioned it in 1740 as a memorial to her late husband, and to provide employment after a harsh winter. The unusual structure of superimposed arches crowned by an obelisk was designed by Richard Castle, architect of Russborough House *(see p124).*

Parlor in Russborough House with original fireplace and stuccowork

# Russborough House ❻

**Road map** D4. Blessington, Co Wicklow.
📞 045 65239. 🚌 65 from Dublin.
🕐 Jun–Aug: daily; Easter–May & Sep–Oct: Sun & public hols. 🏷️ 🎫 ♿

THIS PALLADIAN MANSION, built in the 1740s for Joseph Leeson, Earl of Milltown, is one of Ireland's finest houses. Its architect, an anglicized German called Richard Castle, also designed Powerscourt House (*see pp126–7*) and is credited with introducing the Palladian style to Ireland.

Unlike many grand estates in the Pale, Russborough has survived magnificently, both inside and out. The house claims the longest frontage in Ireland, with a façade adorned by heraldic lions and curved colonnades. The interior is even more impressive. Many rooms feature superb stucco decoration, which was done largely by the Italian Francini brothers, who also worked on Castletown House (*see pp122–3*). The best examples are found in the music room, parlor and library, which are embellished with exuberant foliage and cherubs. Around the main staircase, a riot of Rococo plasterwork

Vernet seascape in the drawing room

depicts a hunt, with hounds clasping garlands of flowers. The stucco moldings in the drawing room were designed especially to enclose marine scenes by the French artist, Joseph Vernet (1714–89). The paintings were sold in 1926, but were tracked down more than 40 years afterward and returned to the house.

Russborough has many other treasures, including finely worked fireplaces of Italian marble, imposing mahogany doorways and priceless collections of silver, porcelain and Gobelins tapestries.

Such riches aside, one of the principal reasons to visit Russborough is to see the **Beit Art Collection**, famous for its Flemish, Dutch and Spanish Old Master paintings. These include fine works by Goya, Velázquez, Hals, Rubens and Vermeer. Sir Alfred Beit, who bought the house in 1952, inherited the pictures from his uncle – also named Alfred Beit and co-founder of the de Beer diamond mining empire in South Africa. In 1974, several masterpieces were taken by the IRA, but they were later retrieved. Several pictures are still missing, following a second robbery in 1986. Only a selection of paintings is on view in the house at any one time, while

## THE HISTORY OF THE PALE

The term "Pale" refers to an area around Dublin that marked the limits of English influence from Norman to Tudor times. The frontier fluctuated, but at its largest the Pale stretched from Dundalk in County Louth to Waterford town. Gaelic chieftains outside the area could keep their lands provided they agreed to bring up their heirs within the Pale.

The Palesmen supported their rulers' interests and considered themselves the upholders of English values. This widened the gap between the Gaelic majority and the Anglo-Irish, a fore-taste of England's doomed involvement in the country. Long after its fortifications were dismantled, the idea of the Pale lived on as a state of mind. The expression "beyond the pale" survives as a definition of those outside the bounds of civilized society.

An 18th-century family enjoying the privileged lifestyle typical within the Pale

**Tourist road train on the beachfront esplanade at Bray**

others are on permanent loan to the National Gallery in Dublin *(see pp68–9)*.

Russborough enjoys a fine position near the village of **Blessington**, with a good view across to the Wicklow Mountains. The house lies amid wooded parkland rather than elaborate flower gardens. As Alfred Beit said of Irish Palladianism, "Fine architecture standing in a green sward was considered enough."

**ENVIRONS:** The **Poulaphouca Reservoir**, which was formed by the damming of the River Liffey, extends south from Blessington. The placid lake is popular with watersports enthusiasts, while other visitors come simply to enjoy the lovely mountain views.

## Powerscourt ❼

*See pp126–7.*

## Bray ❽

**Road map** D4. Co Wicklow.
🚶 27,000. 🚆 *DART.* 🚌 ℹ️ *Old Court House, Main St (01 2867128).*

ONCE A REFINED Victorian resort, Bray is nowadays a brash vacation town, with amusement arcades and fish and chip shops lining the seafront. Its beach attracts large crowds in summer, including many young families. Anyone in search of peace and quiet can escape to nearby Bray

Head, where there is room for bracing cliffside walks. Bray also makes a good base from which to explore Powerscourt Gardens, the Wicklow Mountains and the delightful coastal villages of Killiney and Dalkey *(see p101).*

## Killruddery House ❾

**Road map** D4. Bray, Co Wicklow.
📞 *01 2863405.* 🕐 *May–Jun & Sep: daily (pm only).* 🎟️ 🚻 *limited.*

KILLRUDDERY HOUSE lies just to the south of Bray, in the shadow of Little Sugar Loaf Mountain. Built in 1651, it has been the family seat of the Earls of Meath ever since, although the original mansion was remodeled in an Elizabethan Revival style in the early 19th century.

The house contains some good carving and stuccowork, but it is a rather faded stately home. The real charm of Killruddery stems from the 17th-century formal gardens, which are regarded as the finest French Classical gardens in the country. They were laid out in the 1680s by a French gardener named Bonet, who also worked at Versailles.

The gardens, planted with great precision, feature romantic parterres, a whole array of different hedges and many fine trees and shrubs, both native and foreign. The sylvan theater, a small enclosure surrounded by a bay hedge, is the only known example of its kind in Ireland.

The garden centers on the Long Ponds, a pair of canals which extend 165 m (550 ft) and were once used to stock fish. Beyond, a pool enclosed by two circular hedges leads to a Victorian arrangement of paths flanked by statues and neat hedges of yew, beech, lime and hornbeam.

**View across the Long Ponds to Killruddery House**

# Powerscourt 7

**Bamberg Gate**
*Made in Vienna in the 1770s, this gilded wrought-iron gate was brought to Powerscourt by the 7th Viscount from Bamberg Cathedral in Bavaria.*

**Laocoon statue on upper terrace**

THE GARDENS AT POWERSCOURT are probably the finest in Ireland, both for their design and their dramatic setting at the foot of Great Sugar Loaf Mountain. The house and grounds were commissioned in the 1730s by Richard Wingfield, the 1st Viscount Powerscourt. The gardens fell into decline, but in 1840 the original plan was revived. New ornamental gardens were completed in 1858–75 by the 7th Viscount, who added gates, urns and statues collected during his travels in Europe. The house was gutted by an accidental fire in 1974, but the splendid gardens, maintained with meticulous care, can still be enjoyed.

**The Walled Gardens** include a formal arrangement of clipped laurel trees but are also used for growing plants for Powerscourt's nursery.

**Entrance**

**Statue of Laocoon**

**The Pets' Cemetery** contains the graves of Wingfield family dogs, cats and even horses and cattle.

**Dolphin Pond**
*This pool, designed as a fish pond in the 18th century, is enclosed by exotic conifers in a lovely secluded garden.*

## POWERSCOURT HOUSE

The Palladian mansion at Powerscourt, a burned-out shell since 1974, was built in 1731 on the site of a Norman castle. It was designed, like the original gardens, by Richard Castle, architect also of Russborough House *(see p124)*. Now owned by the Slazenger family, the house at Powerscourt may yet be restored. Some of the rubble left from the fire has been cleared, but the huge task of restoring the building to its former glory has still to begin in earnest.

**Powerscourt on fire in 1974**

### ★ The Perron
*This magnificent Italianate stairway, added in 1874, leads down to the Triton Lake, which is guarded by two statues of Pegasus – the winged horse of Greek myth and the emblem of the Wingfield family.*

## VISITORS' CHECKLIST

**Road map** D4. Enniskerry, Co Wicklow. 📞 01 2867676. 🚌 85 from Bray, 44 from Dublin to Enniskerry. **Gardens** ○ mid-Mar–Oct: 9:30am–5:30pm daily. 🅿 📷 ♿ 🍴

**The Italian Garden**
is laid out on terraces that were first cut into the steep hillside in the 1730s.

### Pebble Mosaic
*Many tons of pebbles were gathered from nearby Bray beach to build the Perron and to make this mosaic on the terrace.*

**The Pepper Pot Tower** was built in 1911.

### ★ Triton Lake
*Made for the first garden, the lake takes its name from its central fountain, which is modeled on a 17th-century work by Bernini in Rome.*

### ★ Japanese Gardens
*These enchanting Edwardian gardens, created out of bogland, contain Chinese conifers and bamboo trees.*

## STAR FEATURES

★ The Perron

★ Japanese Gardens

★ Triton Lake

Powerscourt Gardens with Great Sugar Loaf Mountain beyond ▷

# A Tour of the Military Road ⑩

**Red squirrel**

THE BRITISH BUILT the Military Road through the heart of the Wicklow Mountains during a campaign to flush out Irish rebels after an uprising in 1798 *(see p141)*. Now known as the R115, this road takes you through the emptiest and most rugged landscapes of County Wicklow. Fine countryside, in which deer and other wildlife flourish, is characteristic of the whole of this tour.

### Glencree ①
The former British barracks in Glencree are among several found along the Military Road.

### Powerscourt Waterfall ⑨
The River Dargle cascades 130 m (425 ft) over a granite escarpment to form Ireland's highest waterfall.

### Sally Gap ②
This remote pass is surrounded by a vast expanse of blanket bog dotted with pools and streams.

### Great Sugar Loaf ⑧
The granite cone of Great Sugar Loaf Mountain can be climbed in under an hour from the parking lot on its southern side.

### Glenmacnass ③
After Sally Gap, the road drops into a deep glen where a waterfall spills dramatically over rocks.

### Lough Tay ⑦
Stark, rocky slopes plunge down to the dark waters of Lough Tay. Though it lies within a Guinness-owned estate, the lake is accessible to walkers.

### Roundwood ⑥
The highest village in Ireland, at 238 m (780 ft) above sea level, Roundwood enjoys a fine setting. Its main street is lined with pubs, cafés and craft shops.

### Glendalough ④
This ancient lakeside monastery *(see pp132–3)*, enclosed by wooded slopes, is the prime historical sight in the Wicklow Mountains.

## TIPS FOR DRIVERS

**Length:** 96 km (60 miles).
**Stopping points:** *There are several pubs and cafés in Enniskerry (including Poppies, an old-fashioned tearoom), and also in Roundwood, but this area is better for picnics. There are several marked picnic spots south of Enniskerry. (See also pp355–7.)*

**Map labels:** DUBLIN, Enniskerry, Powerscourt, Glencree, R115, R60, R755, Dargle, Great Sugar Loaf ⑧, R750, Lough Dan, R755, Vartry Reservoir, R115, Annamoe, Glenmacnass, R756, Laragh, R755, Glenmore, Clara, RATHDRUM

0 kilometers        5
0 miles        3

## KEY

━━━ Tour route
═══ Other roads
☆ Viewpoint

### Vale of Clara ⑤
This picturesque wooded valley follows the River Avonmore. It contains the tiny village of Clara, which consists of two houses, a church and a school.

# Wicklow Mountains ⑪

**Road map** D4. 🚌 *to Rathdrum &
Wicklow.* 🚌 *to Enniskerry, Wicklow,
Glendalough, Rathdrum & Avoca.*
ℹ️ *Rialto House, Fitzwilliam Square,
Wicklow (0404 69117).*

STANDING AMID the rugged
wilderness of the Wicklow
Mountains, it can be hard to
believe that Dublin is under
an hour's drive away. The in-
accessibility of the mountains
meant that they once provided
a safe hideout for opponents
of English rule. When much of
the Southeast was obedient to
the English Crown, within an
area known as the Pale *(see
p124)*, warlords such as the
O'Tooles held sway in the
Wicklow Mountains. Rebels
who took part in
the 1798 uprising
*(see p39)* sought
refuge here too.
One of their
leaders, Michael
Dwyer, remained
at liberty in the
hills around Sally
Gap until 1803.

The building of
the **Military Road**,
started in 1800,
made the area more accessible,
but the mountains are still
thinly populated. There is little
traffic to disturb enjoyment
of the exhilarating scenery of
rock-strewn glens, lush forest
and bogland where heather
gives a purple sheen to the
land. Turf-cutting is still a
thriving cottage industry, and

you often see peat stacked up
by the road. Numerous walking trails weave through these
landscapes. Among them is the
**Wicklow Way**, which extends
132 km (82 miles) from Marlay
Park in Dublin to Clonegal in
County Carlow. It is marked
but not always easy to follow,
so do not set out without a
decent map. Although no peak
exceeds 915 m (3,000 ft), the
Wicklow Mountains can be
dangerous in bad weather.

Hiking aside, there is plenty
to see and do in this region. A
good starting point for exploring the northern area is the
picture-postcard estate village
of **Enniskerry**. In summer,
it is busy with tourists who
come to visit the gardens at
Powerscourt *(see pp126–7)*.
From Laragh, to the south, you
can reach Glendalough *(see
pp132–3)* and
the **Vale of
Avoca**, where
cherry trees
are laden with
blossom in the
spring. The
beauty of this
gentle valley
was captured in
the poetry of
Thomas Moore
(1779–1852):
"There is not in the wide world
a valley so sweet as that vale
in whose bosom the bright
waters meet" – a reference to
the confluence of the Avonbeg
and Avonmore rivers, the so-
called **Meeting of the Waters**
beyond Avondale House *(see
p132)*. Nestled among wooded

**Bearnas na Diallaite
SALLY GAP**

⬆ **Bealach Mileata
MILITARY ROAD** ✈

⬅ **Gleann Life
LIFFEY VALLEY** ⤢

**Bealach Fheartire** ➡
**VARTRY DRIVE**

**Road sign in the
Wicklow Mountains**

**Mount Usher Gardens, on the
banks of the River Vartry**

hills at the heart of the valley is
the hamlet of Avoca, where the
**Avoca Handweavers** produce
colorful tweeds in the oldest
hand-weaving mill in Ireland,
in operation since 1723.

Farther north, toward the
coast near Ashford, the River
Vartry rushes through the deep
chasm of the **Devil's Glen**.
On entering the valley, the
river falls 30 m (100 ft) into a
pool known as the Devil's
Punchbowl. There are good
walks around here, with fine
views of the coast.

🏠 **Avoca Handweavers**
Avoca. 📞 *0402 35105.* ⏰ *daily.*
⚫ *Dec 25 & 26.*

# Mount Usher Gardens ⑫

**Road map** D4. Ashford, Co Wicklow.
📞 *0404 40205.* 🚌 *to Ashford.* ⏰
*mid-Mar–Oct: daily.* ♿ 👍 *limited.*

SET BESIDE the River Vartry
just east of Ashford are the
Mount Usher Gardens. They
were designed in 1868 by a
Dubliner, Edward Walpole,
who imbued them with his
strong sense of romanticism.

The gardens contain many
rare shrubs and trees, from
Chinese conifers and bamboos
to Mexican pines and pampas
grass. There is also a Maple
Walk, which is glorious in
autumn. The river provides
the main focus of the Mount
Usher Gardens, and amid the
exotic vegetation you can
glimpse herons on the weirs.

**Colorful moorland around Sally Gap in the Wicklow Mountains**

## Glendalough ⓭

**Road map** D4. Co Wicklow.
 *St. Kevin's Bus from Dublin.*
**Ruins** ⬭ *daily.* 🎫 *in summer.*
**Visitors' Centre** 📞 *0404 45325.*
⬭ *daily.* ● *Dec 23–31.* 📷 ♿

T HE STEEP, WOODED slopes of
Glendalough, the "valley
of the two lakes," harbor one
of Ireland's most atmospheric
monastic sites. Established by
St. Kevin in the 6th century,
the settlement was sacked time
and again by the Vikings but
nevertheless flourished for over
600 years. Decline set in only
after English forces partially
razed the site in 1398, though
it functioned as a monastic
center until the Dissolution of
the Monasteries in 1539 *(see
p36)*. Pilgrims kept on coming
to Glendalough even after that,
particularly on St. Kevin's feast
day, June 3, which was often
a riotous event *(see p28)*.

The age of the buildings is
uncertain, but most date from
the 8th to 12th centuries. Many
were restored during the 1870s.

**Remains of the Gatehouse, the
original entrance to Glendalough**

**View along the Upper Lake at Glendalough**

The main group of ruins lies
east of the Lower Lake, but the
earliest buildings associated
with St. Kevin are by the Upper
Lake. Here, where the scenery
is much wilder, you are better
able to enjoy the tranquillity
of Glendalough and to escape
the crowds which
inevitably descend
on the site. Try to
arrive as early as
possible in the day,
particularly during
the peak tourist
season. You enter
the monastery
through the double
stone arch of the **Gatehouse**,
the only surviving example in
Ireland of a gateway into a
monastic enclosure.

A short walk leads to a
graveyard with a **Round tower**
in one corner. Reaching 33 m
(110 ft) in height, this is one
of the finest of its kind in the
country. Its cap was rebuilt in
the 1870s using stones found
inside the tower. The roofless
**Cathedral** nearby dates mainly
from the 12th century and is

**St. Kevin's Kitchen**

the valley's largest ruin. At
the center of the churchyard
stands the tiny **Priest's House**,
whose name derives from the
fact that it was a burial place
for local clergy. The worn
carving of a robed figure
above the door is possibly
of St. Kevin, flanked by
two disciples. East of
here, **St. Kevin's Cross**
dates from the 12th
century and is one of
the best preserved of
Glendalough's various
High Crosses. Made of
granite, the cross may
once have marked the
boundary of the monastic
cemetery. Below, nestled in
the lush valley, a minuscule
oratory with a steeply pitched
stone roof is a charming sight.
Erected in the 11th century or
earlier, it is popularly known
as **St. Kevin's Kitchen**;
perhaps because its belfry,
thought to be a later addition,
resembles a chimney. One of
the earliest churches at
Glendalough, **St. Mary's**, lies
across a field to the west.

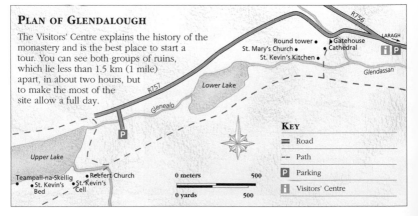

## PLAN OF GLENDALOUGH

The Visitors' Centre explains the history of the
monastery and is the best place to start a
tour. You can see both groups of ruins,
which lie less than 1.5 km (1 mile)
apart, in about two hours, but
to make the most of the
site allow a full day.

LARAGH
Round tower ● ● Gatehouse
St. Mary's Church ● ● Cathedral
St. Kevin's Kitchen ●
Glendassan
R756
R757
Lower Lake
Glenealo
Upper Lake
Teampall-na-Skellig ● Reefert Church
● St. Kevin's ● St. Kevin's
Bed Cell

0 meters        500
0 yards         500

**KEY**

▬ Road
-- Path
P Parking
i Visitors' Centre

**Round tower at Glendalough**

Some traces of Romanesque molding are visible outside the east window. Following the path along the south bank of the river, you reach the Upper Lake. This is the site of more monastic ruins and is also the chief starting point for walks through the valley and to a number of abandoned lead and zinc mines.

Situated in a grove not far from the Poulanass waterfall are the ruins of the **Reefert Church**, a simple Romanesque building. Its unusual name is a corruption of *Righ Fearta*, meaning "burial place of the kings"; the church may mark the site of an ancient cemetery. Near here, on a rocky spur overlooking the Upper Lake, stands **St. Kevin's Cell**, the ruins of a beehive-shaped structure, which is thought to have been the hermit's home.

There are two sites on the south side of the lake that cannot be reached on foot but are visible from the opposite shore. **Teampall-na-Skellig**, or the "church on the rock," was supposedly built on the site of the first church that St. Kevin founded at Glendalough. To the east of it, carved into the cliff, is **St. Kevin's Bed**. This small cave, in reality little more than a rocky ledge, may have been used as a tomb in the Bronze Age, but it is more famous as St. Kevin's favorite retreat. It was from here that the saint allegedly rejected the advances of a naked woman by tossing her into the lake.

## Avondale House 🄎

**Road map** D4. Co Wicklow. 【 *0404 46111*. 🚆 🚌 *to Rathdrum.*
**House** 🄌 *daily.* ● *Good Fri & Dec 23–28.* 🄍 **Grounds** 🄌 *daily.*

LYING JUST south of Rathdrum, Avondale House was the birthplace of the 19th-century politician and patriot, Charles Stewart Parnell *(see p41)*. The Georgian mansion is now a museum dedicated to Parnell and the fight for Home Rule.

The state owns Avondale and runs a forestry school here, but the public is free to explore the grounds. Known as **Avondale Forest Park**, the former estate includes an impressive arboretum first planted in the 18th century and much added to since 1900. There are some lovely walks through the woods, with pleasant views along the River Avonmore.

## Browne's Hill Dolmen 🄏

**Road map** D4. Co Carlow. 🚆 🚌 *to Carlow.* 🄌 *daily.*

IN A FIELD 3 km (2 miles) east of Carlow, along the R726, stands a dolmen boasting the biggest capstone in Ireland. Weighing a reputed 100 tons, this massive stone is embedded in the earth at one end and supported at the other by three much smaller stones. Dating back to 2000 BC, Browne's Hill Dolmen is thought to mark the tomb of a local chieftain. A path leads to it from the road.

**Browne's Hill Dolmen, famous for its enormous capstone**

# Street-by-Street: Kilkenny ⑯

**Kilkenny coat of arms**

**K**ILKENNY is undoubtedly Ireland's loveliest inland city. It rose to prominence in the 13th century, when the Irish Parliament often met at Kilkenny Castle. The Anglo-Norman Butler family came to power in the 1390s and held sway over the city for 500 years. Their power has gone but their legacy is visible in the city's historic buildings, many of which have been restored. Kilkenny is proud of its heritage and every August hosts the Republic's top arts festival.

**To Irishtown, St. Canice's Cathedral**

**PARLIAMENT STREET**

**ST KIERAN'S STREET**

**HIGH STREET**

**Grace's Castle** was built in 1210 and later converted into a jail. Remodeled in the 18th century, it has functioned as a courthouse ever since.

**Marble City Bar**

**Narrow alleyways,** known locally as "slips," are part of Kilkenny's medieval heritage. Several slips survive, and these are currently undergoing restoration.

**Tholsel (City Hall)**

**★ Rothe House**
*This fine Tudor merchant's house, built around two court-yards, is fronted by arcades once typical of Kilkenny's main streets. A small museum inside the house contains a display of local archaeological artifacts and a costume collection.*

**Butter Slip**
*The alley is named after the butter stalls that once lined this small market place.*

**View of the High Street**
*The 18th-century Tholsel, with its distinctive clock tower and arcade, is the main landmark on the High Street. Its elegant Georgian chamber is used by city councillors to this day.*

**STAR SIGHTS**

**★ Kilkenny Castle**

**★ Rothe House**

### Kyteler's Inn

*This medieval coaching inn (see p318) is named after Dame Alice Kyteler, a 14th-century witch who once lived in the building. Like most of the pubs in the city, Kyteler's Inn sells Smithwick's beer, which has been brewed in Kilkenny since 1710.*

### VISITORS' CHECKLIST

**Road map** C4. Co Kilkenny.
🚶 *18,000.* 🚍 *Dublin Road (056 22024).* 🚌 *Dublin Road (056 64933).* 🛈 *Shee Almshouse, Rose Inn St (056 21755).* 🎭 *Kilkenny Arts Week (Aug).* **Rothe House** 📞 *056 22893.* ◻ *Apr–Oct: daily; Nov–Mar: Sat–Sun (pm only).*

**The Shee Almshouse** is one of Ireland's few surviving Tudor poorhouses. Inside, the Cityscope Exhibition illustrates life in 17th-century Kilkenny using a model of the city.

St. Mary's Hall

St. John's Bridge

To train and bus stations, Dublin

★ **Kilkenny Castle**

*Set in a commanding position overlooking the River Nore, this Norman fortress is one of Ireland's most famous castles. The Long Gallery, the finest room in the house, has a striking 19th-century hammer-beam and glass roof.*

CANAL SQ

NORE

ROSE INN STREET

🅿

THE PARADE

PATRICK STREET

**To Cork, Waterford**

0 meters  50

0 yards  50

### KEY

🅿  Parking

🛈  Tourist information

– – –  Suggested route

**Kilkenny Design Centre**
*Housed in Kilkenny Castle's stable block, the center has a nationwide reputation. You can see craftspeople in action and also buy their work.*

## Exploring Kilkenny

In a lovely spot beside a kink in the River Nore, Kilkenny is of great architectural interest, with much use made of the distinctive local black limestone, known as Kilkenny marble. A tour of the town also reveals many unexpected treasures: a Georgian façade often seems to conceal a Tudor chimney, a Classical interior or some other surprise.

The survival of the Irishtown district, now dominated by St. Canice's Cathedral, recalls past segregation in Kilkenny. The area once known as English-town still boasts the city's grandest public buildings.

As a brewery city, Kilkenny is a paradise for avid drinkers. Not counting the popular private drinking clubs, there are about 80 official pubs.

**North side of Kilkenny Castle showing Victorian crenellations**

**Sign of the Marble City Bar on Kilkenny's High Street**

### ♣ Kilkenny Castle
The Parade. **[** 056 21450.
**◯** Apr–Sep: daily; Oct–Mar: Tue–Sun. **●** 10 days at Christmas. **◪**
**◧** obligatory. **&** limited.
Built in the 1190s, Kilkenny Castle was occupied right up until 1935. The powerful Butler family *(see p134)* lived in it from the late 14th century, but because of the exorbitant upkeep, their descendants eventually donated Kilkenny Castle to the nation in 1967. With its drum towers and solid walls, the castle retains its

medieval form, but has undergone many alterations. The Victorian changes made in Gothic Revival style have had the most enduring impact, and are even more impressive since recent restoration work. The castle is a tremendously popular sight, so be prepared to line up during the summer.

High spots of a tour include the library, the wood-paneled dining room and the Chinese bedroom. Best of all, however, is the Long Gallery, rebuilt in the 1820s to house the Butler art collection. Its elaborate painted ceiling has a strong Pre-Raphaelite feel, with many of the motifs inspired by the *Book of Kells (see p62)*.

The castle grounds have shrunk over the centuries, but the French Classical gardens remain, with terraces opening onto a woodland walk and pleasant rolling parkland.

### ⛪ St. Canice's Cathedral
Irishtown. **◯** daily. **Donation. &**
The hilltop cathedral, flanked by a round tower that you can climb for a good view over Kilkenny, was built in the 13th century in an Early English

Gothic style. It was sacked by Cromwell's forces in 1650, but has survived as one of Ireland's medieval treasures. Walls of the local Kilkenny marble and pillars of pale sandstone combine to create an interior of simple grandeur. There is a finely sculpted west door, but the cream of the carving lies inside. An array of splendid 16th-century tombs includes the beautiful effigies of the Butler family in the south transept.

### ⛪ Black Abbey
Abbey St. **[** 056 21279. **◯** daily. **&**
Lying just west of Parliament Street, this Dominican abbey was founded in 1225. It was turned into a courthouse in the 16th century, but is once again a working monastery. The church boasts a fine vaulted undercroft and distinctive, though perhaps overrestored, stonework. There are also some beautiful stained-glass windows, several of which date back to the 14th century.

**ENVIRONS:** Just north of the town lies **Dunmore Cave**, a limestone cavern with an impressive series of chambers, noted for its steep descent and curious rock formations.

**Bennettsbridge**, on the Nore 8 km (5 miles) south of Kilkenny, is famous for its ceramics. The Nicholas Mosse Pottery *(see p327)* specializes in colorful earthenware made from the local clay.

### ⚒ Dunmore Cave
Ballyfoyle. **[** 056 67726. **◯** Mar–mid-Jun: Tue–Sun; mid-Jun–Oct: daily; Nov–Feb: Sat, Sun & public hols. **◪**

**Tomb of 2nd Marquess of Ormonde in St. Canice's Cathedral**

## Jerpoint Abbey 🔟

**Road map** D5. Thomastown, Co
Kilkenny. ☎ 056 24623. 🚌 🚍 to
Thomastown. ☐ mid-Jun–Oct: daily;
Apr–mid-Jun: Tue–Sun. 🎟 🛒 ♿

Lying on the banks of the
Little Arrigle just south of
Thomastown, Jerpoint Abbey
ranks among the finest
Cistercian ruins in Ireland,
despite the loss of many of its
domestic buildings. Founded
in about 1160, the fortified
medieval complex rivaled
nearby Duiske Abbey *(see
p141)* in prestige. Jerpoint
flourished until the Dissolution of the Monasteries *(see
pp34–5)*, when it passed to
the Earl of Ormonde.

The 15th-century cloisters
have not survived as well as
some earlier parts of
the abbey. Even so,
they are the highlight
of Jerpoint, with their
amusing sculptures of
knights, courtly ladies,
bishops and dragons.
The church itself is
well preserved. The
Irish-Romanesque
transepts date back to
the earliest period and
contain several 16th-
century tombs with
exquisite stylized
carvings. The north
side of the nave is
also intact, with a rich
array of decorated
Romanesque capitals.
There are tombs and
effigies of early
bishops and patrons
throughout the abbey. The
battlemented crossing tower
was added during the 1400s.

**Stylized carving of saints on 16th-century tomb in Jerpoint Abbey**

## Lismore 🔟

**Road map** C5. Co Waterford.
🏘 1,100. 🚍 🅸 Apr–Oct: Lismore
Heritage Centre (058 54855).

This genteel riverside town
is dwarfed by **Lismore
Castle**, perched romantically
above the River Blackwater.
Built in 1185 but re-
modeled in the 19th
century, the castle is the
Irish seat of the Duke
of Devonshire and is
closed to the public.
However, you can visit
the sumptuous gardens,
which include a lovely
riverside walk. **Lismore
Heritage Centre** tells
the story of St. Carthage,
who founded a monas-
tic center here in the
7th century. The town
has two cathedrals
dedicated to him. The
Protestant **Cathedral
of St. Carthage** is
the more interesting.
It dates from 1633
but incorporates
older elements and
was later altered to suit the
Neo-Gothic tastes of the
Victorians. There is some fine

**Burne-Jones window
in St. Carthage's
Cathedral, Lismore**

Gothic vaulting, and two
stained-glass windows in the
south transept are by the Pre-
Raphaelite artist, Sir Edward
Burne-Jones.

♣ **Lismore Castle
Gardens** ☎ 058 54424. ☐ May–
Sep: daily (pm only). 🎟 ♿ limited.

**Environs:** From Lismore you
can follow a picturesque
route through the **Blackwater
Valley** *(see p169)*. This runs
from Cappoquin, in an idyllic
woodland setting just east of
Lismore, down to the estuary
at Youghal *(see p171)*.

## Ardmore 🔟

**Road map** C5. Co Waterford. 🏘 380.
🚍 🅸 May–Sep: Main St (024 94444).

Ardmore is a popular seaside
resort with a splendid
beach, lively pubs, good cliff
walks and some interesting
architecture. The hill beside
the village, which provides
fine views of the beach, is the
site of a monastery established
in the 5th century by St. Declan,
the first missionary to bring
Christianity to this area.

Most of the buildings, including the ruined **St. Declan's
Cathedral**, date from the
12th century. The cathedral's
west wall has fine Romanesque
sculptures, arranged in a
series of arcades. The scenes
include The *Archangel
Michael Weighing Souls* in the
upper row, and below this
*The Adoration of the Magi* and
*The Judgment of Solomon*.

The adjacent round tower is
one of the best preserved
examples in Ireland, and rises
to a height of 30 m (95 ft). An
oratory nearby is said to mark
the site of St. Declan's grave.

**St. Declan's Cathedral at Ardmore, with its near-perfect round tower**

# Waterford ⑳

**Waterford city coat of arms**

W ATERFORD WAS FOUNDED in 853 by the Vikings and later extended by the Anglo-Normans. Set in a commanding position by the estuary of the River Suir, it became southeast Ireland's main seaport. From the 18th century, the city's prosperity was consolidated by local industries, including the glassworks for which Waterford is famous. The strong commercial tradition persists today and Waterford's port is still one of Ireland's busiest. While the city has been somewhat tarnished by industrialization, great efforts are now being made to salvage what remains of its heritage, with further excavations of the old Viking city and the creation of pedestrian malls in the historic quarter.

**Reginald's Tower on the quayside**

**Jenkin's Lane, a quiet corner of Waterford off George's Street**

## Exploring Waterford

The extensive remains of the city walls clearly define the area originally fortified by the Vikings. The best-preserved section runs northwest from the **Watch Tower** on Castle Street, although Reginald's Tower, overlooking the river, is the largest structure in the old defenses. In the Reginald Bar *(see p318)* you can see the arches through which boats sallied forth down the river; these sallyports are one of several Viking sections of the largely Norman fortifications.

Although Waterford retains its medieval layout, most of the city's finest buildings are Georgian. Some of the best examples can be seen on the Mall, which runs southwest from Reginald's Tower, and in the lovely Cathedral Square. The latter takes its name from **Christchurch Cathedral**,

which was built in the 1770s to a design by John Roberts, a local architect who contributed much to the city's Georgian heritage. It is fronted by a fine Corinthian colonnade. A grim 15th-century effigy of a rotting corpse is an unexpected sight inside. Heading down toward the river, you pass the 13th-century ruins of **Grey Friars**, often known as the French Church after it became a Huguenot chapel in 1693.

West along the waterfront, a Victorian clock tower stands at the top of Barronstrand Street. Rising above the busy stores is the **Holy Trinity Cathedral**, which has a rich Neo-Classical interior. George's Street, which runs west from here, is dotted with period houses and cozy pubs. It leads to O'Connell Street, whose partially restored warehouses contrast with the shabbier buildings on the quay. In the summer, you can enjoy another view of the waterfront by taking a cruise on the river.

## ♠ Reginald's Tower

The Quay. 📞 *051 73501*. ⏰ *daily*. ⬤ *1 week at Christmas.* 🎫
The Vikings erected a tower on this spot in 1003, but it was the Normans who built the solid structure you see now. With impregnable walls 3 m (10 ft) thick, it is said to be the first Irish building to use mortar, a primitive concoction of blood, lime, fur and mud. The tower has in its time been a fortress, a mint, an arsenal and a prison. Newly restored, it contains Waterford's civic museum.

## 🏛 Waterford Heritage Centre

Grey Friars St. 📞 *051 71227*. ⏰ *Easter–Oct: Mon–Sat*.
This excellent museum tells the story of Waterford using models and a reconstruction of the early city. It has a fine display of Viking and medieval artifacts, which were discovered during recent excavations.

**View of the city of Waterford across the River Suir**

## Waterford Crystal Factory

Kilbarry. **⌞** *051 73311.* **◯** *Apr–Oct: daily; Nov–Mar: Mon–Fri.* ▣ ▣ ▣

A visit to the Waterford Crystal Factory, just 2.5 km (1.5 miles) south of the center, is strongly recommended for the insight it gives into the city's special process of crystalmaking.

The original glass factory was founded in 1783 by two brothers, George and William Penrose, who chose Waterford because of its port. For many

**Craftsman engraving a vase at the Waterford Crystal Factory**

decades their crystal enjoyed an unrivaled reputation, but draconian taxes caused the firm to close in 1851. A new factory was opened in 1947, however, and master blowers and engravers were brought from Europe to train local apprentices. Competition from Tipperary and Galway Crystal hit sales in the early 1990s, but these have revived recently, largely due to an upturn in the North American market.

Visitors can follow all stages of production, observing the process by which sand, lead and potash are transformed by fire into sparkling crystal. The main difference between ordinary glass and crystal is the latter's high lead content, 30 percent in Waterford's case. The glass-blowers require great skill to create walls of the right thickness to take the heavy incisions typical of Waterford Crystal. The factory's other main hallmark is the Waterford signature, which is engraved on the base of each piece

In the gallery showroom, a crystal chandelier lights up a dining table laden with Wedgwood pottery and Waterford glass, tempting visitors to buy.

**VISITORS' CHECKLIST**

**Road map** D5. Co Waterford.
▲ *42,000.* ✈ *6 km (4 miles) S.*
▣ *Plunkett Station, The Bridge (051 73401).* 🚌 *Plunkett Station (051 79000).* ℹ *41 The Quay (051 75788).* 🚢 *(051 21723); Jun–Aug.* 🚢 *Fri.* 🎭 *Operetta Festival (Sep).*

**Ballyhack port, across Waterford Harbour from Passage East**

**ENVIRONS:** The small port of **Passage East**, 12 km (7 miles) east of Waterford, witnessed the landing of the Normans in 1170 (*see p34*), but little has happened since. A car ferry links the village to Ballyhack in County Wexford, providing a scenic shortcut across Waterford Harbour as well as an excellent entry point to the Hook Peninsula (*see p140*).

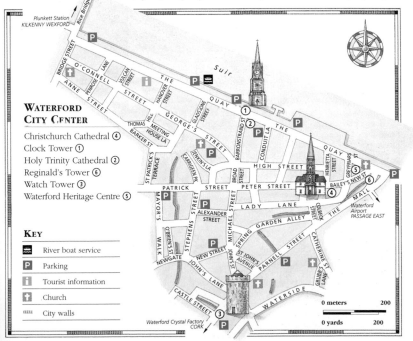

**WATERFORD CITY CENTER**

Christchurch Cathedral ④
Clock Tower ①
Holy Trinity Cathedral ②
Reginald's Tower ⑥
Watch Tower ③
Waterford Heritage Centre ⑤

**KEY**

| 🚢 | River boat service |
| 🅿 | Parking |
| ℹ | Tourist information |
| ✝ | Church |
| ⫼⫼ | City walls |

0 meters 200
0 yards 200

## Dunmore East ㉑

**Road map** D5. Co Waterford.
🏛 *1,100.* ▣

THE APPEAL of Dunmore East, Waterford's most charming fishing village, lies chiefly in its red sandstone cliffs and bustling harbor. Paths run along the foot of the cliffs, but for the best views take the road that winds uphill from the beach, past tidy cottages and the ivy-clad Ship Inn to the Haven Hotel. A gate nearby leads to delightful gardens overlooking the fishing boats below. Climbing up steps cut into the rock, you are rewarded by views of the cliffs and noisy kittiwake colonies.

**Busy fishing harbor at Dunmore East**

## Hook Peninsula ㉒

**Road map** D5. Co. Wexford. ▣ *to Duncannon.* ⛴ *from Passage East to Ballyhack (051 382480).* ℹ *Jun–Sep: Fethard-on-Sea (051 397118).*

THIS TAPERING HEADLAND of gentle landscapes scattered with ancient ruins and quiet villages is perfect for a circular tour. The "Ring of Hook" route begins south of New Ross at **Dunbrody Abbey**, the ruins of a 12th-century Cistercian church, but **Ballyhack** is another good place to start. Once a fortified crossing point into County Waterford, the town still has a ferry service to neighboring Passage East (*see p139*). **Ballyhack Castle**, built by the Knights Templar in about 1450, contains a small museum. About 4 km (2.5 miles) beyond is the small resort of **Duncannon**, with a broad sandy beach and a star-shaped fort, which was built in 1588 in expectation of an attack by the Spanish Armada.

The coast road continues south to **Hook Head**. Here, perched on red sandstone, sits what is almost certainly the oldest lighthouse in Europe, dating from 1172. Paths skirt the coast, which attracts many seabirds and seals and is also famous for its fossils.

Just 2 km (1.5 miles) east is the picturesque village of **Slade**. A ruined 15th-century tower house, **Slade Castle**, presides over the tiny harbor where fishing boats cluster around the slipways. The road proceeds along the rugged coastline, past the resort of Fethard-on-Sea and Saltmills to the dramatic ruin of **Tintern Abbey**. This 13th-century Cistercian foundation was built by William Marshall, Earl of Pembroke, in fulfillment of a vow made when his boat was caught in a storm off the coast nearby. The west end has been restored, but excavation work continues. Fields lead to an old stone bridge and views over **Bannow Bay**, where it is thought the Normans made their first landing in 1169.

🏠 **Dunbrody Abbey**
Campile. 📞 *051 388603.* ⏰ *Apr–Sep: daily.* 🏛

♣ **Ballyhack Castle**
Ballyhack. 📞 *051 389468.* ⏰ *Jul–Aug: daily; Apr–Jun & Sep: Wed–Sun.*

**Norman lighthouse at Hook Head, on the tip of the Hook Peninsula**

## New Ross ㉓

**Road map** D5. Co Wexford. 🏛 *6,000.* ▣ ℹ *mid-Jun–mid-Sep: The Quay (051 21857).* ⛴ *Tue.* **Galley Cruising Restaurants** *The Quay (051 21723).*

LYING ON the banks of the River Barrow, New Ross is one of the oldest towns in the county. Its importance, now as in the past, stems from its status as a port. In summer there is much activity on the river. Cruises run by Galley Cruising Restaurants ply both the Barrow and Nore rivers. Traditional storefronts line the streets, which rise steeply

**Castle ruins and harbor at Slade on the Hook Peninsula**

from the quayside. The **Tholsel**, now the town hall but originally a tollhouse, was occupied by the British during the 1798 rebellion (see pp38–9). Opposite, a monument to a Wexford pikeman commemorates the bravery of the Irish rebels who faced the British cannons.

Nearby is **St. Mary's**, which, when founded in the 13th century, was the largest parish church in Ireland. A modern church occupies the site, but the original (now roofless) south transept remains, as do many medieval tombstones.

**View over Enniscorthy and St. Aidan's cathedral from Vinegar Hill**

**ENVIRONS:** A popular trip up the meandering Barrow goes 16 km (10 miles) north to **Graiguenamanagh**. The main attraction of this market town is **Duiske Abbey**, the largest Cistercian church in Ireland. Founded in 1207, it has been extensively restored and now acts as the parish church. The most striking features include a Romanesque door in the south transept, the great oak roof and traces of a medieval pavement below floor level. There is also a cross-legged statue of the Knight of Duiske, which is one of the finest medieval effigies in Ireland. Outside are two 9th-century granite High Crosses.

Trips along the Nore take you to **Inistioge**. Lying in a deep, wooded valley, this is an idyllic village, with neat 18th-century houses, a square planted with lime trees and a ten-arched bridge spanning the Nore. On a rock above the river stands a ruined Norman fort, a popular place for picnics. From Inistioge you can walk along the river or up to **Woodstock House Demesne**, a national park. Among the

beech woods stands an 18th-century mansion, reduced to a ruin by a fire in 1922.

On a hill 12 km (7.5 miles) south of New Ross, a large area of woodland is enclosed within the **John F Kennedy Park and Arboretum**. Founded in 1968, near the late president's ancestral home in Dunganstown, the park boasts more than 4,500 types of tree and provides splendid panoramic views. There are marked paths and nature trails, and it is also possible to go horseback riding.

🏛 **Duiske Abbey**
Graiguenamanagh, Co Kilkenny.
📞 *0503 24238.* ⏱ *daily.* ♿
🌿 **John F Kennedy Park and Arboretum**
Dunganstown, Co Kilkenny. 📞 *051 388171.* ⏱ *daily.* 📷 ♿

# Enniscorthy ㉔

**Road map** D5. Co Wexford. 🚉 *4,500.* 🚌 🚍 ℹ *County Museum, The Castle (054 35926).*

THE STREETS of Enniscorthy, on the banks of the River Slaney, are full of character and redolent of the town's turbulent past. In 1798, Enniscorthy

witnessed the last stand of the Wexford pikemen, when a fierce battle was fought against a British force of 20,000 on nearby **Vinegar Hill**. The events of that year are told in full at the excellent County Museum inside **Enniscorthy Castle** – an imposing presence in the town, founded by the Normans but altered in the 16th century.

Enniscorthy's other main sight is **St. Aidan's Cathedral**, a Neo-Gothic creation designed in the 1840s by AWN Pugin (1812–52), most famous for his work on the Houses of Parliament in London.

Granaries and mills overlook the Slaney, along with several potteries for which the town is famous. Carley's Bridge was founded in 1654 and is still producing terra-cotta pots.

Enniscorthy's historic pubs are another big attraction. They include the Antique Tavern (see p318), a half-timbered building which is hung with pikes used during the Battle of Vinegar Hill in 1798.

♣ **Enniscorthy Castle**
Castle Hill. 📞 *054 35926.*
⏱ *Mar–Sep: daily; Oct–Feb: Sun.*
📷 ♿ *limited.*

**The inland port of New Ross seen from the west bank of the River Barrow**

**View across the harbor to Wexford town**

# Irish National Heritage Park 25

**Road map** D5. Ferrycarrig, Co Wexford. *from Wexford in summer.* 053 41733. *mid-Mar–mid-Jan: daily.* Dec 25–26 & 31.

**B**UILT ON former marshland near Ferrycarrig, just north of Wexford, the Irish National Heritage Park is a bold open-air museum. Trails lead visitors through woods to replicas of homesteads, places of worship and burial sites. These provide a good introduction to the country's ancient history *(see pp30–31)*, and the section which deals with the Celtic period is particularly interesting. Other highlights include the Viking boatyard, complete with raiding ship, and a 7th-century horizontal watermill.

# Wexford 26

**Road map** D5. Co Wexford. 15,000. Crescent Quay (053 23111).

**W**EXFORD'S name derives from *Waesfjord*, a Norse word meaning "estuary of the mud flats." It thrived as a port for centuries but the silting of the harbor in the Victorian era put an end to most sea traffic. Wexford's quays, from where ships once sailed to Bristol, Tenby and Liverpool, are used today mainly by a fleet of humble mussel dredgers.

Wexford is a vibrant place, packed with fine pubs and

boasting a varied arts scene. The town's singular style is often linked to its linguistic heritage. The *yola* dialect, which was spoken by early settlers, survives in the local pronunciation of certain words.

Wexford retains few traces of its past, but the Viking fish-bone street pattern still exists, with narrow alleys fanning off the meandering Main Street. Keyser's Lane, linking South Main Street with the lively Commodore pub on Paul Quay, is a tiny tunnel-like Viking alley which once led to the Norse water-front. The Normans were responsible for Wexford's town walls, remnants of which include one of the original gateways. This houses the **Westgate Heritage Centre**, which traces the history of Wexford. Behind it lies **Selskar Abbey**, the ruin of a 12th-century Augustinian monastery. King Henry II is said to have done penance here for the murder of Thomas à Becket in 1170.

**Sign of a popular Wexford pub**

Wexford also has several handsome buildings dating from a later period, including the 18th-century market house, known as the **Cornmarket**, on Main Street. The nearby square, the **Bull Ring**, is notable only for its history: it was used for bull-baiting in Norman times and was the scene of a cruel massacre by Cromwell's men in 1649.

Wexford Opera Festival, held in October, is the leading operatic event in the country. Aficionados praise it for its intimate atmosphere – both

during performances and afterward, when artists and audience mingle together in the pubs: the Centenary Stores off Main Street is a favorite, though the Wren's Nest, on Custom House Quay, is better for traditional music.

**m Westgate Heritage Centre**
Westgate. 053 46506. *Jun–Aug: daily; Sep–May: Mon–Sat.* Dec 25 & 26.

**ENVIRONS:** Skirting the shore just east of the town is the **Wexford Wildfowl Reserve**. It covers 100 ha (250 acres) of reclaimed land and is noted in particular for its geese: over a third of the world's entire population of Greenland white-fronted geese winter here between October and April.

The mudflats also attract large numbers of swans and waders, and provide a rich hunting ground for birds of prey. The birds can be viewed from a number of blinds and an observation tower.

**Wexford Wildfowl Reserve**
Wexford. 053 23129. *daily.* *on weekends.*

# Johnstown Castle 27

**Road map** D5. Co Wexford. 053 42888. *to Wexford.* **Gardens** *daily.* Dec 24 & 25.

**Façade of Johnstown Castle**

**J**OHNSTOWN CASTLE, a splendid Gothic Revival mansion, lies amid ornamental gardens and mature woodland 6 km (4 miles) southwest of Wexford. In state hands since 1945, the house now functions as an

**Vast crescent of sand and shingle beach at Rosslare**

agricultural research center. It is not open to the public, but it is possible to visit the **Irish Agriculture Museum**, housed in the castle's farm buildings. Reconstructions illustrate the work of a wheelwright and other traditional trades.

The real glory of Johnstown Castle are the grounds, from the sunken Italian garden and ornamental lakes to the woodlands and shrubberies. Azaleas and camellias flourish alongside an impressive array of trees including Japanese cedars, redwoods and Scots pine.

Hidden among the dense woods west of the house lurk the ruins of **Rathlannon Castle**, a medieval tower house.

🏛 **Irish Agriculture Museum**
Johnstown Castle. ⬜ Apr–mid-Nov.
daily (Sat & Sun pm only); mid-Nov–
Mar: Mon–Fri. 🖼 🔥 limited.

## Saltee Islands ㉘

**Road map** D5. Co Wexford. 🚍 from
Wexford to Kilmore Quay: Wed & Sat.
🚢 from Kilmore Quay: Jul & Aug
(weather permitting). ☎ 053 29684.

THESE ISLANDS off the south coast of Wexford are a haven for sea birds. Great and Little Saltee together form Ireland's largest bird sanctuary, nurturing an impressive array of birds, from gannets and gulls to puffins and Manx shearwaters. Great Saltee is particularly famous for its colonies of cormorants. It also

has more than 1,000 pairs of guillemots and is a popular stopping-off place for spring and autumn migrations. A bird-monitoring and research program is in progress, and a close watch is also kept on the colony of gray seals.

The two uninhabited Islands are privately owned, but visitors are welcome. Boat trips are run in fine weather from **Kilmore Quay**. These leave in late morning and return midafternoon.

Kilmore Quay is a small fishing village built on rare Precambrian gneiss rock – the oldest rock in Ireland. Pretty thatched cottages nestle above a fine sandy beach and the harbor, where a moored lightship houses a **Maritime Museum**. The boat's original fittings are just as interesting as the exhibits.

🏛 **Maritime Museum**
Kilmore Quay. ☎ 053
29655. ⬜ Jun–
Oct: daily (pm
only). 🖼

## Rosslare ㉙

**Road map** D5. Co Wexford. 👥 1,200.
🚍 🚢 ℹ Ferry terminal, Rosslare
Harbor (053 33622).

ROSSLARE REPLACED Wexford as the area's main port after the decline of the original Viking city harbor. The port is so active today that people tend to associate the name Rosslare more with the ferry terminal for France and Wales than with the town lying 8 km (5 miles) further north.

Rosslare town is one of the sunniest spots in Ireland and draws many vacationers. It boasts a fine beach stretching for 9.5 km (6 miles), lively pubs and an excellent golf course fringed by sand dunes. There are good walks north to Rosslare Point.

**ENVIRONS:** At Tagoat, 6 km (4 miles) south of Rosslare, an old farmhouse called **Yola Farmstead** contains displays of traditional crafts such as thatching, glassblowing and bread- and butter-making.

🏛 **Yola Farmstead**
Tagoat. ☎ 053 31111. ⬜ May–Sep:
daily. 🖼 🔥

**Colony of gannets nesting on the cliffs of Great Saltee Island**

# CORK AND KERRY

## CORK · KERRY

**M**AGNIFICENT SCENERY *has attracted visitors to this region since Victorian times. Rocky headlands jut out into the Atlantic and colorful fishing villages nestle in the shelter of the bays. County Kerry offers dramatic landscapes and a wealth of prehistoric and early Christian sites, whereas County Cork's gentle charm has enticed many a casual visitor into becoming a permanent resident.*

Killarney and its romantic lakes are a powerful magnet for tourists, and so are Cork's attractive coastal towns and villages. Yet the region remains remarkably unspoiled, with a friendly atmosphere and authentic culture still alive in Irish-speaking pockets. There is also a long tradition of arts and crafts in the area.

This corner of Ireland used to be the main point of contact with the Continent. In the 17th century, in response to the threat of invasions from France and Spain, the English built a line of forts along the Cork coast, including the massive Charles Fort at Kinsale.

In the 19th century, the city of Cork was an important departure point for people fleeing from the Famine *(see p211)*, with Cobh the main port for emigrants to the New World. Cork's importance as a port has diminished, but it is still the Republic's second city with a lively cultural scene.

Poverty and temperament helped foster a powerful Republican spirit in the southwest. The region saw much guerrilla action in the War of Independence and the subsequent Civil War. In 1920, the center of Cork city was burned in an uncontrolled act of reprisal by the notorious Black and Tans *(see pp42–3)*.

Kerry is known as "the Kingdom" on account of its tradition of independence and disregard for Dublin rule. The Irish recognize a distinctive Kerry character, with a boisterous sense of living life to the full. They also make Kerrymen the butt of countless jokes.

As well as the friendliest people in Ireland, the region has some of the finest scenery. Cork has lush valleys and a beautiful coast while Kerry is wilder and more mountainous. The islands off the Kerry coast appear bleak and inhospitable, but many were once inhabited. Remote, rocky Skellig Michael, for example, was the site of a 6th-century Christian monastery.

**Puffins on the island of Skellig Michael off the coast of Kerry**

◁ **Beach at Barley Cove near Mizen Head, County Cork**

# Exploring Cork and Kerry

KILLARNEY IS A POPULAR BASE with tourists for exploring Cork and Kerry, especially for touring the Ring of Kerry and the archaeological remains of the Dingle Peninsula. Despite the changeable weather, the region attracts many visitors who come to see its dramatic scenery and lush vegetation. As you pass through quiet fishing villages and genteel towns, such as Kenmare, you will always encounter a friendly welcome from the locals. For the adventurous there are plenty of opportunities to go riding, hiking or cycling. Cork city offers a more cosmopolitan atmosphere, with its art galleries and craft shops.

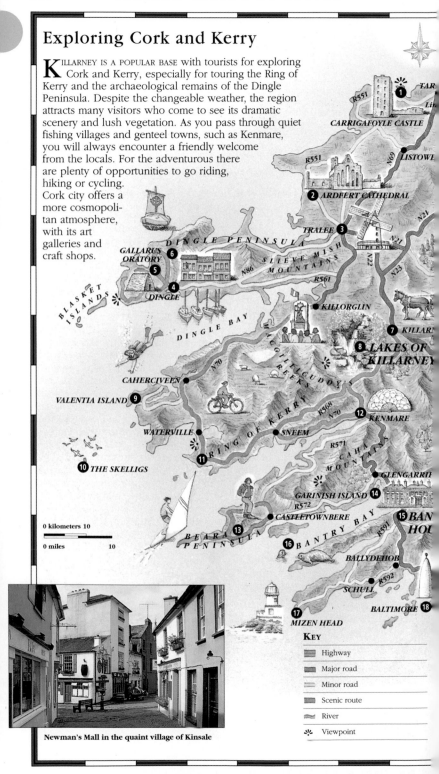

CARRIGAFOYLE CASTLE

LISTOWE

ARDFERT CATHEDRAL

TRALEE

DINGLE PENINSULA

GALLARUS ORATORY

SLIEVE MISH MOUNTAINS

DINGLE

BLASKET ISLANDS

KILLORGLIN

DINGLE BAY

KILLARN

LAKES OF KILLARNEY

MACGILLICUDDY'S REEKS

CAHERCIVEEN

VALENTIA ISLAND

KENMARE

WATERVILLE

SNEEM

RING OF KERRY

THE SKELLIGS

CAHA MOUNTAINS

GLENGARRI

GARINISH ISLAND

CASTLETOWNBERE

BEARA PENINSULA

BANTRY BAY

BAN HOU

BALLYDEHOB

SCHULL

BALTIMORE

MIZEN HEAD

0 kilometers 10

0 miles 10

**KEY**

| | |
|---|---|
| ▨ | Highway |
| ▨ | Major road |
| ▨ | Minor road |
| ▨ | Scenic route |
| ≈ | River |
| ☀ | Viewpoint |

**Newman's Mall in the quaint village of Kinsale**

**Cattle grazing near Ardfert Cathedral**

## SIGHTS AT A GLANCE

Ardfert Cathedral **2**
Baltimore **18**
Bantry Bay **16**
*Bantry House pp160–61* **15**
Beara Peninsula **13**
Blarney Castle **23**
Carrigafoyle Castle **1**
Clonakilty **20**
Cobh **27**
*Cork pp166–9* **25**
Dingle **4**
Drombeg Stone Circle **19**
Gallarus Oratory **5**

Garinish Island **14**
Jameson Heritage Centre **28**
Kenmare **12**
Killarney **7**
*Kinsale pp164–5* **24**
*Lakes of Killarney pp154–5* **8**
Mizen Head **17**
River Blackwater **26**
River Lee **22**
The Skelligs **10**
Timoleague Abbey **21**
Tralee **3**
Valentia Island **9**
Youghal **29**

### Tours
Dingle Peninsula **6**
Ring of Kerry **11**

## GETTING AROUND
To explore the region a car is essential. The N22 connects Cork, Killarney and Tralee while the N71 follows the coastline via Clonakilty, Bantry and on to Killarney. In the more remote parts the road signs may only be written in Irish. Killarney is the base for organized bus tours of the area. The train service from Cork to Dublin is efficient, and trains also connect Killarney with Dublin and Cork, but you may have to change trains en route. Buses run throughout the region, but services to the smaller sights may be infrequent.

### SEE ALSO

• *Where to Stay* pp291–3

• *Restaurants, Cafés and Pubs* pp310–12 & p319

**Kissing the Blarney Stone at Blarney Castle near Cork**

Ardfert Cathedral and the ruins of Teampall na Hoe and Teampall na Griffin

## Carrigafoyle Castle ❶

**Road map** B5. Co Kerry.
🚌 *to Listowel.*

Ruined keep of Carrigafoyle Castle

H IGH ABOVE the Shannon estuary, just west of Ballylongford, this 15th-century castle belonged to the O'Connor clan, who ruled much of northern Kerry. The English besieged or sacked it repeatedly but the body blow was delivered in 1649 by Cromwellian forces *(see p37)*. The ruins include a keep and walled courtyard, with romantic views of the estuary from the top of the tower, reached by a spiral staircase.

## Ardfert Cathedral ❷

**Road map** A5. Co Kerry.
🚌 *to Ardfert.* ◯ *daily.* 🏷️ 🚻

T HIS COMPLEX of churches is linked to the cult of St. Brendan the Navigator *(see p205)*, who was born nearby

in 484 and founded a monastery here. The ruined cathedral dates back to the 12th century and retains a delicate Romanesque doorway and blind arcading. Inside, an effigy of a 14th-century bishop occupies a niche in the northwestern corner. In the graveyard stand the remains of a Romanesque nave-and-chancel church, Teampall na Hoe, and a late Gothic chapel, Teampall na Griffin. The latter is named after the curious griffins carved beside an interior window.

A short walk away are the ruins of a Franciscan friary. It was founded by Thomas Fitzmaurice in 1253, but the cloisters and south chapel date from the 15th century.

**ENVIRONS:** Just northwest of Ardfert is **Banna Strand**. Irish patriot Roger Casement landed here in 1916 on a German U-boat, bringing in rifles for the Easter Rising *(see pp42–3)*. He was arrested as soon as he landed and a memorial stands

on the site of his capture. This beach was also used for the filming of David Lean's *Ryan's Daughter* (1970).

## Tralee ❸

**Road map** B5. Co Kerry. 👥 *17,000.*
🚌 🚉 ⓘ *Ashe Memorial Hall, Dennys St (066 21288).* ◖ *Thu.*

H OST TO the renowned Rose of Tralee International Festival *(see p46)*, Tralee has made great strides in promoting its cultural and leisure facilities. The town's main attraction is **Kerry County Museum** with its theme park, "Kerry the Kingdom." It offers an audiovisual show on Kerry scenery, a display of archaeological finds and interactive models, and a "time travel experience" through Anglo-Norman Tralee, complete with medieval sounds and smells.

Also based in Tralee is the **Siamsa Tíre** folklore theater, an internationally celebrated

Steam train on the narrow gauge railroad between Tralee and Blennerville, with Blennerville Windmill in the background

ambassador for Irish culture. Traditional song and dance performances take place here throughout the summer.

Just outside Tralee is the authentic **Blennerville Windmill**. Built in 1800, it is Ireland's largest working mill and one of Tralee's most popular attractions. The **Steam Railway** connects Blennerville with Tralee along a narrow gauge track. There are trips on the train with multilingual commentary, from Ballyard Station to the windmill.

🏛 **Kerry County Museum**
Ashe Memorial Hall, Dennys St.
📞 066 27777. ⭕ mid-Mar–Dec: daily. ⬤ Dec 25 & 26. 🕮 ♿

🎭 **Siamsa Tire**
Town Park. 📞 066 23055. ⭕ for performances only. 🕮 ♿

🏛 **Blennerville Windmill**
📞 066 21064. ⭕ Apr–Oct: daily. 🕮

🚂 **Steam Railroad**
Ballyard Station. 📞 066 28888.
⭕ Mar–Oct: daily. 🕮 ♿

## Dingle ❹

**Road map** A5. Co Kerry. 🚶 1,300.
🚌 May–Oct: Main St (066 51188).
🚍 Sat.

THIS ONCE REMOTE Irish-speaking town is today a thriving fishing port and an increasingly popular tourist

Gallarus Oratory, a dry-stone early Christian church

center. Brightly painted craft shops and cafés abound, often with slightly hippy overtones.

Dingle Bay is attractive with a somewhat ramshackle harbor lined with fishing trawlers. Along the quayside are lively bars offering music and seafood. The harbor is home to Dingle's biggest star: Fungie, the dolphin, who has been a permanent resident since 1983 and can be visited by boat or on swimming trips.

Although Dingle has few architectural attractions, it makes an engaging base for exploring the archaeological remains on the Dingle Peninsula (see pp150–51).

## Gallarus Oratory ❺

**Road map** A5. Co Kerry.
🚌 to Dingle.

SHAPED LIKE an upturned boat, this miniature church overlooks Smerwick harbor. Gallarus was built some time between the 6th and 9th centuries and is the best preserved early Christian church in Ireland. It represents the apogee of dry-stone corbeling, using techniques first developed by Neolithic tomb-makers. The stones were laid at a slight angle, lower on the outside than the inside, allowing water to run off.

Fishing trawlers moored alongside the quay at Dingle

# A Tour of the Dingle Peninsula 6

**GUINNESS**
**Mar is gnách**

**Pub sign, Ballyferriter**

THE DINGLE PENINSULA offers some of Ireland's most beautiful scenery. To the north rises the towering Brandon Mountain, while the west coast has some spectacular seascapes. A drive around the area, which takes at least half a day, reveals fascinating antiquities ranging from Iron Age stone forts to inscribed stones, early Christian oratories and beehive huts. These are sometimes found on private land, so you may be asked for a small fee by the farmer to see them. Some parts of the peninsula – especially the more remote areas – are still Gaelic-speaking, so many road signs are written only in Irish.

**View from Clogher Head**

### Riasc (An Riasc) 7
This excavated monastic settlement dates from the 7th century. The enclosure contains the remains of an oratory, several crosses and an inscribed pillar stone (see p235).

### Ballyferriter
### (Baile an Fheirtéaraigh) 6
The attractions of this village include the pastel-colored cottages, Louis Mulcahy's pottery and a museum featuring the cultural heritage of the area.

### Blasket Centre
### (Ionad an Bhlascaoid) 5
Overlooking Blasket Sound, the center explains the literature, language and way of life of the inhabitants of the Blasket Islands. The islanders moved to the mainland in 1953.

*Dunquin*
*(Dún Chaoin)*

*Mount Eagle*

*DINGLE BA*

### Dunmore Head
### (Ceann an Dúin Mhoir) 4
Mainland Ireland's most westerly point offers dramatic views of the Blaskets.

### Slea Head
### (Ceann Sléibe) 3
As you round the Slea Head promontory, the Blasket Islands come into full view. The sculpture of the Crucifixion beside the road is known locally as the Cross (An Cros).

### KEY
▬ Tour route
═ Other roads
☼ Viewpoint

0 kilometers    2
0 miles    1

**Kilmalkedar (Cill Maolchéadair)** ⑨
Once a pagan center of worship, Kilmalkedar is home to a ruined Irish Romanesque church with stone carvings. The graveyard still contains primitive pagan stones, a cross and a sundial.

⑨

**Gallarus Oratory (Séipéilín Ghallrois)** ⑧
This tiny, drystone church (see p149) is a relic of early Irish Christianity.

R559

**Dingle (An Daingean)** ①
Dingle, famous for local resident Fungie the dolphin, is a good place to eat, drink or stay the night (see p149).

①

*Dingle Harbour*

TRALEE
N86

bour

**Dunbeg Fort (An Dún Beag)** ②
Dating from the Iron Age, this is one of the best preserved promontory forts in Ireland. Just beyond are the Fahan beehive huts, early Christian huts thought to have been built for pilgrims visiting the area.

DINGLE BAY

### TIPS FOR DRIVERS

**Length:** 40 km (25 miles).
**Stopping-off points:** Most villages on the route, such as Dunquin and Ballyferriter, have friendly bars offering pub meals. There are also many opportunities to stop for a picnic. On the winding coast road around Slea Head stop only at the safe and clearly marked coastal viewing points. (See also pp355–7.)

**Jaunting cars waiting to take visitors to sights around Killarney**

## Killarney ❼

**Road map** B5. Co Kerry. 🏠 7,500.
🚌 🚏 🛈 Town Hall, Main St (064 31633).

KILLARNEY is commonly derided as "a tourist town" but this has not dented the town's open, cheerful atmosphere. The infectious Kerry humor is personified by the wisecracking *jarveys* whose families have run jaunting cars (pony and trap rides) here for generations. The town has much to offer, with stores open until 10pm in summer, several excellent restaurants, and a sprinkling of prestigious hotels around the lake and the heights. From the town visitors can explore the sights around the Lakes of Killarney (see pp154–5) and the surrounding heather-covered hills.

**ENVIRONS:** Overlooking the lakes and a short drive from Killarney is **Muckross House**. This imposing Victorian mansion was built in 1843 in Elizabethan style. Inside, the elegant rooms are decorated with period furnishings. There is also a museum of Kerry Life, with displays on the history of southwest Ireland, and a craft center with numerous workshops. The landscaped gardens are especially beautiful in spring when the rhododendrons and azaleas are in bloom. A short walk away is Muckross Farm – a working farm that still uses traditional farming techniques.

🏛 **Muckross House**
4 km (2.5 miles) S of Killarney.
📞 064 31440. 🕐 daily. ● 10 days at Christmas. 🚫 ♿ ✓

*Stunning mountain scenery near Moll's Gap on the Ring of Kerry* ▷

# Lakes of Killarney ❽

**Fruit of the strawberry tree**

F AMOUS FOR ITS splendid scenery, the area is one of Ireland's most popular tourist attractions. The three lakes are contained within Killarney National Park. Although the landscape is dotted with ruined castles and abbeys, the lakes are the focus of attention: the moody watery scenery is subject to subtle shifts of light and color. The area has entranced many artists and writers including Thackeray, who praised "a precipice covered with a thousand trees and other mountains rising as far as we could see." In autumn, the bright red fruits of the strawberry tree color the shores of the lakes.

**Meeting of the Waters**
*This beautiful spot, best seen from Dinis Island, is where the waters from the Upper Lake meet Muckross Lake and Lough Leane. At the Old Weir Bridge, boats shoot the rapids.*

**Long Range River**

**Torc Waterfall**
*The Owengarriff River cascades through the wooded Friars' Glen into Muckross Lake. A pretty path winds up to the top of this 18-m (60-ft) high waterfall, revealing views of Torc Mountain.*

**Muckross Lake**

**Dinis Island**

**Muckross Abbey** was founded by the Franciscans in 1448, but was burned down by Cromwellian forces in 1653.

**Lough Leane**

**Killarney** *(see p151)* is the main town from which tourists visit the sights around the lakes.

**Innisfallen Island**

**N22 to Tralee** *(see pp148–9)*

**Ross Castle**, built around 1420, was the last stronghold under Irish control to be taken by Cromwellian forces in 1653.

**★ Muckross House**
*The 19th-century manor (see p151) enjoys a lovely location overlooking the lakes. Visit the wildlife center for an introduction to the flora and fauna of the National Park.*

## Upper Lake
*This narrow lake is the smallest of the three lakes. It flows into the Long Range River to the Meeting of the Waters.*

N71 to
Moll's Gap
and Kenmare
(see pp156–8)

### VISITORS' CHECKLIST

**Road map** B5. Killarney, Co Kerry.
✕ *Kerry (066 64644).* 🚌 🚉
**National Park** ⭘ *Jun–Aug:*
*9am–7pm daily; Sep–May: 9am–*
*6pm daily (for access by car).*
ℹ *Muckross House (064 31440).*
**Muckross House** ⭘ *9am–6pm*
*daily.* 📷 🅿 ♿ *in gardens.* 🍴
**Ross Castle** ☎ *064 35851.*
⭘ *Apr & May: 10am–5pm; Jun–*
*Sep: 9am–6pm; Oct: 9am–5pm.*
📷 🎫 *obligatory.* 🚢 *from Ross*
*Castle:* **Destination Killarney**
*(064 32638): daily (weather*
*permitting);* **The Lily of Killarney**
*(064 31068): Mar 17–Oct.*
**Kate Kearney's Cottage** ☎ *064*
*44146.* ⭘ *Easter–Sep: 9am–*
*midnight daily; Oct–Easter:*
*9:30pm–6pm daily.* 🅿 🍴

**Ladies' View** gets its name from the delight it gave Queen Victoria's ladies-in-waiting when they visited the spot in 1861.

**Upper Lake**

**Purple Mountain, 832 m (2,730 ft)**

**★ Gap of Dunloe**
*Glaciers carved this dramatic mountain pass, which is popular with walkers, cyclists and horseback riders. The route through the gap offers fabulous views of the boulder-strewn gorge and three small lakes.*

**Tomie Mountain, 735 m (2,411 ft)**

**Kate Kearney's Cottage** was home to a local beauty who ran an illegal drinking house for passing travelers in the mid-19th century.

**R562 to Killorglin**
**(see pp156–7)**

```
0 kilometers        2
0 miles        1
```

### STAR SIGHTS

★ Muckross House

★ Gap of Dunloe

**Lough Leane**
*The largest lake is dotted with un-inhabited islands and fringed with wooded slopes. Boat trips run between Ross Castle and Innisfallen.*

## Valentia Island ⑨

**Road map** A5. Co Kerry.
▣ to Caherciveen. **ℹ** Jun–Sep:
Caherciveen (066 72589).

ALTHOUGH it feels like the mainland, Valentia is an island, albeit linked by a causeway to Portmagee. It is 11 km (7 miles) long and noted for its water sports,

**Stairway leading to Skellig Michael monastery**

seascapes and views from Geokaun Mountain. Valentia is also popular for its proximity to the Skellig Islands which lie around 15 km (10 miles) southwest of the Iveragh Peninsula.

The **Skellig Experience Centre**, near the causeway linking Valentia to the mainland, houses an audiovisual display about the construction and history of the monastery on Skellig Michael, the largest of the Skellig Islands. Other subjects covered include sea birds and the marine life around the islands, a reminder that the Skellig cliffs lie underwater for a depth of 50 m (165 ft), providing a habitat for giant basking sharks, dolphins and turtles. The center also operates cruises around the islands.

The main village on Valentia is **Knightstown**, which offers accommodation and lively pubs with music and dancing.

The first transatlantic cable was laid from the southwest point of the island to Newfoundland, Canada, in 1866.

**✿ Skellig Experience Centre**
Valentia Island. **【** 066 76306.
◯ Apr–Sep: daily. ▨ ♿

## The Skelligs ⑩

**Road map** A6. Co Kerry. ⛴ Apr–Oct: from Valentia Island. **【** 066 76124 (call a day in advance).

SKELLIG MICHAEL, also known as Great Skellig, is an inhospitable pinnacle of rock rising out of the Atlantic and covering an area of 17 ha (44 acres). Perched on a ledge almost 218 m (714 ft) above sea level and reached by an amazing 1,000-year-old

# A Tour of the Ring of Kerry ⑪

THIS LONG-ESTABLISHED ROUTE around the Iveragh Peninsula, which can be taken in either direction, is always referred to as the Ring of Kerry. Allow a day to see its captivating mountain and coastal scenery, dotted with slate-roofed fishing villages. Set out early to avoid the mass of bus tours that converge on the towns for lunch and tea. There are interesting detours across the spine of the peninsula.

**Caherciveen ④**
The main town on the peninsula is home to a local heritage center.

**Glenbeigh ③**
Stop here to visit the Kerry Bog Village, a cluster of reconstructed cottages dating from the 1800s.

**Beach at Ballinskelligs**

**KEY**

| | |
|---|---|
| ▬▬ | Tour route |
| ═══ | Other roads |
| ⛴ | Boats to the Skelligs |
| ☀ | Viewpoint |

**Derrynane House ⑤**
Dating from the 17th century, the former home of Daniel O'Connell (see p40) now houses a museum featuring his memorabilia.

**Staigue Fort ⑥**
Set on a hill up a narrow track, this Iron Age, drystone fort (caher) is the best preserved in Ireland.

stairway is an isolated early Christian monastery. Monks settled for solitude on Skellig Michael during the 6th century, building a cluster of six corbeled beehive cells and two boat-shaped oratories. These drystone structures are still standing, despite being raked by storms over the centuries. The monks were totally self-sufficient, trading eggs, feathers and seal meat with passing boats in return for cereals, tools and animal skins. The skins were needed to produce the vellum on which the monks copied their religious manuscripts. They remained on this bleak island until the 12th century, when they retreated to the Augustinian priory at Ballinskelligs on the mainland.

Today the only residents on Skellig Michael are the thousands of sea birds that nest

**Gannets flying around the precipitous cliffs of Little Skellig**

and breed on the high cliffs, including storm petrels, puffins and Manx shearwaters. The huge breeding colonies are protected from predators by the sea and rocky shores.

Slightly closer to the mainland is Little Skellig. Covering an area of 7 ha (17 acres), the island has steep cliffs. Home to a variety of sea birds, it has one of the largest colonies of gannets (about 22,000 breeding pairs) in the British Isles.

A cruiser from Valentia Island circles the Skelligs but does not dock. Except for a pier on Skellig Michael, there are no real landing stages on the islands. This is to discourage visitors from disturbing the birdlife, fragile plant cover and archaeological remains.

Atlantic gales permitting, local fishermen may run unofficial trips around the islands from Portmagee or Ballinskelligs, during the summer.

---

TRALEE

**Killorglin ②** This pretty village, sitting on the slopes above a river, is famous for its Puck Fair *(see p47)*.

*Caragh Lake*

R562

*Laune*

*Lakes of Killarney*

CORK N22

M A C G I L L I C U D D Y' S   R E E K S

N71

⑧

R568

*Kenmare*

N71

BANTRY

N70

**Killarney ①**
Visitors touring the Ring of Kerry usually start and finish here. The route passes lovely views of the Lakes of Killarney *(see pp154–5)*.

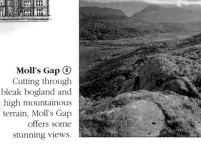

**Moll's Gap ⑧**
Cutting through bleak bogland and high mountainous terrain, Moll's Gap offers some stunning views.

**Sneem ⑦**
Brightly painted cottages line the streets of this charming town, which also has a quaint village green.

| 0 kilometers | 10 |
| 0 miles | 5 |

---

**TIPS FOR DRIVERS**

*Length:* 180 km (112 miles).
*Stopping off points:* Many towns such as Killorglin or Caherciveen offer pub snacks. Finish the day in one of the excellent gourmet restaurants in Kenmare. (See also pp355–7.)

**Lace making at Kenmare**

# Kenmare ⑫

**Road map** B5. Co Kerry. 🏃 *1,400.*
📧 ℹ️ *Apr–Oct: Main St (064
41233).* 🛒 *Wed.*

THIS TOWN, on the mouth of
the River Sheen, was
founded in 1670 by William
Petty, Cromwell's surveyor
general. However, Kenmare's
appearance owes more to his
descendant, the first Marquess
of Lansdowne who, in 1775,
made it a model landlord's
town of neat stone façades
with decorative plasterwork.

Today Kenmare is famous
for its traditional lace. During
the famine years, nuns from
the local convent, St. Clare's,
introduced lace-making to
create work for the women
and girls. Other attractions
include the fine hotels *(see
p292)* and gourmet restaurants
*(p311)*. The town is also an
excellent base for exploring
the Beara Peninsula and the
Ring of Kerry *(see pp156–7)*.

Set in a riverside glade off
Market Street is the **Druid's
Circle**, a prehistoric ring of
15 stones associated with
human sacrifice.

# Beara Peninsula ⑬

**Road map** A6. Co Cork & Co Kerry.
📧 to Glengarriff & Castletownbere
*(Fri only).* ℹ️ *Jun–Sep: Castletownbere
(027 70344).*

DOTTED WITH sparsely
populated fishing villages
surrounded by bleak moor-
land, this peninsula is remote.
It used to be a refuge for
smugglers, with the Irish
getting the better deal in their
exchange of fish for contra-
band French brandy.

The peninsula offers some
spectacular scenery and
wonderful walking country.
From the **Healy Pass**, which
cuts a jagged path across the
spine of the Caha Mountains,
there are some fine views of
Bantry Bay and the rugged
landscape of West Cork. To
the west of the pass is
**Hungry Hill**, the highest
mountain in the Caha range
and popular with hikers.

Encircled by the Caha and
Slieve Miskish Mountains is
**Castletownbere**, the main
town on the peninsula. This
sheltered port was once a
haven for smugglers, but is
now awash with foreign
fishing trawlers. McCarthey's

Bar on Town Square features
an authentic matchmaking
booth, where Cork families
used to agree to marriage
terms until a generation ago.

West of Castletownbere
stands the shell of **Puxley
Mansion**, home of the Puxley
family who owned the mines
at nearby **Allihies**. Center of
the copper-mining district until
the 1930s, it is now a desolate
place, with tall Cornish-style
chimneys and piles of ocher-
colored rubble. Beware of
unmarked mine shafts.

From the tip of the peninsula
a cable car travels across to
**Dursey Island**, with its
ruined castle and colonies of
seabirds. Licensed to carry
three passengers and one cow,
the cable car swings across
the strait, offering views of
Bull, Cow and Calf islands.

From the headland the R757
road back to Kenmare passes
through the pretty villages of
**Eyeries**, noted for its brightly
painted cottages and crafts,
and **Ardgroom**, a center for
mussel farming and a base for
exploring the scenic glacial
valley around **Glenbeg Lough**.

# Garinish Island ⑭

**Road map** B6. Co Cork. 🚤 from
Glengarriff Gardens 📞 027 63040.
⭕ Mar–Oct: daily. 🏷️ 🚻 limited.

ALSO KNOWN as Ilnacullin, this
small island was turned
into an exotic garden in 1910
by Harold Peto for Annan
Bryce, a Belfast businessman.

**View of Caha Mountains from the Healy Pass, Beara Peninsula**

**Italianate garden with lily pool and folly on Garinish Island**

Framed by views of Bantry Bay, the gardens are landscaped with Neo-Classical follies and planted with rich subtropical flora. The microclimate and peaty soil provide the damp, warm conditions needed for these ornamental plants to flourish.

Exotic shrubberies abound especially during the summer months. Throughout May and June, visitors can admire the beautiful camellia beds, azaleas and rhododendrons. There is also a New Zealand fernery and a Japanese rockery, as well as a rare collection of bonsai trees. A Martello tower crowns the island and among the follies are a clock tower and a Grecian temple.

The centerpiece is a colonnaded Italianate garden, with a Classical folly and ornamental lily pool. Much of its charm resides in the contrast between the cultivated lushness of the garden and the glimpses of wild seascape and barren mountains beyond. An added attraction of the boat trip across to this Gulf Stream paradise is the chance to see cavorting seals in Bantry Bay.

# Bantry House **15**

*See pp160–61.*

# Bantry Bay **16**

**Road map** A6. Co Cork. ⊠ to Bantry and Glengarriff. ⓗ Jun–Sep: The Square, Bantry (027 50229).

BANTRY BAY ENCOMPASSES the resorts of **Bantry** and **Glengarriff**. It is also a springboard for trips to Mizen Head and the Beara Peninsula.

Bantry nestles beneath the hills that run down to the bay. Just offshore you can see **Whiddy Island**, the original home of the White family, who moved to Bantry House in the early 18th century. Farther along is **Bere Island**, a British base until World War II, which still boasts Martello towers on its southern side.

Glengarriff at the head the bay, exudes an air of Victorian gentility with its neatly painted storefronts and craft shops. On the coast is the Eccles Hotel, a haunt of Queen Victoria and where George Bernard Shaw supposedly wrote *Saint Joan.*

The wooded hinterland to the north of Glengarriff is set in a bowl of the Caha Mountains. There are some pleasant walks leading to waterfalls.

# Mizen Head **17**

**Road map** A6. Co Cork.
⊠ to Goleen. ⓗ Town Hall, Main St, Skibbereen (028 21766).

MIZEN HEAD, the most southwesterly tip of Ireland, has steep cliffs, which are often battered by storms. There is a lighthouse here, reached via a suspension bridge across a rocky chasm. The lighthouse is not open to the public, but it is still worth the trip for the fine headland walk with views of vertiginous cliffs and Atlantic breakers. The sandy beaches of **Barley Cove** nearby attract swimmers and walkers alike. To the east is **Crookhaven**, a popular yachting harbor lined with painted cottages. From here, there is a walk to Brow Head with views of the lighthouse across the harbor.

Mizen Head can be reached either from Bantry via Durrus or from the market town of **Skibbereen**, on the R592, via the charming crafts center of **Balleydehob** and the village of **Schull**. The latter is the starting point for boat trips to Clear Island *(see p162).*

**Rocky cliffs at Mizen Head**

# Bantry House ⑮

B ANTRY HOUSE has been the home of the White family, formerly Earls of Bantry, since 1739. The original house was built in 1720, but the north façade overlooking the bay was a later addition. Inside there is an eclectic collection of art and furnishings brought from all over Europe by the 2nd Earl of Bantry.

**William and Mary clock in anteroom**
In the carriage house and stable block behind the house is the French Armada Centre, which explains the events surrounding Wolfe Tone's attempted invasion in 1796.

**North façade**

**The anteroom** contains family mementos, china and a collection of 18th-century prints.

**Loggia**

**To parking lot**

**Tearoom and shop**

**Gobelins Room**
*The subject of this 18th-century Gobelins tapestry is* The Bath of Cupid and Psyche. *The room also contains an early 19th-century piano.*

**The Rose Garden**, laid out in the early 18th century, is, in the words of the 1st Earl of Bantry, "a parterre after the English manner."

★ **Dining Room**
*This room is dominated by portraits of King George III and Queen Charlotte by court painter, Allan Ramsay. The Spanish chandelier is decorated with Meissen china flowers.*

## 1ST EARL OF BANTRY (1767–1851)

Richard White, 1st Earl of Bantry, played a leading role in defending Ireland against an attempted invasion by Wolfe Tone and the United Irishmen *(see pp38–9)*. On December 16, 1796, Tone sailed from Brest in Brittany with a fleet of 43 French ships bound for Ireland. White chose strategic spots around Bantry Bay and mustered volunteers to fight. His efforts proved unnecessary as the French fleet was forced back by bad weather. Nonetheless, White was rewarded with a peerage by George III for his "spirited conduct and important services." In 1801 he was made Viscount Bantry, becoming Earl of Bantry in 1816.

**Entrance hall**

★ **Rose Room**
*The rose-colored tapestries (c. 1770) hanging in this room are thought to have been made for Marie Antoinette on her marriage to the Dauphin of France.*

**Statue of Diana (1840)**

**South façade**

**To 1796 French Armada Centre**

**Library**

★ **View of House and Bantry Bay**
*Bantry House enjoys a magnificent location overlooking Bantry Bay. This lovely view, from the terraces above the house, shows the harbor with Whiddy Island and the Caha Mountains beyond.*

**Italian Garden**
*Inspired by the Boboli Gardens in Florence, this garden circles a pool decorated in Classical Grotesque style. It was designed in the early 1850s by the 2nd Earl.*

### STAR FEATURES

★ **View of House and Bantry Bay**

★ **Rose Room**

★ **Dining Room**

**The steps,** known as the "Staircase to the Sky," lead to a series of terraces with fabulous views over the house and across the bay.

## Baltimore ⑱

**Road map** B6. Co Cork. 🚶 *220.*
🚌 🛳 *to Sherkin Island (028 20125);*
*to Clear Island (028 39153).*

**B**ALTIMORE's most bizarre
claim to fame dates back
to 1631 when more than 100
citizens were carried off as
slaves by Algerian pirates.
Today, this village appeals to
both the yachting fraternity
and island-hoppers. Like neighboring Castletownshend and
Schull, the town bustles with
festivals in summer.

Overlooking the harbor is a
ruined 15th-century castle,
once the stronghold of the
O'Driscoll clan. Also worth a
visit are the seafood pubs,
including Bushe's Bar, an
atmospheric inn hung with
nautical memorabilia.

Behind the village, cliff
walks lead to splendid views
of Carbery's Hundred Isles –
mere specks on Roaringwater
Bay. The conical Baltimore
Beacon is an important
marker for boats in the bay.

A short ferry ride away is
**Sherkin Island** with its
sandy beaches in the west, a
ruined 15th-century abbey,
marine station and pubs. The
ferry ride to **Clear Island** is
more dramatic, as the boat
weaves between sharp black
rocks to this remote, Irish-
speaking island, noted for its
bird observatory in the North
Harbor. There are some spectacular views of the mainland
from Clear Island.

**Drombeg Stone Circle, erected about the 2nd century BC**

## Drombeg Stone Circle ⑲

**Road map** B6. Co Cork. 🚌 *to*
*Skibbereen or Clonakilty.*

**S**ITUATED ON the Glandore
road 16 km (10 miles) west
of Clonakilty, Drombeg
is the finest of the
many stone circles
in County Cork.
Dating back to about
150 BC, this circle of
17 standing stones is
9 m (30 ft) in diameter.
At the winter solstice,
the rays of the setting
sun fall on the flat
altar stone which
faces the entrance to
the circle, marked by two
upright stones.

Nearby is a small stream
with a Stone Age cooking pit
(*fulacht fiadh*), similar to one
at Craggaunowen (*see p182*).
A fire was made in the hearth
and hot stones from the fire
were dropped into the cooking pit to heat the water. Once
the water boiled, the meat,
usually venison, was added.

**Sign for Clonakilty
black pudding**

## Clonakilty ⑳

**Road map** B6. Co Cork. 🚶 *3,000.*
🚌 🚊 *Jul–Aug: Astna Street (023
33226) .*

**F**OUNDED as an English out-
post around 1588, this
market town has a typically
hearty West Cork atmosphere.
The **West Cork Regional
Museum**, housed in an old
schoolhouse, pays tribute to
the town's industrial heritage.
A number of the quayside

buildings, linked to the
town's industrial past, have
been restored. Particularly
pleasant is the neat Georgian
nucleus of Emmet Square.

Until the 19th century
Clonakilty was a noted linen
producer. Today, however, it
is renowned for its rich black
puddings, hand-
painted Irish signs
and traditional
music pubs. A
short walk from
the town center is
a model village
exhibition, depict-
ing Clonakilty as it
was during the
1940s. Just east of
town is the recon-
structed **Lisnagun
Ring Fort**, with earthworks,
huts and souterrains (*see p18*).
A causeway links Clonakilty
to **Inchydoney** beach.

🏛 **West Cork Regional
Museum**
Western Road. 🕐 *Mon–Sat.* 🦽 ♿

## Timoleague Abbey ㉑

**Road map** B6. Co Cork.
🚌 *to Clonakilty or Courtmacsherry.*
🕐 *daily.*

**T**IMOLEAGUE ABBEY enjoys a
waterside setting over-
looking an inlet where the
Argideen estuary opens into
Courtmacsherry Bay. Founded
around the late 13th century,
the abbey is a ruined
Franciscan friary. The buildings have been extended at
various times. The earliest
section is the chancel of the
Gothic church. The most

**Distinctive white beacon for boats
approaching Baltimore**

recent addition, the 16th-century tower, was added by the Franciscan Bishop of Ross. The friary was ransacked by the English in 1642 but much of significance remains, including the church, infirmary, fine lancet windows, refectory and a walled courtyard in the west. There are also sections of cloisters and wine cellars. In keeping with Franciscan tradition, the complex is plain to the point of austerity. Yet

**Lancet window in ruined church at Timoleague Abbey**

such restraint belied the friars' penchant for high living; the friary prospered on trade in Spanish wines, easily delivered, thanks to its position on the then navigable creek.

## River Lee ㉒

**Road map** B6. Co Cork. 🚌 🚍 to Cork. ℹ️ Cork (021 273251).

CARVING A COURSE through farm- and woodland to Cork city *(see pp166–9)*, the River Lee begins its journey in the lake of the enchanting **Gougane Barra Park**. The shores of the lake are linked by a causeway to **Holy Island**, where St. Finbarr, the patron saint of Cork, founded a monastery. The Feast of St. Finbarr, on September 25,

signals celebrations that climax in a pilgrimage to the island on the following Sunday.

The Lee flows through several Irish-speaking market towns and villages. Some, such as **Ballingeary**, with its fine lakeside views, have good fishing. The town is also noted for its Irish language college. Farther east, near the town of Inchigeela, stand the ruins of **Carrignacurra Castle**. Farther downstream lies the Gearagh, an alluvial stretch of marsh and woods which has been designated a wildlife sanctuary.

The river then passes through the Sullane valley, home of the thriving market town of **Macroom**. The hulk of a medieval castle, with its restored entrance, lies just off the main square. In 1654, Cromwell granted the castle to Sir William Penn. His son, who gave the state of Pennsylvania its name, also lived there for a time.

Between Macroom and Cork, the Lee Valley passes through a hydroelectric power plant surrounded by artificial lakes, water meadows and wooded banks. Just outside Cork, on the south bank of the river is **Ballincollig**, home to the fascinating Royal Gunpowder Mills museum *(see p169)*.

## Blarney Castle ㉓

**Road map** B5. Blarney, Co Cork. 📞 *021 385252.* 🚌 *to Cork.* 🚍 *to Blarney.* ⭕ *daily.* ⬤ *Dec 24 & 25.* 📷 ♿

VISITORS from all over the world flock to this ruined castle to see the legendary Blarney Stone. Kissing the stone is a long-standing tradition, intended to confer a magical eloquence. It is set in the wall below the castle battlements and, in order to kiss it, the visitor is grasped by the feet and suspended backward under the parapet. Little remains of the castle today except the keep, built in 1446 by Dermot McCarthy. Its design is typical of a 15th-century tower house *(see p18)*. The vaulted first floor was once the Great Hall.

Next to the castle is **Blarney House**, a Scottish baronial mansion and the residence of the Colthurst family since the 18th century. The turreted façade is matched by a period interior, with its grand stairwell, family portraits and Victorian decor. The grounds include an arboretum and landscaped gardens.

Blarney also has a pretty village green with welcoming pubs and craft shops. The **Blarney Woolen Mills** sell quality garments and souvenirs.

🏠 **Blarney House**
Blarney Estate. 📞 *021 385252.* ⭕ *Jun–mid Sep: Mon–Sat (pm only).* 📷 ♿

**Battlemented keep and ruined towers of Blarney Castle**

# Street-by-Street: Kinsale ㉔

**Old office sign in Kinsale**

FOR MANY VISITORS to Ireland, Kinsale heads the list of places to see. One of the prettiest small towns in Ireland, it has had a long and checkered history. The defeat of the Irish forces and their Spanish allies in the Battle of Kinsale in 1601 signified the end of the old Gaelic order. An important naval base in the 17th and 18th centuries, Kinsale today is a popular yachting center. It is also famous for the quality of its cuisine – the town's annual Gourmet Festival attracts food lovers from far and wide. As well as its many wonderful restaurants, the town has pubs and wine bars that cater to all tastes.

**Desmond Castle** was built around 1500. It is known locally as the "French Prison."

★ **Old Courthouse**
*The courthouse, now the regional museum, has a toll board listing the local taxes in 1788.*

**Market Square**

**Kieran's Fo House Inn**

## CHARLES FORT

The star-shaped fort is 3 km (2 miles) east of town in Summercove, but can be reached by taking the well-marked coastal walk from the quayside, past the village of Scilly. The fort was built in the 1670s by the English to protect Kinsale Harbour against foreign naval forces but, because of its vulnerability to land attack, was taken during the siege of 1690 by William of Orange's army. Nevertheless, it remained in service until 1922 when the British forces left the town and handed it over to the Irish Government. Charles Fort remains one of the finest remaining examples of a star-shaped bastion fort in Europe.

**Walls and bastions of Charles Fort**

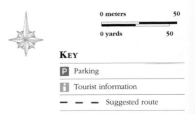

★ **St. Multose Church**
*This much-altered Norman church is named after an obscure 6th-century saint and marks the center of the medieval town.*

| 0 meters | | 50 |
|---|---|---|

| 0 yards | | 50 |
|---|---|---|

**KEY**

| P | Parking |
|---|---|
| i | Tourist information |
| – – – | Suggested route |

**Kinsale Harbour**
*Situated on the estuary of the Bandon River, this is one of Ireland's most scenic harbors. Kinsale is host to a number of international sailing events throughout the year.*

**Mother Hubbard's**, one of Kinsale's most popular cafés, is located in the heart of town on Market Street.

**To Charles Fort**

**The Blue Haven**, easily identified by the ornate clock above the entrance, is one of Kinsale's finest seafood restaurants.

**To Kinsale Harbour, Denis Quay and Compass Hill**

**To Bandon**

## STAR SIGHTS

★ **Old Courthouse**

★ **Main Street**

★ **St. Multose Church**

★ **Main Street**
*Many of Kinsale's best eating and drinking places can be found on this picturesque street.*

# Cork ㉕

**Sign outside a Cork pub**

CORK CITY derives its name from the marshy land on the banks of the River Lee – its Irish name *Corcaigh* means marsh – on which St. Finbarr founded a monastery around AD 650. The narrow alleys, waterways and Georgian architecture gives the city a Continental feel. Since the 19th century, when Cork was a base for the National Fenian movement *(see p41)*, the city has had a reputation for political rebelliousness. Today this mood is reflected in the city's attitude to the arts and its bohemian spirit, much in evidence at the lively October jazz festival.

**Clock tower and weather vane of St. Ann's Shandon**

### ⌂ St. Ann's Shandon

Church St. 021 505906.
☐ daily.
This famous Cork landmark stands on the hilly slopes of the city, north of the River Lee. Built in 1722, the church has a façade made of limestone on two sides, and of red sandstone on the other two. The steeple is topped by a weather vane in the shape of a salmon. The clock face is known by the locals as the "four-faced liar" because, up until 1986 when it was repaired, each face showed a slightly different time. Visitors can climb the tower and, for a small fee, ring the famous Shandon bells.

### ⊞ Butter Exchange

John Redman St. ☐ daily.
Just a short walk away from St. Ann's Shandon is the Butter Exchange. Opened in 1770, it was where butter was graded before it was exported to the rest of the world. It also supplied butter to the British navy. By 1892 the exchange was exporting around 500,000 casks of butter a year, bringing prosperity to the city. The exchange closed in 1924.

Part of the building was re-opened in the 1980s to house the Shandon Craft Centre. Here visitors can watch artists and craft workers, such as crystal cutters and weavers, at work.

### ⊞ Crawford Art Gallery

Emmet Place. 021 273377.
☐ Mon–Sat.
The redbrick and limestone building that houses Cork's major art gallery dates back to 1724. Built as the city's original custom house, it became a school of design in 1850. In 1884, art patron William Horatio Crawford extended the building to accommodate studios, and sculpture and picture galleries. It served as a school and art gallery until the school moved in 1979.

The gallery houses some fine examples of late 19th- and early 20th-century Irish art including paintings by Jack Yeats.

**Detail of stained-glass window** *The Meeting of St. Brendan and the Unhappy Judas* (1911) by Harry Clarke, Crawford Art Gallery

## SIGHTS AT A GLANCE

Butter Exchange ②
Crawford Art Gallery ④
Elizabeth Fort ⑩
English Market ⑥
Father Mathew Statue ⑤
National Monument ⑦
Parliament Bridge ⑧
Red Abbey ⑨
St. Ann's Shandon ①
St. Finbarr's Cathedral ⑪
St. Mary's Dominican Church ③

There are also three excellent windows by Ireland's foremost stained-glass artist, Harry Clarke (1889–1931), including *The Meeting of St. Brendan and the Unhappy Judas* (1911). Another attraction is the small collection by British artists and international works by artists such as Miró and Rouault.

The gallery is well known for its excellent restaurant, which is run by the Ballymaloe cookery school (see p331), the exponents of authentic Irish cooking with a modern twist.

Richly decorated apse ceiling of St. Finbarr's Cathedral

### 🔒 St. Finbarr's Cathedral

Bishop St. 📞 021 963387.
🕐 daily. **Donation**. ♿

Located in a quiet part of town south of the Lee, St. Finbarr's Cathedral is dedicated to the founder and patron saint of the city. Completed in 1878 to the design of William Burges, it is an exuberant

### VISITORS' CHECKLIST

**Road map** C5. Co Cork.
👥 128,000. ✈ 6 km (4 miles) S of Cork. 🚉 Kent Station (021 506766). 🚌 Parnell Place (021 508188). 🛈 Tourist House, Grand Parade (021 273251). 🎭 Cork International Choral Festival (May); Cork Jazz Festival (Oct); Cork Film Festival (Oct).

triple-spired edifice built in Gothic Revival style, and decorated with stone tracery. Inside, the painted and gilded apse ceiling shows Christ in Glory surrounded by angels. The stained-glass windows below tell the story of Christ's life.

### 🏛 Cork City Gaol

Convent Avenue, Sunday's Well.
📞 021 305022. 🕐 daily. 📷 ♿

A pretty, 20-minute walk west of the city center leads to the restored City Gaol, complete with furnished cells. The exhibition and audiovisual display trace the lives of typical inmates during the 19th and 20th centuries, and show some of the harsh punishments they received.

There is also a café which employs an amusing gimmick: visitors can choose between sampling the Victorian prisoners' fare or the superior prison governor's menu.

On weekdays during the winter months, the jail is open only for guided tours.

---

### KEY

| | |
|---|---|
| 🚌 | Bus station |
| 🅿 | Parking |
| 🛈 | Tourist information |
| ✝ | Church |

0 meters 250
0 yards 250

South Channel of the River Lee, looking toward Parliament Bridge

# Exploring Cork

O
NE OF CORK'S great attractions is that it is a city built
on water. Its heart lies on an island between two
arms of the River Lee, and many of today's streets were
in fact once waterways lined with warehouses and
merchants' residences. Although the Dutch canalside
appearance has faded, picturesque quays and bridges
remain. Steep lanes rise to the north and south of the
central island to the city's 19th-century suburbs, offering
wonderful views of the city and its fine buildings.

**Fitzpatrick's secondhand shop
on George's Quay**

### The Quays
Although the river now plays
only a minor part in the city's
economy, much of Cork's
commercial activity still takes
place around the Quays (pronounced "kays" in the Cork
accent). The South Mall,
which covers an arm of the
River Lee, was a water-
way until the late 18th
century. Boats were once
moored at the foot of a
series of stone steps,
some of which are still
intact today. These led
to merchants' domestic
quarters above. The
arches below led to
warehouses where
goods were unloaded.
   Near South Mall is
**Parliament Bridge**,
built in 1806 to com-
memorate the Act of
Union (see p40). Walk
across the bridge to George's
Quay to see Fitzpatrick's
second-hand shop, with its
bizarre display of bicycles,
cartwheels, farm implements
and other assorted bric-a-brac
on its façade. A short walk
away, on Sullivan's Quay, is
the Quay Co-Op, a popular
restaurant and meeting place.
From Sullivan's Quay an
elegant footbridge, built in
1985, crosses the river to the
south end of Grand Parade.

### Grand Parade and
### St. Patrick's Street
   On Grand Parade, also once
a waterway, stands the
grandiose **National
Monument**, recalling the
Irish patriots who died
between 1798 and 1867.
Bishop Lucey Park, off
Grand Parade, has a
section of city walls
and a fine gateway
from the old corn-
market. Between St.
Patrick's Street and
Grand Parade is the
well-restored
**English Market**, a
covered fruit and
vegetable market
established in
1610. Bustling St.
Patrick's Street, the backbone
of the city, was a waterway
until 1800 when boats were
moored under the steps of
gracious houses such as the
Chateau Bar (see p319). A
landmark at the top of the
street, near Patrick Bridge, is
the **Father Mathew Statue**, a
monument to the founder of
Temperance Movement.

**National Monument,
Grand Parade**

### Paul Street
Noted for its ethnic restaurants,
chic bars, bookshops and
trendy boutiques, Paul Street
is the hub of the liveliest
district in town. Just off Paul
Street are the busy backstreets
of Carey's Lane and French
Church Street. In the early 18th
century, Huguenots (French
Protestants) settled in these
streets and set themselves up
as butter exporters, brewers
and wholesale merchants. This
area is Cork's equivalent to
Dublin's Temple Bar (see p76).

### Shandon Quarter
Crossing the Christy Ring
Bridge to Pope's Quay, you
will see on your left **St. Mary's
Dominican Church**, with its
portico of Ionic columns
topped by a huge pediment.
John Redmond Street leads to
the northern slopes of Cork,
dominated by the spire of St.
Ann's Shandon (see p166)
with its fine views of the city.
To the northeast lies the lofty
Montenotte district, once the
epitome of Victorian gentility.

### St. Finbarr's Quarter
South of the river, rising above
the city, this area's distinctive
landmark is St. Finbarr's
Cathedral (see p167). Nearby
is the ivy-clad **Elizabeth Fort**,
a 16th-century structure which
was converted into a prison
in 1835 and later a Garda
(police) station. A short walk
to the east lies the **Red
Abbey**, a 13th-century relic
from an Augustinian abbey –
the oldest building in Cork.

**Selling fruit and vegetables at the English Market**

**ENVIRONS:** Some beautiful countryside surrounds the city of Cork, especially along the lush valley of the River Lee *(see p163).* The landscape of East Cork is much gentler than the wild, rocky coastline of West Cork and County Kerry, and the land is much more fertile. Many local attractions make good day trips and there are also plenty of opportunities for outdoor activities such as walking, riding and fishing.

### ♣ Blackrock Castle
Blackrock. 【 021 357414.
◯ Tue–Sun. & 
On the banks of the River Lee 1.5 km (1 mile) downstream from the city center stands Blackrock Castle. Originally built in 1582 by Lord Mountjoy as a harbor fortification, the castle was destroyed by fire in 1827. It was rebuilt in 1830 to the design of architects J and GR Pain. The riverside castle now houses a banqueting hall which can hold up to 150 guests, a bar and a restaurant. Visitors can admire the fine views from the mock battlements, or enjoy a pleasant walk along the river banks.

**Blackrock Castle standing on the banks of the River Lee**

### ⌂ Dunkathel House
Glanmire. 【 021 821014.
◯ May–mid-Oct: Wed–Sun (pm only).
& ground floor.
Standing just outside the village of Glanmire, 6 km (3.5 miles) northeast of Cork, is this gracious Neo-Classical country house. The building was totally remodeled around 1785 for Abraham Morris, a wealthy Cork merchant, but retains a few features from an earlier

**Copy of *The Three Graces* by Antonio Canova, Dunkathel House**

house, including some Italianate stuccowork. The interior is decorated with Adam fireplaces and a fine collection of Irish furniture. In the spacious entrance hall is an elegant Bath stone staircase with an iron balustrade. On the half landing stands a plaster copy of Canova's *The Three Graces,* thought to have been cast in the early 19th century. The drawing room, hung with Victorian watercolors, offers lovely views of the wooded banks of the River Glanmire. Charming parkland surrounds the house.

### ⛪ Royal Gunpowder Mills
Ballincollig. 【 021 874430.
◯ Apr–Sep: daily. & 
This unusual museum is 10 km (6 miles) west of Cork. Covering 320 ha (130 acres) of landscaped grounds, it is an impressive heritage project featuring canals, weirs, sluice gates, mills and workers' cottages. The mills were established in 1794 and flourished during the Napoleonic Wars, when they were also used as a British military base. By the 1850s, gunpowder production had become one of Cork's foremost industries. The mills finally closed in 1903, at the end of the Boer War. A guided tour covers the production of gunpowder in the main mills, but visitors are free to explore the rest of the fascinating complex on their own.

## River Blackwater ㉖

**Road map** B5. Co Cork. 🚌 to Mallow. 🚌 to Fermoy, Mallow or Kanturk. 🛈 Jun–Sep: 10 Pearse St, Fermoy (025 31811).

THE SECOND LONGEST RIVER in Ireland after the Shannon *(see p177),* the Blackwater rises in high bogland in County Kerry. It then flows eastward through County Cork until it reaches Cappoquin, County Waterford, where it changes course south through wooded sandstone gorges to the sea at Youghal *(see p171).* Much of the valley is wooded, a reminder that the entire area was forested until the 17th century. The river passes some magnificent country houses and pastoral views. However, the region is best known for its fishing – the Blackwater's tributaries are filled with fine brown trout.

The best way to see the valley is to take the scenic Blackwater Valley Drive from Youghal to Mallow. The route passes through **Fermoy**, a town founded by Scottish merchant John Anderson in 1789. Fishing is the town's main appeal, especially for roach, rudd, perch and pike. Farther west is **Mallow**, a prosperous town noted for its fishing, golf and horse racing. Inviting detours along the tributaries include **Kanturk**, a pleasant market town with a castle, on the River Allow.

**Weirs and bridge at Fermoy on the River Blackwater**

# Cobh ㉗

**Road map** C6. Co Cork. 🏠 8,500.
🚇 ℹ️ Old Yacht Club (021 813301).

**C**OBH (pronounced "cove")
lies on Great Island, one
of the three islands in Cork
harbor that are now linked
by causeways. The Victorian
seafront has rows of steeply
terraced houses overlooked
by **St. Colman's**, an imposing
Gothic Revival cathedral.
Following a visit by Queen
Victoria in 1849, Cobh was
renamed Queenstown but
reverted to its original name
in 1921. The town commands
one of the world's largest
natural harbors – the reason
for its rise to prominence as a
naval base in the 18th century.
It was also a major port for
merchant shipping and the
main port from which Irish
emigrants left for America.
Cobh was also a port of call
for luxury passenger liners. In
1838, the *Sirius* made the first
transatlantic crossing under
steam power from here. Cobh
was also the last stop for the
*Titanic*, before its doomed
Atlantic crossing in 1912.
Three years later,
the *Lusitania* was
torpedoed and
sunk by a German
submarine just
off Kinsale *(see
pp164–5)*, south-
west of Cobh. A
memorial on the
promenade is
dedicated to all
those who died
in the attack.

## IRISH EMIGRATION

Between 1848 and 1950 almost six million people emigrated
from Ireland – two and a half million of them leaving from
Cobh. The famine years of 1844–8 *(see p211)* triggered mass
emigration as the impoverished made horrific transatlantic
journeys in cramped, unsanitary conditions. Many headed
for the United States and Canada, and a few risked the
long journey to Australia. Up until the early 20th century,
emigrants waiting to board the ships were a familiar sight
in Cobh. However, by the 1930s world recession and
immigration restrictions in the United States and Canada
led to a fall in the numbers leaving Ireland.

**19th-century engraving of emigrants gathering in Cobh harbor**

## 🏛 The Queenstown Story

Cobh Heritage Centre. 📞 021
813591. ⬜ Feb–Dec: daily. 📷 ♿
Housed in a Victorian railroad
station, *The Queenstown Story*
is an exhibition detailing the
town's marine history. Exhibits
and audiovisual displays recall
the part Cobh played in Irish
emigration and the transportation of convicts. Between 1791
and 1853, 40,000 convicts
were sent to Australian penal
colonies in notorious "coffin
ships"; many prisoners were
also kept in floating jails
in Cork harbor.

On a happier note, the exhibition also documents Cobh's
role as a port of call for
glamorous transatlantic liners.

**ENVIRONS:** North of Cobh is the
280-ha (700-acre) Fota Estate.
Surrounding the Regency
mansion is the **Fota Wildlife
Park and Arboretum**, which
concentrates on breeding and
reintroducing animals to their
natural habitat. The white-
tailed sea eagle is one native
species that has been saved
from extinction in Ireland.
The landscaped park boasts

**Cobh harbor with the steeple of St. Colman's rising above the town**

over 70 species of animals, including giraffes, flamingos and zebras. Only the cheetahs, subject to a long-term breeding program, are restricted in enclosures. A train links the various sections of the park.

The arboretum has rare trees and shrubs from Japan, China, South America, the Himalayas and North America.

### 🐾 Fota Wildlife Park and Arboretum

Carrigtuohill. 📞 *021 812678.*
🏛 *Apr–Oct: daily.* 🎫 ♿

## Jameson Heritage Centre ㉘

**Road map** C5. Distillery Walk, Midleton, Co Cork. 📞 *021 613594.*
🚌 *to Midleton.* 🏛 *Mar–Oct: daily.*
🎫 ♿ 📷

A SENSITIVELY RESTORED 18th-century distillery, Jameson Heritage Centre is part of the vast Irish Distillers group at Midleton. Bushmills *(see p258)* is the oldest distillery in Ireland but Midleton is the largest. It comprises a series of separate distilleries each producing a different brand of Irish whiskey, including Jameson and Tullamore Dew.

The story of Irish whiskey is presented through audiovisual displays, working models and authentic machinery. A tour of the old distillery takes in the mills, maltings, still-houses, kilns, granaries and ware-houses. Visitors can take part in whiskey tasting and try to distinguish between various Irish whiskeys and Scotch. Highlights of the visit include the world's largest pot still, with a capacity of over 30,000 gallons, and the water wheel, which is still in working order.

Clock tower on the main street of Youghal

## Youghal ㉙

**Road map** C5. Co Cork.
🏠 *6,000.* 🚌 🛈 *Market House, Market Square (024 92390).*

YOUGHAL (pronounced "yawl") is a historic walled town and thriving fishing port. The town was granted to Sir Walter Raleigh by Queen Elizabeth I but later sold to the Earl of Cork. In Cromwellian times, Youghal became a closed borough – an English Protestant garrison town.

The picturesque, four-story **Clock tower** was originally the city gate, but was recast as a prison. Steep steps beside the tower lead up to a well-preserved section of the medieval town wall and fine views across the Blackwater estuary. Through the tower, in the somber North Main Street, is the **Red House**. This authentic Dutch mansion was built in 1710. Virtually next door are some forbidding Elizabethan almshouses and, on the far side of the road, a 15th-century tower, known as **Tynte's Castle**.

Nestling in the town walls opposite is **Myrtle Grove**, one of the few unfortified Tudor manor houses to survive in Ireland. It has a triple-gabled façade and exquisite interior oak paneling. Just uphill is the Gothic **Church of St. Mary**. Inside are tomb effigies and stained-glass windows depicting the coats of arms of local families.

Grain truck (c. 1940) at the Jameson Heritage Centre

# THE LOWER SHANNON

## CLARE · LIMERICK · TIPPERARY

*I*N THE THREE COUNTIES *that flank the lower reaches of the Shannon, Ireland's longest river, the scenery ranges from the rolling farmland of Tipperary to the eerie limestone plateau of the Burren. The Shannon's bustling riverside resorts draw many visitors, and there are medieval strongholds and atmospheric towns of great historic interest. The region also boasts a vibrant music scene.*

The River Shannon has long made this area an attractive prospect for settlers. There are several important Stone Age sites, including a major settlement by Lough Gur. From the 5th century on, the region lay at the heart of Munster, one of Ireland's four Celtic provinces. The Rock of Cashel, a remarkable fortified abbey in county Tipperary, was the seat of the Kings of Munster for more than 700 years.

The Vikings penetrated the Shannon in the 10th century, but Gaelic clans put up stern resistance. During the Norman period, the chieftains of these clans built Bunratty Castle and other fortresses that were impressive enough to rival the strongholds erected by the Anglo-Irish dynasties. Foremost among the latter families were the Butlers, the Earls of Ormonde, who held much land in Tipperary, and the Fitzgeralds, the main landowners in the Limerick area.

After the Middle Ages, Limerick was often at the center of events in the Lower Shannon. In 1691, the army of William of Orange laid siege to the town, heralding the Treaty of Limerick that triggered the Catholic nobility's departure for Europe – the so-called "Flight of the Wild Geese."

Lush grassland, which has turned the Lower Shannon into prime dairy country, is typical of the region. In places this gives way to picturesque glens and mountains, such as the Galty range in southern Tipperary. The region's most dramatic scenery, however, is found along the coast of Clare, a county otherwise best known for its thriving traditional music scene.

Ruins of Dysert O'Dea monastery in County Clare with an outstanding 12th-century High Cross

◁ Traditional musicians playing at Feakle in County Clare

# Exploring the Lower Shannon

THE CENTRAL LOCATION of Limerick city makes it a natural focus for visitors to the region. However, there are many charming towns that make pleasanter bases, such as Adare, Cashel and also Killaloe, which is well placed for exploring the River Shannon. Most places of interest in Tipperary lie in the southern part of the county, where historic towns such as Clonmel and Cahir overlook the River Suir. By contrast, County Clare has few towns of any size, though it boasts the major attraction of Bunratty Castle. Beyond Ennis, the landscape becomes steadily bleaker until you reach the Burren.

**Looking up at the Cliffs of Moher**

N67

R477

DOOLIN

R478

Galway

**THE BURREN** ①

② **CLIFFS OF MOHER**

KILFENORA

N67

ENNISTIMON

N85

N18

FEA

**DYSERT O'DEA** ⑦

ENNIS ⑧

CRAGGAUNOWEN ⑩

**KNAPPOGUE CASTLE** ⑨

N67

N68

R483

⑬ **BUNRA CASTLE**

SHANNON ⑥

LIMERICK

KILRUSH ③

R487

④ GLIN

FOYNES ⑤

N69

R521

N21

⑮ ADARE

N20

## GETTING AROUND

Roads extend from Limerick into every corner of the region, providing good access for motorists; the car ferry from Tarbert in Kerry to Killimer, near Kilrush in Clare, is a convenient route across the Shannon. Trains from Limerick serve Cahir, Clonmel and Carrick, but in other areas you must rely on the bus network. This is rather limited, especially in County Clare, although buses to the Burren from Limerick pass the Cliffs of Moher. Some of the most popular sights, such as Bunratty Castle and the Burren, can be reached on bus tours from Limerick.

NEWCASTLE WEST

R522

N21

Cork

MULLAGHAREIRK MOUNTAINS

Tralee

0 kilometers     25

0 miles     25

**KEY**

▬▬ Major road

▭▭ Minor road

▬▬ Scenic route

〜 River

☀ Viewpoint

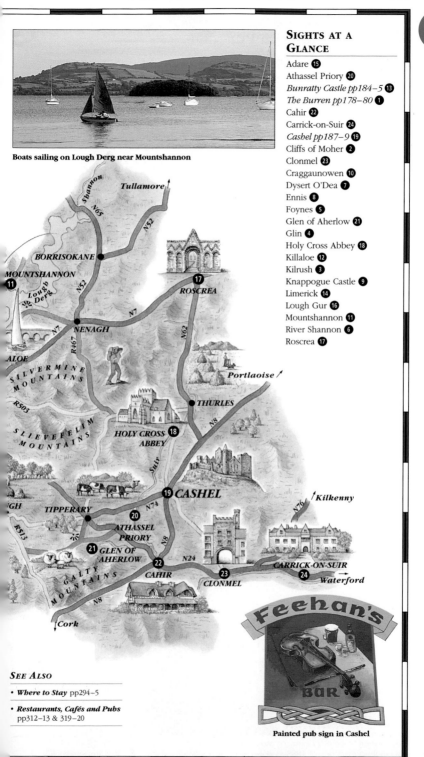

**Boats sailing on Lough Derg near Mountshannon**

## SIGHTS AT A GLANCE

Adare ⑮
Athassel Priory ⑳
*Bunratty Castle pp184–5* ⑬
*The Burren pp178–80* ①
Cahir ㉒
Carrick-on-Suir ㉔
*Cashel pp187–9* ⑲
Cliffs of Moher ②
Clonmel ㉓
Craggaunowen ⑩
Dysert O'Dea ⑦
Ennis ⑧
Foynes ⑤
Glen of Aherlow ㉑
Glin ④
Holy Cross Abbey ⑱
Killaloe ⑫
Kilrush ③
Knappogue Castle ⑨
Limerick ⑭
Lough Gur ⑯
Mountshannon ⑪
River Shannon ⑥
Roscrea ⑰

*Tullamore*

BORRISOKANE

MOUNTSHANNON ⑪

*Lough Derg*

ROSCREA ⑰

...ALOE

NENAGH

SILVERMINE MOUNTAINS

*Portlaoise*

THURLES

SLIEVEFELIM MOUNTAINS

HOLY CROSS ABBEY ⑱

CASHEL ⑲

*Kilkenny*

...GH

TIPPERARY

ATHASSEL PRIORY ⑳

GLEN OF AHERLOW ㉑

GALTY MOUNTAINS

CAHIR ㉒

CLONMEL ㉓

CARRICK-ON-SUIR ㉔

*Waterford*

*Cork*

## SEE ALSO

• *Where to Stay* pp294–5

• *Restaurants, Cafés and Pubs* pp312–13 & 319–20

Feehan's BAR

**Painted pub sign in Cashel**

Looking south along the Cliffs of Moher, one of the most dramatic stretches of Ireland's west coast

## The Burren **❶**

*See pp178–9.*

## Cliffs of Moher **❷**

**Road map** B4. Co Clare. 🚌 *from Ennis & Limerick.* **Visitors' Centre** ☎ *065 81171.* ◯ *Easter–Sep: daily.* **O'Brien's Tower** ◯ *Mar–Oct: daily.* 🖭

Even when shrouded in mist or buffeted by Atlantic gales, the Cliffs of Moher are a breathtaking sight, rising to a height of 200 m (650 ft) out of the sea and extending for 8 km (5 miles). The sheer rock face, with its contrasting layers of black shale and sandstone, provides sheltered ledges where guillemots, kittiwakes and other sea birds nest.

Well-worn paths lead along the cliffs. From the **Visitors' Centre**, 5 km (3 miles) north-west of Liscannor, you can walk south to **Hag's Head** in an hour. To the north, a good alternative is the three-hour walk along the coast between **O'Brien's Tower** – a viewing point built for the benefit of Victorian tourists – and Fisherstreet near **Doolin** *(see p180).*

## Kilrush **❸**

**Road map** B4. Co Clare. 🏠 *2,800.* 🚌 ℹ️ *Heritage Centre, Market House (065 51577).* ◯ *May–Sep.*

With a new marina and the promotion of Kilrush as a heritage town, the fortunes of this 18th-century estate town have been greatly revived. It now has a **Heritage Centre**, where an exhibition covers the Great Famine *(see p211)* and the landlord evictions of 1888

*(see pp40–41).* A well-marked walking trail around the town's historic sights also starts here.

**Environs:** From Kilrush, boats take visitors dolphin-spotting or to nearby **Scattery Island**, site of a medieval monastery. The ruins include five churches and one of the tallest round towers in the country.

The **Loop Head Drive** is a 27-km (17-mile) route that begins at the resort of Kilkee, west of Kilrush. It winds south past dramatic coastal scenery to Loop Head, from where you can enjoy superb views.

## Glin **❹**

**Road map** B5. Co Limerick. 🏠 *600.* 🚌 *from Limerick.*

This charming village on the banks of the Shannon is the seat of the Knights of Glin, a branch of the Fitzgeralds who have lived in the district for seven centuries. Their first medieval castle is a ruin, but west of the village you can see

Rare 18th-century double "flying" staircase in Glin Castle

their newer ancestral home, **Glin Castle**. Originally built in 1780, the Georgian manor succumbed to the vogue for Gothic romance in the 1820s, when it acquired battlements and gingerbread lodges. There is some fine stuccowork and 18th-century furniture inside.

⚓ **Glin Castle**
☎ *068 34173.* ◯ *May–Jun: daily.* 🖭 🅿

## Foynes **❺**

**Road map** B5. Co Limerick. 🏠 *650.* 🚌 *from Limerick.*

Foynes enjoyed short-lived fame in the 1930s and 1940s as the eastern terminus of the first airline passenger route across the Atlantic. **Foynes Flying Boat Museum** presents a detailed history of the seaplane service. The original Radio and Weather Room and a 1940s-style tea room are particularly evocative of the era.

🏛 **Foynes Flying Boat Museum**
Aras Ide, Foynes. ☎ *069 65416.* ◯ *Apr–Oct: daily.* 🖭 ♿

**Environs:** The historic town of **Askeaton**, 11 km (7 miles) east of Foynes, has a castle and Franciscan friary founded by the Fitzgeralds. The friary is particularly interesting, with a 15th-century cloister of black marble. In Rathkeale, 8 km (5 miles) south, **Castle Matrix** is a restored 15th-century tower house renowned for the fine library in the Great Hall.

⚓ **Castle Matrix**
Rathkeale. ☎ *069 64284.* ◯ *May–Sep: Sat–Thu.* 🖭

Fishing on Lough Derg, the largest of the lakes on the Shannon

# River Shannon ➏

**Road map** B4, C4, C3. 🚌 *to Limerick or Athlone.* 🚂 *to Carrick-on-Shannon, Athlone or Limerick.* 🛈 *Arthur's Quay, Limerick (061 317522).*

T HE SHANNON IS the longest river in Ireland, rising in County Cavan and meandering down to the Atlantic. Flowing through the heart of the island, it has traditionally marked the border between the provinces of Leinster and Connaught. In medieval times, castles guarded the major fords from Limerick to Portumna, and numerous monasteries were built along the riverbanks, including the celebrated Clonmacnoise *(see pp242–3).* Work began on the Shannon navigation system in the 1750s, but it fell into disuse with the advent of the railroads. It has since been revived, with an additional boost given by the recent restoration of the Shannon-Erne Waterway *(see p227).*

There are subtle changes of landscape along the length of the river. South of **Lough Allen**, the countryside is covered with the drumlins or low hills typical of the northern Midlands. Towards **Lough Ree**, islands stud the river in an area of ecological importance that is home to otters, geese, gray herons and whooper swans. Continuing south beyond **Athlone** *(see p241),* the river flows through floodplains and bog before reaching **Lough**

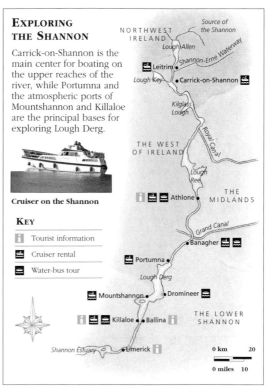

## EXPLORING THE SHANNON

Carrick-on-Shannon is the main center for boating on the upper reaches of the river, while Portumna and the atmospheric ports of Mountshannon and Killaloe are the principal bases for exploring Lough Derg.

Cruiser on the Shannon

### KEY

| 🛈 | Tourist information |
| 🚤 | Cruiser rental |
| 🚢 | Water-bus tour |

0 km        20
0 miles   10

**Derg**, the biggest of the lakes on the Shannon. The scenery is more dramatic here, with the lough's southern end edged by wooded mountains. From **Killaloe** *(see p182)*, the river gains speed on its rush toward **Limerick** *(see p183)* and the sea. The mudflats of the Shannon estuary attract a great variety of birdlife. The port of **Carrick-on-Shannon** *(see p227)* is the cruising center of Ireland, but there are bases all along the river – especially

**Gray heron on the Shannon**

around Lough Derg, which is the lake most geared to boating. Water-buses connect most ports south of Athlone. If you rent a cruiser, inquire about the weather conditions before setting out, particularly on Loughs Ree and Derg, which are very exposed. The calm stretch from **Portumna** *(see p205)* to Athlone is easier for inexperienced sailors.

Walkers can enjoy the Lough Derg Way, a well-marked route around the lake. The woods by **Lough Key** *(see p211)* also provide good walking territory.

Athlone and the southern reaches of Lough Ree

# The Burren ❶

THE WORD BURREN derives from *boireann*, which means "rocky land" in Gaelic – an apt name for this vast limestone plateau in northwest County Clare. In the 1640s, Cromwell's surveyor described it as "a savage land, yielding neither water enough to drown a man, nor tree to hang him, nor soil enough to bury." Few trees manage to grow in this desolate place, yet other plants thrive.

**Dark red helleborine**

The Burren is a unique botanical environment in which Mediterranean and alpine plants rare to Ireland grow side by side. From May to August, an astonishing array of flowers adds splashes of color to the austere landscape. These plants grow most abundantly around the region's shallow lakes and pastures, but they also take root in the crevices of the limestone pavements, which are the most striking geological feature of the rocky plateau. In the southern part of the Burren, limestone gives way to the black shale and sandstone that form the dramatic Cliffs of Moher *(see p176)*.

**Grazing in the Burren**
*A quirk in the local climate means that, in winter, the hills are warmer than the valleys – hence the unusual practice in the Burren of letting cattle graze on high ground in winter.*

## FAUNA OF THE BURREN

The Burren is one of the best places in Ireland for butterflies, with 28 species found in the area. The birdlife is also varied. Skylarks and cuckoos are common on the hills and in the meadows, while the coast is a good place for razorbills, guillemots, puffins and other sea birds. Mammals are harder to spot. Badgers, foxes and stoats live here, but you are much more likely to see a herd of shaggy-coated wild goats or an Irish hare.

**Turloughs** are shallow lakes which are dry in summer but flood in winter, when they attract wildfowl and waders.

**Spring gentian**

**The pearl-bordered fritillary**, *one of a number of fritillaries found in the Burren, can be seen in no other part of Ireland.*

**An Irish hare's** *white and brown winter coat turns to reddish brown in the summer.*

**Whooper swans** *from Iceland flock to the wetlands of the Burren in winter.*

**The hooded crow** *is easily identified by its gray and black plumage.*

**Bloody Cranesbill**
*This alpine plant, common in the Burren, is a member of the geranium family. It flowers in June.*

**Limestone Pavement**
*Glaciation and wind and rain erosion have formed limestone pavements with deep crevices known as "grykes." The porous rock is easily penetrated by rainwater, which has gouged out an extensive cave system beneath the rocky plateau.*

**Hawthorn** is one of the few trees that manages to grow in the Burren, although the plants are usually twisted and stunted.

**Exposed layers of limestone**

**Stone-built Burren cottage**

**Dry-stone wall**

**Limestone slabs, or "clints"**

**The hoary rock rose** is one of several rare plants to grow abundantly in the Burren.

**Holly trees** can gain a foothold in the pavement, but grazing and wind restrict their growth.

**Maidenhair fern** thrives in the damp crevices of the Burren.

**Mountain Avens**
*Normally a mountain plant, this flower grows here at sea level.*

### Exploring the Burren

If you are interested in the unique geology and natural history of the Burren, head for **Mullaghmore**, which is one of the wildest parts of the plateau and has some of the best limestone pavements in the area. A proposal to build a visitors' center here is now causing a major controversy.

A good place to begin a tour of the more accessible parts of the Burren is at the **Cliffs of Moher** (see p176). From here it is a short drive north to **Doolin**, near the port for the Aran Islands (see pp206–7). This rather spread-out village is famous for its traditional music; Gus O'Connor's pub (see p320) acts as a focus for music lovers in the area. The coastal road runs north from Doolin to a desolate limestone outcrop at **Black Head**, while turning inland you will reach **Lisdoonvarna**. The Victorians developed the town as a spa, but it is now most renowned for its colorful pubs and its matchmaking festival (see p48).

**Poulnabrone Dolmen in the heart of the Burren's limestone plateau**

**Music shop in Doolin**

To the north along the N67 lies **Ballyvaughan**, a fishing village dotted with slate-roofed cottages and busy with tourists in summer. It is well placed for reaching a number of sights. Nearby **Bishop's Quarter** has a sheltered beach with glorious views across a lagoon to- wards Galway Bay. **Aillwee Cave**, to the south, is just one of thousands of caves in the Burren, but is the only one open to the public. It consists of a tunnel that opens into a series of caverns. In the first, known as Bear Haven, the remains of hibernation pits used by bears are still visible.

Ruined forts and castles and numerous prehistoric sites dot the landscape. Just west of Aillwee Cave is **Cahermore Stone Fort**, with a linteled doorway, and to the south

**Gleninsheen Wedge Tomb**, a style of grave that marks the transition between Stone and Bronze Age cultures. The more famous **Poulnabrone Dolmen** nearby is a striking portal tomb dating back to 2500–2000 BC. Continuing south you reach the ghostly shell of **Leamaneagh Castle**, a 17th-century mansion that incorporates an earlier tower house built by the O'Briens.

On the southern fringe of the Burren lies **Kilfenora**, a Catholic diocese that by a curious historical quirk has the Pope for its bishop. The village's modest cathedral, one of many 12th-century churches in the Burren, has a roofless chancel with finely sculpted capitals. Kilfenora, however, is more famous for its High Crosses, of which there are several in the graveyard. Best preserved is the Doorty Cross, with a carving of a bishop and two other clerics on the east face. Next door, the **Burren Centre** offers an excellent introduction to the geology and flora of the region, as well as to man's impact on the landscape. The displays include a model of the limestone plateau.

**Carved capital in Kilfenora Cathedral**

---

🏛 **Aillwee Cave**
Ballyvaughan. 【 065 77036.
🕐 mid-Mar–Nov: daily. 🅿 ♿

🏛 **Burren Centre**
Kilfenora. 【 065 88030. 🕐 Mar–Oct: daily. ♿

---

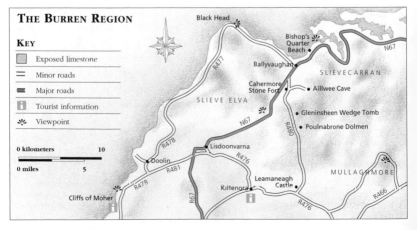

## The Burren Region

### Key

| | |
|---|---|
| ▨ | Exposed limestone |
| = | Minor roads |
| ▬ | Major roads |
| 𝐢 | Tourist information |
| ☀ | Viewpoint |

0 kilometers    10
0 miles    5

Black Head
Bishop's Quarter Beach
Ballyvaughan
SLIEVECARRAN
Cahermore Stone Fort
Aillwee Cave
SLIEVE ELVA
Gleninsheen Wedge Tomb
Poulnabrone Dolmen
R477
R478
N67
Lisdoonvarna
R476
R480
R478
Doolin
R481
Leamaneagh Castle
MULLAGHMORE
R466
Cliffs of Moher
R67
Kilfenora
R476

## Dysert O'Dea ⑦

**Road map** 4B. Corrofin, Co Clare.
🚌 from Ennis. **Archaeology Centre**
☎ 065 37722. ◯ May–Sep: daily.

DYSERT O'DEA CASTLE stands on a rocky outcrop 9 km (6 miles) north of Ennis. This tower house, erected in the 15th century, is home to the **Archaeology Centre**, which includes a small museum and also marks the start of a trail around nearby historic sights. A map of the path, designed for both walkers and cyclists, is available from the tea room.

Across a field from the castle is a monastic site said to have been founded by the obscure St. Tola in the 8th century. The ruins are overgrown and rather worn, but the Romanesque carving above one doorway is still clear, and there is also an impressive 12th-century High Cross, with a bishop sculpted on the east side *(see p235)*.

Farther south, the trail leads past the remains of two stone forts, a ruined castle and the site of a 14th-century battle.

## Ennis ⑧

**Road map** 4B. Co Clare. 🏘 16,000.
🚌 🛈 Clare Rd (065 28366).

CLARE'S COUNTY TOWN, on the banks of the River Fergus, is a charming place. Narrow, winding lanes are particularly characteristic and recall Ennis's medieval beginnings. The town is also known for its painted storefronts and folk music festivals (known as *fleadh* in Gaelic). It abounds in "singing" pubs and traditional music shops.

Colorful exterior of Michael Kerins pub in Ennis

Ennis can trace its origins to the 13th century and to the O'Briens, Kings of Thomond, who were the area's feudal overlords in the Middle Ages. The Franciscan friary that they founded here in the 1240s is now the town's main attraction. Dating largely from the 14th and 15th centuries, the ruined **Ennis Friary** is famous for its rich carvings and decorated tombs in the chancel – above all the 15th-century MacMahon tomb, whose carved alabaster panels have been incorporated into the later Creagh tomb.

Next door to the friary is a delightful 17th-century house, now Cruise's restaurant *(see p312)*, and on the corner of nearby Francis Street stands the Queen's Hotel – featured in James Joyce's *Ulysses*. To the south, O'Connell Square has a monument to Daniel O'Connell *(see p40)*, who was elected MP for Clare in 1828. He also gave his name to the town's main street, where, among the pubs and shops, you can spot a medieval tower, a Jacobean chimney stack and an 18th-century arch.

Finely carved Romanesque doorway at Dysert O'Dea

🔒 **Ennis Friary**
Abbey St. ☎ 065 22464. ◯ May–Sep: daily. 🎫 ♿

**ENVIRONS:** The area around Ennis is rich in monastic ruins. Just 3 km (2 miles) south of the town is **Clare Abbey**, an Augustinian foundation set up by the O'Briens in 1189 but dating mainly from the 1400s.
**Quin Franciscan Friary**, set in meadows 13 km (8 miles) southeast of Ennis, was also built in the 15th century, and incorporates the romantic ruins of a Norman castle. The well-preserved cloister is one of the finest of its kind in Ireland.

## Knappogue Castle ⑨

**Road map** 4B. Quin, Co Clare.
☎ 061 360788. 🚌 to Ennis.
◯ Mar–Oct: daily. 🎫 ♿

A POWERFUL LOCAL CLAN called the MacNamaras erected Knappogue Castle in 1467. Apart from a ten-year spell in Cromwellian times, it stayed in their hands until 1815. During the War of Independence *(see pp42–3)*, the castle was used by the revolutionary forces.

Knappogue, now owned by Texans, has been restored with meticulous care and is one of the country's most charmingly furnished castles. The central tower house is original, but the rest is Neo-Gothic. Inside are fine Elizabethan fireplaces and linenfold wood paneling.

Medieval banquets are staged in the castle *(see p330)*, with storytelling and singing forming part of the entertainment.

## Craggaunowen ⑩

**Road map** B4. Kilmurry, Co Clare.
🚌 🚊 to Ennis. 📞 061 367178.
🕐 Apr–Oct: daily. 🅿️ ♿

THE CRAGGAUNOWEN PROJECT, known as "Craggaunowen: the Living Past" and designed to bring Bronze Age and Celtic culture to life, is a shining example of a recreated pre-historic site. The center was created in the grounds of Craggaunowen Castle in the 1960s by John Hunt, a noted archaeologist who had been inspired by his excavations at Lough Gur *(see p186)*. The castle's tower house contains bronzes and other objects from Hunt's archaeological collection, the rest of which can be seen in Limerick.

At Craggaunowen, people in costume act out particular trades, such as spinning or potting, or serve as guides. A French slave describes how communities lived in the ring fort, a typical early Christian homestead. You can also see meat being prepared in the *fulacht fiadh*, a traditional hunter's cooking hole.

The complex includes part of a *togher*, an original Iron Age timber road that was dis-covered in Longford. The most eye-catching sight, however, is the crannog *(see p31)*, a man-made island enclosing wattle and daub houses – a style of defensive homestead that survived until around 1600.

Another interesting exhibit is a leather-hulled boat built in the 1970s by the explorer, Tim Severin. He used it to retrace

**A woman in peasant costume spinning wool at Craggaunowen**

the route that legend says St. Brendan took in a similar vessel across the Atlantic in the 6th century *(see p25)*.

## Mountshannon ⑪

**Road map** C4. Co Clare. 🏠 240.

THIS PRETTY VILLAGE on the banks of Lough Derg *(see p177)* seems to have its back turned to the lake but is never-theless a major angling center. Solid 18th-century stone houses and churches cluster around the harbor, together with some good pubs: Madden's is a prime spot for Irish music.

Mountshannon is well placed for exploring the lake's western shores, with opportunity for walks and bike rides. Fishing boats are available for rental, and in summer you can go by boat to **Holy Island**, the site of a monastery founded in the 7th century. The ruins include four chapels and a graveyard of medieval tombs.

## Killaloe ⑫

**Road map** C4. Co Clare. 🏠 950.
🚌 ℹ️ Jun–Sep: Heritage Centre, The Bridge (061 376866).

KILLALOE, which enjoys a beautiful setting close to where the Shannon emerges from Lough Derg, is the lake's most prosperous pleasure port. An attractive 17th-century stone bridge divides Killaloe in two, with its twin town of Ballina lying on the opposite bank in Tipperary. Ballina has better pubs, including Goosers on the waterfront *(see p320)*, but Killaloe is the main boating center *(see p335)* and also has more of historical interest.

Killaloe's best site is **St. Flannan's Cathedral**, founded in around 1182. A rather plain, solid church, it has a richly carved Romanesque doorway, which was rescued from an earlier chapel. The church also has an ancient Ogham Stone *(see p32)*, unusual because the inscription is in both Nordic runes and Ogham. Outside stands St. Flannan's Oratory, built around the same time as the cathedral.

The **Heritage Centre**, in a converted boathouse on the bridge, contains an exhibition about the Shannon and Lough Derg, and is the starting point for a marked walk along sections of the old Killaloe Canal. It is also possible to arrange for local fishermen to take you out on the lake.

**Bicycle rental and boat trips at Mountshannon**

## Bunratty Castle ⑬

See pp184–5.

# Limerick ⓐ

**Road map** B4. Co Limerick. 80,000.
Shannon. Arthur's
Quay (061 317522). Sat.

THE THIRD LARGEST CITY in the Republic, Limerick was founded by the Vikings. Given its strategic point on the River Shannon, it thrived under the Normans, but later bore the brunt of English oppression. After the Battle of the Boyne (see p236), remnants of the defeated Jacobite army withdrew here. The siege which followed has entered Irish folklore as a heroic defeat, sealed by the Treaty of Limerick in 1691. English treachery in reneging on most of the terms of the treaty still rankles. It is no coincidence that Catholicism and nationalism are strong in the city.

Limerick has a reputation for high unemployment, crime and general neglect. However, it is fast acquiring a new image as a commercial city, revitalized by new industries and laudable restoration projects. Even so, visitors may still have to dig a little to appreciate its charm.

The city center consists of three historic districts. King's Island was the first area to be settled by the Vikings and was later the heart of the medieval city, when it was known as Englishtown. The island boasts Limerick's two main landmarks, King John's Castle and St. Mary's Cathedral. The old Irishtown, south of the Abbey River, has its fair share of drab houses and shops, but also has its own historic

**Carved misericord in St. Mary's Cathedral**

buildings and a pocket of Georgian elegance in St. John's Square. Near here is Limerick's most conspicuous sight, St. John's Cathedral, built in 1861. Its 85-m (280-ft) spire is the tallest in the country.

The most pleasant part of Limerick in which to stroll is Newtown Pery – a grid of gracious Georgian terraces focused on O'Connell Street.

## ⚓ King John's Castle

Nicholas St. 061 411201. Apr–Oct: daily; Nov–Mar: Sun.
Supposedly founded by King John in 1200, not long after the Normans arrived, this castle is an imposing sight with five drum towers and solid curtain walls. Architecturally, the castle is less interesting inside, but it houses a good exhibition on the history of the city. Replicas of siege machinery are based on finds from the castle. Ongoing excavations have unearthed jewelry and pots, and you can also see Viking houses and later fortifications. One of the most dramatic discoveries was a soldier's diary recording the horrors of the Siege of Limerick.

Across the nearby Thomond Bridge, the Treaty Stone marks the spot where the Treaty of Limerick was signed in 1691.

## ⛪ St. Mary's Cathedral

Bridge Street. 061 416238.
daily (mid-Sep–mid-Jun: am only).
Built in 1172, this is the oldest structure in the city. Except for a fine Romanesque doorway and the nave, however, little remains of the early church.

**Characteristic Georgian doorway in St. John's Square**

The 15th-century misericords in the choir stalls are the pride of St. Mary's, with superb carvings in black oak of angels, griffins and other creatures both real and imaginary.

Nearby, George's Quay is a pleasant street with restaurants and outdoor cafés and good views across the river.

## 🏛 Hunt Museum

Rutland St. Mon–Sat.
Recently moved from Limerick University to the Old Customs House, this museum has one of the greatest collections of antiquities in Ireland, gathered by the archaeologist, John Hunt. The best exhibits, dating from the Bronze Age, include gold jewelry, weapons and a magnificent shield. Among the other artifacts are Celtic brooches and the Antrim Cross, a masterpiece of 9th-century metalwork.

## 🏛 Limerick Museum

St. John's Sq. 061 417826. Tue–Sat. 10 days at Christmas.
A handsome Georgian house provides a fine setting for the city museum. Its displays cover Limerick's history, its traditions and passions, from silver- and lace-making to rugby.

**View of Limerick showing Thomond Bridge across the Shannon and King John's Castle**

# Bunratty Castle ⓑ

T HIS FORMIDABLE CASTLE, built in the 15th century, is
one of Ireland's major tourist attractions. Its most
important residents were the O'Briens, Earls of
Thomond, who lived here from around 1500 until
the 1640s. The present interior looks much as it did
under the so-called "Great Earl," who died in 1624.
Abandoned last century, the castle was in ruins
when Lord Gort bought it in the 1950s, but it
has been beautifully restored to its original state.
The adjacent Folk Park and mock medieval
banquets held in the castle attract many bus
tours, giving Bunratty a rather
commercialized atmosphere,
but it is still well
worth visiting.

**The chimney** is a
replica in wood of
the stone original. It
provided a vent for
the smoke given off
by the fire in the
center of the
Great Hall.

**★ North Solar**
*This 17th-century German
chandelier is the most curious
feature in the Great Earl's private
apartments. The term "solar" was
used during the Middle Ages to
describe an upper chamber.*

**The Murder Hole** was
designed for pouring
boiling water or pitch onto the heads of attackers.

**North Front**
*Bunratty Castle is unusual
for the high arches on both
the north and south sides
of the keep. However, the
entrance, designed to deter
invaders, was typical of
castles of the period.*

**Entrance**

**The basement**, with
walls 3 m (10 ft) thick,
was probably used for
storage or as a stable.

**STAR FEATURES**

★ **Great Hall**

★ **Main Guard**

★ **North Solar**

### VISITORS' CHECKLIST

**Road map** B4. Off N18, Limerick-
Ennis Road, Co Clare. 061
360788. Shannon. from
Ennis, Limerick, Shannon. **Castle**
9:30am–4:45pm daily (last
adm: 4:15pm). Dec 23–26.
**Folk Park** 9:30am–7pm (Sep–
May: 5:30pm). to
Folk Park. **Banquets** see p330.

**★ Main Guard**
*Now used for medieval-style
banquets, this was the room where
Bunratty's soldiers ate, slept
and relaxed. Music
was played to them
from the Minstrels'
Gallery, and a gate
in one corner gave
instant access to
the dungeons.*

**Anteroom**

**The Robing Room**
was where the earls
put on their gowns
before an audience
in the Great Hall.
They also used it for
private interviews.

**South Solar**
*These guest apartments have
fine linenfold wood paneling,
a form of decoration popular
during the Tudor period. The
elaborate fan-vaulted ceiling
is partly a reconstruction.*

**A spiral
staircase** is
found in each
of the four
towers.

### BUNRATTY FOLK PARK

A meticulous re-creation of rural life in Ireland at the
turn of the century, this Folk Park began with the
reconstruction of a farmhouse, which was saved during
the building of nearby Shannon Airport. It now consists
of a complete village, incorporating shops and a whole
range of domestic architecture from a laborer's cottage
to an elegant Georgian house. Other buildings include
a farmhouse typical of the Moher region in the Burren
*(see p176)* and a working corn mill. During the main
summer season, people in authentic costume wander
through the streets and demonstrate traditional crafts
and trades from weaving to buttermaking.

**★ Great Hall**
*This Tudor standard
was among the many
furnishings that Lord
Gort brought to the
castle. It stands in the
Great Hall, once the
banqueting hall and
audience chamber,
and still Bunratty's
grandest room.*

**Main street of Bunratty Folk Park village**

**Typical thatched cottage in the village of Adare**

# Adare ⓯

Road map B5. Co Limerick. 🏛 900.
📷 ℹ️ *Heritage Centre, Main St (061 396255).*

ADARE IS BILLED as Ireland's prettiest village. Cynics call it the prettiest "English" village since its manicured perfection is at odds with normal notions of national beauty. Originally a fief of the Fitzgeralds, the Earls of Kildare, Adare owes its present appearance more to the Earls of Dunraven, who restored the estate village in the 1820s and 1830s. The long, thin village is a picture of neat stonework and thatched roofs punctuated by picturesque ruins, all in a woodland setting.

The tourist office is at the new **Heritage Centre**, which includes a good exhibition on Adare's monastic history. Next

door is the **Trinitarian Priory**, founded by the Fitzgeralds in 1230 and overrestored by the first Earl of Dunraven; it is now a Catholic church and convent. Opposite, by a stone-arched bridge, is the Washing Pool, a restored washhouse site.

By the main bridge, on the Limerick road, is the **Augustinian Priory** which was founded by the Fitzgeralds in 1315. Also known as Black Abbey, this well-restored priory has a central tower, subtle carvings, delightful cloisters and a graceful sedilia – a carved triple seat. Just over the bridge, from where it is best viewed, is **Desmond Castle**, a 13th-century feudal castle set on the banks of the River Maigue.

Nearby stands the main gate to **Adare Manor**, a luxury hotel and golf course *(see p294)*. Within its 900 ha (365 acres) of parkland lie two evocative

ruins. The **St. Nicholas Church** and **Chantry Chapel** date back to the 12th century; both are accessible by path. The graceful 15th-century **Franciscan Abbey**, however, is surrounded by the golf course, though it can be seen clearly from the pathway.

In the heart of the village is the elegant Dunraven Arms Hotel *(see p294)* from where the local hunt rides to hounds. Some of the nearby cottages, originally built by the Earl of Dunraven in 1828 for his estate workers, have been converted into restaurants, including the cozy Inn-Between *(see p312)*.

# Lough Gur ⓰

Road map B5. Co Limerick. 📷
**Visitors' Center** 📞 *061 385186.*
⏱ *May–Sep: daily.* 📷 ♿

THIS STONE AGE settlement, 26 km (16 miles) south of Limerick, was extensively inhabited in 3000 BC. Today the horseshoe-shaped lough and surrounding hills enclose an intriguing if rather inscrutable archaeological park. All around Lough Gur are standing stones and burial mounds, including megalithic tombs. One of the most impressive sights is the 4,000-year-old **Great Stone Circle**, just outside the park, by the Limerick–Kilmallock road. Excavations in the 1970s unearthed rectangular, oval and rounded Stone Age huts with stone foundations. The

**Colorfully painted storefronts on Main Street in Adare**

**Façade of Cashel Palace Hotel**

interpretive center, which is housed in mock Stone Age huts on the site of the original settlement, offers a range of audiovisual displays, models of stone circles, burial chambers, and tools and weapons.

As well as the various prehistoric sights scattered all over the Knockadoon Peninsula, there are also some sights from more modern times. Beside the lough are two castle ruins, the 15th-century **Bourchier's Castle** and **Black Castle**, a 13th-century seat of the Earls of Desmond.

## Roscrea ⑰

**Road map** C4. Co Tipperary.
🚶 4,200. 🚌 🚋 ℹ *Heritage Center, Castle St (0505 21850).*

THIS MONASTIC TOWN on the banks of the River Bun-now, though marred by heavy through traffic, has an interesting historic center. The 13th-century Anglo-Norman **Roscrea Castle** consists of a gate tower, curtain walls and two corner towers. In the courtyard stands Damer House, a Queen Anne-style residence with a magnificent staircase and Georgian garden. Just over the river lies **St. Cronan's Monastery** with a High Cross, Romanesque church gable and a truncated round tower. There are remains of a 15th-century **Franciscan Friary** on Abbey Street and nearby in St. Cronan's churchyard is **Roscrea Pillar**, an enigmatic early Christian stone.

**♠ Roscrea Castle**
Castle Street. ⬭ *Jun–Sep: daily; Oct–May: Sat & Sun.* ♿

## Holy Cross Abbey ⑱

**Road map** C5. Thurles, Co Tipperary.
🚋 *0504 43241.* 🚌 🚋 *to Thurles.*
⬭ *May–Sep: daily; Oct–Apr: Sun.* ♿

FOUNDED IN 1169 by the Benedictines, Holy Cross was supposedly endowed with a splinter from the True Cross, hence its name. Now it has been completely restored, and the church is once again a popular place of worship and pilgrimage. Most of the present structure dates from the 15th century. It was built by the Cistercians, who took over the abbey in 1180. This gracious cruciform church, embellished with mullioned windows and sculpted pillars, is one of the finest examples of late Gothic architecture in Ireland

The chancel has fine ribbed vaulting and, in the south wall, an exquisitely carved sedilia, which is rather oddly called "the tomb of the Good Woman's son." The abbey complex, set in some charming cloistered gardens, also houses an old-fashioned pub.

**Crucifixion carving at Holy Cross Abbey**

## Cashel ⑲

**Road map** C5. Co Tipperary.
🚶 2,500. 🚋 ℹ *Apr–Oct: Town Hall (062 61133).*

THE GREAT TOURIST attraction of the town is the magnificent medieval **Rock of Cashel** (*see pp188–9*). Many people stay overnight to enjoy the eerie floodlit views of the Rock. A private path leads to it from **Cashel Palace Hotel** (*see p294*), an opulent Queen Anne residence that was once the Bishop's Palace. Nearby, a 15th-century tower house has been turned into Grant's Castle Hotel. In the evening you can sample traditional Irish culture at the **Brú Ború Heritage Centre**. Named after Brian Boru, the 10th-century king of Munster (*see pp32–3*), the center offers folk theater, traditional music, banquets, and a craft shop.

At the foot of the Rock is the 13th-century **Dominican Friary**. This austere sandstone church has a fine west door, a 15th-century tower and lancet windows. On farmland outside Cashel lic the scant remains of **Hore Abbey**, a 13th-century Cistercian foundation. The abbey was remodeled and a tower was added in the 15th century, but the barrel-vaulted sacristy, nave, choir and chapter house are original.

**🎭 Brú Ború Heritage Centre**
Cashel. 🚋 *062 61122.* ⬭ *daily (mid-Sep–mid-May: Mon–Fri).* ♿
**♦ Dominican Friary**
Dominic Street. 🚋 *062 61166.* ♿ *limited.*

**Ruins of Hore Abbey (1272) with the Rock of Cashel in the background**

# Rock of Cashel

THIS ROCKY STRONGHOLD, which rises dramatically out of the Tipperary plain, was a symbol of royal and priestly power for more than a millennium. From the 5th century on it was the seat of the Kings of Munster, whose kingdom extended over much of southern Ireland. In 1101, they handed Cashel over to the Church, and it flourished as a religious center until a siege by a Cromwellian army in 1647 culminated in the massacre of its 3,000 occupants. The abbey was finally abandoned in the late 18th century. Today, the Rock of Cashel is besieged by visitors. A good proportion of the medieval complex is still standing, and Cormac's Chapel is one of the most outstanding examples of Romanesque architecture in the country.

**★ St. Patrick's Cross**
*The carving on the east face of this cross is said to be of St. Patrick, who visited Cashel in 450. The cross is a copy of the original that stood here until 1982 and is now in the museum.*

**Hall of the Vicars' Choral**
*This hall was built in the 15th century for Cashel's most privileged choristers. The ceiling, a modern reconstruction based on medieval designs, features several decorative corbels including this painted angel.*

**Dormitory block**

**Entrance**

**The Museum**
in the undercroft contains a display of stone carvings, including the original St. Patrick's Cross.

**Outer wall**

**Limestone rock**

**★ Cormac's Chapel**
*Superb Romanesque carving adorns this chapel – the jewel of Cashel. The tympanum over the north door shows a centaur in a helmet aiming his bow and arrow at a lion.*

**STAR FEATURES**

★ Cormac's Chapel

★ St. Patrick's Cross

★ Cathedral

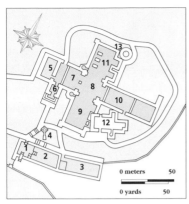

## KEY

☐ **12th Century**

4  St. Patrick's Cross (replica)
12  Cormac's Chapel
13  Round tower

☐ **13th Century**

6  Cathedral porch
7  Nave
8  Crossing
9  South transept
10  Choir
11  North transept

☐ **15th Century**

1  Ticket office
2  Hall of the Vicars' Choral (museum)
3  Dormitory
5  Castle

0 meters     50

0 yards     50

### VISITORS' CHECKLIST

Road map C5. Cashel. **(** *062 61437.* **🚉** *to Thurles.* **🚌** *to Cashel.* **◯** *mid-Jun–mid-Sep: 9am–7:30pm: daily; mid-Sep– mid-Mar: 9:30am–4:30pm; mid-Mar–mid-Jun: 9:30am–5:30pm.* **●** *Dec 24–28.* 🎫 🄾 ♿ 🖾

### The Rock

*The 28-m (92-ft) round tower, the oldest and tallest building on the rock, enabled Cashel's inhabitants to scour the surrounding plain for potential attackers.*

**Round tower**

**Crossing**

**The Choir** contains the 17th-century tomb of Miler Magrath, who caused a scandal by being both a Protestant and a Catholic archbishop at the same time.

**Graveyard**

**The O'Scully Monument**, an ornate memorial erected in 1870 by a local landowning family, was damaged during a storm in 1976.

### North Transept

*Panels from three 16th-century tombs in the north transept are decorated with remarkably fresh and intricate carvings. This one, against the north wall, features a vine-leaf design and strange stylized beasts.*

### ★ Cathedral

*The roofless Gothic cathedral has thick walls riddled with hidden passages; in the north transept these are seen emerging at the base of the windows.*

## Athassel Priory ⑳

**Road map** C5. 8 km (5 miles) W of
Cashel, Co Tipperary. 🚌 to Tipperary.
⭕ daily.

THIS RUINED Augustinian priory
is situated on the west bank
of the River Suir. The tomb of
William de Burgh, the Norman
founder of the priory, lies in
the church. Established in 1192,
Athassel is believed to have
been the largest medieval priory
in Ireland until it burned down
in 1447. The scattered monastic
site conveys a tranquil atmosphere, from the gatehouse
and church to the remains of
the cloisters and chapter
house. The church has a fine
west doorway, nave and
chancel walls, as well as a
15th-century central tower.

**The ruins of Athassel Priory, on the banks of the River Suir**

## Glen of Aherlow ㉑

**Road map** C5. Co Tipperary. 🚌 to
Bansha or Tipperary. ℹ️ Coach Road
Inn, on R663 8 km (5 miles) E of
Galbally (062 56240).

THE LUSH VALLEY of the River
Aherlow runs between the
Galty Mountains and the
wooded ridge of Slievenamuck.
Bounded by the villages of
**Galbally** and **Bansha**, the
glen was historically an important pass between Limerick
and Tipperary and a notorious
hideout for outlaws.
 Today there are opportunities
for riding, cycling, hiking and
fishing. Lowland walks follow

the trout-filled river along the
valley floor. More adventurous
walkers will be tempted by the
Galty range, which offers
more rugged hiking, past
wooded foothills, mountain
streams, tiny corrie lakes and
splendid sandstone peaks.

## Cahir ㉒

**Road map** C5. Co Tipperary.
👥 2,100. 🚌 🚉 ℹ️ Apr–Sep: Castle
Street (052 41453). 🛒 Fri.

ONCE A GARRISON and mill
town, Cahir is today a
busy market town. The pub-
lined Castle Street is the most
appealing area. It leads to the
Suir River, Cahir Castle and the
well-marked rural walk to the
Swiss Cottage.
 On the edge of town lies
the ruined **Cahir Abbey**, a
13th-century Augustinian
priory. Its fine windows are
decorated with carved heads.

### ⚜ Cahir Castle

Castle Street. 📞 052 41011.
⭕ daily. 🚫 ♿ limited.
Built on a rocky island in the
River Suir, Cahir is one of the
most formidable castles in
Ireland and a popular film set.
This well-preserved fortress
dates from the 13th century
but is inextricably linked to its
later owners, the Butlers. A
powerful family in Ireland since
the Anglo-Norman invasion,
they were considered trusty
lieges of the English crown and
were granted the Cahir barony
in 1375. Under their command,
the castle was renovated and
extended throughout the 15th
and 16th centuries. It remained
in the Butler family until 1964.
 The castle is divided into
outer, middle and inner wards,
with a barbican at the outer
entrance. The inner ward is on
the site of the original Norman
castle; the foundations are 13th
century, as are the curtain walls
and keep. The restored interior
includes the striking great hall,
which dates largely from the
1840s, although one of the
walls is original and the windows are 15th century. From
the ramparts there are views
over the river and millrace.

### 🎪 Swiss Cottage

Ardfinnan Road, Cahir. 📞 052 41144.
⭕ May–Sep: daily; Mar–Apr &
Oct–Nov: Tue–Sun. 🚫
The Swiss Cottage is a superb
example of a *cottage orné*, a
rustic folly. It was designed
for the Butlers by the Regency
architect John Nash in 1810.
Here, Lord and Lady Cahir
played at bucolic bliss, enjoying
picnics dressed as peasants.
Fashion dictated a *cottage
orné* should blend in with the

**View across the unspoiled Glen of Aherlow**

countryside and all designs
should be drawn from nature
with nothing matching, so the
windows and sloping eaves
are all of different sizes and
design. The enchantingly
furnished cottage contains a
tea room, gracious music
room and two bedrooms, all
beautifully restored.

## Clonmel ㉓

**Road map** C5. Co Tipperary.
🚶 17,500. 🚆 🚌 🛈 *Chamber
Buildings (052 22960).*

SET ON THE RIVER SUIR and
framed by the Comeragh
Mountains, Clonmel is
Tipperary's main town. This
Anglo-Norman stronghold was
a fief of the Desmonds and
eventually of the Butlers. Its
prosperity was founded on mil-
ling and brewing; attractive
mills still line the quays.
Today, Clonmel is a bustling,
brash town with quirky architecture and lively nightlife.
   The **Franciscan Friary** by
the quays was remodeled in
Early English style in Victorian
times but retains a 15th-century
tower and houses 16th-century
Butler tomb effigies. Nearby is
O'Connell Street, Clonmel's
main shopping street, which
is straddled by the West
Gate, built in 1831.
Visitors to **Hearn's**

**Clonmel's mock Tudor West Gate,
spanning O'Connell Street**

**The Swiss Cottage at Cahir, beautifully restored to its original state**

**Hotel** on Parnell Street can see
memorabilia of Charles
Bianconi (1786 –1875), including pictures of the horse-drawn
coach service he established
between Clonmel and Cahir.
Eventually this developed into
a nationwide passenger service.

## Carrick-on-Suir ㉔

**Road map** C5. Co Tipperary.
🚶 5,100. 🚌

THIS SLEEPY MARKET TOWN has
a distinctly old-fashioned
air. In the 15th century, it was
a strategic site commanding
access west to Clonmel and
southeast to Waterford, but
after Tudor times the town
sank into oblivion. Apart from
Ormond Castle, there are few
specific sights. However, you
can stroll by the old waterside warehouses or shop for
Tipperary Crystal *(see p323)*,
which is made nearby.

### ♣ Ormond Castle

Castle Park. 📞 *051 640787.*
◯ *Jun–Sep: daily.* 🎦 🔼 *limited.*
Although once a fortress,
Ormond Castle is the finest
surviving Tudor manor house
in Ireland. It was built by the
powerful Butler family, the
Earls of Ormonde, who were
given their title by the English
crown in 1328. The castle has
a gracious Elizabethan façade
overlaying the medieval original; the battlemented towers
on the south side sit oddly
with the gabled façade and its
mullioned and oriel windows.
   The finest room is the Long
Gallery, which has a stuccoed
ceiling studded with heraldic
crests, and two ornately
carved fireplaces. The Elizabethan section was added by

Black Tom Butler, the 10th
Earl of Ormonde, a loyal
subject to Elizabeth Tudor.
On his death, the Ormondes
abandoned Carrick for
Kilkenny *(see pp134 –6)*.

**Intricate wood carving on a four-
poster bed at Ormond Castle**

ENVIRONS: In the churchyard
at **Ahenny**, about 10 km
(6 miles) north of Carrick, stand
two magnificent High Crosses
*(see p235)*. Both are crowned
by "caps" or "bishops' miters"
and have intricate cable, spiral
and fret patterns.
   At **Kilkieran**, 5 km (3 miles)
north of Carrick, are three
other interesting High Crosses,
dating from the 9th century.
The Plain Cross is unadorned
but capped; the West Cross is
profusely ornamented though
weathered; the Long Shaft
Cross has an odd design of
stumpy arms on a long shaft.

# THE WEST OF IRELAND

MAYO · GALWAY · ROSCOMMON

THIS IS THE HEART OF CONNAUGHT, *Ireland's historic western province. The West lives up to its image as a traditional, rural, sparsely populated land, with windswept mountains and countryside speckled with low stone walls and peat bogs. Yet it also encompasses Galway, a fast-growing university town whose youthful population brings life to the medieval streets and snug pubs.*

The rugged Atlantic coastline of the West has been occupied for over 5,000 years. It is rich in prehistoric sites such as the land enclosures of Céide Fields and the ring forts on the Aran Islands. Evidence of the monastic period can be seen in the mysterious and beautiful remains at Kilmacduagh and Clonfert; and the region's religious associations still exert an influence, apparent in the pilgrimages to Knock and Croagh Patrick in County Mayo.

In medieval times, the city of Galway was an Anglo-Norman stronghold, surrounded by warring Gaelic clans. After the Cromwellian victories of the 1640s, many Irish were dispossessed of their fertile lands and dispatched "to hell or Connacht." Landlords made their mark in the 17th and 18th centuries, building impressive country houses at Clonalis, Strokestown Park and Westport. During the Great Famine, the West – especially County Mayo – suffered most from emigration, a trend that continues to this day. In spite of this, strong Gaelic traditions have survived in County Galway, the country's largest Gaeltacht *(see p221)*, where almost half the population speaks Irish as a first language.

The bracken browns and soft violets of Connemara in the west of Galway and the fertile farmland, extensive bogs and placid lakes of County Roscommon are in striking contrast to the magnificent cliff scenery of the remote islands off the coast. This region is often shrouded in a misty drizzle or else battered by Atlantic winds and accompanying heavy downpours.

Summer is a time for festivities: the Galway Races in July, traditional sailing ship races off Kinvarra in August and the Galway Oyster Festival in September are all lively events that attract a stream of visitors.

Swans by the quayside of the Claddagh area of Galway

Typical Connemara landscape dominated by the peaks of the Twelve Bens

# Exploring the West of Ireland

GALWAY CITY, CLIFDEN AND WESTPORT make the best bases for exploring the region, with cozy pubs, good walks and access to the scenic islands. Connemara and the wilds of County Mayo attract nature lovers, while the islands of Achill, Aran, Clare and Inishbofin appeal to watersports enthusiasts and ramblers. The lakes of County Roscommon are popular with anglers, and Lough Corrib and Lough Key offer relaxing cruises.

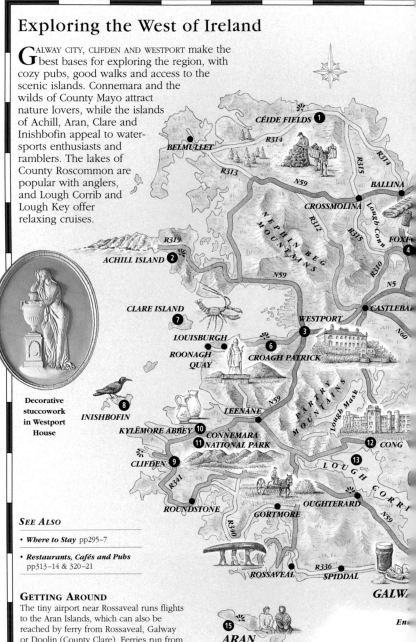

Decorative stuccowork in Westport House

## SEE ALSO

- *Where to Stay* pp295–7

- *Restaurants, Cafés and Pubs* pp313–14 & 320–21

## GETTING AROUND

The tiny airport near Rossaveal runs flights to the Aran Islands, which can also be reached by ferry from Rossaveal, Galway or Doolin (County Clare). Ferries run from Cleggan to Inishbofin and Louisburgh to Clare. There is no rail service between Galway and Westport but the towns are linked by reliable (if slow) buses. Connemara is reached by Bus Éireann services from Galway and Clifden (via Oughterard or Cong) or can be explored on day-long minibus tours also from Galway or Clifden.

0 kilometers 20

0 miles 10

**River valley at Delphi in northern Connemara**

## SIGHTS AT A GLANCE

Achill Island ❷
*Aran Islands pp206–7* ⓯
Boyle ㉕
Céide Fields ❶
Clare Island ❼
Clifden ❾
Clonalis House ㉓
Clonfert Cathedral ⓴
Cong ⓬
Connemara National Park ⓫
Croagh Patrick ❻
Foxford ❹
*Galway pp202–3* ⓮
Inishbofin ❽
Kilmacduagh ⓱
Kinvarra ⓰
Knock ❺
Kylemore Abbey ❿
Lough Corrib ⓭
Portumna ⓳
Roscommon ㉒
Strokestown Park House ㉔
Thoor Ballylee ⓲
Turoe Stone ㉑
Westport ❸

**Colorful storefronts lining
Quay Street, Galway**

## KEY

| | |
|---|---|
| ▬▬ | Major road |
| ▭▭ | Minor road |
| ▬▬ | Scenic route |
| 〜 | River |
| ※ | Viewpoint |

**Bogwood centerpiece in Céide Fields interpretative center**

# Céide Fields ●

**Road map** B2. 8 km (5 miles) W of Ballycastle, Co Mayo. **C** 096 43325. **□** from Ballycastle. **○** mid-Mar–Oct: daily. **☒** **☒** ground floor.

SURROUNDED by heather-clad moorlands and mountains along a bleak, dramatic stretch of north Mayo coastline is Europe's largest Stone Age land enclosure. Over 10 sq km (4 sq miles) were enclosed by walls to make fields suitable for growing wheat and barley, and grazing cattle. Remains of farm buildings indicate that it was an extensive community. The fields were slowly buried below the creeping bog formation, where they have been preserved for 5,000 years.

Part of the bog has been cut away to reveal the collapsed stone walls of the ancient fields. The remains are simple rather than spectacular, but excellent guides help visitors find and recognize key features. Stone Age pottery and a primitive plow have been found in recent excavations. The striking, pyramid-shaped interpretative center has a viewing platform overlooking the site, audiovisual presentations and displays on local geology and botany.

**ENVIRONS:** Scattered around the wilderness of the spectacular north Mayo coast from Ballina to the end of the Mullet peninsula is a series of sculptures forming the **North Mayo Sculpture Trail**. Created by 12 sculptors from three continents, the 15 works, often on a huge scale, are made from earth, stone and other natural materials; additional sculptures are planned. They aim to highlight the coast's grandeur and enduring nature.

# Achill Island ●

**Road map** A3. Co Mayo. **□** from Westport. **i** Jul–Aug: The Sound (098 45384).

IRELAND'S largest island, 22 km (13.5 miles) long and 19 km (12 miles) wide, is reached by a road bridge that can be raised for boats to pass through. Achill offers moorland, mountains, rugged cliffs and long beaches, and is a popular spot for fishing and water sports.

For motorists, the best introduction is the **Atlantic Coast Drive**, a circular, marked route from Achill Sound, by the bridge. The road goes to the island's southern tip, then north around the rest of Achill. Between Doeega and Keel in the southwest, run the dramatic Minaun Cliffs and Cathedral Rocks. In the north is Slievemore, a mountain overlooking the village of Slievemore, which was abandoned during the Great Famine (see p211). Sharks can be spotted from Keem Bay in the west.

# Westport ●

**Road map** B3. Co Mayo. **⌖** 3,700. **☒** **☒** **i** The Mall (098 25711). **☒** Thu.

**The *Angel of Welcome* above the marble staircase at Westport House**

WESTPORT is a neat landlord town and has a prosperous air. In the 1770s, architect James Wyatt laid out the wide, tree-lined streets, including the North and South Mall on either side of Carrowbeg River. The town traded in yarn, cloth, beer and slate, but industrialization and the Great Famine (see p211) spelled long-term decline. The trend was reversed only in the 1950s when new industry and visitors were attracted to the area.

Beyond the South Mall is Bridge Street, lined with cafés and pubs; the most appealing is Matt Molloy's (see p320), named after and owned by the flautist from The Chieftains.

**⌂ Westport House**
Off Louisburgh Rd. **C** 098 25141. **○** May–Sep: daily. **☒**
Just west of the town is the Carrowbeg estuary and Clew Bay. At the head of the bay stands Westport House, the

**The deserted village of Slievemore on Achill Island**

**Statue of St. Patrick at the foot of Croagh Patrick, looking out to Clew Bay**

seat of the Earls of Altamont, descendants of the Browne family, who were Tudor settlers. The town of Westport itself was started in the 1750s by John Browne, first Lord Altamont, to complement the house. Designed in 1732 by Richard Castle, and completed by James Wyatt in 1778, the limestone mansion stands on the site of an O'Malley castle. Its imposing interior includes a sweeping marble staircase and an elegant James Wyatt dining room and is adorned with family portraits, antique Waterford chandeliers and 18th-century Chinese wallpaper. Recently the estate has become heavily commercialized, with a small boating lake, miniature railway, children's zoo, an amusement arcade and several stores.

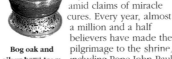

**Bog oak and silver bowl from Westport House**

## Foxford ❹

Road map B3. Co Mayo. 🏘 1,000. 🚌 from Galway. 🚹 Westport (098 25711).

THIS TRANQUIL market town is known for good angling in nearby Lough Conn and for its woven rugs and tweeds. In the town center is **Foxford Woollen Mills**, founded in 1892 by an Irish nun, Mother Arsenius (originally named Agnes). The thriving mill now supplies top fashion houses. An audiovisual tour traces the mill's history, and visitors can see craftspeople at work.

🏭 **Foxford Woollen Mills**
St. Joseph's Place. 📞 094 56756. ◯ daily. ● Good Fri, Dec 24 & 25. 🅿 🔲

## Knock ❺

Road map B3. Co Mayo. 🏘 440. 🛫 15 km (9 miles) N of Knock. 🚌 🚹 May–Sep: Knock (094 88193).

IN 1879, two local women saw an apparition of the Virgin, St. Joseph and St. John the Evangelist by the gable of the Church of St. John the Baptist. The vision was witnessed by 13 more onlookers and validated by the Catholic Church amid claims of miracle cures. Every year, almost a million and a half believers have made the pilgrimage to the shrine, including Pope John Paul II in 1979 and Mother Teresa in 1993. Its focal point is the gable where the apparition was seen, which is now covered over to form a chapel. Nearby is the Basilica of Our Lady, a monolithic modern basilica and Marian

**Bottles of holy water for sale at the shrine in Knock**

shrine. **Knock Folk Museum**, beside the basilica, portrays life in 19th-century rural Ireland with reconstructions of a cottage and schoolroom. An Apparition section covers the background to the miracle.

🏛 **Knock Folk Museum**
📞 094 88100. ◯ May–Oct: daily; Nov–Apr: by appt. 🅿 🔲

## Croagh Patrick ❻

Road map B3. Murrisk, Co Mayo. 🚌 from Westport.

IRELAND'S holy mountain, named after the national saint (see p273), is one of Mayo's best-known landmarks. From the bottom it seems cone-shaped, an impression dispelled by climbing to its flat peak. This quartzite, scree-clad mountain has had a history of pagan worship since 3000 BC. However, in AD 441, St. Patrick is said to have spent 40 days on the mountain fasting and praying for the Irish.

Since then, penitents, often barefoot, have made the pilgrimage to the summit in his honor, especially on Reek or Garland Sunday, the last in July. From the start of the trail at Campbell's Pub in Murrisk, where there is a huge statue of the saint, it is a two-hour climb to the top, at 765 m (2,510 ft). Mass is celebrated there in the modern chapel. There are also panoramic views over Clew Bay. Recently, there have been controversial proposals to mine for gold and bauxite on the mountain.

## Clare Island ❼

**Road map** A3. Co Mayo. 👥 *180.* ⛴
*from Roonagh Quay, 6.5 km (4 miles)*
*W of Louisburgh.* ℹ *Westport.*

**The ferry to Inishbofin leaving Cleggan Harbour**

CLARE ISLAND, set in Clew Bay, is dominated by two hills, and a square 15th-century castle commands the headland and harbor. In the 16th century the island was the stronghold of Grace O'Malley, pirate queen and patriot, who held sway over the western coast. According to Tudor state papers, she was received at Queen Elizabeth I's court, even though she stood out against English rule until her death in her seventies in 1603. She is buried here in a tiny Cistercian abbey decorated with medieval murals and inscribed with her motto: "Invincible on land and sea."

The island is dotted with Iron Age huts and field systems as well as promontory forts and Bronze Age cooking sites *(see p162).* Clare is rich in bog flora and fauna, making it popular with walkers. Animal lovers come to see the seals, dolphins, falcons and otters.

**ENVIRONS:** The mainland coastal village of **Louisburgh** offers rugged Atlantic landscape, sheltered coves, sea angling and water sports. It is also home to the **Granuaile Centre** which celebrates the exploits of Grace O'Malley (*Granuaile* in Gaelic) and has displays on Mayo folklore and archaeology.

🏛 **Granuaile Centre**
St. Catherine's Church, Louisburgh.
☎ *098 66195.* ○ *May–Oct: daily.*
🖼 ♿

## Inishbofin ❽

**Road map** A3. Co Galway. 👥 *200.*
⛴ *from Cleggan.* ℹ *Clifden.*

THE NAME Inishbofin means "island of the white cow." This mysterious, often mist-swathed island was chosen for its remoteness by the exiled 7th-century St. Colman, English Abbot of Lindisfarne. On the site of his original monastery is a late medieval church, graveyard and holy well. At the sheltered harbor entrance lies a ruined castle, occupied in the 16th century by Spanish pirate Don Bosco in alliance with Grace O'Malley. In 1653 it was captured by Cromwellian forces and used as a prison for Catholic priests. Inishbofin was later owned by a succession of absentee landlords and now survives on farming and lobster-fishing.

Surrounded by reefs and islets, the island's landscape is characterized by stone walls, small abandoned cottages, reed-fringed lakes and hay meadows, where the corncrake *(see p16)* can be seen or heard. Inishbofin's beaches offer bracing walks.

## Clifden ❾

**Road map** A3. Co Galway. 👥 *800.*
🚌 ℹ *May–Sep: Market St (095 21163).* 🛒 *Tue.*

FRAMED by the grandeur of the Twelve Bens mountain range and with a striking skyline dominated by two church spires, this early 19th-century market town passes for the capital of the Connemara region and is a good base for exploring. Clifden was founded in 1812 by John d'Arcy, a local landowner and High Sheriff of Galway, to create a pocket of respectability within the lawlessness of Connemara. The family eventually went bankrupt trying to bring prosperity and order to the town. The Protestant church contains a copy of the Cross of Cong *(see p65).*

Today craft shops have taken over much of the town. In the center is the Square, a place for lively pubs such as EJ Kings *(see p320).* Nearby is O'Grady's Seafood Restaurant *(see p313),* one of the finest in Galway. Connemara is noted for its *sean-nos*

**Clifden against a backdrop of the Twelve Bens mountains**

## CONNEMARA

This wild region in the west of Galway encompasses bogs, mountains and a rugged coastline. Major sights include the Connemara National Park and Kylemore Abbey *(see p200)*. For those without a car, bus tours are available from Galway and Clifden *(see p360)*.

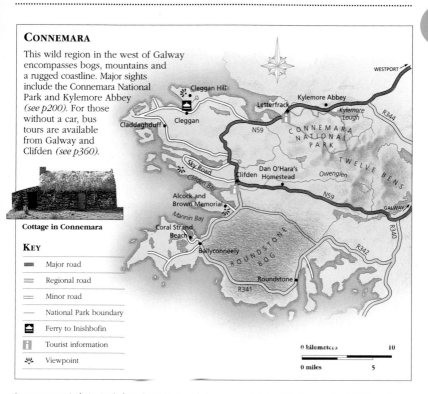

**Cottage in Connemara**

### KEY

| | |
|---|---|
| ▬▬ | Major road |
| ══ | Regional road |
| ══ | Minor road |
| — | National Park boundary |
| ⛴ | Ferry to Inishbofin |
| ℹ | Tourist information |
| ✺ | Viewpoint |

0 kilometres 10
0 miles 5

---

(unaccompanied singing), but in Clifden, general traditional music is more common.

Jutting out into **Clifden Bay** is a sand spit and beach, well-marked from Clifden Square. South of Clifden, at the start of the Roundstone Road, is Owenglen Cascade where, in May, salmon leap on their way to spawn upstream.

**ENVIRONS:** The **Sky Road** is an 11-km (7-mile) circular route with stunning ocean views. The road goes northwest from Clifden and passes desolate scenery and the narrow inlet of Clifden Bay. Clifden Castle, John d'Arcy's Gothic Revival ruin, lies just off the Sky Road, as do several beaches.

The coastal road north from Clifden to **Cleggan**, via Claddaghduff, is spectacular, passing former smuggling coves. Cleggan, an attractive fishing village, nestles into the head of Cleggan Bay. From here boats leave for Inishbofin and Inishturk. **Cleggan Hill** has a ruined Napoleonic Martello tower at the top and a megalithic tomb at the foot.

To the south of Clifden, the lovely coastal route to Round-stone skirts a large area of open bogland pitted with tiny lakes. The **Alcock and Brown Memorial** overlooks the bog landing site of the first trans-atlantic flight made by Alcock and Brown in 1919. Nearby is the site of Marconi's wireless station, which exchanged the first transatlantic radio messages with Nova Scotia in 1907. The **Ballyconneely** area is distinguished by craggy islands and the beautiful **Coral Strand Beach**. The village of **Round-stone** is best seen during the summer regatta of traditional Galway *hookers (see p203)*.

A short drive to the east of Clifden is **Dan O'Hara's Homestead**. In a wild, rocky setting, this organic farm recreates the rough conditions of life in Connemara before the 1840s. The folksy air of Connemara is accentuated by pony and trap rides and traditional music.

🏛 **Dan O'Hara's Homestead**
Heritage Centre, Lettershea, off N59. ▣ 095 21246. ◯ Apr–Sep: daily.

**View of the coast from the Sky Road**

**The imposing Kylemore Abbey on the shores of Kylemore Lough**

## Kylemore Abbey ⑩

**Road map** A3. Connemara, Co
Galway. **(** 095 41146. **⊟** from
Galway and Clifden. **◯** Mar–Oct:
daily. **▧** **⭑** limited.

SHELTERED BY THE SLOPES OF
the Twelve Bens, this lakeside castle is a romantic, battlemented Gothic Revival fantasy.
It was built as a present for
his wife by Mitchell Henry
(1826–1911), who was a
Manchester tycoon and later
Galway MP. The Henrys also
purchased a huge area of
moorland, drained the boggy
hillside and planted thousands
of trees as a windbreak for
their new orchards and exotic
walled gardens. After the
sudden deaths of his wife and
daughter, Henry left Kylemore
and the castle was sold.

It became an abbey when
Benedictine nuns, fleeing from
Ypres in Belgium during World
War I, sought refuge here.
The nuns now run the abbey
as a select girls' boarding
school. Visitors are restricted
to the grounds, restaurant and

craft shop where they can
watch the abbey pottery being
hand-decorated and fired. The
cream earthenware pottery is
painted with a fuchsia motif.

In the grounds, rhododen-
drons and fuchsias enhance
lakeside walks. By the lakeshore stands a Neo-Gothic
chapel, a miniature copy of
Norwich Cathedral.

## Connemara National Park ⑪

**Road map** A3. Letterfrack, Connemara,
Co Galway. **(** 095 41054. **Visitors'
Centre** **◯** May–Sep: daily. **▧** **⭑**

A COMBINATION of bogland,
lakes and mountains
makes up this National Park
in the heart of Connemara.
Within its more than 2,000 ha
(5,000 acres) are four of the
Twelve Bens, including Benbaun, the highest mountain in
the range at 730 m (2,400 ft),
and the peak of Diamond Hill.
At the centre is the valley of
Glanmore with the Polladirk
River flowing through it.

Visitors come for some of the
most spectacular landscape in
the region and to glimpse the
famous Connemara ponies.

Part of the land originally
belonged to the Kylemore
Abbey estate. In 1980 it became a National Park. There
are traces of the land's previous
uses all over the park: megalithic tombs, nearly 4,000 years
old, can be seen as well as old
ridges marking former grazing
areas and arable fields.

The park is open all year,
while the Visitors' Centre near
the entrance, just outside
Letterfrack, is open only in
the summer months. It has
displays on how the landscape
developed and was used and
on local flora and fauna. There
is also an audiovisual theater
and an indoor picnic area.
Two marked paths start from
the Visitors' Centre. In
summer there are guided
walks, some led by botanists,
and various children's activities.
Climbing the Twelve Bens
should be attempted only by
experienced hikers equipped
for all weather conditions.

### CONNEMARA WILDLIFE

The blanket bogs and moorlands of
Connemara are a botanist's paradise,
especially for unusual bog and
heathland plants. Birdlife is also
varied with hooded crows, which
can be recognized by their gray and
black plumage, stonechats, peregrines
and merlins – the smallest falcons in the
British Isles. Red deer have been
successfully reintroduced into the
area and a herd now lives in
the National Park. Badgers, foxes,
stoats and otters may also be
seen, as well as gray seals
along the rocky coast.

**The merlin** nests in old
clumps of heather and feeds
mainly on small birds.

**St. Dabeoc's heath**, a pretty
heather, grows nowhere else in
Ireland or Great Britain.

# Cong ⑫

**Road map** B3. Co Mayo. 🚗 *200*.
🚌 ℹ️ *Galway (091 63081)*.

THIS PICTURESQUE VILLAGE lies on the shores of Lough Corrib, just within County Mayo. Cong means isthmus – the village lies on the strip of land between Lough Corrib and Lough Mask. During the 1840s, as a famine relief project, a canal was built linking the two lakes, but the water drained through the porous limestone bed. Stone bridges and stone-clad locks are still in place along the dry canal.

**Cong Abbey** lies close to the main street. The Augustinian abbey was founded in the early 12th century by Turlough O'Connor, King of Connaught and High King of Ireland, on the site of a 6th-century monastery established by St. Fechin. The abbey has doorways in a style transitional between Romanesque and Gothic, stone carvings and restored cloisters. The Cross of Cong, an ornate processional cross intended for the abbey, is now in Dublin's National Museum *(see pp64–5)*. The most fascinating remains are the Gothic chapter house, stone bridges and the monks' fishing-house overhanging the river – the monks devised a system so that a bell rang in the kitchen when a fish took the bait.

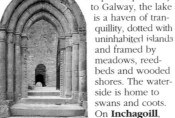
**Carved 12th-century doorway of Cong Abbey**

Just south of Cong is **Ashford Castle**, rebuilt in Gothic Revival style in 1870 by Lord Ardilaun of the Guinness family. One of Ireland's best hotels *(see p284)*, its grounds can be visited by boat from Galway and Oughterard. Cong was the setting for *The Quiet Man*, the 1950s' film starring John Wayne. "Quiet Man" tours cover locations near the castle.

# Lough Corrib ⑬

**Road map** B3. Co Galway. 🚌 *from Galway and Cong*. 🚢 *from Oughterard and Wood Quay, Galway.* ℹ️ *Oughterard (091 82808).*

AN ANGLER'S PARADISE, Lough Corrib offers the chance to fish with local fishermen for brown trout, salmon, pike, perch and eels. Despite its proximity to Galway, the lake is a haven of tranquillity, dotted with uninhabited islands and framed by meadows, reed-beds and wooded shores. The waterside is home to swans and coots. On **Inchagoill**, one of the largest islands, stand the ruins of an early Christian monastic settlement and a Romanesque church.

The lake's atmosphere is best appreciated on a cruise. From Galway, the standard short cruise winds through the marshes to the site of an Iron Age fort, limestone quarries and the battlemented Menlo Castle. Longer cruises continue to Cong or include picnics on the islands.

**ENVIRONS:** On the banks of Lough Corrib, **Oughterard** is known as "the gateway to Connemara." The village has craft shops, thatched cottages and friendly pubs. It is also an important center for golf, fishing, hiking and pony trekking. Other country pursuits include riverside walks, a stroll to a waterfall west of the village and cycle rides.

About 4 km (2.5 miles) southeast of Oughterard (off the N59) is **Aughnanure Castle**. This well-restored six-story tower house clings to a rocky island on the River Drimneen. The present castle, built by the O'Flaherty clan, is on the site of one dating from 1256. The clan controlled West Connaught from Lough Corrib to Galway and the coast in the 13th to 16th centuries. From this castle the feuding O'Flaherty chieftains held out against the British in the 16th century. In 1545 Donal O'Flaherty married the pirate Grace O'Malley *(see p198)*. The tower house has an unusual double bawn *(see p18)* and a murder hole from which missiles could be dropped on invaders.

**View over Lough Corrib from the shore northwest of Oughterard**

⛪ **Aughnanure Castle**
Oughterard. 📞 *091 82214.*
🕐 *mid-Jun – mid-Sep: daily.* 🎫
♿ *limited.*

*Connemara ponies roam semi-wild and are fabled to be from Arab stock that came ashore from Spanish Armada wrecks.*

*Fuchsias grow profusely in the hedgerows of Connemara, thriving in the mild climate.*

# Galway

**Sign with Claddagh ring design**

GALWAY IS BOTH THE CENTER for the Irish-speaking regions in the West and a lively university city. Under the Anglo-Normans, it flourished as a trading post. In 1396 it gained a Royal Charter and for the next two centuries was controlled by 14 merchant families, or "tribes." The city prospered under English influence, but this allegiance to the Crown cost Galway dear when, in 1652, Cromwell's forces wreaked havoc. After the Battle of the Boyne *(see p236)*, Galway fell into decline, unable to compete with east-coast trade. In recent years, as a developing center for high-tech industry, the city's profile has been revived.

**Inside The Quays seafood restaurant and pub**

**Houses on the banks of the Corrib**

## Exploring Galway

The center of the city lies on the banks of the River Corrib, which flows down from Lough Corrib *(see p201)* widening out as it reaches Galway Bay. Urban renewal since the 1970s has led to extensive restoration of the narrow, winding streets of this once-walled city. Due to its compact size, Galway is easy to explore on foot, and a leisurely pace provides plenty of opportunity to stop off at its shops, pubs and historic sights.

## Eyre Square

The square encloses a pleasant park lined with imposing, mainly 19th-century, buildings. On the northwest of the square is the **Browne Doorway**, a 17th-century entrance from a mansion in Abbeygate Street Lower. Beside it are two cannons from the Crimean War and a fountain adorned with a sculpture of a Galway *booker* boat. The **Eyre Square Centre**, overlooking the park, is a modern shopping mall built to incorporate sections of the historic city walls. Walkways link Shoemakers and Penrice towers, two of the wall towers that used to ring the city in the 17th century.

## Latin Quarter

From Eyre Square, William Street and Shop Street are the main routes into the bustling "Latin Quarter." On the corner of Abbeygate Street Upper and Shop Street stands **Lynch's Castle**, now a bank, but still the grandest 16th-century town house in Galway. It was owned by the Lynch family, one of the 14 "tribes."

A side street leads to the **Collegiate Church of St. Nicholas**, Galway's finest medieval building. The church, founded in 1320, was extended in the 15th and 16th centuries, but then damaged by the Cromwellians, who used it to stable horses. The west porch is from the 15th century and there are some finely carved gargoyles under the parapet.

**Lynch family crest on Lynch's Castle**

Quay Street is lined with restaurants and pubs, including **The Quays** *(see p320)*. Tí Neachtain is a town house that belonged to "Humanity Dick," an 18th-century MP who promoted laws against cruelty to animals. Today, it too is a restaurant and pub *(see p320)*. Nearby are the Taibhdhearc and Druid theaters *(see p328)*.

## North Galway

The **Cathedral of St. Nicholas** (1965), made from local limestone and Connemara marble, stands on the west bank. From here you can see Wood Quay, where Lough Corrib cruises start *(see p201)*. **University College Galway**, farther west,

**Outside dining at one of the cosmopolitan cafés in Shop Street**

## GALWAY HOOKERS

Galway's traditional wooden sailing boats, featured on the city's coat of arms, were known as *pucans* and *gleotogs* – hookers in English. They have broad black hulls, thick masts and white or rust-colored sails. Once common in the Claddagh district, they were also used along the Atlantic coast to ferry peat, cattle and beer. Hookers can be seen in action at the Cruinniú na mBád festival in Kinvarra *(see p204).*

**Small Galway hooker sailing by the old quays and Spanish Arch**

## VISITORS' CHECKLIST

**Road map** B4. Co Galway.
52,000. ✈ Carnmore, 11 km (7 miles) NE of Galway. 🚆 Ceannt Station (091 64222). 🚌 Ceannt Station (091 63555). 🛈 Victoria Place, Eyre Square (091 63081). 🚢 Sat. ☼ Galway Arts Festival (late Jul); Galway Races (late Jul); Galway Oyster Festival (late Sep).

is a sprawling campus with a 1849 Gothic Revival quad. Salmon Weir Bridge links the two banks. Shoals of salmon rest under the bridge on their way upstream to spawn.

### The Old Quays

The **Spanish Arch**, where the river opens out, was built in 1584 to protect the harbor, which was then outside the city walls. Here, Spanish traders unloaded their ships. The old quays are a tranquil spot for a stroll down the Long Walk to the docks.

### The Claddagh

Beyond the Spanish Arch, on the west bank of the Corrib, lies the Claddagh. The name comes from *An Cladach*, meaning "flat, stony shore." From medieval times on, this fiercely independent fishing community beyond the city walls was governed by a "king" or "mayor," the last of whom died in 1954. The only remnants of this once close-knit, Gaelic-speaking community

are friendly pubs and Claddagh rings, betrothal rings traditionally handed down from mother to daughter *(see p326).*

**ENVIRONS:** Just west of the city is **Salthill**, Galway's seaside resort. The beaches at Palmer's Rock and Grattan Road are particularly popular with families in summer. A bracing walk along the promenade is still a Galway tradition.

**Spanish Arch on the site of the former docks**

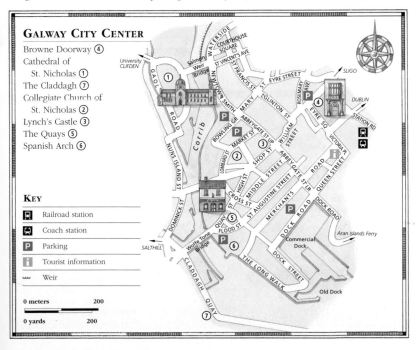

## GALWAY CITY CENTER

Browne Doorway ④
Cathedral of
 St. Nicholas ①
The Claddagh ⑦
Collegiate Church of
 St. Nicholas ②
Lynch's Castle ③
The Quays ⑤
Spanish Arch ⑥

### KEY

🚆 Railroad station

🚌 Coach station

🅿 Parking

🛈 Tourist information

〰 Weir

0 meters         200

0 yards          200

**Mural in the center of Kinvarra depicting a storefront**

## Aran Islands ⑮

*See pp206–7.*

## Kinvarra ⑯

**Road map** B4. Co Galway. 🏠 430.
🚍 ℹ️ *Galway (091 63081).*

ONE OF the most charming fishing villages on Galway Bay, Kinvarra's appeal lies in its sheltered, seaweed-clad harbor and traditional seafaring atmosphere. From medieval times, its fortunes were closely linked to Kilmacduagh, the powerful monastery and bishopric upon which the village depended.

The pier is bordered by a row of fishermen's cottages. Kinvarra remains a popular port of call for sailors of traditional Galway hookers *(see p203)* and is known for the Cruinniú na mBád (gathering of the boats) festival in August. Rambles include historical and nature trails. Birdwatchers may spot teal, curlews and oystercatchers by the shore.

**ENVIRONS:** North of Kinvarra, on a promontory on the shore of Galway Bay, lies **Dunguaire Castle**. It is perched just beyond some quaint thatched cottages and a stone bridge. The castle is named after the 7th-century King Guaire of Connaught, whose court here was renowned as the haunt of bards and balladeers. Although the medieval earthworks survive, the present castle was built in the 16th century, a quintessential tower house *(see p18)* with sophisticated machicolations. The banqueting hall is still used for "medieval banquets" where guests are entertained with Celtic harp music and the poetry of Yeats.

### 🏰 Dunguaire Castle
📞 *091 37108.* ⏰ *mid-Apr–Sep.* 📷

## Kilmacduagh ⑰

**Road map** B4. Outside Gort on Corofin Rd, Co Galway. 🚍 *to Gort.* ⏰ *daily.*

THIS MONASTIC SETTLEMENT is in a remote location on the borders of counties Clare and Galway, roughly 5 km (3 miles) southwest of Gort. The sense of isolation is accentuated by the stony moonscape of the Burren to the west *(see pp178–80)*. Reputedly founded by St. Colman MacDuagh in the early 7th century, Kilmacduagh owes more to the monastic revival that led to rebuilding from the 11th century onward.

The centerpiece of the extensive site is a large, slightly leaning 11th- or 12th-century round tower and a roofless church, known as the cathedral or Teampall. The cathedral is a pre-Norman structure, which was later remodeled in Gothic style, with flamboyant tracery and fine tomb carvings. In the surrounding fields lie the remains of several other churches that once depended on the monastery. To the northeast of the Teampall is the late medieval Glebe or Abbot's House, a variant of a 14th- or 15th-century tower house *(see p18)*.

## Thoor Ballylee ⑱

**Road map** B4. Gort, Co Galway.
📞 *091 31436.* 🚍 *to Gort.* ⏰ *Easter–Sep: daily.* 📷 ♿ *limited.*

FOR MUCH of the 1920s, this beguiling tower house was a summer home to the poet WB Yeats *(see pp20–21)*. Yeats was a regular visitor to nearby Coole Park, the home of his friend Lady Gregory (1852–1932), who was a cofounder of the Abbey Theatre *(see p86)*.

On one visit Yeats came upon Ballylee Castle, a 14th-century de Burgo tower adjoining a cozy cottage with a walled garden and stream. In 1902, both the tower and the cottage became part of the Gregory estate and Yeats bought them in 1916. From 1919 onward, his family divided their time between

**Round tower and cathedral, the most impressive monastic remains at Kilmacduagh**

Dublin and their Galway tower. Yeats used the name Thoor Ballylee as the address, using the Irish word for tower to "keep people from suspecting us of modern gothic and a deer park." His collection, *The Tower* (1928), includes several poems inspired by Thoor Ballylee.

Today, the audiovisual tour includes readings from Yeats's poetry, but the charm of a visit lies in the tower itself, with its spiral stone steps and views from the battlements over forest and farmland.

**ENVIRONS:** Just to the north of Gort is **Coole Park**, which was once the home of Lady Gregory. Although the house was demolished in the 1950s, the estate farm has been restored and the fine gardens survive. In particular, there is the "autograph tree," a spreading copper beech carved with the initials of George Bernard Shaw, JM Synge *(see pp20–21)*, Jack Yeats *(see p68)* and other famous visitors. In the farm buildings is an audiovisual display. The emphasis of the visitors' center is on natural rather than literary history: it is the start of two well-marked walks, one around the gardens and the other through beech, hazel, birch and ash woodland to Coole Lake.

### ✕ Coole Park
3 km (2 miles) NE of Gort. 🚌 091 31804. ☐ mid-Apr–Sep. 📷 ♿ limited.

Gentle hills and woodland by Coole Lake in Coole Park

## Portumna ⑲

**Road map** C4. Co Galway. 🚶 *1,000.*
🚌 ℹ️ *Galway (091 63081).* 🛒 *Fri.*

PORTUMNA is a historic market town with various sights, many of which are newly restored. Situated on Lough Derg, it is a convenient base for cruising the River Shannon *(see p177)* and has a modern marina. **Portumna Castle**, built in the early 17th century, was the main seat of the de Burgo family. Now partially restored, it has a symmetrical façade and some elaborate interior stonework. The façade surveys formal gardens. Near the castle is **Portumna Priory**. Most of the remains date from around 1414 when the priory was founded by the Dominicans, but traces can also be found of the Cistercian abbey that was previously on the site. The large de Burgo estate to the west of the town now forms **Portumna Forest Park**, with picnic sites and marked woodland trails leading to Lough Derg.

## Clonfert Cathedral ⑳

**Road map** C4. Clonfert, Co Galway.
☐ *daily.* ♿

SITUATED near a bleak stretch of the Shannon bordering the boglands of the Midlands, Clonfert is one of the jewels of Irish-Romanesque architecture.

**Human heads carved on the tympanum at Clonfert Cathedral**

The tiny cathedral occupies the site of a monastery, which was founded by St. Brendan in AD 563 and is believed to be the burial place of the saint.

Although a great scholar and enthusiastic founder of monasteries, St. Brendan is best known as the "great navigator." His journeys are recounted in *Navigatio Sancti Brendani*, written in about 1050, which survives in medieval manuscripts in several languages including Flemish, Norse and French. The account seems to describe a voyage to Wales, the Orkneys, Iceland and conceivably the east coast of North America. His voyage and his boat *(see p182)*, have been recreated by modern explorers in an attempt to prove that St. Brendan may have preceded Columbus by about 900 years.

The highlight of Clonfert is its intricately sculpted sandstone doorway. The round arch above the door is decorated with animal and human heads, geometrical shapes, foliage and symbolic motifs. The carvings on the triangular tympanum above the arch are of strange human heads. In the chancel, the 13th-century east windows are fine examples of late Irish-Romanesque art. The 15th-century chancel arch is adorned with sculptures of angels and a mermaid. Although Clonfert was built over several centuries and altered in the 17th century, the church has a profound sense of unity.

**Thoor Ballylee tower house, the summer home of WB Yeats**

# Aran Islands ⑮

**Jaunting car on Inishmore**

INISHMORE, INISHMAAN and Inisheer, the three Aran Islands, are formed from a limestone ridge. The largest, Inishmore, is 13 km (8 miles) long and 3 km (2 miles) wide. The attractions of these islands include the austere landscape crisscrossed with dry-stone walls, stunning coastal views and several large prehistoric stone forts. In the 5th century, St. Enda brought Christianity to the islands, starting a long monastic tradition. Protected for centuries by their isolated position, the islands today are a bastion of traditional Irish culture. Farming, fishing and tourism are the main occupations of the islanders.

**Looking over the cliff edge at Dún Aonghasa**

**Clochán na Carraige** is a large, well-preserved beehive hut *(see p19)*, probably built by early Christian settlers on the islands.

The Seven Churches
*(Na Seacht dTeampaill)*

Clochán na Carraige

Dún Eoghanachta

**Dún Eoghanachta** is a 1st-century BC circular stone fort with a single wall terraced on the inside.

Dun Aengus
*(Dún Aonghasa)*

KILMURVY
*(Cill Mhuirbhi*

I N I S H M O R E

## Na Seacht dTeampaill

*The so-called Seven Churches make up a monastic settlement dedicated to St. Brecan. Built between the 9th and 15th centuries, some are probably domestic buildings.*

## ★ Dún Aonghasa

*This Iron or Bronze Age promontory fort (see p18), has four concentric stone walls. It is also protected by a chevaux de frise, a ring of razor-sharp, pointed stone stakes.*

---

## ARAN TRADITIONS

**Colorful Aran costume**

The islands are famous for their distinctive knitwear *(see p324)* and for the traditional Aran costume that is still worn; for women this consists of a red flannel skirt and crocheted shawl; for men it includes a sleeveless tweed jacket and a colorful knitted belt. From time to time you also see a *currach* or low rowing boat, the principal form of transportation for centuries. Landmaking, the ancient and arduous process of creating soil by covering bare rock with sand and seaweed, continues to this day.

**Currach made from canvas coated in tar**

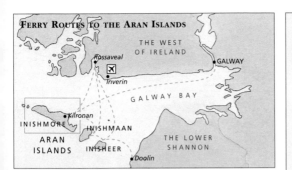

THE WEST OF IRELAND

Rossaveal

GALWAY

Inverin

GALWAY BAY

Kilronan

INISHMORE

INISHMAAN

ARAN ISLANDS

INISHEER

THE LOWER SHANNON

Doolin

## VISITORS' CHECKLIST

**Road map** A4, B4. Co Galway.
🏠 *1,500.* ✈ *from Connemara Airport, Inverin (091 93034).*
⛴ *from Rossaveal:* **Island Ferries** *(091 61767),* **Aran Ferries** *(091 68903); from Galway:* **O'Brien Shipping** *(091 67676), Aran Ferries; from Doolin:* **Doolin Ferry Company** *(065 74455). Ferries depart at least once daily in winter, several times daily in summer; some go to all three main islands. Call for details. Cars cannot be taken to the islands. From Kilronan, you can rent bicycles and jaunting cars, or go on minibus tours (099 61169).* ℹ *May–Sep: Kilronan, Inishmore (099 61263).* **Aran Heritage Centre** *Kilronan.* ☎ *099 61355.* 🕐 *Jun–Sep: 10am–7pm daily; Apr, May & Oct: 11am–5pm daily.* 📷 ♿ 🎁

### Kilmurvy Beach

*The attractive sandy beach east of Kilmurvy offers safe swimming in a sheltered cove. The town itself is a quiet place to stay near a number of the island's most important sights.*

**Teampall Chiaráin**, dedicated to St. Ciaran, is a ruined 12th-century church with striking doorways. Nearby are several stones inscribed with crosses.

Teampall Chiaráin

Dún Eochla

KILRONAN (Cill Rónáin)

Dún Duchathair

I n i s

M ó r

**Dún Eochla** is a circular Bronze Age fort standing close to the highest point on Inishmore.

### KEY

━━ Main road

━━ Minor road

--- Track

▦ Beach

✈ Airport

⛴ Ferry service

ℹ Tourist information

⚟ Viewpoint

0 kilometers    2

0 miles    1

### ★ Kilronan

*The Aran Islands' main port is a busy place, with jaunting cars (ponies and two-wheeled carts) and minibuses waiting by the pier to give island tours; bicycles can also be rented. Nearby, the Aran Heritage Centre is dedicated to the disappearing Aran way of life.*

### ★ Dún Duchathair

*Built on a headland, this Iron Age construction is known as the Black Fort. It has drystone ramparts.*

## STAR SIGHTS

★ Kilronan

★ Dún Aonghasa

★ Dún Duchathair

Farmer on Inishmore, largest of the Aran Islands ▷

**East wall and gatehouse at Roscommon Castle**

# Turoe Stone ㉑

**Road map** B4. Turoe, Bullaun, Loughrea, Co Galway. [C] *0905 42140.* [O] *Apr–Oct: daily; Nov–Mar: groups by appt.* 🖾 🕭

THE TUROE STONE stands at the center of a large area of parkland, the Turoe Pet Farm and Leisure Park, near the village of Bullaun (on the R350). The white granite boulder, which stands about 1 m (3 ft) high, dates back to the 3rd or 2nd century BC. Its top half is carved with curvilinear designs in a graceful Celtic style, known as La Tène, also found in Celtic parts of Europe, particularly Brittany. The lower half has a smooth section and a band of step-pattern carving. The stone was originally found at an Iron Age ring fort nearby, and is thought to have been used there in fertility rituals.

The park around the Turoe Stone is designed mainly for children. The Pet Farm has some small fields containing farm animals and a pond with several varieties of ducks and geese. There is also a wooded

**The Celtic Turoe Stone carved with graceful swirling patterns**

riverside walk (wear heavy shoes or hiking boots – it's often muddy), a picnic area, tea rooms and a playground.

# Roscommon ㉒

**Road map** C3. Co Roscommon. 🕭 *3,500.* 🚆 🚌 🚏 *Jun–Sep: Harrison Hall (0903 26342).* 🗓 *Fri.*

THE COUNTY CAPITAL is a busy market town with various sights. In Main Street is the former jail, celebrated for having a woman as its last executioner. "Lady Betty," as she came to be known, was sentenced to death for the murder of her son in 1780, but negotiated a pardon by agreeing to become a hangwoman. She continued for 30 years.

South of the town center, just off Abbey Street, is the **Dominican Friary**, founded in 1253 by Felim O'Conor, King of Connaught. Set in the north wall of the choir is a late 13th-century effigy of the founder.

**Roscommon Castle**, an Anglo-Norman fortress north of the town, was built in 1269 by Robert d'Ufford, Lord Justice of Ireland, and rebuilt 11 years later after being destroyed by the Irish led by Hugh O'Conor, King of Connaught. The rectangular castle has 16th-century mullioned windows.

# Clonalis House ㉓

**Road map** B3. Castlerea, Co Roscommon. [C] *0907 20014.* [O] *Jun–mid-Sep: Tue–Sun.* 🖾 🕭 *ground floor.*

THIS VICTORIAN manor just outside Castlerea is the ancestral home of the O'Conors, the last High Kings of Ireland

and Kings of Connaught. This old Gaelic family can trace its heritage back 1,500 years. The ruins of their gabled 17th-century home are visible on the grounds. On the lawn lies the O'Conor inauguration stone, dating from 90 BC.

The interior includes a Venetian hallway, a library of many books and documents recording Irish history, a tiny private chapel and a gallery of family portraits spanning 500 years. In the billiard room is the harp once played by Turlough O'Carolan (1670– 1738), blind harpist and last of the Gaelic bards *(see p22)*.

# Strokestown Park House ㉔

**Road map** C3. Strokestown, Co Roscommon. 🏠 **House and Museum** [C] *078 33013.* [O] *May– Sep: Tue–Sun.* 🖾 🕭 *museum only.*

STROKESTOWN PARK HOUSE, the greatest Palladian mansion in County Roscommon, was built in the 1730s for Thomas Mahon, an MP whose family was granted the lands by Charles II after the Restoration. It incorporates an earlier 17th-century tower house *(see p18)*. The design of the new house owes most to Richard Castle, architect of Russborough *(see p124)*. The galleried kitchen, paneled stairwell and groin-vaulted stables are undoubtedly his work, tailoring Palladian principles to the requirements of the Anglo-Irish gentry.

The house stayed in the family's hands until 1979, when major restoration began. In its heyday, the estate encompassed ornamental parkland, a deer park, folly, mausoleum and the town of

Roscommon itself. By 1979, the estate's original 12,000 ha (30,000 acres) had dwindled to 120 ha (300 acres), but recent replanting restores a sense of spaciousness. The original decor and furnishings of the house are intact.

Set in the stable yards, the **Famine Museum** commemorates the 1840s Famine. During the crisis, landlords divided into two camps: the charitable, some of whom started up Famine Relief schemes, and the callous, like the Mahons of Strokestown. Major Denis Mahon, landlord in the 1840s, was murdered after forcing two-thirds of the starving peasantry off his land by a combination of eviction and assisted passages in "coffin ships" to North America. The exhibition uses the Strokestown archives to tell the story of tenants and landlords during the Famine. A section deals with continuing famine and malnutrition worldwide.

## Boyle ㉕

**Road map** C3. Co Roscommon.
🚌 *2,200.* 🚍 🛈 *Jun–mid-Sep:*
*The Courthouse, Market Street (079 62145).* 🚍 *Fri.*

COUNTY ROSCOMMON'S most charming town, Boyle is blessed with fine Georgian and medieval architecture. **Boyle Abbey** is a well-preserved Cistercian abbey founded in 1161 as a sister house to Mellifont in County Louth *(see p237).* It survived raids by Anglo-Norman barons and Irish chieftains, as well as the 1539 suppression of the

### THE GREAT FAMINE

The failure of the Irish potato crop in 1845, 1846 and 1848, due to potato blight, had disastrous consequences for the people of Ireland, many of whom relied on this staple crop. More than a million died of starvation and disease, and by 1856 over two and a half million had been forced to emigrate. The crisis was worsened by unsympathetic landlords who often continued collecting rents. The Famine had far-reaching effects: mass emigration became a way of life *(see pp40–41)* and many rural communities, particularly in the far west, were decimated.

**Peasants lining up for soup during the Famine (1847)**

monasteries. In 1659 it was turned into a castle. The abbey is still remarkably intact, with a church, cloisters, cellars, sacristy and even kitchens. The nave of the church has both Romanesque and Gothic arches and there are well-preserved 12th-century capitals. The visitors' center is housed in the old gatehouse.

The **Kings of Connaught Interpretative Centre** covers the history of Boyle and the Connaught chieftains. It is in King House, a Palladian mansion and the ancestral home of the Anglo-Irish King family, later Earls of Kingston.

**ⓐ Boyle Abbey**
⭘ *mid-May–Oct: daily.* 🏷

**Carved capital in the nave at Boyle Abbey**

**🏛 Kings of Connaught Interpretative Centre**
King House, Main St. 🕿 *079 63242.*
⭘ *May–Sep: Tue–Sun; Apr & Oct: Sat & Sun.* 🏷

**ENVIRONS:** Lough Key is often called the loveliest lake in Ireland. The island-studded lake and surrounding woodland make a glorious setting for the **Lough Key Forest Park**. The 320-ha (790-acre) park formed part of the Rockingham estate until 1957. In that year Rockingham House, a John Nash design, burned down, but farm buildings and estate houses remain. The extensive woods were added by 18th-century landlords. Other features of the park include nature trails, an observation tower, a 17th-century ice house, a deer enclosure and, by the lake, a 17th-century gazebo known as the Temple. The park also has several ring forts *(see p18).* From the jetty, cruisers ply the Boyle River. A river bus visits Church and Trinity Islands, which both contain medieval ruins, and Castle Island, which has a 19th-century folly.

**🐾 Lough Key Forest Park**
N4 8 km (5 miles) E of Boyle.
⭘ *daily.* 🏷 *Easter–Sep.* ♿

**The gatehouse and remains of the nave at Boyle Abbey**

# NORTHWEST IRELAND

## DONEGAL · SLIGO · LEITRIM

**T**OWERING CLIFFS, *deserted golden beaches and rocky headlands abound along the rugged coast of Donegal, which incorporates some of Ireland's wildest scenery. To the south, Sligo is steeped in prehistory and Celtic myth, with its legacy of ancient monuments and natural beauty enriched by associations with the poet, WB Yeats. By contrast, Leitrim is a quiet county of unruffled lakes and waterways.*

In Celtic mythology Sligo was the power base of the warrior Queen Maeve of Connaught *(see p24)*, and the county's legacy of prehistoric sites shows that the area was heavily populated in Celtic times. Later, however, both County Sligo and neighboring County Leitrim often seemed to be little affected by events taking place in the rest of Ireland. The Normans, for example, barely disturbed the rule of local Gaelic clans.

Donegal, on the other hand, was part of Ulster until 1921 and played an active role in that province's history. The O'Donnells held sway over most of Donegal in the Middle Ages, but they fled to Europe in 1607 following their ill-fated stand against the English alongside the O'Neills *(see p247)*. Protestant settlers moved onto land confiscated from the two clans, but they left much of Donegal and its poor soil to the native Irish, who lived there in isolation from the rest of Ulster. This remote corner of the province remained largely Catholic and, at the time of Partition in 1921, Donegal was excluded from the new Protestant Northern Ireland.

County Donegal has little in common with its neighbors in the Republic, either geographically or historically. It is one of the most remote parts of Ireland, and it is no coincidence that Donegal boasts the country's largest number of Gaelic speakers.

While the beauty of Donegal lies mainly along the coast, Sligo's finest landscapes are found inland, around Lough Gill and among the sparsely populated Bricklieve Mountains.

The 19th-century interior of Hargadon's bar in Sligo town, with its original counter and stout jars

w across to Falcarragh from Bloody Foreland in County Donegal

# Exploring Northwest Ireland

THE SUPREME APPEAL of Donegal lies in the natural beauty of its coast, with windswept peninsulas, precipitous cliffs and a host of golden beaches. There is a scattering of small seaside resorts that make good bases, and Donegal town is well placed for exploring the southern part of the county. The cultural heartland of the Northwest lies in and around Sligo, the only size-able town in the region, from where you can reach several prehistoric remains and other historic sights. Farther south, lovely scenery surrounds Lough Gill and the more remote Lough Arrow. In Leitrim, a county of lakes and rivers, the main center of activity is the lively boating resort of Carrick-on-Shannon.

**Procession during the Mary of Dunloe beauty contest in July**

## SEE ALSO

- *Where to Stay pp297–8*

- *Restaurants, Cafés and Pubs* pp314–15 & p321

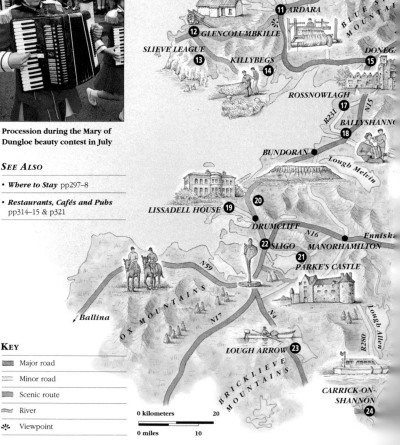

TORY ISLAND ①

BLOODY FORELAND
HORN HE
② R257 DUNFANAG

BUNBEG

③

ARANMORE ISLAND  THE ROSSES ⑩
BURTONPORT
DUNGLOE

DERRYVEAG
MOUNTAIN
N56

R253

ARDARA ⑪
BLUE STA
MOUNTAIN

GLENCOLUMBKILLE ⑫
SLIEVE LEAGUE
⑬   KILLYBEGS ⑭
DONEGA ⑮

ROSSNOWLAGH ⑰
R231 N15
BALLYSHANNO
⑱

BUNDORAN  Lough Melvin

LISSADELL HOUSE ⑲
⑳
DRUMCLIFF N16 Enniski
⑫ SLIGO MANORHAMILTON
⑳ PARKE'S CASTLE

N59
OX MOUNTAINS
N17
Ballina
N4
Lough Allen
R280

LOUGH ARROW ㉓
BRICKLIEVE MOUNTAINS

CARRICK-ON-SHANNON ㉔

## KEY

| | |
|---|---|
| ▬▬ | Major road |
| ═══ | Minor road |
| ▬▬ | Scenic route |
| ≈≈ | River |
| ✸ | Viewpoint |

0 kilometers                    20

0 miles            10

CARNDONAGH

BUNCRANA

INISHOWEN PENINSULA

RATHMELTON

ACRENAN

GRIANÁN OF AILEACH

LETTERKENNY

N15

FANAD PENINSULA

Lough Swilly

R240

R238

Foyle

N13

N56

## GETTING AROUND

The N56, linking Letterkenny and Donegal, provides access to much of the Northwest's best scenery, with minor roads branching off it around the coast's rocky peninsulas. A few buses serve this route, but traveling around without a car is easier farther south, with buses running daily from Donegal along the N15 to Sligo via Ballyshannon. The rail network barely reaches the Northwest, though there are daily trains between Sligo and Carrick-on-Shannon.

**Thatched cottage near Malin Head on Inishowen Peninsula**

## SIGHTS AT A GLANCE

Ardara **11**
Ballyshannon **18**
Bloody Foreland **2**
Carrick-on-Shannon **24**
Derryveagh Mountains **3**
Donegal **15**
Fanad Peninsula **6**
Glencolumbkille **12**
Grianán of Aileach **8**
Horn Head **4**
Killybegs **14**
Letterkenny **9**
Lissadell House **19**
Lough Arrow **23**

Lough Derg **16**
Lough Rynn Estate **25**
Parke's Castle **21**
Rosguill Peninsula **5**
The Rosses **10**
Rossnowlagh **17**
Slieve League **13**
Sligo **22**
Tory Island **1**

**Tours**
Inishowen Peninsula **7**
Yeats Country **20**

OUGH DERG

TTIGO

R202

erne Waterway

RYNN ESTATE

rd

**View from Carrowkeel Bronze Age cemetery above Lough Arrow**

**Quartzite cone of Errigal, the highest of the Derryveagh Mountains**

# Tory Island ❶

**Road map** C1. Co Donegal. 🏠 140.
🚢 from Magheraroarty Pier near Gortahork (074 35061) and Bunbeg (075 31991): daily in summer, weather permitting in winter.

THE TURBULENT Tory Sound separates this windswept island from the northwestern corner of mainland Donegal. Given that rough weather can cut off the tiny island for days, it is not surprising that Tory's inhabitants have developed a strong sense of independence. Most of the islanders speak Gaelic and they even have their own monarch: the powers of this nonhereditary position are minimal, but the current incumbent is heavily involved in promoting the interests of his "subjects" and in attracting visitors to the island.

During the 1970s, the Irish government tried to resettle most of the islanders on the mainland, but they refused to move. Their campaign of resistance was led by Tory's school of Primitive artists. The school emerged after 1968, inspired by a local man, James Dixon, who claimed he could do better than a visiting English painter, Derek Hill. Since then, the school of artists has drawn a growing number of tourists; the new **Dixon Gallery** opened recently in the main village of West Town.

There are ruins of a monastery founded by St. Columba (see p32) nearby, or else you can explore the island's dramatic cliffs and seabird rookeries.

🏛 **Dixon Gallery**
West Town. 🕿 074 35011.
🕐 May–Sep: daily.

# Bloody Foreland ❷

**Road map** C1. Co Donegal. 🚌 to Bunbeg from Letterkenny or Dungloe.

BLOODY FORELAND, which gets its name from the rubescent glow of the rocks at sunset, boasts magnificent scenery. The R257 road skirts the coast around the headland, providing lovely views. The most scenic viewpoint is on the north coast and looks across to the cliffs of nearby offshore islands, including Tory. A short distance farther south, the tiny village of **Bunbeg** has a pretty harbor, but elsewhere the rocky landscape is spoiled by a blanket of vacation bungalows.

# Derryveagh Mountains ❸

**Road map** C1. Co Donegal.

THE WILD BEAUTY of these mountains provides one of the high spots of a visit to Donegal. Errigal Mountain, the range's tallest peak at 751 m (2,466 ft), attracts avid hikers, but the cream of the mountain scenery lies within **Glenveagh National Park**. Covering nearly 10,000 ha (25,000 acres), this takes in the beautiful valley occupied by Lough Veagh and Poisoned Glen, a marshy valley enclosed by dramatic cliffs. The park also protects the largest herd of red deer in the country.

**Glenveagh Castle** stands on the southern shores of Lough Veagh, near the visitors' center. This splendid granite building was constructed in 1870 by John Adair, notorious for his eviction of many families from the area after the Famine (see p211). The castle was given to the nation in the 1970s by its last owner, a wealthy art dealer from Pennsylvania.

Minibuses whisk you up the private road to the castle from the visitors' center. You can go on a guided tour of the sumptuous interior or just stroll

**Glenveagh Castle overlooking Lough Veagh**

**Looking across to Dunfanaghy, gateway to the Horn Head peninsula**

through the formal gardens and rhododendron woods. Trails weave all around the castle grounds; one path climbs steeply to reward you with a lovely view over Lough Veagh.

**Glebe House and Gallery** overlooks Lough Gartan 6 km (4 miles) south of the visitors' center. This modest Regency mansion was the home of the painter and enthusiastic collector, Derek Hill. The house reveals his varied tastes, with William Morris wallpapers, Islamic ceramics and paintings by Tory Island artists. The gallery contains works by Picasso, Renoir and Jack B Yeats among others.

**Fountain at Glenveagh**

The **Colmcille Heritage Centre**, a short distance south, uses stained glass and illuminated manuscripts to trace the life of St. Columba (Colmcille in Gaelic), who was born in nearby Church Hill in AD 521 (*see p32*). A flagstone in the village is said to mark the site of the saint's birthplace.

🌿 **Glenveagh National Park and Castle**
Off R251, 16 km (10 miles) N of Church Hill. 📞 074 37090. **Park** ☐ daily. **Castle** ☐ Easter–Oct: daily. 🞳 🞳 🞳 limited.
🏛 **Glebe House and Gallery**
📞 074 37071. ☐ Easter & May–Sep: Sat–Thu. 🞳 🞳 limited.
🏛 **Colmcille Heritage Centre**
📞 074 37306. ☐ Easter & May–Sep: daily. 🞳

## Horn Head ❹

**Road map** C1. Co Donegal. 🚌 to Dunfanaghy from Letterkenny.
ℹ️ The Workhouse, Dunfanaghy (074 36540).

CARPETED IN HEATHER and rich in birdlife, Horn Head is the most scenic of the northern Donegal headlands. It rises 180 m (600 ft) straight out of the Atlantic and gives lovely views out to sea and inland toward the mountains. The appeal of the area is enhanced by **Dunfanaghy**, a delightful town with an air of affluence and Protestantism unusual in this area. The local beach, **Killahoey Strand**, offers excellent swimming.

## Rosguill Peninsula ❺

**Road map** C1. Co Donegal.

ROSGUILL PENINSULA juts out into the Atlantic Ocean between Sheephaven and Mulroy bays. The simplest way to see it is to follow the 11-km (7-mile) Atlantic Drive, a circular route that skirts the clifftops at the tip of the headland.

**Doe Castle**, 5 km (3 miles) north of Creeslough village, is worth a visit as much for its setting on a promontory overlooking Sheephaven Bay as for its architectural or historical interest. Even so, it is still a substantial ruin – the remains of a castle erected in the 16th century by the MacSweeneys, a family of Scottish mercenaries.

## Fanad Peninsula ❻

**Road map** C1. Co Donegal. 🚌 to Rathmelton & Portsalon from Letterkenny.

A PANORAMIC ROUTE winds between the hilly spine and rugged coast of this tranquil peninsula. The eastern side is by far the most enjoyable and begins at **Rathmelton,** a charming Plantation town founded in the 17th century. Elegant Georgian homes and handsome old warehouses flank its tree-lined Main Street.

Farther north, **Portsalon** offers safe swimming and great views from nearby Saldanha Head. Near **Doaghbeg**, on the way to Fanad Head in the far north, the cliffs have been eroded into arches and other dramatic shapes.

**Doe Castle on Rosguill Peninsula, with its 16th-century battlements**

# A Tour of the Inishowen Peninsula ❼

INISHOWEN, THE LARGEST of Donegal's northern peninsulas, is an area laden with history, from early Christian relics to strategically positioned castles and forts. The most rugged scenery lies in the west and north, around the the steep rock-strewn landscape of the Gap of Mamore and the spectacular cape of Malin Head, the northernmost point in Ireland. Numerous beaches dot the coastline and cater to all tastes, from the remote Isle of Doagh to the busy family resort of Buncrana. From the shores, there are views to Donegal's Derryveagh Mountains in the west and the Northern Ireland coast in the east. The Inishowen Peninsula can be explored by car as a leisurely day trip.

**Tower on Banba's Crown, Malin Head**

**Carndonagh Cross** ④
This 7th-century early Christian cross is carved with human figures and interlacing lines.

**Gap of Mamore** ③
The road between Mamore Hill and the Urris Hills is 250 m (820 ft) above sea level and offers panoramic views.

**Dunree Head** ②
On the headland, Dunree Fort overlooks Lough Swilly. It was built in 1798 to counter the threat of French invasion. Since 1986, it has been a military museum.

**Buncrana** ①
Buncrana has 5 km (3 miles) of sandy beaches and two castles. Buncrana Castle was rebuilt in 1718 and the intact keep of O'Doherty Castle dates from Norman times.

### KEY

| | |
|---|---|
| ▬▬ | Tour route |
| ═══ | Other roads |
| ☀ | Viewpoint |

**Shores of Lough Swilly near Dunree Fort**

**Grianán of Aileach** ⑦
At the neck of the Inishowen Peninsula, perched on a hilltop, stands this formidable circular stone fort. The solid structure that can be seen today is the result of extensive restoration in the 1870s.

## Tips for Drivers

**Tour length:** *157 km (98 miles).*
**Stopping points:** *Malin, Greencastle and Carndonagh all have pubs and eating places; picnic sites are dotted around the coast. The Guns of Dunree Military Museum has a café. There is a 3 km (1.5 mile) scenic walk between Moville and Greencastle. (See also pp355–7.)*

Enjoying the views from the ramparts of the Grianán of Aileach

### Malin Head ⑤

This traditional cottage makes a good stop for tea after enjoying the superb Atlantic views from Malin Head. At the highest point, Banba's Crown, stands a tower built in 1805 to monitor shipping.

R241 ⑥ Inishowen Head

### Greencastle ⑥

A resort and fishing port, Greencastle is named after the overgrown castle ruins just outside town. Built in 1305 by Richard de Burgo, Earl of Ulster, the castle guarded the entrance to Lough Foyle.

| 0 kilometers | 5 |
| 0 miles | 5 |

# Grianán of Aileach ⑧

**Road map** C1. Co Donegal. 🚌 *from Letterkenny or Londonderry.*
🛈 *Burt (077 68512).*

DONEGAL'S most impressive and intriguing ancient monument stands just 10 km (6 miles) west of Londonderry *(see pp250–51)* at the entrance to the Inishowen Peninsula. Overlooking Lough Swilly and Lough Foyle, the circular stone structure, measuring 23 m (77 ft) in diameter, is believed to have been built as a pagan temple around the 5th century BC, although the site was probably a place of worship before this date. Later, Christians adopted the fort: St. Patrick is said to have baptized Owen, founder of the O'Neill dynasty, here in AD 450. The fort became the royal residence of the O'Neills, but was damaged in the 12th century by the army of Murtagh O'Brien, King of Munster.

The fort was restored in the 1870s. Two doorways lead from the outside through 4-m (13-ft) thick defenses into a grassy arena ringed by three terraces. The most memorable feature of the fort, however, is its magnificent vantage point, which affords stunning views in every direction.

At the foot of the hill stands an attractive church, dedicated to St. Aengus and built in 1967. Its circular design echoes that of the Grianán.

# Letterkenny ⑨

**Road map** C1. Co Donegal. 🚶 *7,100.*
🚌 🛈 *Derry Rd (074 21160).*

STRADDLING the river Swilly, with the Sperrin Mountains to the east and the Derryveagh Mountains *(see pp216–17)* to the west, Letterkenny is Donegal's largest town. It is also the region's main business center, a role it took over from Londonderry after partition in 1921. The likeable town makes a good base from which to explore the northern coast of Donegal and, for anglers, is well placed for access to the waters of Lough Swilly.

Letterkenny has one of the longest main streets in Ireland, which is dominated by the 65-m (215-ft) steeple of **St. Eunan's Cathedral.** A Neo-Gothic creation built in the late 19th century, it contains Celtic-style stonework, a rich marble altar and vivid stained-glass windows. The **County Museum** is small but has informative displays on local history and a collection of archaeological artifacts found in Donegal, some of them dating from the Iron Age.

Every August, the center of Letterkenny is taken over for four days by the International Folk Festival, when traditional and folk musicians play in the bars and hotels, and dancing competitions are held.

### 🏛 County Museum

High Rd. 🖀 *074 24613.* 🕐 *Tue–Sat.* ⬤ *10 days at Christmas and public hols.* ♿

The imposing spire of St. Eunan's Cathedral in Letterkenny

Isolated cottage near Burtonport in the Rosses

# The Rosses ⑩

**Road map** C1. Co Donegal. 🚌 *to Dungloe or Burtonport from Letterkenny.* ℹ️ *Jun–Sep: Main St, Dungloe (075 21297).* ⛴️ *to Aranmore from Burtonport (075 20532).*

A ROCKY HEADLAND dotted with more than 100 lakes, the Rosses is one of the most picturesque and unspoiled corners of Donegal. It is also a strong Gaeltacht area, with many Gaelic-speaking people.

The hub of the Rosses, at the southern end of the headland, is **Dungloe**, a bustling market town and major fishing center.

**ENVIRONS:** There is a glorious sheltered beach 8 km (5 miles) west of Dungloe at **Maghery Bay**. From here you can also walk to nearby **Crohy Head**, known for its caves, arches and unusual cliff formations. From Burtonport, 8 km (5 miles)

north of Dungloe, car ferries sail daily to Donegal's largest island, **Aranmore**. This rugged place is ideal for clifftop walks, particularly in the northwest, and from the south coast you can enjoy fine views across to the Rosses. Most of Aranmore's population of 1,000 lives in Leabgarrow. The village's thriving pub culture is due partly to lax licensing laws.

# Ardara ⑪

**Road map** C2. Co Donegal. 🚶 *700.* 🚌 *from Killybegs or Donegal.* ℹ️ *Easter–Sep: Heritage Centre, The Diamond (075 41704).*

THE TOWN of Ardara is the weaving capital of Donegal and it has a proliferation of shops selling locally made tweeds and hand-knitted sweaters. Some larger stores put on displays of hand-loom

weaving. There is not much to Ardara otherwise, but it is a tidy place whose main street is lined with pubs much loved for their fiddle sessions.

**ENVIRONS:** There is superb scenery between Ardara and **Loughros Point**, 10 km (6 miles) west of the town: the drive along the narrow peninsula provides dramatic coastal views. Another picturesque route runs southwest from Ardara to Glencolumbkille, going over **Glengesh Pass**, a series of bends through a wild, deserted landscape.

Hand-loom worker in Ardara

# Glencolumbkille ⑫

**Road map** B2. Co Donegal. 🚶 *260.* 🚌 *from Killybegs.* ℹ️ *Donegal (073 21148).*

GLENCOLUMBKILLE, a quiet, grassy valley scattered with brightly colored cottages, feels very much like a backwater, in spite of the sizable number of visitors who come here.

The "Glen of St. Colmcille" is a popular place of pilgrimage due to its associations with the saint more commonly known as St. Columba. Just north of the valley's main village of Cashel, on the way to Glen Head, there is a tiny church where St. Columba worshiped. It is said that between prayers the saint slept on the two stone slabs still visible in one corner.

Another attraction here is the **Folk Village Museum**, which depicts rural Donegal lifestyles through the ages. It was started in the 1950s by a local priest called Father James

Old irons at the Folk Village Museum in Glencolumbkille

**Slieve League, the highest sea cliffs in Europe**

MacDyer. Concerned about the high rate of emigration from this poor region, he sought to provide jobs and a sense of regional pride, partly by encouraging people to set up craft cooperatives. The Folk Village shop sells local wares, and has a good stock of wine – made of anything from seaweed to fuchsias.

There is plenty to explore in the valley, which is littered with cairns, dolmens and other ancient monuments. The nearby coast is lovely too, the best walks taking you west across the grassy foreland of **Malinbeg**. Beyond the small resort of Malin More, steps drop down to an idyllic sandy cove hemmed in by cliffs.

🏛 **Folk Village Museum**
Cashel. 🔲 073 30017. ◯ Easter & May–Sep: daily. 🌐 🎫

## Slieve League ⓭

**Road map** B2. Co Donegal. 🚌 to Carrick from Glencolumbkille or Killybegs.

Tʜᴇ ʜɪɢʜᴇsᴛ cliff face in Europe, Slieve League is spectacular not just for its sheer elevation but also for its color: at sunset the rock is streaked with changing shades of red, amber and ocher. The 8-km (5-mile) drive to the eastern end of Slieve League from **Carrick** is bumpy but well worth enduring. Beyond Teelin, the road becomes a

series of alarming switchbacks before reaching **Bunglass Point** and Amharc Mor, the "good view." From here, you can see the whole of Slieve League, its sheer cliffs rising dramatically out of the ocean.

Only experienced hikers should attempt the treacherous ledges of **One Man's Pass**. This is part of a trail which climbs westward out of Teelin and up to the highest point of Slieve League – from where you can admire the Atlantic Ocean shimmering 598 m (1,972 ft) below. The path then continues on to Malinbeg, 16 km (10 miles) west. During the summer, for a less strenuous but safer and equally rewarding excursion, pay a boat-owner from Teelin to take you out to see Slieve League from the sea.

## Killybegs ⓮

**Road map** C2. Co Donegal. 🚶 1,700. 🚌 from Donegal. ℹ️ Donegal (073 21148).

Nᴀʀʀᴏᴡ ᴡɪɴᴅɪɴɢ streets give Killybegs a timeless feel, which contrasts sharply with the industriousness of this small town. The sense of prosperity stems in part from the manufacture of the Donegal carpets for which the town is famous, and which adorn Dublin Castle (see pp74–5) and other palaces around the world.

Killybegs is one of Ireland's busiest fishing ports and the quays are well worth seeing when the trawlers arrive to unload their catch: gulls squawk overhead and the smell of fish fills the air. Trawlermen come from far and wide – so do not be surprised if you hear Eastern European voices as you wander around the town.

**Trawler crew in Killybegs relaxing after unloading their catch**

## Tʜᴇ Iʀɪsʜ Gᴀᴇʟᴛᴀᴄʜᴛs

The term "Gaeltacht" refers to Gaelic-speaking areas of Ireland. Up to the 16th century, virtually the entire population

**Gaelic pub sign in Gaeltacht region**

spoke the native tongue. British rule, however, undermined Irish culture, and the Famine (see p211) drained the country of many of its Gaelic-speakers. The use of the local language has fallen steadily since. Even so, in the Gaeltachts 75 percent of the people still speak it, and road signs are exclusively in Irish – unlike most other parts of Ireland.

The Donegal Gaeltacht stretches almost unbroken along the coast from Fanad Head to Slieve League and boasts the largest number of Irish-speakers in the country. Ireland's other principal Gaeltachts are in Galway and Kerry.

Donegal town, overlooked by the ruins of its 15th-century castle

8 km (5 miles) north of the border village of Pettigo. The island is completely covered by a religious complex, which includes a basilica, built in 1921, and hostels for pilgrims.

The pilgrimage season runs from June to mid-August. People spend three days on the island, eating just one meal of dry bread and black tea per day. Although only pilgrims can visit Station Island, it is interesting to go to the jetty to savor the atmosphere and get a good view of the basilica near the shore.

## Donegal ⓯

**Road map** C2. Co Donegal. 🏃 *2,300.* 🚌 ℹ️ *Kiosk, Quay St (073 21148).*

DONEGAL MEANS "Fort of the Foreigners," after the Vikings who built a garrison here. However, it was under the O'Donnells that the town began to take shape. The ruins of **Donegal Castle** in the town center incorporate the gabled tower of a fortified house built by the family in the 15th century. The adjoining house and most other features are Jacobean – added by Sir Basil Brooke, who moved in after the O'Donnells were ousted by the English in 1607 *(see pp36–7)*. The castle has recently been partly restored.

Brooke was also responsible for laying out the market square, which is known as the **Diamond**. An obelisk in the center commemorates four Franciscans who wrote the *Annals of the Four Masters* in the 1630s. This manuscript traces the history of the Gaelic people from 40 days before the Great Flood up to the end of the 16th century. Part of it was written at **Donegal Abbey**, south of the market square along the River Eske. Built in 1474, little now remains of the abbey but a few Gothic

windows and cloister arches. About 1.5 km (1 mile) farther on is **Donegal Craft Village**, a showcase for the work of local craftspeople.

While there is not a huge amount to explore in Donegal town, it has some pleasant hotels *(see p298)* and makes a good base for exploring the southern part of the county.

⚓ **Donegal Castle**
Tirchonaill St. 📞 *073 22405.* ⭘ *mid-Jun–Sep: daily.* 🚫 🚹 *limited.*

⭘ **Donegal Craft Village**
Ballyshannon Rd. ⭘ *May–Sep: daily.* 🚹 *limited.*

## Lough Derg ⓰

**Road map** C2. Co Donegal. 🚤 *Jun–mid-Aug (pilgrims only).* 🚌 *to Pettigo from Donegal.*

PILGRIMS HAVE made their way to Lough Derg ever since St. Patrick spent 40 days praying on one of the lake's islands in an attempt to rid Ireland of all evil spirits. The Pilgrimage of St. Patrick's Purgatory began in around 1150 and still attracts thousands of Catholics every summer. Their destination is the tiny **Station Island**, close to Lough Derg's southern shore and reached by boat from a jetty

## Rossnowlagh ⓱

**Road map** C2. Co Donegal. 🏃 *55.* 🚌 *from Bundoran & Donegal.* ℹ️ *May–mid-Sep: Main St, Bundoran (072 41350).*

Vacationers enjoying the fine sandy beach at Rossnowlagh

AT ROSSNOWLAGH, Atlantic waves break on to one of Ireland's finest beaches, drawing crowds of both bathers and surfers to this tiny place. Even so, the village remains far more peaceful than the resort of Bundoran, 14 km (9 miles) south. The cliffs at Rossnowlagh provide opportunity for exhilarating coastal walks. Away from the sea, you can visit the **Donegal Historical Society Museum**, housed in a striking Franciscan friary

Basilica on Station Island viewed from the shores of Lough Derg

**Lissadell House dining room with Gore-Booth family portraits**

built in the 1950s. The tiny but fascinating collection includes displays of Stone Age flints, Irish musical instruments and other local artifacts.

Rossnowlagh never fails to make the news on July 12, when it hosts the only parade to take place in the Republic by the Protestant organization, the Orange Order *(see p47)*.

🏛 **Donegal Historical Society Museum**
📞 *072 51342.* ⬜ *daily.* ⬤ *Dec 25.*

## Ballyshannon ⑱

**Road map** C2. Co Donegal. 🏠 *2,600.* 🚌 *from Bundoran & Donegal.*

IN BALLYSHANNON, well-kept Georgian homes jostle for space along hilly streets on the banks of the River Erne, near where it flows into Donegal Bay. This is a bustling town, full of character and off the main tourist track – though it gets packed during August's festival of traditional music, which is one of the best of its kind in the country.

The festival apart, Ballyshannon is most famous as the birthplace of poet William Allingham (1824–89), who recalled his home town in the lines "Adieu to Ballyshanny and the winding banks of the Erne." He lies buried in the graveyard of St. Anne's Church, off Main Street. There is a fine view over the river from here: you can see the small island of **Inis Saimer** where, according to legend, Greeks founded the first colony in Ireland after the Great Flood. Beyond, you can glimpse a large Irish Army base; Ballyshannon's position on a steeply rising bluff overlooking the River Erne has always made the town a strategic military site.

About 1.5 km (1 mile) northwest of town lie the scant ruins of **Assaroe Abbey**, founded by Cistercians in 1184. A graveyard with some ancient burial slabs and headstones remains. Nearby, two waterwheels installed by the monks have been restored and incorporated into an interpretive center called the **Water Wheels**. One of the wheels now powers a generator.

**Mural of the family dog in Lissadell's dining room**

🏛 **Water Wheels**
Assaroe Abbey. 📞 *072 51580.* ⬜ *May–Aug: daily; Sep–Apr: Sun pm.*

## Lissadell House ⑲

**Road map** B2. Carney, Co Sligo.
📞 *071 63150.* 🚌 *or* 🚌 *to Sligo.*
⬜ *Jun–mid-Sep: Mon–Sat.* 🎨 ♿

A LATE GEORGIAN mansion built in the 1830s, Lissadell is famous more for its occupants than its architecture. It was once the home of the Gore-Booths who, unlike some of the Anglo-Irish gentry, contributed much to the region. During the Famine *(see p211)*, Sir Robert mortgaged the house to help feed his employees.

The most famous member of the Gore-Booth family was Sir Robert's granddaughter, Constance Markievicz (1868–1927). She was a leading revolutionary who took part in the 1916 Rising *(see pp42–3)* and was the first woman to be elected to the British House of Commons. WB Yeats, a regular visitor to the house, immortalized Constance and her sister, Eva, in one of his poems, describing them as "Two girls in silk kimonos, both beautiful, like a gazelle." The house is still in the hands of the Gore-Booth family.

Built of gray limestone, the exterior of Lissadell House is rather austere. The interior, on the other hand, has an appealing atmosphere of faded grandeur, with peeling paintwork and copious memorabilia of the building's former occupants. The finest rooms are the gallery (previously the music room) and the dining room, which is decorated with extraordinary full-length murals of the Gore-Booth family, their servants and their dog. Painted directly on to the wall, they were the work of Constance's husband, Count Casimir Markievicz.

Both the house and the overgrown estate are slowly being restored. There are plans, for example, to open up the woodland vistas to recreate the sweeping views down to the lake. You can already explore along paths skirting the lakeshore, and there is also a wildlife preserve, which is a popular winter refuge for barnacle geese.

# A Tour of Yeats Country ⑳

**Yeats tour sign**

EVEN FOR PEOPLE unfamiliar with the poetry of WB Yeats, Sligo's engaging landscapes are reason enough to make a pilgrimage. This tour follows a route through varied scenery, taking you past sandy bays and dramatic limestone ridges, through forest and alongside rivers and lakes. The delightful Lough Gill lies at the heart of Yeats country, enclosed by wooded hills crisscrossed by hiking trails. In summer, boats ply the length of the lough, or you can head to one of the northwest's best beaches, at Rosses Point.

**Ben Bulben ⑤**
The eerie silhouette of Ben Bulben rises abruptly out of the plain. You can climb to the top, but go carefully.

**Lissadell House ④**
Yeats was a close friend of the Gore-Booth sisters who lived at Lissadell. You can see the room where the poet slept as a guest (see p223).

**Drumcliff ③**
Although he died in France, in 1948 Yeats's body was laid to rest in Drumcliff churchyard. The ruins of an old monastic site include a fine High Cross.

**Rosses Point ②**
Yeats and his brother used to spend their summers at this pretty resort. It stands at the entrance to Sligo Bay, and a steady flow of boats passes by.

**Sligo ①**
This town is a good place to begin a tour of Yeats country. It has many connections with the poet and his family, whose literary and artistic legacy has helped to inspire Sligo's thriving arts scene (see p226).

## TIPS FOR DRIVERS

**Length:** 88 km (55 miles).
**Stopping-off points:** Outside Sligo, the best choice of eating places is at Rosses Point, although there are good pubs in Drumcliff and Dromahair, and Parke's Castle has a café. Lough Gill provides most choice in terms of picnic spots.
**Boat trips:** Wild Rose Water Bus (071 64266 or 088 598869). (See also pp355–7.)

## KEY

| | |
|---|---|
| ▬▬ | Tour route |
| ═══ | Other roads |
| ⌸ | Boat trips |
| ☀ | Viewpoint |

## WB YEATS AND SLIGO

As a schoolboy in London, Yeats (*see p21*) longed for his native Sligo, and as an adult he often returned here. He lovingly describes the county in his *Reveries over Childhood and Youth*, and the lake-studded landscape haunts his poetry. "In a sense," Yeats said, "Sligo has always been my home," and it is here that he wished to be buried. His gravestone in Drumcliff bears an epitaph he penned himself: "Cast a cold eye on life, on death. Horseman pass by."

**WB Yeats (1865–1939)**

Parke's Castle viewed from across the calm waters of Lough Gill

## Parke's Castle ㉑

**Road map** C2. 6 km (4 miles) N of Dromahair, Co Leitrim. 📞 *071 64149.* 🚌 *or* 🚌 *to Sligo .* ⏰ *Easter–May: Tue–Sun; Jun–Oct: daily.* 🏛 ♿ 🎫

### Glencar Lough ⑥

"There is a waterfall … that all my childhood counted dear," wrote Yeats of the cataract that tumbles into Glencar Lough. A path leads down to it from the road.

### Parke's Castle ⑦

This 17th-century fortified manor house commands a splendid view over the tranquil waters of Lough Gill. It is a starting point for boat trips around the lough.

### Isle of Innisfree ⑧

"There midnight's all a glimmer, and noon a purple glow," is how Yeats once described Innisfree. There is not much to see on this tiny island but it is a romantic spot. In summer, a boatman ferries visitors here.

### Dooney Rock ⑨

A steep path leads from the road to Dooney Rock, from where glorious views extend over the lough to Ben Bulben. Trails weave through the surrounding woods and by the lake.

0 kilometers  3

0 miles  2

Tʜɪs ғᴏʀᴛɪғɪᴇᴅ ᴍᴀɴᴏʀ ʜᴏᴜsᴇ dominates the eastern end of Lough Gill. It was built in 1609 by Captain Robert Parke, an English settler who later became MP for Leitrim. It has been beautifully restored by the Office of Public Works using 17th-century building methods and native Irish oak.

Parke's Castle was erected on the site of a 16th-century tower house belonging to the O'Rourkes, a powerful local clan, and stones from this earlier structure were used in the new building. The original foundations and part of the moat were incorporated, but otherwise Parke's Castle is the epitome of a Plantation manor house (*see p37*). It is protected by a large enclosure or *bawn*, whose sturdy wall includes a gatehouse and two turrets as well as the house itself.

Among the most distinctive architectural features of Parke's Castle are the diamond-shaped chimneys, mullioned windows and the parapets. There is also a curious stone hut, known as the "sweathouse," which was an early Irish sauna. Inside, an exhibition and audiovisual presentation cover Parke's Castle and various historic and prehistoric sites in the area, with photographs and archaeological finds. There is also a working forge.

Boat trips around sights on Lough Gill that are associated with the poet, WB Yeats, leave from outside the castle walls.

Hargadon's bar, one of Sligo town's most famous watering holes

# Sligo ②

**Road map** C2. Co Sligo. 🏃 *18,000.*
🚉 🚌 🛈 *Aras Reddan, Temple St*
*(071 61201).* 🚢 *Fri.*

THE PORT of Sligo sits at the mouth of the Garavogue, sandwiched between the Atlantic and Lough Gill. The largest town in the northwest, it rose to prominence under the Normans, being well placed as a gateway between the provinces of Ulster and Connaught. The appearance of Sligo today is mainly the result of growth during the late 18th and 19th centuries.

Sligo is perfectly situated for touring the striking countryside nearby, and it is also a good center for traditional music. While the town itself can seem rather somber, the quiet back streets are reasonably atmospheric.

Sligo's link with the Yeats family is the main source of the town's appeal. WB Yeats (*see pp224–5*), Ireland's best-known poet, was born into a prominent local family. The Pollexfen warehouse, at the western end of Wine Street, has a rooftop turret from which the poet's grandfather would observe his merchant fleet moored in the docks.

The town's sole surviving medieval building is **Sligo Abbey**, founded in 1253. Some original features remain, such as the delicate lancet windows in the choir, but this ruined Dominican friary dates mainly from the 15th century. The best features are a beautifully carved altar and the cloisters.

A short distance west from the abbey is O'Connell Street, with the town's main stores

**Bronze statue
of WB Yeats**

and Hargadon's bar – an old Sligo institution complete with a dark, wooden interior, booths and a grocery counter. Near the junction with Wine Street, overlooking Hyde Bridge, is the Yeats Memorial Building. This houses the Yeats Society and the **Sligo Art Gallery**, which puts on shows by foreign and Irish artists. The Yeats International Summer School is held here too: Sligo's fame as the arts capital of northwest Ireland rests partly on this annual festival of readings and lectures on the poet's life and work.

The Yeatsian associations continue on the other side of the river. The first thing you see on crossing Hyde Bridge is a statue of the poet, engraved with lines from his own verse. From here, it is just a short walk east to **Sligo County Museum and Art Gallery**. The museum has a small selection of Yeatsian memorabilia, while the gallery includes evocative Sligo landscapes by WB Yeats's brother, Jack, and several portraits by his father, John B Yeats.

---

🏛 **Sligo Abbey**
Abbey St. ⭕ *daily.* 🎫 *mid-Jun–Sep.*
🏛 **Sligo Art Gallery**
Hyde Bridge. 📞 *071 45847.*
⭕ *Mon–Sat (for exhibitions only).*
🏛 **Sligo County Museum
and Art Gallery**
Stephen St. 📞 *071 42212.*
⭕ *Apr–Oct: Mon–Sat (Apr–May &
Oct: am only).* ♿ *to museum.*

**ENVIRONS:** In a most unlikely setting in the suburbs of Sligo, **Carrowmore Megalithic Cemetery** once boasted the country's largest collection of Stone Age tombs. Quarrying has destroyed many graves, but about 40 passage tombs (*see pp238–9*) and dolmens (*see p30*) survive. They lie scattered among abandoned gravel pits and quarries, in private gardens and some even protruding from cottages.

Dwarfing these tombs from atop **Knocknarea** mountain is a huge, unexcavated cairn, which dates back about 5,000 years and is said to contain the tomb of the legendary Queen Maeve of Connaught (*see p24*). You can climb the mountain in about an hour; the path starts 4 km (2.5 miles) west of Carrowmore.

**Tobernalt**, by Lough Gill 5 km (3 miles) south of Sligo, means "cliff well," after a nearby spring with alleged curative powers. It was a holy site in Celtic times and later became a Christian shrine. Priests came here to celebrate Mass in secret during the 18th century, when Catholic worship was illegal. The Mass rock, which is still visible next to an altar erected at the turn of the century, remains a place of pilgrimage.

Altar by the holy well at Tobernalt, overlooking Lough Gill in Sligo

# Lough Arrow ㉓

**Road map** C3. Co Sligo. 🚌 *to Ballinafad.* 🛈 *Jul–Aug: Main St, Ballinafad (079 66232).*

Pᴇᴏᴘʟᴇ ɢᴏ to Lough Arrow to sail and fish for the local trout, and also simply to enjoy the glorious countryside. You can explore the lake by boat, but the views from the shore are the real joy of Lough Arrow. A full circuit of the lake is recommended, but for the most breathtaking views head for the southern end around **Ballinafad**. This small town lies in a gorgeous spot, enclosed to the north and south by the Bricklieve and Curlew Mountains.

The **Carrowkeel Passage Tomb Cemetery** occupies a remote and eerie spot in the Bricklieve Mountains to the north of Ballinafad. The best approach is up the single lane road from Castlebaldwin, 5 km (3 miles) northeast of the site.

The 14 Neolithic passage graves, which are scattered around a hilltop overlooking Lough Arrow, are elaborate corbeled structures. One is comparable with Newgrange *(see pp238–9)*, except that the burial chamber inside this cairn is lit by the sun on the day of the summer solstice (June 21) as opposed to the winter solstice. On a nearby ridge are the remains of Stone Age huts, presumably those occupied by the farmers who buried their dead in the Carrowkeel passage graves.

**Passage tomb in Carrowkeel cemetery above Lough Arrow**

# Carrick-on-Shannon ㉔

**Road map** C3. Co Leitrim. 🏛 *1,900.* 🚌 🚂 🛈 *Apr–Sep: The Marina (078 20170).*

Tʜᴇ ᴛɪɴʏ ᴄᴀᴘɪᴛᴀʟ of Leitrim, one of the least populated counties in Ireland, stands in a lovely spot on a tight bend of the Shannon.

The town's location by the river and its proximity to the Grand Canal were crucial to Carrick's development. They are also the main reasons for its thriving tourist industry. There is a colorful, modern marina, which in summer fills up with private launches and boats available for rent.

Already a major boating center, Carrick has benefited from the reopening of the Shannon-Erne Waterway, one end of which begins 6 km (4 miles) north at Leitrim. The channel was restored in a cross-border joint venture billed as a symbol of peaceful cooperation between Northern Ireland and the Republic.

Away from the bustle of the marina, Carrick-on-Shannon is an old-fashioned place, with 19th-century churches and convents mixed in with more refined Georgian houses and storefronts. The town's most curious building is the quaint **Costello Chapel** on Bridge Street. One of the smallest of its kind anywhere in the world, the chapel was built in 1877 by local businessman, Edward Costello, to house the tombs of himself and his wife.

# Lough Rynn Estate ㉕

**Road map** C3. Mohill, Co Leitrim. 📞 *078 31427.* 🚌 *or* 🚂 *to Carrick-on-Shannon.* 🕐 *April–mid-Sep: daily.* 🎫 🚻 ♿

Tʜɪs ᴠᴀsᴛ ᴇsᴛᴀᴛᴇ, lying 3 km (2 miles) south of Mohill, was the ancestral seat of the Clements family, Earls of Leitrim. The baronial-style house, constructed in 1832 and full of hunting trophies and grandiose furniture, is of less interest than the grounds. These extend across 40 ha (100 acres) of land and more than 240 ha (600 acres) of lakes. There is a lot to explore, including ornamental gardens, water meadows, lush woodland and an arboretum with California redwoods and other exotic trees. The ruins of a 16th-century castle overlook one of the lakes, and you can also walk up to the remains of a Neolithic burial site.

## Sʜᴀɴɴᴏɴ-Eʀɴᴇ Wᴀᴛᴇʀᴡᴀʏ

This labyrinthine system of rivers and lakes passes through unspoiled border country, linking Leitrim on the Shannon and Upper Lough Erne in Fermanagh. It follows the course of a canal which was completed and then abandoned in the 1860s. The channel was reopened in 1993, enabling the public to enjoy both the Victorian stonework (including 34 bridges) and the state-of-the-art technology used to operate the 16 locks.

**Cruiser negotiating a lock on the Shannon-Erne Waterway**

# THE MIDLANDS

CAVAN · MONAGHAN · LOUTH · LONGFORD · WESTMEATH
MEATH · OFFALY · LAOIS

*T*HE CRADLE *of Irish civilization and the Celts' spiritual home, the Midlands encompass some of Ireland's most sacred and symbolic sites. Much of the region is ignored, but the ragged landscapes of lush pastures, lakes and bogland reveal ancient Celtic crosses, gracious Norman abbeys and Gothic Revival castles.*

The fertile Boyne Valley in County Meath was settled during the Stone Age and became the most important center of habitation in the country. The remains of ancient sites from this early civilization fill the area and include Newgrange, the finest Neolithic tomb in the country. In Celtic times, the focus shifted south to the Hill of Tara, the seat of the High Kings of Ireland and the Celts' spiritual and political capital. Tara's heyday came in the 3rd century AD, but it retained its importance until the Normans invaded in the 1100s.

Norman castles, such as the immense fortress at Trim in County Meath, attest to the shifting frontiers around the region of English influence known as the Pale *(see p124)*. By the end of the 16th century, this area incorporated nearly all the counties in the Midlands.

The Boyne Valley returned to prominence in 1690, when the Battle of the Boyne ended in a landmark Protestant victory over the Catholics *(see pp36–7)*.

Although part of the Republic since 1921, historically Monaghan and Cavan belong to Ulster, and the former retains strong links with the province. The rounded hills called drumlins, found in both counties, are typical of the border region between the Republic and Northern Ireland.

Grassland and bog dotted with lakes are most characteristic of the Midlands, but the Slieve Bloom Mountains and the Cooley Peninsula provide good walking country. In addition to Meath's ancient sites, the historical highlights of the region are monasteries like Fore Abbey and Clonmacnoise, this last ranking among Europe's greatest early Christian centers.

**Carlingford village and harbor, with the hills of the Cooley Peninsula rising behind**

◁ **Temple Finghin round tower at Clonmacnoise monastery on the banks of the Shannon**

# Exploring the Midlands

D ROGHEDA IS THE OBVIOUS BASE from which to explore the Boyne Valley and neighboring monastic sites, such as Monasterboice. Trim and Mullingar, to the southwest, are less convenient but make pleasanter places in which to stay. The northern counties of Monaghan, Cavan and Longford are quiet backwaters with a patchwork of lakes that attract many anglers. To the south, Offaly and Laois are dominated by dark expanses of bog, though there is a cluster of sights around the attractive Georgian town of Birr. For a break by the sea, head for the picturesque village of Carlingford on the Cooley Peninsula.

**West doorway of Nuns' Church at Clonmacnoise**

## KEY

| | |
|---|---|
| ▬▬ | Highway |
| ▬▬ | Major road |
| ▭▭ | Minor road |
| ▭▭ | Scenic route |
| ～ | River |
| 🔅 | Viewpoint |

## SEE ALSO

• **Where to Stay** p299

• **Restaurants, Cafés and Pubs** pp315–16 & p321

## GETTING AROUND

In the Midlands, there is an extensive network of roads and rail lines fanning out across the country from Dublin. As a result, getting around on public transportation is easier than in most other areas. The Dublin–Belfast railroad serves Dundalk and Drogheda, while Mullingar and Longford town lie on the Dublin–Sligo route. The railroad and N7 road between Dublin and Limerick give good access to Laois and Offaly. For motorists, roads in the Midlands are often flat and straight but also potholed.

Enniskillen
Sligo
R200
Shannon-Erne Waterway
DRUMLANE 2
Lough Oughter
CAVAN
Sligo
CARRIGGLAS MANOR 3
R194
LONGFORD
Galway
Royal Canal
N55
TULLYNALLY CASTLE 4
Lough Derravaragh
R390
MULLING
Lough Ree
ATHLONE 18
N6
KILBEGGAN 17
CLONMACNOISE 19
N62
Grand C
TULLAMC
SHANNONBRIDGE BOG RAILWAY 20
Shannon
N52
R440
SLIEVE BLOOM MOUNTAINS
BIRR 21
22
PORTLAC
N62
N7
Thurles
N7
Limerick
Cashel

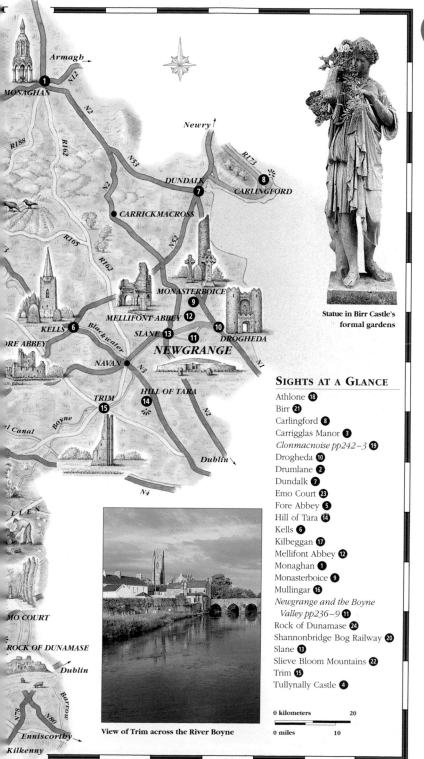

Statue in Birr Castle's formal gardens

## SIGHTS AT A GLANCE

Athlone 18
Birr 21
Carlingford 8
Carrigglas Manor 3
*Clonmacnoise pp242–3* 19
Drogheda 10
Drumlane 2
Dundalk 7
Emo Court 23
Fore Abbey 5
Hill of Tara 14
Kells 6
Kilbeggan 17
Mellifont Abbey 12
Monaghan 1
Monasterboice 9
Mullingar 16
*Newgrange and the Boyne Valley pp236–9* 11
Rock of Dunamase 24
Shannonbridge Bog Railway 20
Slane 13
Slieve Bloom Mountains 22
Trim 15
Tullynally Castle 4

View of Trim across the River Boyne

0 kilometers    20

0 miles    10

**Rossmore Memorial drinking fountain in Monaghan**

# Monaghan ❶

**Road map** D2. Co Monaghan.
🏠 *6,000.* 🚌 🛈 *Market House,
Market Square (047 81122).*

THE NEAT AND THRIVING town
of Monaghan is the urban
highlight of the northern Midlands. Established by James I
in 1613 *(see p37)*, it developed
into a prosperous industrial
center as a result of the local
manufacture of linen. A crannog *(see p31)* off Glen Road
is the sole trace of the town's
Celtic beginnings.

Monaghan centers on three
almost contiguous squares.
The main attraction in Market
Square is the 18th-century
**Market House**, a squat but
charming building with the
original oak beams still visible.
It is now home to the tourist
office. To the east lies Church
Square, very much the heart of
modern Monaghan and lined
with dignified 19th-century
buildings, such as the Classical-
style courthouse. The third
square, which is known as the
Diamond, was the original
marketplace. It contains the
**Rossmore Memorial**, a large
Victorian drinking fountain
with an ornate stone canopy
supported by marble columns.

Do not miss the excellent
**County Museum**, just off
Market Square, which tells the
story of Monaghan's linen and
lace-making industries. The
pride of its historical collection
is the Cross of Clogher, an
ornate bronze altar cross which
dates from around 1400.

The Gothic Revival Cathedral
of St. Macartan perches on a
hilltop south of the town, from
where you can enjoy a fine
view over Monaghan.

**🏛 County Museum**
Hill St. 📞 *047 82928.* ⏰ *Tue–Sat.*
⬤ *public hols.* 🚻 *limited.*

# Drumlane ❷

**Road map** C3. 1 km (0.5 miles) S of
Milltown, Co Cavan. 🚌 *to Belturbet.*

STANDING ALONE by the Erne,
the medieval church and
round tower of Drumlane
merit a visit as much for their
delightful setting as for the
ruins themselves. The abbey
church, founded in the early
13th century but significantly
altered about 200 years later,
features fine Romanesque
carvings. The nearby round
tower has lost its cap but is
unusual for the well-finished
stonework, with carvings of
birds on the north side.

# Carrigglas Manor ❸

**Road map** C3. Co Longford. 📞 *043
45165.* 🚌 *to Longford.* ⏰ *Jun–Sep:
Thu–Mon.* 🚗 🎫 🚻 *limited.*

CARRIGGLAS MANOR has been
the seat of the Lefroys, a
family of Huguenot descent,
ever since its construction in
1837. It has changed little in
the intervening years and is a
fine example of the Tudor
Revival style. The Victorian
atmosphere is still very much
alive inside, where the rooms
are decorated with pseudo-
Gothic paneling and ornate

**Drawing room in Carrigglas Manor with original 19th-century features**

**Authentic Victorian kitchen in Tullynally Castle**

plasterwork ceilings. The stable block, by contrast, is a grand Neo-Classical building by James Gandon, the architect of Dublin's Custom House *(see p86)*; it contains a costume museum. The manor is set in pleasant grounds consisting primarily of woodland.

**ENVIRONS:** Just 14 km (9 miles) south of Carrigglas Manor, **Ardagh** is considered the most attractive village in Longford, with pretty stone cottages gathered around a green.

## Tullynally Castle **❹**

**Road map** C3. Castle Pollard, Co Westmeath. **☎** *044 61159.* **🚌** to Mullingar. **Castle ◯** *mid-Jun–mid-Aug: daily (pm only).* 🖼 ☑️ *obligatory.* ♿ **Grounds ◯** *May–Sep: daily (pm only).* 🖼 ♿ *limited.*

THIS HUGE STRUCTURE, adorned with numerous turrets and battlements, is one of Ireland's largest castles. The original 17th-century tower house was given a Georgian gloss, but this was all but submerged under later Gothic Revival changes. The Pakenham family have lived at Tullynally since 1655. Thomas Pakenham, son of the present Earl of Longford, now manages the estate.

The imposing great hall leads to a fine paneled dining room hung with family portraits. Of equal interest are the Victorian kitchen and laundry rooms and the adjacent drying room, complete with its immense boiler. The 8,000-volume library looks out onto rolling wooded parkland, much of which was landscaped in the 1760s. The grounds include Victorian terraces, walled kitchen and flower gardens, and two small lakes where black swans have recently been introduced.

## Fore Abbey **❺**

**Road map** C3. Fore, Castle Pollard, Co Westmeath. **🚌** *to Castle Pollard.* **◯** *daily.*

THE RUINS of Fore Abbey lie in glorious rolling countryside about 8 km (5 miles) east of Tullynally Castle. St. Fechin set up a monastery here in 630, but what you see now are the remains of a large Benedictine priory founded about 1200. Located on the northern border of the Pale *(see p124)*, Fore Abbey was heavily fortified in the 15th century as protection against the native Irish.

The ruined church was part of the original Norman priory, but the cloister and refectory date from the 1400s. On the hill opposite lies St. Fechin's Church, a Norman building said to mark the site of the first monastery. The tiny church nearby incorporates a 15th-century anchorite's cell.

## Kells **❻**

**Road map** D3. Co Meath. **👥** *3,500.* **🚌** **ℹ** *Mill St, Trim (046 37111).*

LABELED by its Irish name, Ceanannus Mór, this modest town provides an unlikely backdrop to the monastery for which it is so famous.

**Kells Monastery** was set up by St. Columba in the 6th century, but its heyday came after 806, when monks fled here from Iona. They may have been the scribes who illuminated the superb *Book of Kells,* now kept at Trinity College, Dublin *(see p62).*

Lying in the west of town, the monastery centers on an 18th-century church. This is a rather gloomy building, but the displays in the gallery that relate to Kells are worth seeing. A decapitated round tower stands guard outside, and you can also see several 9th-century High Crosses; the South Cross is in the best condition.

Just north of the enclosure is **St. Columba's House**, a tiny steep-roofed stone oratory, similar to St. Kevin's Kitchen at Glendalough *(see p132).*

In Cross Street, in the town center, you can see a High Cross that was moved from the monastery and used as gallows during the uprising in 1798 *(see p39).* The battle scene on the base is a subject rarely used in High Cross art.

**Ruins of Fore Abbey, a medieval Benedictine priory**

**Thatched cottage in Carlingford on the mountainous Cooley Peninsula**

# Dundalk **❼**

**Road map** D3. Co Louth. 🚶 30,000. 🚌 🏛 ℹ *Market Square (042 35484).* 🚃 *Thu.*

DUNDALK once marked the northernmost point of the Pale, the area controlled by the English during the Middle Ages (*see p124*). Now, lying midway between Dublin and Belfast, it is the last major town before the Northern Ireland border.

Dundalk is the gateway to the magnificent countryside of the Cooley Peninsula, but there is little worth stopping for in the town itself. However, the **County Museum**, which is housed in an 18th-century distillery, gives an insight into some of Louth's traditional industries such as beermaking.

🏛 **County Museum**
Jocelyn St. 🕿 042 27056. ◯ *Tue–Sat.* ● *Dec 25 & 26 & Jan 1.* 🎟 ♿

# Carlingford **❽**

**Road map** D3. Co Louth. 🚶 650. 🚌 ℹ **Holy Trinity Heritage Centre** *Churchyard Rd (042 73454).* **Carlingford Adventure Centre** *Tholsel St (042 73100).*

THIS IS A PICTURESQUE fishing village, beautifully located between the mountains of the Cooley Peninsula and the waters of Carlingford Lough. The border of Northern Ireland runs right through the center of this drowned river valley, and from the village you can look across to the Mountains of Mourne on the Ulster side (*see pp276–7*). Carlingford is an interesting place to explore, with its

pretty whitewashed cottages and ancient buildings clustered along medieval alleyways. The ruins of **King John's Castle**, built by the Normans to protect the entrance to the lough, still dominate the village, and there are other impressive fortified buildings, including the Mint. The **Holy Trinity Heritage Centre**, which is housed in a medieval church, traces the history of the port from Anglo-Norman times.

Carlingford is the country's oyster capital, and its oyster festival in August draws a large crowd. The lough is a popular watersports center too, and in summer you can go on cruises around the lough from the village quayside.

Carlingford is well placed for hikes around the Cooley Peninsula. The **Carlingford Adventure Centre** provides information for walkers and also organizes its own tours.

**ENVIRONS:** A scenic route weaves around the **Cooley Peninsula**, skirting the coast and then cutting right through the mountains. The section along the north coast is the most dramatic: just 3 km (1.5 miles) northwest of Carlingford, in the **Slieve Foye Forest Park**, a corkscrew road climbs to give a gorgeous panoramic view over the hills and lough.

The Tain Trail, which you can join at Carlingford, is a 30-km (19-mile) circuit through some of the peninsula's most rugged scenery, with cairns and other prehistoric sites scattered over the moorland. Avid hikers will be able to walk it in a day.

# Monasterboice **❾**

**Road map** D3. Co Louth. 🚌 *to Drogheda.* ◯ *daily.*

FOUNDED in the 5th century by an obscure disciple of St. Patrick called St. Buite, this monastic settlement is one of the most famous religious sites in the country. The ruins of the medieval monastery are enclosed within a graveyard in a lovely secluded spot north of Drogheda. The site includes a roofless round tower and two churches, but Monasterboice's greatest treasures are its 10th-century High Crosses.

Muiredach's High Cross is the finest of its kind in Ireland, and its sculpted biblical scenes are still remarkably fresh. They depict the life of Christ on the west face, while the east face, described in detail opposite, features mainly Old Testament scenes. The cross is named after an inscription on the base: "A prayer for Muiredach by whom this cross was made," which is perhaps a reference to the abbot of Monasterboice. The 6.5-m (21-ft) West Cross, also known as the Tall Cross, is one of the largest in Ireland. The carving has not lasted as well as on Muiredach's Cross, but you can make out scenes from the Death of Christ. The North Cross, which is the least notable of the three, features a Crucifixion and a carved spiral pattern.

**Detail from a tomb in Monasterboice graveyard**

**Round tower and West High Cross at Monasterboice**

# Ireland's High Crosses

**H**IGH CROSSES exist in Celtic parts of both Britain and Ireland. Yet in their profusion and craftsmanship, Irish High Crosses are exceptional. The distinctive ringed cross has become a symbol of Irish Christianity and is still imitated today. The beautiful High Crosses associated with medieval monasteries were carved between the 8th and 12th centuries. The early crosses bore only geometric motifs, but in the 9th to 10th centuries a new style emerged when sculpted scenes from the Bible were introduced. Referred to as "sermons in stone," these later versions may have been used to educate the masses. In essence, though, the High Cross was a status symbol for the monastery or a local patron.

*Pillar stones* inscribed with crosses, like this 6th-century example at Riasc (see p150), were precursors of the High Cross.

Capstone, showing St. Anthony and St. Paul meeting in the desert

*The High Cross at Abenny* (see p191) is typical of 8th-century "ornamental" crosses. These were carved with interlacing patterns and spirals similar to those used in Celtic metalwork and jewelry.

Tenon

## MUIREDACH'S CROSS
Each face of this 10th-century cross at Monasterboice features scenes from the Bible, including the east face seen here. The 5.5-m (18-ft) cross consists of three blocks of sandstone fitted together by means of tenons and sockets.

**The Last Judgment** shows Christ in Glory surrounded by a crowd of resurrected souls. The devil stands on his right clutching a pitchfork, ready to chase the damned souls into Hell.

Angle molding

Adoration of the Magi

David struggling with Goliath

**The ring** served a functional as well as a decorative purpose, providing support for the head and arms of the stone cross.

**Moses** smites the rock to obtain water for the Israelites.

*The Dysert O'Dea Cross* (see p181) dates from the 1100s and represents the late phase of High Cross art. It features the figures of Christ and a bishop carved in high relief.

Socket

*The Fall of Man* shows Adam and Eve beneath an apple-laden tree, with Cain slaying Abel alongside. Both scenes are frequently depicted on Irish High Crosses.

Base

Tenon

# Drogheda ⑩

**Road map** D3. Co Louth. 🏛 25,000.
🚃 🚌 ℹ West St (041 37070).
🎪 Sat.

IN THE 14TH CENTURY, this historic Norman port near the mouth of the River Boyne was one of Ireland's most important towns. However, the place seems never to have recovered from the trauma of a vicious attack by Cromwell in 1649 *(see p37)*, in which 2,000 citizens were killed. Although it now looks rather dilapidated, the town has retained its original street plan and has a rich medieval heritage.

Little remains of Drogheda's medieval defenses but **St. Lawrence Gate**, a fine 13th-century barbican, has survived. Nearby, there are two churches called **St. Peter's**. The one belonging to the Church of Ireland, built in 1753, is the more striking and has some splendid grave slabs. The Catholic church is worth visiting to see the embalmed head of Oliver Plunkett, an archbishop martyred in 1681.

South of the river you can climb Millmount, a Norman motte topped by a Martello tower. As well as providing a good view, this is the site of the **Millmount Museum**,

**Drogheda viewed from Millmount across the River Boyne**

which contains a display of historical artifacts, a genealogy center and craft workshops.

### 🏛 Millmount Museum
Duleek St. 🎫 041 33097. ⬜ Tue–Sun. 🌑 10 days at Christmas. 🎦 ♿

# Newgrange and the Boyne Valley ⑪

**Road map** D3. Co Meath. 🚌 to Drogheda. 🚌 to Slane or Drogheda. ℹ Mar–Oct: Newgrange (041 24274).

KNOWN AS Brugh na Boinne, the "Palace of the Boyne," this river valley was the cradle of Irish civilization. The fertile soil supported a sophisticated society in Neolithic times and much evidence of this early habitation survives, in the form of ring forts, barrows, passage graves and sacred enclosures.

The most important Neolithic monuments in the valley are three passage graves: supreme among these is **Newgrange** *(see pp238–9)*, but **Dowth** and **Knowth** are significant too. The Boyne Valley also encompasses the Hill of Slane and the Hill of Tara *(see p240)*, both of which are major sites in Celtic mythology. Indeed, this whole region is rich in associations with Ireland's

**River Boyne near the site of the Battle of the Boyne**

---

## THE BATTLE OF THE BOYNE

In 1688, the Catholic King of England, James II, was deposed from his throne, to be replaced by his Protestant daughter, Mary, and her husband, William of Orange. Determined to win back the crown, James sought the support of Irish Catholics, and challenged William at Oldbridge by the River Boyne west of Drogheda. The Battle of the Boyne took place on July 1, 1690, with James's poorly trained force of 25,000 French and Irish Catholics facing William's hardened army of 36,000 French Huguenots, Dutch, English and Scots. The Protestants triumphed and James fled to France, after a battle that signaled the beginning of total Protestant power over Ireland. It ushered in the confiscation of Catholic lands and the suppression of Catholic interests, sealing the country's fate for the next 300 years.

**William of Orange leading his troops at the Battle of the Boyne, July 1, 1690**

prehistory. With monuments predating Egypt's pyramids, the Boyne Valley is marketed as the Irish "Valley of the Kings." A new interpretative center is due to open near Newgrange in 1996. This will cover the area's Stone Age heritage and include a reconstruction of Newgrange passage grave.

## ⋔ Dowth

Off N51, 3 km (2 miles) E of New-grange. ● *to the public.*
The passage grave at Dowth was plundered by Victorian souvenir hunters and has not been fully excavated. You cannot approach the tomb, but it can be seen from the road.

## ⋔ Knowth

Off N51, 1.5 km (1 mile) NW of New-grange. █ *041 24824.* ○ *May–Oct: daily.* 🖼 ♿ 🎟
Knowth outdoes Newgrange in several respects, above all in the quantity of its treasures, which form the greatest concentration of megalithic art in Europe. In addition, the site was occupied for a much longer period – from Neolithic times right up until about 1400.

Unusually, Knowth has two passage tombs rather than one. These are closed during excavation work, which has been going on since 1962. However, while just a third of the site is open, you can see into several of the 17 satellite tombs. Some of the curbstones, many of them finely carved, are also on display.

Slane Castle in grounds landscaped by Capability Brown

## Mellifont Abbey ⓬

**Road map** D3. Cullen, Co Louth.
█ *041 26459.* 🚌 *to Drogheda.*
🚌 *to Drogheda or Slane.* ○ *May–Oct: daily.* 🖼

ON THE BANKS of the River Mattock, 10 km (6 miles) west of Drogheda, lies the first Cistercian monastery to have been built in Ireland. Mellifont was founded in 1142 on the orders of St. Malachy, the Archbishop of Armagh. He was greatly influenced

**Glazed medieval tiles at Mellifont Abbey**

by St. Bernard who, based at his monastery at Clairvaux in France, was behind the success of the Cistercian Order in Europe. The archbishop introduced not only Cistercian rigor to Mellifont but also the formal style of monastic architecture used on the continent. His new monastery became a model for other Cistercian centers built in Ireland, retaining its supremacy over them until 1539, when the abbey was closed and turned into a fortified house. William of Orange used Mellifont as his headquarters during the Battle of the Boyne in 1690. The abbey is now a ruin, but it is still possible to appreciate the scale and ground

plan of the original complex. Not much survives of the abbey church, but to the south of it, enclosed by what remains of the Romanesque cloister, is the most interesting building at Mellifont: a unique 13th-century lavabo where monks came to wash their hands in a fountain before meals. Four of the building's original eight sides survive, each with a graceful Romanesque arch. On the eastern side of the cloister stands the 14th-century chapter house. It has an impressive vaulted ceiling and a floor laid with glazed medieval tiles taken from the abbey church.

## Slane ⓭

**Road map** D3. Co Meath. 🚶 *700.* 🚌

SLANE IS AN ATTRACTIVE estate village, centered on a quartet of Georgian houses. The Boyne flows through it and skirts the grounds of **Slane Castle**, set in glorious gardens laid out in the 18th century by Capability Brown. Sadly, the Gothic Revival castle has been closed since a fire in 1991.

Just to the north rises the **Hill of Slane** where, in 433, St. Patrick is said to have lit a Paschal (Easter) fire as a challenge to the pagan High King of Tara *(see p240).* The event is endowed with symbolic importance as the triumph of Christianity over paganism.

**Ruined lavabo at Mellifont Abbey**

# Newgrange

**Tri-spiral carving on entrance stone**

THE ORIGINS of Newgrange, one of the most important passage graves in Europe, are steeped in mystery. According to Celtic lore, the legendary kings of Tara *(see p240)* were buried here, but Newgrange predates them. Built in around 3200 BC, the grave was left untouched by all invaders (though not by tomb robbers) and was eventually excavated in the 1960s. Archaeologists then discovered that on the winter solstice (December), rays of sun enter the tomb and light up the burial chamber, making it the oldest solar observatory in the world. Newgrange receives a flood of visitors and, if you go in summer, be prepared for long lines. The new interpretive center nearby *(see p237)* will hopefully relieve some of the pressure on the site.

**Basin Stone**
*The chiseled stones, found in each recess, would have once contained funerary offerings and the bones of the dead.*

**The chamber** has three recesses or side chambers: the north recess is the one struck by sunlight on the winter solstice.

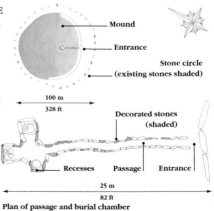

**Chamber Ceiling**
*The burial chamber's intricate corbeled ceiling, which reaches a height of 6 m (20 ft) above the floor, has survived intact. The overlapping slabs form a conical hollow, topped by a single capstone.*

## CONSTRUCTION OF NEWGRANGE

The tomb at Newgrange was designed by people with clearly exceptional artistic and engineering skills, who had use of neither the wheel nor metal tools. About 200,000 tons of loose stones were transported to build the mound, or cairn, which protects the passage grave. Larger slabs were used to make the circle around the cairn (12 out of a probable 35 stones have survived), the curb and the tomb itself. Many of the curbstones and the slabs lining the passage, the chamber and its recesses are decorated with zigzags, spirals and other geometric motifs. The grave's corbeled ceiling consists of smaller, unadorned slabs and has proved almost completely waterproof for the last 5,000 years.

Mound

Entrance

Stone circle
(existing stones shaded)

100 m
328 ft

Decorated stones
(shaded)

Recesses    Passage    Entrance

25 m
82 ft
**Plan of passage and burial chamber**

## Restoration of Newgrange

*Located on a low ridge north of the Boyne, Newgrange took more than 70 years to build. Between 1962 and 1975 the passage grave and mound were restored as closely as possible to their original state.*

**The standing stones** in the passage are slabs of slate which would have been collected locally.

**Passage**

*At dawn on December 21, a beam of sunlight shines through the roof box (a feature unique to Newgrange), travels along the 19-m (62-ft) passage and hits the central recess in the burial chamber.*

**The retaining wall** around the front of the cairn was rebuilt using the white quartz and granite stones found scattered around the site during excavations.

**Entrance**

*Newgrange's most elaborately carved curbstone originally covered the tomb entrance. It now stands just in front, forming part of the curb of huge slabs around the cairn.*

**Roof box**

**Trim Castle set in water meadows beside the River Boyne**

# Hill of Tara ⓮

**Road map** D3. Nr Killmessan Village, Co Meath. 📞 046 25903. 🚌 to Navan. ◯ daily. 📷 for Interpretative Center. 📷

A SITE of mythical importance, Tara was the political and spiritual center of Celtic Ireland and the seat of the High Kings until the 11th century. The spread of Christianity, which eroded the importance of Tara, is marked by a statue of St. Patrick. The symbolism of the site was not lost on Daniel O'Connell (see p40), who chose Tara for a rally in 1843, attended by over one million people.

Tours from the Interpretative Center point out a Stone Age passage grave and Iron Age hill forts, though to the untutored eye, these earthworks look like mere hollows and grassy mounds. Clearest is the Royal Enclosure, an oval fort, in the center of which is Cormac's House containing the "stone of destiny" (Lialh Fail), an ancient fertility symbol and inauguration stone of the High Kings. However, all this is secondary to the poignant atmosphere and views over the Boyne Valley.

# Trim ⓯

**Road map** D3. Co Meath. 🏠 4,000. 🚌 ℹ️ Mill St (046 37111). 🛒 Fri.

T RIM IS ONE of the most pleasing Midlands market towns. A Norman stronghold on the River Boyne, it marked a boundary of the Pale (see p124). Trim runs efficient heritage and genealogy centers

while the **Duchas Trim Folk Theatre** provides rousing summer entertainment. (This popular company is at present in search of new premises.) Equally engrossing is the Nun Run, a bizarre summer horse race with nuns as jockeys, which takes place near **Trim Castle**. The castle was founded in 1173 by Hugh de Lacy, a Norman knight, and is one of the largest medieval castles in Ireland. It makes a spectacular backdrop so is often used as a movie set, most recently seen in Mel Gibson's Braveheart (1995). Over the river is **Talbot Castle**, an Augustinian abbey converted to a manor house in the 15th century. Just north of the abbey, **St. Patrick's Cathedral** incorporates part of a medieval church with a 15th-century tower and sections of the original chancel.

**Butterstream Gardens**, on the edge of town, are the best in the county. A fine herbaceous bed is the centerpiece, but equally pleasing are the exotic woodland, rose and white gardens. The design is enhanced by pergolas, pools and bridges.

🏰 **Trim Castle**
◯ daily.
🌷 **Butterstream Gardens**
Kildalkey Rd. 📞 046 36016.
◯ May–Sep: Tue–Sun (pm only). 📷

# Mullingar ⓰

**Road map** C3. Co Westmeath.
🏠 12,000. 🚌 🚆 ℹ️ Dublin Rd (044 48650). 🛒 Sat.

T HE COUNTY TOWN of Westmeath is a prosperous but unremarkable market town circled by the Royal Canal

**Aerial view of Iron Age forts on the Hill of Tara**

*(see p99)*, which with its 46 locks links Dublin with the River Shannon. The cost of building the canal bankrupted its investors and it was never profitable. Although Mullingar's main appeal is as a base to explore the surrounding area, pubs such as Con's and the cheery Canton Casey's can make a pleasant interlude.

**ENVIRONS:** Recent restoration of the Dublin to Mullingar stretch of the Royal Canal has created attractive towpaths for walkers, and angling facilities.

Just off the Kilbeggan road from Mullingar stands **Belvedere House**, a romantic Palladian villa overlooking Lough Ennel. The house, built in 1740 by Richard Castle and decorated with Rococo plasterwork, is being restored, but the wonderful gardens are open.

Shortly after the house was built, the first Earl of Belvedere accused his young wife of having an affair with his brother, and imprisoned her for 31 years in a neighboring house. In 1755, the Earl built a Gothic folly – the Jealous Wall – to block the view of his second brother's more opulent mansion across the lake. The Jealous Wall remains, as does an octagonal gazebo and other follies.

Charming terraces, framed by urns and yews, descend to the lake; on the other side of the house is a picturesque walled garden, enclosed by an arboretum and rolling parkland.

### 🏛 Belvedere House
6.5 km (4 miles) S of Mullingar. [ 044 42820. **House** ⬤ for restoration. **Gardens** ◯ Apr–Oct: daily. 🖼 🚹

**The Jealous Wall at Belvedere House, near Mullingar**

**Athlone Castle below the towers of the church of St. Peter and St. Paul**

## Kilbeggan ⑰

**Road map** C4. Co Westmeath. 🚶 600. 🚉

SITUATED BETWEEN Mullingar and Tullamore, this pleasant village has a small harbor on the Grand Canal. However, the main point of interest is **Locke's Distillery**. Founded in 1757, it claims to be the oldest licensed pot still distillery in the world. Unable to compete with Scotch whisky manufacturers, the company went bankrupt in 1954, but the aroma hung in the warehouses for years and was known as "the angel's share." The distillery was reopened as a museum in 1987. The building is authentic, a solid structure complete with water wheel and inside steam engine. A tour traces the process of Irish whiskey-making, from the mash tuns to the vast fermentation vats and creation of wash (rough beer) to the distillation and maturation stages. At the tasting stage, workers would sample the whiskey in the can pit room. Visitors can still taste whiskeys in the bar but, unlike the original workers, cannot bathe in the whiskey vats.

**Miniature whiskey bottles at Locke's Distillery in Kilbeggan**

### 🏛 Locke's Distillery
Main Street. [ 0506 32134. ◯ daily. 🖼

## Athlone ⑱

**Road map** C3. Co Westmeath. 🚶 15,000. 🚉 🚌 🚹 The Castle, Market Square (0902 94630). 🚉 Fri.

THE TOWN owes its historical importance to its position by a natural ford on the River Shannon. **Athlone Castle** is a much altered 13th-century fortress, which was badly damaged in the Jacobite Wars *(see pp36–7)*. It lies in the shadow of the 19th-century church of St. Peter and St. Paul. The neighboring streets offer several good pubs as well as docks lined with warehouses. Across the river from the castle, boats depart for Clonmacnoise *(see pp242–3)* or Lough Ree.

### ⚓ Athlone Castle
Market Square. [ 0902 94630. ◯ May–Oct: daily. 🖼 🚹 limited.

**ENVIRONS:** The **Lough Ree Trail** starts 8 km (5 miles) northeast of Athlone, at Glasson. The route passes picturesque views and unspoiled countryside. The trail is a popular cycling tour.

# Clonmacnoise ⓲

**Detail on a grave slab**

THIS MEDIEVAL MONASTERY, in a remote spot by the River Shannon, was founded by St. Ciaran in 545–548. Clonmacnoise lay at a crossroads of medieval routes, linking all parts of Ireland. Known for its scholarship and piety, it thrived from the 7th to the 12th century. Many kings of Tara and of Connaught were buried here. Plundered by the Vikings and Anglo-Normans, it fell to the English in 1552. Today, a group of stone churches (temples), a cathedral, two round towers and three High Crosses remain.

**Last Circuit of Pilgrims at Clonmacnoise**
*This painting (1838), by George Petrie, shows pilgrims walking the traditional route three times around the site. Pilgrims still do this every year on September 9, St. Ciaran's Day.*

**The Pope's Shelter** was where John Paul II conducted Mass during his visit in 1979.

**Cross of the Scriptures**
*This copy of the original 9th-century cross (now in the museum) is decorated with biblical scenes, but the identity of most of the figures is uncertain.*

## VISITING CLONMACNOISE

The Visitors' Center is housed in three buildings modeled on beehive huts *(see p19)*. The museum section contains early grave slabs and the three remaining High Crosses, replicas of which now stand in their original locations. The Nuns' Church, northeast of the main site, has a Romanesque doorway and chancel arch.

### KEY

| | |
|---|---|
| **1** South Cross | **7** Cathedral |
| **2** Temple Dowling | **8** North Cross |
| **3** Temple Hurpan | **9** Cross of the Scriptures |
| **4** Temple Melaghlin | **10** Round Tower |
| **5** Temple Ciaran | **11** Temple Connor |
| **6** Temple Kelly | **12** Temple Finghin |

0 meters        50
0 yards         50

Pilgrim path to Nuns' Church

Entrance

Pope's Shelter

To Visitors' Center

### Whispering Door

*Above the cathedral's 15th-century north doorway are carvings of saints Francis, Patrick and Dominic. The acoustics of the doorway are such that even a whisper is carried inside the building.*

**The Shannonbridge Bog Railway passing an area of cut bog**

# Shannonbridge Bog Railway ⑳

**Road map** C4. 5 km (3 miles) E of
Shannonbridge, Co Offaly. ☎ 0905
74114. 🚆 to Athlone. ◯ Apr–Oct:
daily; Nov–Mar: groups by appt. 🖼 🅱

**The Round Tower** *(see p18)* is over 19 m (62 ft) high with its doorway above ground level.

### Temples Dowling, Hurpan and Melaghlin

*Built as a family crypt, Temple Hurpan was a 17th-century addition to the early Romanesque Temple Dowling. The 13th-century Temple Melaghlin has two fine round-headed windows.*

S TARTING near Shannonbridge, this guided tour by train is run by the Irish Peat Board (Bord na Móna). The 45-minute tour covers 9 km (6 miles) of bogland and gives a fascinating insight into the history and development of the Blackwater raised bogs – an area of great ecological importance, parts of which are protected.

Tour guides describe the transformation from lake to marshy fen and thence to bog *(see p244)*, and explain that in several hundred years the bog will become fields and woodland. They also point out the area's distinctive flora and fauna, from dragonflies to bog cotton, bog asphodel and sphagnum moss. The small lakes and pools that punctuate the bog provide excellent habitats for wetland birds.

Bog oaks – old trees which have been preserved in the bog – are visible in the places where the peat has been harvested. For centuries, peat has been the main source of fuel in rural Ireland, and visitors can watch peat being cut by hand using the traditional tool known as a "slane". Modern peat-harvesting machines in use nearby supply the power station at Shannonbridge. There is a craft shop and also a machinery museum close to where the train ride begins.

# The Raised Bogs of the Midlands

**P**EATLAND OR BOG, which covers about 15 percent of the Irish landscape, exists in two principal forms. Most extensive is the thin blanket bog found chiefly in the west, while the dome-shaped raised bogs are more characteristic of the Midlands – notably in an area known as the Bog of Allen.

**Four-spotted chaser dragonfly**

Although Irish boglands are some of the largest in Europe, the use of peat for domestic fuel and fertilizer has greatly reduced their extent. This has threatened not only the shape of the Irish landscape but also the survival of a unique habitat and the unusual plants and insects it supports.

Unspoiled expanse of the Bog of Allen

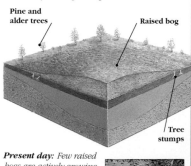

***Peat cutters*** *still gather turf (as peat is known locally) by hand in parts of Ireland. It is then set in stacks to dry. Peat makes a good fuel, because it is rich in partially decayed vegetation, laid down over thousands of years.*

**Fen plants**   **Birch and willow scrub**   **Moraine (glacial deposits)**

***8000 BC:*** *Shallow meltwater lakes that formed after the Ice Age gradually filled with mud. Reeds, sedges and other fen plants began to dominate in the marshy conditions.*

**Fen plants (reeds and sedges)**   **Fen peat**   **Mud**

***6000 BC:*** *As the fen vegetation died, it sank to the lake bed but did not decompose fully in the waterlogged conditions, forming a layer of peat. This slowly built up and spread outward.*

**Fen peat**   **Fresh sphagnum peat**   **Buried tree stumps**

***3000 BC:*** *As the peat built up and the lake slowly disappeared, plant life in the developing bog had to rely almost exclusively on rainwater, which is acid. Fen plants could not survive in these acidic conditions and gave way to bog mosses, mainly species of sphagnum. As these mosses died, they formed a layer of sphagnum peat on the surface of the bog which, over the centuries, attained a distinctive domed shape.*

**Pine and alder trees**   **Raised bog**   **Tree stumps**

***Present day:*** *Few raised bogs are actively growing today. Those that remain contain a fascinating historical record of the landscape. The survival of ancient tree stumps shows how well plants are preserved in peat.*

**Sphagnum moss**

# Birr ㉑

**Road map** 4C. Co Offaly. 🏃 *4,100.*
🚌 ℹ️ *May–Sep: Rosse Row (0509 20110).*

BIRR, A GENTRIFIED estate town, grew up in the shadow of the castle where the Earls of Rosse have resided for almost four centuries. It is famous for its authentic Georgian layout, with houses displaying original fanlights, door paneling and iron railings. Two particularly elegant streets are Oxmantown Mall, designed by the 2nd Earl of Rosse, and John's Mall. Emmet Square may have sold its Georgian soul to commerce, but Dooly's Hotel is still a fine example of an old coaching inn. Foster's bar, on nearby Connaught Street, is one of many traditional storefronts to have been restored in Birr.

### 🏰 Birr Castle

Rosse Row. 📞 *0509 20056.*
**Gardens** 🕐 *daily* 🕐 *Dec 25.* 🎫 ♿

Birr Castle was founded in 1620 by the Parsons, later Earls of Rosse, and is still the family seat. They have been most noted for their contribution to astronomy – a telescope, built by the 3rd Earl in 1845, was the largest in the world at the time. The 17-m (56-ft) wooden tube, supported by two walls, can be seen in the grounds and is currently being restored to its original condition.

The castle is closed to the general public, but the glory of Birr lies in its grounds. First landscaped in the 18th century, these are famous for their 9-m (30-ft) boxwood hedges and for the exotic trees and shrubs that were gathered during foreign expeditions sponsored

by the 6th Earl. The magnolias and maples are particularly striking. The gardens overlook the meeting of two rivers, and water greatly influenced the planning of the grounds. There is a charming riverside garden and a small suspension bridge.

# Slieve Bloom Mountains ㉒

**Road map** D4. Co Offaly and Co Laois.
🚌 *to Mountmellick.* ℹ️ *May–Sep: Rosse Row, Birr (0509 20110).*

THIS LOW RANGE of mountains rises unexpectedly from the bogs and plains of Offaly and Laois, providing a welcome change in the predominantly flat Midlands. You can walk along the **Slieve Bloom Way**, a 30-km (19-mile) circular trail through an unspoiled landscape of open vistas, wooded glens and mountain streams. There are other marked paths too. Good starting points are **Cadamstown**, with an attractive old mill, and the pretty village of **Kinnitty** – both in the northern foothills.

An alcove in the front hall of Emo Court with a *trompe l'oeil* ceiling

# Emo Court ㉓

**Road map** D4. 13 km (8 miles) NE of Portlaoise, Co Laois. 📞 *0502 26110.*
🚌 *to Monasterevin or Portlaoise.*
**House** 🕐 *mid-Jun–Sep: daily.*
**Gardens** 🕐 *daily.* 🎫 ♿ *limited.*

EMO COURT, commissioned by the Earl of Portarlington in 1790, represents the only foray into domestic architecture by James Gandon, designer of the Custom House in Dublin *(see p86).* The monumental Neo-Classical mansion has a splendid façade featuring an Ionic portico. Inside, the centerpiece is a magnificent gilded rotunda and there are fine stuccowork ceilings in the dining room and library.

Emo Court's current owner, who restored the house with great care, has now turned his attention to the grounds. These are adorned with fine statuary and include a lakeside walk.

# Rock of Dunamase ㉔

**Road map** D4. 5 km (3 miles) E of Portlaoise, Co Laois. 🚌 *to Portlaoise.*

THE ROCK OF DUNAMASE, which looms dramatically above the plains east of Portlaoise, has long been a military site. Originally crowned by an Iron Age ring fort, the 13th-century castle that succeeded it is now more prominent – though it was virtually destroyed by Cromwellian forces in 1650. You can reach the battered keep by climbing up banks and ditches through two gateways and a fortified courtyard.

**Rock of Dunamase viewed from Stradbally to the east**

# NORTHERN IRELAND

LONDONDERRY · ANTRIM · TYRONE · FERMANAGH
ARMAGH · DOWN

NORTHERN IRELAND *has sights from every era of Ireland's history as well as magnificently varied coastal and lakeland scenery. In the past, it has received fewer visitors than the Republic as a result of the "Troubles." Following the cease-fire of 1994, there seems every chance that this area will at last attract the attention it deserves.*

The province of Northern Ireland was created after partition of the island in 1921. Its six counties (plus Donegal, Monaghan and Cavan) were part of Ulster, one of Ireland's four traditional kingdoms. It was most probably in Ulster that Christianity first ousted the old Celtic pagan beliefs. In 432 St. Patrick landed at Saul in County Down, later founding a church at Armagh, which is still the spiritual capital of Ireland.

The dominant political force in early Christian times was the Uí Néill clan. Their descendants, the O'Neills, put up fierce resistance to English conquest in the late 16th century. Hugh O'Neill, Earl of Tyrone, had some notable successes against the armies of Elizabeth I, but was defeated. In 1607 he fled to Europe with other Irish lords from Ulster, in what became known as the "Flight of the Earls." Vacant estates were granted to individuals and companies, who planted them with English and Scottish Protestants *(see p37).* Many Plantation towns, such as Londonderry, preserve their 17th-century layout around a central square or "diamond." The arrival of new settlers meant that Irish Catholics were increasingly marginalized, thereby sowing the seeds of 400 years of conflict.

In the relative tranquility of the 18th century, the Anglo-Irish nobility built stately homes, such as Mount Stewart House on the Ards Peninsula and Castle Coole near Enniskillen. Ulster also enjoyed prosperity in the 19th century through its shipbuilding, linen and ropemaking industries.

Though densely populated and industrialized around Belfast, the region away from the capital is primarily agricultural. It also has areas of outstanding natural beauty, notably the rugged Antrim coastline around the Giant's Causeway, the Mountains of Mourne in County Down and the Erne lakeland in the west of the region.

Belfast's City Hall (1906), symbol of the city's civic pride

◁ **Carrick-a-rede Rope Bridge, an unusual tourist attraction on the Causeway Coast**

# Exploring Northern Ireland

THE STARTING POINT for most visitors to the province is Belfast. The capital has grand Victorian buildings, good pubs and the excellent Ulster Museum. However, Northern Ireland's greatest attractions lie along its coast. These range from the extraordinary volcanic landscape of the Giant's Causeway to Carrickfergus, Ireland's best preserved Norman castle. There are also Victorian resorts, like Portstewart, tiny fishing villages and unspoiled sandy beaches, such as Benone Strand. Ramblers are drawn to the Mountains of Mourne, while anglers and boating enthusiasts can enjoy the lakeland of Lower Lough Erne.

**Harbor and promenade at the seaside resort of Portstewart**

CAUSEW
CO

BENONE STRAND 2    PORTSTE 3 4

MUSSENDEN
TEMPLE    COLE

Letterkenny

Lough Foyle

A2

1
**LONDONDERRY**

Roe

Foyle

A6

STRABANE    B48    SPERRIN MOUNTAINS

Derg

BEAGHMORE
STONE CIRCLES    13

ULSTER HISTORY PARK

14

15    A505    COOKSTOWN 12

**ULSTER-AMERICAN
FOLK PARK**

A29

OMAGH

0 kilometers    10

0 miles    5

A47    DUNGANNON 22

Sligo    16    17    **LOWER
LOUGH
ERNE**

A32

**BELLEEK
POTTERY**

A4

DEVENISH 18
ISLAND    19

ARMAG

**ENNISKILLEN**

A4    A509    Upper Lough Erne    A34

MARBLE 20
ARCH CAVES    21    Monaghan

FLORENCE
COURT

## GETTING AROUND

Belfast is the transportation hub of Northern Ireland. From here the limited train network runs northwest to Londonderry and south to Dublin. In most parts of the province you have to rely on buses, but fortunately, even in rural areas, these are fairly frequent and punctual. However, a car is essential if you want to go off the beaten track in search of ancient monuments or tour the coast at leisure. Depending on the security situation, you may still encounter temporary checkpoints set up by the army and police (see p343).

**KEY**

| | |
|---|---|
| | Highway |
| | Major road |
| | Minor road |
| | Scenic route |
| | River |
| 🌿 | Viewpoint |

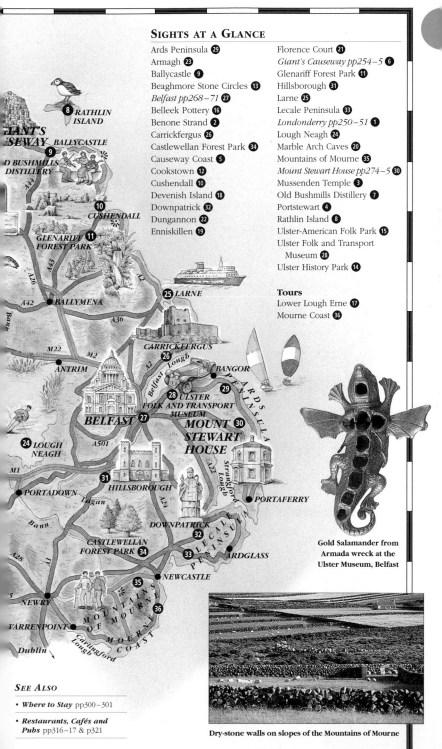

## SIGHTS AT A GLANCE

Ards Peninsula 29

Armagh 23

Ballycastle 9

Beaghmore Stone Circles 13

*Belfast pp268–71* 27

Belleek Pottery 16

Benone Strand 2

Carrickfergus 26

Castlewellan Forest Park 34

Causeway Coast 5

Cookstown 12

Cushendall 10

Devenish Island 18

Downpatrick 32

Dungannon 22

Enniskillen 19

Florence Court 21

*Giant's Causeway pp254–5* 6

Glenariff Forest Park 11

Hillsborough 31

Larne 25

Lecale Peninsula 33

*Londonderry pp250–51* 1

Lough Neagh 24

Marble Arch Caves 20

Mountains of Mourne 35

*Mount Stewart House pp274–5* 30

Mussenden Temple 3

Old Bushmills Distillery 7

Portstewart 4

Rathlin Island 8

Ulster-American Folk Park 15

Ulster Folk and Transport
  Museum 28

Ulster History Park 14

**Tours**

Lower Lough Erne 17

Mourne Coast 36

**Gold Salamander from
Armada wreck at the
Ulster Museum, Belfast**

**Dry-stone walls on slopes of the Mountains of Mourne**

**SEE ALSO**

• *Where to Stay* pp300–301

• *Restaurants, Cafés and
  Pubs* pp316–17 & p321

# Londonderry ❶

**Carving on Shipquay Gate**

S<small>T</small>. C<small>OLUMBA</small> founded a monastery here beside the River Foyle in 546. He called the place Doire or "oak grove," later anglicized as Derry. In 1613, the city was selected as a major Plantation project *(see pp36–7)*, organized by London livery companies. As a result, it acquired the prefix London, though most people still call it Derry. When British troops shot dead 13 demonstrators in 1972, Derry hit the world's headlines. Today, with an end to the Troubles in sight, the city council has undertaken several admirable heritage projects.

### ★ Tower Museum
*The excellent displays on local history in this new museum include one on the mapping of the area during the reign of Elizabeth I.*

**Shipquay Gate**

**The Craft Village** was opened in 1992 as part of the city's plans to bring the center back to life.

**Butcher's Gate**

### The Diamond
*The war memorial in the Diamond or main square was erected in 1927. It was originally made for the city of Sheffield in England.*

**Court House**

**Army post**

**Bishop's Gate**

### ★ St. Columb's Cathedral
*The nave's wooden ceiling dates from 1862. The corbels are carved with the heads of former bishops and deans.*

**New Gate**

**The Playhou**

**K**EY

| | |
|---|---|
| **P** | Parking |
| **i** | Tourist information |
| – – – | Suggested route |

**Road Map** C1. Co Londonderry.
95,000. ✈ 11 km (7 miles) E.
🚉 Waterside, Duke Street (01504
42228). 🚌 Foyle Street (01504
262261). ℹ 8 Bishop Street
(01504 267284). 🚢 Sat. 🎭 Two
Cathedrals Music Festival (Oct);
Hallowe'en Festival (Oct 31).

## VISITORS' CHECKLIST

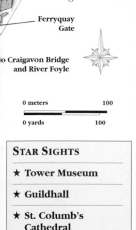

★ **Guildhall**
*This stained-glass
window shows
St. Columba.
Others feature
incidents from
the siege of Derry,
including the
apprentice boys
shutting the city
gates in 1688.*

— **Ferryquay
Gate**

o Craigavon Bridge
and River Foyle

0 meters        100

0 yards         100

### STAR SIGHTS

★ **Tower Museum**

★ **Guildhall**

★ **St. Columb's
Cathedral**

### 🕇 St. Columb's Cathedral

St. Columb's Court. 📞 01504 267313.
◯ Mon–Sat. 🎥 ♿
Built between 1628 and 1633,
in "Planters' Gothic" style, St.
Columb's was the first cathedral to be founded in
the British Isles after
the Reformation.
The interior was
extensively rebuilt
in the 19th century.
A small museum in
the Chapter House
contains relics from the
siege of 1689 (*see
pp36–7*), including
the 17th-century
locks and keys of the city. In
the vestibule is a hollow mortar
cannonball that was fired into
the city by James II's army. It
carried terms for capitulation,
but the reply of the Protestants
within the walls was a defiant
"No surrender," a phrase used
by Loyalists to this day.

**Lock of city gate in
St. Columb's Cathedral**

### 🏛 Tower Museum

Union Hall Place. 📞 01504 372411.
◯ Jul & Aug: daily; Sep–Jun: Tue–Sat.
● Mar 17, Good Fri, Dec 25 & 26.
🎥 ♿
Housed in O'Doherty Tower
(a replica of the original 16th-
century building on this site),
the museum traces the history
of the city from its foundation
to the recent Troubles using
multimedia displays. Upstairs,
an exhibition about the 1688
Spanish Armada includes
artifacts from ships wrecked
in nearby Kinnagoe Bay.

### ⚓ Walls of Derry

Access from Magazine Street.
Among the best preserved city
fortifications in Europe, the
city walls rise to a height of
8 m (26 ft) and in places are
9 m (30 ft) wide. Completed
in 1618 to defend the new
merchant city from Gaelic
chieftains in Donegal, the walls
have never been breached, not
even during the siege of 1689,
when 7,000 out of a population
of 20,000 perished from disease
or starvation. Extensive
restoration work
means that it should
soon be possible to
walk all around the
walls for the first
time in decades.
Just outside the old
fortifications, beyond
Butcher's Gate, is the
Bogside, a Catholic
area with a famous
mural that announces "You
are now entering free Derry."

### 🏛 Guildhall

Guildhall Square. 📞 01504 365151.
◯ Mon–Fri. 🎥 Jul & Aug.
Standing between the walled
city and the River Foyle, this
Neo-Gothic building was constructed in 1890, but a fire in
1908 and a bomb in 1972
necessitated substantial repairs.
Stained-glass windows – copies
of the originals – recount the
history of Derry. To the rear
of the Guildhall is Derry Quay,
from where Irish emigrants
sailed to America in the 18th
and 19th centuries.

**ENVIRONS:** Just off the B194,
on the way to Muff, stands a
memorial to American aviator
Amelia Earhart, the first woman
to complete a transatlantic solo
flight. She had intended to fly
to Paris, but in May 1932
landed in a field outside Derry.
A sculpture marks the spot and
the nearby **Earhart Centre**
contains a small exhibition.

### 🏛 Earhart Centre

Ballyarnet. 📞 01504 354040.
◯ Jun–Sep: daily; Oct–May: Mon–Fri.

**The old walled city viewed across the River Foyle**

Terraced houses behind the promenade at Portstewart

## Benone Strand ➋

**Road map** D1. Co Londonderry.
🅸 Jul & Aug: Benone Tourist Complex, 53 Benone Ave, Seacoast Rd, Magilligan (015047 50555).

T HE WIDE, golden sands of Ireland's longest beach, also known as Magilligan Strand, sweep along the Londonderry coastline for more than 10 km (6 miles). The magnificent beach has been given an award for its cleanliness. Marking the western extremity of the beach is **Magilligan Point** where a Martello tower, built during the Napoleonic wars, stands guard over the bottleneck entrance to Lough Foyle. To get to the point, renowned for its rare shellfish and sea birds, you have to drive over ramps below the watchtowers and listening devices of a huge army base. The experience is rather unsettling, but well worth the trouble.

## Mussenden Temple ➌

**Road map** D1. Co Londonderry.
🅲 01265 848728. 🅾 Jul–Aug: daily (pm only); Apr–Jun & Sep: Sat, Sun & public hols.

T HE ODDEST SIGHT along the Londonderry coast is this small, domed rotunda perched precariously on a windswept headland outside the family resort of Castlerock. The temple was built in 1785 by Frederick

Augustus Hervey, the eccentric Earl of Bristol and Protestant Bishop of Derry, as a memorial to his cousin Mrs. Frideswide Mussenden. The design was based on the Temple of Vesta at Tivoli outside Rome.

The walls, made of basalt faced with sandstone, open out at the four points of the compass to three windows and an entrance. Originally designed for use as a library (or, as some stories go, an elaborate boudoir for the bishop's mistress), the structure is now maintained by the National Trust and remains in excellent condition.

The bishop allowed the local priest to say Mass for his Roman Catholic tenants in the basement. Today, this contains artifacts from the bishop's former residence, the nearby Downhill Castle, which was gutted by fire and is now little more than an impressive shell.

The surrounding area offers some good glen and cliff walks and there are some magnificent views of the Londonderry and Antrim coastline. Below the temple is Downhill Strand, where the bishop used to sponsor horse racing between his clergy.

## Portstewart ➍

**Road map** D1. Co Londonderry.
🅸 5,500. 🅿 to Coleraine or Portrush.
🅿 🅸 Jul & Aug: Town Hall, The Crescent (01265 832286).

A POPULAR HOLIDAY destination for Victorian middle-class families, the resort still emits a sedate, old-fashioned air. Its long, crescent-shaped seafront promenade is sheltered by rocky headlands. Just west of town, and accessible by road or by a cliffside walk, stretches **Portstewart Strand**, a magnificent, long, sandy beach, protected by the National Trust.

On Ramore Head, just to the east, lies **Portrush**, a brasher resort with an abundance of souvenir shops and amusement arcades. The East Strand is backed by sand dunes and runs parallel with the world-class **Royal Portrush Golf Links**. You can stroll along the beach to White Rocks – limestone cliffs carved by the wind and waves into caves and arches.

To the south is the university town of **Coleraine**. The North West 200 (see p26), the world's fastest motorcycle road race, is run between Portstewart, Coleraine and Portrush. The race is held in May in front of 100,000 people.

Mussenden Temple set on a cliff top on the Londonderry coast

# Causeway Coast ⑤

**Road map** D1. Co Antrim. 🚹 *Giant's Causeway (012657 31855).* **Carrick-a-rede Rope Bridge** 📞 *012657 31159.* ⭕ *Easter & May–Aug: daily; Sep: Sat & Sun.* 🅿 *for parking.*

**The roofless ruins of 13th-century Dunluce Castle**

THE FAME of the **Giant's Causeway** *(see pp254–5),* Ireland's only World Heritage Site, overshadows the other attractions of this stretch of North Antrim coast. When visiting the Causeway, it is well worth investigating the sandy bays, craggy headlands and dramatic ruins that punctuate the rest of this inspirational coastline.

Approaching the Causeway from the west, you pass the eerie ruins of **Dunluce Castle** perched vulnerably on a steep crag – a storm once blew its kitchen into the sea. Dating back to the 13th century, it was the main fortress of the MacDonnells, chiefs of Antrim. Although the roof has gone, it is still well preserved, with its twin towers, gateway and some original cobbling intact.

**Dunseverick Castle** can be reached by road or a lengthy hike from the Causeway. It is a much earlier fortification than Dunluce and only one massive wall remains. Once the capital of the kingdom of Dalriada, it was linked to Tara *(see p240)* by a great road and was the departure point for 5th-century Irish raids on Scotland.

Just past the attractive, sandy **White Park Bay**, a tight switchback road leads down to the picturesque harbor of **Ballintoy**, reminiscent – on a good day – of an Aegean fishing village. **Sheep Island**, a rocky outcrop just offshore, is a cormorant colony. Local boat owners run trips past it in the summer.

Just east of Ballintoy is one of the most unusual and scary tourist attractions in Ireland, the **Carrick-a-rede Rope Bridge**. The bridge hangs 25 m (80 ft) above the sea and wobbles and twists as soon as you stand on it. Made of planks strung between wires, it provides access to the salmon fishery on the tiny island across the 20-m (65-ft) chasm. There are strong handrails and safety nets, but it's not for those with vertigo. Farther east along the coast lies **Kinbane Castle**. Little remains of this 16th-century ruin but the views from it are spectacular.

⛫ **Dunluce Castle**
⭕ *Apr–Sep: daily; Oct–Mar: Tue–Sun.* 🅿

**Fishing boats moored in the shelter of Ballintoy harbor**

**Carrick-a-rede Rope Bridge**

## THE NORTH ANTRIM COASTLINE

### KEY

| | | | |
|---|---|---|---|
| ═══ | Minor road | 🅿 | Parking |
| ▬▬▬ | Major road | 🚹 | Tourist information |

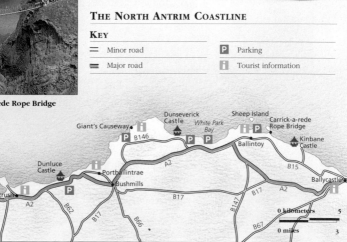

# Giant's Causeway ❻

T HE SHEER STRANGENESS of this place and the bizarre regularity of its basalt columns has made the Giant's Causeway the subject of numerous legends. The most popular tells how the giant, Finn MacCool (*see pp24–5*), laid the causeway to provide a path across the sea to his lady love, who lived on the island of Staffa in Scotland – where similar columns are found. The Giant's Causeway attracts many tourists, who are taken by the busload from the Visitors' Centre down to the shore. Nothing, however, can destroy the magic of this place, with its looming gray cliffs and shrieking gulls; paths along the coast allow you to escape the crowds.

**Chimney stacks**

**Aird's Snout**
*This nose-shaped promontory juts out from the 120-m (395-ft) basalt cliffs that soar above the Giant's Causeway.*

## THE FORMATION OF THE CAUSEWAY

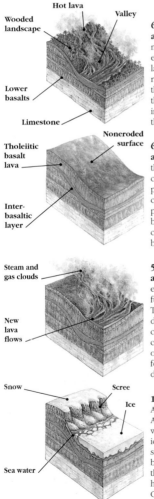

**Hot lava**
**Wooded landscape**
**Valley**
**Lower basalts**
**Limestone**

**61 million years ago:** In a series of massive volcanic eruptions, molten lava poured from narrow fissures in the ground, filling in the valleys and burning the vegetation that grew there.

**Tholeiitic basalt lava**
**Noneroded surface**
**Inter-basaltic layer**

**60 million years ago:** This layer of tholeiitic basalt lava cooled rapidly. In the process it shrank and cracked evenly into polygonal-shaped blocks, forming columnar jointing beneath the surface.

**Steam and gas clouds**
**New lava flows**

**58 million years ago:** New volcanic eruptions produced further lava flows. These had a slightly different chemical composition from earlier flows and, once cool, did not form such well-defined columns.

**Snow**
**Scree**
**Ice**
**Sea water**

**15,000 years ago:** At the end of the Ice Age, when the land was still frozen, sea ice ground its way slowly past the high basalt cliffs, eroding the foreshore and helping to form the Giant's Causeway.

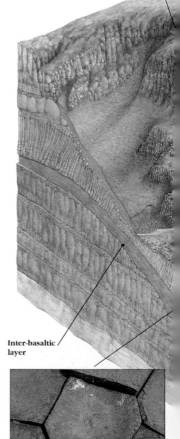

**Inter-basaltic layer**

**Shape of the Columns**
*Most columns are hexagonal, but some have four, five, eight or ten sides. They generally measure about 30 cm (12 in) across.*

## Giant's Causeway and the North Antrim Coast

*Millions of years of geological activity can be witnessed in the eroded cliffs flanking the Causeway. The striking band of reddish rock is the interbasaltic layer, which formed during a long period of temperate climatic conditions. The high iron content explains the rock's rich ocher color.*

### Middle Causeway

*This section of the Middle Causeway is known as the Honeycomb. Like other unusual rock formations along the coast, it was christened by local guides during Victorian times.*

Road

Little Causeway

## GIANT'S CAUSEWAY TODAY

It has been estimated that 37,000 basalt columns extend from the cliffs down into the sea. Close to the shore, they have been eroded to form the Grand, Middle and Little Causeways.

**Plant debris** is trapped between the lava flows.

### Wishing Chair

*Myth has it that this rocky seat was made for Finn MacCool when he was a boy, and that wishes made here will come true.*

Lower basalts

Grand Causeway

**Visitors exploring the Giant's Causeway at low tide** ▷

## Old Bushmills Distillery 7

**Road map** D1. Bushmills, Co Antrim. 012657 31521. from Coleraine & Giant's Causeway. Jun–Aug: Mon–Sat; Sep–May: Mon–Fri (Fri: am only). 1 week in Oct; 2 weeks at Christmas. obligatory.

Murlough Bay, on the coast facing Scotland to the east of Ballycastle

THE SMALL TOWN of Bushmills has an attractive square and an excellent river for salmon and trout fishing, but its main claim to fame is whiskey. The Old Bushmills plant on the outskirts of the town prides itself on being the oldest distillery in the world. Its Grant to Distill was given in 1608, though the spirit was probably made here at least 200 years before that.

In 1974 Bushmills joined the Irish Distillers Group based at the Jameson plant *(see p171)* in Midleton, but its products have retained their unique character. Most brands are a blend of many different whiskeys; Old Bushmills, in contrast, is made from a blend of a single malt and a single grain.

The tour of the distillery ends with a sampling session in the Potstill Bar in the former malt kilns, where there is also a minimuseum with old distilling equipment.

Whiskey barrel at Bushmills Distillery

## Rathlin Island 8

**Road map** D1. Co Antrim. 120. daily from Ballycastle (012657 63915). Ballycastle (012657 62024).

RATHLIN IS SHAPED rather like a boomerang – 11 km (7 miles) in length and at no point more than 1.6 km (1 mile) wide. The island is just a 50-minute boat ride from Ballycastle. About 30 families remain on Rathlin Island, making a living from fishing, farming and a little tourism. Facilities are limited, amounting to just a café, a pub and a guesthouse. The fierce, salty Atlantic winds ensure that the landscape on Rathlin is virtually treeless.

High white cliffs encircle much of the island, and at craggy **Bull Point** on the westerly tip, tens of thousands of seabirds, including kittiwakes, puffins and razorbills, make their home. A local minibus service will take visitors to view the birds. At the opposite end of the island is **Bruce's Cave**, where, in 1306, Robert Bruce, King of Scotland, supposedly watched a spider climbing a thread. The spider's perseverance inspired the dejected Bruce to return and win back his kingdom.

## Ballycastle 9

**Road map** D1. Co Antrim. 4,000. Sheskburn House, 7 Mary St (012657 62024). Sat.

A MEDIUM-SIZED resort town, Ballycastle boasts an attractive harbor and a central sandy beach. Near the harbor stands a memorial to Guglielmo Marconi. The great inventor's assistant transmitted the first-ever wireless message across water from here to Rathlin Island in 1898.

Ballycastle's annual Oul' Lammas Fair, held in late August, is one of the oldest traditional fairs in Ireland. It features noisy livestock sales and stalls selling yellowman (honeycomb toffee) and dulce (dried, heavily salted seaweed).

On the outskirts of town, the ruined 15th-century **Bonamargy Friary** houses the remains of Sorley Boy MacDonnell, former chieftain of this part of Antrim. Sections of the church, gatehouse and cloisters are well preserved.

## IRISH WHISKEY

The word whiskey comes from the Gaelic *uisce beatha*, meaning water of life. Distillation was probably introduced to Ireland by monks from Asia over 1,000 years ago. Small-scale production became part of the Irish way of life, but in the 17th century, the English introduced a licensing system and started to close down stills. In the 19th century, post famine poverty and the Temperance movement combined to lower demand. The result was that Scotch whisky (with no "e") took advantage of the situation, but in recent years, thanks to lower production costs, improved marketing and the rise in popularity of Irish coffee, sales have been increasing.

**Poster showing the Old Bushmills Distillery beside the River Bush**

**ENVIRONS:** Off the A2, 5 km (3 miles) east of town, a narrow scenic road starts to wind its way along the coast to Cushendall. First stop is **Fair Head**, where a poorly marked path meanders across heathery marshland to towering cliffs 200 m (650 ft) above the sea. From here there are stunning views of Rathlin and the islands off the Scottish coast.

To the lee side of the headland lies **Murlough Bay**, the prettiest inlet along the coast. This can be reached by road. Further to the southeast stands **Torr Head**, a peninsula that reaches to within 21 km (13 miles) of the Mull of Kintyre making it the closest point in Ireland to Scotland.

Carnlough harbor, a popular stop south of Cushendall

## Cushendall ⑩

**Road map** D1. Co Antrim. ⚄ *1,400.* 🚌 ℹ *Jul & Aug: 4b Mill St (012667 71180).*

THREE OF THE NINE Glens of Antrim converge toward Cushendall, earning it the unofficial title of "Capital of the Glens." This attractive village has brightly painted houses and a distinctive tower made of local red sandstone,

known as the Curfew Tower. It was erected in the early 19th century as a lockup for local thieves and idlers.

**ENVIRONS:** About 1.5 km (1 mile) north of the village stands **Layde Old Church**. It can be reached by a pretty walk along the cliffs. Founded by the Franciscans, it was a parish church from 1306 to 1790 and contains many monuments to the local chieftains, the MacDonnells.

Just over 3 km (2 miles) west of Cushendall, on the slopes of Tievebulliagh mountain, lies **Ossian's Grave**, named after the legendary warrior-poet and son of the giant Finn MacCool *(see pp24–5)*.

It is in fact a Neolithic court tomb: the area was a major center of Stone Age toolmaking and axheads made of Tievebulliagh's hard porcellanite rock have been found at a wide range of sites all over the British Isles.

Other attractive villages farther south along the coast road include **Carnlough**, which has a fine sandy beach and a delightful harbor, and **Ballygally**, whose 1625 castle is now a hotel *(see p300)*.

## Glenariff Forest Park ⑪

**Road map** D1. Co Antrim. 📞 *012667 58232.* ◯ *daily.* 🅿 *for car park.* ♿ *limited.*

NINE RIVERS have carved deep valleys through the Antrim Mountains to the sea. Celebrated in song and verse, the Glens of Antrim used to be the wildest and most remote part of Ulster. This region was not "planted" with English and Scots settlers in the 17th century and was the last place in Northern Ireland where Gaelic was spoken.

Today the Antrim coast road brings all the glens within easy reach of the tourist. Glenariff Forest Park contains some of the most spectacular scenery. The main scenic path runs through thick woodland and wildflower meadows and around the sheer sides of a gorge, past three waterfalls. There are also optional trails to distant mountain viewpoints. William Makepeace Thackeray, the 19th-century English novelist, called the landscape "Switzerland in miniature."

Glenariff Forest Park

**Stone circle and stone rows at Beaghmore**

# Cookstown ⑫

**Road map** D2. Co Tyrone. 🏠 *11,000.*
🚌 ℹ️ *Easter–Sep: 48 Molesworth St*
*(016487 66727).* 🚍 *Sat.*

COOKSTOWN STICKS in the
memory for its fine
central thoroughfare –
2 km (1.25 miles) long
and perfectly straight.
The road is about
40 m (130 ft) wide
and, as you look
to the north, it
frames the bulky
outline of Slieve
Gallion, the highest of
the Sperrin Mountains.
A 17th-century
Plantation town *(see
pp36–7)*, Cookstown
takes its name from its
founder, Alan Cook.

**ENVIRONS:** The countryside around Cookstown is
rich in Neolithic and early
Christian monuments. To the
east, on a desolate stretch of
Lough Neagh shoreline, the

**Ardboe**
**Cross**

**Ardboe Cross** stands on the
site of a 6th-century monastery. Although eroded, the
10th-century cross is one of
the best examples of a High
Cross *(see p235)* in Ulster: its
22 sculpted panels depict Old
Testament scenes on the east
side and New Testament
ones on the west. The
**Wellbrook Beetling Mill**,
west of Cookstown, is a
fascinating relic of
Ulster's old linen
industry. "Beetling"
was the process of
hammering the cloth
to give it a sheen. Set
amid trees beside the fast-
flowing Ballinderry River,
the mill dates from 1768
and is now a popular
tourist attraction. The
National Trust has restored
the whitewashed two-
story building and its
waterwheel. Inside, working
displays demonstrate just how
loud "beetling" could be. From
the mill, there are pleasant
walks along the river banks.

**🏛 Ardboe Cross**
Off B73, 16 km (10 miles) E of
Cookstown.
**🏭 Wellbrook Beetling Mill**
Off A505, 6.5 km (4 miles) W of
Cookstown. **☎** *016487 51715.* **🕐** *Jul
& Aug: Wed–Mon (pm only); Apr–Jun
& Sep: Sat, Sun & public hols.* 🏷

# Beaghmore Stone Circles ⑬

**Road map** D2. Co Tyrone. Off A505,
14 km (9 miles) NW of Cookstown.

ON A STRETCH of open
moorland in the foothills
of the Sperrin Mountains lies
a vast collection of stone
monuments, dating from
between 2000 and 1200 BC.
There are seven stone circles,
several stone rows and a
number of less prominent
features, possibly collapsed
field walls of an earlier
period. Their exact purpose
remains unknown, though in
some cases their alignment
correlates with movements of
the sun, moon and stars.
Three of the rows, for
example, are clearly aligned
with the point where the sun
rises at the summer solstice.
　The individual circle stones
are small – none is more than
1.20 m (4 ft) in height – but
their sheer numbers make
them a truly impressive sight.
As well as the circles and
rows, there are a dozen
round cairns (burial mounds).
Up until 1945, the whole
complex, one of Ulster's
major archaeological finds,
had lain buried beneath a
thick layer of peat.

---

## ULSTER'S HISTORIC LINEN INDUSTRY

The rise in Ulster's importance as a linen
producer was spurred on by the arrival from
France of refugee Huguenot weavers
at the end of the 17th century.
Linen remained a flourishing
industry for two more
centuries, but today it is
produced only in small
quantities for the luxury
goods market. Hundreds
of abandoned mills dot
the former "Linen Triangle"
bounded by Belfast, Armagh
and Dungannon. One of the
reasons why the material

**18th-century print, showing flax
being prepared for spinning**

diminished in popularity was the expensive
production process: after cutting, the flax
had to be retted, or soaked, in
large artificial ponds so that
scutching – the separation
of the fibers – could
begin. After combing,
the linen was spun and
woven before being
bleached in the sun,
typically in fields along
river banks. The final stage
was "beetling," the process
whereby the cloth was
hammered to give it a sheen.

**Copy of Iron Age Celtic stone head at the Ulster History Park**

# Ulster History Park ⑭

**Road map** C2. Co Tyrone. 📞 01662 648188. 🚌 from Omagh. ○ Apr–Sep: daily; Oct–Mar: Mon–Fri. ● Jan 1, Dec 25 & 26. 📷 ♿

NESTLING AT THE EDGE of the Sperrin Mountains, the Ulster History Park is filled with full-scale models of structures built by successive waves of settlers in Ireland. They range from a Mesolithic hunter/gatherer's hut covered with animal pelts, dating from 7000 BC, to a 17th-century Plantation village *(see pp36–7)*. There are also megalithic burial tombs, a crannog *(see p31)* from the early Christian period and a Norman motte and bailey (a wooden fortress built on a high mound). An exhibition center helps put the exhibits in perspective.

# Ulster-American Folk Park ⑮

**Road map** C2. Co Tyrone. 📞 01662 243292. 🚌 from Omagh. ○ Easter–Sep: daily; Oct–Easter: Mon–Fri exc public hols. 📷 ♿

ONE OF THE BEST open-air museums of its kind, the Folk Park grew up around the restored boyhood home of Judge Thomas Mellon (founder of the Pittsburgh banking dynasty). The Park's permanent exhibition, called "Emigrants," examines why two million people left Ulster for America during the 18th and 19th centuries. It also shows what became of them, following stories of both fortune and failure, including the grim lives of indentured servants and the 15,000 Irish vagrants and convicts trans-ported to North America in the mid-18th century.

The park has more than 30 historic buildings, some of them original, some replicas. There are settler homesteads (including that of John Joseph Hughes, the first Catholic Archbishop of New York), churches, a schoolhouse and a forge, some with craft displays, all with costumed interpretative guides. There's also an Ulster streetscape, a reconstructed emigrant ship and a Pennsylvania farmstead,

complete with log barn, corn crib and smokehouse. The six-roomed farmhouse is based on the one built by Thomas Mellon and his father in the early years of their new life in America.

A fully stocked library and database allow visitors to trace their family roots. Popular American festivals such as Independence Day and Hallowe'en are celebrated at the park and there is an Appalachian-Bluegrass music festival in early September.

# Belleek Pottery ⑯

**Road map** C2. Belleek, Co Fermanagh. 📞 013656 58501. 🚌 ○ Mar–Aug: daily; Oct–Feb: Mon–Sat. ● 17 Mar & 10 days at Christmas. 📷 ♿

**Worker at the Belleek factory making a Parian ware figurine**

THE LITTLE BORDER VILLAGE of Belleek would attract few visitors other than anglers were it not for the world-famous Belleek Pottery, founded in 1857. The company's pearly colored china is known as Parian ware. Developed in the 19th century, it was supposed to resemble the famous Parian marble of ancient Greece.

Belleek is now best known for its ornamental pieces of fragile latticework decorated with pastel-colored flowers. These are especially popular in the US. Several elaborate showpieces stand on display in the visitors' center and small museum. There's also a 20-minute video presentation on the company's history, a gift shop and ample parking space for tour buses.

Pennsylvania farmhouse

**Pennsylvania log farmhouse at the Ulster-American Folk Park**

# A Tour of Lower Lough Erne ⑰

THE AREA AROUND Lower Lough Erne boasts a rich combination of both natural and historic sights. From pre-Christian times, settlers sought the security offered by the lough's forests and inlets. Monasteries were founded on several of its many islands in the Middle Ages, and a ring of castles recalls the Plantation era *(see p37)*. The lake is a haven for water birds such as ducks, grebes and kingfishers, and the trout-rich waters attract many anglers. Lough Erne is a delight to explore by land or by boat. In summer, ferries serve several islands, and cruisers are available for rent.

**Kingfisher**

**View across Lower Lough Erne**

### Boa Island ⑤
Two curious double-faced figures stand in Caldragh cemetery, a Christian graveyard on Boa Island. While little is known about the stone idols, they are certainly pre-Christian.

### Belleek ⑦
Northern Ireland's most westerly village, Belleek is famous for its pottery *(see p261)*. There is also a new museum, ExplorErne, which covers most aspects of the region.

### Castle Caldwell Forest Park ⑥
The park's wooded peninsulas are a sanctuary for birds, and you can watch waterfowl from blinds on the shore. You may see great crested grebes, the common scoter duck and perhaps even otters.

← *BALLYSHANNON*
*R230*
*A47*
*Erne*
*A46*
*B52*
*SLIGO*
*B136*
⑤
*Lusty B*
LOWER  LOU
*Cliffs of Magho* ⑥ ⑧

### Lough Navar Forest Drive ⑧
An 11-km (7-mile) drive through pine forest leads to a viewpoint atop the Cliffs of Magho, with a magnificent panorama over Lough Erne and beyond. Trails weave through the woods.

### Tully Castle ⑨
A delightful 17th-century-s herb garden has recently been planted alongside fortified Plantation house whose protective enclos or bawn, is still visible.

## TIPS FOR DRIVERS
**Length:** 110 km (68 miles).
**Stopping points:** Outside Enniskillen, the best places to eat are the pubs in Kesh and Belleek; in summer, a café opens in Castle Archdale Country Park. There are good picnic places all along the route of this tour, including at the Cliffs of Magho viewpoint. (See also pp355–7.)

## KEY
▬ Tour route
═ Other roads
⛴ Boats to islands
☀ Viewpoint

## White Island ④

The Romanesque church on White Island has bizarre pagan-looking figures set into one wall. Of uncertain origin, they probably adorned an earlier monastery on this site. Ferries to the island leave from Castle Archdale Marina in summer.

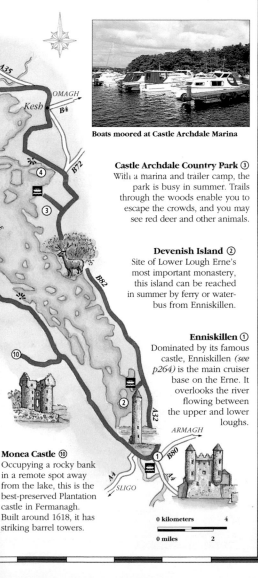

Boats moored at Castle Archdale Marina

### Castle Archdale Country Park ③

With a marina and trailer camp, the park is busy in summer. Trails through the woods enable you to escape the crowds, and you may see red deer and other animals.

### Devenish Island ②

Site of Lower Lough Erne's most important monastery, this island can be reached in summer by ferry or water-bus from Enniskillen.

### Enniskillen ①

Dominated by its famous castle, Enniskillen (*see p264*) is the main cruiser base on the Erne. It overlooks the river flowing between the upper and lower loughs.

### Monea Castle ⑩

Occupying a rocky bank in a remote spot away from the lake, this is the best-preserved Plantation castle in Fermanagh. Built around 1618, it has striking barrel towers.

0 kilometers 4
0 miles 2

Beautifully constructed round tower on Devenish Island

# Devenish Island ⑱

**Road map** C2. Co Fermanagh.
🚢 from Trory Point, 5 km (3 miles) N of Enniskillen (01365 322711): Apr–Sep: Tue–Sat & Sun pm; from Enniskillen (01365 322882): May–Jun: Sun pm; Jul–Aug: daily; Sep: Tue, Sat & Sun.
🎫 for museum and round tower.

ST. MOLAISE, who had 1,500 scholars under his tutelage, founded a monastery on this tiny windswept island in the 6th century. Although raided by Vikings in the 9th century and burned in 1157, it remained an important religious center up to the early 17th century.

Several fine buildings from the medieval monastery have survived, including **Teampall Mor** near the jetty. Built in 1225, this church displays the transition between Romanesque and Gothic styles. On the highest ground stands **St. Mary's Priory**, an Augustinian church that was erected in the 15th century. An intricately carved stone cross close by dates from the same period.

The most spectacular sight on Devenish Island is the 12th-century round tower, which stands some 25 m (82 ft) high. It is perfectly preserved, and the five floors can be reached by internal ladders. Supporting the roof is a cornice with a human face carved above each of the four windows; this is a unique feature in an Irish round tower. A museum covers the history and architecture of the island, and contains a collection of stone carvings and other antiquities discovered at the site.

# Enniskillen ⑲

Road map C2. Co Fermanagh.
🏘 14,000. 🚌 ℹ Wellington Road
(01365 323110). 🚆 Thu.

THE BUSY tourist center of Enniskillen occupies an island between Upper and Lower Lough Erne. The town gained fame for the wrong reason in 1987, when 11 people died in an IRA bomb attack, but it deserves a visit for its setting and sights.

At the west end of town stands **Enniskillen Castle**, which dates back to the 15th century. It houses a heritage center and the Inniskilling Regimental Museum. Its most stunning feature, however, is the Watergate, a fairy-tale twin-turreted tower, best admired from the far bank of the river. Farther west, **Portora Royal School**, founded in 1618, counts among its old boys the playwrights Oscar Wilde and Samuel Beckett *(see pp20–21)*.

The **Cole Monument** stands on a little hill in a pretty Victorian park on the east side of town. It is a tall Doric column with an internal

Enniskillen Castle seen from across the River Erne

spiral staircase that can be climbed for magnificent views of the lake country.

### ⚓ Enniskillen Castle
📞 01365 325000. 🕐 Jul & Aug: daily (Sat–Mon pm only); May–Jun & Sep: Mon–Sat; Oct–Apr: Mon–Fri. 🚫 Jan 1, Dec 25 & 26. ♿ limited.

**ENVIRONS:** Just outside town, set in a park with mature oak woodland overlooking a lake, is **Castle Coole**, one of the finest Neo-Classical homes in Ireland. It has a long Portland stone façade, with a central portico and small pavilions at each end. The stone was shipped from Dorset to Ballyshannon in County Donegal. Many of the fixtures and fittings were also brought from England. The first Earl of Belmore, who commissioned the house in the 1790s, was almost bankrupted by the cost of it. The original design was by Irish architect Richard Johnston, but the Earl then commissioned a second set of drawings by the fashionable English architect James Wyatt. The extravagant Earl died, deep in debt, in 1802 and it was left to his son to complete the decorating and furnishing during the 1820s.

The glory of Castle Coole is that almost all the house's original furniture is still in place. Family portraits from the 18th century line the walls of the dining room. In the lavish State Bedroom there is a bed made specially for King George IV on the occasion of his visit to Ireland in 1821, although in the end he never came here to sleep in it. One of the finest rooms is the oval parlor (or ballroom) at the back of the house. The heavy curtains and richly gilded Regency furniture may not be to everyone's taste, but the spacious oak-floored room produces a magnificent effect of understated luxury.

The parlor at Castle Coole, with original Regency furnishings

### ♦ Castle Coole
Off A4, 1.6 km (1 mile) SE of Enniskillen.
📞 01365 322690. 🕐 Jun–Aug: Fri–Wed (pm only); Apr, May & Sep: Sat, Sun & public hols. 🚫 ♿

# Marble Arch Caves ⑳

**Road map** C2. Marlbank Scenic Loop Rd, Florence Court, Co Fermanagh.
🎫 *01365 348855.* 🚌 *from Enniskillen (Jul & Aug).* 🕐 *Apr–Sep: daily.* ♿ 🎟 *obligatory.*

T HE CAVES are cut by three streams, which flow down the slopes of Cuilcagh Mountain, unite underground and emerge as the Cladagh River. Tours lasting 75 minutes consist of a boat ride into the depths of the cave complex and a guided walk that leads past stalagmites, calcite cascades and other curious limestone formations. The 9-m (30-ft) "Marble Arch" itself stands outside the cave system in the glen where the river gushes out from below ground.

The caves are very popular, so it's best to book ahead. It is also advisable to call to check the local weather conditions before setting out; the caves may be closed because of rain. Whatever the weather, bring a sweater and sensible walking shoes.

**Boat trip through Marble Arch Caves**

# Florence Court ㉑

**Road map** C2. Co Fermanagh.
🎫 *01365 348249.* 🚌 *from Enniskillen (Jul & Aug).* **House** 🕐 *Jun–Aug: Wed–Mon (pm only); Apr–May & Sep: Sat, Sun & public hols.* ♿ ♿ **Grounds** 🕐 *daily.* ♿ *for parking.*

T HIS THREE-STORY Palladian mansion was built for the Cole family in the mid-18th century. The arcades and pavilions, which are of a later date than the main house, were probably added around 1770 by William Cole, first Earl of Enniskillen. The house features flamboyant Rococo plasterwork said to be by the Dublin artist Robert West. Sadly, however, hardly any of what you see today is original as most of the central block was seriously damaged by fire in 1955. The furniture was lost, but the plasterwork was painstakingly recreated from photographs. The finest examples are in the dining room, the staircase and the small Venetian room.

Perhaps more spectacular are the grounds, which occupy a natural amphitheater set between hills and mountains. The area is fairly wild and there are many enjoyable walks and nature trails around the house. One woodland trail leads to the famous Florence Court yew tree, whose descendants are to be found all over Ireland. Closer to the house is a walled garden where pink and white roses make an attractive sight in early summer.

# Dungannon ㉒

**Road map** D2. Co Tyrone. 🏘 *9,500.* 🚌 ℹ *Apr–Sep: Killymaddy Tourist Centre, Ballygawly Rd, 8 km (5 miles) W of town (01868 767259).* 🛒 *Thu.*

D UNGANNON'S HILLY location made an ideal site for the seat of government of the O'Neill dynasty from the 14th century until Plantation *(see pp36–7),* when their castle was razed. The town's **Royal School** claims to be the oldest school in Northern Ireland. Opened in 1614, it moved to its present site on Northland Row in 1789.

Once a major linen center, this busy market town's best-known factory is now **Tyrone Crystal**, the largest concern of its kind in Northern Ireland. Tours of its modern complex cover all stages of production, including glassblowing.

🏭 **Tyrone Crystal**
Coalisland Road. 🎫 *01868 725335.* 🕐 *Mon–Sat.* 🔴 *10 days at Christmas.* 🎟 ♿

**Florence Court, the former seat of the Earls of Enniskillen**

**View of Armagh dominated by St. Patrick's Roman Catholic Cathedral**

## Armagh ㉓

**Road map** D2. Co Armagh.
👥 14,400. 🚉 ℹ️ 40 English St
(01861 527808). 🚌 Tue & Fri.

ONE OF IRELAND'S oldest cities,
Armagh dates back to the
age of St. Patrick *(see p273)* and
the advent of Christianity. The
narrow streets in the city center
follow the ditches that once
ringed the church, founded by
the saint in 455. Two cathedrals, both called **St. Patrick's**,
sit on opposing hills. The more
visually striking is the
huge Roman Catholic
one, a twin-spired
Neo-Gothic build-
ing with seem-
ingly every
inch of wall
covered in mosaic.
The older Protestant
Cathedral dates back
to medieval times. It
boasts the bones of
Brian Boru, the King of Ireland
who defeated the Vikings in
1014 *(see pp32–3)*, and an
11th-century High Cross.

Armagh's gorgeous oval tree-
lined Mall, where cricket is
played in summer, is surrounded by dignified Georgian
buildings. One of these houses
the small **Armagh County
Museum**, which has a good
exhibition on local history. Off
the Mall, **St. Patrick's Trian**
is a heritage center telling the
story of the city. It also has a
"Land of Lilliput" fantasy
center for children, based on
*Gulliver's Travels* by Jonathan
Swift *(see p80)*. Ireland's only
planetarium is on College Hill
in the **Observatory Grounds**,
from where there are splendid
views over the city.

🏛 **Armagh County Museum**
The Mall East. 📞 *01861 523070.*
⬜ *Mon–Sat.* ⬛ *some public hols.*
🏛 **St. Patrick's Trian**
40 English St. 📞 *01861 527808.*
⬜ *daily.* ⬛ *some public hols.* ♿
♣ **Observatory Grounds**
College Hill. 📞 *01861 522928.*
⬜ *Mon–Sat.* **Planetarium**
📞 *01861 523689.*

**ENVIRONS:** To the west of
Armagh stands **Navan Fort**, a
large earthwork on the summit
of a hill. In legend, Navan was
Emain Macha, ceremonial and
spiritual capital of
ancient Ulster,
associated with
tales of the great
warrior Cuchu-
lainn *(see p24)*.
The site may have been
in use as much as 4,000
years ago, but seems

**Skull of Barbary ape
from Navan Fort** to have been most
active around 100 BC
when a huge timber
building, 40 m (130 ft) across,
was erected over a giant
cairn. The whole thing was
then burned and the remains
covered with soil. Archaeological evidence indicates that
this was not an act of war,
but a solemn ritual performed
by the inhabitants of Emain
Macha themselves.

Below the fort, the grass-
roofed **Navan Centre**, built
to blend in with the landscape,
interprets the archaeology and
mythology of the site through
interactive displays and a 25-
minute film. The most unexpected exhibit is the skull of a
Barbary ape, found in the remains of a Bronze Age house.
The animal must have been
brought from Spain or North
Africa, evidence that by 500
BC Emain Macha had already
become an important place
with far-flung trading links.

🏛 **Navan Centre**
On A28 4 km (2.5 miles) W of Armagh.
📞 *01861 525550.* ⬜ *daily.*
⬛ *10 days at Christmas.* ♿ ⬛

## Lough Neagh ㉔

**Road map** D2. Co Armagh, Co
Tyrone, Co Londonderry, Co Antrim.

LEGEND TELLS that the giant
Finn MacCool *(see pp24–5)*
created Lough Neagh by
picking up a piece of turf and
hurling it into the Irish Sea, thus
forming the Isle of Man in the
process. At 400 sq km (153 sq
miles), the lake is the largest
in Britain. Most of it is bordered
by sedgy marshland, so few
roads run along the shore.
The best recreational areas lie
in the south; Oxford Island,
actually a peninsula, has
walking trails, bird lookouts
and the informative **Lough
Neagh Discovery Centre**. In
the southwest corner of the
Lough Neagh basin, a narrow-
gauge railway runs through
the bogs of **Peatlands Park**.

**Navan Fort, the site of Emain Macha, legendary capital of Ulster**

**Blinds for birdwatchers at Oxford Island on the southern shore of Lough Neagh**

Salmon and trout are found in the rivers that flow from Lough Neagh, while the lake itself is famous for its eels. One of the world's largest eel fisheries is at **Toome** on the north shore.

🏛 **Lough Neagh Discovery Centre**
Oxford Island. Exit 10 off M1.
📞 01762 322205. ○ Apr–Sep: daily; Oct–Mar: Wed–Sun.
● Dec 25 & 26. 🅿

🌳 **Peatlands Park**
Exit 13 off M1. 📞 01762 851102.
○ Jun–Aug: daily; Easter–May & Sep: Sat, Sun & public hols.

## Larne 25

**Road map** D1. Co Antrim.
🏠 18,000. �／🚊🅸 Narrow Gauge Rd (01574 260088) & at Ferry Terminal (01574 270517).

INDUSTRIAL LARNE is the arrival point for ferries from Scotland (*see pp352–4*). The town is not the finest introduction to Ulster scenery, but it lies on the threshold of the magnificent Antrim coastline (*see p259*).

The sheltered waters of Larne Lough have been a landing point since Mesolithic times – flint flakes found here provide some of the earliest evidence of human presence on the island – nearly 9,000 years ago. Since then, Norsemen used the lough as a base in the 10th century, Edward Bruce landed his Scottish troops in the area in 1315, and in 1914 the Ulster Volunteer Force landed a huge cache of German arms here during its campaign against Home Rule (*see pp42–3*).

## Carrickfergus 26

**Road map** E2. Co Antrim. 🏠 23,000.
🚉🚊🅸 Antrim St (01960 366455). ● Thu & Sat.

CARRICKFERGUS grew up around the massive castle begun in 1180 by John de Courcy to guard the entrance to Belfast Lough. De Courcy was the leader of the Anglo-Norman force, which invaded Ulster following Strongbow's conquest of Leinster in the south (*see pp34–5*).

**Carrickfergus Castle** was shaped to fit the crag on which it stands overlooking the harbor. The finest and best-preserved Norman castle in Ireland, it even has its original portcullis (*see pp34–5*). Naturally, many changes and adaptations have been made since the 12th century, including wide ramparts to accommodate the castle's cannons. Arms and armor are on display in the large rectangular keep, while life-size model soldiers are posed along the ramparts.

In continuous use up to 1928, the castle has changed hands several times over the years. The Scots, under Edward Bruce, took it in 1315, holding it for three years. In the 17th century James II's army was in control of the castle from 1688 until General Schomberg took it for William III in 1690. William himself stayed at the castle before the Battle of the Boyne (*see p236*) in July 1690.

The history of the town is recreated in a series of audio-visual displays at **Knight Ride**. The exhibition is literally a ride through history as you are transported from scene to scene in small cable cars. This appeals principally to children, who also enjoy the gorier episodes from the history of Carrickfergus.

♦ **Carrickfergus Castle**
📞 01960 351273. ○ daily.
● 25 Dec. 🅿 🅛
🏛 **Knight Ride**
Antrim St. 📞 01960 366455.
○ daily. ● Dec 25. 🅿

**The massive Norman keep of Carrickfergus Castle**

# Belfast ㉗

BELFAST WAS THE ONLY CITY in Ireland to experience the full force of the Industrial Revolution. Its shipbuilding, linen, rope-making and tobacco industries caused the population to rise to almost 400,000 by the end of World War I. The

**Red Hand of Ulster, Linen Hall Library** wealth it enjoyed is still evident in its imposing banks, churches and other public buildings. The Troubles and the decline of traditional industries have since damaged economic life, but Belfast remains a handsome city and most visitors are agreeably surprised by the genuine friendliness of the "Big Smoke."

**Mosaic in St. Anne's Cathedral, showing St. Patrick's journey to Ireland**

**Interior of the Grand Opera House**

## ♟ City Hall

Donegall Square. **(** 01232 320202 ext 2618. **📷** usually Wed (must be booked in advance).

Most of Belfast's main streets (and many major bus routes) radiate out from the hub of Donegall Square. In the center of the square stands the vast rectangular Portland stone bulk of the 1906 City Hall. It has an elaborate tower at each corner and a central copper dome that rises to a height of 53 m (173 ft). Highlight of the tour of the interior is the sumptuous oak-paneled council chamber.

Statues around the building include a glum-looking Queen Victoria outside the main entrance and, on the east side, Sir Edward Harland, founder of the Harland and Wolff shipyard, which built the *Titanic*. A memorial to those who died when the *Titanic* sank in 1912 stands close by.

## 🎭 Grand Opera House

Great Victoria St. **(** 01232 240411. Designed by Frank Matcham, the renowned theater-architect, this exuberant late-Victorian building opened its doors in 1894. The sumptuous interior, with its gilt, red plush and intricate plasterwork, was restored to its full glory in 1980. On occasions, bombings of the adjacent Europa Hotel disrupted business at the theater, but it survives as a major venue for plays and concerts. In 1984, Belfast-born singer Van Morrison recorded a famous live album here.

## ✝ St. Anne's Cathedral

Donegall St. **(** 01232 328332. The Neo-Romanesque façade of this Protestant cathedral, consecrated in 1904, fails to make much of an impression. The interior is far more attractive, especially the vast, colorful mosaics executed by the two Misses Martin in the 1920s. The one covering the baptistry ceiling contains over 150,000 pieces. The wide nave is paved with Canadian maple and the aisles with Irish marble. Lord Carson (1854– 1935), implacable leader of the campaign against Home Rule *(see p42)*, is buried in in the south aisle.

**Detail of *Titanic* Memorial outside City Hall**

**ARMAGH** DONEGALL RD SANDY ROW GREAT VICTORIA SHAFTESBURY SQUARE DUBLI DONEGALL PA UNIVERSITY ROAD BOTANIC AVENUE CROMWELL RD ⑦ UNIVERSITY STREET FITZROY AVENUE ROAD ⑧ UNIVERSITY AVENUE ORME STRANMILLS ⑨ AGINCOURT AVENUE BALFOUR AVENUE EMBANKMENT RIDGEWAY ST STRANMILLS EMBANKMENT ANNADALE EMBANKMENT Giant's Ring PARK ROAD

## SIGHTS AT A GLANCE

Albert Memorial Clock Tower ⑩
Botanical Gardens ⑨
City Hall ③
Crown Liquor Saloon ②
The Entries ⑤
Grand Opera House ①
Lagan Weir Lookout ⑪
Linen Hall Library ④
Queen's University ⑦
St. Anne's Cathedral ⑥
Ulster Museum ⑧

| 0 meters | | 500 |
| --- | --- | --- |
| 0 yards | | 500 |

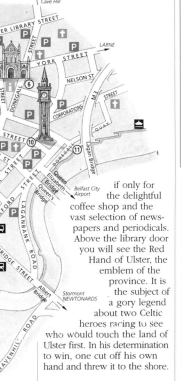

*Belfast International Airport Cave Hill*

LARNE

*Belfast City Airport*

Stormont NEWTONARDS

## VISITORS' CHECKLIST

**Road map** D2. Co Antrim.
305,000. ✈ *Belfast City Airport, 6.5 km (4 miles) E; Belfast International, 29 km (18 miles) NW.* 🚉 *Central Station, East Bridge St (01232 899411); Great Victoria St Station.* 🚌 *Europa Buscentre, Great Victoria St & Oxford St (01232 333000).* 🛈 *59 North St (01232 231221).* *Royal Ulster Agricultural Show & Lord Mayor's Show (May); Belfast Festival at Queen's (Nov).*

if only for the delightful coffee shop and the vast selection of newspapers and periodicals. Above the library door you will see the Red Hand of Ulster, the emblem of the province. It is the subject of a gory legend about two Celtic heroes racing to see who would touch the land of Ulster first. In his determination to win, one cut off his own hand and threw it to the shore.

### ⚑ The Entries

The Entries are a series of narrow alleys between Ann Street and High Street. They feature some of the best pubs in the city, including White's Tavern (*see p321*), reputedly the oldest bar in Belfast. The Globe in Joy's Entry and the Morning Star on Pottinger's

Entry both serve excellent lunches. In 1791, the United Irishmen, a radical movement inspired by the new ideas of the French Revolution, was founded in a tavern on Crown Entry. Its most famous member was Wolfe Tone (*see pp38–9*).

### ⚑ Crown Liquor Saloon

Great Victoria St. ☎ *01232 325368.* ◯ *daily.*
Even teetotallers should make a detour to the multicolored tiled façade of this flamboyant Victorian drinking palace. The Crown, which dates back to the 1880s, is the only pub owned by the National Trust. The lovingly restored interior features stained and painted glass, lots of marbling and mosaics and a splendid ceiling with scrolled plasterwork. The wooden snugs facing the long bar have their original gas lamps: the perfect place for a pint of Guinness or Bass and some Strangford Lough oysters.

### ⚑ Linen Hall Library

17 Donegall Square North.
☎ *01232 321707.* ◯ *Mon–Sat.*
Founded as the Belfast Society for Promoting Knowledge in 1788, the library has thousands of rare, old books in its dark wooden stacks. There is also extensive documentation of political events in Ireland since 1968 and a vast database of genealogical information. Even if you have no special reason for visiting the library, it is still well worth going inside,

## KEY

| | |
|---|---|
| 🚉 | Railroad station |
| 🚌 | Bus station |
| ⚓ | Ferry port |
| P | Parking |
| 🛈 | Tourist information |
| ✝ | Church |

**The ornate Victorian interior of the Crown Liquor Saloon**

# Exploring Belfast

Away from the city center, Belfast has many pleasant suburbs unaffected by the civil strife of recent times. The area around Queen's University to the south of the city has two major attractions in the Ulster Museum and the Botanic Gardens. To the north, there are splendid views to be enjoyed from the heights of Cave Hill, while visitors interested in Belfast's industrial heritage will be eager to see both the old docks and the Harland and Wolff working shipyards.

**Interior of the Victorian Palm House at the Botanic Gardens**

### 🏛 Ulster Museum

Botanic Gardens. ☎ *01232 381251.*
⭘ *daily (Sat & Sun: pm only).*
● *some public hols.* ♿

This four-floor bunker of a museum covers all aspects of Ulster, from local history, archaeology, antiquities and art to geology, natural history and technology. Especially prized treasures include gold and silver jewelry recovered from the *Girona*, a Spanish Armada ship that sank off the Giant's Causeway in 1588 *(see p249)*. One of the most interesting exhibits is of Belfast industry, featuring some crude turn-of-the-century textile machinery.

In the top-floor gallery is a collection of paintings mostly by British and Irish artists, including a large number by Belfast-born Sir John Lavery (1856–1941).

In addition to the Irish collections, there are exhibits ranging from ancient Egyptian mummies to dinosaurs. The museum also holds frequent temporary exhibitions on a wide variety of themes.

### 🌸 Botanic Gardens

Stranmillis Rd. ☎ *01232 324902.*
⭘ *daily.*

Backing on to the university, the Botanic Gardens provide a quiet refuge from the bustle of campus. The 1839 Palm House is a superb example of curvilinear glass and cast-iron work. The Tropical Ravine, or Fernery, is another fine piece of Victorian garden architecture. Visitors can look down from the balcony to a sunken glen of exotic plants.

### 🎓 Queen's University

University Rd. ☎ *01232 245133.*

A 15-minute stroll south from Donegall Square, through the lively entertainment district known as the Golden Mile, leads to Northern Ireland's most prestigious university. The main building, designed in Tudor-style red and yellow brick by Charles Lanyon in 1849, bears similarities to Magdalene College, Oxford. A towered gateway leads to a colonnaded quadrangle.

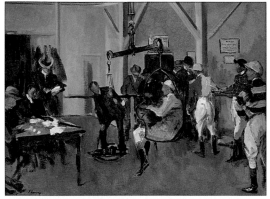

*Weighing Room, Hurst Park* (1924) by Sir John Lavery, Ulster Museum

## THE POLITICAL MURALS OF WEST BELFAST

**Republican mural in the Falls Road**

Ever since the onset of the "Troubles" in 1968, popular art has played a conspicuous role in proclaiming the loyalties of Belfast's two most intransigent working-class communities, on the Protestant Shankill Road and the Catholic Falls Road. The gable walls of dozens of houses in these areas have been decorated with vivid murals expressing local political and paramilitary affiliations. Likewise, curbstones on certain streets are painted either in the red, white and blue of the United Kingdom or the green, white and gold of Ireland. Whatever the outcome of the current peace process, many are likely to remain. Some tourists make the journey out to West Belfast just to see the murals. The simplest way to do this is to take a taxi from the center; cabs that go to the Falls Road leave from Castle Street, while those for the Shankill Road leave from North Street.

**Protestant Loyalist mural**

## ♛ Albert Memorial Clock Tower

Queen's Square.
One of Belfast's best-known monuments, the clock tower was designed by WJ Barre. Prince Albert, Queen Victoria's consort, had no personal connection with Belfast, but memorials to him were built in many British cities in the decade following his death in 1861. Today, the tower arouses most interest because it leans slightly as a result of subsidence. Beyond it, facing the river, stands the Custom House (1854) designed by Charles Lanyon, architect of Queen's University.

**Belfast cityscape showing the giant cranes, Samson and Goliath**

## 🏛 Lagan Weir Lookout

Donegall Quay. 📞 01232 315444. ◯ daily (Sat & Sun: pm only). 🖼
Belfast's once thriving harbor area, five minutes' walk from Donegall Square, can best be viewed from the footbridge alongside the new Lagan Weir development. Five computer-controlled steel gates, unveiled in 1994, maintain a fixed water level, getting rid of the smelly mudbanks produced by varying tide levels and creating possibilities for angling and watersports along the river. The Visitors' Center, on the footbridge, explains how it all works and tells some good tales of modern Belfast folklore. At night, the weir is lit by gas-filter blue light that shimmers across the water.

Unfortunately, the new Cross-Harbour Road and Rail Link bridge partly obscure the view across to the giant yellow cranes – appropriately named Samson and Goliath – of the once-mighty Harland and Wolff shipyards.

**The unmistakable profile of Cave Hill above the roofs of Belfast**

**ENVIRONS:** The best place for an overall view of Belfast and Belfast Lough is the 360-m (1,118-ft) summit of Cave Hill, the most distinctively shaped of the hills encircling the city.

## ⛰ Cave Hill

Antrim Rd, 6.5 km (4 miles) N of city center. **Heritage Centre** 📞 01232 776925. ◯ daily. ● Dec 25. ♿ **Zoo** 📞 01232 774625. ◯ daily. ● Dec 25. 🖼 ♿
It was on Cave Hill, next to the remains of MacArt's Fort (named after an Iron Age chieftain), that Wolfe Tone (see p39) and the northern leaders of the United Irishmen met in 1795 to pledge themselves to rebellion. The five artificial caves near the fort were carved out during the Neolithic period.

On the thickly wooded, eastern slopes of the hill stands the baronial pile of Belfast Castle, built in 1870. Previously home to the Earl of Shaftesbury, the castle now belongs to the city and houses two restaurants and a new heritage center that interprets the area's history. A little farther along the road past the castle is Belfast Zoo, which makes the most of its steep woodland setting.

## ∩ Giant's Ring

Off B23, 5 km (3 miles) S of city center.
Little is known about this awe-inspiring prehistoric enclosure almost 200 m (660 ft) in diameter. It is surrounded by a grassy bank averaging almost 6 m (20 ft) in width and 4.5 m (15 ft) in height. Bones from a Stone Age burial were found under the dolmen in the center. During the 18th century the ring was a popular spot for horse races.

## ♛ Stormont

Newtownards Rd, 8 km (5 miles) SE of city center. ● to the public. 🖼 by arrangement only.
Built between 1928 and 1932, at a cost of £1,250,000, Stormont was designed to house the Northern Ireland Parliament. The huge Anglo-Palladian mass of Portland stone and Mourne granite stands at the end of a majestic avenue, 1.6 km (1 mile) long, bordered by parkland. A statue of Lord Carson (see p42) stands near the front entrance.

Since the parliament was disbanded in 1972, the building has been used as government offices. Its future depends very much on the outcome of the ongoing peace process. The debating chamber was badly damaged in a fire in 1994.

**Stormont in its parkland setting outside Belfast**

# Ulster Folk and Transport Museum 🖭

**Road map** E2. Cultra, near Holywood, Co Down. 📞 *01232 428428.* 🚌 🏠 ◯ *daily.* 🗒 🖢

OZENS of old buildings, including flax-, corn- and sawmills plus various rural dwellings, have been plucked from the Ulster countryside and re-erected in this absorbing folk park. Demonstrations of traditional crafts, industries and farming methods are given all year around.

The A2 road divides the folk museum from the transport section. This is dominated by a hangar that houses the Irish Railway Collection. The smaller Transport Gallery exhibits machinery made in Ulster, including a parlor car from the trolley service that ran from Portrush to Giant's Causeway (*see pp254–5*). Of particular note is a test model of the spectacularly unsuccessful De Lorean car, made in the early 1980s with a huge government subsidy. There's also a popular exhibit on another ill-fated construction – the *Titanic*. It's best to allow half a day to take in most of the attractions.

**1883 trolley car at the Ulster Folk and Transport Museum**

# Ards Peninsula 🖭

**Road map** E2. Co Down. 🚌 🏠 *to Bangor.* 🛈 *34 Quay St, Bangor (01247 270069).*

THE PENINSULA – and some of Northern Ireland's finest scenery – begins east of Belfast at **Bangor**. This resort town has a modern marina and some well-known yacht clubs. A little way south is **Donaghadee**, from where boats sail to the three **Copeland Islands**. These are now populated only

**Scrabo Tower, a prominent landmark of the Ards Peninsula**

by seabirds, as the last human residents left the islands in the 1940s. **Ballycopeland Windmill** (1784), Northern Ireland's only working windmill, stands on a small hill a little farther south, near the town of Millisle.

A short journey across the peninsula is **Newtownards** on the even more stunning Strangford Lough side.

Above the town on a pleasantly wooded hill stands **Scrabo Tower**, built in 1857 as a memorial to the third Marquess of Londonderry. The tower's 122 steps lead up to a great view of Strangford Lough.

Past the grounds of **Mount Stewart House** (*see pp274–5*) is the hamlet of Greyabbey, with its antique shops and Cistercian abbey ruins. Founded in 1193, **Grey Abbey** was used as a parish church until the 17th century. It is idyllically set in lush meadows by a stream and some of its features, particularly the finely carved west doorway, are well preserved.

On the tip of the peninsula, **Portaferry** overlooks the Strangford Narrows (stunning at sunset) across from the Lecale Peninsula (*see p276*).

Portaferry's large aquarium, **Exploris**, displays the surprising diversity of marine life in the Irish Sea and Strangford Lough.

🌀 **Ballycopeland Windmill**
On B172 1.6 km (1 mile) W of Millisle. 📞 *01247 861413.* ◯ *Easter–Sep: Tue–Sun; Oct–Mar: Sat & Sun.* 🗒

🌀 **Scrabo Tower**
Near Newtownards. 📞 *01247 811491.* ◯ *Easter & Jun–Sep: Sat–Thu.*

🛈 **Grey Abbey**
Greyabbey village. ◯ *Apr–Sep: Tue–Sun.* 🗒 🖢

🐟 **Exploris**
Castle Street, Portaferry. 📞 *012477 28062.* ◯ *daily.* ⬤ *Dec 25.* 🗒 🖢

**Ballycopeland Windmill, which dates back to 1784**

## Mount Stewart House ③⓪

*See pp274–5.*

## Hillsborough ③①

**Road map** D2. Co Down. 🏠 *2,400.*
🚌 ℹ️ *The Square (01846 682477).*

**D**OTTED WITH antique shops and restaurants, this show-piece Georgian town lies less than 16 km (10 miles) from Belfast. Its most impressive building is the massive **Hillsborough Castle**, where visiting dignitaries to Northern Ireland stay. Though not open to the public, its elaborate wrought-iron gates and coat of arms are worth seeing.

Across from the 18th-century Market House in the town square, and next to the pleasant Forest Park, is **Hillsborough Fort**. An artillery fort dating from 1650, it was remodeled in the 18th century for feasts held by the descendants of Arthur Hill, founder of the town.

**♠ Hillsborough Fort**
Access from town square or car park at Forest Park. 📞 *01846 683285.*
🕐 *Tue–Sun.*

## Downpatrick ③②

**Road map** E2. Co Down. 🏠 *10,300.*
🚌 ℹ️ *74 Market St (01396 612233).* 🚌 *Sat.*

**W**ERE IT NOT for its strong links with St. Patrick, Downpatrick would attract few visitors. The Protestant **Down Cathedral**, high on the Hill of Down, dates in its present form from the early 19th century – many previous incarnations have been razed to the ground. In the churchyard is a well-worn 10th-century cross and the reputed burial place of St. Patrick, marked by a granite slab (placed here this century) with the inscription "Patric."

**Down County Museum**, which is housed in the 18th-century Old County Gaol, features refurbished cells and exhibits relating to St. Patrick, while close by is the **Mound of Down**, a large Norman motte and bailey.

**Terraced houses in the town of Hillsborough**

**🏛 Down County Museum**
The Mall. 📞 *01396 615218.*
🕐 *Jul–mid-Sep: daily (Sat & Sun: pm only); mid-Sep–Jun: Tue–Sat & public hols.* ⬛ *Dec 25 & 26.*

**ENVIRONS:** There are several sights associated with St. Patrick on the outskirts of Downpatrick. **Struell Wells**, believed to be a former pagan place of worship that the saint blessed, has a ruined church, 17th-century bath houses and good potential for a picnic. Farther out and to the north at **Saul**, where St. Patrick landed and began his Irish mission in 432, is a small memorial church.

The nearby hill of **Slieve Patrick** is an important place of pilgrimage and has a granite figure of the saint at its summit. An open-air mass is celebrated here every June.

Not far from the banks of the River Quoile is the Cistercian **Inch Abbey**, founded by John de Courcy in about 1180. Its attractive marshland setting is probably more memorable than its scant remains, but it's worth a visit nonetheless.

**♠ Inch Abbey**
5 km (3 miles) NW of Downpatrick.
🕐 *Apr–Sep: Tue–Sun.* 🎟️

### THE LIFE OF ST. PATRICK

Little hard information is known about St. Patrick, the patron saint of Ireland, but he was probably not the first missionary to visit the country – a certain Palladius was sent by Pope Celestine in 431. Most stories say that Patrick was kidnapped from Britain by pirates and brought to Ireland to tend sheep. From here he escaped to France to study Christianity. In 432, he sailed to Saul in County Down, where he quickly converted the local chieftain. He then traveled throughout the island convincing many other Celtic tribes of the truth of the new religion. The fact that Ireland has no snakes is explained by a legend that St. Patrick drove them all into the sea.

**19th-century engraving showing St. Patrick banishing all snakes from Ireland**

# Mount Stewart House ⑳

**Lord Castlereagh**
**(1769–1822)**

THIS GRAND 19TH-CENTURY HOUSE has a splendid interior, but it is the magnificent gardens which are the main attraction. These were planted only in the 1920s, but the exotic plants and trees have thrived in the area's subtropical microclimate. Now owned by the National Trust, Mount Stewart used to belong to the Londonderry family, the most famous of whom was Lord Castlereagh, British Foreign Secretary from 1812 until his death in 1822.

**The Sunk Garden**
consists of symmetrical beds that in summer are full of rich blue, yellow and orange flowers, complemented by purple foliage.

**Stone pergola**

★ **Shamrock Garden**
*A yew hedge in the shape of a shamrock encloses this topiary Irish harp and a striking flower-bed designed in the form of a red hand, emblem of Ulster.*

**The Music Room**
has a beautiful inlaid floor of mahogany and oak.

**Italian Garden**
*The flowers in the Italian Garden, the largest of the formal gardens, are planted so that strong oranges and reds on the east side contrast with the softer pinks, whites and blues on the west.*

**Fountain**

### THE TEMPLE OF THE WINDS

This banqueting pavilion looks over Strangford Lough to the east of the house. It was built in 1785 by James "Athenian" Stuart, a renowned pioneer of Neo-Classical architecture, who took his inspiration from the Tower of the Winds in Athens. Restored in the 1960s and now being worked on once more, the building's finest features are the spiral staircase and the upper room's plasterwork ceiling and exquisite inlaid floors.

**The Spanish Garden** is framed by a neat arcade of clipped cypress trees.

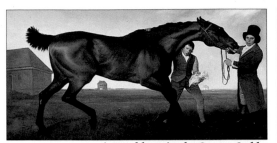

**★ Hambletonian by George Stubbs**
*This picture of the celebrated racehorse at Newmarket, painted in 1799, hangs halfway up the main staircase.*

## Visitors' Checklist

**Road map** E2. 3 km (2 miles) N of Greyabbey, Co Down. *012477 88387. to Newtownards from Belfast.* **House** *Apr–Oct: 1–5pm Wed–Mon.* **Gardens** *Mar: 1–5pm Sun; Apr–Oct: 10:30am–5:30pm daily.* **Temple of the Winds** *for restoration until 1996. in house.*

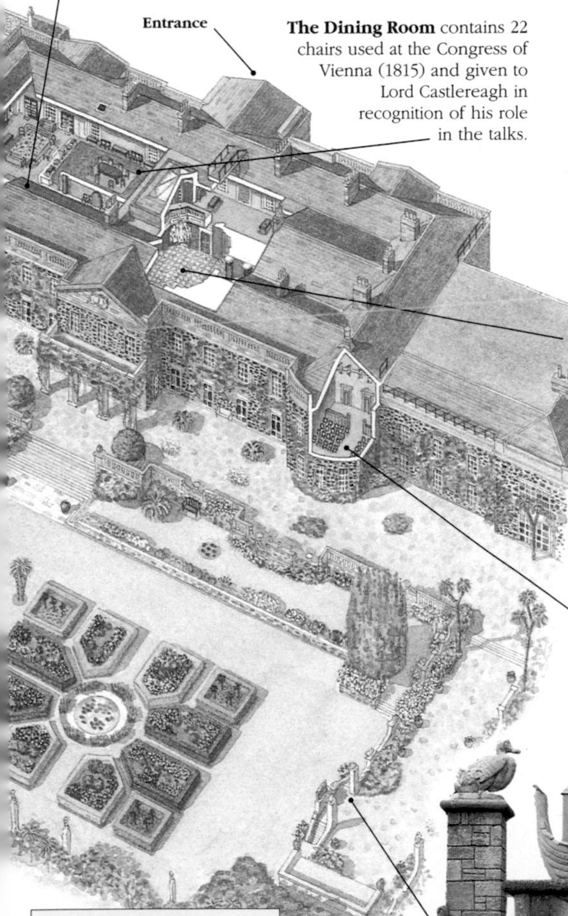

**Entrance**

**The Dining Room** contains 22 chairs used at the Congress of Vienna (1815) and given to Lord Castlereagh in recognition of his role in the talks.

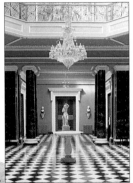

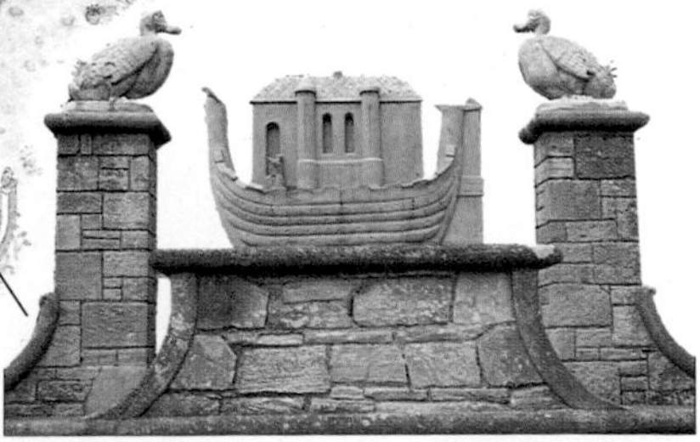

**The Chapel,** converted from a sitting room in 1884, is still used by the Londonderry family.

**Entrance Hall**
*The most austere room in the house, this hall features Ionic stone pillars which have been painted to resemble green marble. It is lit by an impressive glass dome.*

**★ Dodo Terrace**
*The stone dodos and ark on this terrace relate to the Ark Club, a social circle set up by Lady Londonderry in London during World War I. Each member was given an animal nickname.*

## Star Features

- ★ Dodo Terrace
- ★ Shamrock Garden
- ★ Hambletonian by George Stubbs

Lady Bangor's Gothic boudoir in Castle Ward on the Lecale Peninsula

# Lecale Peninsula ❸

**Road map** E2. Co Down. 🚌 to
Ardglass. 🛈 Downpatrick (01396
612233).

A GOOD WAY to get to this part
of County Down is to take
the short but scenic car ferry
from Portaferry on the Ards
Peninsula to Strangford. Just
outside this tiny port is **Castle
Ward**, the intriguing estate of
Lord and Lady Bangor, who
seemed to argue about everything – including the design
of their mansion, built in the
1760s. His choice, Palladian,
can be seen at the front, while
her favorite Gothic style
influences the garden façade.
Likewise, the interior is a mix
of Classical and Gothic fantasy.
Look out for Lady Bangor's
cluttered boudoir, with its
extravagant fan-vaulted ceiling
based on Henry VIII's chapel
in Westminster Abbey. Around
the extensive grounds are fine
gardens, gentle walking trails
and a lakeside farmyard with
a working grain mill.
    About 4 km (2.5 miles) south
of Strangford, the A2 passes
**Kilclief Castle**, which dates
from the 15th century and is
one of the oldest tower houses
(see p18) in Ireland. The road
continues to **Ardglass**, now a
small fishing village but once
Ulster's busiest harbor. A
cluster of castles was erected
between the 14th and 16th
centuries to protect the port,
of which six remain. Only one
of these is open to the public,

**Jordan's Castle**. The finest
view in the area is from **St.
John's Point**, 6 km (3.5 miles)
southwest of Ardglass, which
provides a sweeping panorama
over Dundrum Bay.

🚏 **Castle Ward**
On A25, 2.5 km (1.5 miles) W of
Strangford. 🕻 01396 881204.
**House** 🕐 May–Aug: Fri–Wed (pm
only); Apr, Sep & Oct: Sat, Sun & public
hols. 🖾 🕭 **Grounds** 🕐 daily.
🖾 for parking lot.
🛥 **Jordan's Castle**
Ardglass. 🕐 May–Aug: Tue–Sun. 🖾

# Castlewellan
Forest Park ❸

**Road map** D2. Main St, Castlewellan,
Co Down. 🕻 013967 78664. 🕐 daily.
🖾 for parking lot.

T HE OUTSTANDING FEATURE of
Castlewellan Forest Park,
in the foothills of the Mourne
Mountains, is its magnificent
arboretum. This has grown far
beyond the

original walled garden, begun
in 1740, and now comprises
hothouses, dwarf conifer beds
and a rhododendron wood.
    Elsewhere in the park are a
19th-century Scottish baronial-
style castle (now a conference
center), a lake and pleasant
woodlands; these are at their
most colorful in autumn.

# Mountains of
Mourne ❸

**Road map** D2. Co Down. 🚌 to
Newry. 🚌 to Newcastle. 🛈 10 Central
Promenade, Newcastle (013967 22222).

T HESE MOUNTAINS occupy just
a small corner of County
Down, with no more than a
dozen peaks higher than 600 m
(2,000 ft), and yet they attract
thousands of visitors each year.
    Only one road of any size,
the B27 between Kilkeel and
Hilltown, crosses the Mournes,
making this ideal territory for
hikers. A popular but tough
trail runs from **Newcastle**, the
main gateway to the area, up
to the peak of **Slieve Donard**:
at 848 m (2,796 ft), this is the
highest mountain in the range.
Part of the route follows the
**Mourne Wall**, which was
erected in 1904–22 to enclose
the catchment area of the two
reservoirs in the **Silent Valley**.
    Over 20 other short hikes are
described in the *St. Patrick's
Vale Walks* booklet, available
from local tourist offices. These
range from easy strolls around
Rostrevor Forest to rather more
arduous treks up Slieve Muck
and other Mourne peaks.
    Some 35 km (22 miles) north
of Newcastle, but still within
the Mountains of Mourne, the
**Legananny Dolmen** *(see p30)*
is one of the finest and most
photographed ancient sights
in the country.

**Rounded peaks of the Mountains of Mourne**

# A Tour of the Mourne Coast ⊛

Newcastle, where, in the words of the 19th-century songwriter Percy French, "the Mountains of Mourne sweep down to the sea," makes a good base from which to explore this area. Driving up and down the dipping roads of the Mournes is one of the highlights of a trip to Northern Ireland. Along the coast, the road skirts between the foothills and the Irish Sea, providing lovely views and linking a variety of fishing villages and historic castles. Heading inland, you pass through an emptier landscape of moorland, purple with heather. The Silent Valley, with a visitors' center and well-marked paths, is the only area to have been developed especially for tourists.

**Dundrum ②**
The town is overlooked by the ruins of a Norman castle, and from the nearby bay you can see the mountains rising in the distance.

**Tollymore Forest Park ③**
This attractive park is dotted with follies like the Gothic Gate that formed part of the original 18th-century estate.

**Spelga Dam ④**
There are stunning views north from the Spelga Dam over the Mourne foothills.

**Newcastle ①**
A popular resort since the early 19th century, Newcastle has a promenade overlooking a sweeping, sandy beach.

**Rostrevor with Slieve Martin behind**

**Silent Valley ⑦**
The valley is closed to traffic, but you can walk to the top of Ben Crom Mountain from the parking lot, or in summer go by bus.

**Rostrevor ⑤**
This tranquil and leafy Victorian resort nestles below the peak of Slieve Martin, on the shores of Carlingford Lough.

**Green Castle ⑥**
Erected in the 13th century, Green Castle lies at the end of a single track road on a rocky outcrop at the entrance to Carlingford Lough.

## Tips for Drivers

**Length:** 85 km (53 miles).
**Stopping-off points:** Newcastle has the biggest choice of pubs and restaurants. Dundrum, Annalong, Kilkeel and Rostrevor all have pubs, and a café opens in the Silent Valley in summer. The Spelga Dam and Tollymore Forest Park are good picnic spots. (See also pp355–7.)

0 kilometers 5
0 miles 3

### Key

▬▬▬ Tour route
═══ Other roads
🌟 Viewpoint

# TRAVELERS' NEEDS

WHERE TO STAY 280-301

RESTAURANTS, CAFÉS AND PUBS 302-321

SHOPPING IN IRELAND 322-327

ENTERTAINMENT IN IRELAND 328-335

# WHERE TO STAY

**W**HETHER YOU ARE STAYING in exclusive luxury or modest efficiency accommodations, one thing you can be certain of in Ireland is that you'll receive a warm welcome. The Irish are renowned for their friendliness. Even in big corporate hotels, where you might expect the reception to be more impersonal, the staff go out of their way to be hospitable. The choice is enormous: you can stay in an elegant 18th-century country house, a luxurious (or slightly run-down) castle, a Victorian town house, an old-fashioned commercial hotel, a cozy village inn, or

*Waterford Castle doorman*

on a working farm. For the hardier visitor there are good hostels, plenty of trailer and camping sites, or even your own horse-drawn caravan. We give details here on the various types of accommodations available, tourist board ratings and the choices for efficiencies. Our listings on pages 286–301 recommend over 200 hotels around the country – all places of quality, ranging from simple bed-and-breakfast to unashamed luxury accommodation. Bord Fáilte (the Irish Tourist Board) and the Northern Ireland Tourist Board both publish comprehensive guides.

Entrance hall of the Delphi Lodge *(see p296)* in Connemara

## HOTELS

**A**T THE TOP of the price range there are a handful of expensive, luxury hotels in castles and stately country houses. Magnificently furnished and run, they offer maximum comfort, delicious food and a wide range of sports facilities – either owned by the hotel or available close by. Salmon fishing, foxhunting and shooting can be arranged as well as riding, golf, sailing and cycling.

If your priority is a full range of indoor facilities, such as a gym, sauna and swimming pool, the modern hotel chains will best cater to your needs. **Jury's**, **Great Southern Hotels** and **Irish Welcome** offer this standard of accommodation in the Republic, as do **Hastings Hotels** and Irish Welcome in Northern Ireland. However,

these establishments can lack the charm and individuality of privately run hotels.

Coastal resort hotels usually offer a range of sports activities, or can advise you on the best places to go. In smaller towns, the main hotel is often the social center of the area with a lively public bar, popular with locals and guests alike.

The shamrock symbols of both the Northern Ireland Tourist Board and Bord Fáilte are displayed by hotels (and other forms of accommodation) that have been inspected and officially approved.

## COUNTRY HOUSE ACCOMMODATION

**V**ISITORS WISHING to stay in a period country home and sample authentic Irish country life can contact a special

organization called **Hidden Ireland**. However, this type of accommodation may not suit everybody. The organization emphasizes the houses they offer are not guesthouses, hotels or bed-and-breakfast establishments, but private residences. You should therefore not expect the facilities and service usually found in a hotel, such as a swimming pool, elevators, televisions, porters or room service. Instead, the experience is a very intimate one; guests dine together with their host and hostess as if at a private dinner party. Many of the houses have been in the same family for hundreds of years and the history attached to them can be fascinating. Prices reflect the type of house and the standard of accommodation, but

The entrance to the Shelbourne Hotel in Dublin *(see p287)*

**Bar at the Hunter's Hotel** *(see p290)* in Rathnew, County Wicklow

all offer excellent bargains and a first-hand experience of an aspect of the Irish way of life.

In addition to the houses that are part of the Hidden Ireland group, there are many other private residences that also take paying guests. Local tourist boards throughout Ireland can supply listings and will make reservations with those residences that they have officially approved.

## GUESTHOUSES

MOST GUESTHOUSES are found in cities and large towns. They are usually converted family homes and have an atmosphere all of their own. Most offer a good-value evening meal and all give you a delicious full Irish breakfast *(see p304)*. Top-of-the-line guesthouses can be just as good, and sometimes even better, than hotels. You will see a much more personal side of a town or city while staying at a guesthouse. If you are looking for anonymity, however, a guesthouse may not suit you – both the proprietor and your fellow guests are likely to make attempts to draw you into conversation.

There are plenty of good guesthouses to choose from in the Dublin area and the prices are usually extremely reasonable. The **Irish Hotel Federation** publishes a useful booklet with guesthouse listings that cover the whole of Ireland including Dublin. The Northern Ireland Tourist Board publishes a similar

booklet, *Where to Stay in Northern Ireland*. This includes a comprehensive list of approved guesthouses updated annually. However, it is hard to beat personal recommendations that you might receive from fellow guests.

**Bedroom at Enniscoe House** *(see p295)*, Crossmolina in County Mayo

## PRICES

ROOM RATES advertised in both Northern Ireland and the Republic are inclusive of tax and service. In general, prices in the Republic are marginally cheaper than

in the North. Hotel rates can vary by as much as 40 percent depending on the time of year; country house rates also vary a great deal according to the season. Guesthouse prices are influenced more by their location in relation to tourist sights and transportation.

For those on a tight budget, farmhouse accommodations represent excellent bargains, although the best option, if you want privacy, is to rent an efficiency cottage *(see p282)*.

## TIPPING

TIPPING IN IRELAND is a matter of personal discretion but is not common practice, even at the larger hotels. Tasks performed by staff are considered part of the service. Tipping is not expected, for example, for carrying bags to your room or for serving drinks. However, it is usual to tip the waiting staff in hotel restaurants: the standard tip is around 10 percent and anything over 15 percent of the bill would be considered generous.

## BOOKING

IT IS WISE to reserve your accommodation during the peak season and public holidays *(see p49)*, particularly if your visit coincides with a local festival or major sporting event *(see pp26–7)*. Bord Fáilte can offer advice and make reservations through its nationwide accommodation service; the Northern Ireland Tourist Board runs a similar service. Central reservation facilities are available at the hotel chains that have been listed here.

**Façade of the Londonderry Arms** *(see p300)* in Carnlough, County Antrim

A bed-and-breakfast on the River Corrib in Galway

## BED-AND-BREAKFASTS

IRELAND has the reputation for the best B&Bs in Europe. You will never be far from a place to stay, even in the most remote spots. Your welcome will always be friendly and the food and company excellent. Even if the house is no architectural beauty, the comfort and atmosphere will more than compensate. Not all bedrooms have bathrooms *en suite*. When one is available, you may have to pay a little extra, but considering the inexpensive rates, the surcharge is negligible.

The Irish swear by their B&Bs and many stay in them by choice rather than suffer the impersonality and prices of the mainstream hotels; frequent visitors to Ireland agree. The **Town and Seaside House Association** will provide details of bed-and-breakfast accommodation in Northern Ireland, while the **Town and Country Homes Association** covers the Republic.

## FARMHOUSES

FARMHOUSE VACATIONS are a popular tradition in Ireland. The **Farmhouse Association** provides lists of farmhouses in the Republic that take paying guests. You can stay for one night or longer, and they make an excellent base for touring the countryside. As with most things in Ireland, it is the hospitality and friendliness of the people that makes staying on a farm so memorable. You get a feel of rural Ireland with its rich agricultural heritage, and the families are determined you will enjoy every moment of your stay.

## HOUSE AND APARTMENT RENTALS

VACATIONS SPENT in rental houses are an increasingly popular option in Ireland and there are properties to rent all over the country. You are likely to have more choice in the south and west since these areas have traditionally attracted the majority of tourists. Bord Fáilte has a small section in its general accommodation guide, but local tourist offices have lists of apartments and houses to rent in their area. It is also worth looking for ads in the newspapers, both local and international. Accommodations can range from quaint, stone cottages, converted barns and stable yards to more modern bungalows. All will generally have adequate facilities, with simple but comfortable furnishings, modern kitchen equipment and televisions.

An organization called **Rent an Irish Cottage** runs a popular form of self-catering. Its cottages are built in traditional style with whitewashed walls inside and out, and painted roofs and windows; the decor is also traditional – simple and attractive. Locations are generally superb; the only possible criticism is if you want to be "away from it all," the cottages are built in clusters of about ten, so there isn't much privacy.

At the other end of the scale, you could rent a castle or country house, furnished with paintings and antiques. In some cases, the properties are fully staffed. A company called **Elegant Ireland** has a selection of such properties.

## CAMPING, TRAILERS AND MOTOR HOMES

A LIST of fully inspected camping and trailer parks is given in the Bord Fáilte accommodation guide. Many of the camp sites and parks offer additional facilities – such as a store, restaurant or café/snack bar, an indoor game room, laundry, tennis court and miniature golf course. The standard and condition of these facilities

A farmhouse in Clonakilty, County Cork

**Traditional painted horse-drawn caravan from Slattery's in Tralee**

will vary but you can be reliably guided by the tourist board's star ratings: four-star parks have a large range of facilities with a high standard of management; three-star parks have good facilities and management; two-star parks offer limited facilities and good management and the one-star parks have the minimum facilities required for registration with Bord Fáilte. A complete list of approved camping sites in the North is produced by the Northern Ireland Tourist Board.

If you want to experience the Irish countryside at a more leisurely pace, it is possible to rent a traditional horse-drawn caravan. Two of the best companies specializing in this type of vacation are **Kilvahan Caravans**, based at Portlaoise in the Midlands, and **Slattery's Travel Agency** in Tralee, County Kerry.

## YOUTH HOSTELS

THERE ARE 40 youth hostels registered with **An Óige** (Irish Youth Hostel Association), set in some wonderfully scenic areas of Ireland in buildings ranging from castles to military barracks. Accommodation is generally provided in simple dormitories with comfortable beds and basic cooking facilities. You can only use these hostels if you are a member of An Óige or

another youth organization affiliated to the International Youth Hostel Federation. Charges vary according to standard, location and season. Northern Ireland is covered by the **Youth Hostel Association of Northern Ireland**, which is also affiliated with the international body and has over 30 registered hostels.

There are many independent hostels and places, such as universities, that offer similar inexpensive accommodation. Tourist boards have listings of those they recommend.

## DISABLED TRAVELERS

A FACT SHEET for disabled visitors is produced by Bord Fáilte and in their main accommodation guide there is a symbol for wheelchair accessibility. A similar symbol is used in the accommodation listings in this book *(see pp286–301)*. The National Rehabilitation Board *(see p340)* publishes two free guides *Accommodation for Disabled Persons* and *Dublin: A Guide for Disabled Persons*, both in conjunction with the tourist board. The annual publication *Holidays in the British Isles* caters specifically for the disabled traveler and covers Northern Ireland. There is also a guide, with comprehensive listings, available from the Northern Ireland Tourist Board entitled *Accessible Accommodation*.

**Bord Fáilte sign for approved accommodations**

**Typical bed-and-breakfast sign in Pettigo, County Donegal**

# Ireland's Best: Hotels

THE HOTELS featured here are a selection from our lists of recommended places to stay on pages 286–301. They give an indication of the very best that Ireland has to offer, ranging from private establishments that are members of the Hidden Ireland group *(see p280)* to the efficiency and luxury of five-star hotels or the romance of historic castles. All are impressive places, both for their setting and the buildings themselves.

**St. Ernan's House**
*This elegant, pink Regency country house is situated on its own private island not far from Donegal.*
(See p298.)

NORTHWEST IRELAND

**Delphi Lodge**
*The atmosphere at this comfortable, well-run fishing lodge is extremely relaxing. The River Delphi and nearby loughs provide plenty of sport.* (See p296.)

THE WEST OF IRELAND

**Ashford Castle**
*This huge Gothic-style edifice is set on the shores of Lough Corrib. The standard of service is impeccable and the food is excellent.*
(See p296.)

THE LOWER SHANNON

**Adare Manor**
*Set in a large estate beside one of the prettiest villages in the country, this luxurious hotel occupies a magnificent Victorian Gothic mansion.*
(See p294.)

CORK AND KERRY

**Bantry House**
*The spacious library in this 18th-century house looks out on to the gardens. Many of the bedrooms enjoy superb views of Bantry Bay. (See pp160–61 and p291.)*

**Streeve House**
*This 18th-century dower house is a member of the Hidden Ireland group. A stay here gives access to the stunning gardens of Drenagh House, which include the hidden Moon Garden. (See p301.)*

NORTHERN IRELAND

**Hunter's Hotel**
*Cobbled courtyards, paddocks and a magnificent garden are only a few of the attractions of this friendly and comfortable inn. The building dates back to 1720, and is owned and run by the fourth generation of the Hunter family. (See p290.)*

THE MIDLANDS

**Roundwood House**
*This fine, small Palladian house is set in chestnut and beech woods. The Slieve Bloom Mountains are close by, and you can fish and play golf locally. The lovely rooms are filled with antiques, books and pictures, and the atmosphere is one of relaxed informality. (See p299.)*

SOUTHEAST IRELAND

0 kilometers 50

0 miles 25

**Waterford Castle**
*The ultimate in "getting away from it all," this 15th-century castle sits on a beautifully located island in the estuary of the River Suir. The hotel is reachable only by its own private ferry. (See p291.)*

# Choosing a Hotel

THESE HOTELS have been selected across a wide price range for their good value, facilities and location; they are listed by region, starting with Dublin. Use the color-coded thumb tabs, which indicate the regions covered on each page, to guide you to the relevant section of the chart. For Dublin map references see pages 110–11; for road map references see the inside back cover.

| | Credit Cards | Children's Facilities | Parking Facilities | Restaurant | Public Bar |
|---|---|---|---|---|---|
| **DUBLIN** | | | | | |
| **SOUTHEAST DUBLIN:** *Fitzwilliam* €€<br>41 Fitzwilliam St Upper, Dublin 2. **Map** E5. **[** 01 6600448. **FAX** 01 6767488.<br>A friendly, unpretentious guest house on an attractive Georgian street, with simple, elegant decor and comfortable bedrooms. **📻 TV** *Rooms: 12* | MC V AE DC | | ■ | | |
| **SOUTHEAST DUBLIN:** *Georgian House* €€<br>20–21 Baggot St Lower, Dublin 2. **Map** F5. **[** 01 6618832. **FAX** 01 6618834.<br>A short walk from St. Stephen's Green, this small, stylish hotel is the perfect base for exploring Dublin. The bedrooms are large and very comfortable, and there's a good seafood restaurant in the basement. **📻 TV** *Rooms: 33* | MC V | ● | ■ | ● | ■ |
| **SOUTHEAST DUBLIN:** *The Grey Door Hotel* €€<br>22–23 Pembroke St Upper, Dublin 2. **[** 01 6763286. **FAX** 01 6763287.<br>This centrally located Georgian house has immaculately decorated, well-equipped rooms and an excellent restaurant. **📻 TV** *Rooms: 7* | MC V AE DC | ● | | ● | |
| **SOUTHEAST DUBLIN:** *Harcourt* €€<br>60 Harcourt St, Dublin 2. **Map** D5. **[** 01 4783677. **FAX** 01 4752013.<br>Just off St. Stephen's Green, this hotel is close to many of the city's main sights. The bedrooms are modern and well-equipped; there is a popular bar, a restaurant for evening meals and a nightclub. **📻 TV** *Rooms: 40* | MC V AE | ● | | ● | ■ |
| **SOUTHEAST DUBLIN:** *Kilronan House* €€<br>70 Adelaide Rd, Dublin 2. **[** 01 4755266. **FAX** 01 4782841.<br>A reasonably priced, small guest house on a quiet street in the center. Charming owners and delicious breakfasts. **📻 TV** *Rooms: 11* | MC V | ● | ■ | | |
| **SOUTHEAST DUBLIN:** *Leeson Court* €€<br>26–27 Leeson St Lower, Dublin 2. **Map** E5. **[** 01 6763380. **FAX** 01 6618273.<br>Spread across two Georgian houses, this cheerfully decorated hotel has a relaxed, informal atmosphere and the service is good. St. Stephen's Green is only a few minutes' walk away. **📻 TV** *Rooms: 20* | MC V AE DC | ● | ■ | ● | ■ |
| **SOUTHEAST DUBLIN:** *Longfields* €€<br>Fitzwilliam St Lower, Dublin 2. **Map** F5. **[** 01 6761367. **FAX** 01 6761542.<br>Two Georgian town houses have been joined together to create this stylish hotel with an attractive sitting room and smart, pretty bedrooms. There is a very good restaurant in the basement. **📻 TV** *Rooms: 28* | MC V AE DC | ● | | ● | ■ |
| **SOUTHEAST DUBLIN:** *Russell Court* €€<br>21–25 Harcourt St, Dublin 2. **Map** D5. **[** 01 4784066. **FAX** 01 4781576.<br>Jolly, welcoming hotel with young staff and a lively atmosphere in the evenings. There's a choice of bars and a more formal restaurant. Bedrooms are neat and well-equipped. **📻 TV** *Rooms: 42* | MC V AE | ● | ■ | ● | ■ |
| **SOUTHEAST DUBLIN:** *Buswells* €€€<br>Molesworth St, Dublin 2. **Map** E4. **[** 01 6764013. **FAX** 01 6762090.<br>A great old favorite in the center of Dublin, still run by members of the Duff family, who first opened it in 1928. Traditional in style and atmosphere, it is a friendly, comfortable place to stay. **📻 TV 🔥** *Rooms: 67* | MC V AE DC | ● | | ● | ■ |
| **SOUTHEAST DUBLIN:** *Mont Clare* €€€<br>Merrion Square, Dublin 2. **Map** F4. **[** 01 6616799. **FAX** 01 6615663.<br>Not as grand as the Davenport opposite, but with the same clublike feel. A busy, traditional pub takes up most of the ground floor. **📻 TV** *Rooms: 74* | MC V AE DC | ● | ■ | ● | ■ |
| **SOUTHEAST DUBLIN:** *Temple Bar* €€€<br>Fleet St, Temple Bar, Dublin 2. **Map** D3. **[** 01 6773333. **FAX** 01 6773088.<br>This new hotel, located in a trendy area of Dublin, is a popular meeting place with its theme bar "Buskers" attracting a lively crowd. Bedrooms are comfortable but lack character. **📻 TV 🔥** *Rooms: 108* | MC V AE DC | ● | | ● | ■ |

| | | CREDIT CARDS | CHILDREN'S FACILITIES | PARKING FACILITIES | RESTAURANT | PUBLIC BAR |
|---|---|---|---|---|---|---|

**Price categories** are for a standard double room (not per person) for one night, including tax, service charges and breakfast.
**£** under IR£50
**££** IR£50–100
**£££** IR£100–150
**££££** IR£150–200
**£££££** over IR£200

**CHILDREN'S FACILITIES**
Cribs and high chairs are available and some hotels will also provide a baby-sitting service.
**PARKING FACILITIES**
Parking provided by the hotel in either a private parking lot or a private garage close by.
**RESTAURANT**
The hotel has a restaurant for residents, which also welcomes nonresidents – usually only for evening meals.
**PUBLIC BAR**
The hotel has a bar that is open to nonresidents and residents alike.

| | CREDIT CARDS | CHILDREN'S FACILITIES | PARKING FACILITIES | RESTAURANT | PUBLIC BAR |
|---|---|---|---|---|---|
| **SOUTHEAST DUBLIN:** *Davenport* **££££**<br>Merrion Square, Dublin 2. **Map** F4. ( 01 6616800. FAX 01 6615663.<br>The grand proportions of the Neo-Classical façade are carried through into the lobby – a vast, marble-floored atrium. Opened in 1994, it is elegant but rather like a gentleman's club. 🛏 TV ♿ *Rooms: 120* | MC<br>V<br>AE<br>DC | ● | ■ | ● | ■ |
| **SOUTHEAST DUBLIN:** *Stephen's Hall* **££££**<br>Leeson St Lower, Dublin 2. **Map** E5. ( 01 6610585. FAX 01 6610606.<br>All the rooms are suites and represent good value for families who want smart, comfortable accommodations in the center of the city, near St. Stephen's Green. Cooking facilities are available. 🛏 TV ♿ *Rooms: 37* | MC<br>V<br>AE<br>DC | ● | ■ | | |
| **SOUTHEAST DUBLIN:** *Westbury Hotel* **££££**<br>Grafton St, Dublin 2. **Map** D4. ( 01 6791122. FAX 01 6797078.<br>You couldn't get much closer to the center of things than here, only seconds from Dublin's major shopping street. It is a stylish, ritzy hotel with lots of shiny floors and heavily coordinated bedrooms. 🛏 TV ♿ *Rooms: 203* | MC<br>V<br>AE<br>DC | ● | ■ | ● | ■ |
| **SOUTHEAST DUBLIN:** *Conrad Hotel* **£££££**<br>Earlsfort Terrace, Dublin 2. **Map** D5. ( 01 6765555. FAX 01 6765424.<br>This international-style hotel near St. Stephen's Green, is geared to business people for whom there are excellent facilities. A jolly pub with a large terrace is the only concession to traditional Dublin. 🛏 TV *Rooms: 191* | MC<br>V<br>AE<br>DC | ● | ■ | ● | ■ |
| **SOUTHEAST DUBLIN:** *Shelbourne Hotel* **£££££**<br>27 St. Stephen's Green, Dublin 2. **Map** D4. ( 01 6766471. FAX 01 6616006.<br>The Shelbourne has been the city's most distinguished hotel since it opened in the 19th century. Although it has every facility for the business traveler, it manages to retain a personal atmosphere. 🛏 TV ♿ *Rooms: 164* | MC<br>V<br>AE<br>DC | ● | ■ | ● | ■ |
| **SOUTHWEST DUBLIN:** *Avalon House* **£**<br>55 Aungier St, Dublin 2. **Map** C4. ( 01 4750001. FAX 01 4750303.<br>This cheap and cheerful budget accommodation is centrally located and has clean bedrooms and a self-service restaurant. *Rooms: 38* | MC<br>V<br>AE | | | ● | |
| **SOUTHWEST DUBLIN:** *Grafton Plaza* **££**<br>Johnson's Place, Dublin 2. **Map** D4. ( 01 4750888. FAX 01 4750908.<br>This newly constructed hotel, with a Georgian façade, is neat and tastefully decorated throughout. Only a few minutes' walk from Grafton Street, it makes an excellent city base. 🛏 TV ♿ *Rooms: 75* | MC<br>V<br>AE<br>DC | ● | | ● | ■ |
| **SOUTHWEST DUBLIN:** *Jury's Christchurch Inn* **££**<br>Christchurch Place, Dublin 8. **Map** B4. ( 01 4750111. FAX 01 4750488.<br>The Jury's group "inns" offer stylish modern facilities. This "inn," 15 minutes from St. Stephen's Green, has a good bar and restaurant, and neat, well-equipped rooms at reasonable prices. 🛏 TV ♿ *Rooms: 183* | MC<br>V<br>AE<br>DC | ● | | ● | ■ |
| **SOUTHWEST DUBLIN:** *Blooms* **£££**<br>Anglesea St, Dublin 2. **Map** D3. ( 01 6715622. FAX 01 6715997.<br>Near Trinity College in the heart of Dublin, this modern hotel is convenient for exploring the city but its reception areas are limited. 🛏 TV *Rooms: 86* | MC<br>V<br>AE<br>DC | ● | ■ | ● | |
| **SOUTHWEST DUBLIN:** *Central* **£££**<br>1–5 Exchequer St, Dublin 2. **Map** D5. ( 01 6797302. FAX 01 6797303.<br>As its name suggests, one of the great advantages of this hotel is its location. Molly Malone's Tavern, on the ground floor, offers music most nights, so choose your neat, functional bedroom carefully. 🛏 TV *Rooms: 70* | MC<br>V<br>AE<br>DC | ● | | ● | ■ |
| **SOUTHWEST DUBLIN:** *Clarence* **£££££**<br>6–8 Wellington Quay, Dublin 2. **Map** C3. ( 01 6623066. FAX 01 6623077.<br>The hotel was recently bought by the rock band U2 and has been completely refurbished. The stylish restaurant sets the standard for the rest of the hotel. 🛏 TV ♿ *Rooms: 50* | MC<br>V<br>AE<br>DC | ● | | ● | ■ |

<table>
<tr><td>

**Price categories** are for a standard double room (not per person) for one night, including tax, service charges and breakfast.

£ under IR£50
££ IR£50–100
£££ IR£100–150
££££ IR£150–200
£££££ over IR£200

</td><td>

**CHILDREN'S FACILITIES**
Cribs and high chairs are available and some hotels will also provide a baby-sitting service.

**PARKING FACILITIES**
Parking provided by the hotel in either a private parking lot or a private garage close by.

**RESTAURANT**
The hotel has a restaurant for residents, which also welcomes nonresidents – usually only for evening meals.

**PUBLIC BAR**
The hotel has a bar that is open to nonresidents and residents alike.

</td></tr>
</table>

| | Price | CREDIT CARDS | CHILDREN'S FACILITIES | PARKING FACILITIES | RESTAURANT | PUBLIC BAR |
|---|---|---|---|---|---|---|
| **NORTH OF THE LIFFEY:** *Isaacs*<br>Frenchman's Lane, Dublin 1. **Map** E2. **(** 01 8749321. **FAX** 01 8741574.<br>Recently developed alongside an older hostel of the same name, the hotel is reasonably priced, well-run and centrally located. ▣ TV **Rooms:** 25 | £ | MC<br>V | ● | | ● | ■ |
| **NORTH OF THE LIFFEY:** *Royal Dublin*<br>40 O'Connell St Upper, Dublin 1. **Map** D1. **(** 01 8733666. **FAX** 01 8733120.<br>Modern hotel on one of Dublin's most famous streets. It has well-equipped rooms and is stylish, though lacking in atmosphere. ▣ TV ♿ **Rooms:** 117 | ££ | MC<br>V<br>AE<br>DC | ● | ■ | ● | ■ |
| **NORTH OF THE LIFFEY:** *Gresham Hotel*<br>23 O'Connell St Upper, Dublin 1. **Map** D1. **(** 01 8746881. **FAX** 01 8787175.<br>One of Dublin's oldest and best known hotels. It is a popular rendezvous spot so the public areas are always busy. The bedrooms are comfortable and there is ample safe parking. ▣ TV **Rooms:** 200 | £££ | MC<br>V<br>AE<br>DC | ● | ■ | ● | ■ |
| **BALGRIFFIN:** *Belcamp Hutchinson*<br>Malahide Rd, Balgriffin, Dublin 17. **(** 01 8460843. **FAX** 01 8485703.<br>Poorly located for central Dublin but only ten minutes from the airport, it's a comfortable, pleasant place to stay with good food. ▣ TV **Rooms:** 5 | ££ | MC<br>V | | ■ | | |
| **BALLSBRIDGE:** *Anglesea Town House*<br>63 Anglesea Rd, Dublin 4. **(** 01 6683877. **FAX** 01 6683461.<br>This Edwardian house is beautifully decorated and furnished. It has a lovely drawing room, very comfortable bedrooms and offers a superb breakfast – all within ten minutes' drive of the center. ▣ TV **Rooms:** 7 | ££ | MC<br>V<br>AE<br>DC | ● | ■ | | |
| **BALLSBRIDGE:** *Ariel House*<br>Lansdowne Rd, Ballsbridge, Dublin 4. **(** 01 6685512. **FAX** 01 6685845.<br>Near Lansdowne Road Station, this Victorian house is elegantly decorated, with comfortable bedrooms and good breakfasts. ▣ TV ♿ **Rooms:** 28 | ££ | MC<br>V<br>AE | | ■ | | |
| **BALLSBRIDGE:** *Glenogra Guesthouse*<br>64 Merrion Rd, Ballsbridge, Dublin 4. **(** 01 6683661. **FAX** 01 6683661.<br>Attractive, stylish guest house convenient both for Dun Laoghaire and the center. The bedrooms are charming and very comfortable. ▣ TV **Rooms:** 10 | ££ | MC<br>V<br>AE | ● | ■ | | |
| **BALLSBRIDGE:** *Mount Herbert Hotel*<br>Herbert Rd, Ballsbridge, Dublin 4. **(** 01 6684321. **FAX** 01 6607077.<br>A Victorian hotel close to Lansdowne Road stadium. The rooms are light, with modern furnishings, and it is reasonably priced. ▣ TV ♿ **Rooms:** 140 | ££ | MC<br>V<br>AE<br>DC | ● | ■ | ● | |
| **BALLSBRIDGE:** *Hibernian*<br>Eastmoreland Place, Ballsbridge, Dublin 4. **(** 01 6687666. **FAX** 01 6602655.<br>Tucked away on a quiet street but close to the center, this impressive turn-of-the-century building opened as a stylish, comfortable hotel in 1993. Elegant, luxurious rooms. ▣ TV ♿ **Rooms:** 29 | £££ | MC<br>V<br>AE<br>DC | ● | ■ | ● | ■ |
| **BALLSBRIDGE:** *Berkeley Court Hotel*<br>Lansdowne Rd, Dublin 4. **(** 01 6601711. **FAX** 01 6617238.<br>The very stylish lobby area sets the standard for this luxury hotel, which is well located for Lansdowne Road stadium. ▣ TV ♿ **Rooms:** 188 | ££££ | MC<br>V<br>AE<br>DC | ● | ■ | ● | ■ |
| **BALLSBRIDGE:** *Jury's Hotel & The Towers at Jury's*<br>Pembroke Rd, Ballsbridge, Dublin 4. **(** 01 6605000. **FAX** 01 6605540.<br>A modern hotel, popular with business people and tourists, a short distance from the center, with all the facilities you'd expect from a five-star hotel. The Towers is an exclusive wing with deluxe bedrooms. ▣ TV ♿ **Rooms:** 390 | £££££ | MC<br>V<br>AE<br>DC | ● | ■ | ● | ■ |
| **BOOTERSTOWN:** *Doyle Tara*<br>Merrion Rd, Dublin 4. **(** 01 2694666. **FAX** 01 2691027.<br>Conveniently located for Dun Laoghaire, the hotel has recently undergone refurbishment, with a number of new rooms added. ▣ TV ♿ **Rooms:** 113 | £££ | MC<br>V<br>AE<br>DC | ● | ■ | ● | ■ |

**DONNYBROOK:** *Morehampton Townhouse* ££ MC V
46 Morehampton Rd, Donnybrook, Dublin 4. ( 01 6602106. FAX 01 6602566.
Attractively decorated Victorian town house, ten minutes' drive from the center, with great hospitality and delicious breakfasts. 🔲 TV **Rooms:** 6

**DONNYBROOK:** *Doyle Montrose* £££ MC V AE DC
Stillorgan Rd, Dublin 4. ( 01 2693311. FAX 01 2691164.
One of the Doyle group of good city hotels. This one, like the Tara, has undergone major refurbishment, including the addition of a second bar and a buffet. It lies south of the city on the main road. 🔲 TV 🔲 **Rooms:** 179

**RATHMINES:** *Clara House* ££ MC V
23 Leinster Rd, Rathmines, Dublin 6. ( 01 4975904. FAX 01 4975904.
In an attractive area, ten minutes' walk from the center, this Georgian house is a comfortable B&B with a friendly atmosphere. 🔲 TV **Rooms:** 13

## SOUTHEAST IRELAND

**BAGENALSTOWN:** *Lorum Old Rectory* £ MC V
Co Carlow. **Road map** D4. ( 0503 75282. FAX 0503 75455.
Set beneath the Blackstairs Mountains, with a cozy atmosphere and log fires, and an inspired five-course dinner. Member of Hidden Ireland. 🔲 **Rooms:** 5

**BALLYMACARBRY:** *Clonanav Farm Guesthouse* £ MC V AE
Clonmel, Co Waterford. **Road map** C5. ( 052 36141. FAX 052 36141.
A friendly welcome and lots of outdoor activities are offered at this bunga-low farmhouse; there's an evening meal and a full breakfast. 🔲 **Rooms:** 10

**BALLYMURN:** *Ballinkeele House* £ MC V
Co Wexford. **Road map** D5. ( 053 38105. FAX 053 38468.
The comfortable rooms overlook its parkland setting. Delicious dinners are served in the original dining room. Member of Hidden Ireland. 🔲 **Rooms:** 5

**BLESSINGTON:** *Tulfarris House & Country Club* ££ MC V AE DC
Blessington Lakes, Co Wicklow. **Road map** D4. ( 045 64574. FAX 045 64423.
In a lovely location overlooking Poulaphouca Lake, the hotel offers stylish comfort and the many facilities of the Country Club. 🔲 TV 🔲 **Rooms:** 21

**CAPPOQUIN:** *Richmond House* ££ MC V
Co Waterford. **Road map** C5. ( 058 382520. FAX 058 54988.
Lovely, 18th-century, Georgian country house, charmingly decorated and furnished with antiques, set in peaceful parkland. 🔲 **Rooms:** 10

**CASTLEDERMOT:** *Kilkea Lodge* ££
Co Kildare. **Road map** D4. ( 0503 45112. FAX 0503 45112.
A member of Hidden Ireland, this attractive house is popular with racegoers since the Curragh, Punchestown and Naas are in easy reach. 🔲 **Rooms:** 7

**CLONEA:** *Clonea Strand Hotel* ££ MC V
Dungarvan, Co Waterford. **Road map** C5. ( 058 42416. FAX 058 42880,
A large, modern resort hotel without huge charm but located next to a lovely beach and with lots of facilities – great for families. 🔲 TV **Rooms:** 59

**DUNMORE EAST:** *Church Villa* £
Co Waterford. **Road map** D5. ( 051 383390.
Located in the village, this attractive house is an excellent-value, simple B&B. Very friendly owners and neat, comfortable bedrooms. 🔲 **Rooms:** 5

**ENNISKERRY:** *Enniscree Lodge* ££ MC V AE DC
Glencree Valley, Enniskerry, Co Wicklow. **Road map** D4.
( 01 2863542. FAX 01 2866037.
Set in a wonderful location, with stunning views from most of the rooms, it's a friendly place with country-style furnishings. 🔲 TV **Rooms:** 10

**INISTIOGE:** *Cullintra House* £
The Rower, Inistioge, Co Kilkenny. **Road map** D5. ( 051 23614. FAX 051 23614.
An attractive farmhouse set in woods and farmland, very cozy, with open fires and a relaxed atmosphere. Member of Hidden Ireland. 🔲 **Rooms:** 6

**KILBRIDE:** *The Manor* ££ MC V
Blessington, Co Wicklow. **Road map** D4. ( 01 4582105. FAX 01 4582607.
A member of the Hidden Ireland group, The Manor has large comfort-able rooms, log fires and is surrounded by over 16 ha (40 acres) of gardens complete with a lake full of trout. Open April to October. 🔲 🔲 **Rooms:** 5

**Price categories** are for a standard double room (not per person) for one night, including tax, service charges and breakfast.
£ under IR£50
££ IR£50–100
£££ IR£100–150
££££ IR£150–200
£££££ over IR£200

**CHILDREN'S FACILITIES**
Cribs and high chairs are available and some hotels will also provide a baby-sitting service.

**PARKING FACILITIES**
Parking provided by the hotel in either a private parking lot or a private garage close by.

**RESTAURANT**
The hotel has a restaurant for residents, which also welcomes nonresidents – usually only for evening meals.

**PUBLIC BAR**
The hotel has a bar that is open to nonresidents and residents alike.

| | CREDIT CARDS | CHILDREN'S FACILITIES | PARKING FACILITIES | RESTAURANT | PUBLIC BAR |
|---|---|---|---|---|---|
| **KILKENNY:** *Butler House* ££<br>Patrick St, Kilkenny, Co Kilkenny. **Road map** C4. 056 65707. **FAX** 056 65626.<br>The former dower house of Kilkenny Castle is right in the heart of town, has been restored by the Civic Trust. The 18th-century building has fine proportions and is stylishly decorated throughout. **Rooms:** 13 | MC V AE DC | ● | ■ | | |
| **KILKENNY:** *Lacken House* ££<br>Dublin Rd, Kilkenny, Co Kilkenny. **Road map** C4. 056 61085. **FAX** 056 62435.<br>Within easy reach of the center, this Victorian house is a very comfortable place to stay and has a highly regarded restaurant. **Rooms:** 9 | MC V AE DC | ● | ■ | ● | |
| **RATHASPECK:** *Rathaspeck Manor* £<br>Co Wexford. **Road map** D5. 053 42661/45148.<br>This 300-year-old Georgian manor has an 18-hole, par-three golf course and a tennis court. Offering B&B only, the bedrooms are large and comfortable and the breakfast is excellent. **Rooms:** 7 | | | ■ | | |
| **RATHNEW:** *Hunter's Hotel* ££<br>Co Wicklow. **Road map** D4. 0404 40106. **FAX** 0404 40338.<br>This inn on the old Dublin coaching road dates back to 1720 and is run by the fourth generation of the Hunter family. Comfortable and relaxing if a little eccentric, it's a great place to stay and the food is delicious. **Rooms:** 16 | MC V AE DC | ● | ■ | ● | ■ |
| **RATHNEW:** *Tinakilly House, Hotel and Restaurant* £££<br>Co Wicklow. **Road map** D4. 0404 69274. **FAX** 0404 67806.<br>The many outstanding features of this Victorian house include lovely views over the coast and large, attractive gardens. Comfort is assured with a mix of antiques and modern facilities. **Rooms:** 29 | MC V AE DC | ● | ■ | ● | ■ |
| **RATHVILLY:** *Lisnavagh House* £££<br>Co Carlow. **Road map** D4. 503 61104.<br>A member of Hidden Ireland. Built in Victorian-Gothic style in 1848, the house has been remodeled but retains great character. The atmosphere is relaxed and guests have a vast estate at their disposal. **Rooms:** 5 | MC V | | ■ | | |
| **ROSSLARE:** *Kelly's Resort Hotel* ££<br>Co Wexford. **Road map** D5. 053 32114. **FAX** 053 32222.<br>This hotel on the beach is ideal for families who don't care about lack of character but want lots of leisure and sports facilities. **Rooms:** 99 | MC V AE | ● | ■ | ● | ■ |
| **STRAFFAN:** *Kildare Hotel & Country Club* £££££<br>Co Kildare. **Road map** D4. 01 6273333. **FAX** 01 6273312.<br>Parts of this exclusive hotel building date back to the 17th century. As well as luxurious bedrooms and a grand drawing room, it boasts a one-star Michelin restaurant, The Byerley Turk. Excellent facilities include a championship golf course and extensive fishing. **Rooms:** 43 | MC V AE DC | ● | ■ | ● | ■ |
| **TACUMSHANE:** *Furziestown House* £<br>Co Wexford. **Road map** D5. 053 31376.<br>An attractive, peaceful spot, with access to local beaches and lakes, it offers cozy farmhouse rooms at very reasonable prices. **Rooms:** 3 | | ● | ■ | | |
| **THOMASTOWN:** *Mount Juliet Estate* £££<br>Co Kilkenny. **Road map** D5. 056 24455. **FAX** 056 24522.<br>One of Ireland's luxury hotels but retaining the character and style of a grand family house. Set on an estate of over 450 ha (1,100 acres) with lots of sports facilities including an 18-hole golf course. **Rooms:** 64 | MC V AE DC | ● | ■ | ● | ■ |
| **WATERFORD:** *Foxmount Farm* £<br>Passage East Rd, Waterford, Co Waterford. **Road map** D5.<br>051 74308. **FAX** 051 54906.<br>An attractive, 17th-century house, full of antiques and personality. The atmosphere is homey, and you can bring your own wine to dinner. **Rooms:** 6 | | ● | ■ | | |

**WATERFORD:** *Waterford Castle Hotel* ££££££
The Island, Ballinakill, Waterford, Co Waterford. **Road map** D5.
[ 051 78203. **FAX** 051 79316.
Guests are ferried across the river to this romantically placed 15th-century castle. Log fires blaze in lofty rooms, and both the large suites and the smaller cozy bedrooms are truly luxurious. **Rooms:** 19
*MC V AE DC*

**WEXFORD:** *Newbay Country House* ££
Newbay, Wexford, Co Wexford. **Road map** D5. [ 053 42779. **FAX** 053 46318.
This country house hotel is a member of Hidden Ireland. Part Georgian and part early Victorian, the house is very comfortable and relaxing, with peat fires and interesting antiques. **Rooms:** 6
*MC V*

**WEXFORD:** *White's Hotel* ££
George St, Wexford, Co Wexford. **Road map** D5. [ 053 2231. **FAX** 053 45000.
Centrally located, this former coaching inn is neat and reasonably comfortable with a choice of formal or country-style restaurant. There is also a fitness and leisure center with gym and solarium. **Rooms:** 82
*MC V AE DC*

**WICKLOW:** *The Old Rectory Country House* ££
Co Wicklow. **Road map** D4. [ 0404 67048. **FAX** 0404 69181.
A pretty house offering great comfort and good cooking. Guests can walk to the harbor and town center. Open April to November. **Rooms:** 5
*MC V AE*

## CORK AND KERRY

**BALLINADEE:** *Glebe Country House* £
Bandon, Co Cork. **Road map** B6. [ 021 778294. **FAX** 021 778456.
Only ten minutes from Kinsale, with lots of sports opportunities close by, this attractive Georgian rectory is beautifully furnished and makes a great base for the area. Book by noon if you want dinner. **Rooms:** 3
*MC V*

**BALLYLICKEY:** *Ballylickey Manor House* £££
Bantry Bay, Co Cork. **Road map** B6. [ 027 50071. **FAX** 027 50124.
A 17th-century shooting lodge that has been completely refurbished over recent years. It's an attractive place to stay with lovely, comfortable rooms and delicious food. **Rooms:** 11
*MC V AE*

**BANTEER:** *Clonmeen Lodge* ££
Co Cork. **Road map** B5. [ 029 56238. **FAX** 029 56294.
A popular countryside spot, located on the banks of the River Blackwater. There are lots of lovely riding trails and walks and a very friendly, relaxed atmosphere. Breakfast is served when you want it. **Rooms:** 6
*MC V DC*

**BANTRY:** *Bantry House* £££
Co Cork. **Road map** B6. [ 027 50047. **FAX** 027 50795.
An outstanding, 18th-century, stately home *(see pp160–61)*, which has been open to the public since 1946, it has a fine collection of pictures, furniture and works of art. The comfortable bedrooms with *en suite* bathrooms are in the east and west wings. **Rooms:** 9
*MC V AE DC*

**CARAGH LAKE:** *Caragh Lodge* ££
Co Kerry. **Road map** A5. [ 066 69115. **FAX** 066 69316.
Colonial-style fishing lodge in magnificent, award-winning gardens bordering the lake. All rooms are neatly decorated and furnished with antique and period furniture. Open Easter to mid-October. **Rooms:** 10
*MC V*

**CARAGH LAKE:** *Ard-na-Sidhe* £££
Co Kerry. **Road map** A5. [ 066 69105. **FAX** 066 69282.
This attractive Victorian mansion enjoys a wonderfully peaceful setting beside the lake. The ambience is somewhat old-fashioned, reinforced by the neat period furnishings. Open May to September. **Rooms:** 20
*MC V AE DC*

**CLONAKILTY:** *O'Donovan's Hotel* £
Co Cork. **Road map** B6. [ 023 33250. **FAX** 023 33250.
A traditional, centrally located, family-run hotel in the old commercial mold. The decor and furnishings are unremarkable but the place is friendly. There are two restaurants and occasionally Irish music in the bar. **Rooms:** 16
*MC V AE DC*

**CORK:** *Jury's Cork Inn* ££
Anderson's Quay, Cork, Co Cork. **Road map** C5.
[ 021 276444. **FAX** 021 276144.
A fixed-room-rate hotel with modern, attractive furnishings and good facilities for reasonable prices – particularly good for families. **Rooms:** 133
*MC V AE DC*

For key to symbols see back flap

**Price categories** are for a standard double room (not per person) for one night, including tax, service charges and breakfast.
**€** under IR£50
**€€** IR£50–100
**€€€** IR£100–150
**€€€€** IR£150–200
**€€€€€** over IR£200

**CHILDREN'S FACILITIES**
Cribs and high chairs are available and some hotels will also provide a baby-sitting service.

**PARKING FACILITIES**
Parking provided by the hotel in either a private parking lot or a private garage close by.

**RESTAURANT**
The hotel has a restaurant for residents, which also welcomes nonresidents – usually only for evening meals.

**PUBLIC BAR**
The hotel has a bar that is open to nonresidents and residents alike.

| | CREDIT CARDS | CHILDREN'S FACILITIES | PARKING FACILITIES | RESTAURANT | PUBLIC BAR |
|---|---|---|---|---|---|
| **CORK:** *Lotamore House* €€<br>Tivoli, Cork, Co Cork. **Road map** C5. 021 822344. FAX 021 822219.<br>This Georgian manor converted into a guest house is surrounded by lovely grounds with good views of the harbor and Blackrock Castle. Five minutes' drive from the city center. **Rooms:** 20 | MC V AE | ● | ■ | | |
| **CORK:** *Seven North Mall* €€<br>7 North Mall, Cork, Co Cork. **Road map** C5. 021 397191. FAX 021 300811.<br>This stylish 18th-century house overlooks the River Lee and is a convenient base for exploring the city and surrounding areas. **Rooms:** 5 | MC V | | ■ | | |
| **DINGLE:** *Benners Hotel* €€<br>Main St, Dingle, Co Kerry. **Road map** A5. 066 51638. FAX 066 51412.<br>American-owned hotel right in the center of town. The old building has been converted to provide an efficient hotel with a choice of bars, a restaurant and comfortable bedrooms. **Rooms:** 24 | MC V AE DC | ● | ■ | ● | ■ |
| **DINGLE:** *Doyle's Seafood Bar and Townhouse* €€<br>John St, Dingle, Co Kerry. **Road map** A5. 066 51174. FAX 066 51816.<br>Famous for its delicious seafood, Doyle's also provides first-class accommodations. Stylish bedrooms with luxurious bathrooms and an attractive sitting room. Informal, relaxed atmosphere. **Rooms:** 8 | MC V DC | ● | | ● | ■ |
| **INISHANNON:** *Inishannon House* €€<br>Co Cork. **Road map** B6. 021 775121. FAX 021 775609.<br>This 18th-century house is very romantic, with lovely gardens and parkland leading down to the River Bandon. The bedrooms are individual both in shape and decor and look out over the river or the garden. **Rooms:** 14 | MC V AE DC | ● | ■ | ● | ■ |
| **KANTURK:** *Assolas Country House* €€€<br>Co Cork. **Road map** B5. 029 50015. FAX 029 50795.<br>An elegant, 17th-century house, run like a glorified family home with cozy decor and an excellent restaurant. Open April to November. **Rooms:** 9 | V AE | ● | ■ | ● | |
| **KENMARE:** *Park Hotel* €€€€€<br>Co Kerry. **Road map** B5. 064 41200. FAX 064 41402.<br>Built in 1897 in a stunning setting by Kenmare Bay, the Park is rated one of Ireland's finest hotels, luxurious with an individual style and lots of original touches. The facilities include an 18-hole golf course. Open Easter to October and for Christmas and New Year's. **Rooms:** 50 | MC V AE DC | ● | ■ | ● | ■ |
| **KENMARE:** *Sheen Falls Lodge* €€€€€<br>Co Kerry. **Road map** B5. 064 41600. FAX 064 41386.<br>The new hotel blends in well with the original 17th-century house. Luxurious, spacious bedrooms with great views over the falls or the huge grounds. Closed January to mid-February. **Rooms:** 40 | MC V AE DC | ● | ■ | ● | ■ |
| **KILLARNEY:** *Dunloe Castle* €€<br>Co Kerry. **Road map** B5. 064 44111. FAX 064 44583.<br>A member of the Historic Castles and Gardens Association. The modern buildings are on lovely grounds by the ruins of the 13th-century castle. Excellent facilities. Open April to September. **Rooms:** 120 | MC V AE DC | ● | ■ | ● | ■ |
| **KILLARNEY:** *Royal Hotel* €€<br>College St, Killarney, Co Kerry. **Road map** B5. 064 31853. FAX 064 34001.<br>A short walk from the center of town, this traditional hotel is a stylish, comfortable place to stay. **Rooms:** 49 | MC V | ● | | ● | ■ |
| **KILLARNEY:** *Hotel Europe* €€€<br>Co Kerry. **Road map** B5. 064 31900. FAX 064 32118.<br>Huge five-star resort hotel with stunning views of the Lakes of Killarney and the mountains, with every facility from beauty salon to Olympic-size pool and lots of outdoor sports. Open April to October. **Rooms:** 205 | MC V AE DC | ● | ■ | ● | ■ |

**KILLARNEY:** *Killarney Park Hotel* £££ · MC V AE DC
Kenmare Place, Killarney, Co Kerry. **Road map** B5. ☎ 064 35555. FAX 064 35266.
This modern hotel is conveniently located in the center of town. It has been extremely well built and is tastefully decorated. 🛏 📺 *Rooms: 66*

**KILLEAGH:** *Ballymakeigh House* £ · V
Co Cork. **Road map** C5. ☎ 024 95184. FAX 024 95370.
This attractive 18th-century farmhouse is a comfortable, reasonably priced base to explore the area. Cozy bedrooms and good food. 🛏 *Rooms: 5*

**KINSALE:** *Old Presbytery* £
Cork St, Kinsale, Co Cork. **Road map** B6. ☎ 021 772027.
A comfortable, relaxing place to stay on a quiet street in the town center. Bedrooms are simple but stylish, furnished mainly with Victorian pieces. The small restaurant offers an excellent dinner. 🛏 *Rooms: 6*

**KINSALE:** *The Blue Haven* ££ · MC V AE DC
3–4 Pearse St, Kinsale, Co Cork. **Road map** B6. ☎ 021 772209. FAX 021 774268.
Attractive, small hotel right in the center of Kinsale, built on the site of the old fish market. It is stylish throughout, after a recent refurbishment, and has a very popular restaurant. 🛏 📺 *Rooms: 19*

**KINSALE:** *Old Bank House* ££ · MC V AE
11 Pearse St, Kinsale, Co Cork. **Road map** B6. ☎ 021 774075. FAX 021 774296.
Right in the center of town, the Old Bank House used to be a branch of the Munster and Leinster Bank. A listed Georgian building, it has finely proportioned, comfortable rooms and excellent staff. 🛏 📺 *Rooms: 9*

**KINSALE:** *Scilly House* ££ · MC V AE
Co Cork. **Road map** B6. ☎ 021 772413. FAX 021 774629.
Very attractive old house overlooking Kinsale Bay and the harbor. The charming bedrooms and reception rooms are full of interesting and original furniture. Open April to November. 🛏 *Rooms: 7*

**MALLOW:** *Longueville House* £££ · MC V AE DC
Co Cork. **Road map** B5. ☎ 022 47156. FAX 022 47459.
The main part of the house is Georgian; the rooms are elegant and individually decorated, many with huge old-style beds. The hotel's Presidents' Restaurant has won a number of awards. 🛏 📺 *Rooms: 21*

**MIDLETON:** *Bailick Cottage* ££
Co Cork. **Road map** C5. ☎ 021 631244.
A charming, vinecovered cottage with a pretty, informal garden, ten minutes' walk from the town. Bedrooms and reception rooms are attractively decorated and furnished with antiques. 🛏 *Rooms: 6*

**PARKNASILLA:** *Great Southern Hotel* £££ · MC V AE DC
Co Kerry. **Road map** A6. ☎ 064 45122. FAX 064 45323.
Amid acres of subtropical gardens, the main building is Victorian. Recreation and conference facilities have been added, including a 9-hole golf course. All the rooms are stylishly coordinated. 🛏 📺 🏊 ♿ *Rooms: 84*

**SHANAGARRY:** *Ballymaloe House* £££ · MC V AE DC
Midleton, Co Cork. **Road map** C6. ☎ 021 652531. FAX 021 652021.
The house is charming with plenty of places to relax and lots for children to do. The farm provides the food, supplemented by local seafood, for the restaurant – one of Ireland's best. 🛏 🏊 ♿ *Rooms: 32*

**TAHILLA:** *Tahilla Cove Country House* ££ · MC V AE DC
Co Kerry. **Road map** A6. ☎ 064 45204. FAX 064 45104.
A friendly guest house spread over two houses and set in lovely gardens. Views from the rooms are either of the sea or mountains. The bar is open to nonresidents and is a great focus of hospitality. 🛏 📺 ♿ *Rooms: 9*

**WATERVILLE:** *The Smugglers' Inn* £ · MC AE DC V
Cliff Rd, Waterville, Co Kerry. **Road map** A6. ☎ 066 74330. FAX 066 74422.
A 100-year-old, modernized, whitewashed inn on the Ring of Kerry. It is an unpretentious, jolly place with comfortable bedrooms, a friendly bar and a good restaurant. 🛏 ♿ *Rooms: 12*

**YOUGHAL:** *Aherne's Seafood Restaurant* ££ · MC V AE DC
163 North Main St, Youghal, Co Cork. **Road map** C5. ☎ 024 92424. FAX 024 93633.
Run by the Fitzgibbon family, this well-known fish restaurant also has smart, comfortable bedrooms. 🛏 📺 ♿ *Rooms: 10*

For key to symbols see back flap

**Price categories** are for a standard double room (not per person) for one night, including tax, service charges and breakfast.

ⓔ under IR£50
ⓔⓔ IR£50–100
ⓔⓔⓔ IR£100–150
ⓔⓔⓔⓔ IR£150–200
ⓔⓔⓔⓔⓔ over IR£200

**CHILDREN'S FACILITIES**
Cribs and high chairs are available and some hotels will also provide a baby-sitting service.

**PARKING FACILITIES**
Parking provided by the hotel in either a private parking lot or a private garage close by.

**RESTAURANT**
The hotel has a restaurant for residents, which also welcomes nonresidents – usually only for evening meals.

**PUBLIC BAR**
The hotel has a bar that is open to nonresidents and residents alike.

| | CREDIT CARDS | CHILDREN'S FACILITIES | PARKING FACILITIES | RESTAURANT | PUBLIC BAR |
|---|---|---|---|---|---|

## THE LOWER SHANNON

**ADARE:** *Dunraven Arms*  ⓔⓔⓔ
Co Limerick. **Road map** B5. ☎ 061 396633. FAX 061 396541.
Set in the extremely pretty village of Adare, this inn was established in 1792 and is a great touring base for the southwest. The bedrooms are luxurious and the restaurant is outstanding. 🚗 TV **Rooms:** 66

| MC V AE DC | ● | ■ | ● | ■ |

**ADARE:** *Adare Manor*  ⓔⓔⓔⓔⓔ
Co Limerick. **Road map** B5. ☎ 061 396566. FAX 061 396124.
This huge, Victorian-Gothic mansion was the former seat of the Earls of Dunraven. It was built in 1720 but was elaborated and enlarged in the 19th century. It's both tasteful and luxurious throughout. 🚗 TV 🏊 & **Rooms:** 64

| MC V AE DC | ● | ■ | ● | ■ |

**AGLISH:** *Ballycormac House*  ⓔⓔ
Borrisokane, Co Tipperary. **Road map** C4. ☎ 067 21129. FAX 067 21200.
Located in a quiet rural setting, this cozy, 300-year-old house has a relaxed, informal atmosphere with lots of activities offered, including riding and golf. Dinner is by reservation only. 🚗 **Rooms:** 5

| MC V | ● | | | |

**AHERLOW:** *Aherlow House*  ⓔⓔ
Glen of Aherlow, Co Tipperary. **Road map** C5. ☎ 062 56153. FAX 062 56212.
In a wonderful setting in the middle of a pine forest with a view of the mountains, this comfortable and welcoming hunting lodge is a delight to stay in. 🚗 TV & **Rooms:** 30

| MC V AE DC | | ■ | ● | ■ |

**BALLYVAUGHAN:** *Hylands*  ⓔⓔ
Co Clare. **Road map** B4. ☎ 065 77037. FAX 065 77131.
Dating back to the 18th century, this family run hotel is traditional in style, with simple but pretty bedrooms. Irish music in the bar. 🚗 TV **Rooms:** 19

| MC V AE | ● | ■ | ● | ■ |

**BALLYVAUGHAN:** *Gregans Castle*  ⓔⓔⓔ
Co Clare. **Road map** B4. ☎ 065 77005. FAX 065 77111.
This is a marvelous place to stay in the middle of the Burren, with views toward Galway Bay. Very comfortably furnished. 🚗 **Rooms:** 22

| MC V | ● | ■ | ● | ■ |

**CASHEL:** *Cashel Palace*  ⓔⓔⓔ
Main St, Cashel, Co Tipperary. **Road map** C5. ☎ 062 61411. FAX 062 61521.
Beautiful Palladian house originally built as an archbishop's palace in the 1730s. Right in the center of town but surrounded by a peaceful garden, it is an extremely civilized place to stay. 🚗 TV **Rooms:** 20

| MC V AE DC | ● | ■ | ● | ■ |

**CLARECASTLE:** *Carnelly House*  ⓔⓔⓔ
Co Clare. **Road map** B4. ☎ 065 28442. FAX 065 29222.
A lovely Queen Anne house designed by Francis Bindon and set in delightful grounds. A member of Hidden Ireland, it is elegantly and tastefully furnished, and has a relaxed atmosphere. 🚗 **Rooms:** 5

| MC V AE | | ■ | | |

**CLONMEL:** *Clonmel Arms Hotel*  ⓔⓔ
Sarsfield St, Clonmel, Co Tipperary. **Road map** C5. ☎ 052 21233. FAX 052 21526.
A predictable but comfortable central hotel. The bars and restaurants are popular with the locals. Particularly helpful staff. 🚗 TV & **Rooms:** 31

| MC V AE DC | ● | ■ | ● | ■ |

**FEAKLE:** *Smyths Village*  ⓔ
Co Clare. **Road map** B4. ☎ 061 924002. FAX 061 924244.
A complex made up of modern cottages and a restaurant. Set in lovely countryside, it is a simple, cheap and pleasant place to stay. 🚗 **Rooms:** 12

| MC V AE DC | ● | ■ | ● | ■ |

**GLIN:** *Glin Castle*  ⓔⓔⓔ
Co Limerick. **Road map** B5. ☎ 068 34173. FAX 068 34364.
Though it's described as a historic Irish house and not a hotel, you can stay here either as individuals or in a group. Built in the 1780s, this magnificent building is still owned and lived in by the Knight of Glin. 🚗 **Rooms:** 6

| MC V DC | ● | ■ | | |

**KILNABOY:** *Fergus View* £
Corrofin, Co Clare. **Road map** B4. 065 37606. FAX 065 37192.
This very good-value, friendly guest house is a useful base for exploring the Burren. Recently refurbished, it is pristine and comfortable. Dinner is available only if prebooked. **Rooms:** 6

**LIMERICK:** *Woodfield House* ££
Ennis Rd, Limerick, Co Limerick. **Road map** B4. 061 453022. FAX 061 326755.
Located just out of town, this traditional hotel has been recently refurbished but still retains its friendly, informal family atmosphere. Smart, well-equipped bedrooms. TV **Rooms:** 22
MC V AE DC

**LIMERICK:** *Jury's Hotel* £££
Ennis Rd, Limerick, Co Limerick. **Road map** B4.
061 327777. FAX 061 326400.
Reliable part of the Jury's chain, with good quality furnishings and dependable service. Lovely location on 2 ha (5 acres) of garden on the banks of the River Shannon. TV **Rooms:** 95
MC V AE DC

**LISDOONVARNA:** *Sheedy's Spa View* £
Co Clare. **Road map** B4. 065 74026. FAX 065 74555.
This house has been in the Sheedy family for five generations and has now been converted into a very comfortable, efficient hotel by the present owners. **Rooms:** 11
MC V AE DC

**LISMACUE:** *Lismacue House* ££
Bansha, Co Tipperary. **Road map** C5. 062 54106. FAX 062 54126.
The house is part of the Hidden Ireland group. It's a classically beautiful, Irish country house built at the beginning of the 19th century; it has particularly fine reception rooms and comfortable bedrooms. **Rooms:** 5
MC AE

**NEWMARKET-ON-FERGUS:** *Dromoland Castle* £££££
Co Clare. **Road map** B4. 061 368144. FAX 061 363355.
Sister hotel to Ashford Castle in Cong, you can expect a high standard of luxury here, too. The castle dates back to the 16th century and has a fascinating history. The grounds cover 150 ha (370 acres). TV **Rooms:** 73
MC V AE DC

**QUIN:** *Ballykilty Manor* ££
Co Clare. **Road map** B4. 065 25627. FAX 065 25654.
Lovely Georgian manor surrounded by 20 ha (50 acres) of woodland. Spacious reception rooms with blazing fires and comfortable bedrooms. Very friendly owners. **Rooms:** 10
MC V AE DC

## THE WEST OF IRELAND

**BALLINA:** *Mount Falcon* ££
Co Mayo. **Road map** B2. 096 70811. FAX 096 71517.
This 19th-century castle, surrounded by over 40 ha (100 acres) of woods and parkland, is a peaceful, friendly place to stay. Bedrooms are light and spacious. There's fishing on local loughs and the River Moy **Rooms:** 10
MC V AE DC

**BALLYNAHINCH:** *Ballynahinch Castle* £££
Recess, Connemara, Co Galway. **Road map** A3. 095 31006. FAX 095 31085.
A magnificent castle, once owned by a maharaja, in a superb location. The hotel is well-run, and has a friendly feel. There is an excellent restaurant and lots of hunting possibilities. TV **Rooms:** 28
MC V AE DC

**CASHEL BAY:** *Zetland House* £££
Connemara, Co Galway. **Road map** A3. 095 31111. FAX 095 31117.
A professionally run, stylishly decorated, 19th-century shooting lodge. Set on the edge of Cashel Bay in lovely gardens, most of the bedrooms and the dining room share the superb views. **Rooms:** 20
MC V AE DC

**CASHEL BAY:** *Cashel House* ££££
Connemara, Co Galway. **Road map** A3. 095 31001. FAX 095 31077.
In a stunning location at the head of Cashel Bay, this is a great place to stay. Extremely comfortable, relaxing rooms, full of interesting antiques. Very welcoming hosts. TV **Rooms:** 32
MC V AE DC

**CLIFDEN:** *Erriseask House* ££
Connemara, Co Galway. **Road map** A3. 095 23553. FAX 095 23639.
This modern farmhouse is stylishly decorated, with light, comfortable bedrooms. It's set in a beautiful spot, only a short walk away from the sea and the food is superb. **Rooms:** 13
MC V AE DC

For key to symbols see back flap

| | CREDIT CARDS | CHILDREN'S FACILITIES | PARKING FACILITIES | RESTAURANT | PUBLIC BAR |
|---|---|---|---|---|---|

**Price categories** are for a standard double room (not per person) for one night, including tax, service charges and breakfast.

£ under IR£50
££ IR£50–100
£££ IR£100–150
££££ IR£150–200
£££££ over IR£200

**CHILDREN'S FACILITIES**
Cribs and high chairs are available and some hotels will also provide a baby-sitting service.

**PARKING FACILITIES**
Parking provided by the hotel in either a private parking lot or a private garage close by.

**RESTAURANT**
The hotel has a restaurant for residents, which also welcomes nonresidents – usually only for evening meals.

**PUBLIC BAR**
The hotel has a bar that is open to nonresidents and residents alike.

---

**CLIFDEN:** *Rock Glen Manor House* ££
Connemara, Co Galway. **Road map** A3. ☎ 095 21035. FAX 095 21737.
Just outside Clifden, in a lovely location overlooking the bay, this traditional hotel used to be a shooting lodge for Clifden Castle. Comfortable rooms and reliable, friendly service. 🛏 TV **Rooms:** 29

| MC V AE DC | ● | ■ | ● | |

---

**CONG:** *Ashford Castle* £££££
Co Mayo. **Road map** B3. ☎ 092 46003. FAX 092 46260.
A mixture of 13th-century and Gothic Revival, this magnificent castle is set on the shore of Lough Corrib. Rich wall-to-wall carpeting kills a lot of the historical atmosphere, but it is undoubtedly luxurious. 🛏 TV 🛗 **Rooms:** 83

| MC V AE DC | ● | ■ | ● | |

---

**CROSSMOLINA:** *Enniscoe House* ££
Castlehill, Crossmolina, Co Mayo. **Road map** B2. ☎ 096 31112. FAX 096 31773.
This fine Georgian house, set on magnificent grounds that lead down to Lough Conn, is full of beautiful antiques and has a relaxed, lived-in feel, with attractive bedrooms and good food. Member of Hidden Ireland. 🛏 **Rooms:** 6

| MC V AE | ● | ■ | | |

---

**GALWAY:** *Hazlewood House* £
Oranmore, Galway, Co Galway. **Road map** B4. ☎ 091 94275. FAX 091 94608.
Set on secluded grounds a short drive from town, this is a friendly place to stay. Pleasant rooms, good cooking and lots of activities locally. **Rooms:** 6

| MC V AE DC | ● | ■ | | |

---

**GALWAY:** *Ardilaun House* ££
Taylor's Hill, Galway, Co Galway. **Road map** B4. ☎ 091 21433. FAX 091 521546.
A short distance from the city center and quite close to Salthill, this hotel is popular with business people and tourists. Stylish decor, friendly, efficient service and comfortable rooms. 🛏 TV 🛗 **Rooms:** 89

| MC V AE DC | ● | ■ | | |

---

**GALWAY:** *Great Southern Hotel* £££
Eyre Sq, Galway, Co Galway. **Road map** B4. ☎ 091 64041. FAX 091 66704.
The rooftop swimming pool is an unusual feature of this large and rambling Victorian hotel in the heart of the city. The rooms are comfortable and there are plenty of facilities. 🛏 TV ≋ 🛗 **Rooms:** 114

| MC V AE DC | ● | ■ | | ■ |

---

**KINGSTOWN:** *Kille House* £
Clifden, Connemara, Co Galway. **Road map** A3. ☎ 095 21849. FAX 095 21849.
Set in lovely, peaceful surroundings, this dignified 19th-century house specializes in B&B. Evening meals by arrangement only. 🛏 **Rooms:** 4

| | ● | ■ | | |

---

**KNOCKFERRY:** *Knockferry Lodge* £
Roscahill, Co Galway. **Road map** B3. ☎ 091 80122. FAX 091 80328.
Situated in a tranquil spot on the western shore of Lough Corrib, the prices reflect the simple rooms with plain decor and furnishings. The atmosphere is very friendly and the food good. 🛏 **Rooms:** 12

| MC V AE DC | | ■ | | |

---

**LETTERFRACK:** *Rosleague Manor House* ££
Connemara, Co Galway. **Road map** A3. ☎ 095 41101. FAX 095 41168.
A substantial Georgian house overlooking Ballinakill Bay and well located for the Connemara National Park with only a short walk to the sea. Comfortable and relaxed, with an excellent restaurant. 🛏 **Rooms:** 20

| MC V AE | ● | ■ | ● | ■ |

---

**LEENANE:** *Delphi Lodge* ££
Co Galway. **Road map** B3. ☎ 095 42211. FAX 095 42296.
A sporting lodge in a lovely setting by a lough surrounded by mountains. Informal atmosphere with plenty of fishing on the loughs and River Delphi. A member of Hidden Ireland. Open February to November. 🛏 **Rooms:** 11

| MC V | | ■ | | |

---

**MOYARD:** *Crocnaraw Country House* ££
Connemara, Co Galway. **Road map** A3. ☎ 095 41068.
Lovely Georgian house on Ballinakill Bay surrounded by award-winning gardens. Very attractively furnished, with a friendly, relaxed atmosphere and comfortable bedrooms. 🛏 🛗 **Rooms:** 8

| MC V AE DC | ● | ■ | ● | ■ |

**NEWPORT:** *Newport House*
Co Mayo. **Road map** B3. **C** 098 41222. **FAX** 098 41613.
A stay at this historic, creeper-covered Georgian house is extremely comfortable and civilized. It stands beside the River Newport, renowned as a great fishing center. *Rooms: 19*
£££ | MC V AE DC

**OUGHTERARD:** *Currarevagh House*
Connemara, Co Galway. **Road map** B3. **C** 091 82312. **FAX** 091 82731.
In an isolated, peaceful spot on the shores of Lough Corrib and surrounded by woods, parkland and gardens, this Victorian country house is traditionally run with a cozy, slightly old-fashioned atmosphere. *Rooms: 15*
££

**OUGHTERARD:** *Ross Lake House*
Rosscahill, Oughterard, Co Galway. **Road map** B3.
**C** 091 80109. **FAX** 091 80184.
This 18th-century house, surrounded by gardens, is nicely decorated throughout and feels neat and efficient. Fishing is available in nearby loughs and you can play tennis in the hotel grounds. *Rooms: 13*
££ | MC V AE DC

**PONTOON:** *Healy's*
Foxford, Co Mayo. **Road map** B3. **C** 094 56443. **FAX** 094 56572.
In a stunning location on the shores of Lough Conn and Lough Cullen, this traditional old stone hotel is a great spot for bird-watchers. Simple, neat bedrooms and good Irish cooking. *Rooms: 10*
££ | MC V

**RENVYLE:** *Renvyle House*
Connemara, Co Galway. **Road map** A3. **C** 095 43511. **FAX** 095 43515.
A very relaxed family hotel on the edge of the Atlantic, it offers lots of sporting activities as well as comfort and good food. Beams and polished wooden floors with rugs, give atmosphere and style. *Rooms: 65*
££ | MC V AE DC

**ROSTURK:** *Rosturk Woods*
Mulrany, Westport, Co Mayo. **Road map** B3. **C** 098 36264. **FAX** 098 36264.
In a wonderfully quiet spot by the sea, 11 km (7 miles) from Newport, this stylishly furnished guest house is an extremely attractive and comfortable place to stay. *Rooms: 4*
£ | MC V

**WESTPORT:** *Olde Railway*
The Mall, Westport, Co Mayo. **Road map** B3. **C** 098 25166. **FAX** 098 25090.
Situated in the center of town, this traditional hotel is comfortable and reliable and has recently been attractively refurbished. It makes an excellent base for the area. *Rooms: 25*
££ | MC V AE

## NORTHWEST IRELAND

**ARDARA:** *Woodhill House*
Co Donegal. **Road map** C2. **C** 075 41112. **FAX** 075 41516.
The house dates back to the 17th century but is predominantly Victorian in appearance. The reasonably comfortable rooms are good value and it is a good base for exploring the surrounding area. *Rooms: 9*
£ | MC V AE D

**BALLYMOTE:** *Temple House*
Co Sligo. **Road map** B3. **C** 071 83329. **FAX** 071 83808.
Lovely Georgian house, owned by the Perceval family since 1665, set in 420 ha (1,000 acres) of parkland. Comfortable sitting rooms, large bedrooms and good food. Member of Hidden Ireland. *Rooms: 5*
££ | MC V AE

**BRUCKLESS:** *Bruckless House*
Co Donegal. **Road map** C2. **C** 073 37071. **FAX** 073 37070.
Set on 7 ha (17 acres) of attractive grounds on the shores of Bruckless Bay, this 18th-century farmhouse is a comfortable and relaxing place to stay, with friendly hosts and good food. *Rooms: 4*
£ | MC V AE

**CASTLEBALDWIN:** *Cromleach Lodge Country House*
Ballindoon, Boyle, Co Sligo. **Road map** C3. **C** 071 65155. **FAX** 071 65455.
Its superb location in the hills above Lough Arrow provides all the spacious bedrooms in this house with magnificent views. The lodge has an excellent restaurant and a high standard of comfort. *Rooms: 10*
£££ | MC V AE DC

**COLLOONEY:** *Markree Castle*
Co Sligo. **Road map** C2. **C** 071 67800. **FAX** 071 67840.
The castle has been in the Cooper family since 1640 but it has only recently been restored and turned into a hotel. It has stately rooms and lovely grounds and the atmosphere is very civilized and relaxing. *Rooms: 14*
££ | MC V AE DC

**Price categories** are for a standard double room (not per person) for one night, including tax, service charges and breakfast.

£ under IR£50
££ IR£50–100
£££ IR£100–150
££££ IR£150–200
£££££ over IR£200

**CHILDREN'S FACILITIES**
Cribs and high chairs are available and some hotels will also provide a baby-sitting service.

**PARKING FACILITIES**
Parking provided by the hotel in either a private parking lot or a private garage close by.

**RESTAURANT**
The hotel has a restaurant for residents, which also welcomes nonresidents – usually only for evening meals.

**PUBLIC BAR**
The hotel has a bar that is open to nonresidents and residents alike.

| | Credit Cards | Children's Facilities | Parking Facilities | Restaurant | Public Bar |
|---|---|---|---|---|---|
| **DONEGAL: St. Ernan's House** £££<br>Co Donegal. Road map C2. 073 21065. FAX 073 22098.<br>Located on a small island linked to the mainland by a causeway, this attractive, pink-painted, 19th-century house is elegantly furnished but retains a relaxed, informal atmosphere. **Rooms: 12** | MC V | | ■ | ● | |
| **DRUMCLIFF: Urlar House** £<br>Co Sligo. Road map C2. 071 63110.<br>In a peaceful, secluded spot in the shadow of Ben Bulben, this attractive farmhouse offers good, simple accommodations and makes a perfect base for exploring Yeats Country. **Rooms: 5** | AE | ● | ■ | | |
| **DUNKINEELY: Castle Murray House** £<br>Co Donegal. Road map C2. 073 37022. FAX 073 37330.<br>Stunningly located on a cliff with views down the Donegal coast, this small hotel is a wonderful place to stay. The decor is simple but stylish and the restaurant offers a delicious menu. **Rooms: 10** | V AE | ● | ■ | ● | |
| **LETTERKENNY: Castle Grove Country House** ££<br>Co Donegal. Road map C1. 074 51118. FAX 074 51384.<br>Approached down a long avenue through lovely parkland, this 17th-century house looks out on Lough Swilly and is a peaceful and relaxing place to stay. **Rooms: 8** | MC V AE DC | ● | ■ | ● | |
| **LOUGH ESKE: Ardnamona House** ££<br>Co Donegal. Road map C2. 073 22650. FAX 073 22819.<br>A member of Hidden Ireland, this Edwardian house is in a beautiful spot, surrounded by famous gardens and backed by the Blue Stack Mountains. Comfortable rooms and a hospitable, informal atmosphere. **Rooms: 5** | MC V DC | ● | ■ | | |
| **LOUGH ESKE: Harvey's Point** £££<br>Donegal, Co Donegal. Road map C2. 073 22208. FAX 073 22352.<br>Swiss-style hotel on the banks of Lough Eske. Neat, modern furnishings, excellent restaurant and lots of sports facilities. Most rooms overlook the lough. **Rooms: 20** | MC V AE DC | | ■ | ● | ■ |
| **MOHILL: Glebe House** £<br>Ballinamore, Mohill, Co Leitrim. Road map C3. 078 31086. FAX 078 31886.<br>This early-19th-century former rectory is set on 20 ha (50 acres) of parkland, woods and farmland, and is peaceful and attractive. **Rooms: 7** | MC V AE | ● | ■ | | |
| **RIVERSTOWN: Coopershill House** ££<br>Co Sligo. Road map C2. 071 65108. FAX 071 65466.<br>Very civilized, elegant 17th-century house surrounded by a vast estate. Fine rooms with lovely antiques, huge bedrooms and excellent food. **Rooms: 7** | MC V AE DC | ● | ■ | ● | |
| **ROSSNOWLAGH: Smuggler's Creek** £<br>Co Donegal. Road map C2. 072 52366.<br>This is a very cozy place in a wonderful spot on top of the cliff looking down over the Rossnowlagh beach. There's a choice of bar food or the restaurant, and all the bedrooms have sea views. **Rooms: 5** | MC V | ● | ■ | ● | ■ |
| **ROSSNOWLAGH: Sand House** ££<br>Co Donegal. Road map C2. 072 51777. FAX 072 52100.<br>An imposing, white castellated building right on a sandy beach overlooking Donegal Bay, this long-established hotel is very comfortable and well decorated and has a relaxed atmosphere. **Rooms: 39** | MC V AE DC | ● | ■ | ● | ■ |
| **STRANORLAR: Kee's Hotel** ££<br>Ballybofey, Co Donegal. Road map C2. 074 31018. FAX 074 31917.<br>A coaching inn and mail staging post in the 19th century, the hotel maintains a tradition of generous hospitality. Freshly refurbished with a new recreation center. Well located for exploring Donegal. **Rooms: 36** | MC V AE DC | ● | ■ | ● | ■ |

# THE MIDLANDS

**ARDEE:** *Red House* £)£
Co Louth. **Road map** D3. ( 041 53523. FAX 041 53523.
This very attractive Georgian manor house is a member of Hidden Ireland.
The rooms are comfortable and there is a floodlit tennis court. **Rooms:** 3
MC V

**BIRR:** *Tullanisk* £)£
Co Offaly. **Road map** C4. ( 0509 20572. FAX 0509 21783.
This well-restored, 18th-century dower house for Birr Castle is a member
of the Hidden Ireland group. It is a comfortable, relaxing place to stay,
with large, stylishly decorated bedrooms. **Rooms:** 7
MC V

**CARLINGFORD:** *McKevitt's Village Hotel* £
Market Sq, Carlingford, Co Louth. **Road map** D3. ( 042 73116. FAX 042 73144.
Popular village inn at the heart of the local scene. Rooms have real fires
and a great atmosphere; bedrooms are pristine and pretty. TV **Rooms:** 13
MC V AE DC

**CARLINGFORD:** *Viewpoint* £
Omeath Rd, Carlingford, Co Louth. **Road map** D3. ( 042 73733. FAX 042 73144.
Motel-style, modern accommodations. Well-equipped bedrooms with
wonderful views across Carlingford Lough. TV **Rooms:** 8
V

**CLONES:** *Hilton Park* £)£)£
Co Monaghan. **Road map** C2. ( 047 56007. FAX 047 56033.
Superb mansion in magnificent parkland. A member of Hidden Ireland
and extremely civilized. The rooms have a relaxed grandeur. **Rooms:** 5
MC V

**CROSSDONEY:** *Lisnamandra Farmhouse* £
Lisnamandra, Crossdoney, Co Cavan. **Road map** C3. ( 049 37196. FAX 049 37111.
Simple but comfortable accommodations in hospitable 17th-century
farmhouse. Plenty of activities on the farm and nearby. **Rooms:** 6
MC V

**DROGHEDA:** *Boyne Valley* £)£
Co Louth. **Road map** D3. ( 041 37737. FAX 041 39188.
A much extended and refurbished 18th-century manor house. Although
most of the decor and furnishings are modern, the hotel preserves much
of the house's traditional feel. TV **Rooms:** 37
MC V AE DC

**DULEEK:** *Annesbrook* £)£
Co Meath. **Road map** D3. ( 041 23293. FAX 041 23024.
This 17th-century house is a member of Hidden Ireland. It has a lovely
welcoming atmosphere and spacious, comfortable bedrooms. **Rooms:** 5
MC V

**KILMESSAN:** *Station House* £)£
Co Meath. **Road map** D3. ( 046 25239 FAX 046 25588.
The railroad used to run through Kilmessan, but now this Victorian station
building is a comfortable hotel with a good restaurant. TV **Rooms:** 10
MC V AE DC

**LONGFORD:** *Carrigglas Manor* £)£)£
Co Longford. **Road map** C3. ( 043 45165. FAX 043 41026.
The magnificent ancestral home of the Lefroys *(see pp232–3)* is a member
of Hidden Ireland. Being treated as private guests and staying in lovely
surroundings make for a special stay. Open May to October. **Rooms:** 6
MC V AE

**MOUNTRATH:** *Roundwood House* £)£
Co Laois. **Road map** C4. ( 0502 32120. FAX 0502 32711.
A beautiful, 18th-century Palladian villa set in lovely grounds close to the
Slieve Bloom Mountains. Civilized but informal atmosphere. **Rooms:** 10
MC V AE DC

**MULLINGAR:** *Bloomfield House* £)£
Co Westmeath. **Road map** C3. ( 044 40894. FAX 044 43767.
A manor house on Lough Ennell with great views. Traditional in atmosphere
but recently refurbished, it's comfortable and friendly. TV **Rooms:** 33
MC V AE DC

**MULLINGAR:** *Greville Arms* £)£
Co Westmeath. **Road map** C3. ( 044 48563. FAX 044 48052.
Centrally located, this traditional hotel caters to both locals and tourists.
Good facilities with a large bar and restaurant. TV **Rooms:** 40
MC V AE DC

**SLANE:** *Conyngham Arms* £)£
Co Meath. **Road map** D3. ( 041 24155. FAX 041 24205.
In the heart of the estate village, this traditional family hotel is welcoming
and comfortable. Good base for touring the Boyne Valley. TV **Rooms:** 16
MC V DC

For key to symbols see back flap

**Price categories** are for a standard double room (not per person) for one night, including tax, service charges and breakfast.

£ under £50
££ £50–100
£££ £100–150
££££ £150–200
£££££ over £200

**CHILDREN'S FACILITIES**
Cribs and high chairs are available and some hotels will also provide a baby-sitting service.

**PARKING FACILITIES**
Parking provided by the hotel in either a private parking lot or a private garage close by.

**RESTAURANT**
The hotel has a restaurant for residents, which also welcomes nonresidents – usually only for evening meals.

**PUBLIC BAR**
The hotel has a bar that is open to nonresidents and residents alike.

## NORTHERN IRELAND

| | CREDIT CARDS | CHILDREN'S FACILITIES | PARKING FACILITIES | RESTAURANT | PUBLIC BAR |
|---|---|---|---|---|---|
| **ANNALONG:** *Glassdrumman Lodge* **££**<br>Mill Rd, Annalong, Co Down. **Road map** D2. 📞 013967 68451. 📠 013967 67041.<br>Set deep in the "Kingdom of Mourne," the hotel looks out on the region's famous drystone walls. Excellent reputation for food. 🚪 📺 ♿ **Rooms:** 10 | MC V AE DC | | ■ | ● | |
| **ARMAGH:** *Charlemont Arms* **£**<br>Co Armagh. **Road map** D2. 📞 01861 522028. 📠 01861 526979.<br>A country-style hotel perfectly located for the major attractions. What it lacks in luxury it makes up for in the warmth of its welcome. 🚪 📺 ♿ **Rooms:** 14 | MC V | ● | ■ | ● | ■ |
| **BALLYGALLY:** *Ballygally Castle* **££**<br>274 Coast Rd, Ballygally, Co Antrim. **Road map** D1.<br>📞 01574 583212. 📠 01574 583681.<br>Reputedly haunted, the castle showpiece is the Ghost Room, a tiny old tower bedroom with a macabre legend. Musicians provide a more friendly atmosphere in the Dungeon Bar of the old fortress. 🚪 📺 **Rooms:** 30 | MC V AE DC | | ■ | ● | ■ |
| **BALLYMENA:** *Galgorm Manor* **£££**<br>Co Antrim. **Road map** D1. 📞 01266 881001. 📠 01266 880080.<br>The River Maine sweeps past the hotel, enhancing the view from many of the rooms. Fishing and riding are available on the magnificent estate. There is a first-rate restaurant and a traditional, Irish-style bar. 🚪 📺 ♿ **Room:** 23 | MC V AE DC | ● | ■ | ● | ■ |
| **BANGOR:** *Clandeboye Lodge* **££**<br>10 Estate Rd, Bangor, Co Down. **Road map** E2. 📞 01247 853777. 📠 01247 852772.<br>Resembling a Victorian church school, the hotel has reasonably priced rooms and a stylish dining room with a great menu. 🚪 📺 ♿ **Rooms:** 43 | MC V AE DC | ● | ■ | ● | ■ |
| **BELFAST:** *Duke's Hotel* **££**<br>65 University St, Belfast BT7. **Road map** D2. 📞 01232 236666. 📠 01232 237177.<br>A modern hotel offering comfort, style and international cuisine in the heart of the city. It has a good public bar. 🚪 📺 ♿ **Rooms:** 21 | MC V AE DC | | | ● | ■ |
| **BELFAST:** *Malone Lodge Hotel* **££**<br>60 Eglantine Ave, Belfast BT9. **Road map** D2. 📞 01232 382409. 📠 01232 382706.<br>Centrally located, it's ideal for business people and tourists. Modern and functional, with good bedroom facilities. 🚪 📺 ♿ **Rooms:** 33 | MC V AE DC | ● | ■ | ● | |
| **BELFAST:** *Europa Hotel* **£££**<br>Great Victoria St, Belfast BT2. **Road map** D2. 📞 01232 327000. 📠 01232 327800.<br>An imposing building in the heart of the Golden Mile, ideal for business people and tourists, with a very good restaurant. 🚪 📺 ♿ **Room:** 184 | MC V AE DC | ● | ■ | ● | ■ |
| **BELFAST:** *Stormont Hotel* **£££**<br>587 Upper Newtownards Rd, Belfast BT4. **Road map** D2.<br>📞 01232 658621. 📠 01232 480240.<br>Close to Stormont and the airport, it's excellent for business people. Modern and functional, with an award-winning restaurant. 🚪 📺 ♿ **Rooms:** 109 | MC V AE DC | ● | ■ | ● | ■ |
| **CARNLOUGH:** *Londonderry Arms Hotel* **££**<br>20 Harbour Rd, Carnlough, Co Antrim. **Road map** D1.<br>📞 01574 885255. 📠 01574 885263.<br>Winston Churchill once owned this ivy-covered inn next to the harbor of Carnlough in a breathtaking setting at the foot of Glencloy. Family owned, it has a genuine warmth of welcome. 🚪 📺 **Rooms:** 21 | MC V AE DC | ● | ■ | ● | ■ |
| **COLERAINE:** *Blackheath House* **££**<br>112 Killeague Rd, Blackhill, Coleraine, Co Londonderry.<br>**Road map** D2. 📞 01265 868433. 📠 01265 868433.<br>A Georgian country house in a magnificent setting with landscaped gardens. Its restaurant, MacDuffs, offers award-winning cooking. 🚪 📺 **Rooms:** 5 | MC V AE DC | ● | ■ | ● | |

**CRAWFORDSBURN:** *The Old Inn at Crawfordsburn* ⓔⓔ
Co Down. **Road map** E2. 01247 853255. FAX 01247 852775.
One of Ireland's oldest hostelries, this thatched 16th-century inn offers
quality and comfort with roaring log fires and four-poster beds in some
rooms. A good Irish menu and an excellent wine list. *Rooms: 33*
MC V

**DUNGANNON:** *Grange Lodge* ⓔⓔ
Grange Rd, Dungannon, Co Tyrone. **Road map** D2.
018687 84212. FAX 018687 723891.
The hotel is set in pleasant surroundings and offers good Ulster
home-style cooking and a hospitable family welcome. *Rooms: 5*
MC V AE DC

**ENNISKILLEN:** *Killyhevlin Hotel* ⓔ
Dublin Rd, Enniskillen, Co Fermanagh. **Road map** C2.
01365 323481. FAX 01365 324726.
The grounds sweep down to Lower Lough Erne and many bedrooms look
out on the lough, but you must pay extra for the view. *Rooms: 45*
MC V AE

**ENNISKILLEN:** *Manor House* ⓔⓔ
Killadeas, Enniskillen, Co Fermanagh. **Road map** C2.
013656 21561. FAX 013656 21545.
Located on the shores of Lough Erne, this country hotel has a rich interior,
with antiques and paintings, a warm atmosphere and friendly staff. The emphasis is on healthy eating using local seasonal produce. *Rooms: 46*

**FIVEMILETOWN:** *Blessingbourne* ⓔⓔ
Co Tyrone. **Road map** C2. 013655 21221.
An Elizabethan-style Victorian mansion with breathtaking views from its
mullioned windows. One bedroom has a four-poster bed and they all have
an appealing elegance. A member of the Hidden Ireland group. *Rooms: 4*
MC V AE DC

**HOLYWOOD:** *The Culloden Hotel* ⓔⓔⓔ
142 Bangor Rd, Holywood, Co Down. **Road map** E2.
01232 425223. FAX 01232 426777.
A very fine hotel, set in gardens and woodlands by Belfast Lough.
Originally the palace of the Bishops of Down, it retains its opulence
with many fine antiques and valuable paintings. *Rooms: 91*
MC V

**KILKEEL:** *The Kilmorey Arms Hotel* ⓔ
41 Greencastle St, Kilkeel, Co Down. **Road map** D3.
016937 62220. FAX 016937 65399.
An excellent base for the Mourne area. The rooms are well furnished and
the Smugglers' Bar's ambience fits well with the area. *Rooms: 28*
MC V AE DC

**LIMAVADY:** *Streeve House* ⓔⓔ
Co Londonderry. **Road map** D1. 015047 66563. FAX 015047 66563.
This 18th-century dower house on the Drenagh estate is a good base for
the area. The gardens at Drenagh House are exquisite. Plenty of sports
opportunities nearby. Member of Hidden Ireland. *Rooms: 3*
MC V

**LONDONDERRY:** *Beechill Country House* ⓔⓔ
32 Ardmore Rd, Londonderry, Co Londonderry. **Road map** C1.
01504 49279. FAX 01504 45366.
Good service and food and a real "home away from home" atmosphere.
The bedrooms, some with beautiful pieces of Victorian furniture, give
the feel of a grand old country home. *Rooms: 17*
MC V AE

**NEWCASTLE:** *Burrendale Hotel and Country Club* ⓔⓔ
51 Castlewellan Rd, Co Down. **Road map** E2.
013967 22599. FAX 013967 22328.
An excellent base for climbing, horseback riding and golf. Good wheelchair accesss, and a comfortable bar and restaurant. *Rooms: 51*
MC V AE DC

**NEWCASTLE:** *Slieve Donard Hotel* ⓔⓔ
Downs Rd, Newcastle, Co Down. **Road map** E2.
0139 67 23681. FAX 0139 67 24830.
A stunning redbrick building overlooking the beach and the famous Royal
County Down Golf Course. Good efficient service. *Rooms: 120*
MC V AE DC

**PORTAFERRY:** *Portaferry Hotel* ⓔⓔ
The Strand, Portaferry, Co Down. **Road map** E2.
0124 77 28231. FAX 012477 28999.
This waterside inn on the Ards Peninsula overlooks Strangford Lough. A
pleasant atmosphere and an award-winning restaurant. *Rooms: 14*
MC V AE DC

For key to symbols see back flap

# RESTAURANTS, CAFÉS AND PUBS

ALTHOUGH the highest concentration of top gourmet restaurants is in Ireland's main cities, equally fine cuisine can be found in some very un-likely, remote locations around the country. Good, plain cooking is offered at moderately priced, family-style restaurants all over Ireland. The restaurants listed on pages 306–17 are recommended for their high standards of service, quality of food and good

Restaurant sign in Kinsale

value. To supplement these listings, look for the useful *Dining in Ireland* booklet published by Bord Fáilte, the Irish Tourist Board. Pub lunches are one of Ireland's top travel bargains, offering generous portions of fresh vegetables and prime meats, and can often serve as the main meal of the day for a very reasonable price. Light meals, bar food and a variety of carryouts are also widely available.

## IRISH EATING PATTERNS

TRADITIONALLY, the Irish have started the day with a huge breakfast: bacon, sausages, black pudding, eggs, tomatoes and brown bread. In Northern Ireland this, plus potato cakes and soda farls *(see p304)*, is known as an "Ulster Fry." The main meal, dinner, was served at midday, with a lighter "tea" in the early evening.

Although continental break-fasts are now available, you will be hard-pressed to escape the traditional breakfast, which is included in almost all hotel and bed-and-breakfast rates. Increasingly, however, even the Irish settle for a light salad or soup and sandwiches at midday and save their main meal for the evening. Vestiges of the old eating patterns remain in the huge midday platefuls still served in pubs.

Enjoying breakfast at the Adare Manor Hotel *(see p294)*

Arriving at a café in Kinvarra *(see p204)*

## TIPS ON EATING OUT

ELEGANT DINING becomes considerably more afford-able when you make lunch your main meal of the day. In many of the top restaurants, the fixed-price lunch and dinner menus offer much the same, but lunch will usually come to about half the price. House wines are quite drink-able in most restaurants and can reduce the total cost of your meal. If you are traveling with children, shop around for one of the many restaurants that provide a less expensive children's menu.

Lunch is usually served between noon and 2:30pm, with dinner between 6:30 and 10pm, although many ethnic and city-center restaurants stay open later. Bed-and-breakfast hosts will often provide an ample home-cooked evening meal if given advance notice, and many will serve tea and scones in the late evening at no extra charge.

In top restaurants, men are expected to wear a jacket, though not necessarily a tie, and women to wear a dress or pants suit. Elsewhere, the dress code is pretty informal, stopping short of bare chests and short-shorts.

Visa (V) and Mastercard/Access (MC) are the most commonly accepted credit cards, with Diners Club (DC) and American Express (AE) also in use. The abbreviations in brackets are used in the restaurant listings to indicate which cards are accepted.

## GOURMET AND ETHNIC DINING

THIS ONCE gourmet-poor land now sports restaurants that rank among Europe's very best, with chefs trained in outstanding domestic and continental institutions. There is a choice of Irish, French, Italian, Chinese and even Russian cuisines, with styles ranging from traditional to regional to *nouvelle cuisine*. Locations vary as widely as the cuisine, from hotel dining rooms, town house basements and city mansions to castle hotels and tiny village cafés tucked away by the sea. The small County Cork town of Kinsale has established itself as the "Gourmet Capital of Ireland." Outstanding chefs also reign over the gracious houses listed in *Ireland's Blue Book of Country Houses and Restaurants*, available from tourist offices.

Selection of cakes served at Bantry House café *(see pp160–61)*

## BUDGET DINING

IT IS QUITE POSSIBLE to eat well on a small budget wherever you are in Ireland. In both city and rural locations, there are small cafés, tea rooms and family-style restaurants with inexpensive meals. Even if a café or tea room is at a main tourist attraction, such as Bantry House, you can still expect good, homemade food and freshly baked bread and cakes. Sandwiches are usually made with thick, tasty slices of cheese or meat (not processed); salad plates feature smoked salmon, chicken, ham, pork and beef; and hot meals usually come with large helpings of vegetables, with the beloved potato often showing up roast, boiled and mashed, all on one plate.

## PUB FOOD

IRELAND'S PUBS have moved into the food field with a vengeance. In addition to bar snacks (soup, sandwiches and

so on), available from noon until late, salads and hot meals are served from midday to 2:30pm. At rock-bottom prices, hot plates all come heaped with mounds of fresh vegetables, potatoes in one or more versions, and good portions of local fish or meat. Particularly good bargains are the pub carveries that offer a choice of joints, sliced to your preference. In recent years, the international staples of spaghetti, lasagna and quiche have also appeared on pub menus. For a list of recommended pubs, see pages 318–21.

Café sign at Baltimore

## FISH AND CHIPS AND OTHER FAST FOODS

THE IRISH, from peasant to parliamentarian, love their "chippers," immortalized in Roddy Doyle's novel *The Van*, and any good pub night will end with a visit to the nearest

fish-and-chip shop. At virtually any time of day, however, if you pass by Leo Burdock's in Dublin, there will be a long line for this international institution *(see p307)*. With Ireland's long coastline, wherever you choose, the fish will usually be the freshest catch of the day – plaice, cod, haddock, whiting or ray (a delicacy). The many other fast-food outlets include a host of familiar international names, such as McDonald's and Kentucky Fried Chicken, as well as numerous burger and kebab shops. Relatively new arrivals on the scene are several quite good pasta and pizza chains, such as Pasta Fresca and the Chicago Pizza Pie Factory.

## PICNICS

IRELAND IS GLORIOUS picnic country. Farmhouse cheeses and flavorsome tomatoes are picnic treats, or stop by one of the many small shops that offer sandwiches made with fresh local ingredients. As for where to picnic, the long, indented coast is ringed with wide, sandy beaches; with over 400 forest areas, many with picnic tables; great views add to the pleasure of mountainside picnics; and there are often pull-offs in scenic spots. Turn off a main road onto almost any country lane and you will soon find a picnic spot by a lakeside, riverbank or the shady edge of a field.

The 1601 pub in Kinsale *(see p319)*

# What to Eat in Ireland

Irish coffee

IRELAND'S rich pastureland, unpolluted rivers and extensive coastline provide tender lamb, beef and pork, an array of fish and seafood and fresh fruit and vegetables. From hearty rural fare that makes the most of ingredients available, Irish cooking has evolved into the gourmet cuisine created by internationally trained chefs. Often you will find the best of both worlds, with Irish stew or ham and cabbage on the same menu as more exotic dishes. The ideal end to a meal is an Irish coffee – coffee, cream and whiskey.

**Wheaten bread**      **Soda bread**

**Soda farl**      **Potato cake**

*Bread, invariably baked daily, comes in different guises. Soda bread may be brown or white. In Northern Ireland, brown soda bread is called wheaten bread.*

**Sausage**      **Bacon**

**Soda farl**      **Grilled tomato**

**Potato cake**      **Fried egg**

**Black pudding**

*An Ulster fry consists of home-baked soda farls (soft bread cakes leavened with soda and buttermilk) and potato cakes (bread made from mashed potato, butter and flour), as well as the basic ingredients of a fried meal. The ultimate Irish breakfast, the "fry" is a perfect way to set yourself up for the day. Without the soda farls and potato cakes, meals like this are consumed with relish all over Ireland at any time of day.*

*Mushroom soup makes a wholesome appetizer or snack. It is normally made with freshly picked local mushrooms and a generous amount of cream.*

*Smoked salmon, available all over Ireland and very popular, is generally served as simply as possible – enabling you to enjoy the full flavor of the fish.*

*Mussel soup is a substantial dish made with fresh local mussels in a creamy fish stock flavored with vegetables and herbs. Try it with wheaten bread.*

*Fresh oysters, here served on a bed of seaweed and cracked ice, make a light but delicious lunch – especially when accompanied by a glass of Guinness.*

*Dublin coddle, a traditional Saturday night supper dish, consists of chopped sausages and ham or bacon cooked in stock with potatoes and onions.*

***Irish stew***, *originally a peasant dish, is a thick casserole made with lamb or mutton, onions, and parsley, topped with potatoes.*

***Fresh salmon*** *is often poached in fish stock or wine and herbs. Galway salmon is particularly sought after for its fine taste.*

***Lamb cutlets*** *are usually served with mint sauce or jelly. Lamb from Kerry and Wicklow is famous for its tenderness.*

***Vegetables*** *are served in generous portions, usually as an accompaniment to the main course. It is not uncommon to be given potatoes in a number of different forms – roast, boiled, mashed, baked or fried – together with whichever vegetables happen to be fresh and in season.*

Mashed potato

Roast potatoes

Broccoli

Boiled potatoes

Carrots

***Baked ham***, *coated with cloves and brown sugar, is commonly served with buttered boiled cabbage and eaten at Christmas or on other festive occasions.*

***Strawberries and cream*** *are the archetypal summer dessert. They are sometimes sweetened with honey rather than sugar.*

***Porter cake***, *a classic Irish cake made with dried fruit, is most famous for the inclusion of stout, usually in the form of Guinness.*

***Apple tart***, *or "cake" as the Irish often call it, is eaten all year round but is traditionally associated with Hallowe'en.*

## CHEESES

For centuries, cheese has been made in farms and monasteries throughout Ireland. Cheese-making has expanded in the last 25 years and Ireland now produces cheeses with a worldwide reputation, from semisoft ones such as Cashel Blue and St. Killian, which is similar to Camembert, to Gouda-like Carrigaline and smoked Durrus.

St. Killian

Carrigaline

**Cashel Blue**　**Durrus**

***Tea-time*** *favorites include ladyfingers, fruit cakes and white or brown scones, made with or without fruit. Barm brack, a doughy, fruity bread, is traditionally eaten at Hallowe'en and on All Saint's Day, when a ring is hidden in the cake. Traditionally, the finder of the ring will marry by the following Easter.*

Brown scone

Fruit scone

Plain scone

Barm brack

# Choosing a Restaurant

THIS CHART LISTS restaurants, selected for their good value, food and location, by region, starting with Dublin. Use the color-coded thumb tabs, which indicate the regions covered on each page, to guide you to the relevant section of the chart. For Dublin map references, see the map on pages 110–11; for road map references, see the inside back cover.

## DUBLIN

| | Credit Cards | Open Lunchtime | Open Late | Fixed-Price Menu | Good Wine List |
|---|---|---|---|---|---|
| **SOUTHEAST DUBLIN:** *Bewley's Oriental Café* (£)<br>78–79 Grafton St, Dublin 2. **Map** D4. 01 6776761.<br>This Dublin institution is open from breakfast time onward. Its breads, pastries and homemade soups are superb. | MC V AE DC | ● | ■ | | |
| **SOUTHEAST DUBLIN:** *Kilkenny Shop Restaurant* (£)<br>The Kilkenny Shop, 6–10 Nassau St, Dublin 2. **Map** E4. 01 6777066.<br>A busy restaurant, overlooking Trinity College playing fields, offering traditional Irish cooking and an extensive cheeseboard. | MC V AE DC | ● | | | ■ |
| **SOUTHEAST DUBLIN:** *Ante Room* (£)(£)(£)<br>20 Baggot St Lower, Dublin 2. **Map** F5. 01 6618832.<br>Lobster, oysters and clams are served fresh from their seawater tanks in this cozy basement restaurant in the Georgian House Hotel. | MC V AE DC | ● | | ● | ■ |
| **SOUTHEAST DUBLIN:** *Gotham Café* (£)(£)(£)<br>8 Anne St South, Dublin 2. **Map** D4. 01 6795266.<br>The American-style menu at this bright, friendly café includes "Bowery," "Upper East Side" and "Central Park" gourmet pizzas. | MC V AE DC | ● | ■ | | |
| **SOUTHEAST DUBLIN:** *Pier 32* (£)(£)(£)<br>23 Pembroke St Upper, Dublin 2. 01 6761494.<br>The regularly changing menu includes seafood and regional dishes. Try hare and champ (mashed potatoes, spring onions and butter). | MC V | ● | ■ | | ■ |
| **SOUTHEAST DUBLIN:** *Rajdoot Tandoori* (£)(£)(£)<br>26–28 Clarendon St, Dublin 2. **Map** D4. 01 6794274.<br>This North Indian restaurant serves mildly spiced curries and, from the clay oven, tandoori barbecued beef, chicken and lamb. | MC V AE DC | ● | ■ | ● | |
| **SOUTHEAST DUBLIN:** *Sandbank Seafood Bar* (£)(£)(£)<br>Westbury Hotel, Grafton St, Dublin 2. **Map** D4. 01 6791122.<br>There is a delightful buzz about this pub and restaurant full of maritime memorabilia. Try the fresh oysters washed down with Guinness. | MC V AE DC | ● | ■ | | ■ |
| **SOUTHEAST DUBLIN:** *The Commons* (£)(£)(£)(£)<br>Newman House, St. Stephen's Green South, Dublin 2. **Map** D5. 01 4780530.<br>Specially commissioned paintings by Irish artists share the honors in this tasteful restaurant with gourmet specialties. | MC V AE DC | ● | ■ | ● | ■ |
| **SOUTHEAST DUBLIN:** *Dobbin's Wine Bistro* (£)(£)(£)(£)<br>15 Stephen's Lane, Mount St Upper, Dublin 2. **Map** F5. 01 6764679.<br>An intimate, friendly bistro with an innovative monthly menu and one of Dublin's best wine lists. | MC V AE DC | ● | ■ | | ■ |
| **SOUTHEAST DUBLIN:** *L'Ecrivain* (£)(£)(£)(£)<br>109 Baggot St Lower, Dublin 2. **Map** F5. 01 6611919.<br>In the heart of Georgian Dublin, French classics here have an Irish touch, such as breast of guinea fowl with a black pudding mousse. | MC V AE DC | ● | ■ | | ■ |
| **SOUTHEAST DUBLIN:** *The Grey Door* (£)(£)(£)(£)<br>Grey Door Hotel, 23 Pembroke St Upper, Dublin 2. 01 6763286.<br>Award-winning Russian-Scandinavian cuisine in elegant surroundings. Specialties include blini with caviar, borscht and gravlax. | MC V AE DC | ● | ■ | ● | ■ |
| **SOUTHEAST DUBLIN:** *La Stampa* (£)(£)(£)(£)<br>35 Dawson St, Dublin 2. **Map** D4. 01 6778611.<br>This upscale Italian restaurant in the heart of Dublin is noted for its sumptuous, highly ornate Georgian decor. Service is efficient and there is a lively atmosphere. Be sure to book on weekends. | MC V AE DC | ● | ■ | ● | ■ |

<table>
<tr>
<td>
Average prices for a three-course meal for one, half a bottle of house wine and unavoidable charges such as service and cover:<br>
(£) under IR£10<br>
(£)(£) IR£10–15<br>
(£)(£)(£) IR£15–25<br>
(£)(£)(£)(£) IR£25–50
</td>
<td>
OPEN LUNCHTIME<br>
Many restaurants open only in the evening, but those in large towns and attached to pubs often open at lunch time.<br>
OPEN LATE<br>
Restaurant remains open with the full menu available after 10pm.<br>
FIXED-PRICE MENU<br>
A good-value fixed-price menu is offered at lunch, dinner or both, usually with three courses.<br>
GOOD WINE LIST<br>
Denotes a wide range of good wines, or a more specialized selection of wines.
</td>
</tr>
</table>

| | Price | Credit Cards | Open Lunchtime | Open Late | Fixed-Price Menu | Good Wine List |
|---|---|---|---|---|---|---|
| **SOUTHWEST DUBLIN:** *Leo Burdock's*<br>2 Werburgh St, Dublin 8. **Map** C4. ☎ 01 4540306.<br>Dublin's oldest fish-and-chip takeaway attracts a mix of patrons. The fish are fresh, and the fries made from top-grade Irish potatoes. 🚶 | (£) | | ● | ■ | | |
| **SOUTHWEST DUBLIN:** *Elephant and Castle*<br>18 Temple Bar, Dublin 2. **Map** D3. ☎ 01 6793121.<br>This boisterous American-style restaurant serves upscale fast food from tortillas to hamburgers. It is popular for brunch on Sunday. 🚶 | (£)(£) | MC<br>V<br>AE<br>DC | ● | ■ | | |
| **SOUTHWEST DUBLIN:** *Les Frères Jacques*<br>74 Dame St, Dublin 2. **Map** C3. ☎ 01 6794555.<br>This French restaurant next to the Olympia Theatre adds Irish flair to many of its classical French dishes. Live piano music on weekends. 🚶 ✂ | (£)(£)(£)(£) | MC<br>V<br>AE | ● | ■ | ● | ■ |
| **SOUTHWEST DUBLIN:** *Lord Edward*<br>23 Christchurch Place, Dublin 8. **Map** B4. ☎ 01 4542420.<br>Dublin's oldest seafood restaurant serves lunch in the ground-floor pub and evening meals in the upstairs restaurant. Service is courteous. ✂ | (£)(£)(£)(£) | MC<br>V<br>AE<br>DC | ● | ■ | | ■ |
| **NORTH OF THE LIFFEY:** *Conway's Pub and Restaurant*<br>70 Parnell St, Dublin 1. **Map** D1. ☎ 01 8732474.<br>Decor in this pub reflects its 1745 origin, and its patrons include Dubliners and actors from the Gate Theatre as well as visitors. The menu features unexpected items, such as tiger shrimp in phyllo pastry. ♿ V | (£) | | ● | ■ | ● | ■ |
| **NORTH OF THE LIFFEY:** *Flanagan's Restaurant*<br>61 O'Connell St Upper, Dublin 1. **Map** D2. ☎ 01 8731388.<br>A popular family restaurant, Flanagan's provides exceptional value for money with an extensive menu ranging from burgers and salads to hot meals including vegetarian and pasta choices. 🚶 ✂ V | (£)(£) | MC<br>V | ● | ■ | ● | ■ |
| **NORTH OF THE LIFFEY:** *101 Talbot*<br>100–102 Talbot St, Dublin 1. **Map** E2. ☎ 01 8745011.<br>Vegetarians have a wide choice in this bright restaurant near the Abbey Theatre. Try the broccoli, fennel, zucchini and blue cheese strudel. ✂ V | (£)(£)(£) | MC<br>V<br>AE<br>DC | ● | ■ | | ■ |
| **NORTH OF THE LIFFEY:** *Chapter One Restaurant*<br>Dublin Writers Museum, Parnell Square, Dublin 1. **Map** C1. ☎ 01 8732266.<br>The decor features Irish writers. Deep-fried Parmesan and sage gnocchi and king scallops with leeks and mussels are on the menu. 🚶 ✂ V | (£)(£)(£)(£) | AE<br>DC<br>MC<br>V | ● | ■ | ● | ■ |
| **BALLSBRIDGE:** *Conservatory Restaurant*<br>Berkeley Court Hotel, Lansdowne Rd, Dublin 4. ☎ 01 6601711.<br>In this bright, conservatory-style room in one of the city's most luxurious hotels, meals from the extensive menu provide excellent value for money. Very popular with Dubliners. ♿ 🚶 ✂ V | (£)(£) | MC<br>V<br>AE<br>DC | ● | ■ | | ■ |
| **BALLSBRIDGE:** *Roly's Bistro*<br>7 Ballsbridge Terrace, Dublin 4. ☎ 01 6682611.<br>Lively bistro with Irish cuisine, including seasonal delights such as venison pie with juniper berries and wood mushrooms. Book ahead. ♿ ✂ V | (£)(£)(£) | MC<br>V<br>AE<br>DC | ● | | ● | ■ |
| **BALLSBRIDGE:** *Le Coq Hardi*<br>35 Pembroke Rd, Dublin 4. ☎ 01 6689070.<br>French classical cuisine uses the best Irish ingredients in this lovely restaurant, winner of countless awards. Book ahead for dinner. ✂ V | (£)(£)(£)(£) | MC<br>V<br>AE<br>DC | ● | ■ | ● | ■ |
| **DUN LAOGHAIRE:** *Restaurant Na Mara*<br>1 Harbour Rd. ☎ 01 2806767.<br>This restaurant, overlooking the harbor, serves the best just-caught seafood in the area. Nonfish dishes are also available. ♿ 🚶 ✂ V | (£)(£)(£)(£) | MC<br>V<br>AE<br>DC | ● | ■ | ● | ■ |

**Average prices** for a three-course meal for one, half a bottle of house wine and unavoidable charges such as service and cover:

£ under IR£10
££ IR£10–15
£££ IR£15–25
££££ IR£25–50

**OPEN LUNCHTIME**
Many restaurants open only in the evening, but those in large towns and attached to pubs often open at lunch time.

**OPEN LATE**
Restaurant remains open with the full menu available after 10pm.

**FIXED-PRICE MENU**
A good-value fixed-price menu is offered at lunch, dinner or both, usually with three courses.

**GOOD WINE LIST**
Denotes a wide range of good wines, or a more specialized selection of wines.

| | | Credit Cards | Open Lunchtime | Open Late | Fixed-Price Menu | Good Wine List |
|---|---|---|---|---|---|---|
| **HOWTH:** *Abbey Tavern* <br> Abbey St. 01 8390307. <br> A 16th-century tavern overlooking Howth Harbour and specializing in seafood. Its Irish music session is an institution. Book ahead. | £££ | MC V AE DC | ● | | ● | ■ |
| **HOWTH:** *King Sitric Fish Restaurant* <br> East Pier. 01 8325235. <br> Howth crab and lobster star on the menu in this elegant restaurant. In summer, a seafood bar serves lunch. Reserve for dinner. | ££££ | MC V AE DC | ● | ■ | ● | ■ |
| **MALAHIDE:** *Eastern Tandoori* <br> 1 New St. 01 8454154. <br> Decor and cuisine are authentically Indian in this restaurant located by the marina. Flavors to suit all tastes are served. | £££ | MC V AE DC | | ■ | ● | ■ |
| **MALAHIDE:** *Roches Bistro* <br> 12 New St. 01 8452777. <br> Daily menu changes ensure freshness in this cozy bistro, and a French influence is seen in dishes such as crab soufflé *à la crème*. | £££ | MC V AE DC | ● | ■ | ● | ■ |

## SOUTHEAST IRELAND

| | | Credit Cards | Open Lunchtime | Open Late | Fixed-Price Menu | Good Wine List |
|---|---|---|---|---|---|---|
| **BALLYHACK:** *Neptune Bistro Restaurant* <br> Ballyhack Harbour. **Road map** D5. 051 389284. <br> Next to Ballyhack Castle, this attractive bistro specializes in fresh seafood such as poached hake in lobster sauce. | £££ | MC V AE DC | | | ● | ■ |
| **CAPPOQUIN:** *Richmond House* <br> Cappoquin. **Road map** C5. 058 54278. <br> On the banks of the Blackwater River, this 18th-century country home serves French dishes and local salmon and trout. | ££££ | MC V | | | ● | ■ |
| **CARLOW:** *The Beams Restaurant* <br> 59 Dublin St. **Road map** D4. 0503 31824. <br> A family-run restaurant with beamed ceilings and an old wall oven. Dishes include wild Atlantic salmon with white wine sauce, plus a huge choice of Irish cheeses. | £££ | MC V | | ■ | ● | ■ |
| **DUNGARVAN:** *Merry's* <br> Main St. **Road map** C5. 058 41974. <br> Set in an atmospheric 19th-century wine merchant's shop, Merry's menu features shellfish and other seafoods, plus game in season. | £££ | MC V DC | ● | | | ■ |
| **FERRYCARRIG BRIDGE:** *Conservatory Restaurant* <br> Ferrycarrig Hotel. **Road map** D5. 053 22999. <br> One of the best restaurants in County Wexford, this relaxed room filled with greenery overlooks the Slaney estuary. Book ahead. | ££££ | MC V AE DC | ● | | ● | ■ |
| **GOREY:** *Marlfield House* <br> Courtown Rd. **Road map** D4. 055 21124. <br> This Regency mansion houses one of the Southeast's premier dining rooms. Only organically grown vegetables are used. | ££££ | MC V DC | ● | | ● | ■ |
| **KILDARE:** *Silken Thomas* <br> The Square. **Road map** D4. 045 22232. <br> Located near the Norman castle keep in the town center, this restaurant includes beef stroganoff and Gaelic steak on its menu. | £££ | MC V AE | | | | ■ |
| **KILKENNY:** *Kilkenny Design Centre Restaurant* <br> Castle Yard. **Road map** C4. 056 22118. <br> A bright, self-service restaurant with home-cooked casseroles and other hot dishes, plus salads, quiches, soups and patés. | £ | MC V AE DC | ● | | | |

**KILKENNY:** *Edward Langton Restaurant and Bar*　£££
69 John St. **Road map** C4. [ *056 65133.*
At Langton's, each of several small rooms has its own distinctive
decor. Stuffed mussels are among local favorites. 🅰 🅺 **V**
*MC V DC* — ● ● ■

**LEIGHLINBRIDGE:** *Lord Bagenal Inn*　£££
Main St. **Road map** D4. [ *0503 21668.*
This riverside restaurant has an old-world air and award-winning wine
list. Wild Irish salmon and game dishes appear in season. 🅺 🗲 **V**
*MC V DC* — ● ■ ● ■

**LISMORE:** *Eamonn's Place*　£
Main St. **Road map** C5. [ *058 54025.*
In summer, meals in the stone-walled beer garden here are delightful,
while a cheerful turf fire adds a glow to winter meals inside. 🅰 🅺 **V**
● ● ■

**NAAS:** *Manor Inn*　££
Main St. **Road map** D4. [ *045 97471.*
A hangout of bettors en route to and from the nearby Curragh
racecourse. Fish, steaks, pasta and grills feature on the menu. 🅰 🅺 **V**
*MC V AE DC* — ● ■ ● ■

**RATHNEW:** *Hunter's Hotel*　£££
Rathnew. **Road map** D4. [ *0404 40106.*
Cheerful hotel dining room attracting patrons from Dublin and nearby,
with its friendly ambience and superb meat and fish dishes. 🅰 🅺
*MC V AE DC* — ● ● ■

**ROSSLARE:** *The Lobster Pot*　£££
Carne. **Road map** D5. [ *053 31110.*
Lobster and oysters come straight from sea tanks in this
traditional pub and restaurant near Rosslare ferry harbor. 🅺 **V**
*MC V AE* — ● ■

**THOMASTOWN:** *The Loft*　£££
Mount Juliet Estate. **Road map** D5. [ *056 24455.*
Traditional Irish cuisine, such as Irish stew and bacon and cabbage,
is the order of the day in this informal restaurant. 🅰 🅺 🗲 **V**
*MC V AE DC* — ● ● ■

**THOMASTOWN:** *Lady Helen McCalmont Room*　££££
Mount Juliet Estate. **Road map** D5. [ *056 24455.*
The menu, as elegant as the decor, includes chicken breast with fennel
stuffing in a tomato and red pepper sauce. Book ahead. 🅰 🅺 🗲 **V**
*MC V AE DC* — ● ■

**WATERFORD:** *The Munster Bar*　£
Bailey's New St. **Road map** D5. [ *051 74656.*
One Munster specialty popular among locals is a "blaa" (meat, onion,
tomato and lettuce on a small roll), found only in Waterford City. Other
traditional dishes are featured on the extensive menu. 🅰 🅺 **V**
*MC V DC* — ● ■

**WATERFORD:** *The Olde Stand Pub and Restaurant*　££
45 Michael St. **Road map** D5. [ *051 79488.*
A glowing fireplace adds to the ambience upstairs in this Victorian-style
restaurant. More casual meals are served downstairs. Skip dessert and
indulge in one of their connoisseur coffees. 🅰 🅺 🗲 **V**
*MC V* — ● ● ■

**WATERFORD:** *Prendiville's Restaurant*　£££
Cork Rd. **Road map** D5. [ *051 78851.*
Chef Paula Prendiville has perfected her culinary creations in
this bright restaurant near the Waterford Crystal factory. 🅰 🗲 **V**
*MC V AE DC* — ● ● ■

**WATERFORD:** *Waterford Castle Hotel*　££££
The Island, Ballinakill. **Road map** D5. [ *051 78203.*
A small car ferry crosses to Waterford Castle on its River
Suir estuary island. Fish and seafood are the specialties in
the magnificent wood-paneled dining room. 🅰 🅺 🗲 **V**
*MC V AE DC* — ● ● ■

**WEXFORD:** *The Granary*　£££
Westgate. **Road map** D5. [ *053 23935.*
Once a grain store, this is now an inviting restaurant specializing in
fresh seafood such as Wexford mussels and Kilmore scallops. 🅺 🗲 **V**
*MC V AE DC* — ● ■

**WICKLOW:** *The Old Rectory*　££££
Wicklow. **Road map** D4. [ *0404 67048.*
The pretty dining room is the setting for gourmet meals centered
around pure health foods, organically grown vegetables and edible
flowers, local meats and seafood. Book in advance. 🅺 🗲 **V**
*MC V AE* — ● ■

*For key to symbols see back flap*

**Average prices** for a three-course meal for one, half a bottle of house wine and unavoidable charges such as service and cover:
- £ under IR£10
- ££ IR£10–15
- £££ IR£15–25
- ££££ IR£25–50

**OPEN LUNCHTIME**
Many restaurants open only in the evening, but those in large towns and attached to pubs often open at lunch time.

**OPEN LATE**
Restaurant remains open with the full menu available after 10pm.

**FIXED-PRICE MENU**
A good-value fixed-price menu is offered at lunch, dinner or both, usually with three courses.

**GOOD WINE LIST**
Denotes a wide range of good wines, or a more specialized selection of wines.

## CORK AND KERRY

| Restaurant | Price | Credit Cards | Open Lunchtime | Open Late | Fixed-Price Menu | Good Wine List |
|---|---|---|:-:|:-:|:-:|:-:|
| **BALLYFERRITER:** *Tig an Tobair*<br>Ballyferriter. **Road map** A5. ( 066 56404.<br>A glassed-over wishing-well is the centerpiece of the small "House of the Well" restaurant. The chef always uses local fish. & ⊼ ⇆ **V** | £££ | MC V | ● | | | ■ |
| **BALLYLICKEY:** *Sea View House Hotel*<br>Bantry Bay. **Road map** B6. ( 027 50073.<br>The award-winning cuisine at this charming restaurant concentrates on fresh fish from Bantry Bay as well as local meat and produce. & ⊼ **V** | £££ | MC V AE | | | ● | ■ |
| **BANTRY:** *O'Connor's Seafood Restaurant*<br>The Square. **Road map** B6. ( 027 50221.<br>Bantry Bay's famed mussels are the specialty of this established restaurant. Mountain lamb and steaks are also excellent. ⇆ **V** | £££ | MC V | ● | | | ■ |
| **BLARNEY:** *Phelan's Woodview House*<br>Tweedmount. **Road map** B5. ( 021 385197.<br>This intimate restaurant often draws diners from nearby Cork. Make sure you sample chef Billy Phelan's hot seafood bundle. & ⊼ ⇆ **V** | £££ | MC V | | ■ | ● | ■ |
| **CASTLETOWNSHEND:** *Mary Ann's*<br>Skibbereen. **Road map** B6. ( 028 36146.<br>Local seafood stars on the menu of this 150-year-old bar. Try the filleted sole stuffed with fish forcemeat and Mornay sauce glaze. ⊼ **V** | £££ | MC V | ● | | ● | |
| **CORK:** *Beecher's Inn*<br>Faulkner's Lane. **Road map** C5. ( 021 273144.<br>A little hard to find, Beecher's is in a lane between St. Patrick's Street and Emmet Place. Superb homemade lunches make it worth the effort. ⊼ **V** | £ | MC V AE DC | ● | | | |
| **CORK:** *Arbutus Lodge Hotel Gallery Bar*<br>Montenotte. **Road map** C5. ( 021 501237.<br>This informal bar provides some of the best-value lunchtime food in Cork. The more formal restaurant in the same hotel offers gourmet dinners mixing Irish, French and other international cuisines. **V** | ££ | MC V AE DC | ● | ■ | | ■ |
| **CORK:** *Isaac's Restaurant*<br>48 MacCurtain St. **Road map** C5. ( 021 503805.<br>The menu in this converted warehouse is extensive. Try the tagliatelle with red pepper sauce, cream cheese and smoked bacon. & ⊼ ⇆ **V** | £££ | MC V AE DC | ● | ■ | | |
| **CORK:** *Clifford's*<br>18 Dyke Parade. **Road map** C5. ( 021 275333.<br>Chef Michael Clifford changes his menu monthly. His creations include monkfish tails *en papillote* with ginger and spring onions. ⇆ | ££££ | MC V DC | ● | ■ | ● | ■ |
| **DINGLE:** *Beginish*<br>Green St. **Road map** A5. ( 066 51588.<br>This award-winning restaurant offers specialties such as breast of duck with honey and mustard sauce. Efficient and friendly service. ⊼ ⇆ **V** | £££ | MC V AE DC | ● | | | ■ |
| **DINGLE:** *Half Door Restaurant*<br>3 John St. **Road map** A5. ( 066 51600.<br>A combination of stone and light woods creates a relaxed ambience at the Half Door. The day's catch determines the menu. & ⊼ ⇆ **V** | £££ | MC V AE DC | ● | | | ■ |
| **DURRUS:** *Blair's Cove House Restaurant*<br>Blair's Cove. **Road map** B6. ( 027 61127.<br>In this romantic waterside restaurant on the shores of Dunmanus Bay, both wine list and cheeseboard are exceptional. & ⊼ **V** | ££££ | MC V AE DC | | | ● | ■ |

**KANTURK:** *Assolas Country House* ££££ | MC V AE
Kanturk. **Road map** B5. 029 50015.
Hazel Bourke's culinary expertise and emphasis on freshness has gained this lovely 17th-century home an international reputation. Choose from her seasonal menu or from the dishes of the day. **V**

**KENMARE:** *The Purple Heather* £
Henry St. **Road map** B5. 064 41016.
This town-center pub and restaurant serves up tasty, hearty food. Dishes include chicken liver terrine and Cumberland sauce. **& V**

**KENMARE:** *Lime Tree Restaurant* £££ | MC V
Shelbourne St. **Road map** B5. 064 41225.
Housed in a charming 1830s school, the Lime Tree offers an imaginative choice of dishes. Try the goats' cheese potato cakes. **& ♿**

**KENMARE:** *Packie's Food and Wine* £££ | MC V
Henry St. **Road map** B5. 064 41508.
On the eclectic menu here, you're likely to find touches of Californian or Mediterranean cuisine along with traditional Irish dishes, such as casserole of beef with Guinness and mushrooms. **& ♿ V**

**KILLARNEY:** *Dingle's Restaurant* £££ | MC V AE DC
40 New St. **Road map** B5. 064 31079.
Glowing open fires, oak and leather paneling and exposed stone create an inviting decor at Dingle's. Irish stew is a specialty, and there's a terrific vegetarian casserole. **V**

**KILLARNEY:** *Gaby's* ££££ | MC V AE DC
High St. **Road map** B5. 064 32519.
Gaby's is the best seafood restaurant in town. Its interior incorporates seafaring memorabilia. Specialties include lobster, shellfish, oysters and Atlantic salmon. There is a fixed-price menu at lunchtime. **♿**

**KILLARNEY:** *The Strawberry Tree* ££££ | MC V AE DC
24 Plunkett St. **Road map** B5. 064 32688.
No chemically treated meats or vegetables are used here. The wild Atlantic salmon with a sorrel sauce is simple and delicious. **♿ ✈ V**

**KILLORGLIN:** *Nick's Restaurant* £££ | MC V AE DC
Lower Bridge St. **Road map** A5. 066 61219.
Chef Nick Foley's background as a butcher ensures that only the best cuts of meat reach the table. The same care goes into seafood offerings. There are open fires and a pianist plays regularly. **♿ ✈ V**

**KINSALE:** *The Blue Haven* £££ | MC V AE DC
3–4 Pearse St. **Road map** B6. 021 772209.
A pleasant family restaurant, the Blue Haven offers a wide variety of food, from bar lunches to substantial meals. There's always a good selection of farmhouse cheeses. **& ♿ ✈ V**

**KINSALE:** *Max's Wine Bar* £££ | MC V
Main St. **Road map** B6. 021 772443.
For more than 20 years, Max's has been in the forefront of Kinsale's gourmet restaurants. Among its culinary specialties is rack of lamb with red wine and rosemary sauce. **✈ V**

**KINSALE:** *Man Friday* ££££ | MC V AE DC
Scilly. **Road map** B6. 021 772260.
Overlooking Kinsale Harbour, this restaurant has won culinary awards galore. No wonder, with specialties such as black sole with seafood stuffing and roast lamb with mint and rosemary sauce. **♿ ✈ V**

**LEAP:** *Friskey's Restaurant* £££ | MC V
The Leap Inn. **Road map** B6. 028 33307.
Traditional Irish dishes (Irish stew, bacon and cabbage, roast stuffed chicken) feature on lunchtime menus in this delightful country inn. Locally caught seafoods are also a specialty. **& ♿ ✈**

**MALLOW:** *Presidents' Restaurant* ££££ | MC V AE DC
Longueville House. **Road map** B5. 022 47156.
Portraits of Irish presidents line the walls in this Georgian mansion. An excellent white wine from their own vineyard is available. **& ✈ V**

For key to symbols see back flap

**Average prices** for a three-course meal for one, half a bottle of house wine and unavoidable charges such as service and cover:
£ under IR£10
££ IR£10–15
£££ IR£15–25
££££ IR£25–50

**OPEN LUNCHTIME**
Many restaurants open only in the evening, but those in large towns and attached to pubs often open at lunch time.

**OPEN LATE**
Restaurant remains open with the full menu available after 10pm.

**FIXED-PRICE MENU**
A good-value fixed-price menu is offered at lunch, dinner or both, usually with three courses.

**GOOD WINE LIST**
Denotes a wide range of good wines, or a more specialized selection of wines.

| | CREDIT CARDS | OPEN LUNCHTIME | OPEN LATE | FIXED-PRICE MENU | GOOD WINE LIST |
|---|---|---|---|---|---|
| **PARKNASILLA:** *Pygmalion Restaurant* ££££<br>Great Southern Hotel. **Road map** A6. 064 45122.<br>Overlooking Kenmare Bay on the Ring of Kerry, the Pygmalion's elegant decor and polished service set off a gourmet cuisine. | MC V AE DC | | | ● | ■ |
| **SHANAGARRY:** *Ballymaloe House* ££££<br>Shanagarry, Midleton. **Road map** C6. 021 652531.<br>At Ballymaloe House, acclaimed for its Irish and French classics, vegetables and meats come from their own farm, and seafood is local. | MC V AE DC | ● | | ● | ■ |
| **YOUGHAL:** *Aherne's Seafood Restaurant* ££££<br>163 North Main St. **Road map** C5. 024 92424.<br>Chef David Fitzgibbon's seafood chowder is positively addictive. His sumptuous platter of six fish and four shellfish recently won Aherne's the prestigious Seafood Dish of the Year Award. | MC V AE DC | ● | | ● | ■ |

## THE LOWER SHANNON

| | CREDIT CARDS | OPEN LUNCHTIME | OPEN LATE | FIXED-PRICE MENU | GOOD WINE LIST |
|---|---|---|---|---|---|
| **ADARE:** *The Inn-Between* £££<br>Dunraven Arms Hotel, Main St. **Road map** B5. 061 396633.<br>A charming restaurant in a thatched cottage, with informal service and a cozy atmosphere. Lunch features soups and soda bread. | MC V AE | ● | | ● | |
| **ADARE:** *The Mustard Seed at Echo Lodge* ££££<br>Ballingarry. **Road map** B5. 069 68508.<br>The Mustard Seed's move from Adare to a country house nearby means a change of scene but no change to the excellent food, with seasonal dishes prepared with the freshest of ingredients. | MC V AE DC | | | ● | ■ |
| **BUNRATTY:** *MacCloskey's* ££££<br>Bunratty House Mews. **Road map** B4. 061 364082.<br>Downstairs in this 1846 mansion, the original kitchen, staff quarters and wine cellars form one of the best restaurants in the country. | MC V DC | | | ● | ■ |
| **CAHIR:** *Malone's* ££<br>The Galtee Inn, The Square. **Road map** C5. 052 41247.<br>The all-day menu in this family-run restaurant offers prime beef with rich sauces, roasts and seafood dishes as well as light meals. | MC V | ● | ■ | | ■ |
| **CASHEL:** *Chez Hans* ££££<br>Rockside. **Road map** C5. 062 61177.<br>At the foot of the Rock of Cashel, Chez Hans occupies a former Wesleyan chapel. For several years, Hans-Peter Matthiä has created wonderfully innovative versions of traditional dishes. | MC V | | | | ■ |
| **CLONMEL:** *Michael's* £££<br>Clonmel Arms Hotel, Sarsfield St. **Road map** C5. 052 21233.<br>Michael's is a bright, airy hotel dining room, decorated with strong colors, lots of brass and some interesting art. The European-influenced menu changes with the seasons. | MC V AE DC | ● | ■ | | ■ |
| **DOOLIN:** *Bruach na hAille* £££<br>Roadford. **Road map** B4. 065 74120.<br>This charming, cottage-style restaurant (its name means "banks of the river") uses local produce in unexpected ways, such as fillets of sole in cider served with shellfish in a cream sauce. | MC V AE | | | ● | ■ |
| **ENNIS:** *Cruise's Pub and Restaurant* ££<br>Abbey St. **Road map** B4. 065 41800.<br>The 17th-century building's low, beamed ceilings and the open fires in winter create a cozy ambience in this restaurant. Several nights a week, meals are served with traditional music. | MC V AE | ● | | ● | |

**LIMERICK:** *Bridges Restaurant*                £££   MC
Jury's Hotel, Ennis Rd. **Road map** B4. ( 061 327777.   V
All-day service makes this bright hotel restaurant one of the most con-   AE
venient in Limerick. Light snacks share the menu with full meals. The more   DC
formal Copper Room serves gourmet and traditional Irish dishes. 🚫 🏃 **V**

**LIMERICK:** *The Silver Plate*                £££   MC
74 O'Connell St. **Road map** B4. ( 061 316311.   V
Freshness is the keynote in this Georgian city-center house where you   AE
can select your own lobster and oysters from a seawater tank. 🚫 **V**   DC

**NENAGH:** *Gurthalougha House*                ££££   MC
Ballinderry. **Road map** C4. ( 067 22080.   V
The candlelit dining room in this country home, reached by land or   AE
water, overlooks a lake. The menu features homegrown produce. 🚫   DC

**NEWMARKET-ON-FERGUS:** *Earl of Thomond Room*      ££££   MC
Dromoland Castle. **Road map** B4. ( 061 368144.   V
A traditional Irish harper accompanies evening meals in this elegant   AE
dining room. The "Taste of Ireland" set menu has no less than six courses.   DC
Try the hot brown-bread soufflé and the creamy lamb ravioli. 🚫 **V**

## THE WEST OF IRELAND

**ACHILL ISLAND:** *The Boley House Restaurant*        £££   MC
Keel. **Road map** A3. ( 098 43147.   V
Owner Tom McNamara uses only the freshest ingredients, with seafood
from local waters. Roasted free-range duckling is a favorite. 🚫 🚫 **V**

**ARAN ISLANDS:** *Dún Aonghasa Restaurant*         £££   MC
Kilronan, Inishmore. **Road map** B4. ( 099 61104.   V
Overlooking the harbor, in a setting of stone, wood and open fires,
chef Grace Flaherty bases her menu on fish fresh from Galway Bay.
Choices include creamy seafood chowder and grilled shark 🚫 🏃 🚫 **V**

**BARNA:** *Donnelly's Seafood Restaurant and Bar*      £££   MC
Seapoint **Road map** B4. ( 091 592487.   V
Fresh seafood is a specialty in this rustic restaurant. Among non-   AE
seafood dishes is chicken supreme, Gaelic-style. 🏃 🚫 **V**   DC

**CLARINBRIDGE:** *Moran's Oyster Cottage*            ££   MC
The Weir. **Road map** B4. ( 091 96113.   V
Known as "Moran's of the Weir," this 200-year-old restaurant   AE
in a thatched cottage is loved by both locals and celebrities,
especially during the annual Clarinbridge Oyster Festival. 🏃

**CLIFDEN:** *O'Grady's Seafood Restaurant*         ££££   MC
Market St. **Road map** A3. ( 095 21450.   V
Award-winning O'Grady's offers delicious seafood, such as baked   AE
fillet of cod with a Calvados cream glaze, as well as superb vegetarian
choices including an avocado and blue cheese mousse in puff pastry. **V**

**CLIFDEN:** *Rock Glen Restaurant*                ££££   MC
Rock Glen Manor House. **Road map** A3. ( 095 21035.   V
A converted Connemara shooting lodge is the setting for gracious dining   AE
here, with friendly service enhancing an excellent cuisine. 🚫 🏃 🚫 **V**   DC

**CONG:** *Connaught Room*                ££££   MC
Ashford Castle. **Road map** B3. ( 092 46003.   V
Only the best local ingredients come to table in this   AE
wood-paneled dining room. Its menu includes rack of   DC
Connemara hill lamb and fillet of turbot with scallops. 🚫 🚫 **V**

**GALWAY:** *Eyre House and Park*                £££   MC
Forster St, Eyre Sq. **Road map** B4. ( 091 64924.   V
A tasteful restaurant offering good value and a wide-ranging menu that   DC
features grilled sea trout, honey-glazed rack of lamb and other Irish
specialties prepared from local ingredients. 🚫 🚫 **V**

**GALWAY:** *Hooker Jimmy's Steak and Seafood Bar*      £££   MC
The Fishmarket, Spanish Arch. **Road map** B4. ( 091 68351.   V
This bar serves meals outside in fine weather. Galway salmon   AE
and shellfish from their own boat are on the menu. 🚫 🏃 🚫 **V**   DC

For key to symbols see back flap

**Average prices** for a three-course meal for one, half a bottle of house wine and unavoidable charges such as service and cover:
£ under IR£10
££ IR£10–15
£££ IR£15–25
££££ IR£25–50

**OPEN LUNCHTIME**
Many restaurants open only in the evening, but those in large towns and attached to pubs often open at lunch time.

**OPEN LATE**
Restaurant remains open with the full menu available after 10pm.

**FIXED-PRICE MENU**
A good-value fixed-price menu is offered at lunch, dinner or both, usually with three courses.

**GOOD WINE LIST**
Denotes a wide range of good wines, or a more specialized selection of wines.

| | Credit Cards | Open Lunchtime | Open Late | Fixed-Price Menu | Good Wine List |
|---|---|---|---|---|---|
| **GALWAY:** *Rabbitt's Bar and Restaurant* £££ <br> 23–25 Forster St, Eyre Sq. **Road map** B4. 091 66490. <br> Dating back to 1872, this atmospheric bar-restaurant has a menu as traditional as its decor. Irish stew with local lamb is excellent. | MC V DC | ● | | | ■ |
| **MOYCULLEN:** *Drimcong House* £££ <br> Moycullen. **Road map** B4. 091 85115. <br> This top restaurant is in a 17th-century lakeside house. The menu changes weekly, and there is a five-course set vegetarian menu. | MC V AE DC | | ■ | ● | |
| **ROSCOMMON:** *Abbey Hotel* £££ <br> Galway Rd. **Road map** C3. 0903 26250. <br> Set dinners in this 18th-century turreted mansion feature steak prepared in different ways, grilled sea trout and other fish dishes. | MC V AE DC | ● | | ● | |
| **WESTPORT:** *The Asgard Tavern and Restaurant* £££ <br> The Quay. **Road map** B3. 098 25319. <br> The lively bar here dishes up award-winning lunches. Evening meals include a superb seafood chowder and garlic steak. | MC V AE | ● | | | ■ |

## NORTHWEST IRELAND

| | Credit Cards | Open Lunchtime | Open Late | Fixed-Price Menu | Good Wine List |
|---|---|---|---|---|---|
| **BALLYSHANNON:** *Sweeney's White Horse Bar* £ <br> Assaroe Rd. **Road map** C2. 072 51452. <br> Sweeney's set bar menu offers good food in an inviting atmosphere. There is traditional music in the Cellar Bar on Friday nights. | | ● | ■ | ● | |
| **CASTLEBALDWIN:** *Cromleach Lodge Country House* ££££ <br> Ballindoon, Boyle. **Road map** C3. 071 65155. <br> Fabulous views of Lough Arrow and the Bricklieve Mountains form a backdrop for gourmet dining in this hilltop country house. | MC V AE DC | | | ● | ■ |
| **COLLOONEY:** *Glebe House Restaurant* £££ <br> Collooney. **Road map** C2. 071 67787. <br> At this Georgian house, there's an emphasis on organically grown produce and imaginative use of local fish and meats. Friendly service. | MC V AE | | | ● | ■ |
| **INISHOWEN PENINSULA:** *Bree Inn* £ <br> Malin Head. **Road map** C1. 077 70161. <br> At the northernmost point in Ireland, this lively country inn serves home-cooked meals all day. The place is a favorite with locals. | | ● | ■ | | |
| **INISHOWEN PENINSULA:** *Restaurant St John's* £££ <br> Fahan. **Road map** C1. 077 60289. <br> An atmospheric restaurant on the shores of Lough Swilly offering five- and six-course set menus, with excellent fish dishes and desserts. | MC V DC | | | ● | ■ |
| **KILLYBEGS:** *Sail Inn* £££ <br> Main St. **Road map** C2. 073 31130. <br> Food is served all day at this traditional inn. Bar food is good value, and fish from the town's fleet is served in the upstairs restaurant. | MC V | ● | | | |
| **LETTERKENNY:** *Carolina House Restaurant* £££ <br> Milford Rd. **Road map** C1. 074 22480. <br> Chef Mary Prendergast's approach to fish dishes (that fish must swim three times: in water, butter and wine) makes for superb dining. Vegetables and herbs come from the kitchen garden. | MC V AE DC | | | | ■ |
| **RATHMULLAN:** *Pavilion Restaurant* ££££ <br> Rathmullan Country House. **Road map** C1. 074 58188. <br> The Pavilion offers gourmet food in a glass-walled setting. Sample the seaweed-based dessert of carrageen moss with stewed fruits. | MC V AE DC | | | ● | ■ |

**SLIGO:** *Gulliver's Restaurant*    £££
24 Grattan St. **Road map** C2. 071 42030.
A nautical theme dominates the decor here. The menu ranges from
burgers, salads and sandwiches to prime meats and fresh fish. 🏃 🍽 V

MC
V
AE
DC

**SLIGO:** *Truffles Restaurant*    £££
11 The Mall. **Road map** C2. 071 44226.
Whimsical *trompe l'oeil* decorations share honors with a traditional peat
fire in this restaurant. The New Age pizza menu has a Mediterranean
flavor, with Californian and Mexican influences. 🖤 🍽 V

**TOBERCURRY:** *Killoran's Traditional Restaurant*    £££
Teeling St. **Road map** B3. 071 85111.
Irish stew, boxty (potato pancakes) and crubeens (pickled pigs' feet) are
on the traditional menu. Snacks and full meals served all day. 🖤 🏃 🍽 V

MC
V
AE
DC

## THE MIDLANDS

**ARDEE:** *The Gables*    £££
Dundalk Rd. **Road map** D3. 041 53789.
The accent here is definitely French, using the freshest local ingredients
available. Choose from classics like snails with garlic butter. V

MC
V
AE
DC

**ATHLONE:** *L'Escale Restaurant*    ££££
The Hodson Bay Hotel. **Road map** C3. 0902 92444.
Cuisine is a blend of French and Irish. A typical dish is Dublin Bay shrimp
with shallots, mushrooms and tomato, flamed in whiskey. 🖤 🏃 V

MC
V
AE
DC

**BUTLER'S BRIDGE:** *Derragarra Inn*    £££
Butler's Bridge. **Road map** C3. 049 31003.
A thatched cottage inn decorated with relics of rural Ireland by the River
Annalea. The restaurant menu is available in the bar all day. 🖤 🏃 🍽 V

MC
V

**CARLINGFORD:** *Jordan's Town House Restaurant*    £££
Newry St. **Road map** D3. 042 73223.
A renovated 19th-century warehouse overlooking the harbor is the
setting for culinary gems with organically grown local ingredients. 🍽 V

MC
V
AE

**CARRICKMACROSS:** *Nuremore Hotel*    ££££
Carrickmacross. **Road map** D3. 042 61438.
This beautiful restaurant has an imaginative menu, including
French and Irish cuisine, served in a tranquil setting. 🖤 🏃 V

MC
V
AE
DC

**DUNDALK:** *Quaglino's Restaurant*    £££
88 Clanbrassil St. **Road map** D3. 042 38567.
This bright, town-center restaurant features superb Continental
dishes, which the menu lists in no less than four languages. 🏃 🍽 V

MC
V
AE
DC

**KELLS:** *Monaghan's*    £
Kells. **Road map** D3. 046 40100.
Monaghan's is a moderately priced family restaurant. Only local,
hormone-free meats are used. Children welcome until 9pm. 🖤 🏃 V

MC
V

**MONAGHAN:** *Andy's Restaurant*    £££
Market St. **Road map** D2. 047 82277.
This restaurant in Monaghan town center is above an award-winning
pub. The extensive menu includes sirloin steak in whiskey and beer
sauce and half a dozen vegetarian dishes. 🖤 🏃 🍽 V

MC
V

**MOUNTRATH:** *Roundwood House*    £££
Mountrath. **Road map** C4. 0502 32120.
Prebooking is a must in this gracious Palladian mansion. Its compulsory
four-course set menu changes daily. Superb Sunday lunches. 🏃 V

MC
V
AE
DC

**MULLINGAR:** *Crookedwood House*    £££
Crookedwood. **Road map** C3. 044 72165.
This 200-year-old restaurant changes its menu with the seasons. A summer
specialty is River Moy salmon with hollandaise sauce. 🏃 🍽 V

MC
V
AE
DC

**TULLAMORE:** *Moorhill Country House*    £££
Clara Rd. **Road map** C4. 0506 21395.
Stone walls, oak beams and open fires welcome you to this
traditional but imaginative restaurant in renovated stables. 🖤 🏃 V

MC
V
AE

For key to symbols see back flap

**Average prices** for a three-course meal for one, half a bottle of house wine and unavoidable charges such as service and cover:
£ under £10
££ £10–15
£££ £15–25
££££ £25–50

**OPEN LUNCHTIME**
Many restaurants open only in the evening, but those in large towns and attached to pubs often open at lunch time.

**OPEN LATE**
Restaurant remains open with the full menu available after 10pm.

**FIXED-PRICE MENU**
A good-value fixed-price menu is offered at lunch, dinner or both, usually with three courses.

**GOOD WINE LIST**
Denotes a wide range of good wines, or a more specialized selection of wines.

## NORTHERN IRELAND

| | | CREDIT CARDS | OPEN LUNCHTIME | OPEN LATE | FIXED-PRICE MENU | GOOD WINE LIST |
|---|---|---|---|---|---|---|
| **ARMAGH:** *Pilgrim's Table* <br> 38–40 English St. **Road map** D2. 01861 527808. <br> Fine home cooking makes use of the best fresh local produce. Non-fussy dishes, especially the soups (such as potato and leek or chicken and bacon), are tasty, filling and superb value. | £ | | ● | | | |
| **BALLYCASTLE:** *Wysner's Restaurant* <br> 16 Anne St. **Road map** D1. 01265 762372. <br> Wysner's serves excellent meat and fish dishes. Downstairs is in the style of a French café, while upstairs is a more expensive restaurant where the Bushmills Malt cheesecake is a must. | £££ | MC V | ● | | ● | ■ |
| **BELFAST:** *Crown Liquor Saloon* <br> 46 Great Victoria St. **Road map** D2. 01232 249476. <br> Centrally located with Victorian decor, this bar's snuglike booths provide the table space for a bowl of Irish stew or champ – a local specialty of potatoes, spring onions and butter. | £ | MC V DC | ● | | | ■ |
| **BELFAST:** *Duke of York* <br> 11 Commercial Court. **Road map** D2. 01232 241062. <br> Pub grub, including chili, steak and lasagne is the typical fare at this very reasonably priced restaurant. Near St. Anne's Cathedral, it is Irish in style and carefully cluttered with Belfast memorabilia. | £ | | ● | | | |
| **BELFAST:** *Pierre Victoire* <br> 30 University Rd. **Road map** D2. 01232 315151. <br> A bicycle hangs over the door of this simple French restaurant where the menu changes daily. Portions are adequate rather than generous. The French onion soup is well worth sampling. | ££ | MC V | ● | ■ | ● | ■ |
| **BELFAST:** *Malone House* <br> Barnett Demesne. **Road map** D2. 01232 681246. <br> Clare Connery is one of Northern Ireland's top chefs and uses only the best Ulster produce for her traditional and modern Irish cuisine. Vegetarian dishes are often the house specialty. | £££ | MC V DC | ● | | ● | ■ |
| **BELFAST:** *Nick's Warehouse* <br> 35–39 Hill St. **Road map** D2. 01232 439690. <br> Nick Price's converted warehouse, tucked away in the cobbled backstreets of city-center Belfast, gets top marks for atmosphere. The menu regularly includes Nick's latest culinary innovations. | £££ | MC V AE DC | ● | | ● | ■ |
| **BELFAST:** *Antica Roma* <br> 67 Botanic Ave. **Road map** D2. 01232 311121. <br> The Roman atmosphere and first-rate service complement the Italian menu featuring creative pasta dishes such as tagliatelle with a rich lamb sauce. There is a resident pianist. | ££££ | MC V AE | ● | ■ | | ■ |
| **BELFAST:** *Roscoff* <br> 7 Lesley House, Shaftesbury Sq. **Road map** D2. 01232 331532. <br> Classical French cuisine with Californian influence combine to make Roscoff a wonderful eating experience. Its Michelin star guarantees use of the freshest local produce and great service. Try the fillet of Glenarm salmon with horseradish sauce and chive cream. | ££££ | MC V AE DC | ● | ■ | ● | ■ |
| **BELLEEK:** *Rooney's Bar and Restaurant* <br> Main St. **Road map** C2. 01365 658279. <br> This cozy pub and restaurant offers huge portions of simply cooked fresh food. Steaks, roast ham or rack of Irish lamb are all on the menu, served with vegetables and potatoes. | ££ | MC V AE | ● | | ● | ■ |

**DUNDRUM:** *The Buck's Head*
77 Main St. **Road map** E2. ( *01396 751868.*
Open fires and hospitable, friendly service make this an excellent stop
for lunch or dinner. There is a conservatory and beer garden. ⓑ 🕆 Ⓥ
£££ | MC V AE

**DUNGANNON:** *Viscount's Great Food Hall*
10 Northland Row. **Road map** D2. ( *01868 753800.*
A Victorian church has been converted into a medieval-style banqueting
hall with the emphasis on fun as much as food. The large menu caters
to all appetites and is popular with families in the daytime. ⓑ 🕆 ⚡ Ⓥ
£££ | MC V

**ENNISKILLEN:** *Tullyhona Farm Restaurant*
59 Marble Arch Rd, Florencecourt. **Road map** C2. ( *01365 348452.*
Beside Marble Arch caves, this farm restaurant offers great food and
service. Produce fresh from the farm is used, and desserts such as
lemon soufflé and fresh fruit pavlova are a specialty. ⓑ 🕆 ⚡ Ⓥ
£

**ENNISKILLEN:** *Franco's Pizzeria*
Queen Elizabeth Rd. **Road map** C2. ( *01365 324185.*
A warren of nooks and crannies, this hospitable restaurant often has
live traditional music. Franco's vast menu offers Italian food with an
Irish influence. Seafood dishes include fresh lobster and mussels. ⓑ 🕆 Ⓥ
££ | MC V AE DC

**ENNISKILLEN:** *The Sheelin*
Bellanaleck. **Road map** C2. ( *01365 348232.*
This thatched cottage restaurant on the shores of Lower Lough
Erne is a gourmet experience. Favorites include ham in a honey
and fruit marinade followed by Baileys Cream cheesecake. ⓑ 🕆 Ⓥ
££ | MC V AE

**HOLYWOOD:** *Iona Bistro*
27 Church Rd. **Road map** E2. ( *01232 425655.*
Roughcast walls and tightly packed tables make this restaurant,
owned by Dutchman Bart Brave, homey and welcoming. He
offers four-course surprise menus. Bring your own wine. 🕆 Ⓥ
££ | MC V

**LONDONDERRY:** *The Metro*
3–4 Bank Pl. **Road map** C1. ( *01504 267401.*
Shadowed by Derry's city walls, this is a favorite with locals. The food,
from soup and sandwiches to beef stew in Guinness, is first rate. ⓑ 🕆 Ⓥ
£

**LONDONDERRY:** *Schooners*
59 Victoria Rd. **Road map** C1. ( *01504 311500.*
Overlooking Lough Foyle, Schooners is a maritime restaurant.
Try the "Captain's Catch" – baked fillet of trout served with
hazelnut butter. Plenty of nonfish options too. ⓑ 🕆 ⚡ Ⓥ
££ | MC V

**NEWCASTLE:** *Pavilion Restaurant*
36 Downs Rd. **Road map** E2. ( *01396 726239.*
Overlooking miles of sandy beach, this is one of Newcastle's best
restaurants. Lunchtime snacks are served in the downstairs bar
while in the evening a more elaborate menu is offered. ⓑ 🕆 Ⓥ
£££ | MC V AE

**NEWCASTLE:** *Percy French*
Downs Rd. **Road map** E2. ( *01396 723175.*
The Tudor-style bar and restaurant offer generous portions of dishes
from plowman's cheese and pickle to à la carte choices. ⓑ 🕆 ⚡ Ⓥ
£££ | MC V AE DC

**PORTBALLINTRAE:** *Sweeny's Wine Bar*
6b Seaport Ave. **Road map** D1. ( *01265 732404.*
Prices here are cheap and cheerful and the food creatively prepared.
Situated on the Causeway Coast, Sweeny's occupies a converted stable
block overlooking Portballintrae Harbour. ⓑ 🕆 Ⓥ
££

**PORTRUSH:** *The Ramore Restaurant*
The Harbour. **Road map** D1. ( *01265 824313.*
The Ramore looks over Portrush Harbour and is one
of the finest restaurants in Northern Ireland, with excellent
presentation. Gourmet food includes fried squid with salad. ⓑ Ⓥ
£££ | MC V

**STRANGFORD:** *The Lobster Pot*
The Square. **Road map** E2. ( *01396 881288.*
Only the finest local catches are served in this predominantly
fish restaurant overlooking Strangford Lough. ⓑ 🕆 Ⓥ
£££ | MC V AE DC

For key to symbols see back flap

# Pubs in Ireland

THE ARCHETYPAL IRISH PUB is celebrated for its convivial atmosphere, friendly locals, genial bar staff and the "crack" – the Irish expression for fun. Wit is washed down with whiskey or Guinness, the national drinks. Irish pubs date back to medieval taverns, coaching inns and shebeens, illegal drinking dens that flourished under colonial rule. In Victorian times, brewing and distilling were major industries. The sumptuous Edwardian or Victorian interiors of some city pubs are a testament to these times, furnished with mahogany and marble bar counters. Snugs, partitioned-off booths, are another typical feature of Irish pubs. Traditional pubs can be boldly painted, thatched or "black-and-white" – beamed with a white façade and black trim. Some rural pubs double as grocery stores.

Good pubs are not evenly distributed throughout the country: in the Southeast, Kilkenny is paradise for pub-lovers, while Cork and Kerry possess some of the most picturesque pubs. The Lower Shannon region is noted for its boisterous pubs, especially in County Clare where spontaneous music sessions are common. The West has an abundance of typical Irish pubs, and the many tourists and students guarantee a profusion of good pubs in Galway. The listings below cover a selection of pubs throughout Ireland; for Dublin pubs, see pages 104–7.

## SOUTHEAST IRELAND

**Dunmore East:** *The Ship Inn*
Road map D5. **C** 051 383141.
This old, ivy-covered pub lies above the harbor, away from the crowds on the beach. It is noted both for its seafood. Inside, nautical memorabilia and half-barrel seats abound in the front bar. The small garden is an appealing spot for drinking in the summer. Lemon sole, turbot and brill are on the menu. 🍴 🎵

**Enniscorthy:** *The Antique Tavern*
14 Slaney St. Road map D5.
**C** 054 33428.
This traditional, timbered, black-and-white pub is charming. The dark, intimate bar contains relics such as pikestaffs from Vinegar Hill, the decisive battle in the 1798 uprising that was fought outside town. Pub lunches and local chat are offered. In good weather, you can sit on the balcony. 🎵

**Enniscorthy:** *The Cotton Tree*
Slaney Place. Road map D5.
**C** 054 33179.
Although this is essentially a work-aday pub with few pretensions, its site makes it worth a visit – it is built into the base of an old quarry, and a vertical cliff forms part of the back wall of the bar. Snacks are available all day, and there are impromptu music sessions.

**Kilkenny:** *Kyteler's Inn*
27 St. Kieran's St. Road map C4.
**C** 056 21064.
In good weather you can sit in the courtyard of this historic coaching inn and cellar bar. Food is served all day, and meals are served in the restaurant downstairs until 9:45pm (last orders). An effigy of a witch sits in the window frame, a reminder of the story of a former resident, Dame Alice Kyteler. In 1324, Alice and her maid were pronounced guilty of witchcraft after four of Alice's husbands had died in mysterious circumstances; although pardoned, Alice was again accused but escaped, leaving her maid to burn at the stake. 🍴 🎵

**Kilkenny:** *Langton's*
69 John St. Road map C4.
**C** 056 65133.
Langton's is noted for its black-and-white exterior, Edwardian ambience (most of the time) and the stylish glass interior at the back. The front bar is cozy with a low ceiling. Pub food is offered, and there's music and dancing three or four nights a week; Tuesday is disco night.

**Kilkenny:** *Maggie Holland's*
St. Kieran's St. Road map C4.
**C** 056 62273.
Set in a central spot near the river, this dimly lit but welcoming pub is the best place for live music. Traditional music sessions on Tuesday evenings draw plenty of locals. 🎵

**Kilkenny:** *Marble City Bar*
66 High St. Road map C4.
**C** 056 62091.
Marble City Bar, the most famous pub in town, is named after the local limestone, which becomes black when polished. This four-story building has a bright Edwardian façade, adorned with a sign lit by an atmospheric gas lamp.

**Kilkenny:** *Tynan's Bridge House Bar*
2 John's Bridge. Road map C4.
**C** 056 21291.
This is the most genuine old-world pub in town, with an intimate interior lit by charming lamps. Quaint relics of the former grocery store and pharmacy are on display, from a set of old scales to the drawers labeled with names of nuts and spices. No food, no music, no TV; as proprietor Michael puts it, "a chat bar."

**Kilmore Quay:** *The Wooden House*
Road map D5. **C** 053 29804.
This traditional – if over-restored – thatched pub is full of nautical memorabilia and quirky sayings, while the small terrace is decorated with anchors. Hearty pub fare is served. 🍴 🎵

**Waterford:** *T and H Doolin*
George's St. Road map D5.
**C** 051 72764.
Set in the city's most charming pedestrianized street, this traditional, 18th-century black-and-white pub offers an intimate atmosphere and good "crack." Traditional folk music sessions are held on Tuesday evenings. 🎵

**Waterford:** *The Reginald Bar*
The Mall. Road map D5.
**C** 051 55087.
Set beside Reginald's Tower, the pub incorporates part of the Viking city walls and the medieval sallyports (attack exits), which are still visible. The service is rather brusque but the pub offers both reasonable bar snacks (noon–7:30pm) and a restaurant menu (5:30–10:30pm). There is also an adjoining nightclub. 🍴

**Wexford:** *Centenary Stores*
Charlotte St. Road map D5.
**C** 053 24424.
Tucked away in a converted warehouse, this cozy, dimly lit pub is the most charming in Wexford. The friendly bar staff and a mixed local and bohemian crowd chat in the wood-panelled bar. Drinkers are often entertained with impromptu sessions of traditional music. 🎵

**Wexford:** *Westgate Tavern*
Westgate. **Road map** D5.
【 053 22086.
Licensed since 1761, this distinctive, timbered tavern faces the path leading to the famous Selskar Abbey and Westgate Heritage Centre. Simple snacks are available in the welcoming bar, and there is traditional music on weekends. 🎵

## CORK AND KERRY

**Clonakilty:** *De Barra's*
**Road map** B6. 【 023 33381.
This is one of the best-known pubs in West Cork, with a traditional folk club open most nights; many musicians come from the Gaeltacht *(see p221)*. The bar is lovingly restored, with hand-painted signs and traditional whiskey jars. Simple snacks are served from 11:30am–2:30pm. 🍴 🎵

**Cork:** *Chateau Bar*
St. Patrick's St. **Road map** C5.
【 021 270370.
This bar in the heart of the city occupies a striking building that was once on the quayside. Founded in 1793, this elegant pub has a stylish Victorian interior and offers good quality bar fare.

**Cork:** *Chimes*
27 Church St. **Road map** C5.
【 021 304136.
Set in the hilly, old-world Shandon district, this convivial working-class pub attracts a mixed, friendly crowd, from local pensioners to sports fans and students. Simple bar food is sometimes offered, and on Thursday, Saturday and Sunday nights there's music, usually accordion or keyboard soloists. 🎵

**Cork:** *Henchy's*
40 St. Luke's Cross. **Road map** C5.
【 021 507833.
This traditional pub, located close to Chimes *(see above)*, dates from 1884 and has retained much of its Victorian ambience, enhanced by the mahogany bar, stained glass and a snug (a private room in this case, with a separate entrance). It has long been associated with poets and is where young hopefuls often recite their work. A varied bar menu is offered at lunchtime.

**Cork:** *The New Oyster*
Market Lane, off St. Patrick's St.
**Road map** C5. 【 021 272716.
Founded in the 18th century, this tavern was slightly refurbished by the new management in 1994. Bar and restaurant are now open-plan, with bar food served from 12:30–2pm, and more substantial dinners from 6–10pm, but the main attraction is still the oysters. 🍴

**Dingle:** *Dick Mack's*
Green St. **Road map** A5.
【 066 51960.
This individualistic spot is part shoe store, part pub, and retains the original shop and drinking counters. The pub is a hangout of local artists, eccentrics and extroverts. In the evening, regulars often congregate around the piano. 🎵

**Dingle:** *Doyle's Townhouse*
John St. **Road map** A5.
【 066 51174.
This charming bar and restaurant is celebrated for its delicious seafood (visible in a tank). The pub's rustic, yet cozy, stone interior is an appealing place for a fish or seafood lunch. 🍴

**Dunquin:** *Krugers*
**Road map** A5. 【 066 56127.
Situated close to the quays for the Blasket Islands, this well-known family pub is also a guest house. The pub is decorated with family memorabilia and stills from the films made in the neighborhood, such as *Ryan's Daughter*. 🎵

**Killarney:** *Buckley's Bar*
College St. **Road map** B5.
【 064 31037.
This oak-paneled bar is noted for its regular traditional music sessions and its filling meals. The pub was opened in 1926 when Tom Buckley, a homesick emigrant, returned from New York. Bar food is served until 9pm. 🍴 🎵

**Killarney:** *The Laurels*
Main St. **Road map** B5.
【 064 31149.
This claims to be Killarney's liveliest pub and is popular with the young locals as well as Irish-Americans who enjoy listening to the ballads and singing along. The pub provides excellent bar snacks or good meals (steak, mussels, oysters, fish) in a separate restaurant area. Ballads are performed nightly from 9:15pm between April and October, and more sporadically over the winter. 🍴 🎵

**Killorglin:** *The Old Forge*
**Road map** A5. 【 066 61231.
Set on the popular Ring of Kerry, this thatched pub is delightfully old-fashioned and authentic. Expect it to be packed during the Puck Fair in August *(see p47)*. 🎵

**Kinsale:** *Kieran's Folk House Inn*
Guardwell. **Road map** B6.
【 021 772382.
This convivial corner of old Kinsale draws locals and visitors alike, including anglers and divers. The interior is snug and

welcoming, with live music on Friday, Saturday and Sunday evenings. The inn also houses a pleasant guest house and a noted restaurant, the Bacchus Brasserie, open for lunch and dinner between April and October. 🍴 🎵

**Kinsale:** *The Lord Kingsale*
Main St. **Road map** B6.
【 021 772371.
This beamed, old-fashioned pub attracts a quiet, genteel crowd. Although the pub is several hundred years old, the interior is, in part, a clever fake. In summer, live music is usually performed on weekends. 🎵

**Kinsale:** *The 1601*
Pearse St. **Road map** B6.
【 021 772529.
The front bar is bedecked as a tribute to the Battle of Kinsale *(see p164)* while the back bar incorporates an ever-changing art gallery. The bar food (served at lunchtime and evenings) is tasty and eclectic, but the pub tends to get rather crowded. On Monday or Tuesday evenings you might find live modern or traditional music performed in the pub. 🍴 🎵

**Kinsale:** *The Spaniard Inn*
Scilly. **Road map** B6.
【 021 772436.
Set on a hairpin bend above the village of Scilly, this popular fishermen's pub has the air of a smugglers' inn. There is often live traditional music in one of the bars every night during the summer. Expect crowds around the log fire on weekends. Bar food is simple, but excellent. 🍴 🎵

## THE LOWER SHANNON

**Ballyvaughan:** *Monk's Pub*
The Pier. **Road map** B4.
【 065 77059.
This quaint, cozy pub is located on the quay. Inside, country furniture and peat fires are matched by home-cooked seafood and pies served until 6pm in the winter, 9pm in the summer. There's live music most evenings; call for details. 🍴 🍴 🎵

**Bunratty:** *Durty Nelly's*
**Road map** B4. 【 061 364072.
Set beside Bunratty Castle, this touristy, extremely commercialized pub appeals to locals as well as tourists. The 17th-century atmosphere is sustained by the warren of rooms, inglenook fireplaces and historical portraits. Traditional music is performed most evenings, and wholesome food is available both from the bar and from the two restaurants. 🍴 🍴 🎵

**Doolin:** *O'Connor's*
**Road map** B4. ( 065 74168.
This famous pub is known to lovers of traditional music all over the world. The pub has been in the O'Connor family for over 150 years and combines an authentic grocery store with a lively pub. This is the place for spontaneous music, simple bar food, young company and great "crack." 🍴 🎵

**Ennis:** *The Cloister*
Abbey St. **Road map** B4.
( 065 29521.
This historic pub is located by the famous Ennis Friary. The pub's cozy, atmospheric interior is complemented by a patio for summer dining. Bar food is available as well as more refined dishes in the restaurant, from Ballyvaughan mussels to fresh fish from Donegal. 🍴

**Ennistimon:** *The Archway Bar*
Main St. **Road map** B4.
( 065 71080.
This imposing old pub, situated on the main street, has several homey bars and a terrace overlooking the trout-rich river, waterfall and stone-arched bridge. On summer evenings, sessions of spontaneous traditional music often take place. The adjoining restaurant serves such filling dishes as stew, pasta and chicken. 🍴 🍴 🎵

**Killaloe:** *Goosers*
Ballina. **Road map** C4.
( 061 376791.
This delightfully picturesque waterfront pub on the Ballina side of the river has a thatched roof, traditional interior and a welcoming atmosphere. Noted for its cuisine, Goosers serves fairly pricey seafood in the restaurant and satisfying "pub grub" in the rustic bar. 🍴 🍴

**Limerick:** *The Locke*
3 George's Quay. **Road map** B4.
( 061 413733.
Set on a quay on the Shannon, this is a typical black-and-white pub. In summer, it is a favorite port of call for riverside strollers. In winter, blazing fires and snugs make it a cozy spot. There's live traditional music on Tuesday and Sunday nights, and bar snacks are served all day. 🍴 🎵

**Limerick:** *Nancy Blake's*
Upper Denmark St. **Road map** B4.
( 061 416443.
As Limerick's best-known bar, Nancy Blake's has much to offer in the way of good "crack" and traditional music. If you prefer rhythm and blues, try the adjoining Outback Bar. The cozy main bar serves soup and sandwiches at lunchtime. Music is played from Sunday to Wednesday. 🍴 🎵

## THE WEST OF IRELAND

**Aran Islands:** *Joe Watty's Pub*
Kilronan, Inishmore. **Road map** B4.
( 099 61155.
Set along the road between Kilronan and Kilmurvy Bay, this island pub is noted for its informality and huge, hearty portions of food. Cyclists and hikers appreciate the lamb stews, soups, sandwiches and stout. 🍴 🎵

**Clarinbridge:** *Moran's Oyster Cottage*
The Weir, Kilcolgan. **Road map** B4.
( 091 96113.
Set in a thatched cottage, this bar was a regular port of call for crews from passing "hookers" (traditional ships). Nowadays, you can sample all kinds of seafood here, though Moran's is best known as an oyster bar – the owner holds the local speed record for shelling oysters. You can watch fishers at work from the terrace tables. 🍴 🍴

**Clarinbridge:** *Paddy Burke's Oyster Inn*
**Road map** B4. ( 091 96226.
Founded in 1835, this authentic thatched pub has leaded windowpanes and a charming beamed interior. Apart from the renowned Clarinbridge oysters and buffet lunches, gourmet menus are also offered some evenings. 🍴

**Clifden:** *EJ Kings*
The Square. **Road map** A3.
( 095 21330.
This spacious, bustling pub is located on several floors, with the ground floor the most appealing. Seafood platters or varied pub fare can be enjoyed by the peat fire. In summer, live music is often offered, especially folk and ballads. The staff, mainly students, are exceptionally friendly. 🍴 🍴 🎵

**Galway:** *Cooke's Thatch Bar*
Cooke's Corner, 2 Newcastle Rd.
**Road map** B4. ( 091 21714.
Located on the outskirts of Galway, this traditional thatched inn has been in the same family for six generations and is renowned for its friendliness. Bar food is available, with over 20 wines for sale as well as beer and spirits. There is a beer garden and barbecue, and customers can use the piano if the spirit moves them. 🍴

**Galway:** *The King's Head*
15 High St. **Road map** B4.
( 091 63771.
Founded in 1649, this historic pub is adorned with a bow-fronted façade. The homey interior

contains authentic 17th-century fireplaces. Simple lunch snacks are served in the main bar. In the back bar, live theater at lunchtime, jazz on Sunday at lunchtime, and various live bands playing in the evenings attract a youthful crowd. 🍴 🎵

**Galway:** *O'Flaherty's*
Great Southern Hotel, 15 Eyre Sq.
**Road map** B4. ( 091 64041.
This solid cellar bar began as wine cellars but now offers cozy snugs and railroad memorabilia. The popular pub provides a contrast to the more sophisticated hotel cocktail bar on the floor above. A buffet lunch is offered daily in the bar, while on weekends live music sessions (from traditional music to jazz) draw large audiences of locals and visitors. 🍴 🎵

**Galway:** *The Quays*
11 Quay St. **Road map** B4.
( 091 68347.
This cavernous pub is the highlight of a Galway pub crawl. Set in an old stone mansion in Galway's "Latin Quarter," the sprawling pub is noted for its old-world charm, choice of bars and variety of live music. The quaint front bar retains its authenticity, while the rest of the pub has been sensitively converted, using old materials. The tasty and filling cooked pub meals are popular with locals. 🍴 🎵

**Galway:** *The Slate House*
Cross St Upper. **Road map** B4.
( 091 68820.
This barnlike city pub occupies several stories, including the shell of a 16th-century convent on the top floor. Regular live music sessions in the evenings ensure that it is popular with local students. Television and a pool table are available on the ground floor. 🎵

**Galway:** *Tí Neachtain*
Quay St. **Road map** B4.
( 091 68820.
Set in the "Latin Quarter," this 17th-century town house boasts a distinctive oriel window. Inside, a musty wood interior is home to old-world snugs and friendly service. Traditional music can often be heard. Upstairs is one of Galway's best restaurants, run by a Swiss chef. 🍴

**Maam Cross:** *Keogh's Tavern*
**Road map** B3. ( 091 82306.
Next to a replica of the traditional cottage used in the 1950s John Wayne film *The Quiet Man*, this modern pub is highly popular with locals. Standard pub food is available, as well as steaks barbecued over the turf fire. 🍴 🎵

**Westport:** *The Asgard Tavern*
The Quay. **Road map** B3.
[C] 098 25319.
This old inn facing the pier and
Clew Bay is decorated with a
nautical theme. Both the main
downstairs back bar and the upstairs restaurant provide excellent
seafood and salads. The small
downstairs front bar is the most
atmospheric. 🍴 📷 🎵

**Westport:** *Matt Molloy's*
Bridge St. **Road map** B3.
[C] 098 26655.
Founded by the flutist from the
traditional Irish folk band The
Chieftains, this deceptively
spacious pub is designed along
equally traditional lines. There is
live music in the back room most
evenings, when the pub is packed.
No children after 9pm. 🎵

## NORTHWEST IRELAND

**Crolly:** *Leo's Tavern*
Menaleck. **Road map** C1.
[C] 075 48143.
Owned by the father of modern
folk musicians Clannad and of the
singer Enya, this friendly pub
attracts locals and tourists for its
sing-alongs around the accordion,
and traditional music nights. 🎵

**Dromahair:** *Stanford's Inn*
Main St. **Road map** C2.
[C] 0716 4140.
Set in a picturesque village, this
traditional pub has been in the
same family for generations. The
tiny, quaint Biddy's Bar remains
unchanged, adorned with family
portraits and old grocery jars. The
main bar contains mellow brick-
work and flagstones from a ruined
castle, the rustic effect reinforced
by tweed lampshades. Delicious
food is offered all day, and in
summer there are often impromptu
evening music sessions. 📷 🎵

**Rossnowlagh:** *Smugglers'
Creek Inn*
**Road map** C2. [C] 072 52366.
On a clifftop overlooking Donegal
Bay, this pub is popular with surfers
and other water-sports enthusiasts.
There is traditional music on
weekends, and the beer garden
offers panoramic views. 🍴 📷 🎵

**Sligo:** *Beezie's*
45 O'Connell St. **Road map** C2.
[C] 071 45030.
The pub is dedicated to Beezie
Gallagher, a hospitable and much-
loved Sligo character who regularly
rowed from her home on Cottage
Island to Sligo until her death in
1951. A Victorian mood is re-created
by the old-fashioned stained glass,
skylights and fireplaces.

**Sligo:** *Hargadon's*
4–5 O'Connell St. **Road map** C2.
[C] 071 70933.
A scruffy, rather ramshackle
exterior reveals the most traditional pub in town. The timeless
atmosphere is enhanced by the
old-fashioned stove, uneven floors
and wooden grocery drawers.
The pub is lined with cozy snugs,
all individually designed. During
the summer, dinner is served in
the beer garden. 🍴 📷

## THE MIDLANDS

**Abbeyleix:** *Morrissey's*
Main St. **Road map** C4.
[C] 0502 31233.
If driving through County Laois, it
is worth stopping at this genuinely
traditional pub. The 18th-century
inn was remodeled in the Victorian
era and has stayed the same ever
since. The grocery section survives
while the plain but unpretentious
bar serves simple bar snacks.

**Carlingford:** *PJ O'Hare's
Anchor Bar*
Tholsel St. **Road map** D3.
[C] 042 73106.
Known locally as PJ's, this atmospheric pub and grocery store is
popular with sailors and locals
alike. A friendly and often eccentric
welcome is matched by bar food
such as oysters and sandwiches. 📷

**Kilbeggan:** *Locke's Distillery
Museum*
Mullingar. **Road map** C3.
[C] 0506 32307.
As well as being the oldest licensed
pot still distillery in the world
(established in 1757), this historic
complex has a tiny whiskey bar –
the ideal place to sample a few
brands of whiskey before buying
(see p241). The adjoining restaurant
is closed in the evening. 🍴

**Portlaoise:** *Tracey's Pub and
Restaurant*
The Heath, Dublin Rd. **Road map** C4.
[C] 0502 46539.
This charming thatched cottage
pub and restaurant is 5 km (3 miles)
outside of the town, but is well
worth the drive. It is the oldest
family-run pub in these parts, and
there is a good range of pub grub
(roasts, fish, salads) as well as
prime steak at amazingly
reasonable prices. 🍴 📷

## NORTHERN IRELAND

**Bangor:** *Jenny Watt's*
41 High St. **Road map** E2.
[C] 01247 460682.
Likeable and very popular, this bar
with Victoriana trimmings is found
in the center of town. The walls

are adorned with local photos and
memorabilia. There's live jazz at
Sunday at lunchtime, and folk
music on Tuesday nights. Bar
food is served until 9:30pm, and
there's a beer garden. 📷 🎵

**Belfast:** *Crown Liquor Saloon*
46 Great Victoria St. **Road map** D2.
[C] 01232 325368.
This Victorian gin palace ranks as
one of the most gorgeous bars in
Ireland (see p269). Lunch includes
several local specialties including
Strangford Lough oysters, which
are almost too good to believe.
The recently renovated Robinson's
pub next door is particularly lively
in the evening. 🍴

**Belfast:** *Lavery's Gin Palace*
12–14 Bradbury Place. **Road map** D2.
[C] 01232 328205.
Yet another of Belfast's fine old
gin palaces. This one regularly
has discos in the evenings and is
particularly popular with students
from Queen's University.

**Belfast:** *White's Tavern*
Winecellar Entry. **Road map** D2.
[C] 01232 243080.
Just one of several daylight-free
pubs tucked away in the Entries
(see p269) sector of Belfast city
center, that are best at lunchtime
when decent, reasonably priced
pub food is served. White's claim
to be the oldest bar in the city.
Other pubs in this series of alleys
that are worth a look include the
Morning Star and the Globe. 🎵

**Bushmills:** *Bushmills Inn*
25 Main St. **Road map** D1.
[C] 01265 732339.
Set in an old coaching inn, this
cozy bar is lit by gaslights. There
is also an excellent restaurant on
the premises, with patio tables for
summer dining. 🍴 📷

**Enniskillen:** *Blake's of the
Hollow*
6 Church St. **Road map** C2.
[C] 01365 322143.
One of a number of popular town-
center pubs, Blake's dates back to
Victorian days and has many of its
original fittings to prove it.

**Hillsborough:** *Plough Inn*
The Square. **Road map** D2.
[C] 01846 682985.
Dating back to the 1750s, this
quintessential village pub has
wooden ceiling beams and a
selection of crockery, china and
other ornaments on the walls.
There's a bistro upstairs open
during the day, serving oysters,
and a good beer garden. The
Hillside, just down the main street,
is also worth a visit. 🍴 📷

# SHOPPING IN IRELAND

IRELAND OFFERS a wide range of handmade goods, usually regionally based and highly individual. Its most renowned products include chunky Aran sweaters, Waterford crystal, demure Irish linen, hand-loomed Donegal tweed and tasty farmhouse cheeses. The thriving crafts industry is based on traditional products with an innovative twist. Typical of contemporary Irish crafts are good design, quality craftsmanship and a range spanning

**Linen shirt and tweed waistcoat**

Celtic brooches and bone china, knitwear and designer fashion, carved bogwood and books of Irish poetry. Kitsch souvenirs also abound, from leprechauns and shamrock emblems to Guinness tankards and garish religious memorabilia. In the directory on page 325, a map reference is given for each address. Dublin references are to the map on pages 110–11; road map references are to the towns and cities shown on the inside back cover.

**Fruit and vegetable market in Moore Street, Dublin**

## WHERE TO SHOP

THE CHOICE of places to shop in Ireland ranges from tiny workshops to large factory outlets, from elegant boutiques to chain stores. Bargains can often be had at bric-a-brac shops and local markets, although the banter is sometimes the best thing available. This guide lists market days for every town featured. For last-minute purchases of traditional Irish goods and foods, try the airport duty-free shops.

## SHOPPING IN DUBLIN

IN DUBLIN there are two major shopping quarters: the more plebeian north side of the Liffey, centered on O'Connell and Henry Streets, and the more prestigious south side, around Grafton and Nassau Streets. The Temple Bar area contains a number of trendy craft shops. The two main markets are Mother Redcap's indoor flea market in Christchurch on weekends, and the

fruit and vegetable market on Moore Street from Monday to Saturday. Dublin's largest shopping center is **St. Stephen's Green Shopping Centre,** full of clothes and craft shops. Near chic Grafton Street is the Powerscourt Townhouse Shopping Centre (see p76), encased by a Georgian shell. Traditional department stores in the city include **Brown Thomas** and **Clery's**.

## WHEN TO SHOP

MOST STORES are open from Monday to Saturday, 9am to 5:30 or 6pm. In shopping centers and large towns, stores tend to have at least one late-night opening, usually Thursday or Friday (Thursday in Dublin). In tourist areas, craft shops are generally open on Sundays too. Stores are closed on Easter and Christmas and on St. Patrick's Day but are open on most other public holidays. In Killarney, Ireland's tourist capital, most stores are open until 10pm in summer.

## HOW TO PAY

MAJOR CREDIT CARDS are generally accepted in department stores and larger retail outlets, but smaller stores prefer cash. Most traveler's checks are accepted in major stores with a passport as identification. Eurocheques are slightly less acceptable in stores but can be cashed at certain banks (see p347).

## SALES TAX AND REFUNDS

MOST PURCHASES are subject to VAT (sales tax) at 21 percent, a sum included in the sales price. However, visitors from outside the European Union (EU) can reclaim VAT prior to departure. If you are shipping goods overseas, refunds can be claimed at the point of purchase. If taking your goods with you, look for the CashBack logo in shops, fill in the special voucher, then visit CashBack offices at Dublin or Shannon Airport.

**A traditional fiddlemaker in his workshop in Dingle**

**Colorful bric-a-brac shop in Kilkenny**

## BOOKS

READING is a national passion so bookshops are generally good. In larger shops expect solid sections on Irish archaeology and architecture, folklore, history, politics and cuisine. **Eason and Son** is one of the biggest bookshops in Dublin with a wide range of Irish literature and national and international newspapers; seek out the smaller "Irish interest" shops too. In Galway, **Kennys Bookshop and Art Gallery** is full of both new and second-hand Irish books.

## MUSIC

TRADITIONAL MUSICAL instruments (see pp22–3) are made in many regions, especially County Clare, known as "the singing county." Handmade harps are a specialty in Mayo and Dublin. In Dublin, several shops sell musical instruments, such as handcrafted bodhráns (traditional goatskin handheld drums) and uillean pipes (bagpipes). **Waltons** sells traditional instruments and sheet music, while **Claddagh Records** sells Irish folk and traditional music.

## CRAFTS

CRAFTS are a flourishing way of life in rural Ireland. The **Crafts Council of Ireland**, with branches in Dublin and Kilkenny, recommends good small-scale outlets, and tourist offices provide lists of local

workshops, where you can often watch the production process. Many craft shops, such as the **Kilkenny Design Centre** and **Bricín**, and especially those at large tourist sights, sell good examples of several different crafts. Some regions are traditionally associated with specific crafts. In Cork and Kerry there is an abundance of workshops; the *Guide to Craft Outlets* is available from local tourist offices. Distinctive products from this area are traditional tiles based on designs found in Kilkenny Cathedral and nearby medieval abbeys. Further west, Connemara marble, green mottled stone, is made into "worry stones," small charms like worry beads. Also made in Connemara, particularly Clifden, are wall hangings, handknits and woollen rugs.

**Kylemore Abbey teapot**

Other crafts in Ireland include metalwork, leatherwork and carpentry. Local woods are used for ash or beech furniture, blackthorn walking sticks and sculptures made of 1,000-year-old bogwood.

## CERAMICS AND CHINA

ESTABLISHED in 19th-century Ulster, the Belleek Pottery (see p261) produces creamy china with a lustrous sheen and subtle decorative motifs, including shamrocks and flowers. **Royal Tara China**, in Galway, is Ireland's leading fine bone china manufacturer, with designs incorporating Celtic themes. Also in County Galway, Kylemore Abbey produces handpainted pottery (see p200). **Louis Mulcahy's Pottery** in Ballyferriter is noted for its fine decorative glazes, while **Nicholas Mosse Pottery** in Bennettsbridge, County Kilkenny, is well known for its colorful handpainted designs. Enniscorthy in County Wexford is another center for ceramics.

## CRYSTAL AND GLASSWARE

IN THE WAKE of Waterford Crystal (see p139), the brand leader, come countless followers. The price depends on reputation, the quantity of lead used in the glass and the labor-intensiveness of the design. In the North, **Tyrone Crystal** is rated almost as highly as Waterford but is less expensive. Like Waterford, the factory runs an illuminating tour. **Tipperary Crystal** offers a number of lines, including trophies, lamps and gifts. **Galway Irish Crystal** is another elegant brand.

In County Kilkenny, the famous Jerpoint Abbey inspires local designs by **Jerpoint Glass**. Decorated with simple yet stylish motifs, the small vases, candlesticks, jugs and bowls make pleasing gifts. Most stores will pack and send glassware overseas for you.

**Pottery display in Kilkenny Design Centre**

**Sign for the linen department at Dublin's Brown Thomas store**

## JEWELRY

**I**N ITS GOLDEN AGE, Celtic metalwork was the pride of Ireland (see pp30–33). Many contemporary craftspeople are still inspired by traditional designs on Celtic chalices and ornaments. Handcrafted or factory-made silver, gold, enamel and ceramic jewelry is produced all over Ireland in a huge variety of designs. The Claddagh ring from Galway is the most famous – the lovers' symbol of two hands cradling a crowned heart. In Dublin's Powerscourt Townhouse Shopping Centre (see p76), stores display handmade and antique jewelry. Ceramic Design, a studio that produces Celtic-influenced brooches, is based here. Gold- and silversmiths can also be seen at work in the shopping center.

## KNITWEAR AND TWEED

**A**RAN SWEATERS are sold all over Ireland, but particularly in County Galway and on the Aran Islands themselves. One of Ireland's best

buys, these oiled, off-white sweaters used to be handed down through generations of Aran fishermen. Legend has it that each family used its own motifs so that if a fisherman was lost at sea and his body unidentifiable, his family could recognize him by his sweater.

Given the Irish experience of wet weather, warm and waterproof clothes are generally of good quality, from waxed jackets and duffel coats to sheepskin jackets. Knitwear is on sale all over Ireland, with **Avoca Handweavers** and **Blarney Woollen Mills** the best-known outlets. Good buys include embroidered sweaters and waistcoats and hand-woven shawls and scarves.

Donegal tweed is a byword for quality, noted for its texture, tension and subtle colors (originally produced by dyes made from lichens, local plants and minerals). Tweed caps, hats, scarves, ties, jackets and suits are sold in outlets such as **Magee and Co** in Donegal.

**Secondhand furniture shop in Kenmare**

## LINEN

**D**AMASK LINEN was brought to Armagh by Huguenot refugees fleeing French persecution. As a result, Belfast became the world linen capital. Ulster is still the place for linen, with sheets and double-damask table linen on sale in Belfast – at **Smyth's Irish**

**Linen**, for example – and in other towns. There are also outlets in the Republic. Hand-embroidered linen is made in County Donegal. Linenmaking can be seen at Wellbrook Beetling Mill (see p260).

## FASHION

**I**NSPIRED by a predominantly young population, Ireland is fast acquiring a name for fashion. Conservatively cut tweed and linen suits continue to be models of classic good taste, while younger designers are increasingly experimental, using bold lines and mixing traditional fabrics.

**A-Wear** is an upscale boutique with branches in major cities. Here, and in the Design Centre in Powerscourt Townhouse Shopping Centre in Dublin, are clothes by the best Irish designers including John Rocha, Paul Costelloe, Louise Kennedy and Mariad Whisker. Sizes run smaller than American ones, so the best guide is to try things on.

## FOOD AND DRINK

**S**MOKED SALMON, home-cured bacon, farmhouse cheeses, soda bread, preserves and handmade chocolates make perfect last-minute gifts. Several shops will package and send Irish salmon overseas.

Bewley's teas and coffees are sold in **Bewley's Oriental Café** and Bewley shops all over Ireland. Guinness travels less well and is best drunk in Ireland. Irish whiskey is hard to beat as a gift or souvenir. Apart from the cheaper Power and Paddy brands, the big names are Bushmills (see p258) and Jameson (see p171). Rich Irish liqueurs include Irish Mist and Baileys Irish Cream.

**Selection of handknitted sweaters at a craft shop in Dingle**

## DIRECTORY

### DEPARTMENT STORES AND SHOPPING CENTERS

**Brown Thomas**
88–92 Grafton St, Dublin 2.
**Dublin map** D4.
📞 01 6795666.

**Clery's**
18–27 O'Connell St
Lower, Dublin 1.
**Dublin map** D2.
📞 01 8786000.

**St. Stephen's Green Shopping Centre**
St. Stephen's Green West,
Dublin 2. **Dublin map** D4.

### BOOKS

**Eason and Son**
80 Abbey St Middle,
Dublin 1. **Dublin map** D2.
📞 01 8733811.

**Fred Hanna**
27–29 Nassau St, Dublin 2.
**Dublin map** E4.
📞 01 6771255.

**Kennys Bookshop and Art Gallery**
High St, Galway.
**Road map** B4.
📞 091 62739.

**Waterstone's**
7 Dawson St, Dublin 2.
**Dublin map** D4.
📞 01 6791415.

### MUSIC

**Claddagh Records**
2 Cecilia St, Temple Bar,
Dublin 2. **Dublin map** C3.
📞 01 6770262.

**J McNeill**
140 Capel St, Dublin 1.
**Dublin map** C2.
📞 01 8722159.

**Waltons**
2–5 Frederick St North,
Dublin 1.
📞 01 8747805.

### CRAFTS

**Bricín**
26 High Street, Killarney,
Co Kerry. **Road map** B5.
📞 064 34902.

**Connemara Marble Factory**
Moycullen, Co Galway.
**Road map** B4.
📞 091 85102.

**Crafts Council of Ireland**
Powerscourt Townhouse
Shopping Centre, William
St South, Dublin 2.
**Dublin map** D4.
📞 01 6797368.
Crescent Workshop,
Castleyard, Kilkenny.
**Road map** C4.
📞 056 61804.

**Craftsworks Gallery**
13 Linenhall St, Belfast.
**Road map** D2.
📞 01232 236334.

**Doolin Crafts Gallery**
Ballyvoe, Doolin, Co Clare.
**Road map** B4.
📞 065 74309.

**Kilkenny Design Centre**
Castle Yard, Kilkenny.
**Road map** C4.
📞 056 22118.

**The Kilkenny Shop**
6 Nassau St, Dublin 2.
**Dublin map** E4.
📞 01 6777066.

**Standuin**
Spiddal, Co Galway.
**Road map** B4.
📞 091 83357.

**Tower Enterprise Centre**
Pearse St, Dublin 2.
📞 01 6775655.

### CERAMICS AND CHINA

**Cré Irish Porcelain**
Wellpark, Galway.
**Road map** B4.
📞 091 52788.

**Hogg's**
10 Donegal Sq West,
Belfast. **Road map** D2.
📞 01232 243898.

**Louis Mulcahy's Pottery**
Clogher Strand, Ballyferriter,
Tralee, Co Kerry.
**Road map** A5.
📞 066 56229.

**Nicholas Mosse Pottery**
Bennettsbridge, Co
Kilkenny. **Road map** D5.
📞 056 27126.

**Royal Tara China**
Tara Hall, Mervue, Galway.
**Road map** B4.
📞 091 751301.

**Treasure Chest**
William St, Galway.
**Road map** B4.
📞 091 67237.

### CRYSTAL AND GLASSWARE

**Galway Irish Crystal**
Merlin Park, Galway.
**Road map** B4.
📞 091 757311.

**Jerpoint Glass**
Stoneyford, Co Kilkenny.
**Road map** D5.
📞 056 24350.

**Sligo Crystal**
Grange, Co Sligo.
**Road map** C2.
📞 071 63251.

**Tipperary Crystal**
Ballynoran, Carrick-on-
Suir, Co Tipperary.
**Road map** C5.
📞 051 641188.

**Tyrone Crystal**
Killybrackey, Coal Island Rd,
Dungannon, Co Tyrone.
**Road map** D2.
📞 01868 725335.

**Waterford Crystal**
Kilbarry, Waterford.
**Road map** D5.
📞 051 73311.

### JEWELRY

**Brian de Staic**
18 High St, Killarney,
Co Kerry. **Road map** B5.
📞 064 33822.

**Hilser Brothers**
Grand Parade, Cork.
**Road map** C5.
📞 021 270382.

**Saller's Jewellers**
Williamsgate St, Galway.
**Road map** B4.
📞 091 61226.

### KNITWEAR AND TWEED

**Avoca Hand-weavers**
Kilmacanogue, Bray, Co
Wicklow. **Road map** D4.
📞 01 2867466.

**Blarney Woollen Mills**
Blarney, Co Cork.
**Road map** B5.
📞 021 385280.

**Exclusively Irish**
14–15 O'Connell St Upper,
Dublin 1. **Dublin map** D2.
📞 01 8746064.

**Magee and Co**
The Diamond, Donegal.
**Road map** C2.
📞 073 21100.

**Quills Woollen Market**
1 High St, Killarney, Co
Kerry. **Road map** B5.
📞 064 32277.

**Studio Donegal**
Kilcar, Co Donegal.
**Road map** B2.
📞 073 38194.

### LINEN

**Forgotten Cotton**
Savoy Centre, 117–119 St
Patrick's St, Cork.
**Road map** C5.
📞 021 276098.

**Smyth's Irish Linen**
65 Royal Ave, Belfast.
**Road map** D2.
📞 01232 242232.

### FASHION

**A-Wear**
26 Grafton St, Dublin 2.
**Dublin map** D4.
📞 01 6717200.

### FOOD AND DRINK

**Bewley's Oriental Café**
78 Grafton St, Dublin 2.
**Dublin map** D4.
📞 01 6776761.

**Butler's Irish Hand-made Chocolates**
51 Grafton St, Dublin 2.
**Dublin map** D4.
📞 01 6710599.

# What to Buy in Ireland

**St Brigid's cross**

Hundreds of gift and craft shops scattered throughout Ireland make it easy to find Irish specialties to suit all budgets. The best buys include linen, tweeds and crystal from factory shops which invariably offer an extensive choice of good quality products. Local crafts make unique souvenirs, from handmade jewelry and ceramics to traditional musical instruments. Religious artifacts are also widely available. Irish food and drink are evocative reminders of your trip.

**Traditional hand-held drum (bodhrán) and beater**

**Connemara marble "worry stone"**

**Traditional Claddagh ring**

**Enamel brooch**

**Bronzed resin Celtic figurine**

*Modern jewelry and metalwork* draw on a long and varied tradition. Craftspeople continue to base their designs on sources such as the Book of Kells (see p62) and Celtic myths. Local plants and wildlife are also an inspiration. County Galway produces Claddagh rings – traditional betrothal rings – in gold and silver, as well as "worry stones."

**Fuchsia earring from Dingle**

**Celtic-design enamel brooch**

**Donegal tweed jacket and waistcoat**

**Tweed skirt and jacket**

*Clothing* made in Ireland is usually of excellent quality. Tweed-making still flourishes in Donegal where tweed can be bought ready-made as clothing or hats or as lengths of cloth. Knitwear is widely available all over the country in large factory outlets and local craft shops. The many hand-knitted items on sale, including Aran sweaters, are expensive but should give years of wear.

**Tweed cap**

**Tweed fisherman's hat**

**Aran sweater**

*Irish linen* is world-famous and the range unparalleled. There is a huge choice of table and bed linen, including extravagant bedspreads and crisp, formal tablecloths. On a smaller scale, tiny, intricately embroidered hand-kerchiefs make lovely gifts as do linen table napkins. Tea towels printed with colorful designs are widely available. You can also buy linen goods trimmed with fine lace, which is still handmade in Ireland, mainly in Limerick and Kenmare.

**Set of linen placemats and napkins**

**Nicholas Mosse plate**

**Belleek teapot**

**Nicholas Mosse cup**

**Fine linen handkerchiefs**

*Irish ceramics* come in traditional and modern designs. You can buy anything from a full dinner service by established factories, such as Royal Tara China or the Belleek Pottery, to a one-of-a-kind contemporary piece from local potters.

**Book of Irish Proverbs**

*Irish crystal*, hand-blown and hand-cut, can be ordered or bought in many shops in Ireland. Visit the outlets of the principal manu-facturers, such as Waterford Crystal, Tyrone Crystal and Jerpoint Glass, to see the full range – from glasses and decanters to elaborate chandeliers.

*Books and stationery* are often beautifully illustrated. Museums and bookstores stock a wide range.

**Celtic-design cards**

**Waterford crystal tumbler and decanter**

*Food and drink* will keep the distinctive tastes of Ireland fresh long after you arrive home. Whiskey connoisseurs should visit the Old Bushmills Distillery (see p258) or the Jameson Heritage Centre (see p171) to sample their choice of whiskeys. Good regional food can be found at local shops all over Ireland. Try the dried seaweed, which is eaten raw or added to cooked dishes.

**Jameson whiskey**

**Bushmills whiskey**

**Fruit cake made with Guinness**

**Jar of Irish marmalade**

**Packet of dried seaweed**

# ENTERTAINMENT IN IRELAND

I F THERE IS ONE SPHERE in which Ireland shines, it is entertainment. For details about entertainment in Dublin, see pages 102–7. Elsewhere in Ireland, nightclubs and concerts by international entertainers tend to be concentrated in large cities, but many other events including theater, arts festivals, traditional music and dance, cultural holidays and even medieval banquets take place all over the country. Most towns and cities also have one or two theaters showing the most recent movies. Not to be overlooked is

Morris Minor van advertising the Clonakilty Folk Club

the free entertainment (planned or spontaneous) provided by a night in a pub. For more active forms of entertainment, covered on pages 332–5, the list is even longer, from golf to pony trekking and cycling to scuba diving. Those who prefer their sports sitting down can go along as spectators to Ireland's famous horse race meetings, as well as Gaelic football, hurling, soccer and rugby matches. Best of all, a happy mix of these activities can easily be put together with almost any itinerary.

Ulster Symphony Orchestra at the Ulster Hall in Belfast

## INFORMATION SOURCES

THE TOURIST BOARD for the Republic, **Bord Fáilte**, and the **Northern Ireland Tourist Board** both publish a yearly *Calendar of Events* that lists major events around the country, and all the regional tourist offices have information about happenings in each locality. To supplement these listings, check regional newspapers and inquire locally to find on-the-spot entertainment.

## BOOKING TICKETS

TICKETS can usually be bought at the door on the day or evening of most events. Advance booking is a must, however, for popular concerts and plays. Many cultural and arts festivals require tickets only for the key performances, but for internationally famous festivals, such as the Wexford Opera Festival, you will need to book well in advance through the festival office for all performances.

Credit-card bookings for major plays, concerts and other events around the country can be made by telephone through **Keith Prowse Travel (IRL) Ltd** and **HMV** in Dublin.

## MAJOR VENUES

I N MANY IRISH CITIES, the main theaters host a huge variety of events. In Cork, the **Opera House** presents predominantly Irish plays during the summer months, with musical comedy, opera and ballet at other times of year. The city's **Everyman Palace Theatre** stages plays by local and visiting companies interspersed with concerts of both classical and popular music. Sligo's **Hawks Well Theatre** and Limerick's **Belltable Arts Centre** are the spots for drama and concerts. In the center of Belfast, the **Grand Opera House**, **Arts Theatre** and **Lyric Theatre** present a varied program that includes Irish and international plays, experimental drama, pantomime and opera.

## THEATER

F ROM INTERNATIONAL TOURS to amateur productions, there is excellent theater to be seen in virtually every location in Ireland. In Galway, the **Druid Theatre** specializes in avant-garde plays, new Irish plays and Anglo-Irish classics, with frequent lunchtime and late-night performances, while Gaelic drama, Irish music, singing and dancing have all thrived at the **Taibhdhearc Theatre** since 1928. Waterford boasts its resident Red Kettle Theatre Company which performs at the **Garter Lane Theatre**, while the **Theatre Royal** brings amateur drama and musicals to the city.

Keep an eye out for small theater groups performing in local halls around the country. Many of them are superb and they have spawned several of Ireland's leading actors.

Home of the Druid Theatre Company in Galway (see p202)

**The Moscow Ballet at Belfast's Grand Opera House** *(see p268)*

## CLASSICAL MUSIC, OPERA AND DANCE

**M**AJOR VENUES for classical music include the **Crawford Art Gallery**, Opera House and Everyman Palace in Cork; the Theatre Royal in Waterford; the Hawks Well Theatre in Sligo; and the Belltable Arts Centre in Limerick. Belfast's **Ulster Hall** hosts concerts from rock bands to the Ulster Symphony Orchestra.

Opera lovers from around the world arrive in great numbers for the **Wexford Opera Festival** in October and November and the **Waterford Festival of Light Opera** in late September and early October. At Wexford, neglected operas are revived, while Waterford selects more mainstream operas and musicals. Elsewhere, opera is performed in Cork's Opera House and in Belfast's Grand Opera House.

Ireland has no resident ballet or avant-garde dance companies, but leading international companies perform occasionally at the major venues around the country.

## ROCK, JAZZ AND COUNTRY

**W**HEN INTERNATIONAL rock and pop stars such as Prince tour in Ireland, concerts outside Dublin are held at large outdoor sites. **Semple Stadium** in County Tipperary and Slane Castle *(see p237)* in County Meath are popular places. Tickets and information are available from HMV.

Musical pubs *(see pp318–21)* are your best bet for good rock and jazz performed by Irish groups. Check local tourist offices and newspapers for rock and jazz nights, which usually take place midweek, with country and traditional music on weekends. For some of Ireland's "big band" jazz music, keep an eye out for Waterford's Brass and Co. who play at dances around the country. Jazz lovers have a field day at the **Cork Jazz Festival** in late October, when music pours from every pub and international jazz greats play in the city's theaters.

**Pub scene at Feakle Traditional Music Weekend, County Clare**

## TRADITIONAL MUSIC AND DANCE

**T**HE COUNTRY PUB has helped keep Irish music alive and provided the setting for the musical revival that began in the 1960s. Today, sessions of informal or impromptu music are still commonplace. In pubs, traditional music embraces ballads and rebel songs, as well as the older *sean-nos* – unaccompanied, understated stories, often sung in Irish.

Nights of Irish music and song are scheduled in many pubs, such as The Laurels and the Danny Mann in Killarney, the Yeats Tavern in Drumcliff, near Sligo, and An Phoenix and The Lobby in Cork. In Derry, the Gweedore Bar, Castle Bar and Dungloe Bar are among the cluster of musical pubs along Waterloo Street. Wherever you are, ask the locals and they will send you off to the nearest musical pub. For more pub listings, see pages 318–21.

In Tralee, **Siamsa Tire**, the National Folk Theatre, stages marvelous folk drama incorporating traditional music, singing and dance. The Barn, in Bunratty Folk Park, is the setting for the **Shannon Ceili** – traditional music nights during the summer months.

**Comhaltas Ceoltóirí Éireann**, in Monkstown near Dublin, has branches around the country and organizes traditional music and dance nights all year. Traditional Irish dancing can be stylish step dancing or joyous set dancing. Visitors are usually encouraged to join in the fun.

The **Fleadh Cheoil** (national traditional music festival) is a weekend of music, dance, song and stage shows that spill over into colorful street entertainment. It takes place at the end of August in a different town each year. Earlier in August, the **Feakle Traditional Music Weekend** in County Clare is a more intimate celebration of traditional music, song and dance.

**A large audience for open-air music at the Cork Jazz Festival**

**Knappogue banquet at Knappogue Castle, County Clare**

## FESTIVALS

THE IRISH are experts at organizing festivals, staging a week of street entertainment, theater, music and dance to celebrate almost everything under the sun *(see pp46–9)*.

In mid-July the lively town of Galway is host to the **Galway Arts Festival**, one of the largest festivals in Ireland. Here you will find Irish and international theater and music, street entertainment and events for children. Taking place over two weeks in late July and early August is the **Boyle Arts Festival**. The events here include art exhibitions, poetry and drama performances as well as classical, traditional, folk and jazz concerts. Creative workshops are run for both adults and children.

**Kilkenny Arts Week** in August, another major festival, features poetry, classical music concerts, movies and a range of crafts. The **Cork Film Festival** takes place in the first week of October when international feature, documentary and short movies are screened at venues all over the city. The **Belfast Festival at Queen's** is held for three weeks in mid- to late November. The lively and cosmopolitan program includes a mixture of drama, ballet, comedy, cabaret, music and film. These take over the Queen's University campus plus theaters and other venues throughout Belfast.

In May and June, the **County Wicklow Gardens Festival** entices gardening enthusiasts to the county's

most beautiful gardens. In mid-June, the **Music Festival in Great Irish Houses** opens the doors to many of Ireland's historic homes to which the public seldom has access, with classical music performed by top-rate musicians. Venues include Strokestown Park House *(see pp210–11)*, Mount Stewart House *(see pp274–5)* and University College, Cork.

**Kilkenny Arts Week street theater**

## TRADITIONAL BANQUETS WITH ENTERTAINMENT

IRELAND'S BANQUETS have gained international fame and are great fun. Each of the banquets features costumed waiters and performers, as well as traditional food and drink of the chosen period.

Most famous are the medieval banquets – the one at Bunratty Castle *(see pp184–5)* was the first and is the liveliest, with year-round performances. From May to October, there is a glittering pageant at Knappogue Castle *(see p181)*, and at Dunguaire Castle *(see p204)* there is a quieter, more intimate program of music and poetry. From March until November, the highly enjoyable Killarney Manor Banquet, held at the stately manor on the Loreto road just south of Killarney, creates an early 19th-century atmosphere.

## CULTURAL VACATIONS

A VACATION IN IRELAND focused on any one of the cultural aspects of Irish life is enriching as well as fun. Choose from a variety of cultural topics and study courses: Irish music and literature, great houses and gardens, Irish language and folklore, crafts and cooking.

One of the most fascinating possibilities is the exploration of Ireland's 5,000-year history as revealed in the many relics strewn across the landscape. The **Achill Archaeological Summer School** in County Mayo, for example, runs a course that includes the active excavation of ancient sites.

To learn the secret of Irish cooking, there is no better place than the **Ballymaloe School of Cookery** in County Cork; it is run by Darina Allen, Ireland's most famous cook.

For literature enthusiasts, the **Yeats International Summer School** studies the works of Yeats and his contemporaries, while **Listowel Writers' Week** brings together leading writers for lectures and workshops.

**Folk dancers in traditional Irish costume**

## DIRECTORY

### INFORMATION SOURCES

**Bord Fáilte**
Baggot St Bridge,
Dublin 2.
☎ 01 6765871.

**Northern Ireland Tourist Board**
St Anne's Court, 59 North St, Belfast.
☎ 01232 231221.

### BOOKING TICKETS

**HMV**
65 Grafton St, Dublin 2.
☎ 01 6797817.

**Keith Prowse Travel (IRL) Ltd**
10 St Stephen's Green, Dublin 2.
☎ 01 6795444.

### MAJOR VENUES

**Arts Theatre**
Botanic Ave, Belfast.
☎ 01232 324936.

**Belltable Arts Centre**
69 O'Connell St, Limerick.
☎ 061 319866.

**Everyman Palace Theatre**
MacCurtain St, Cork.
☎ 021 501673.

**Grand Opera House**
Great Victoria St, Belfast.
☎ 01232 240411.

**Hawks Well Theatre**
Temple St, Sligo.
☎ 071 61526.

**Lyric Theatre**
55 Ridgeway St, Belfast.
☎ 01232 381081.

**Opera House**
Emmet Place, Cork.
☎ 021 270022.

### THEATER

**Druid Theatre**
Chapel Lane, Galway.
☎ 091 68617.

**Garter Lane Theatre**
22A O'Connell St, Waterford.
☎ 051 77153.

**Taibhdhearc Theatre**
Middle St, Galway.
☎ 091 62024.

**Theatre Royal**
The Mall, Waterford.
☎ 051 74402.

### CLASSICAL MUSIC, OPERA AND DANCE

**Crawford Art Gallery**
Emmet Place, Cork.
☎ 021 273377.

**Ulster Hall**
Bedford St, Belfast.
☎ 01232 323900.

**Waterford Festival of Light Opera**
60 Morrissons Ave, Waterford.
☎ 051 75437.

**Wexford Opera Festival**
Theatre Royal, High St, Wexford.
☎ 053 22144.

### ROCK, JAZZ AND COUNTRY

**Cork Jazz Festival**
Guinness House,
St Patrick's St, Cork.
☎ 021 270463.

**Semple Stadium**
Thurles, Co Tipperary.

### TRADITIONAL MUSIC AND DANCE

**Comhaltas Ceoltóirí Éireann**
32 Belgrave Sq,
Monkstown, Co Dublin.
☎ 01 2800295.

**Feakle Traditional Music Weekend**
Maghera, Caher, Co Clare.
☎ 061 925125.

**Fleadh Cheoil**
32 Belgrave Sq,
Monkstown, Co Dublin.
☎ 01 2800295.

**Shannon Ceili**
Bunratty Castle and Folk Park, Bunratty, Co Clare.
☎ 061 360788.

**Siamsa Tire**
National Folk Theatre,
Tralee, Co Kerry.
☎ 066 23055.

### FESTIVALS

**Belfast Festival at Queen's**
Festival House, 25 College Gardens, Belfast.
☎ 01232 667687.

**Boyle Arts Festival**
Festival Office, Boyle,
Co Roscommon.
☎ 079 63085.

**Cork Film Festival**
Hatfield House, Tobin St, Cork.
☎ 021 271711.

**County Wicklow Gardens Festival**
St Manntan's House,
Kilmantin Hill, Wicklow.
☎ 0404 66058.

**Galway Arts Festival**
6 Upper Dominic St, Galway.
☎ 091 583800.

**Kilkenny Arts Week**
Rose House, Parliament St, Kilkenny.
☎ 056 63663.

**Music Festival in Great Irish Houses**
31 Beechwood Lawn,
Dun Laoghaire,
Co Dublin.
☎ 01 2852838.

### CULTURAL VACATIONS

**Archaeology**
**Achill Archaeological Summer School**
St O'Hara's Hill, Tullamore,
Co Offaly.
☎ 0506 21627.

**Belcoo Archaeology Summer School**
Enterprise Centre, Belcoo,
Co Fermanagh.
☎ 01365 386536.

**Oideas Gael**
Glencolumbkille,
Co Donegal.
☎ 073 30248.

**Cooking**
**Ballymaloe School of Cookery**
Shanagarry, Midleton,
Co Cork.
☎ 021 646785.

### Crafts
**Ardess Craft Centre**
Ardess House, Kesh,
Co Fermanagh.
☎ 01365 631267.

**Great Houses and Gardens**
**Irish Heritage Properties**
Hillsbrook, Dargle Village,
Bray, Co Wicklow.
☎ 01 2862777.

**National Trust**
Rowallane House,
Saintfield, Ballynahinch,
Co Down.
☎ 01238 510721.

**Irish Language**
**Irish Conversation Courses**
Oidhreacht Chorca
Dhuibhne, Ballyferriter,
Co Kerry.
☎ 066 56100.

**Literary**
**Goldsmith Summer School**
Rackmore, Ballymahon,
Co Longford.
☎ 0902 32374.

**James Joyce Summer School**
University College Dublin,
Belfield, Dublin 4.
☎ 01 7068480.

**Listowel Writers' Week**
PO Box 147, Listowel,
Co Kerry.
☎ 068 21074.

**William Carleton Summer School**
Leisure Services Dept,
Dungannon District
Council, Circular Rd,
Dungannon, Co Tyrone.
☎ 018687 25311.

**Yeats International Summer School**
Yeats Society, Yeats
Memorial Building, Douglas
Hyde Bridge, Sligo.
☎ 071 42693.

**Music**
**South Sligo Summer School of Traditional Music, Song and Dance**
Tubbercurry, Co Sligo.
☎ 071 85010.

**Willie Clancy Summer School**
Miltown Malbay, Co Clare.
☎ 065 84148.

# Sports and Outdoor Activities

**E**VEN IN THE LARGEST CITIES, the country-side is never far away, and it beckons to all lovers of the outdoors. Topping the list of spectator sports is Ireland's famous horse racing, while hurling, Gaelic football and soccer also make for exciting viewing. Those who want to do more than just watch can choose from fishing, golf, horse-back riding, cruising, cycling, hiking and water sports. Entire vacations can be based around any of these activities. In addition to the contacts on page 335, Bord Fáilte in the Republic, the Northern Ireland Tourist Board and all local tourist offices have information on spectator and participant sports. For details of the main events in Ireland's sporting calendar, see pages 26–7.

**Horse riding in Killarney**

**Fishing in the canal at Robertstown, County Kildare** *(see p120)*

## SPECTATOR SPORTS

**T**HE IRISH PASSION for horse racing is legendary. Major courses include the Curragh *(see p121),* where the Irish Derby is held, Fairyhouse, the site of Ireland's Grand National, and Leopardstown. Apart from these Dublin-based courses, there are smaller ones al over the Republic (and two in Northern Ireland), where the atmosphere is exciting and informal. Galway Race Week in late July is a great social event. A racing calendar that covers all of Ireland, available from the **Irish Horse Racing Authority**, enables you to choose from both National Hunt and flat race meets, which are scheduled for over 230 days of the year.

In Dublin, **Croke Park** hosts Gaelic football and hurling matches *(see pp26–7),* while international rugby and soccer matches are held at Lansdowne Road Stadium. Ticket details for soccer internationals are available from the **Football Association of Ireland**.

For keen golfers, the annual highlight is the Irish Open Golf Championship in July. The location varies from year to year. For tickets and the latest information, contact the **Irish Open Office**.

**Sign outside a fishing tackle shop in Donegal**

## FISHING

**T**HE CLAIM that Ireland is a paradise for anglers is no exaggeration. Coarse, game and sea fishing all enjoy widespread popularity. The lakes and rivers are home to bream, pike, perch and roach. The **Kingfisher Angling Centre**, near the River Bann, is one of many centers to provide accommodations for anglers on vacation. Coastal rivers yield the famous Irish salmon, and, among other game fish, sea trout and brown trout also offer anglers a real challenge.

Flounder, whiting, mullet, bass and coalfish tempt the sea angler; deep-sea excursions chase abundant supplies of dogfish, shark, skate and ling. You can organize sea-angling trips from many different places – the Cork and Kerry coastline being a particularly popular starting point.

Maps and information on fishing locations are provided by the **Central Fisheries Board** and Bord Fáilte in the Republic, and the **Department of Agriculture (Fisheries)** and Northern Ireland Tourist Board. Check permit requirements before you go.

## GOLF

**O**F THE 300 or more golf courses in the whole of Ireland, over 50 are championship class, and many are by spectacular stretches of coast. Mount Juliet's world-class, Jack Nicklaus-designed course in County Kilkenny has won international acclaim, and many others are also kept in top condition. Northern Ireland's best-known courses are Royal Portrush and Royal

**Golfers at Portstewart in Northern Ireland** *(see p252)*

**Walking in the Gap of Dunloe, Killarney** *(see p155)*

County Down. The **Golfing Union of Ireland** and the tourist boards have information on courses, conditions and greens fees throughout the Republic and Northern Ireland. Some have clubs for rent, but it is better to bring your own.

**Golfing Ireland** organizes customized golfing vacations for individuals and groups in the Republic, while **Golfers Abroad** does the same for Northern Ireland.

## CYCLING

CYCLING is one of Ireland's most popular sports. There is an exhilarating range of countryside to be explored and the comparatively traffic-free roads make cycling a pleasure. Limerick, Waterford and Galway make good bases for cycling vacations. Several organizations, such as **Celtic Cycling**, will plan an itinerary and book accommodations.

If you bring your own bike, you can transport it around the country fairly inexpensively by train or bus.

Alternatively, try the many **Raleigh Rent-a-Bike** dealers with depots in the Republic and Northern Ireland, or the **Bike Store**, based in Dublin and with branches in several cities in the Republic.

## HORSEBACK RIDING AND PONY TREKKING

THE IRISH ARE rightly proud of their fine horses. Many riding centers, both residential and nonresidential, offer trail riding and trekking along woodland trails, deserted beaches, country lanes and mountain routes. Dingle, Donegal, Connemara, and Killarney are all renowned areas for trail riding. There are two types of trail riding – post-to-post and based. Post-to-post trails follow a series of routes with accommodations in a different place each night. Based trail rides follow different routes in one area and you stay at the same

place for the whole trip. Also offered at many riding centers are lessons for everyone from beginners to more advanced riders to those who want to learn show jumping.

Bord Fáilte and the Northern Ireland Tourist Board publish details of riding centers and courses. **Equestrian Holidays Ireland** organizes vacations for riders of various abilities.

## HIKING AND MOUNTAINEERING

A HIKING TRIP puts you in the very middle of the glorious Irish landscape. The network of marked trails all over the country takes you to some of the loveliest areas. Information on long-distance walks is available from Bord Fáilte and the Northern Ireland Tourist Board. Routes include the Wicklow Way *(see p131)*, Dingle Way, Munster Way, Kerry Way and Barrow Towpath. All may be split into shorter sections for less experienced walkers or those short of time. The 800-km (500-mile) Ulster Way circles Northern Ireland, passing through a wide range of locations from the spectacular coastal scenery around the Giant's Causeway *(see pp254–5)* to the peaks of the Mountains of Mourne *(see pp276–7)*. **Celtic Journeys** offers guided walking tours both in Northern Ireland and the Republic.

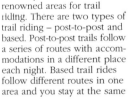

**Sign for the Ulster Way, the trail around Northern Ireland**

Hill walking, rock climbing and mountaineering trips are also available. For specialized information, contact the **Association for Adventure Sports**. Always make sure that you go well-equipped for the notoriously changeable Irish weather.

**Cycling through the Muckross House estate near Killarney** *(see p151)*

**Surfing at Bundoran** *(see p222)*

## WATER SPORTS

WITH A COASTLINE of over 4,800 km (3,000 miles), there's small wonder that water sports are among Ireland's favorite recreational activities. Surfing, windsurfing, scuba diving, water-skiing and canoeing are the most popular, and there are facilities for all of these around the coastline.

Conditions in Donegal are the best in Ireland for surfing, but many other coastal locations offer good conditions. The **Irish Surfing Association** will put you in touch with surf clubs all over the Republic and Northern Ireland. Windsurfing centers are mainly found near Dublin, Cork and Westport in County Galway.

There is a wide range of diving conditions off the coast of Ireland – visibility is particularly good on the west coast. The **Irish Underwater Council** will put you in touch with courses and facilities. **DV Diving** organizes scuba diving courses and offers accommodations near Belfast Lough and the Irish Sea where there are a number of historic wrecks to be explored.

Inland, Lower Lough Erne *(see pp262–3)* and Killaloe by Lough Derg *(see p182)* are popular vacation centers. The **Lakeland Canoe Centre**, between Upper and Lower Lough Erne, gives canoeing courses and organizes canoeing vacations (with overnight camping), including one down

the Shannon-Erne Waterway *(see p227)*. **Irish Canoeing Holidays** rents canoeing equipment, with or without a guide, for trips on the Shannon and Barrow rivers.

## CRUISING AND SAILING

A TRANQUIL CRUISING trip is an ideal alternative to the stress and strain of driving, and Ireland's 14,500 km (9,000 miles) of rivers and some 800 lakes offer a huge variety of conditions for those who want a waterborne vacation. Stopping over at waterside towns and villages puts you in touch with the Irish on their home ground. Whether you opt for Lough Derg or elsewhere on the Shannon *(see p177)*, or the Grand Canal *(see p99)* from Dublin to the Shannon, a unique view of the Irish countryside opens up all along the way.

Running between Carrick-on-Shannon in County Leitrim and Upper Lough Erne in Fermanagh is the **Shannon-Erne Waterway** *(see p227)*, an unused canal reopened in 1993. From here it is simple to continue through Upper and Lower Lough Erne to Belleek *(see p262)*. **Emerald Star** has a fleet of cruisers for use on the waterway.

A popular sailing area is between Cork and the Dingle Peninsula. The **International Sailing Centre**, near Cork, offers lessons. In Carrickfergus the **Ulster Cruising School** provides lessons at all levels; more experienced sailors can charter a yacht and sail up to the western coast of Scotland.

## HUNTING AND SHOOTING

IRELAND'S HUNTING season runs from October to March, and although foxhunting predominates, stag and hare hunts also take place. Clay-pigeon (year-round) and pheasant (from November to January) shooting are increasing in popularity. **Mount Juliet Estate**, in County Kilkenny, offers both with guns and cartridges for rent. For details, contact the **Irish Master of Foxhounds Association** in the Republic and, in Northern Ireland, the **Irish Fieldsports Agency**.

**Yachting off Rosslare** *(see p143)*

## SPORTS FOR THE DISABLED

SPORTS ENTHUSIASTS with a disability can obtain details of facilities for the disabled from the **Irish Wheelchair Association**. Central and local tourist boards and many of the organizations listed in the directory under each sport will also advise on available facilities. The **Share Centre** provides a range of activity vacations for people with and without disabilities.

**Boats moored at Carnlough Harbour on the Antrim coast** *(see p259)*

## DIRECTORY

### SPECTATOR SPORTS

**Croke Park**
Dublin 3.
☎ 01 8363222.

**Football Association of Ireland**
80 Merrion Sq, Dublin 2.
☎ 01 6766864.

**Irish Horse Racing Authority**
Leopardstown Racecourse,
Foxrock, Dublin 18.
☎ 01 2892888.

**Irish Open Office**
35 Upper Mount St,
Dublin 2.
☎ 01 6622433.

### FISHING

**Central Fisheries Board**
Balnagowan House,
Mobhi Boreen, Glasnevin,
Dublin 9.
☎ 01 8379206.

**Department of Agriculture (Fisheries)**
Stormont, Belfast.
☎ 01232 523434.

**Irish Federation of Sea Anglers**
67 Windsor Drive,
Monkstown, Co Dublin.
☎ 01 2806901.

**Kingfisher Angling Centre**
24 Hiltonstown Rd,
Portglenone, Ballymena,
Co Antrim.
☎ 01266 821301.

### GOLF

**Golfers Abroad**
6 Park St, Wombwell,
Barnsley, S Yorks. England.
☎ 01226 751704.

**Golfing Ireland**
18 Parnell Sq, Dublin 1.
☎ 01 8726711.

**Golfing Union of Ireland**
Glencar House, 81
Eglinton Rd, Dublin 4.
☎ 01 2694111.

### CYCLING

**Ardclinis Activity Centre**
High St, Cushendall,
Co Antrim.
☎ 01266 771340.

**Bike Store**
58 Lower Gardiner St,
Dublin 1.
☎ 01 8725399.

**Celtic Cycling**
Lorum Old Rectory,
Bagenalstown, Co Carlow.
☎ 0503 75282.

**Raleigh Rent-a-Bike**
PO Box 3520, Raleigh
House, Kylemore Rd,
Dublin 10.
☎ 01 6261333.

### HORSEBACK RIDING AND PONY TREKKING

**Association of Irish Riding Establishments**
11 Moore Park,
Newbridge, Co Kildare.
☎ 045 31584.

**British Horse Society**
House of Sport, Upper
Malone Rd, Belfast.
☎ 01232 381222.

**Equestrian Holidays Ireland**
1 Sandyford Office Park,
Foxrock, Dublin 18.
☎ 01 2958928.

### HIKING AND MOUNTAINEERING

**Association for Adventure Sports**
House of Sport, Longmile
Rd, Dublin 12.
☎ 01 4509845.

**Celtic Journeys**
Carrick-a-rede Cottage,
111 White Park Rd,
Ballycastle, Co Antrim.
☎ 01265 769651.

**Countryside Tours**
Chamber of Commerce
House, 10 Prince of Wales
Terrace, Quinsboro Rd,
Bray, Co Wicklow.
☎ 0404 2760733.

**Out and Out Activities**
Garrison,
Co Fermanagh.
☎ 01365 658105.

### WATER SPORTS

**Ballyronan Marina**
Watersports Centre,
Ballyronan, Co
Londonderry.
☎ 01868 722528.

**DV Diving**
138 Mountstewart Rd,
Newtownards,
Co Down.
☎ 01247 464671.

**Irish Canoeing Holidays**
Multifarnham,
Co Westmeath.
☎ 044 71324.

**Irish Surfing Association**
1 Ardeelan Dale,
Rossnowlagh,
Co Donegal.
☎ 072 52522.

**Irish Underwater Council**
78a Patrick St, Dun
Laoghaire, Co Dublin.
☎ 01 2844601.

**Irish Water Ski Federation**
91 South Mall, Cork.
☎ 021 271962.

**Irish Windsurfing Association**
Surfdock Marketing Ltd,
Grand Canal Dockyard,
South Dock Rd, Ringsend,
Dublin 4.
☎ 01 6683945.

**Lakeland Canoe Centre**
Castle Island, Enniskillen,
Co Fermanagh.
☎ 01365 324250.

### CRUISING AND SAILING

**Athlone Cruisers**
Jolly Mariner, Athlone,
Co Westmeath.
☎ 0902 72892.

**Derg Line Cruisers**
Killaloe, Co Clare.
☎ 061 376364.

**Emerald Star**
47 Dawson St, Dublin 2.
☎ 01 6798166.

**Erne Marine**
Bellanaleck, Enniskillen,
Co Fermanagh.
☎ 01365 348267.

**International Sailing Centre**
East Beach, Cobh, Cork.
☎ 021 811237.

**Lough Melvin Holiday Centre**
Garrison, Co Fermanagh.
☎ 01365 658142.

**Shannon-Erne Waterway**
Ballinamore, Co Leitrim.
☎ 078 44855.

**Silver Line Cruisers**
The Marina, Banagher,
Co Offaly.
☎ 0509 51112.

**Ulster Cruising School**
The Marina, Carrickfergus,
Co Antrim.
☎ 01960 368818.

### HUNTING AND SHOOTING

**Irish Fieldsports Agency**
174 Castlereagh Rd,
Belfast.
☎ 01232 459248.

**Irish Master of Foxhounds Association**
Thornton, Dunlavin,
Co Kildare.
☎ 045 51294.

**Mount Juliet Estate**
Thomastown, Co Kilkenny.
☎ 056 24455.

### SPORTS FOR THE DISABLED

**Irish Wheelchair Association**
Aras Chuchulain,
Blackheath Drive,
Clontarf, Dublin 3.
☎ 01 8338241.

**Share Centre**
Smith's Strand, Lisnaskea,
Co Fermanagh.
☎ 01365 722122.

# SURVIVAL
# GUIDE

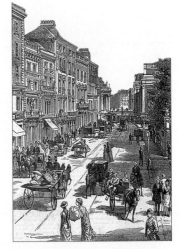

PRACTICAL INFORMATION 338-349
TRAVEL INFORMATION 350-361

# PRACTICAL INFORMATION

A LTHOUGH IRELAND is quite a small island, visitors should not expect to see everything in a short time, since many of the country's most magnificent attractions are in rural areas. In remote parts of the island the roads are narrow, the pace of life is very slow, banks often open for only one or two days of the week and public transport tends to be infrequent. However, although the Republic of Ireland remains one of

**Bord Fáilte logo**

Europe's most unspoilt nations, its economy is developing fast. Any decent-sized town in the Republic is likely to have a tourist information centre and offer a full range of facilities for the traveller. Northern Ireland has its own tourist board with offices in most towns. The standard of facilities available to those travelling in the North equals that across the border and, as with the Republic, the level of hospitality is first-rate.

## TOURIST INFORMATION

I N BOTH THE REPUBLIC and Northern Ireland there is an impressive network of tourist information offices. As well as providing lots of free local information, the tourist offices in large towns sell maps and guide books and can reserve accommodation for a nominal charge. There are also tourist information points in some of the smaller towns and villages. The opening hours can be somewhat erratic and many are open only during the summer season. The local museums and libraries often stock a selection of useful tourist literature.

Before leaving for Ireland you can get information from **Bord Fáilte** (Irish Tourist Board) or **Northern Ireland Tourist Board** (NITB) offices, which will supply you with maps and leaflets. Bord Fáilte offices can be found in major cities all over the world – a reflection of the universal appeal of Ireland. It's also worth contacting the regional tourist offices in Dublin, Cork, Limerick and Galway for more information on destinations, including accommodation and car rental. If you call at a tourist office in the Republic and pick up a list of places to stay, you shouldn't expect every local hotel and guesthouse to be included – these lists recommend only those establishments that have been approved by Bord Fáilte.

The OPW-run Parke's Castle in County Sligo *(see p225)*

## ADMISSION CHARGES

M OST OF IRELAND'S major sights, including ancient monuments, museums and national parks, have an admission fee. For each place of interest in this guide, we specify whether or not there is a charge. The entrance fees in the Republic of Ireland are normally between IR£1

**Heritage card giving access to historic sites**

and IR£5 with discounts for students and the elderly. The **Office of Public Works** (OPW) maintains parks, museums, monuments and inland waterways and issues a Heritage Card which allows unlimited access to all its managed sites

**Northern Ireland Tourist Board logo**

for a year. At IR£15 for adults, IR£10 for senior citizens and IR£6 for children and students, the card is a good investment. Popular OPW sites include the historic Kilkenny Castle *(see pp134–6)*, the monastery at Clonmacnoise *(see pp242–3)* and the passage tomb at Newgrange *(see pp238–9)*. Entrance fees in Northern Ireland are about the same as in the Republic, with discounts for students and senior citizens. North of the border the **National Trust** has a scheme similar to the Heritage Card, but membership costs more (around £25 per annum per person or £45 for families) and there are fewer sites. It doesn't represent very good value for money unless you are also intending to visit National Trust sites elsewhere in the UK.

**Interpretative centre at Connemara National Park** *(see p200)*

## OPENING TIMES

THE OPENING DAYS of sights are listed in this guide. Few places are open on a Sunday morning, and some museums are shut on Monday. Opening hours are generally between 10am and 5pm; some sights stay open a little later and others close for lunch.

From June to September all the sights are open but the crowds are at their biggest. In winter many tourist attractions are closed several days per week and keep shorter hours; some close down completely. There are also variations on public holidays – many places open for Easter and then close again until summer.

## INTERPRETATIVE CENTRES

MANY OF IRELAND'S major sights are ruins or Stone Age archaeological sites and can be difficult to appreciate. In recent years, however, money has become available for building interpretative or visitors' centres which explain the historical significance of sites. Entry to the site may be free, but you have to pay to visit the interpretative centre.

In areas of natural beauty, such as Connemara National Park, an interpretative centre acts as a useful focal point. The centre typically provides information leaflets and has reconstructions of sights. Connemara has 3D models and displays, as well as an audiovisual presentation on the development of the local landscape over the last 10,000 years. There is also a shop for postcards, books and posters.

## RELIGIOUS SERVICES

IRELAND is a deeply religious country and for much of the population, churchgoing is a way of life. Because the Republic of Ireland is 95 per cent Roman Catholic, finding a non-Catholic church may sometimes be difficult. In the Republic and Northern Ireland, the tourist offices, hotels and B&Bs all keep a list of local church service times.

### DIRECTORY

**IRISH TOURIST BOARD (BORD FÁILTE) OFFICES**

**Republic of Ireland**
Baggot St Bridge, Dublin 2.
📞 01 6024000.

**United Kingdom**
150 New Bond St, London W1Y 0AQ. 📞 0171 4933201.

**United States**
345 Park Avenue,
New York, NY 10154.
📞 (212) 418-0800.

**NORTHERN IRELAND TOURIST BOARD OFFICES**

**Northern Ireland Tourist Board**
St Anne's Court, 59 North St,
Belfast BT1 1NB.
📞 01232 246609.

**United Kingdom**
11 Berkeley St, London
W1X 5AD.
📞 0171 4930601.

**United States**
551 Fifth Ave, Suite 701,
New York, NY 10176.
📞 (212) 922-0101.

**OTHER USEFUL ADDRESSES**

**National Trust**
Rowallane House, Saintfield,
Ballynahinch, County Down
BT24 7LH. 📞 01238 510721.

**Office of Public Works**
51 St Stephen's Green, Dublin 2.
📞 01 6613111 ext 2386.

## LANGUAGE

The Republic of Ireland is officially bilingual – almost all road signs have place names in both English and Irish. English is the spoken language everywhere apart from a few parts of the far west, called Gaeltachts *(see p221)*, but now and then you may find signs written only in Irish. Here are some of the words you are most likely to come across.

## USEFUL WORDS

*an banc* – **bank**
*an lár* – **town centre**
*an trá* – **beach**
*ar aghaidh* – **go**
*bád* – **boat**
*bealach amach* – **exit**
*bealach isteach* – **entrance**
*bus* – **bus**
*dúnta* – **closed**
*fáilte* – **welcome**
*fir* – **men**
*gardaí* – **police**
*leithreas* – **toilet**

**Sign using old form of Gaelic**

*mná* – **women**
*oifig an poist* – **post office**
*oscailte* – **open**
*óstán* – **hotel**
*siopa* – **shop**
*stop/stad* – **stop**
*ticéad* – **ticket**
*traein* – **train**

# Additional Information

**European Youth Card**

IRELAND IS DIVIDED between the state of the Republic of Ireland, and Northern Ireland – a province of the United Kingdom. Each has a separate currency, postal service and telecommunications system *(see pp344–9)*. However, there are many similarities between them: they are part of the European Union, English is their first language and, both north and south of the border, the tourist industry is well advanced. These two pages describe the regulations that affect the Republic and Northern Ireland, and the special facilities that are available to travelers, including students and the disabled. There is also a general guide to the media in both the North and South as well as a directory of useful names and addresses.

**Students at Trinity College, Dublin**

## VISAS

VISITORS FROM the EU, US, Canada, Australia and New Zealand require a valid passport but not a visa for entry into the Republic or Northern Ireland. All others, including those wanting to study or get a job, should check with their local Irish or British Embassy first. UK nationals born in Great Britain or Northern Ireland do not strictly need a passport to enter the Republic of Ireland but should take one with them for car rental, cashing of traveler's checks and medical services.

## DUTY-FREE GOODS AND CUSTOMS ALLOWANCES

ADULTS TRAVELING between Ireland and countries outside the British Isles can buy duty-free goods at the airport, on the plane or on the ferry. This also applies to those going between the Republic and Great Britain but not between North and South. Duty-free is not available when traveling between Northern Ireland and other parts of the UK. Current allowances include a liter of alcohol, 50 grams of perfume and 200 cigarettes. 1993 EU regulations also allow travelers within the European Union a quantity of duty-paid goods. Present quotas include 55 liters of beer, 45 liters of wine and 800 cigarettes.

## STUDENT TRAVELERS

STUDENTS WITH a valid ISIC card (International Student Identity Card) benefit from numerous travel discounts as well as reduced admission to museums and concerts. Buy a Travelsave stamp from any branch of **USIT** and affix it to your ISIC card to get a 50 percent discount on Irish Rail, NIR train services and Irish Ferries. A Travelsave stamp will also get you discounts on Bus Éireann routes in the South and special rates on commuter tickets (Sep–Jun only) in Dublin, Limerick, Cork, Galway and Waterford. In the North, an ISIC card gives a 15 percent discount on Ulsterbus services and 20 percent on Belfast Citybus "Gold Card" commuter services. ISIC cards can be obtained from branches of USIT travel in Dublin, Belfast and other college towns.

USIT will also supply non-students under 26 with an EYC (European Youth Card) for discounts in restaurants, shops and theaters. The name of the card, which is recognized in over 20 European states, varies from country to country but can be identified by its distinctive logo.

## FACILITIES FOR THE DISABLED

MOST SIGHTS in Ireland have access for wheelchairs. This book gives basic information about disabled access for each sight, but it's worth calling to check details. The Access Department of the **National Rehabilitation Board** provides information for the Republic and publishes county-by-county guides to accommodation, restaurants and amenities. In the North, **Disability Action** can advise on accessibility, while the Open Arts organization has a list of entertainment venues and museums providing wheelchair access.

**Duty-free shop at Shannon Airport**

Relaxing with newspapers in Eyre Square, Galway

## RADIO AND TELEVISION

IRELAND has two television channels, RTE 1 and Network 2. Both are run by the state-controlled RTE. There are three national radio stations, including an Irish-language service, and many local ones.

The four British television channels can be picked up in most parts of Ireland. Cable TV is quite common in the Republic, where most hotels offer this service.

A selection of daily newspapers from North and South

## NEWSPAPERS AND MAGAZINES

THE REPUBLIC of Ireland has six national daily papers and five Sunday papers. Quality dailies include the *Irish Independent*, the *Irish Press*, the *Cork Examiner* and the *Irish Times*, renowned for its journalistic excellence. The newspapers are useful for up-to-date information on theater and concerts. Ireland's daily

tabloid is the *Star*. The North's top local paper is the *Belfast Telegraph*, on sale in the afternoon. The province's morning papers, the *News Letter* and *Irish News*, are less rewarding.

In larger towns throughout Ireland, British tabloids are on sale. Newspapers such as *The Times* are also available and cost less than the quality Irish press. Most towns have a local or regional paper, which will tell you what's on and where.

*USA Today*, *Newsweek* and *Time* magazine are sold in major cities but are very hard to find in the countryside.

## IRISH TIME

THE WHOLE of Ireland is in the same time zone as Great Britain, i.e. five hours ahead of New York and Toronto, one hour behind Germany and France, and ten hours behind Sydney. In both the North and the South, clocks go forward one hour for summer time.

## CONVERSION CHART

### Imperial to Metric
1 inch = 2.5 centimeters
1 foot = 30 centimeters
1 mile = 1.6 kilometers
1 ounce = 28 grams
1 pound = 454 grams
1 US pint = 0.5 liters
1 US gallon = 3.8 liters

### Metric to Imperial
1 millimeter = 0.04 inches
1 centimeter = 0.4 inches
1 meter = 3 feet 3 inches
1 kilometer = 0.6 miles
1 gram = 0.04 ounces
1 kilogram = 2.2 pounds
1 liter = 2.1 US pints

## METRICATION

THE CHANGE towards metrication is slow in Ireland, particularly in the North, where distances are still measured in miles. In the Republic, all new road signs show distances in kilometers, but there are still many old ones that use miles (*see p356*). However, throughout Ireland all speed limits are shown in miles. In both Northern Ireland and the Republic, gasoline is sold in liters but draught beer is always sold in pints. And just to add to the confusion, food may be weighed out either in imperial or in metric measures.

One of the new metric road signs used in the Republic of Ireland

# Personal Security and Health

**Pharmacy in Dublin showing old-fashioned snake and goblet symbol**

I RELAND IS PROBABLY one of the safest places to travel in Europe. Petty theft, such as pickpocketing, is seldom a problem outside certain parts of Dublin and a few other large towns. Tourist offices and hoteliers gladly point out the areas to be avoided. In the recent past, the main security risk in Northern Ireland has been the threat of bombings, though this has hardly ever affected tourists. In fact, crimes against the individual tend to be fewer than in other parts of the UK and Europe.

**Pearse Street Garda Station, Dublin**

## PERSONAL SECURITY

T HE POLICE, should you ever need them, are called the Gardaí in the Republic of Ireland and the Royal Ulster Constabulary (RUC) in Northern Ireland. Violent street crime in Ireland – North or South – is almost unheard of but it's still advisable to take suitable precautions, such as avoiding poorly lit streets in cities and the larger towns. Poverty and a degree of

**Male garda**  **RUC policeman**

heroin addiction in inner-city Dublin has been known to cause a few problems, and Limerick isn't the most inviting of places after dark, but if you avoid the backstreets at night there should be little cause for concern. In some of the larger southern towns you may be approached in the street by people asking for money. This rarely develops into a troublesome situation, but it is still best to avoid eye contact and leave the scene as quickly as possible.

## PERSONAL PROPERTY

B EFORE YOU LEAVE, make sure that your possessions are insured, as it might be difficult and more expensive to do this in Ireland. Travel insurance for the UK will not cover you for the Republic, so make sure you have an adequate policy. Since pickpocketing and purse snatching are problems in some of the larger towns in the Republic, it's best not to carry your passport or large amounts of cash, or leave them in your room. Most hotels have a safe and it makes sense to take advantage of this facility. Those carrying large amounts of money around should use traveler's checks *(see pp346–7)*. While out, use a purse that can be held securely, and be alert in crowded places and restaurants. A money belt may be a good investment.

If traveling by car, be sure all valuables are locked in the trunk and always lock the car, even when leaving it for just a few minutes. If visiting

**Garda Station**

**RUC Station**

Northern Ireland, do not leave any of your bags or packages unattended, as they are likely to result in a security scare.

## LOST PROPERTY

R EPORT ALL LOST or stolen items at once to the police. To make an insurance claim, you'll need to get a copy of the police report. Most rail and bus stations in the Republic operate a lost-property service.

## MEDICAL TREATMENT

V ISITORS TO the Republic of Ireland from all countries outside the European Union (EU) are strongly advised to take out medical insurance against the cost of any emergency hospital care, specialists' fees and repatriation. Residents of countries in the European Union can claim free medical treatment, in both the Republic of Ireland and Northern Ireland, by obtaining form E111 before setting out. Make sure you let the doctor know that you want to be treated under the European Union's social security regulations, then simply show your E111 and a form of identification, such as a driver's license or passport. British citizens need no documentation when visiting Northern Ireland.

> **EMERGENCY NUMBERS**
>
> **Police, Fire, Ambulance and Coast Guard Services**
>
> Dial 999 in both the Republic and Northern Ireland.

## PHARMACIES

A WIDE RANGE of medical supplies is available over the counter at pharmacies. However, many medicines are available only with a prescription authorized by a local doctor. If you are likely to require specialized drugs during your stay, take your own supplies or ask your doctor to write a letter with the generic name of the medicine you require. Always obtain a receipt for insurance claims.

Until recently, condoms were not freely available in the Republic but are now relatively easy to obtain, in the big cities at least. In some of the small towns you may discover that the pharmacist is opposed to contraception and does not sell condoms.

Dublin ambulance

Dublin fire engine

Garda patrol car

RUC patrol car

**Small rural health center in County Donegal**

## PERSONAL SAFETY IN NORTHERN IRELAND

**Checkpoint signs**

Even at the height of the Troubles in Northern Ireland, there was never a significant threat to the tourist, and traveling around the province was deemed to be as safe as in the Republic. As long as peace exists north of the border, no extra precautions need to be taken there, but in the event of the Troubles resurfacing, first-time visitors should be prepared for certain unfamiliar situations. When driving, if you see a sign that indicates you are approaching a checkpoint, slow down and use low beams. To keep fuss down to a minimum in these situations, it is a good idea to keep a passport or some other form of identification close at hand. When parking in the province's towns and cities, be sure to avoid leaving your vehicle unattended in an area that is marked by a Control Zone sign. If you are walking around the city centers of Belfast and Londonderry, you may notice a strong police or military presence. This is unlikely to cause you any inconvenience. Occasionally, however, you may be asked by store security to reveal the contents of your bags – don't be alarmed, this is merely a routine procedure.

**RUC armor-plated Land Rover**

# Local Currency

THE REPUBLIC and Northern Ireland have different currencies. Although punts, or Irish pounds, and pounds sterling are issued in the same bill and coin denominations, they are not interchangeable. Many retailers in the Republic accept sterling if the exchange rate is in their favor, but don't rely on this. When traveling between Northern Ireland and the Republic, there's no shortage of money changers – official and unofficial – in towns on either side of the border. However, for the best exchange rates, avoid stores and gas stations and use the *bureaux de change* or banks.

**Ulster Bank branch in Delvin, County Westmeath**

## CURRENCY IN THE REPUBLIC OF IRELAND

THE UNIT OF CURRENCY in the Republic is the punt (IR£), often called the Irish pound. It is divided into 100 pence (p). Although there are no restrictions on bringing currency into the Republic, you cannot take more than IR£150 in bills out. However, you can take out the same amount of foreign currency as you bring in, up to IR£1,200.

**Banknotes**
*The Republic's bills are issued in denominations of IR£50, IR£20, IR£10 and IR£5. They increase in size according to value and depict many famous figures from the country's past.*

IR£50 bill

IR£20 bill

IR£10 bill

IR£5 bill

**Coins**
*The Republic of Ireland issues the following coins: IR£1, 50p, 20p, 10p, 5p, 2p and 1p. Although the denominations are the same as those used north of the border, the appearance of the coins is very different.*

IR£1

50p

20p

10p

5p

2p

1p

## CURRENCY IN NORTHERN IRELAND

NORTHERN IRELAND uses British currency – the pound sterling (£), which is divided into 100 pence (p). As there are no exchange controls in the UK, there is no limit to the amount of cash you can take into and out of Northern Ireland. In addition to the British currency, four provincial banks issue their own bills, worth the same as their counterparts. To tell them apart, look for the words "Bank of England" on British bills.

### Money

*British bills are issued in the denominations £50, £20, £10 and £5. Their different colors help to make them easily distinguishable.*

£50 bill

£20 bill

£10 bill

£5 bill

### Coins

*Coins come in the following denominations: £1, 50p, 20p, 10p, 5p, 2p and 1p. All have the Queen's head on one side and are the same as those elsewhere in the UK, except that the pound coin has a different detail - a flax plant - on the reverse side.*

### PROVINCIAL MONEY

Bills issued by the four provincial banks are not normally accepted by retailers in other parts of the UK, so if you intend to travel on to Great Britain, exchange them for Bank of England bills. Provincial currency is not legal tender in the Republic of Ireland.

Bank of Ireland £5 bill          Ulster Bank £5 bill

Northern Bank £5 bill          First Trust Bank £10 bill

£1          50p

20p          10p          5p          2p          1p

# Banks in Ireland

THE OPENING TIMES of banks in Ireland vary depending on whether the banks are situated in the town or country, in the Republic or Northern Ireland. Both north and south of the border, banks in small towns are often suboffices where banking services may be provided on only one or two days of the week, so it's advisable to make the most of facilities in the bigger towns whenever you can. Banks throughout Ireland generally provide very good service and, along with many of the larger post offices, will exchange traveler's checks, often without charging commission.

Bank of Ireland suboffice in Sneem, County Kerry

## USING BANKS

THE FIVE RETAIL BANKS in the Republic of Ireland are the Bank of Ireland, the Allied Irish Bank (AIB), the Ulster Bank, the National Irish Bank and the TSB Bank. In Northern Ireland there are four retail banks: the Ulster Bank, the Bank of Ireland, the Northern Bank and the First Trust Bank.

In the Republic of Ireland the usual banking hours are Monday to Friday from 10am to 12:30pm and from 1:30 to 3pm. Some of the larger branches do stay open during lunchtime – a custom that more and more banks are adopting. There is extended opening (till 5pm) on one day of the week. In Dublin, Cork and most other cities and towns, late opening is on Thursdays but in rural areas banks often stay open late on market day instead. Branches of the TSB Bank remain open at lunchtime and until 7pm on Thursdays and up to 5pm on other weekdays. Most of the banks in Northern Ireland open from 10am to 3:30pm, though some of them close for lunch between 12:30 and 1:30pm. In both the Republic and Northern Ireland, all the banks are closed on public holidays, some of which differ from North to South *(see p49)*. Banks in the cities and most of the towns are provided with automated teller machines, or cash dispensers, so if you happen to discover the local bank is closed, it isn't necessarily a major catastrophe.

**Cash dispenser**

**First Trust Bank logo**

## CREDIT CARDS

THROUGHOUT IRELAND you can pay by credit card in most hotels, gas stations, large stores, restaurants and supermarkets. VISA or Mastercard (known also as Access) are the most commonly accepted credit cards. Fewer businesses take American Express and Diners Club cards. Cash can be withdrawn from banks showing the appropriate sign.

## TRAVELER'S CHECKS

TRAVELER'S CHECKS are the safest way to carry large amounts of money. These are best changed at one of the main banks but, failing this, many stores and restaurants accept them – usually for a small charge.

Traveler's checks can be bought before leaving at American Express, Thomas

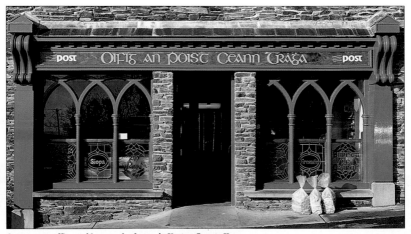

Ornate post office and *bureau de change* in Ventry, County Kerry

Cook or your own bank. In Ireland, traveler's checks can be purchased at banks or from *bureaux de change*, which can be found in the larger cities and at airports.

### EUROCHEQUES

INSTEAD OF traveler's checks, if you have a European bank account, you can use a Eurocheque book and guarantee card. When buying from a store that takes Eurocheques, you make out a check for the exact amount in punts or pounds. The Eurocheque card can also be used to withdraw cash up to your card limit.

**Drawing money from an Allied Irish Bank ATM**

### BUREAUX DE CHANGE

IN ADDITION to the foreign exchange counters at the main banks, there are some private *bureaux de change* in Dublin. As with most other exchange facilities, *bureaux de change* open later than banks. However, it's worth checking their rates before undertaking any transactions.

---

### BUREAUX DE CHANGE

**American Express**
116 Grafton Street, Dublin 2.
( 01 6772874.
Plus offices in Cork, Galway, Killarney, Limerick, Waterford & Belfast.

**Thomas Cook**
118 Grafton Street, Dublin 2.
( 01 6770476.
11 Donegall Place, Belfast.
( 01232 550030.
Branch also at Belfast International Airport and offices in Ballymena, Bangor, Coleraine, Lisburn, Londonderry & Portadown.

---

# Sending a Letter

**Northern Ireland Post Office sign**

MAIN POST OFFICES in the Republic and Northern Ireland are usually open from 9am to 5:30pm during the week and from 9am to around 1pm on Saturdays, although times do vary. Some smaller offices close for lunch on weekdays and do not open on Saturdays. Standard letter and postcard stamps can also be bought from certain newsstands. The Republic of Ireland does not have a first- and second-class system, but sending a postcard is a little less expensive than a letter. Although it is improving all the time, the postal service in the Republic is still quite slow – allow three to four days when sending a letter to Great Britain and at least six days for the United

**Republic of Ireland Post Office logo**

States. In Northern Ireland, letters to other parts of the UK can be sent by either first- or second-class mail. First-class postage is slightly more expensive but most letters sent this way reach their UK destination the next day. A letter to any EU country (including the Republic) costs the same as first-class mail.

### MAILBOXES

MAILBOXES in Ireland come in two colors – green in the Republic and red in the North. Many of Ireland's mailboxes are quite historic. Some of those in the Republic even carry Queen Victoria's monogram on the front, a relic from the days of British rule. Even the smallest towns in Ireland have a mailbox, from which the mail is collected regularly – anything from one to four times daily.

ÉIRE 28    ÉIRE 32    ÉIRE 52

**Postcard, letter and parcel stamps for the Republic of Ireland**

19ᵖ    25ᵖ    41ᵖ

**Second-class, first-class and parcel stamps used in the North**

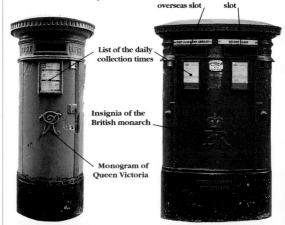

First-class and overseas slot

Second-class slot

List of the daily collection times

Insignia of the British monarch

Monogram of Queen Victoria

**Mailbox in the Republic**

**Northern Ireland double mailbox**

# Using Ireland's Telephones

THE TELEPHONE SYSTEM in the Republic of Ireland is run exclusively by Telecom Eireann and provides a modern and efficient service. Today, TE has a network of up-to-date coin and card telephones. For those intending to spend more than IR£4 ($6) on calls, it can be cheaper to use phonecards since they offer reasonable discounts. Also, there are now more card phones in the Republic than coin phones. Northern Ireland, like the rest of the United Kingdom, has British Telecom coin and card public phones. BT and TE phonecards are available from newsstands, post offices, supermarkets and other retail outlets.

# TELECOM EIREANN

The Telecom Eireann logo

## USING A TE COIN PHONE

1 Lift the receiver and wait for the dial tone.

2 Insert any of the coins below. The illuminated display shows the minimum amount required.

3 Dial the number and wait to be connected.

4 The display indicates how much money you have put in and the credit left. A rapid bleeping noise means your money has run out. Insert more coins.

5 If you want to make another call and you have money left in credit, do not replace the receiver, press the follow-on-call button.

6 When you have finished speaking, replace the receiver and collect your change. Only wholly unused coins are refunded.

## USING A TE CARD PHONE

1 Lift the receiver and wait for the dial tone.

3 The display shows how many units are left. The minimum charge is one unit (20p).

4 Dial the number and wait until you are connected.

5 When your phonecard runs out you will hear a rapid bleeping noise. To continue, press the "change card" button and the old card will come out. Remove it and insert a new card.

6 If you want to make another call and you have money left in credit, do not replace the receiver, press the follow-on-call button.

2 Insert a TE Callcard in the direction of the arrow on the card.

7 To adjust the volume in your earpiece, press the button with the upward-pointing arrow to increase it, and the button with the downward-pointing arrow to decrease it.

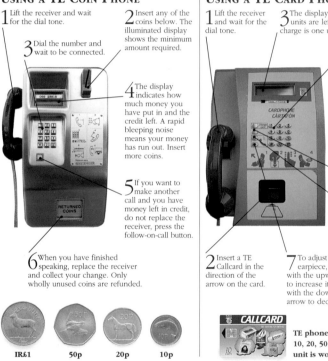

| IR£1 | 50p | 20p | 10p |

**CALLCARD**

TE phonecards come in 10, 20, 50 and 100 units. A unit is worth 20p.

## PHONING FROM THE REPUBLIC OF IRELAND

Bargain-rate calls within the Republic and to the UK are from 6pm to 8am weekdays and all day on weekends. Off-peak times for international calls vary from country to country, but are generally as above.
- To call Northern Ireland: dial 08, then the area code, followed by the number.
- To call the UK: dial 0044, the area code (minus the leading 0), then the number.
- To call other countries: dial 00, followed by the country code (for example, 1 for the US, 61 for Australia), the area code (minus the leading 0), then the number.

- For directory assistance: call 1190 for numbers in the Republic and Northern Ireland, 1197 for numbers in Great Britain and 1198 for numbers in other countries.
- For assistance in making a call: dial 10 for numbers within Ireland and Britain, 114 for international calls.
- Credit cards issued in certain countries including the US, Australia and Canada are accepted as payment for calls to the country from where the card was issued.
- To send a telemessage: dial 196.
- For emergencies: dial 999.

### Telephone booths

*Most of the phone booths in the Republic are modern. There are two styles in Northern Ireland – new ones and the traditional red booths – but both are issued with the same type of telephone. In both North and South, the wording around the top of each booth indicates whether it is a coin, phonecard or credit card phone.*

**Telecom Eireann phone booth**

**Old BT phone booth   New BT phone booth**

## USING A BT COIN PHONE

1 Lift the receiver and wait for the dial tone.

2 Insert any of the coins shown below. The display shows the minimum amount of money you must put in.

3 Dial the number and wait to be connected.

4 The display indicates how much money you have put in and the credit left. A rapid bleeping noise means your money has run out. Insert more coins.

5 If you want to make another call and you have money left in credit, do not replace the receiver, press the follow-on-call button.

6 When you have finished speaking, replace the receiver and collect your change. Only wholly unused coins are refunded.

| £1 | 50p | 20p | 10p |

## USING A BT CARD PHONE

1 Lift the receiver and wait for the dial tone.

3 The display shows how many units you have left. The minimum charge is one unit (10p).

4 Some of the BT phones take credit cards as well as phonecards. With the black strip on the right-hand side and away from you, insert and slide through.

5 Dial the number and wait until you are connected.

6 When your phonecard runs out you will hear a rapid bleeping noise. Press the eject button and remove the old card, replacing it with a new one.

7 If you have credit on your card and want to make another call, just press and quickly release the receiver rest.

2 Insert a BT phonecard, green side up, in the direction of the arrows on the card.

**BT phonecards come in 20, 40, 100 and 200 units. The value of each unit is 10p.**

## PHONING FROM NORTHERN IRELAND

Bargain-rate calls within the province, to other parts of the UK and to the Republic are from 6pm to 8am on weekdays and all day at weekends. Times for off-peak international calls vary from country to country but are generally as above.

• For calls within the UK: dial the area code and the number you require.
• For international calls: dial 00, then the country code (for example, 1 for Canada, 64 for New Zealand), then the area code minus the first 0 and finally, the number you require.

• For calls to the Republic of Ireland: dial 00 353 then the area code minus the first 0, then the number.
• For assistance with making a call: contact the operator on 100 for calls within the UK and 155 for all other countries, including the Republic of Ireland.
• For directory assistance: call 192 for UK and Republic of Ireland numbers and 153 for all other countries.
• For telemessages: dial 0800 190191.
• For the 24-hour speaking clock: call 8081.
• For emergency services: call 999.

# TRAVEL INFORMATION

IRELAND'S THREE main airports, Dublin, Shannon and Belfast, are well served by flights from Britain, the United States and an increasing number of countries around the world. If you are traveling by sea from the UK, there is a very good choice of ferry routes to both the Republic and Northern Ireland. Instead of buying separate tickets, you can purchase combined bus/ferry and rail/ferry tickets from almost all of the towns in mainland Britain. The less-than-comprehensive public transportation systems in both the North and South reflect the rural nature of the island. With this in mind, traveling around Ireland is probably best enjoyed if you embrace the Irish way of thinking and just take your time.

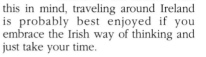
**Aer Lingus Airbus in flight**

**The modern exterior of Dublin International Airport**

## FLYING TO THE REPUBLIC OF IRELAND

FLIGHTS from most of the major cities in Europe arrive at **Dublin Airport**, which is the country's busiest airport. Regular services to the Republic depart from all five of the London airports (Heathrow, City, Gatwick, Luton and Stansted) and 15 other cities in Britain, plus the Channel Islands and the Isle of Man.

The major airline operating scheduled flights between Britain and the Republic is **Aer Lingus**, although since deregulation the rival **Ryanair** firm has grown fast due to its policy of cheap fares from Stansted, Luton, Gatwick and other British airports. Aer Lingus and **Delta Airlines** fly direct from the US to Dublin Airport and **Shannon Airport**, ten miles outside Limerick – gone is the old ruling that all

planes flying eastward to Dublin must first touch down at Shannon. As well as flying from Moscow, **Aeroflot** has nonstop flights from Miami, Chicago and Washington, DC to Shannon Airport.

**Cork Airport** is served by flights from London (Heathrow and Stansted), Birmingham, Manchester, Bristol, Plymouth, Exeter and Newquay. Although there are no direct flights to any of Ireland's airports from Australia and New Zealand, popular connecting points are London and Moscow.

The other airports in the Republic are smaller with fewer regular flights. There are many charter flights for pilgrims to **Knock International Airport**, which also has flights from Dublin, London (Stansted) and Manchester; there are flights into Kerry Airport from Dublin, Luton, Düsseldorf and Munich; Waterford Airport is served by flights from London (Stansted), Luton and Manchester, and at Galway Airport there are twice-daily flights from Dublin.

## GETTING TO AND FROM THE AIRPORT

THE REPUBLIC'S three main airports are all served by regular bus services, whereas the smaller airports depend mainly on local taxi services. An express bus service runs between Dublin Airport and the city's main train and bus stations about every 20 minutes, from early morning to midnight. The journey takes half an hour. At Cork, Bus Éireann provides an express bus service, taking 15 minutes, to get from the airport to the city. Buses run every 45 minutes on weekdays and hourly on the weekends. At Shannon Airport, Bus Éireann has a regular service to Limerick, taking 35 minutes to the city center. Also, several buses a day go to the town of Ennis, about 30 km (18 miles) away. All airports in the Republic have both long- and short-term parking facilities.

**Information signs in the main concourse of Shannon Airport**

**One of the Airlink buses which take passengers from Dublin Airport into the city center**

Passengers checking in at Belfast International Airport

## FLYING TO NORTHERN IRELAND

THERE ARE HOURLY FLIGHTS, operated by either **British Airways** or **British Midland**, from London Heathrow to **Belfast International Airport** (BIA), 30 km (18 miles) northwest of Belfast city center. BIA is also served by flights from Luton and some regional airports like Manchester and Glasgow. There is a daily **KLM** flight from Amsterdam and a weekly **American Trans Air** flight from New York.

**Belfast City Airport** is used by smaller aircraft, but is favored by many because of its location – it is just 6 km (4 miles) from the city center. The airport also has more flights from the UK – around 15 cities plus Gatwick, Stansted and Luton – than BIA. The City of Derry Airport is Northern Ireland's smallest, with one flight daily from Manchester and Glasgow.

## AIRPORT CONNECTIONS IN NORTHERN IRELAND

THE ARRANGEMENTS for getting to and from the airports in Northern Ireland are generally good. BIA's Airbus service will take you from the airport to the Europa Bus-centre via Oxford Street Bus Station and Central Railway Station. This runs every half hour and takes about 30 minutes from end to end. At Belfast City Airport the Number 21 bus passes every half hour, taking around 10 minutes to get to the Belfast City Hall bus depot. There are trains from the airport to Central Station about every 30

minutes. Derry's airport is on a local bus route: the Number 143 goes into the city center every hour (less frequently on weekends). All airports in Northern Ireland have taxi ranks and both long- and short-term parking facilities.

## AIR FARES

AIRLINE OPTIONS between the United States and Ireland are more limited than from the United States to Europe or the UK. In general there are no direct flights from the West Coast and limited nonstop services from the East Coast, so many journeys involve changing carrier at New York or London. For a real bargain try flights from the UK to Ireland via the new London City Airport.

Air fares are at their highest in the peak season from July to September. The best bargains are on flights with fixed dates. It's quite easy to get a round trip flight to Shannon from the East Coast for under $600, but these tickets often restrict your visit to between seven and 30 days. Cheapest flights are between New York and Shannon, with Belfast and Dublin costing as much as $100 more.

Many UK airports service Ireland and airlines offer a host of options on air fares from Great Britain to Ireland. It is easy to get a return flight for less than £100. The cheapest place to fly from is usually London, though fares from Luton and Stansted to both Dublin and Belfast have been particularly low in recent years. Ticket prices increase at Christmas, during the summer season and on bank holidays.

**← Arrivals ↗**
**↑ Shops 🚻 Siopaí**
**Bar 🍴 Beár**
**↑ Snacks ✕ Sólaistí**

**Airport sign in English and Gaelic**

### DIRECTORY

## MAJOR AIRPORTS

**Belfast City Airport**
📞 01232 457745.

**Belfast International**
📞 01849 422888.

**Cork International**
📞 021 313131.

**Dublin Airport**
📞 01 8444900.

**Knock International**
📞 094 67222.

**Shannon Airport**
📞 061 471444.

## AIRLINES WITH FLIGHTS TO IRELAND

**Aer Lingus**
📞 01 7056705.
📞 (800) 223-6537 (US).

**Aeroflot**
📞 061 472299.
📞 (212) 332-1050 (US).

**American Trans Air**
📞 01232 666653 (Northern Ireland).
📞 (800) 221-0924 (US).

**British Airways/BA Express**
📞 (800) 247-9297 (US).
📞 01345 222111 (UK).

**British Midland**
📞 01 2838833.
📞 0345 554554 (UK).

**Delta**
📞 01 6768080 or 1800 768080.
📞 (800) 221-1212 (US).

**KLM**
📞 (800) 374-7747 (US).
📞 020 4747747 (Netherlands).

**Malaysian Airlines**
📞 (212) 697-8994 (US).
📞 0181 7402626 (UK).

**Manx Airlines**
📞 01 2601588.
📞 0345 256256 (UK).

**Qantas**
📞 (800) 227-4500 (US).
📞 02 6913636 (Aus).

**Ryanair**
📞 01 8444411.
📞 0171 4357101 (UK).

**Virgin Atlantic Cityjet**
📞 (800) 862-8621 (US).
📞 01293 747146 (UK).

# Arriving by Sea

Traveling by ferry is a popular way of getting to Ireland, especially for groups or families intending to tour the country by car. Eight ports in Great Britain and four in France provide ferry crossings to Ireland's six ports. All ferries are of the modern drive-on/drive-off variety with lounges, restaurants and, if you're sailing to the Republic, duty-free shops. Crossing the Irish Sea is now faster than ever before, thanks to a new generation of high-speed ferries.

**Logo of Irish Ferries**

both the conventional ferry and the speedier Sea Lynx catamaran-style ferries. Those intending to take a car on Sea Lynx should make sure the measurements of their vehicle, when fully loaded, are within those specified by Stena Sealink. The maximum dimensions allowable per vehicle on Sea Lynx are: height 3 m (10 ft), length 6 m (20 ft) and weight 3 tons.

Irish Ferries operates two crossings to Rosslare from Pembroke all year round, which take about 4½ hours. There are also Irish Ferries services to Rosslare from Le Havre (20 hours), Cherbourg (16½ hours) and Roscoff (15 hours). On all crossings to Rosslare, cabins and berths are available but these should be booked in advance.

**Stena Sea Lynx leaving Dun Laoghaire harbor**

## FERRIES TO DUBLIN AND DUN LAOGHAIRE

There is a good choice of ferry services from Wales to Ireland. **Irish Ferries**, the country's largest shipping company, is the sole operator on the Holyhead–Dublin route and has two crossings a day. Unlike the service to Dun Laoghaire, there is no high-speed service – only the conventional ferry, which takes about 3½ hours. Like most ferry companies, Irish Ferries does not operate on December 25 or 26.

The service from Holyhead to the Dublin suburb of Dun Laoghaire – traditionally the busiest port in Ireland – is operated by **Stena Sealink**. This route is served by conventional ferries and the Stena HSS (High-speed Sea Service) newly introduced into service in September 1995. As the world's largest fast ferry, the HSS has the same passenger and vehicle capacity as the conventional ferries but its jet-engine propulsion gives it twice the speed.

Vehicle loading and unloading times on the Stena HSS are also considerably shorter than with other ferries – the loading time for cars is about 20 minutes as opposed to a

minimum of 30 minutes with most other ferries. Passengers requiring special assistance at ports or on board the ship should contact the company they are booked with at least 24 hours before the departure time. Like most other ferry companies, Irish Ferries and Stena Sealink take bicycles for free, but this should be mentioned when making your reservation.

## FERRIES TO ROSSLARE

Rosslare, in County Wexford, is the main port for crossings from South Wales to Ireland. Stena Sealink runs a service from Fishguard using

## FERRIES TO CORK

The prospect of a 10-hour sea journey could be enough to deter some from taking the ferry to Cork, but for those heading to Southwest Ireland, sailing to the small town of Ringaskiddy, near Cork, can help cut out a cross-Ireland car trip of up to

| FERRY ROUTE | OPERATORS |
|---|---|
| Holyhead–Dun Laoghaire | Stena Sealink |
| Fishguard–Rosslare | Stena Sealink |
| Pembroke–Rosslare | Irish Ferries |
| Stranraer–Belfast | SeaCat Scotland Stena Sealink |
| Stranraer–Larne | Stena Sealink |
| Cairnryan–Larne | P&O European Ferries |
| Swansea–Cork | Swansea Cork Ferries |

Gallery overlooking the quayside at Rosslare harbor

250 miles. During the tourist season, **Swansea Cork Ferries** has up to six crossings per week between the two cities but the service doesn't operate between early January and mid-March. The crossing takes about 10 hours. There are also several routes direct to Cork from France. Between May and September, Irish Ferries operates weekly sailings from Le Havre to Cork, taking about 22 hours, and Roscoff to Cork, which takes

**Directions for ferry passengers**

around 15 hours. Brittany Ferries has a 14-hour Roscoff–Cork service from March to October and an 18-hour St. Malo–Cork crossing during the same period. Cabins and berths are available on routes to Cork but should be booked in advance. There is a small charge for taking bicycles on Swansea Cork Ferries.

## PORT CONNECTIONS

A<small>LL IRELAND'S PORTS</small> have adequate bus and train connections. At Dublin Port, buses are arranged (fare payable) to take all ferry passengers into the city center. From Dun Laoghaire, DART trains run into Dublin every 10 to 15 minutes stopping at Pearse Street, Tara Street and Connolly Stations. These go from the railroad station near the main passenger concourse. Buses run from Dun Laoghaire to Eden Quay and Fleet Street in the city center every 10 to 15 minutes. At all ports, taxis are there to meet arrivals.

Irish Ferries ship loading up at Rosslare Harbour

### DIRECTORY

#### FERRY COMPANIES

**Brittany Ferries**
( 021 277801 (Cork).
( 01752 221321 (UK).
( 98 29 28 00 (France).

**Irish Ferries**
( 01 8552222 (Dublin).
( 0151 2273131 (UK).
( 35 22 50 28 (France).

**Isle of Man Steam Packet Co. Ltd**
( 01624 661661 (Isle of Man).

**Norse Irish Ferries**
( 01232 779090 (Belfast).
( 0151 9441010 (UK).

**P&O European Ferries**
( 1800 409049 (Ireland).
( 0181 5758555 (UK).

**Stena Sealink Line**
( 01 2808844 (Dublin).
( 01233 647047 (UK).

**Swansea Cork Ferries**
( 021 271166 (Cork).
( 01792 456116 (UK).

**SeaCat**
( 01345 523523 (UK).

#### EXPRESS BUS COMPANIES

**Citylink/Ulsterbus**
( 01232 337002 (Belfast).
( 0141 3329191 (UK).

**Eurolines**
( 01 8366111 (Dublin).
( 01582 404511 (UK).

**National Express**
( 0990 808080 (UK).

| ENGTH OF JOURNEY | CROSSINGS TO IRELAND | BUS AND TRAIN CONNECTIONS |
|---|---|---|
| HSS: 1 hr 40 mins<br>Ferry: 3 hrs 30 mins | 6–8 per day | DART train or local bus to Dublin:<br>14 km (9 miles) |
| Sea Lynx: 1 hr 40 mins<br>Ferry: 3 hrs 30 mins | Mid-Jul–mid-Oct: 5–7 per day<br>Mid-Oct–mid-Jul: 2–5 per day | Train or bus to Wexford: 19 km (12 miles);<br>or Dublin: 162 km (101 miles) |
| 4 hrs | 2 per day | Train or bus to Wexford: 19 km (12 miles);<br>or Dublin: 162 km (101 miles) |
| 1 hr 30 mins | Mid-Jun–mid-Sep: 5 per day<br>Mid-Sep–mid-Jun: 4 per day | Local bus to city center: 1 km (0.6 miles) |
| 2 hrs 20 mins | Up to 10 per day | Bus or train to Belfast: 37 km (23 miles) |
| 2 hrs 20 mins | 3–5 per day | Bus or train to Belfast: 37 km (23 miles) |
| 10 hours | Mid-Mar–early Jan: 3–5 per week<br>Early Jan–mid-Mar: no service | Bus to Cork: 18 km (11 miles) |

## FERRIES TO BELFAST AND LARNE

THE FASTEST CROSSING to Northern Ireland is the 90-minute **SeaCat** service from Stranraer to Belfast. This catamaran-style ferry sails four or five times per day, all year round. On the same route, Stena Sealink will introduce the second of their new HSS ferries in spring 1996. The sailing time will be the same as for the SeaCat.

A Liverpool to Belfast service is run by **Norse Irish Ferries**, leaving Liverpool every other evening at 8:30pm and docking around 7am the next day. Crossing the Irish Sea with the **Isle of Man Steam Packet Co.** lets you visit the Isle of Man en route. Leaving from both Liverpool and Heysham, this summer-only service also has the advantage of allowing you to disembark at Dublin and return from Belfast or vice versa. There are two sea routes to Larne – both from ports in Scotland. The ferry service from Stranraer is operated by Stena Sealink, and the route from Cairnryan is served by **P&O European Ferries**. Both of these routes are served by the slower, conventional ferries and take about 140 minutes. In the tourist season there are between 10 and 15 sailings to Larne from Scotland each day.

**Port of Belfast logo**

**Cars and trucks disembarking at Larne Port**

## PORT CONNECTIONS

ALTHOUGH it's only a ten minute walk into the city center from Belfast Port, Flexibus shuttles are available to take ferry passengers into the city center via the Europa Buscentre and Central Railway Station. A regular bus service connects Larne Port to the town's bus station, and from here, buses run every hour into Belfast city center. From Larne Port, there are trains to take ferry passengers to Belfast's Yorkgate and Central railroad stations. At both Belfast and Larne ports, there are usually taxis waiting to meet each arriving ship.

## FARES AND CONCESSIONS

FARES ON FERRY CROSSINGS to Ireland vary dramatically according to the season – prices on certain days during the peak period of mid-June to mid-September can be double those at other times of the year. Prices increase greatly during the Christmas and New Year period, too. It is also advisable to book your journey both ways before departing. Those traveling to ports without a reservation should always check availability before setting out.

Often, the cheapest way for families or groups of adults to travel is to buy a ticket that allows you to take a car plus a maximum number of passengers. At certain times of the

year on particular routes, a round-trip ticket for a car and five adults (two children count as one adult) can cost less than £50. The least expensive crossings are usually those where the passenger must depart and return within a specified period. Fares are normally reduced for midweek, early-morning and late-night travel. Many ferry companies offer discounts for students with an ISIC card *(see p340)* and some have reduced rates for those with InterRail tickets *(see p359)*.

## RAIL AND EXPRESS COACH TICKETS

IT IS POSSIBLE TO TRAVEL from any railroad station in Great Britain to any specified destination in Ireland on a combined sea/rail ticket. This can be bought at most British Rail stations.

**Eurolines** runs an express bus service from about 35 towns in Britain to over 100 destinations in the Republic. **Citylink/Ulsterbus** offers the same service to destinations in Northern Ireland. Tickets for both these coach companies can be booked through **National Express**, which has over 2,000 agents in Great Britain. Travelers from North America, Australia, New Zealand and certain countries in Asia can buy a BritIreland pass. The pass includes round-trip and ferry crossing to Ireland and unlimited rail travel throughout Great Britain and Ireland on any five or ten days in a month.

**Hitchhiker waiting for a lift at Larne Harbour**

# On the Road

ONE OF THE BEST WAYS to see Ireland's magnificent scenery and ancient sites is by car. Driving on the narrow, twisting country roads can be a pleasure; often you don't see another vehicle for miles. It can also be frustrating, especially if you find yourself stuck behind a slow-moving tractor or a herd of cows. If you don't want to take your own vehicle, car rental in Ireland is no problem. All international car-rental firms operate in the Republic and are also well represented in the North. Touring by bicycle is another enjoyable way of seeing the best parts of the island at your own leisurely pace.

**Gaelic road sign instructing motorists to yield or give way**

## TAKING A CAR

IF YOU INTEND to take a rented car across on the ferry *(see pp352–4)* check the car insurance to find out how well you are covered. To prevent a fully comprehensive policy being downgraded to third-party coverage, ask your insurance company for a Green Card. Carry your insurance certificate, Green Card, car registration and, most importantly, a valid driver's license. You should also carry a passport or National ID.

Membership in one of the reputable automobile clubs like the **AA**, **RAC** or **Green Flag National Breakdown** is advisable unless you are undaunted by the prospect of breaking down in remote areas. Nonmembers can join for just the duration of their vacation. Depending on the type of coverage, automobile clubs may offer only limited services in Ireland.

## RENTING A CAR

CAR RENTAL FIRMS do good business in Ireland, so in summer it's wise to book ahead. Car rental – particularly in the Republic – is quite expensive and the best rates are often obtained by renting in advance. Broker companies, such as **Holiday Autos**, uses the major rental companies and will shop around to get you the best deal. Savings can also be made by choosing a fly-drive or even a rail-sail-drive vacation, but always check for hidden extras. Car rental usually includes unlimited mileage plus passenger indemnity insurance and

**One for the road**

coverage for third party, fire and theft, but not damage to the vehicle. If you plan to cross the border in either direction, however briefly, you must tell the rental company, as there may be a small additional insurance premium to be paid.

To rent a car, you must show a full driver's license, which you should have held for two years without violations. Cars are usually rented only to those between ages 23 and 70, but some companies may make exceptions.

## BUYING GASOLINE

UNLEADED GASOLINE and diesel fuel are available almost everywhere in Ireland. Although prices vary from station to station, gas in the Republic is quite expensive. In Northern Ireland it is roughly ten percent cheaper. Almost all gas stations accept VISA and Mastercard, though check before filling up, particularly in rural areas.

## ROAD MAPS

THE ROAD MAP on the inside back cover shows all the towns and villages mentioned in this guide. In addition, each chapter starts with a map of the region showing all the major sights and providing tips on getting around. However, if you plan to do much driving or cycling, you should equip yourself with a more detailed map. Ordnance Survey Holiday Maps are among the best road maps. You can usually get town plans free from tourist offices *(see p338)*. The tourist boards of the Republic and Northern Ireland both issue free lists of suggested routes for cyclists.

**A busy Hertz car-rental desk at Dublin Airport**

The familiar sight of a farmer and cattle on an Irish country road

## RULES OF THE ROAD

E VEN FOR THOSE unused to driving on the left, driving in Ireland is unlikely to pose any great problems. For many, the most difficult aspect of driving on Ireland's roads is getting used to passing on the right and yielding to traffic on the left at traffic circles. On both sides of the border, the wearing of seat belts is required for drivers and all front-seat passengers; where provided, rear seat belts must be worn. All children must have a suitable restraint system. Motorcyclists and passengers must wear helmets. Northern Ireland uses the same Highway Code as Great Britain. The Republic of Ireland's Highway Code is very similar – copies of both are available at bookstores. In Northern Ireland, you will notice some cars carrying a red "R" plate. These identify "restricted" drivers who have passed their driving test within the previous 12 months and have to keep to lower speeds.

## SPEED LIMITS

I N THE REPUBLIC and Northern Ireland the maximum speed limits, which are shown in miles, are more or less the same as those in Britain:
• 30 mph (50 km/h) in built-up areas.
• 60 mph (95 km/h) outside built-up areas.
• 70 mph (110 km/h) on highways.
On certain roads, which are clearly marked, the speed limits are either 40 mph (65 km/h) or 50 mph (80 km/h). Where there is no indication, the speed limit is 60 mph (95 km/h). In the Republic, vehicles towing trailers must not exceed 55 mph (90 km/h) on any road. Speed limits are more strictly enforced in the North than in the Republic.

## ROAD SIGNS

M OST ROAD SIGNS in the Republic are in both Gaelic and English. Ireland is striving toward metrication so all the new-style green and white signs are in kilometers. However, nothing's quite that simple in Ireland, so expect to come across some black-on-white signs showing distances in miles. As in Britain, road signs in the North are always

in miles. One road sign that is unique to the Republic is the "Yield" sign – in the UK this is worded "Give Way." Throughout both the Republic and Northern Ireland, brown signs with white lettering indicate places of historic, cultural or leisure interest.

### SIGNS IN THE REPUBLIC

| | |
|---|---|
| Unprotected quay or river ahead | Junction ahead |
| Children or school ahead | Dangerous curves ahead |

### SIGNS IN NORTHERN IRELAND

**Motorway M1, M2**

Highway direction sign

**Newcastle A 24**

Primary route sign

## ROAD CONDITIONS

N ORTHERN IRELAND'S roads are well surfaced and generally in better condition than those in the Republic, though there are just as many winding stretches requiring extra caution. The volume of traffic, particularly in the South, is much lower than in Britain. On some of the more rural roads you may not come across another driver for miles. Even the major roads can be surprisingly quiet. There are only a few sections of highways in the whole of Ireland, though recent years have seen extensive construction of two-lane highways in the Republic, including rural areas such as County Donegal.

Speed limit signs in mph on a country road in County Cork

## PARKING

PREDICTABLY, in a country with so little congestion, parking is rarely a problem in Ireland. Most towns have at least one free parking lot. Dublin, Belfast and a few other cities have either parking meters or (fairly expensive) parking lots. Parking on the street is allowed, though a single yellow line along the edge of the road means there are some restrictions (there should be a sign nearby showing the permitted parking times). Double yellow lines indicates no parking at any time.

**Parking disk sign**

Disk parking – a version of "pay & display" – operates in most large towns and cities in the Republic of Ireland. Disks can be bought at local newsstands, gas stations, tourist offices and many small shops. In Northern Ireland, almost all towns and villages have Control Zones, which are indicated by large yellow or pink signs. For security reasons, unattended parking in a Control Zone is not permitted at any time of the day.

**Warning sign in Northern Ireland**

## CYCLING

THE QUIET ROADS of Ireland help to make touring by bicycle a real joy. The **Raleigh Rent-a-Bike** network of bike dealers operates a reasonably priced rental scheme throughout Ireland. Also local shops, such as **Rent-a-Bike** in Dublin, rent bikes to tourists and are open at least six days a week. You can often rent a bike in one town and drop it off at another for a small charge. Many dealers can also provide safety helmets, but bring your own lightweight waterproof clothing to help cope with the unpredictable weather. Buses and trains will usually carry bikes for a surcharge.

## SECURITY ROADBLOCKS IN NORTHERN IRELAND

IN THE LATE 1960s, when the Northern Ireland conflicts began, roadblocks were introduced on the roads of the province. These days if you are traveling by road, whether in the center of Londonderry or the remote Sperrin Mountains, you may come across several roadblocks or none at all, depending on the political climate at the time. Checkpoints can be staffed by either the army or the police, who will simply ask for identification. In the unlikely event of being stopped, show your driver's license and insurance certificate or rental agreement when asked and don't make any sudden movements. As long as you are polite, it should be a smooth encounter.

**Cyclists checking their directions in Ballyvaughan, County Clare**

# Traveling by Train

THE REPUBLIC OF IRELAND'S RAILROAD NETWORK is run by **Irish Rail** (Iarnród Éireann) and is state-controlled. The rail network is far from comprehensive and quite expensive, but the trains are generally reliable and comfortable and can be a good way of covering long distances. The service provided by **Northern Ireland Railways** (NIR) is more limited but fares are slightly cheaper. In 1996 the line connecting North to South is being modernized, with high-speed trains taking passengers from Belfast to Dublin in under 95 minutes.

Logo of the Iarnród Éireann InterCity service

## TRAIN SERVICES IN NORTHERN IRELAND

OTHER THAN an express service out to Larne Harbour and a commuter line to Bangor, there are only two main routes out of Belfast: a line westward to Londonderry via Coleraine (for the Giant's Causeway) and Ireland's only cross-border service, operating between Belfast and Dublin six times daily. All trains leave from Central Station except for the Larne Harbour link, which departs from Yorkgate. A new station, Great Victoria Street, opens in September 1995 and intends to bring rail travelers right to the heart of the city's business and shopping district. Bear in mind that there are no baggage room facilities at any of Northern Ireland's train or bus stations.

Platform of Heuston station in Dublin

## TRAIN SERVICES IN THE REPUBLIC OF IRELAND

ALTHOUGH the more rural areas in the Republic of Ireland are not served by railroads, Irish Rail operates a satisfactory service to most of the large cities and towns. Going by rail is probably the fastest and most convenient way of traveling from Dublin to places like Waterford, Cork, Limerick and Galway. However, there are glaring gaps in the rail network; for example, Donegal is totally devoid of train services, so if you are planning to explore the west coast of Ireland using public transportation, you will have to continue westward from towns such as Galway, Sligo, Limerick and Westport using the local bus services.

The two main rail stations in Dublin are Connolly, for trains to the north, northwest and Rosslare, and Heuston, which serves the west, midlands and southwest. These two stations are connected by the No. 90 bus which runs every 10 to 15 minutes and takes a quarter of an hour – traffic permitting. All trains in the Republic of Ireland have standard and super-standard (first-class) compartments. A supplement is charged for all first-class travel. Bicycles can be taken on trains but for this there is a supplement of up to IR£6, depending on the length of the trip. For information on times and routes, InterCity rail timetables are available at most Irish Rail stations and cost around 50p.

## DART SERVICE

THE HANDY electric rail service known as DART (Dublin Area Rapid Transit) serves 25 stations between Howth, County Dublin and Bray, County Wicklow, with several stops in Dublin city center. A Dublin Explorer ticket allows four consecutive days' travel on DART trains as well as Dublin Bus services. Tickets can be purchased at any of the DART Stations. Bikes can be taken on the trains if there is room, but you'll have to pay extra.

**DART** Stáisiún

DART station sign

## DART STATIONS

- ● **HOWTH**
- Sutton
- Bayside
- ● **HOWTH JUNCTION**
- Killbarrack
- Raheny
- Harmonstown
- Killester
- ● **CONNOLLY**
- Tara Street
- ● **PEARSE**
- Lansdowne Road
- Sandymount
- Sydney Parade
- Booterstown
- Blackrock
- Seapoint
- Salthill & Monkstown
- ● **DUN LAOGHAIRE**
- Sandycove & Glasthule
- Glenageary
- Dalkey
- Killiney
- Shankill
- ● **BRAY**

## TICKETS AND FARES

THROUGHOUT IRELAND, train tickets are generally quite expensive, but there are lots of bargain incentive or concessionary passes. Most of these include bus travel, so you can get virtually anywhere in Ireland on one ticket.

The most comprehensive ticket available is the Emerald Card, which can be used on all Irish Rail, Northern Ireland Railways, Dublin Bus and Ulsterbus services. For around IR£100 the Emerald Card gives eight days' unlimited travel in a 30-day period. An eight-day Irish Explorer ticket is slightly cheaper and is valid on all Irish Rail and Bus Éireann transportation. For rail travelers, the Irish Rover ticket can be good value for money. It is valid on all Irish Rail and Northern Ireland Railways trips for five days within a 15-day period.

**The modern ticket office at Belfast's Central Station**

## CONCESSIONS

STUDENTS CAN BUY a Travelsave Stamp *(see p340)* to affix to their ISIC cards for discounts on train fares. F*aircards* give those under 26 a 50 percent discount on Irish Rail one-way tickets, and can be bought from USIT *(see p340).*

Under-26 InterRail passes allow unlimited rail travel for 15 days or one month in the Republic and 25 other European countries. Older travelers can get InterRail Plus 26 cards costing slightly more. However, InterRail cards allow only a one-third discount on Northern Ireland Railways.

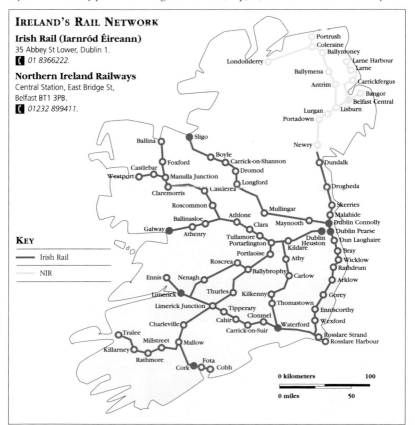

## IRELAND'S RAIL NETWORK

**Irish Rail (Iarnród Éireann)**
35 Abbey St Lower, Dublin 1.
[ *01 8366222.*

**Northern Ireland Railways**
Central Station, East Bridge St,
Belfast BT1 3PB.
[ *01232 899411.*

**KEY**

—— Irish Rail

—— NIR

# Traveling by Bus and Taxi

THE BUS SERVICES THROUGHOUT IRELAND are quite good, for such a rural island. However, longer trips often involve changing buses en route so extra traveling time should be allowed for. Touring by bus is also a good way to see Ireland – local tourist offices have details of tours as well as prices and often take bookings. Taxi services are available in all major cities and towns in Ireland. In the Republic, taxis are usually sedans and are identified by a yellow light on the roof. In the North, cities like Belfast and Londonderry have both minicabs and London-style black cabs.

Boarding a bus at the Europa Buscentre in Belfast

Logo on Bus Éireann local and express buses

## GETTING AROUND BY BUS

THE REPUBLIC OF IRELAND'S national bus company, Bus Éireann, operates a countrywide network of buses serving all the cities and most of the towns. In Dublin, the main bus station is the Busáras on Store Street, a short walk from O'Connell Street. There are also numerous private bus companies that either compete with the national network or provide services on routes not covered by Bus Éireann. In rural Donegal, for example, there are several private bus services. Some are not fully licensed, so it might be best to check whether you would be covered in the unlikely event of an accident. Local tourist offices should be able to point out the most reputable firms.

Ulsterbus runs an excellent service throughout Northern Ireland including express links between all the major towns. Belfast has two main

bus stations – the Europa Buscentre off Great Victoria Street and Oxford Street Station. Check before setting out that you are going to the right one. Note that there are no baggage room facilities at any of the stations in Northern Ireland.

## FARES AND TICKETS

IN THE REPUBLIC, long-distance buses are about half the price of the equivalent rail trip. If you are making the return trip on the same day, ask for a "day-return ticket," which is much cheaper than the normal round-trip fare. Also, between Tuesday and Thursday you can buy a "period" return ticket for the price of a one-way trip. Under 16s pay half the adult fare. Students with a Travelsave stamp *(see p340)* get a 30 percent reduction. For those intending to do a lot of traveling it is best to buy a "Rambler" ticket. This allows unlimited bus travel throughout the Republic for a certain

number of days in a set period, for example, 15 days' travel out of 30 consecutive days.

A "Freedom of Northern Ireland" ticket provides unlimited travel on all Ulsterbus routes for a day or a week. Ulsterbus also offers bargain day-return tickets. Students can get a 15 percent discount by showing their ISIC card. There are also a number of period passes available for all travelers that combine bus and rail travel *(see p359)*.

## BUS TOURS

WHILE THE BUS SERVICES in Ireland are generally adequate for getting from town to town, using public transportation isn't a very practical way of exploring specific areas or regions in great detail – unless you have a lot of spare time. If you find yourself in a remote area like Connemara *(see pp198–201)* but have only a limited amount of time in which to see its main attractions, a local guided tour of the area is a good idea. For about IR£10 per adult you can do the picturesque "figure of eight" circuit by bus, starting from Galway and taking in Spiddal, Kylemore, Letterfrack, Oughterard and then returning to Galway. The bus sets out at 10am and returns around 5:30pm, making regular stops at places of interest. The price does not include admission fees or lunch. Bookings are made at Galway Tourist Information Centre and can be arranged

**Express service bus in Northern Ireland**

in advance or on the day. Four-hour or one-day tours such as this are available in many of Ireland's main tourist areas. Other popular tours of rural Ireland include Glendalough *(see pp132–3)*, Donegal *(see pp216–23)*, and the Ring of Kerry *(see pp156–7)*. In Dublin and other cities in the Republic, Bus Éireann and some local companies run half- and one-day excursions. Dublin Bus (Bus Átha Cliath) runs a Dublin City tour, which leaving from O'Connell Street Upper. This guided tour takes in the city's most famous sights.

In Northern Ireland, Ulsterbus operates a number of tours from the Europa Buscentre in Belfast to all the major places of interest. These tours include the Causeway Coast, the Glens of Antrim, the Ulster-American Folk Park, near Omagh. Ulsterbus prefers bookings to be made in person at their Belfast office rather than over the phone. During the summer, Belfast Citybus operates up to three guided bus tours a week around the city.

### CITY AND LOCAL BUSES

LOCAL BUS SERVICES in cities and large towns throughout the Republic are generally well-run and reasonably priced. Dublin Bus runs all the services in the Greater Dublin area (which includes parts of Wicklow, Kildare and Meath), while city buses in Cork, Galway, Limerick and

**Passengers alighting from a Waterford city bus**

Waterford are operated by Bus Éireann. Buses in Dublin city center run from 6am until 11:30pm. If you're using the bus more than two or three times in a day, it's worth getting a one-day pass, costing around IR£3. In other parts of the Republic the bus services are operated mainly by Bus Éireann. In some places, though, the bus routes connecting towns and villages are served by private companies as well as Bus Éireann. Bus times (and stops) in villages and the more remote places are often best found by asking the locals. All Bus Éireann routes and times can be found in its timetable, which costs 50p and is available at main bus stations.

Except for Belfast, Northern Ireland's bus network is run by Ulsterbus. In the province's capital the comprehensive local service is operated by Citybus. A wide variety of travel passes are available for Citybus and Ulsterbus lines. Regional timetables are available at bus stations.

**Dublin Bus logo**

### TAXIS IN THE REPUBLIC

EXCEPT in the most rural of places, there is usually a local taxi service – your hotel or B&B will provide details. In Dublin, taxis are large sedans. Cruising taxis are a rarity: the best places to find cabs are at train or bus stations, hotels and taxi stands. Prices are based on metered mileage. If your taxi does not have a meter, always ask the fare to your destination.

### TAXIS IN NORTHERN IRELAND

TAXIS IN NORTHERN IRELAND are reasonably priced. Short trips within the center of Belfast usually cost no more than £3 by minicab or black cab. In most decent-sized towns in the North you will find at least one taxi stand where you can line up for a cab. Otherwise, ask for the number of a taxi company at a local hotel or B&B.

---

### DIRECTORY

#### NATIONAL BUS COMPANIES

**Bus Éireann**
( *01 8366111 (including day tour inquiries).*

**Ulsterbus**
( *01232 333000.*
( *01232 337004 (day tours).*

#### CITY BUS COMPANIES

**Dublin Bus**
( *01 8734222 (including day tour inquiries).*

**Belfast Citybus**
( *01232 246485.*
( *01232 458484 (day tours).*

#### BUS TOUR COMPANIES

**Gray Line Tours**
3 Clanwilliam Terrace, Dublin 2.
( *01 6619666.*

**McGeehan Coaches**
Fintown PO, Co Donegal.
( *075 46101.*

**Taxis lined up outside the arrivals building at Dublin Airport**

# General Index

Page numbers in **bold** type refer to main entries.

## A

A-Wear (Dublin) 325
Abbey Theatre (Dublin) **86**, 105
  Dublin's Best: Entertainment 107
  history 42
  Literary Ireland 20–21
  Street-by-Street map 85
Abbeyleix, pubs 321
Abbeys and priories
  Assaroe Abbey (Ballyshannon) 223
  Athassel Priory **190**
  Augustinian Priory (Adare) 186
  Black Abbey (Kilkenny) 136
  Bonamargy Friary 258
  Boyle Abbey 211
  Cahir Abbey 190
  Clare Abbey (Ennis) 181
  Cong Abbey 201
  Donegal Abbey 222
  Duiske Abbey 141
  Dunbrody Abbey 140
  Ennis Friary 181
  Fore Abbey **233**
  Grey Abbey 272
  Holy Cross Abbey **187**
  Hore Abbey 187
  Inch Abbey 273
  Jerpoint Abbey **137**
  Kylemore Abbey **200**
  Mellifont Abbey 33, **237**
  Moore Abbey (Monasterevin) 120
  Muckross Abbey 154
  Portumna Priory 205
  Quin Franciscan Friary 181
  Red Abbey (Cork) 168
  Rock of Cashel **114**
  St. Mary's Abbey (Dublin) **91**
  Selskar Abbey (Waterford) 142
  Sligo Abbey 226
  Timoleague Abbey **162–3**
  Tintern Abbey 140
  *see also* Monasteries
Achill Archaeological Summer
  School 331
Achill Island **196**
  restaurants 313
Act of Union (1800) 38
Adair, John 216
Adams, Gerry 45
Adare 13, **186**
  hotels 294
  restaurants 312
Adare Jazz Festival 46
Adare Manor 284, 302
Admission charges 338
Aer Lingus 350, 351
Aeroflot 351
Aglish, hotels 294
Agricola 31
Ahenny 191
  High Cross 235

Aherlow, Glen of **190**
Aherlow, hotels 294
Aherlow, River 190
Aillwee Cave 180
Air travel 350–51
Aird's Snout 254
Airports
  Belfast City 351
  Belfast International 351
  Cork 351
  Dublin International **350**, 351, 361
  Knock International 351
  Shannon 340, **350**, 351
Albert, Prince Consort 271
Alcock and Brown Memorial 199
Alcohol, duty-free allowances 340
All-Ireland Football Final 27, 48
All-Ireland Hurling Final 27, 48
Allen, Lough 177
Allied Irish Bank (AIB) 346
Allihies 158
Allingham, William 223
Allow, River 169
Altamont, Earls of 197
Altamont, John Browne, 1st Earl 196
Ambulances 342, 343
American Express 347
American Trans Air 351
An Béal Bocht (Dublin restaurant) 105
An Óige 283
*An Taisce* (Irish National Trust) 80
An Tostal 46
Anderson, John 169
Andrews Lane Theatre (Dublin) 105
Anglo-Irish Agreement 45
Anglo-Irish families 117
  The Pale 124
Anglo-Irish Treaty (1921) 42–3
Anglo-Normans **34–5**
  Dublin Castle 71, 74
  invasion of Ireland 29, 117
Animals, wildlife 16–17
Anna Livia Fountain (Dublin) 87
  Street-by-Street map 84
Annalong, hotels 300
*The Annals of the Four Masters* 37
Antrim, County 247
  coastline map 253
  map 248–9
Apprentice boys (Londonderry) 37
Aquariums
  Exploris (Portaferry) 272
Aran Islands 20, **206–7**
  pubs 320
  restaurants 313
Aranmore 220
Áras an Uachtaráin (Dublin) 94
Archaeological holidays 330, 331
Architecture **18–19**
  Georgian terraces **67**
Ardagh 233
Ardagh Chalice 53, 64
Ardara **220**
  hotels 297

Ardboe Cross 260
Ardclinis Activity Centre
  (Cushendall) 335
Ardee
  hotels 299
  restaurants 315
Ardess Crafts Centre (Kesh) 331
Ardfert Cathedral 147, **148**
Ardglass 276
Ardgroom 158
Ardilaun, Lord 58
Ardmore 19, **137**
Ards Peninsula **272**
Argus Rent-a-Car 357
Arkle 121
Armada, French (1796)
  French Armada Centre 160
Armada, Spanish (1588)
  history 36
  treasure 270
  Ulster Museum 270
  wreck 249
Armagh **266**
  Christianity 32
  hotels 300
  restaurants 316
Armagh, County 247
Arrow, Lough 215, **227**
Arsenius, Mother 197
Arts Theatre (Belfast) 331
*Asgard* (ship) 95
Ashford Castle 201, 284
Ashtown Castle (Dublin) 94
Askeaton 176
Assaroe Abbey 223
Association for Adventure Sports 335
Athassel Priory **190**
Athlone 177, **241**
  restaurants 315
Athlone Castle 241
Athlone Cruisers 335
Atlantic Coast Drive
  (Achill Island) 196
Aughnanure Castle 201
Augustinian order 190, 201
Auld Dubliner (Dublin pub) 105
Automobile Association (AA) 357
Autumn in Ireland 48
Avis 357
Avoca 131
Avoca Handweavers (Bray) 131, 325
Avondale Forest Park 133
Avondale House **133**
Avonmore River 130, 133

## B

BA Express 351
Bad Bob's Backstage Bar
  (Dublin) 105
Bagenalstown, hotels 289
Baggot Inn (Dublin) 105
Baily Lighthouse 100
Balgriffin, hotels 288
Balleydehob 159

Ballina 182
  hotels 295
Ballinadee, hotels 291
Ballinafad 227
Ballinasloe Fair 48
Ballincollig 163
Ballinderry River 260
Ballingeary 163
Ballinskelligs 156, 157
Ballintoy 253
Ballsbridge
  hotels 288
  restaurants 307
Ballycastle **258–9**
  restaurants 316
Ballyconneely 199
Ballycopeland Windmill 272
Ballyferriter
  Dingle Peninsula tour 150
  restaurants 310
Ballygally, hotels 300
Ballyhack 140
  restaurants 308
Ballyhack Castle 140
Ballylickey
  hotels 291
  restaurants 310
Ballymacarbry, hotels 289
Ballymaloe School of Cookery 331
  Crawford Art Gallery (Cork) 167
Ballymena, hotels 300
Ballymote, hotels 297
Ballymurn, hotels 289
Ballynahinch, hotels 295
Ballyronan Marina 335
Ballyshannon **223**
  restaurants 314
Ballyshannon International Folk
  Festival 47
Ballyvaughan **180**, 357
  hotels 294
  pubs 319
Baltimore **162**
Banba's Crown 219
Bandon River 165
Bangor 272
  hotels 300
  pubs 321
Bangor, Lord and Lady 276
Bank of Ireland (Dublin) **58**, 346
  Street-by-Street map 56
Banknotes 344–5
Banks 346–7
Banna Strand 148
Bannow Bay 140
Banquets **330**, 331
  Bunratty Castle 184–5, 312
  Knappogue Castle 330
Bansha 190
Banshees 24
Banteer, hotels 291
Bantry 159
  hotels 291
  restaurants 310

Bantry, 1st Earl of (Richard White) 160
Bantry, 2nd Earl of 160, 161
Bantry Bay **159**, 161
Bantry House **160–61**
  hotel 284, 291
Barley Cove 145, 159
Barna, restaurants 313
Barralet, James 99
Barre, WJ 271
Barrow, River 140, 141
Bars, Dublin 104, 105
Battle of the Boyne Day 47
*Beach Scene* (Degas) 89
Beaghmore Stone Circles **260**
Beaker people 30
Bear Island 159
Beara Peninsula **158**
Becket, Thomas à 142
Beckett, Samuel 21, **60**
  Nobel prize 44
  Portora Royal School 264
  Trinity College, Dublin 60
Bed-and-breakfasts 282
Bedell, Bishop 81
Beehive huts 19
Beer
  duty-free allowances 340
  Guinness **96–7**
  Guinness Hop Store (Dublin) **96**
Begging 342
Behan, Brendan 21
  Abbey Theatre 102
  Dublin's pubs 104
  McDaid's (Dublin) 107
Beit, Sir Alfred 124, 125
Beit Art Collection (Russborough
  House) 124–5
Belcoo Archaeology Summer
  School 331
Belfast 247, **268–71**
  Albert Memorial Clocktower 271
  Botanic Gardens 270
  buses 360
  Cave Hill 271
  City Hall 268
  Crown Liquor Saloon 269
  The Entries 269
  ferries 354
  Giant's Ring 271
  Grand Opera House 268
  hotels 300
  Lagan Weir Lookout 271
  Linen Hall Library 269
  map 268–9
  personal safety 343
  political murals 270
  pubs 321
  Queen's University 270
  railway station 359
  restaurants 316
  St. Anne's Cathedral 268
  Stormont 271
  Ulster Museum 270
  Visitors' Checklist 269

Belfast Castle 271
Belfast City Airport 351
Belfast Citybus 361
Belfast Civic Festival and Lord
  Mayor's Show 46
Belfast Festival at Queen's 48, 331
Belfast International Airport 351
Belfast Lough 267, 271
Belfast Music Festival 49
*Belfast Newsletter* 38
Bellaghy 37
Belleek 261
  Lower Lough Erne tour 262
  restaurants 316
Belleek Pottery **261**, 323
Belltable Arts Centre (Limerick) 331
Belmore, 1st Earl of 264
Belvedere, 1st Earl of 241
Belvedere College (Dublin) 88
Belvedere House 241
Ben Bulben 114
  Yeats Country tour 224
Benbaun 200
Benedictine order
  Fore Abbey 233
  Holy Cross Abbey 187
  Kylemore Abbey 200
  St. Mary's Abbey (Dublin) 91
Bennettsbridge 136
Benone Strand **252**
Bernard, St. 237
Bewley's Oriental Café (Dublin)
  58, 325
  Street-by-Street map 56
Bianconi, Charles 40, 191
Bicycles **357**
  cycling holidays **333**, 335
  on trains 358
  renting 335
Bike Store (Dublin) 335
Birds
  The Burren 178
  Castle Caldwell Forest Park 262
  Connemara 200
  Saltee Islands 143
  The Skelligs 156–7
  Wexford Wildfowl Reserve 142
Birr **245**
  hotels 299
Birr Castle 231, 245
Bishop's Quarter 180
Black Castle 187
Black Death 35, 77
Black Head 180
Black, Mary 15, 22
Black and Tans 42
Blackrock Castle 169
Blackwater, River 137, **169**
Blanket bog 17, 244
Blarney Castle 147, **163**
Blarney House 163
Blarney, restaurants 310
Blarney Stone 147, **163**
Blarney Woollen Mills 325

Blasket Centre
  Dingle Peninsula tour 150
Blasket Islands 20, 150, 151
Blennerville Windmill (Tralee)
  148, **149**
Blessing of the Sea 47
Blessington 125, 341
  hotels 289
Bloody Foreland 213, **216**
Bloody Sunday (1972) 44
Bloomsday 21, 46
Blues music, Dublin 103, 105
Boa Island 24
  Lower Lough Erne tour 262
Boats
  cruising and sailing **334**, 335
  *currachs* 206
  ferries 352–4
  Galway hookers 203
*Bodhrán* (drum) 22, 323, 326
Bog of Allen 120, 244
Bogs 17, **244**
  Peatland World 120
  Shannonbridge Bog Railway 243
Bolton, Thomas 64
Bonamargy Friary (Ballycastle) 258
Bonet (gardener) 125
*Book of Durrow* 32, 53, 61
*Book of Kells* **62**, 233
Books
  shops **323**, 325
  What to Buy in Ireland 327
Booterstown, hotels 288
Bord Fáilte 331, **338**, 339
Bosco, Don 198
Bourchier's Castle 187
Boycott, Captain 40
Boyle **211**
Boyle Abbey 211
Boyle family 80
  monument 81
Boyne, Battle of the (1690) 29, **236**
  history 36–7
  Talbot family 100
  tapestry 36
Boyne, River 231, 236, 240
Boyne Valley 229, **236–7**
Brandon Mountain 25, 150
Bray 119, **125**
Bray Head 125
Brazen Head (Dublin pub) 105
Breakfast 302
  Ulster fry 304
Brecan, St 206
Brendan, St. **25**
  Ardfert Cathedral 148
  Clonfert Cathedral 205
  replica boat 182
  voyages 205
Breweries *see* Beer
Brian Boru 32–3, 77
  grave of 266
Bricin (Killarney) 325
Bricklieve Mountains 227

Brigid, St. 120
Bristol, Frederick Augustus Hervey,
  Earl of 252
British Airways 351
British Commonwealth 44
British Horse Society 335
British Midland 351
British Telecom 349
Brittany Ferries 353
Broighter gold boat **31**, 64
Bronze Age 30, 64
Brooke, Sir Basil 222
Brown, Capability 237
Brown Thomas (Dublin) 324, 325
Browne family 197
Browne's Hill Dolmen **133**
Brú Ború *see* Brian Boru
Brú Ború Heritage Centre, Cashel 187
Bruce, Edward 34, 267
Bruce, Robert, King of Scotland 258
Bruce's Cave (Rathlin Island) 258
Bruckless, hotels 297
Bryce, Annan 159
Buite, St. 234
Budget (car hire) 357
Budget restaurants 303
Buncrana
  Inishowen Peninsula tour 218
Buncrana Castle 218
Bundoran 222, 334
Bunglass Point 221
Bunnow, River 187
Bunratty
  pubs 319
  restaurants 312
Bunratty Castle **184–5**
Bunratty Folk Park 185
*Bureaux de change* 344, **347**
Burges, William 167
Burgh, Thomas 75
Burgh, William de 190
Burke, Éamonn 35
Burke, Edmund 60
Burne-Jones, Sir Edward 137
The Burren **178–80**
  map 180
Burtonport 220
Bus Éireann 361
Buses **360–61**
  airport 350
  bus tours 360–61
  through-tickets 354
Bushmills
  Old Bushmills Distillery **258**
  pubs 321
  What to Buy in Ireland 327
Butler family (Earls of Ormonde)
  117, 173
  Cahir Castle 190
  Clonmel 191
  Kilkenny 134
  Kilkenny Castle 115, 136

Butler family (cont)
  Ormond Castle 191
  Swiss Cottage (Cahir) 190–91
  tombs 136
Butler's Bridge, restaurants 315
Butler's Irish Hand-made Chocolates
  (Dublin) 325

## C

Cadamstown 245
Caha Mountains 158, 161
Cahirciveen
  Ring of Kerry tour 156
Cahermore Stone Fort 180
Cahir **190–91**
  restaurants 312
Cahir Abbey 190
Cahir Castle 190
Cahir, Lord and Lady 190
Caldragh cemetery 262
Camcor, River 245
Camogie 27
Camping 282–3
Canals
  Dublin **99**
  Waterways Visitors' Centre
  (Dublin) 99
Canova, Antonio, *The Three
  Graces* 169
Cappoquin
  hotels 289
  restaurants 308
Car rental 355
Caragh Lake, hotels 291
Caravaggio, *The Taking of Christ*
  53, 69
Caravans 282–3
  horse-drawn 283
Carbery's Hundred Isles 162
Carleton (William) Summer School
  (Dungannon) 331
Carlingford 229, **234**
  hotels 299
  pubs 321
  restaurants 315
Carlingford Lough 234
Carlow, County 117
Carlow, restaurants 308
Carndonagh Cross
  Inishowen Peninsula tour 218
Carnlough harbor 259, 334
Carnlough, hotels 300
Carrick (Co Donegal) 221
Carrick-a-rede
  rope bridge 247, 253
Carrickfergus 267
Carrickfergus Castle **34–5**, 267
Carrickmacross, restaurants 315
Carrick-on-Shannon 177, **227**
  Carrick Theatre Festival 48
Carrick-on-Suir 191
Carrigafoyle Castle **148**
Carrigglas Manor **232–3**
Carrignacurra Castle 163

Carrowkeel Passage Tomb Cemetery
215, 227
Carrowmore Megalithic Cemetery 226
Cars **355–7**
 breakdown and recovery services
 355, 357
 buying gasoline 355
 parking 357
 renting **355**, 357
 road conditions 356
 road maps 355
 road signs 356
 rules of the road 356
 security roadblocks 357
 speed limits 356
 taking a car from Britain 355
 *see also* Tours by car
Carson, Edward (Lord Carson) 42
 statue of 271
 tomb of 268
Casement, Roger 148
Cash dispensers 346
Cashel **187**
 hotels 294
 restaurants 312
 Rock of Cashel 114, 187, **188–9**
Cashel Bay, hotels 295
Cashels (stone forts) 19
Castle Archdale Country Park
 Lower Lough Erne tour 263
*Castle of Bentheim* (Ruisdael) 69
Castle Caldwell Forest Park
 Lower Lough Erne tour 262
Castle Clinton 40
Castle Coole 19, 264
Castle Inn (Dublin) 105
Castle Matrix 176
Castle, Richard 19
 Belvedere House 241
 Conolly's Folly, Castletown
 House 123
 Leinster House (Dublin) 63
 Powerscourt 126
 Rotunda Hospital (Dublin) 84, 88
 Russborough House 39, 124
 Strokestown Park House 210
 Westport House 197
Castle Ward 276
Castle Ward Opera 47
Castlebaldwin
 hotels 297
 restaurants 314
Castledermot, hotels 289
Castlereagh, Lord 274, 275
Castles
 Anglo-Norman 34–5
 Ashford Castle 201
 Ashtown Castle (Dublin) 94
 Athlone Castle 241
 Aughnanure Castle 201
 Ballyhack Castle 140
 Belfast Castle 271
 Birr Castle 245
 Black Castle 187

Castles (cont)
 Blackrock Castle 169
 Blarney Castle 147, **163**
 Bourchier's Castle 187
 Buncrana Castle 218
 Bunratty Castle **184–5**
 Cahir Castle 190
 Carrickfergus Castle **34–35**, 267
 Carrigafoyle Castle 148
 Carrignacurra Castle 163
 Castle Matrix 176
 Desmond Castle 164
 Doe Castle 217
 Donegal Castle 222
 Dublin Castle 52, **74–5**
 Dunguaire Castle 204
 Dunluce Castle 253
 Dunseverick Castle 253
 Dysert O'Dea 181
 Enniscorthy Castle 141
 Enniskillen Castle 264
 Glenveagh Castle 216
 Green Castle 277
 Hillsborough Castle 273
 Howth Castle 100
 Johnstown Castle **142–3**
 Jordan's Castle 276
 Kilclief Castle 276
 Kilkenny Castle 115, **136**
 Kinbane Castle 253
 King John's Castle
 (Carlingford) 234
 King John's Castle (Limerick) 183
 Knappogue Castle 181
 Kylemore Abbey 200
 Leamaneagh Castle 180
 Lismore Castle 137
 Malahide Castle 100
 Monea Castle 263
 O'Doherty Castle 218
 Ormond Castle 191
 Parke's Castle **225**, 338
 Portumna Castle 205
 Rathlannon Castle 143
 Reginald's Tower (Waterford) 138
 Rock of Dunamase 245
 Roscommon Castle 210
 Roscrea Castle 187
 Ross Castle 154
 Slade Castle 140
 Slane Castle 237
 tower houses 18–19
 Trim Castle 240
 Tully Castle 262
 Tullynally Castle 233
Castletown House **122–3**
 stucco 19, 117
Castletownbere 158
Castletownshend, restaurants 310
Castlewellan Forest Park 276
Cathedrals
 Ardfert 147, **148**
 Christ Church (Dublin) 52,
 72, **78–9**

Cathedrals (cont)
 Christchurch (Waterford) 138
 Clonfert **205**
 Down (Downpatrick) 273
 Glendalough 132
 Holy Trinity (Waterford) 138
 Rock of Cashel 189
 St. Aidan's (Enniscorthy) 141
 St. Anne's (Belfast) 268
 St. Brigid's (Kildare) 120–21
 St. Canice's (Kilkenny) 136
 St. Carthage (Lismore) 137
 St. Colman's (Cobh) 170
 St. Columb's (Londonderry)
 250, **251**
 St. Declan's (Ardmore) 137
 St. Eunan's (Letterkenny) 219
 St. Finbarr's (Cork) 167
 St. Flannan's (Killaloe) 182
 St. John's (Limerick) 183
 St. Macartan (Monaghan) 232
 St. Mary's (Limerick) 183
 St. Mary's Pro-Cathedral (Dublin)
 85, **87**
 St. Nicholas (Galway) 202
 St. Patrick's (Armagh) 266
 St. Patrick's (Dublin) 52, **80–81**
 St. Patrick's (Trim) 240
 *see also* Churches in Dublin
Catholic Church 14
 Battle of the Boyne 236
 emancipation 39
 Protestant conquest 36–7
Catholic Emancipation Act 40
Catholic University of Ireland 59
Causeway Coast 247, **253**
Cavan, County 229
Caves
 Aillwee Cave 180
 Bruce's Cave (Rathlin Island) 258
 Dunmore Cave 136
 Marble Arch Caves 265
Céide Fields **196**
Celestine, Pope 273
Celtic Cycling (Bagenalstown) 335
Celtic Journeys (Ballycastle) 335
Celts
 Celtic heritage 24–5
 Christianity 32–3
 High Crosses 235
 history 30–31
Central Fisheries Board 335
Ceramics
 Belleek Pottery 261
 shops **323**, 325
 What to Buy in Ireland 327
Chambers, Sir William
 Castletown House 122
 Marino Casino (Dublin) 98
 Trinity College, Dublin 60
Charlemont, 1st Earl of 39, 98
Charles II, King of England 210
Charles Fort 164
Charlotte, Queen 160

Cheeses 305
Chester Beatty, Sir Alfred 99
Chester Beatty Library and Gallery of Oriental Art (Dublin) **99**
Chesterfield, Lord 94
The Chieftains 15, 22
Children of Lir 25
*Children of Lir* (Kelly) 89
Children, in restaurants 302
Children's Cultural Centre (Dublin) 76
China shops **323**, 325
Christ Church Cathedral (Dublin) 52, **78–9**
  Street-by-Street map 72
Christianity
  Celtic 32–3
  St. Patrick 29
Churches
  religious services 339
  *see also* Cathedrals
Churches in Dublin
  Church of the Most Holy Trinity 74, 75
  St. Ann's 56, **59**
  St. Audoen's **77**
  St. Audoen's Roman Catholic Church 77
  St. Michan's Church **90**
  St. Werburgh's 72, **75**
  University Church 59
  Whitefriar Street Carmelite Church **81**
Ciaran, St. 242
CIE 76
Cigarettes, duty-free allowances 340
Cinema *see* Films
Cistercian order 33
  Assaroe Abbey 223
  Boyle Abbey 211
  Duiske Abbey 141
  Holy Cross Abbey 187
  Hore Abbey 187
  Inch Abbey 273
  Jerpoint Abbey 137
  Mellifont Abbey 237
  Portumna Priory 205
  St. Mary's (Dublin) 91
  Tintern Abbey 140
City Art Centre (Dublin theater) 105
City Hall (Dublin) **75**
  Street-by-Street map 72
Citylink 353
Civil War 42, 43
Cladagh River 265
Claddagh Records (Dublin) 325
Clan na Gael 41
Clancy (Willie) Summer School (Miltown Malbay) 331
Clannad 15
Clara, Vale of *see* Vale of Clara
Clare Abbey 181
Clare, County 173
Clare Island **198**

Clare, Richard de *see* Strongbow
Clarecastle, hotels 294
Clarendon 81
Clarinbridge
  pubs 320
  restaurants 313
Clarke, Harry, *The Meeting of St. Brendan and the Unhappy Judas* 166, 167
Clarke, Tom 43
Clear Island 159, 162
Cleggan 199
Clements family 227
Clery's (Dublin shop) 325
Clifden **198–9**
  hotels 295–6
  pubs 320
  restaurants 313
Cliffs of Magho 262
Cliffs of Moher **176**, 180
Climate 46–9
Clochán na Carraige 206
Clogher Head 150
Clonakilty **162**, 282
  hotels 291
  pubs 319
Clonakilty Folk Club 328
Clonalis House **210**
Clonea, hotels 289
Clones, hotels 299
Clonfert Cathedral **205**
Clonmacnoise **242–3**
  Nuns' Church 33, 230
  Temple Finghin round tower 229
Clonmacnoise Crozier 33
Clonmel **191**
  hotels 294
  restaurants 312
Clontarf, Battle of (1014) 32, 33
  Viking in Dublin 77
Clothes
  in restaurants 302
  shops **324**, 325
  What to Buy in Ireland 326
Coastguards 342
Coasts 16
Cobh **170–71**
Coins 344–5
Cole family 265
Coleraine 252
Collins, Michael 43
Collooney
  hotels 297
  restaurants 314
Colman, St. 198, 204
Colmcille Heritage Centre 217
Colmcille, St. *see* Columba, St.
Colthurst family 163
Columba, St. (Colmcille) 32
  Glencolumbkille 220
  Kells Monastery 233
  Londonderry 250, 251
  Tory Island 216

Columbanus, St. 32
Columbus, Christopher 205
Comeragh Mountains 191
Comhaltas Ceoltóirí Éireann (Monkstown) 331
Comyn, John, Archbishop of Dublin 80
Condoms 343
Cong **201**
  hotels 296
  restaurants 313
Cong Abbey 201
Connaught 177, 193
Connemara 193
  map 199
Connemara Marble Factory (Moycullen) 325
Connemara National Park 114, **200**, 339
Connemara ponies 200, 201
Connolly, James 43, 95
Connolly, Katherine 123
Conolly, William 122
Conolly's Folly, Castletown House 123
Conversion chart 341
Cook, Alan 260
Cook, Thomas 347
Cookery holidays 331
Cookstown 260
Coole Park 205
Cooley Peninsula 229, 234
Cooley, Thomas 75
Copeland Islands 272
Cork **166–9**
  Blackrock Castle 169
  Butter Exchange 166
  Cork City Gaol 167
  Crawford Art Gallery 166–7
  Dunkathel House 169
  ferries 352–3
  hotels 291–2
  map 166–7
  pubs 319
  the Quays 168
  restaurants 310
  Royal Gunpowder Mills 169
  St. Ann's Shandon 166
  St. Finbarr's Cathedral 167
  Visitors' Checklist 167
Cork Airport 351
Cork Choral Festival 46
Cork, County 145
Cork, Earls of 80, 171
Cork Film Festival 48, 331
Cork Jazz Festival 48, 329, 331
Cork, Katherine Boyle, Countess of 80
Cork and Kerry **145–71**
  hotels 291–3
  pubs 319
  restaurants 310–12
Cork Regatta Week 27, 47
Cormac's Chapel (Cashel) 33

Corrib, Lough **201**
Corrib, River 202, 282
Corrigan, Mairead 45
Costello, Edward 227
Costello, John A 44
Cottages 18
Country house accommodation 280–81
Country houses 19
  Avondale House 133
  Bantry House **160–61**, 284, 291
  Belvedere House 241
  Blarney House 163
  Carrigglas Manor **232–3**
  Castle Coole 264
  Castle Ward 276
  Castletown House 117, **122–3**
  Clonalis House **210**
  Derrynane House 156
  Dunkathel House 169
  Emo Court **245**
  Florence Court **265**
  Glin Castle 176
  Johnstown Castle **142–3**
  Killruddery House **125**
  Lissadell House **223**, 224
  Mount Stewart House 115, 272, **274 5**
  Muckross House 151
  Parke's Castle **225**
  Powerscourt 115, **126–7**
  Puxley Mansion 158
  Russborough House **124–5**
  Strokestown Park House **210–11**
  Talbot Castle 240
  Westport House 194, 196–7
Country music **329**, 331
  Dublin 103, 105
Countryside Tours (Rathdrum) 335
County Wexford Strawberry Fair 47
County Wicklow Garden Festival 46, 331
Courbet, Gustave 89
Courcy, John de 34, 267, 273
Covered Market (Dublin)
  Street-by-Street map 73
Crafts
  cultural holidays 331
  shops **323**, 325
  What to Buy in Ireland 326–7
Crafts Council of Ireland (Dublin) 325
Craftsworks Gallery (Belfast) 325
Craggaunowen **182**
Cramillion, Bartholomew 88
The Cranberries 15
Crannogs 19, **31**
Crawford Art Gallery (Cork) 331
Crawford, William Horatio 166
Crawfordsburn, hotels 300
Cré Irish Porcelain (Galway) 325
Credit cards 322, 346
Crime 342–3
Croagh Patrick **197**
Crohy Head 220

Croke Park (Dublin) 335
Crolly, pubs 321
Cromwell, Oliver
  destruction of buildings 18
  history 36
  Macroom Castle 163
  sacks Galway 202
  sacks Kilkenny 136
  siege of Drogheda 37, 236
Crookhaven 159
Cross of Cong 65, 201
Crossdoney, hotels 299
Crosses see High Crosses
Crossmolina, hotels 296
Cruinniú na mBad 47
Cruising **334**, 335
Crystal
  shops **323**, 325
  Waterford Crystal **139**, 325
  What to Buy in Ireland 327
Cuchulainn **20**, 24, 87
Cuilcagh Mountains 265
Cultural holidays **330**, 331
Culture 15
Cumann na nGaedheal 43
*Currachs* (rowing boats) 206
Curragh racecourse 26, 121
Currency 344–5
Curtain walls 19
Cushendall 259
Custom House (Dublin) 53, 83, **86**
  history 39
  Street-by-Street map 85
Customs allowances 340
Cycling see Bicycles

**D**

*Dáil Éireann* **63**
  history 42
  Mansion House (Dublin) 59
Dalkey **101**
Dalkey Island 101
Dan O'Hara's Homestead (Lettershea) 199
Dance **329**, 331
  Dublin 103, 105
  traditional 23, **329**, 331
D'Arcy, John 198, 199
Dargle, River 130
DART rail service 93, 358
Davitt, Michael 41
Davy Byrne's (Dublin pub) 105
Dawson, Joshua 59
De Burgo family 205
De Burgo, Richard 205
De Lorean car factory 45, 272
De Valera, Eamon **43**, 59
  Anglo-Irish Treaty 42
  elected as President 44
  imprisonment 95
de Vos, Paul
  *The Boar Hunt* 123
Deane, Sir Thomas 63, 64
Declan, St. 137

Deerfield (Dublin) 94
Degas, Edgar 69
  *Beach Scene* 89
Delaney, Edward 59
Delphi 195
Delphi Lodge (Connemara) 280, 284
Delta (airline) 351
Department of Agriculture 335
Department stores 325
Derg, Lough 175, 177, 182, **222**
Derg Line Cruisers (Killaloe) 335
Derry see Londonderry
Derrynane House
  Ring of Kerry tour 156
Derryveagh Mountains **216–17**
DESIGNyard (Dublin) 76
Desmond Castle (Kinsale) 164
Desmond, Earls of 187
Desmond family, 191
Desmond rebellion 36
Devenish Island 33, **263**
  Lower Lough Erne tour 263
Devil's Glen 131
Devil's Punchbowl 131
Devonshire, Duke of 137
Dialling codes 348
Diamond Hill 200
Dingle **149**
  Dingle Peninsula tour 151
  hotels 292
  pubs 319
  restaurants 310
Dingle Peninsula
  tour of **150–51**
  wildlife 16
Dinis Island 154
Disability Action 341
Disabled travelers 340
  hotels 283
  sports **334**, 335
Discounts
  students 340
  travel concessions 359
Dixon, James 216
Doaghbeg 217
Doctors 342
Doe Castle 217
Doheny and Nesbitt (Dublin pub) 105
Dolmens 30
  Browne's Hill **133**
  Carrowmore Megalithic Cemetery 226
  Leganannny Dolmen 276
  Poulnabrone Dolmen 180
Dominican order 34, 205, 226
Donaghadee 272
Donegal **222**
  hotels 298
Donegal Abbey 222
Donegal Castle 222
Donegal Craft Village 222
Donegal, County 213
Donnybrook, hotels 289

Doolin 176, 180
  pubs 320
  restaurants 312
Doolin Crafts Gallery (Doolin) 325
Dooney Rock
  Yeats Country tour 225
Down, County 247
  map 248–9
Downhill Castle 252
Downpatrick 273
Dowth 236, **237**
Doyle, Roddy 21, 303
Drink *see* Food and drink
Drogheda **236**
  hotels 299
  siege of (1649–52) 37
Drogheda, Earls of 120
Dromahair 236
Drombeg Stone Circle **162**
Druid Theatre (Galway) 328, 331
Druids 24
Druid's Circle (Kenmare) 158
Drumcliff
  hotels 298
  Yeats Country tour 224
Drumlane **232**
Dublin **51–111**
  *Book of Kells* **62**
  buses 360, 361
  canals 99
  Christ Church Cathedral **78–9**
  DART rail service 93, 358
  Dublin Castle **74–5**
  entertainments 102–7
  Farther Afield 92–101
  ferries 352
  Georgian terraces 67
  hotels 286–9
  maps *see Maps*
  millennium 45
  National Gallery **68–9**
  National Museum **64–5**
  North of the Liffey 82–91
  restaurants 306–8
  shops 322
  Southeast Dublin 54–69
  Southwest Dublin 70–81
  train services 358
  Trinity College **60–61**
Dublin Airport 361
Dublin Bus 361
Dublin Castle **52**
  Street-by-Street map 72
Dublin Civic Museum **75**
  Street-by-Street map 73
Dublin Exhibition (1853) 41
Dublin Film Festival 49, 105
Dublin Horse Show 27, 47
Dublin International Airport **350**, 351
Dublin Literary Pub Crawl 105
Dublin Marathon 27
Dublin Theatre Festival 48, 105
Dublin Writers Museum 19, **89**
The Dubliners 103

Dublinia **77**
  Street-by-Street map 72
Duiske Abbey 141
Duleek, hotels 299
Dún Aonghasa 206
Dún Duchathair 207
Dún Eochla 207
Dún Eoghanachta 206
Dun Laoghaire **100–101**
  ferries 352
  restaurants 307
Dunamase, Rock of *see* Rock of
  Dunamase
Dunbeg Fort
  Dingle Peninsula tour 151
Dunbrody Abbey 140
Duncannon 140
Dundalk **234**
  County Museum 234
  restaurants 315
Dundrum
  Mourne Coast tour 277
  restaurants 317
Dunfanaghy 217
Dungannon **265**
  hotels 301
  restaurants 317
Dungarvan, restaurants 308
Dungloe 220
Dunguaire Castle 204
Dunkathel House 169
Dunkineely, hotels 298
Dunloe, Gap of *see* Gap of Dunloe
Dunluce Castle 253
Dunmore Cave 136
Dunmore East 117, **140**
  hotels 289
  pubs 318
Dunmore Head 151
  Dingle Peninsula tour 150
Dunquin, pubs 319
Dunraven, Earls of 186
Dunree Head
  Inishowen Peninsula tour 218
Dunseverick Castle 253
Durrus, restaurants 310
Dursey Island 158
Duty-free goods 340
DV Diving (Newtownards) 335
Dwyer, Michael 131
Dysert O'Dea 173, **181**
  High Cross 235

**E**
Earhart, Amelia 251
Eason and Son (Dublin) 325
Easter Rising (1916) **42–3**
  flag 64
  Garden of Remembrance
    (Dublin) 89
  General Post Office 84, **87**
  O'Connell Street 84
Edgeworth, Maria 20
Edwards, Hilton 88

Eida, Minoru 121
Eida, Tassa 121
Éire 43
Elegant Ireland 283
Elizabeth I, Queen of England
  171, 247
  and Grace O'Malley 198
  Trinity College, Dublin 60
Embassies 341
Emerald Card 359
Emerald Star (Dublin) 335
Emergency numbers 342
Emigration 40–41, **170**
  Ulster-American Folk Park 261
Emmet, Robert 58, **75**
  grave 90
  imprisonment 95
  uprising 40
Emo Court 19, 39, **245**
Enda, St. 206
Ennel, Lough 241
Ennis **181**
  pubs 320
  restaurants 312
Enniscoe House (Castle Hill) 281
Enniscorthy **141**
  pubs 318
Enniscorthy Castle 141
Enniskerry 131
  hotels 289
Enniskillen **264**
  hotels 301
  Lower Lough Erne tour 263
  pubs 321
  Remembrance Day bombing 45
  restaurants 317
Enniskillen Castle 264
Enniskillen, William Cole, 1st Earl
  of 265
Ennistimon, pubs 320
Ensor, John 66, 88
Entertainment **328–35**
  banquets **330**, 331
  booking tickets **328**, 331
  classical music, opera and dance
    **329**, 331
  cultural holidays **330**, 331
  Dublin 102–7
  festivals **330**, 331
  information sources **328**, 331
  major venues **328**, 331
  rock, jazz and country **329**, 331
  theater **328**, 331
  traditional music and dance
    **329**, 331
Equestrian Holidays Ireland
  (Dublin) 335
Erne, Lough 227
  Lower Lough Erne tour **262–3**
Erne Marine (Enniskillen) 335
Erne, River 16, 223, 232, 264
Errigal Mountain 216
Ethnic restaurants 302–3
Eurocheques 322, 347

EuroDollar 357
Eurolines 353
Europcar/InterRent 357
European Union 14, 44
European Youth Card (EYC) 340
Everyman Palace Theatre (Cork) 331
Exclusively Irish (Dublin) 325
Exploris (Portaferry) 272
Eyeries 158

### F

Fair Head 259
Fairies 24
Fairyhouse 26
Falcarragh 213
Famine see Great Famine
Fanad Peninsula 217
Farmhouse accommodations 282
Farrell, Michael 89
Fashion shops 324, 325
Fast foods 303
Feakle 173
  hotels 294
Feakle Traditional Music Weekend
  329, 331
The Feast of St. Kevin amid the ruins
  of Glendalough (Peacock) 29
Fechin, St. 201, 233
Feis Ceoil 46
Fenian risings 41
Fergus, River 181
Fermanagh, County 247
Fermoy 169
Ferries 352–4
  Ballyhack 119
  Killimer 174, 176
Ferrycarrig 142
Ferrycarrig Bridge, restaurants 308
Festivals 15, 46–9, 330, 331
Fianna 24–5
Fianna Fáil 15, 43
Field, John 75
Films 21
  Dublin 104, 105
  festivals 48, 49
Finbarr, St. 163, 166
Fine Gael 15, 43
Finn MacCool 24–5
  Giant's Causeway 115, 254–5
  Lough Neagh 266
Fire services 342, 343
First Trust Bank 346
Fish and chips 303
Fishing 49, 332, 335
  The Sporting Year 26
Fitzgerald family 117, 173, 176
Fitzgerald, Lord Edward 75
Fitzgerald, "Silken Thomas" 36, 77, 91
Fitzgibbon, Marjorie
  statue of James Joyce 85
Fitzmaurice, Thomas 148
Fitzwilliam Square (Dublin) 66
Five Nations Rugby Tournament
  26, 49

Fivemile Town, hotels 301
Fleadh Cheoil (Monkstown) 331
Fleadh Nua 46
"Flight of the Earls" 247
"Flight of the Wild Geese" 173
Florence Court 265
Flying Boat Museum, Foynes 176
Foley, John
  The Houseless Wanderer 68
  monument to Daniel O'Connell 85
  statue of Edmund Burke 60
  statue of Henry Grattan 58
Folklore 24–5
Food and drink
  fast foods 303
  fish and chips 303
  Guinness 96–7
  picnics 303
  pubs and bars 104, 105
  shops 324, 325
  What to Buy in Ireland 327
  What to Eat in Ireland 304–5
  see also Pubs; Restaurants
Football Association of Ireland
  26, 335
Football (soccer) 26–7, 332
For the Road (J Yeats) 68
Fore Abbey 233
Forgotton Cotton (Cork) 325
Forts (Iron Age) 18–19
  Cahermore Stone Fort 180
  Dún Aonghasa 206
  Dún Duchathair 207
  Dún Eochla 207
  Dunbeg Fort 151
  Grianán of Aileach 218, 219
  Hill of Tara 240
  Lisnagun Ring Fort 162
  Navan Fort 266
  Staigue Fort 156
Forts (modern)
  Charles Fort 164
  Elizabeth Fort (Cork) 168
  Hillsborough Fort 273
Fota Wildlife Park and Arboretum
  170–71
Four Courts (Dublin) 90–91
Foxford 197
Foxford Woollen Mills 197
Foyle, Lough 219
Foyle, River 36, 53, 250, 251
Foynes 176
Francini, Paolo and Filippo 19
  Newman House (Dublin) 59
  Russborough House 124
Franciscan order
  Annals of the Four Masters 222
  Ennis Friary 181
  Muckross Abbey 154
  Quin Franciscan Friary 181
  Timoleague Abbey 162–3
French, Percy 277
Friel, Brian 21
  Abbey Theatre (Dublin) 86, 107

Fry, Cyril 100
Fry Model Railway 100
Fungie (dolphin) 149
Fusilier's Arch (Dublin)
  Street-by-Street map 56

### G

Gaelic Athletic Association 27, 41
Gaelic football 27
Gaelic language 15, 25, 339
  cultural holidays 331
  Gaeltachts 221, 339
Gaelic literature 20
Gaeltachts 221, 339
Gaiety Theatre (Dublin) 105
Galbally 190
Galilei, Alessandro 122
Gallarus Oratory 149
  Dingle Peninsula tour 151
Galleries see Museums and galleries
Galty Mountains 173, 190
Galway 195, 202–3
  hotels 296
  map 203
  pubs 320
  restaurants 313–14
Galway Arts Festival 47, 331
Galway, County 193
Galway hookers 203
Galway Irish Crystal (Galway) 325
Galway Oyster Festival 48
Galway Races 27
Gandon, James
  Bank of Ireland (Dublin) 58
  Carrigglas Manor 233
  Custom House (Dublin) 39, 53, 86
  Emo Court 39, 245
  Four Courts (Dublin) 90–91
  King's Inns (Dublin) 90
Gap of Dunloe 155, 333
Gap of Mamore
  Inishowen Peninsula tour 218
Garage (Dublin pub) 105
Garavogue, River 226
Gardai 342, 343
Garden of Remembrance (Dublin) 89
Gardens see Parks and gardens
Gardiner, Luke 86
Garinish Island 158–9
Garryduff Gold Bird 33
Garter Lane Theatre (Waterford) 331
Gate Theatre (Dublin) 88, 105
  Dublin's Best: Entertainment 106
  Street-by-Street map 84
Geese, Wexford Wildfowl
  Reserve 142
Geldof, Bob 45
General Post Office (Dublin) 87
  Easter Rising 43
  Street-by-Street map 84
General strike (1913) 42
Geokaun Mountain 156
George III, King of England 160
George IV, King of England 264

Georgian country houses **19**
Georgian terraces, Dublin 67
Giant's Causeway 115, **254–5**
  Causeway Coast 253
  legends 25
Giant's Ring 271
Gibson, Mel 240
Gifford, Grace 95
Gill, Lough 225, 226
Giraldus Cambrensis 63
Gladstone, WE 41
Glasnevin Cemetery (Dublin) 98
Glassware
  shops **323**, 325
  Tyrone Crystal 265
  Waterford Crystal 139
  What to Buy in Ireland 327
Glen of Aherlow **190**
Glenariff Forest Park **259**
Glenbeg Lough 158
Glenbeigh
  Ring of Kerry tour 156
Glencar Lough
  Yeats Country tour 225
Glencolumbcille Health Centre 343
Glencolumbkille **220–21**
Glencree
  Military Road tour 130
Glendalough 32, 49, **132–3**
  Military Road tour 130
Glengarriff 159
Glengesh Pass 220
Gleninsheen Gorget **30–31**, 64
Gleninsheen Wedge Tomb 180
Glenmacnass
  Military Road tour 130
Glenveagh Castle 216
Glenveagh National Park 216
Glin **176**
  hotels 294
Glin Castle 176
Glin, Knights of 176
Gobelins tapestries 160
Gogarty, Oliver St. John 101
  Dublin pub 105
Goldsmith, Oliver 20, 60
Goldsmith Summer School
  (Ballymahon) 331
Golf 27, **332–3**, 335
Golfing Ireland (Dublin) 335
Golfing Union of Ireland 335
Gore-Booth, Eva 223, 224
Gore-Booth family 223
Gore-Booth, Sir Robert 223
Gorey, restaurants 308
Gort, Lord 184, 185
Gougane Barra Park 163
Gourmet restaurants 302–3
Government of Ireland Act (1920)
  29, 42
Goya y Lucientes, Francisco José de
  69, 124
Grafton Street (Dublin) **58**
  Street-by-Street map 56

Graham, Patrick 89
Graiguenamanagh 118, **141**
Grand Canal 99, 120, 227
Grand Canal Company 120
Grand Opera House
  (Belfast) **268**, 329, 331
Granuaile Centre 198
Grattan, Henry 38, 58
Gray Line Tours 361
Great Charter Roll of Waterford 35
Great Famine (1845–8) 40–41, **211**
  emigration 13, 29
  Famine Museum (Strokestown
    Park House) 211
Great Island 170
Great Saltee Island 143
Great Seal of Ireland 37
Great Stone Circle (Lough Gur) 186
Great Sugar Loaf Mountain 126
  Military Road tour 130
Green Card 355
Green Castle
  Mourne Coast tour 277
Greencastle
  Inishowen Peninsula tour 219
Green Flag National Breakdown 357
Gregory, Lady Augusta 88
  Abbey Theatre (Dublin) 20, 86
  Coole Park 204, 205
Gregory XVI, Pope 81
Grey Abbey 272
Greyhound racing 27
Grianán of Aileach **219**
  Inishowen Peninsula tour 218
Gris, Juan, *Pierrot* 68
Guaire, King of Connacht 204
Guesthouses 281
Guinness, Arthur 39, 96, **97**
Guinness, Sir Benjamin 80
Guinness Brewery 39, **96–7**
Guinness, Desmond 80
Guinness family
  Iveagh House 59
  memorials 75
Guinness Hop Store (Dublin) **96**
Gundestrup Cauldron 24
Gunpowder Mills (Cork) 169
Gur, Lough **186–7**

## H

Habermel, Erasmus 65
Hag's Head 176
Hallowe'en (Shamhana) 48, 305
Halpin, Robert 101
Hals, Frans 124
*Hambletonian* (Stubbs) 275
Handel, George Frederick 90
  *Messiah* 38, 79
Hanly, Daithí 89
Hanna, Fred (Dublin) 325
Ha'penny Bridge (Dublin) **91**
Harland, Sir Edward 268
Harland and Wolff 268, 271
Harp 22–3

Hastings Hotels 283
Hawks Well Theatre (Sligo) 331
Health 342–3
Healy Pass 158
Heaney, Séamus 21
Henry II, King of England 29, 34, 142
Henry VIII, King of England 276
  breaks with Catholic Church 29
  Christ Church Cathedral
    (Dublin) 79
  Silken Thomas's rebellion 36, 91
Henry, Mitchell 200
Heraldic Museum (Dublin) 63
Hertz 357
Heuston, Sean J 42
Heuston station (Dublin) 358
Hiberno-Romanesque style 19
Hidden Ireland 283
High Crosses **235**
  Ahenny 191, 235
  Ardboe 260
  Clonmacnoise 242
  Dysert O'Dea 181, 235
  Glendalough 132
  Kells 233
  Kilfenora 180
  Kilkieran 191
  Monasterboice 234, 235
  Rock of Cashel 188
High King 32
Hill, Arthur 273
Hill, Derek 216, 217
Hill of Slane 237
Hill of Tara 32, 238, **240**
Hillsborough **273**
  pubs 321
Hillsborough Castle 273
Hillsborough Fort 273
Hilser Brothers (Cork) 325
History **29–45**
HMV (Dublin shop) 105, 331
Hobbema, Meindert 69
Hogg's (Belfast) 325
Holiday Autos 357
Holidays, public 49
Holy Cross Abbey **187**
Holy Island 163, 182
Holywood
  hotels 301
  restaurants 317
Home Rule 29, 40, 41
Hook Head 140
Hook Peninsula 139, **140**
Hooker Sailing 47
Hookers, Galway 203
Hore Abbey (Cashel) 187
Horn Head **217**
Horse Ploughing Match and Heavy
  Horse Show 46
Horses
  horse-drawn caravans 283
  National Stud 120, 121
  racing 15, 26–7, **121**, 332
  riding and pony trekking **333**, 335

Hotels **280–301**
  booking 281
  chain hotels 283
  Cork and Kerry 291–3
  disabled travelers 283
  Dublin 286–9
  Ireland's Best 284–5
  Lower Shannon 294–5
  Midlands 299
  Northern Ireland 300–301
  Northwest Ireland 297–8
  prices 281
  Southeast Ireland 289–91
  tipping 281
  West of Ireland 295–7
Houghton, Ray 45
*The Houseless Wanderer*
  (Foley) 68
Howth **100**
  restaurants 308
Howth Head 93, 100
Hugh Lane Municipal Gallery of
  Modern Art (Dublin) **89**
  concerts 105
Hughes, John Joseph, Archbishop of
  New York 261
Huguenots
  in Cork 168
  linen industry 39, 260
  St. Patrick's Cathedral (Dublin) 80
"Humanity Dick" 202
Hungry Hill 158
Hunt, John 182, 183
Hunter's Hotel (Rathnew) 281, 285
Hunting **334**, 335
Hurling 27, 332
Hyde, Douglas 59
  memorial 81

**I**

Iarnród Éireann (Irish Rail) 358, 359
Ilnacullin 158
Inch Abbey 273
Inchagoill 201
Inchydoney 162
Industrial Revolution 268
Inis Saimer 223
Inishannon, hotels 292
Inishbofin **198**
Inisheer 206
Inishmaan 206
Inishmore 206
Inishowen Peninsula 215
  restaurants 314
  tour of **218–19**
Inistioge 141
  hotels 289
Innisfallen Island 154
Innisfree, Isle of *see* Isle of Innisfree
Insurance
  cars 355
  travel 342
International Bar (Dublin) 105
International Rally of the Lakes 26

International Sailing Centre
  (Cobh) 335
International Student Identity Card
  (ISIC) 340
Interpretive centers 339
Iona 62
Ireland's Eye 100
Irish Agriculture Museum (Johnstown
  Castle) 143
Irish Canoeing Holidays
  (Multifarnham) 335
Irish Champion Hurdle 26
Irish Citizen Army 87
Irish Conversation Courses
  (Ballyferriter) 331
Irish Derby 26, 121
Irish Distillers Group 171, 258
Irish Explorer tickets 359
Irish Federation of Sea Anglers 335
Irish Ferries 353
Irish Fieldsports Agency (Belfast) 335
Irish Film Centre (Dublin) 76, 105
Irish Football League 26
Irish Free State 13, 29
  Anglo-Irish Treaty (1921) 42
  civil war 43
  Parliament 63
Irish Georgian Society 122
Irish Gold Cup 26
Irish Grand National 26
Irish Heritage Properties
  (Dalkey) 331
Irish Horse Racing Authority 335
Irish Horse Federation 283
*Irish Life* 87
Irish Master of Foxhounds
  Association 335
Irish Museum of Modern Art 95
Irish National Heritage Park **142**
Irish National Trust 80
Irish Open Golf Championship 27
Irish Open Office (Dublin) 335
Irish Peat Board 243
Irish Rail 358–9
Irish Republican Army (IRA) 124
  Enniskillen bomb 264
  history 43
  Troubles 44, 45
Irish Republican Brotherhood 41
Irish Revival 20
Irish Rover tickets 359
Irish Surfing Association 335
Irish Tourist Board **338**, 339
Irish Underwater Council 335
Irish Volunteers (18th century) 39
Irish Volunteers (20th century)
  Easter Rising 87
  Garden of Remembrance
  (Dublin) 89
Irish Water Ski Federation 335
Irish Welcome 283
Irish Wheelchair Association 335
Irish Whiskey Corner (Dublin) **90**
Irish Windsurfing Association 335

Iron Age 30
  *see also* Forts (Iron Age)
Isle of Innisfree
  Yeats Country tour 225
Isle of Man Steam Packet Co Ltd 353
Iveagh House (Dublin) 59
Iveragh Peninsula 156

**J**

James I, King of England 37, 232
James II, King of England
  Battle of the Boyne 29, 36, 236
  Carrickfergus Castle 267
  siege of Derry 37
Jameson Heritage Centre
  (Midleton) **171**
Japanese Gardens (Kildare) 121
Jazz **329**, 331
  Dublin 103, 105
  festivals 46, 48
Jerpoint Abbey 35, **137**
Jerpoint Glass (Thomastown) 325
Jewelry
  shops **324**, 325
  What to Buy in Ireland 326
John the Evangelist, St. 197
John, King of England 183
John Paul II, Pope 197
  at Clonmacnoise 242
  in Phoenix Park (Dublin) 45, 94
Johnson, Ester (Stella) 80, 81
Johnston, Denis 88
Johnston, Francis 74, 90
Johnston, Richard 264
Johnstown Castle **142–3**
Jordan's Castle 276
Joseph, St. 197
Joyce, James 59, **88**
  bust of 58
  and Ennis 181
  James Joyce Cultural Centre
  (Dublin) 84, **88**
  James Joyce Tower (Sandycove,
  Dublin) **101**
  National Library (Dublin) 63
  statues of 83, 85
  Summer School (Dublin) 331
  *Ulysses* 20, 21, 46, 88, 104
*Judith with the Head of Holofernes*
  (Mantegna) 69
Jury's Hotel (Dublin) 105

**K**

Kanturk 169
  hotels 292
  restaurants 311
Kate Kearney's Cottage 155
Kavanagh, Patrick 21, 104
Kearney, Kate 155
Kehoe's (Dublin pub) 105
Kells **233**
  monastery 33, 233
  restaurants 315
  *see also* Book of Kells

Kelly, Oisín, *Children of Lir* 89
Kenmare **158**
 hotels 292
 restaurants 311
 shops 324
Kenmare, Earl of 88
Kennedy, John F 44
 John F Kennedy Park and
  Arboretum 141
Kennys Bookshop and Art Gallery
 (Galway) 325
Kerry *see* Cork and Kerry
Kerry Bog Village 156
Kerry, County 145
Kerry, Ring of **156–7**
Kevin, St. 132–3
Key, Lough 211
Kilbeggan **241**
 pubs 321
Kilbride, hotels 289
Kilclief Castle 276
Kildare **120–21**
 restaurants 308
Kildare, County 117
Kildare, Earls of 72, 186
Kildare, 8th Earl of 35, 36
 feud with Earl of Ormonde 81
 and Lambert Simnel 35, 79
Kilfenora 180
Kilkeel, hotels 301
Kilkenny 25, **134–6**
 hotels 290
 pubs 318
 restaurants 308–9
 shops 323
 Street-by-Street map 134–5
Kilkenny Arts Week 47, 330, 331
Kilkenny Castle 115, **136**
 Street-by-Street map 135
Kilkenny, County 117
Kilkenny Design Centre 323, 325
Kilkenny Shop (Dublin) 325
Kilkenny, Statute of (1366) 35
Kilkieran 191
Killahoey Strand 217
Killaloe 177, **182**
 pubs 320
Killarney **151**, 332
 hotels 292–3
 pubs 319
 restaurants 311
 Ring of Kerry tour 157
Killarney, Lakes of 114, **154–5**
Killarney National Park 154
Killeagh, hotels 293
Killiney **101**
Killorglin
 pubs 319
 restaurants 311
 Ring of Kerry tour 157
Killruddery House **125**
Killybegs **221**
 restaurants 314
Kilmacduagh **204**

Kilmainham Gaol (Dublin) 43, **95**
Kilmalkedar
 Dingle Peninsula tour 151
Kilmessan, hotels 299
Kilmore Quay 143
 pubs 318
Kilmurvy Beach 207
Kilnaboy, hotels 295
Kilronan 207
Kilrush 176
Kinbane Castle 253
King family 211
King's Inns (Dublin) **90**
Kingfisher Angling Centre
 (Ballymena) 335
Kingstown, hotels 296
Kinnitty 245
Kinsale **146**
 hotels 293
 pubs 303, 319
 restaurants 302, 311
 Street-by-Street map 164–5
Kinsale Gourmet Festival 48
Kinvarra **204**
 cafés 302
Kitchen (Dublin nightclub) 105
KLM 351
Knappogue Castle **181**
 banquets 330
Knights of St. Patrick 52, 74
Knights Templar 140
Knightstown 156
Knitwear shops **324**, 325
Knock **197**
Knock International Airport 351
Knockferry, hotels 296
Knocknarea 226
Knowth 236, **237**
Koralek, Paul 61
Koran 99
Kylemore Abbey **200**
Kyteler, Dame Alice 135, 318

**L**

La Tène culture 31, 210
Lacy, Hugh de 240
"Lady Betty" 210
Lakeland Canoe Centre
 (Enniskillen) 335
Lakes
 Landscape of Ireland 16
Lakes of Killarney **154–5**
Land League 41
Land War 41
Landscape of Ireland 16–17
Lane, Sir Hugh
 Hugh Lane Municipal Gallery of
  Modern Art (Dublin) 89
Language *see* Gaelic language
Lansdowne, 1st Marquess of 158
Lanyon, Sir Charles
 Custom House (Belfast) 271
 Queen's University (Belfast) 270
 Trinity College, Dublin 60

Laois, County 229
Larkin, James, statue of 84, 87
Larne **267**
 ferries 354
*Last Circuit of Pilgrims at
 Clonmacnoise* (Petrie) 242
Lavery, Sir John 270
Lawless, Matthew James
 *The Sick Call* 69
Laytown Beach Races 46, 47
Leamaneagh Castle 180
Lean, David 148
Leane, Lough 155
Leap, restaurants 311
Lecale Peninsula 276
Lee, River **163**, 166, 167
 Cork environs 169
 Exploring Cork 168
Lee, Sir Thomas 36
Leenane, hotels 296
Lefroy family 232
Legananny Dolmen 30, 276
Legends 24–5
Leighlinbridge, restaurants 309
Leinster 177
Leinster Aqueduct 120
Leinster, Duke of 63
Leinster House (Dublin) **63**
 Street-by-Street map 57
Leitrim, County 213, 227
Leitrim, Earls of 227
Leixlip Castle 39
Lennox, Lady Louisa 122–3
Lennox, Tom 122
Leopardstown 26, 49, 121
Leprechauns 24
Letterfrack, hotels 296
Letterkenny **219**
 County Museum 219
 hotels 298
 restaurants 314
Letterkenny Folk Festival 47
Lever Brothers 72
Libraries
 Chester Beatty Library and Gallery
  of Oriental Art (Dublin) 99
 Linen Hall Library (Belfast) 269
 Marsh's Library (Dublin) 81
 National Library (Dublin) 57, **63**
 Old Library, Trinity College
  (Dublin) 53, 55, 61
Liffey Bridge (Dublin) 91
Liffey, River 125
Light House (Dublin cinema) 105
Lillie's Bordello (Dublin nightclub) 105
Limavady, hotels 301
Limerick **183**
 history 33
 hotels 295
 pubs 320
 restaurants 313
 River Shannon 177
 siege of 173, 183
Limerick, County 173

Limestone pavement,
  The Burren 179
Linen 39, **260**
  shops **324**, 325
  What to Buy in Ireland 327
Lir, King 25
Lisdoonvarna 180
  hotels 295
Lisdoonvarna Matchmaking
  Festival 48
Lismacue, hotels 295
Lismore **137**
  restaurants 309
Lismore Castle 137
Lisnagun Ring Fort 162
Lissadell House **223**
  Yeats Country tour 224
Listings magazines, entertainments
  102, 103
Listowel Writers' Week 331
Liszt, Franz 88
Literature **20–21**
  cultural holidays 330, 331
  Literary Pub Crawl (Dublin) 104
Little Arrigle 137
Little Skellig 16, 157
Live Aid 45
Livingstone, Dr David 66
Locke, Josef 22
Locke's Distillery (Kilbeggan) 241
Loftus, Adam 37
Londonderry **250–51**
  hotels 301
  map 250
  personal safety 343
  restaurants 317
  siege of (1689) 37, 251
Londonderry, 3rd Marquess of 272
Londonderry Arms (Carnlough) 281
Londonderry, County 247
Londonderry family 274–5
Londonderry, Lady 274–5
The Long Hall (Dublin pub) 105
  Street-by-Street map 73
Long Range River 154
Longford, County 229
Longford, hotels 299
Loop Head 176
Lost property 342
Lough Eske, hotels 298
Lough Key Forest Park 211
Lough Melvin Holiday Centre
  (Garrison) 335
Lough Navar Forest Drive
  Lower Lough Erne tour 262
Lough Ree Trail 241
Lough Rynn Estate **227**
Loughros Point 220
Louisburgh 198
Louth, County 229
Lower Shannon **173–91**
  hotels 294–5
  map 174–5
  restaurants 312–13

Lughnasa Fair 47
*Lusitania* (liner) 89, 170
Lynch family 202
Lyric Theatre (Belfast) 331

# M

Maam Cross, pubs 320
Mac Liammóir, Micheál 88
McBride, Major John 42
McCarthy, Dermot
  King of Munster 163
McCausland Car Hire 357
McCormack, John F **22**
  Moore Abbey 120
  St. Mary's Pro-Cathedral 87
McDaid's (Dublin pub) 105
  Dublin's Best: Entertainment 107
MacDonnell family 253
MacDonnell, Sorley Boy 258
McDonough, Thomas 42
MacDyer, Father James 220–21
McEvoy, Eleanor 22
McGeehan Coaches 361
McGuigan, Barry 45
Mack, Robert 76
Maclise, Daniel
  *Marriage of Strongbow* 34
McMurrough, Art, King of Leinster 35
McMurrough, Dermot, King of
  Leinster 33, 34
MacNamara clan 181
MacNeice, Louis 21
McNeill, J (Dublin) 325
Macroom 163
MacSweeney family 217
Maeve, Queen of Connaught 213
  and Cuchulainn 24
  Knocknarea 226
Magazines 341
Magee and Co (Donegal) 325
Maghery Bay 220
Magho, Cliffs of *see* Cliffs of Magho
Magilligan Point 252
Magilligan Strand *see* Benone Strand
Mahon, Major Denis 211
Mahon, Derek 21
Mahon, Thomas 210
Mail services 347
Malachy, St. 237
Malahide, restaurants 308
Malahide Castle 93, **100**
Malaysia Airlines 351
Malin Head 215
  Inishowen Peninsula tour 219
Malinbeg 221
Mallow 169
  hotels 293
  restaurants 311
Malone, Molly, statue of 56, 58
Mamore, Gap of *see* Gap of Mamore
Mansion House (Dublin) **59**
  Street-by-Street map 56
Mantegna, Andrea, *Judith with the
  Head of Holofernes* 69

Manx Airlines 351
Maps
  Aran Islands 206–7
  Belfast 268–9
  The Burren 180
  Celtic Ireland 32
  Connemara 199
  Cork 166–7
  Cork and Kerry 146–7
  Dingle Peninsula tour 150–51
  Dublin at a Glance 52–3
  Dublin, North of the Liffey 83, 84–5
  Dublin, Southeast 55, 56–7
  Dublin, Southwest 71, 72–3
  Dublin Street Finder 108–11
  Galway 203
  Glendalough 132
  Great Famine 40
  Greater Dublin 11, 93
  Inishowen Peninsula tour 218–19
  Ireland 10–11
  Ireland at a Glance 114–15
  Kilkenny 134–5
  Kinsale 164–5
  Lakes of Killarney 154–5
  Londonderry 250
  Lower Lough Erne tour 262–3
  Lower Shannon 174–5
  Midlands 230–31
  Military Road tour 130
  Mourne Coast tour 277
  North Antrim coastline 253
  Northern Ireland 248–9
  Northwest Ireland 214–15
  Phoenix Park (Dublin) 94
  Ring of Kerry tour 156–7
  Shannon, River 177
  Southeast Ireland 118–19
  Waterford 139
  West of Ireland 194–5
  Yeats Country tour 224–5
Maracycle 46
Marble Arch Caves 265
Marconi, Guglielmo 199
  Ballycastle memorial 258
Marie Antoinette, Queen of
  France 161
Marino Casino (Dublin) 38–9, **98**
Markets in Dublin
  Covered Market 73
  Moore Street Market 84
Markievicz, Count Casimir 223
Markievicz, Countess Constance
  Easter Rising 59
  elected first woman MP 42
  Lissadell House 223
*Marriage of Strongbow* (Maclise) 34
Marsh, Narcissus, Archbishop of
  Dublin 81
Marsh's Library (Dublin) **81**
Martello towers
  Cleggan 199
  Dalkey Island 101
  Drogheda 236

Martello towers (cont)
Howth Head 93
James Joyce Tower 101
Magilligan Point 252
Martin, Misses 268
Mary I, Queen of England 36
Mary II, Queen of England 236
Mary from Dungloe International
Festival 47, 214
Mask, Lough 201
Mason, James 88
Matcham, Frank 268
Mathew, Father Theobald
statues of 87, 168
temperance crusade 40
Matisse, Henri 101
Matt Molloy's pub (Westport) 15, 196
Mattock, River 237
Mayo, County 193
Maze Prison (Belfast) 45
Meath, County 229
Meath, Earls of 125
Medical treatment 342
Medieval Trust 77
The Meeting of St. Brendan and the
Unhappy Judas (Clarke) 166, 167
Meeting of the Waters 131
Mellifont Abbey 33, 237
Mellifont, Treaty of (1603) 37
Mellon, Judge Thomas 261
Merrion Square (Dublin) 66
Metal Bridge (Dublin) 91
Metric system 341
Midlands 229–45
hotels 299
map 230–31
pubs 321
restaurants 315
Midleton, hotels 293
Military Road 131
tour of 130
Millstreet Indoor International
showjumping event 27
Milltown, Joseph Leeson, Earl of 124
Minot, Archbishop 80
Miró, Joan 167
Mizen Head 145, 159
Moher, Cliffs of see Cliffs of Moher
Mohill, hotels 298
Molaise, St. 263
Molloy, Matt 196
Moll's Gap
Ring of Kerry tour 157
Monaghan 232
restaurants 315
Monaghan, County 229
County Museum 232
Monasterboice 234
Monasterevin 120
Monasteries 29
Celtic 32–3
Clonmacnoise 229, 230, 242–3
Devenish Island 263
Glendalough 32–3, 132–3

Monasteries (cont)
Kells 33, 233
Kilmacduagh 204
Monasterboice 234
round towers 18–19
St. Cronan's Monastery
(Roscrea) 187
see also Abbeys
Monea Castle
Lower Lough Erne tour 263
Monet, Claude 69, 89
Money 344–5
Monuments
Alcock and Brown 199
Daniel O'Connell 85, 87
O'Scully (Rock of Cashel) 189
Parnell 84, 87
Strongbow 78
Wolfe Tone 59
Moore Abbey 120
Moore, Brian 21
Moore, Henry 58
Reclining Connected Forms 60
Moore Street Market (Dublin)
shopping 322
Street-by-Street map 84
Moore, Thomas 131
Morris, Abraham 169
Morris, William 217
Morrison, Van 22, 107, 268
Mosse, Dr Bartholomew 88
Mosse (Nicholas) Pottery
(Bennettsbridge) 136, 325
What to Buy in Ireland 327
Mother Redcap's Tavern (Dublin) 105
Motte and bailey 19
Mount Juliet Estate
(Thomastown) 335
Mount Stewart House 115,
272, 274–5
Mount Usher Gardens 131
Mountaineering 333, 335
Mountains of Mourne 249, 276
Mountains, wildlife 17
Mountjoy, Lord 169
Mountrath
hotels 299
restaurants 315
Mountshannon 175, 182
Mourne, Mountains of see Mountains
of Mourne
Mourne Coast tour 277
Mourne Wall 276
Movies see Films
Moyard, hotels 296
Moycullen, restaurants 314
Mr Pussy's Café de Luxe
(Dublin pub) 105
Muckross Abbey 154
Muckross House 151, 333
Muckross Lake 154
Muiredach's Cross 234, 235
Mulcahy (Louis) Pottery (Ballyferriter)
150, 325

Mullaghmore 180
Mulligan's (Dublin pub) 105
Mullingar 240–41
hotels 299
restaurants 315
Munster 173
Munster, Kings of 188
Murals, Belfast 270
Murlough Bay 259
Museums and galleries
admission charges 338
Armagh County Museum 266
Avondale House 133
Beit Art Collection (Russborough
House) 124–5
Blennerville Windmill (Tralee)
148, 149
Bunratty Folk Park 185
Burren Display Centre 180
Chester Beatty Library and Gallery
of Oriental Art (Dublin) 99
Cobh Heritage Centre 170
Colmcille Heritage Centre 217
Cork City Gaol 167
Crawford Art Gallery (Cork) 166–7
Dan O'Hara's Homestead
(Lettershea) 199
Derrynane House 156
Dixon Gallery (Tory Island) 216
Donegal Historical Society Museum
(Rossnowlagh) 222–3
Down County Museum
(Downpatrick) 273
Dublin Civic Museum 73, 75
Dublin Writers Museum 89
Dublinia 72, 77
Dysert O'Dea 181
Earhart Centre (Londonderry) 251
Famine Museum (Strokestown Park
House) 211
Folk Village Museum
(Glencolumbkille) 220–21
Foynes Flying Boat Museum 176
French Armada Centre (Bantry
House) 160
Glebe House and Gallery (Lough
Gartan) 217
Granuaile Centre (Louisburgh) 198
Guinness Hop Store (Dublin) 96
Heraldic Museum (Dublin) 63
Holy Trinity Heritage Centre
(Carlingford) 234
Horse Museum (National
Stud) 121
Hugh Lane Municipal Gallery of
Modern Art (Dublin) 89, 105
Hunt Museum (Limerick) 183
Irish Agriculture Museum
(Johnstown Castle) 143
Irish Museum of Modern Art
(Kilmainham) 95
Irish National Heritage Park
(Ferrycarrig) 142
Irish Whiskey Corner (Dublin) 90

Museums and galleries (cont)
Jameson Heritage Centre
(Midleton) **171**
Kerry County Museum (Tralee)
148, 149
Kings of Connaught Interpretative
Centre (Boyle) 211
Knight Ride (Carrickfergus) 267
Knock Folk Museum 197
Lagan Weir Lookout (Belfast) 271
Limerick Museum 183
Lough Neagh Discovery
Centre 266, 267
Maritime Museum (Kilmore
Quay) 143
Millmount Museum (Drogheda)
236
National Gallery (Dublin) 53, **68–9**
National Maritime Museum (Dun
Laoghaire) 101
National Museum (Dublin)
53, **64–5**
Natural History Museum
(Dublin) **66**
Navan Centre (Armagh) 266
Rock of Cashel 188
Royal Gunpowder Mills (Cork) 169
Royal Hibernian Academy
(Dublin) 66
St. Patrick's Trian (Armagh) 266
Skellig Experience Centre 156
Sligo Art Gallery **226**
Sligo County Museum and Art
Gallery 226
Tower Museum (Londonderry)
250, **251**
Ulster-American Folk Park (Co
Tyrone) **261**
Ulster Folk and Transport Museum
(Cultra) **272**
Ulster History Park (Co
Tyrone) **261**
Ulster Museum (Belfast) 270
Water Wheels (Assaroe Abbey) 223
Waterford Heritage Centre 138
West Cork Regional Museum
(Clonakilty) 162
Westgate Heritage Centre
(Wexford) 142
Yola Farmstead (Rosslare) 143
Music 15, **22–3**
classical music, opera and dance
103, 105, **329**, 331
cultural holidays 331
festivals 46–9
rock, jazz, blues and country 103,
105, **329**, 331
shops **323**, 325
traditional music and dance 22–3,
103, 105, **329**, 331
Music in Great Irish Houses 47, 331
Mussenden, Frideswide 252
Mussenden Temple **252**
Myths **24–5**

# N

Naas, restaurants 309
Napoleon I, Emperor 40, 101
Nash, John 190, 211
National Botanic Gardens
(Dublin) **98**
National Breakdown, Green Flag 357
National Concert Hall (Dublin) 105
Dublin's Best: Entertainment 107
National Express 353
National Gallery (Dublin) 53, **68–9**
National Irish Bank 346
National Library (Dublin) **63**
Street-by-Street map 57
National Monument (Cork) 168
National Museum (Dublin) 53, **64–5**
Street-by-Street map 57
National Rehabilitation Board 341
National Stud 120, 121
National Symphony Orchestra 107
National Trust 331, 339
Crown Liquor Saloon (Belfast) 269
Mount Stewart House 274–5
Mussenden Temple 252
Portstewart Strand 252
Wellbrook Beetling Mill 260
Natural History Museum (Dublin) **66**
Navan Fort 266
Neagh, Lough **266–7**
Neary's (Dublin pub) 105
Nelson Pillar (Dublin) 75
Nenagh, restaurants 313
Neo-Classical architecture 19
Neolithic 30
New Ross **140–41**
New York, Irish immigration 41
Newcastle 276
hotels 301
Mourne Coast tour 277
restaurants 317
Newgrange 30, 31, 236–7, **238–9**
Newman, John Henry 59
Newmarket-on-Fergus
hotels 295
restaurants 313
Newport, hotels 297
Newspapers 341
Newton, Lord 59
Newtownards 272
Nightclubs, Dublin 103, 105
Nobel prizes 43, 44, 45
Nore, River 136
Norse Irish Ferries 353
The Norseman (Dublin pub) 105
North Mayo Sculpture Trail 196
North West 200 (motorcycle race)
26, 252
Northern Bank 346
Northern Ireland **247–77**
Anglo-Irish Treaty (1921) 42
banks 346
buses 360, 361
coach tours 361
currency 345

Northern Ireland (cont)
history 29
hotels 300–301
map 248–9
personal safety 343
pubs 321
restaurants 316–17
security roadblocks 357
taxis 361
telephones 349
terrorism 342
train services 358
Troubles 13, 44–5, 343
Northern Ireland Civil Rights
Association 44
Northern Ireland Railways 359
Northern Ireland Tourist Board 331,
338, 339
Northwest Ireland **213–27**
hotels 297–8
pubs 321
restaurants 314–15

# O

O'Brien, Donach 184
O'Brien, Edna 21
O'Brien family
Bunratty Castle 184
Clare Abbey 181
and Ennis 181
Leamaneagh Castle 180
O'Brien, Flann 21
O'Brien, Murtagh, King of
Munster 219
O'Brien's Tower (Cliffs of Moher) 176
O'Carolan Harp and Traditional Music
Festival 47
O'Carolan, Turlough **22**
death 38
harp 210
memorial 81
O'Casey, Sean 20, 85
Abbey Theatre (Dublin) 86, 102
O'Connell, Daniel
Catholic emancipation 40
Derrynane House 156
grave 98
Hill of Tara 240
Merrion Square (Dublin) 66
monuments to 85, 87, 181
National Library (Dublin) 63
O'Connell Street (Dublin) 53, **86–7**
Street-by-Street map 84–5
O'Connor, Sinéad 22
O'Conor family 148, 210
O'Conor, Felim, King of
Connaught 210
O'Conor, Hugh, King of
Connaught 210
O'Conor, Turlough, King of
Connaught 201
Octoberfest (Londonderry) 48
O'Doherty Castle 218
O'Donnell family 213, 222

O'Donoghue's (Dublin) 103, 105
O'Driscoll clan 162
O'Faolain, Seán 21
Offaly, County 229
Office of Public Works 339
   Heritage Card 338
O'Flaherty, Donal 201
O'Flaherty clan 201
Ogham Stones 32, 182
Oideas Gael (Glencolumbkille) 331
Old Bushmills Distillery **258**
Oliver St. John Gogarty (Dublin pub)
   104, 105
Olympia Theatre (Dublin) 102, 105
O'Malley, Grace
   Achill Island 196
   Clare Island 198
   marriage 201
One Man's Pass 221
O'Neill, Brian 34
O'Neill family 213
   Dungannon 265
   Grianán of Aileach 219
   and Protestant conquest 36, 247
O'Neill, Owen 219
Opening hours
   banks 346
   shops 322
   sights 339
Opera **329**, 331
   Dublin 103, 105
   Wexford Opera Festival 142
Opera House (Cork) 331
*Ór – Ireland's Gold* exhibition 64
Orange Order (Orangemen) 36,
   39, 47
Ormond Castle (Carrick-on-Suir) 191
Ormonde, 2nd Marquess of
   tomb of 136
Ormonde, Black Tom Butler, 10th
   Earl of 191
Ormonde, Earls of 81, 94, 137,
   173, 191
O'Rourke family 225
O'Scully Monument 189
Ossian 25
Ossian's Grave 31
O'Toole family 131
O'Toole, St. Laurence, Archbishop of
   Dublin 78, 79, 87
Oughter, Lough 16
Oughterard 201
   hotels 297
Oul' Lammas Fair 47
Out and Out Activities (Garrison) 335
Oxford Island 267
Oxmanstown 77

# P

P&O European Ferries 353
Pain, J and GR 169
Paisley, Rev Ian 44
Pakenham family 233
Pakenham, Thomas 233

The Pale 34, **124**
Palestrina Choir 87
Palladian architecture 19
   Castletown House 122
   Florence Court 265
   Marino Casino 39
   Powerscourt 126
   Russborough House 124–5
   Strokestown Park House 210–11
Palladius 32, 273
Pan Celtic Festival 46
Pantomimes 49
Papal Cross (Dublin) 94
Parian ware 261
Parke, Captain Robert 225
Parke's Castle **225**, 338
   Yeats Country tour 225
Parking 357
Parknasilla
   hotels 293
   restaurants 312
Parks and gardens
   cultural holidays 331
   Avondale Forest Park 133
   Bantry House 161
   Birr Castle 245
   Botanic Gardens (Belfast) 270
   Butterstream Gardens (Trim) 240
   Castle Archdale Country Park 263
   Castle Caldwell Forest Park 262
   Castlewellan Forest Park 276
   Connemara National Park 200
   Coole Park 205
   County Wicklow Garden
   Festival 46
   Emo Court 245
   Florence Court 265
   Fota Wildlife Park and Arboretum
   170–71
   Garden of Remembrance
   (Dublin) 89
   Garinish Island 158–9
   Glenariff Forest Park 259
   Glenveagh Castle 217
   Glenveagh National Park 216
   Gougane Barra Park 163
   Irish National Heritage Park 142
   Japanese Gardens (Kildare) 121
   Johnstown Castle 143
   Kennedy (John F) Park and
   Arboretum 141
   Killruddery House 125
   Kylemore Abbey 200
   Lismore Castle 137
   Lissadell House 223
   Lough Key Forest Park 211
   Lough Rynn Estate 227
   Merrion Square (Dublin) 66
   Mount Stewart House 115, **274–5**
   Mount Usher Gardens 131
   Muckross House 151
   National Botanic Gardens
   (Dublin) 98
   Phoenix Park (Dublin) 94

Parks and gardens (cont)
   Portumna Forest Park 205
   Powerscourt 115, **126–7**
   St. Stephen's Green (Dublin)
   56, **58–9**
   Slane Castle 237
   Slieve Foye Forest Park 234
   Tollymore Forest Park 277
   Tully Castle 262
   Woodstock House Demesne 141
Parliament **63**
   Bank of Ireland building
   (Dublin) 58
   history 34, 42
   Leinster House (Dublin) 63
Parnell, Charles Stewart 41
   Avondale House 133
   grave 98
   Home Rule campaign 40, 41
   imprisonment 41, 95
   monument to 87
Parnell Monument (Dublin)
   Street-by-Street map 84
Parsons family 245
Passage East 139
Passage graves
   Carrowkeel Passage Tomb
   Cemetery 227
   Carrowmore Megalithic
   Cemetery 226
   Dowth 236, **237**
   Hill of Tara 240
   Knowth 236, **237**
   Newgrange 236–7, **238–9**
Passports 340, 342
Pasture 17
Patrick, St. 268, **273**
   Armagh 32, 247, 266
   Croagh Patrick 197
   Downpatrick 273
   Grianán of Aileach 219
   Hill of Slane 237
   Hill of Tara 240
   Lough Derg 222
   mission to Ireland 29, 32
   St. Patrick's Bell 65
   St. Patrick's Cathedral (Dublin) 80
   St. Patrick's Cross (Cashel) 188
   *St Patrick* (Smyth) 74
Pavarotti, Luciano 107
Payne-Townsend, Charlotte 98
Peacock, Joseph, *The Feast of St.
   Kevin amid the ruins of
   Glendalough* 29
Peacock Theatre (Dublin) 86
Pearce, Edward Lovett 58
Pearse, Patrick 42, 59, 87
Peat **244**
   Shannonbridge Bog Railway 243
Peatland World **120**
Peatlands Park 266, 267
Pedroza, Eusebio 45
Pembroke, William Marshall, Earl
   of 140

Penn, Sir William 163
Penrose, George 139
Penrose, William 139
People's Garden, Phoenix Park
    (Dublin) 94
Perfume, duty-free allowances 340
Personal security 342–3
Peto, Harold 158–9
Petrie Crown 57
Petrie, George, *Last Circuit of
    Pilgrims at Clonmacnoise* 242
Petrol 355
Pettigo 283
Petty, William 158
Pharmacies 342, **343**
*Phoenix* 36
Phoenix Column (Dublin) 94
Phoenix Park (Dublin) 45, **94**
Phonecards 348–9
Picasso, Pablo 217
Picnics 303
Picts 31
*Pierrot* (Gris) 68
Pillar stones 235
Pioneer Total Abstinence
    Movement 87
Place names 25
Planetarium, Observatory Grounds
    (Armagh) 266
Plantation 36, **37**
Plunkett, Joseph 43, 95
Plunkett, Oliver 236
POD (Dublin nightclub) 105
Point Theatre (Dublin) 105
    Dublin's Best: Entertainment 107
Police 342, 343
Political murals, Belfast 270
Pomodoro, *Sphere within Sphere*
    57, 61
Pontoon, hotels 297
Pony trekking **333**, 335
Portaferry **272**
    hotels 301
Portal tombs 30
Portarlington, Earl of 245
Portballintrae, restaurants 317
Portlaoise, pubs 321
Portrush 252
    restaurants 317
Ports 352–3
Portsalon 217
Portstewart 248, **252**
    golf 332
Portstewart Strand 252
Portumna 177, **205**
Portumna Castle 205
Portumna Forest Park 205
Portumna Priory 205
Post offices 347
Postage stamps 347
Postal services 347
Postboxes 347
Pottery *see* Ceramics
Poulaphouca Reservoir 125

Poulnabrone Dolmen 180
Poussin, Nicolas 69
Powerscourt 115, **126–7**
Powerscourt, Richard Wingfield, 1st
    Viscount 126
Powerscourt, 7th Viscount 126
Powerscourt Townhouse (Dublin) **76**
    Street-by-Street map 73
Powerscourt Waterfall
    Military Road tour 130
Poynings, Edward 35
Prehistoric Ireland **30–31**
    interpretative centres 339
    Beaghmore Stone Circles **260**
    Boyne Valley **236–7**
    Browne's Hill 133
    Carrowkeel Passage Tomb
        Cemetery 215, 227
    Carrowmore Megalithic
        Cemetery 226
    Cave Hill (Belfast) 271
    Céide Fields **196**
    Connemara National Park 200
    Craggaunowen **182**
    Drombeg Stone Circle **162**
    Dún Aonghasa 206
    Dún Duchathair 207
    Dún Eochla 207
    Giant's Ring 271
    Gleninsheen Wedge Tomb 180
    Great Stone Circle
        (Lough Gur) 186
    Grianán of Aileach 218, **219**
    Hill of Tara **240**
    Knocknarea 226
    Legananny Dolmen 276
    Lough Gur **186–7**
    Navan Fort 266
    Newgrange 236–7, **238–9**
    Poulnabrone Dolmen 180
    Turoe Stone **210**
    *see also* Forts (Iron Age)
Prime Minister 63
Priories *see* Abbeys and priories
Project Arts Theatre (Dublin)
    76, 105
Promontory forts 18
Prospect Cemetery (Dublin) 98
Protestant Church of Ireland 80
Protestants
    Battle of the Boyne 236
    Protestant Ascendancy 38–9
    Protestant Conquest 36–7
Prowse (Keith) Travel (IRL) Ltd
    (Dublin) 331
Ptolemy 31
Public holidays 49
Public Records Office (Dublin) 91
Pubs **318–21**
    Cork and Kerry 319
    Dublin 104, 105
    Dublin's Best: Entertainment 106–7
    food in 303
    Lower Shannon 319–20

Pubs (cont)
    Midlands 321
    Northern Ireland 321
    Northwest Ireland 321
    Southeast Ireland 318–19
    traditional music 103, 105, 329
    West of Ireland 320–21
Puck Fair 47
Pugin, AWN 141
Punchestown 26, 121
Purple Mountain 155
Puxley Mansion 158

**Q**

Qantas 351
Queen's (Dublin pub) 105
Queen's University, Belfast 270
Quills Woollen Market (Killarney) 325
Quin, hotels 295
Quin Franciscan Friary 181

**R**

Racing, horse 26–7, **121**, 332
Radio 341
Railroads *see* Trains
Rainfall 48
Raised bogs 244
Raleigh, Sir Walter 171
Raleigh Rent-a-Bike (Dublin) 335, 357
Ramsay, Allan 160
Rathaspeck, hotels 290
Rathlannon Castle 143
Rathlin Island 258
Rathmelton 217
Rathmines, hotels 289
Rathmullan, restaurants 314
Rathnew
    hotels 290
    restaurants 309
Rathvilly, hotels 290
Reagh, MacCarthy, Lord of
    Carbery 162
Red Abbey (Cork) 168
Ree, Lough 177
Reformation 81
*The Relief of Derry* (Sadler) 37
Religion
    Celtic Christianity 32–3
    religious services 339
    *see also* Abbeys and priories;
        Cathedrals; Churches in Dublin;
        Monasteries
Rembrandt 69
Renoir, Pierre Auguste 217
Rent-a-Bike 357
Rent an Irish Cottage 283
Renting a car 355
Renvyle, hotels 297
Restaurants **302–17**
    budget dining 303
    Cork and Kerry 310–12
    Dublin 306–8
    gourmet and ethnic dining 302–3
    Irish eating patterns 302

Restaurants (cont)
  Lower Shannon 312–13
  Midlands 315
  Northern Ireland 316–17
  Northwest Ireland 314–15
  Southeast Ireland 308–9
  West of Ireland 313–14
  What to Eat in Ireland 304–5
Ri-Rá (Dublin nightclub) 105
Riasc
  Dingle Peninsula tour 150
Richard II, King of England 35
Riding **333**, 335
Riding for the Disabled, Association
  of Ireland 335
Ring forts 18–19
Ring of Kerry tour **156–7**
Riverbank Theatre (Dublin) 105
Rivers 16
Riverstown, hotels 298
Road maps 355
Road signs 356
Roadblocks, security 357
Roberts, John 138
Robertstown **120**, 332
Robinson, Mary 14, 44, 45
Robinson, Sir William
  Dublin Castle 74
  Marsh's Library (Dublin) 81
  Royal Hospital Kilmainham 95
Roche, Steven 45
Rock of Cashel 114, 187, **188–9**
Rock of Dunamase **245**
Rock Garden (Dublin) 105
Rock music **329**, 331
  Dublin 103, 105
Rockingham estate 211
Rodin, Auguste 89
Romans 31
Roscommon **210**
  restaurants 314
Roscommon Castle 210
Roscommon, County 193
Roscrea **187**
Roscrea Castle 187
Rose of Tralee Festival 47
Rosguill Peninsula **217**
Ross, Bishop of 163
Ross Castle 154
Rosse, 2nd Earl of 245
Rosse, 3rd Earl of 245
Rosse, 6th Earl of 245
The Rosses **220**
Rosses Point
  Yeats Country tour 224
Rosslare **143**, 334
  ferries 352
  hotels 290
  restaurants 309
Rossnowlagh **222–3**
  hotels 298
  pubs 321
Rostrevor
  Mourne Coast tour 277

Rosturk, hotels 297
Rotunda Hospital (Dublin) 38, **88**
  Street-by-Street map 84
Rouault, Georges 167
Round Ireland Yacht Race 26
Round towers 18–19
Roundstone 199
Roundwood
  Military Road tour 130
Roundwood House 285
Royal Automobile Club (RAC) 357
Royal Canal 40, 99, 240–41
Royal College of Surgeons
  (Dublin) 59
Royal Cork Yacht Club 27
Royal Dublin Society 38, 63, 105
Royal Gunpowder Mills (Cork) 169
Royal Hibernian Academy
  (Dublin) **66**
Royal Hospital Kilmainham **95**
  concerts 105
Royal Tara China (Galway) 325
Royal Ulster Agriculture Society
  Show 46
Royal Ulster Constabulary (RUC) 342
Rubens, Peter Paul 69, 124
Rugby 26, 332
Ruisdael, Jacob van, *Castle of
  Bentheim* 69
Rules of the road 356
Russborough House 39, **124–5**
  Milltown collection 68
  stucco 19
Rutland Fountain (Dublin) 66
Ryanair 351
Rynhart, Jean, *Molly Malone* 58

**S**

Sadler, William II, *The Relief of
  Derry* 37
Safety 342–3
Sagas 20
Sailing 26–7, **334**, 335
  regattas 47
St. Ann's Church (Dublin) **59**
  Street-by-Street map 56
St. Audoen's Church (Dublin) 77
St. Audoen's Roman Catholic Church
  (Dublin) 77
St. Ernan's House 284
St. James's Gate Brewery (Dublin) 39
St. John Ambulance Brigade 79
St. John's Point 276
St. Mary's Abbey (Dublin) **91**
St. Mary's Pro-Cathedral (Dublin) **87**
  Street-by-Street map 85
St. Michael's Tower (Dublin) 77
St. Michan's Church (Dublin) 90
St. Patrick's Cathedral (Dublin) 52,
  **80–81**
St. Patrick's Day 46
St. Stephen's Day 49
St. Stephen's Green (Dublin) **58–9**
  Street-by-Street map 56

St. Stephen's Green Shopping Centre
  (Dublin) 325
St. Werburgh's Church (Dublin) **75**
  Street-by-Street map 72
Sales tax 322
Saller's Jewellers (Galway) 325
Sally Gap 131
  Military Road tour 130
Salmon fishing 26, 49
Saltee Islands **143**
Salthill 203, 341
Sandel, Mount 30
Sands, Bobbie 45
Saul 273
Saxons 31
Sayers, Peig 20
Scattery Island 176
Schomberg, General 267
Schull 159
Scrabo Tower 272
Screen (Dublin) 105
Sculpture
  High Crosses 235
  North Mayo Sculpture Trail 196
Scurlogstown Olympiad Celtic
  Festival 46–7
Sea travel 352–4
Sea trout fishing 49
SeaCat 353
*Seanad Éireann* 63
Security roadblocks 357
Self-catering accommodation 282
Selskar Abbey (Wexford) 142
Semple Stadium (Thurles) 331
Seven Churches (Aran Islands) 206
Severin, Tim 182
Shaftesbury, Earl of 271
Shaikh, Ahmad 99
Shanagarry
  hotels 293
  restaurants 312
Shannon Airport 340, **350**, 351
Shannon Ceili (Bunratty) 331
Shannon-Erne Waterway 177,
  **227**, 335
Shannon hydro-electric scheme 43
Shannon, River 16, **177**
  Lower Shannon 173
  map 177
Shannonbridge Bog Railway **243**
Share Centre (Lisnaskea) 335
Shaw, George Bernard 20, 98, 106
  Coole Park 205
  National Gallery (Dublin) 68
  National Library (Dublin) 63
  Nobel prize 43
  *Saint Joan* 159
Shaw's Birthplace (Dublin) **98**
Sheares, Henry and John 90
Sheen, River 158
Sheep Island 253
Shelbourne Bar (Dublin) 105
Shelbourne Hotel (Dublin) 59, 280
  Street-by-Street map 57

Sheridan, Richard Brinsley 20
Sherkin Island 162
Shooting **334**, 335
Shopping **322–7**
    books **323**, 325
    ceramics and china **323**, 325
    crafts **323**, 325
    crystal and glassware **323**, 325
    department stores 325
    Dublin 322
    fashion **324**, 325
    food and drink **324**, 325
    how to pay 322
    jewelry **324**, 325
    knitwear and tweed **324**, 325
    linen **324**, 325
    music **323**, 325
    opening hours 322
    sales tax and refunds 322
    What to Buy in Ireland 326–7
    where to shop 322
Siamsa Tíre folklore theatre
    148–9, 331
*The Sick Call* (Lawless) 69
Silent Valley 276
    Mourne Coast tour 277
Silver Line Cruisers (Banagher) 335
Simnel, Lambert 35, 79
Sinn Féin
    cease-fire (1994) 45
    Custom House fire 86
    history 42
*Sirius* (liner) 170
Sirr, Major Henry 75
Sitric Silkenbeard 33
Skellig Experience Centre 156
Skellig Michael 145, **156–7**
The Skelligs **156–7**
Skibbereen 159
Sky Road 199
Slade 140
Slade Castle 140
Slane **237**
    hotels 299
Slane Castle 237
Slane, Hill of *see* Hill of Slane
Slaney, River 141
Slattery's (Dublin) 105
Slattery's Travel Agency (Tralee) 283
Slazenger family 126
Slea Head
    Dingle Peninsula tour 150
Slieve Bloom Mountains **245**
Slieve Bloom Way 245
Slieve Donard 276
Slieve Foye Forest Park 234
Slieve Gallion 260
Slieve League **221**
Slieve Patrick 273
Slievemore 196
Sligo 213, **226**
    pubs 321
    restaurants 315
    Yeats Country tour 224–5

Sligo Abbey 226
Sligo Arts Festival 48
Sligo, County 213
    Yeats Country tour 224–5
Sligo Crystal (Grange) 325
Sligo International Choral Festival 48
Smith, John Charles 197
Smithfield (Dublin) **90**
Smyth, Edward
    Church of the Most Holy Trinity
        sculptures 74
    Custom House sculpture 85, 86
    King's Inns sculptures 90
    Marino Casino lions 38
    *St. Patrick* 74
Smyth's Irish Linen (Belfast) 325
Sneem 346–7
    Ring of Kerry tour 157
Soccer 26–7, 332
South Sligo Summer School of
    Traditional Music, Song and
    Dance 331
Southeast Ireland **117–43**
    hotels 289–91
    map 118–19
    pubs 318–19
    restaurants 308–9
Southern Hotels 283
Spanish Armada 36
Speed limits 356
Spelga Dam
    Mourne Coast tour 277
Sperrin Mountains 260
*Sphere within Sphere* (Pomodoro)
    57, 61
Sports **332–5**
    The Sporting Year 26–7
Spring in Ireland 46
Stag's Head (Dublin pub) 105
    Dublin's Best: Entertainment 106
Staic, Brian de (Killarney) 325
Staigue Fort
    Ring of Kerry tour 156
Stamps, postage 347
Standun (Spiddal) 325
Stapleton, Michael 19
    Belvedere College (Dublin) 88
    James Joyce Cultural Centre
        (Dublin) 88
    Powerscourt Townhouse
        (Dublin) 76
    Trinity College, Dublin 60
Station Island 222
Stena Sealink 353
Stewart, Richard 75
Stoker, Bram 59
Stone Age 173
    interpretive centers 339
    *see also* Prehistoric Ireland
Stone circles
    Beaghmore Stone Circles 260
    Drombeg Stone Circle 162
    Great Stone Circle (Lough Gur) 186
Stormont 271

Stradbally 245
Stradbally Steam-engine Rally 47
Straffan, hotels 290
Strangford, restaurants 317
Stranorlar, hotels 298
Street, George 78
Streeve House 285
Strokestown Park House **210–11**
Strongbow (Richard de Clare)
    Christ Church Cathedral
        (Dublin) 78
    invades Ireland 71, 77
    marriage 34
    monument to 78
Struell Wells 273
Stuart, James "Athenian" 274
Stubbs, George, *Hambletonian* 275
Stucco 19
Student information 340
Students, travel concessions 359
Studio Donegal (Kilcar) 325
Suir, River 138, 190, 191
Summer Cabaret (Limerick) 331
Summer in Ireland 46–7
Sunlight Chambers (Dublin)
    Street-by-Street map 72
Sunshine 47
Swans 25
Swansea Cork Ferries 353
Swift, Jonathan 20, **80**
    Dean of St. Patrick's Cathedral 38
    *Gulliver's Travels* 266
    marble bust 55
    memorials 52, 81
    *A Modest Proposal* 38
Swilly, Lough 218, 219
Swilly, River 219
Synge, John Millington 20–21, 85
    Abbey Theatre (Dublin) 86, 102

## T

Tacumshane, hotels 290
Tahilla, hotels 293
Taibhdhearc Theatre (Galway) 331
Tailors' Hall (Dublin) **80**
Tain Trail 234
*The Taking of Christ* (Caravaggio)
    53, 69
Talbot Castle 240
Talbot family 100
*Tánaiste* 63
*Taoiseach* 63
Tara, Hill of *see* Hill of Tara
Tara Brooch 65
"A Taste of Baltimore" Shellfish
    Festival 46
Tax, sales (VAT) 322
Taxis 360–61
Tay, Lough
    Military Road tour 130
*Teachta Dála* (TDs) 63
Telecom Eireann 348
Telephones 348–9
Television 341

Temperance crusade 40
Temperatures 49
Temple Bar (Dublin) 71, **76**
  Dublin's Best: Entertainment 106
  Street-by-Street map 73
Temple Bar Blues Festival (Dublin)
  103, 105
Teresa, Mother 197
Terrorism 342
  see also Troubles
Thackeray, William Makepeace
  154, 259
Theater **328**, 331
  Dublin 102, 105
  Dublin's Best: Entertainment 106–7
  festivals 48
Theatre Royal (Waterford) 331
Them 22
Thin Lizzy 22, 103
Thomastown
  hotels 290
  restaurants 309
Thomond, Earls of 184
Thoor Ballylee **204–5**
The Three Graces (Canova) 169
Thrifty Car Rentals 357
Ticket Shop (Dublin) 105
Tickets
  air travel 351
  buses 360
  for entertainments 102, 105,
  **328**, 331
  ferries 354
  trains 359
Time zone 341
Timoleague Abbey **162–3**
Tintern Abbey 140
Tipperary, County 173
Tipperary Crystal (Carrick-on-Suir)
  325
Tipping, in hotels 281
Titanic 42, 170, 272
  Titanic Memorial (Belfast) 268
Tobercurry, restaurants 315
Tobernalt 226
Tola, St. 181
Tollymore Forest Park
  Mourne Coast tour 277
Tombs see Passage graves
Tone, Wolfe 269
  Cave Hill (Belfast) 271
  French Armada Centre (Bantry
  House) 160
  marriage 59
  monument 59
  portraits 100
  rebellion 38, 39, 160
  Tailors' Hall rally 80
  "Tonehenge" 59
Toner's (Dublin pub) 105
Toome 267
Torc Mountain 154
Torc Waterfall 154
Torr Head 259

Tory Island **216**
Tour de France 45
Tourist information offices 338
Tours by car
  Dingle Peninsula 150–51
  Inishowen Peninsula 218–19
  Lower Lough Erne 262–3
  Military Road 130
  Mourne coast 277
  Ring of Kerry 156–7
  Yeats Country 224–5
Tower Enterprise Centre (Dublin) 325
Tower houses 18–19
Towers, round 18–19
Town and Country Homes
  Association 283
Town and Seaside House
  Association 283
Traditional music and dance **329**, 331
  Dublin 103, 105
Trains **358–9**
  Shannonbridge Bog Railway 243
  Steam Railway (Tralee) 149
  student discounts, 340
  through-tickets, 354
Tralee **148–9**
Travel **350–61**
  air 350–51
  buses 360–61
  cars 355–7
  Cork and Kerry 147
  getting to Ireland 10
  insurance 342
  Lower Shannon 174
  Midlands 230
  Northern Ireland 248
  Northwest Ireland 215
  sea 352–4
  Southeast Ireland 119
  taxis 360–61
  trains 358–9
  Ulster Folk and Transport
  Museum 272
  West of Ireland 194
Traveler's checks 322, 346–7
Treasure Chest (Galway) 325
Trevor, William 21
Trim 231, **240**
Trim Castle 240
Trinity College, Dublin 13,
  **60–62**, 340
  Book of Kells 62
  history 36
  Old Library 53, 55, 61
  Street-by-Street map 57
The Troubles 13, 44–5
  personal safety 343
  political murals 270
TSB Bank 346
Tullamore, restaurants 315
Tully Castle
  Lower Lough Erne tour 262
Tullynally Castle **233**
Turloughs 178

Turner, Richard 98
Turoe Stone **210**
Tweed shops **324**, 325
Twelve Bens 193, 198, 200
Tympanum 19
Tyrone, County 247
Tyrone, Hugh O'Neill,
  Earl of 37, 247
Tyrone Crystal (Dungannon) 265, 325

**U**
U2 (band) 15, 22, 103
Ufford, Robert d' 210
Uí Néill clan 247
Ulster see also Northern Ireland
Ulster Bank 344
Ulster Cruising School
  (Carrickfergus) 335
Ulster Folk and Transport
  Museum 272
Ulster Hall (Belfast) 331
Ulster History Park 261
Ulster Peace Movement 45
Ulster, Red Hand of 268–9
Ulster, Richard de Burgo, Earl of 219
Ulster Volunteer Force 42, 267
Ulster Way 333
Ulster-American Folk Park 261
Ulsterbus 353, 361
Unionist Party 42
United Irishmen
  attempted invasion of Ireland 160
  foundation of 269
  rebellion 38, 39
United Nations 44
United States, Irish immigration
  41, 170
University Church (Dublin) 59
USIT 341

**V**
Valdré, Vincenzo 74
Vale of Avoca 131
Vale of Clara
  Military Road tour 130
Valentia Island **156**
Valentine, St. 81
Vanhomrigh, Hester 80
Vartry, River 131
VAT (sales tax) 322
Veagh, Lough 216
Velázquez, Diego de Silva y 124
Ventry 346–7
Vermeer, Jan 124
Vernet, Joseph 124
Victoria, Queen of England
  Cobh 170
  Glengarriff 159
  Lakes of Killarney 155
  opens Dublin Exhibition 41
  statues of 44, 268
Vikings 32
  Donegal 222
  Dublin 71, **77**

Vikings (cont)
  invasions of Ireland 29, 33, 117
  Limerick 183
  Lower Shannon 173
  National Museum exhibition 65
  Waterford 138
  Wexford 142
  Wood Quay (Dublin) 72, **76**
Vinegar Hill 141
Vintners Company 37
Virgin Atlantic Cityjet 351
Virgin Mary 197
Visas 340

# W

Walking **333**, 335
Walpole, Edward 131
Waltons (Dublin) 325
Warbeck, Perkin 35
Water sports **334**, 335
Waterfalls
  Glencar Lough 225
  Powerscourt 130
  Torc 154
Waterford 35, **138–9**
  hotels 290–91
  pubs 318
  restaurants 309
Waterford Castle 280, 285
Waterford, County 117
Waterford Crystal 68, 72, **139**, 325
Waterford Festival of Light Opera
  48, 331
Waterfront Rock Bar (Dublin) 105
Waterstone's (Dublin) 325
Waterville, hotels 293
Waterways Visitors' Centre
  (Dublin) **99**
Waugh, Samuel 41
Wavertree, Lord 121
Wayne, John 21, 201
Weather 46–9
Wellbrook Beetling Mill 260
Welles, Orson 88
Wellington, Duke of 58, 66
Wellington Testimonial (Dublin) 94
West of Ireland **193–211**
  hotels 295–7
  pubs 320–21
  restaurants 313–14
West, Robert 265
Westmeath, County 229
Westport **196–7**
  hotels 297
  pubs 321
  restaurants 314
Westport House 194, 197
Wetlands 16

Wexford **142**
  hotels 291
  pubs 318–19
  restaurants 309
Wexford, County 117
Wexford Opera Festival 48, 142, 331
Wexford Wildfowl Reserve 142
Wheelchair access *see* Disabled
  travelers
Whelan's (Dublin) 105
Whiddy Island 159, 161
Whiskey **258**
  Irish Whiskey Corner (Dublin) 90
  Jameson Heritage Centre
    (Midleton) 171
  Locke's Distillery 241
  Old Bushmills Distillery 258
Whitby, Synod of (664) 32
White family 159, 160
White Island
  Lower Lough Erne tour 263
White Park Bay 253
Whitefriar Street Carmelite Church
  (Dublin) **81**
Whyte, Samuel 58
Wicklow, County 117
Wicklow Mountains 17, 117, **131**
  Military Road tour 130
Wicklow Town
  hotels 291
  restaurants 309
Wicklow Way 131
"Wild Geese, Flight of the" 173
Wilde, Oscar 20
  *The Importance of Being Oscar* 88
  Merrion Square (Dublin) 66
  Portora Royal School 264
Wildlife 16–17
Wildlife reserves
  The Burren 178–9
  Castle Caldwell Forest Park 262
  Connemara 200–201
  Fota Wildlife Park and Arboretum
    170–71
  Peatlands Park 266, 267
  Shannonbridge Bog Railway
    243
  Wexford Wildfowl Reserve 142
William of Orange
  Battle of the Boyne 29, 36, 236
  Carrickfergus Castle 267
  Mellifont Abbey 237
  siege of Kinsale 164
  siege of Limerick 173
  throne 74
Williams, Betty 45
Wilton, Joseph 98
Windsor, John 91

Wine, duty-free allowances 340
Wingfield family 127
Winter in Ireland 49
Wood Quay (Dublin) **76**
  Street-by-Street map 72
Woodstock House Demesne
  141
World Cup (football) 45
World War I 42
World War II 43
Wyatt, James 19
  Castle Coole 264
  Westport 196
  Westport House 197

# Y

Yeats, Jack
  Coole Park 205
  Crawford Art Gallery (Cork) 166
  *For the Road* 68
  Glebe House and Gallery 217
  Sligo County Museum and Art
    Gallery 226
Yeats, John 226
Yeats, WB **20**
  Abbey Theatre (Dublin) 86, 102
  *Cathleen ni Houlihan* 13
  Country Tour **224–5**
  and Constance Markievicz 223
  Easter Rising 87
  grave 224–5
  Irish Revival 21
  memorial 58
  Merrion Square (Dublin) 66
  Nobel prize 43
  and Sligo **225**, 226
  statue of 226
  Thoor Ballylee 204–5
  Yeats Country 114, **224–5**
  Yeats International Summer School
    (Sligo) 331
Yola Farmstead (Rosslare) 143
Youghal **171**
  hotels 293
  restaurants 312
Young Ireland Uprising 41
Youth Hostel Association of
  Northern Ireland 283
Youth hostels 283

# Z

Zoos
  Belfast Zoo 271
  Fota Wildlife Park and Arboretum
    170–71
  Zoological Gardens, Phoenix Park
    (Dublin) 94
Zurbarán, Francisco 69

# Acknowledgments

DORLING KINDERSLEY would like to thank the following people whose contributions and assistance have made the preparation of this book possible.

## MAIN CONTRIBUTORS

LISA GERARD-SHARP is a writer and broadcaster who has contributed to numerous travel books, including the *Eyewitness Travel Guide to France*. She is of Irish extraction, with roots in County Sligo and County Galway, and a regular visitor to Ireland.

TIM PERRY, from Dungannon, County Tyrone, writes on travel and popular music for various publishers in North America and the British Isles.

## ADDITIONAL CONTRIBUTOR
Douglas Palmer.

## ADDITIONAL PHOTOGRAPHY
Mike Linley, Joe Cornish, Michael Diggin, Anthony Haughey, Peter Anderson, Clive Streeter, Steve Gorton, Stephen Oliver, Matthew Ward.

## ADDITIONAL ILLUSTRATIONS
Richard Bonson, Brian Craker, John Fox, Paul Guest, Stephan Gyapay, Ian Henderson, Claire Littlejohn, Gillie Newman, Chris Orr, Kevin Robinson, John Woodcock, Martin Woodward.

## ADDITIONAL PICTURE RESEARCH
Miriam Sharland.

## EDITORIAL ASSISTANCE
Marion Broderick, Margaret Chang, Guy Dimond, Fay Franklin, Caroline Radula-Scott.

## DESIGN ASSISTANCE
Martin Cropper, Yael Freudmann, Sally Ann Hibbard, Annette Jacobs, Erika Lang, Michael Osborn.

## INDEX
Hilary Bird.

## SPECIAL ASSISTANCE
Dorling Kindersley would like to thank all the regional and local tourist offices in the Republic and in Northern Ireland for their valuable help. Particular thanks also to: Ralph Doak and Egerton Shelswell-White at Bantry House, Bantry, Co Cork; Vera Greif at the Chester Beatty Library and Gallery of Oriental Art, Dublin; Alan Figgis at Christ Church Cathedral, Dublin; Labhras Ó Murchu at Comhaltas Ceoltóirí Éireann; Catherine O'Connor at Derry City Council; Patsy O'Connell at Dublin Tourism; Tanya Cathcart at Fermanagh Tourism, Enniskillen; Peter Walsh at the Guinness Hop Store, Dublin; Gerard Collet at the Irish Shop, Covent Garden, London; Dónall P Ó Baoill at ITE, Dublin; Pat Cooke at Kilmainham Gaol, Dublin; Angela

Shanahan at the Kinsale Tourist Office; Bill Maxwell, Adrian Le Harivel and Marie McFeely at the National Gallery of Ireland, Dublin; Philip McCann at the National Library of Ireland, Dublin; Willy Cumming at the National Monuments Divison, Office of Public Works, Dublin; Eileen Dunne and Sharon Fogarty at the National Museum of Ireland, Dublin; Joris Minne at the Northern Ireland Tourist Office, Belfast; Dr Tom MacNeil at Queen's University, Belfast; Sheila Crowley at St. Mary's Pro-Cathedral, Dublin; Paul Brock at the Shannon Development Centre; Tom Sheedy at Shannon Heritage and Banquets, Bunratty Castle, Co Clare; Angela Sutherland at the Shannon-Erne Waterway, Co Leitrim; Máire Ní Bháin at Trinity College, Dublin; Anne-Marie Diffley at Trinity College Library, Dublin; Pat Maclean at the Ulster Museum, Belfast; Harry Hughes at the Willie Clancy School of Traditional Music, Miltown Malbay, Co Clare.

## ADDITIONAL ASSISTANCE
Kathleen Crowley, Rory Doyle, Peter Hynes, David O'Grady, Mary O'Grady, Madge Perry, Poppy.

## PHOTOGRAPHY PERMISSIONS
THE PUBLISHER would like to thank all those who gave permission to photograph at various cathedrals, churches, museums, restaurants, hotels, shops, galleries and other sights too numerous to list individually.

## PICTURE CREDITS
tl = top left; tc = top center; tr = top right; cla = center left above; ca = center above; cra = center right above; cl = center left; c = center; cr = center right; clb = center left below; cb = center below; crb = center right below; bl = bottom left; bc = bottom center; br = bottom right.

Every effort has been made to trace the copyright holders and we apologize in advance for any unintentional omissions. We would be pleased to insert the appropriate acknowledgments in any subsequent edition of this publication.

Works of art have been reproduced with the permission of the following copyright holders: © DACS, London 1995 68tr, 88tr.

The publisher would like to thank the following individuals, companies and picture libraries for permission to reproduce their photographs:

AER LINGUS/AIRBUS INDUSTRIE: 350tc; AKG, LONDON: National Museum, Copenhagen/Erich Lessing 24cl; ALLSPORT: David Rogers 26cb; Steve Powell 45tc; APPLETREE PRESS LTD, BELFAST (*Irish Proverbs* © illustrations Karen Bailey) 327cl.

BORD FÁILTE/IRISH TOURIST BOARD: 22–23, 23tl, 238tl, 238tr, 330c; © BRISTOL CITY MUSEUMS AND ART GALLERY: 30bl; © BRITISH LIBRARY: *Richard II's Campaigns in Ireland* Ms.Harl.1319, f.18 35tl; © BRITISH MUSEUM: 31bl; © BUSHMILLS LTD: 258bl.

© CENTRAL BANK OF IRELAND: *Lady Lavery as Cathleen ni Houlihan*, John Lavery 13ca, 344 (all banknotes and coins except for tr), 345; © CHESTER BEATTY LIBRARY, DUBLIN: 99tr; © CLASSIC DESIGNS/LJ YOUNG LTD, BLARNEY: 327c; BRUCE COLEMAN LTD: Frances Furlong 16tl; Gordon Langsbury 16cl; Patrick Clement 16clb, 16bl; Uwe Walz 16cr; MR Phicton 16crb; Adrian Davies 16br; George McCarthy 17tl, 17bl, 17br, 130tl; Kim Taylor 17tc; Mark Boulton 17tr; Hans Reinhard 17tcb, 154tl; Rodney Dawson 17cl; Pekka Helo 17cr; Dr Eckhart Pott 17cb; R Wanscheidt 17cbr; Uwe Walz 177cb; © CORK EXAMINER: 27tl; © CORK PUBLIC MUSEUM: 33cla; JOE CORNISH: 8–9, 17cla, 133br, 204b, 215br, 262tr, 336–7; CRAWFORD MUNICIPAL ART GALLERY: *The Meeting of St. Brendan and the Unhappy Judas*, Harry Clarke 166bl.

DERRY CITY COUNCIL: 250tr; MICHAEL DIGGIN: 18tl, 145b, 155cr, 156cla, 157tr, 198bl, 217t, 218tr, 218cl, 219cra, 332tl, 333tl, 333b, 339br, 343cl, 346b, 356bl; BILL DOYLE: 206bl; GA DUNCAN: 44cb, 44bl; © DUNDEE ART GALLERIES AND MUSEUMS: *The Children of Lir*, John Duncan 25tc.

ET ARCHIVE: 25bl; MARY EVANS PICTURE LIBRARY: 9 (inset), 22tl, 24tr, 24bl, 24br, 25cla, 32bl, 35bc, 36bl; 42bl, 51 (inset), 75cl, 87bl, 113 (inset), 273br, 279 (inset), 337 (inset).

© STEPHEN FALLER LTD, GALWAY: 326cla; © FAMINE MUSEUM CO ROSSCOMMON: 211tr; JIM FITZPATRICK: 77bl.

GILL AND MACMILLAN PUBLISHERS, DUBLIN: 43bl; TIM GRAHAM: 94tr; RONALD GRANT ARCHIVE: *The Commitments*, Twentieth Century Fox 21br; © GUINNESS IRELAND LTD: 96bl, 97tl, 97bl, 97br.

HULTON DEUTSCH COLLECTION: 20clb, 21tr, 40br, 44crb, Reuter 45crb, 60bl.

ILLUSTRATED LONDON NEWS PICTURE LIBRARY: 40cra; IMAGES COLOUR LIBRARY: 53tl; 221bc; INPHO, DUBLIN: 26cla, Billy Stickland 26br, Lorraine O'Sullivan 27br; IRISH PICTURE LIBRARY, DUBLIN: 36cla, 39tl, 42tl; © IRISH TIMES: 126br; © IRISH TRADITIONAL MUSIC ARCHIVE, DUBLIN: 23bl.

JARROLD COLOUR PUBLICATIONS: JA Brooks 60br; MICHAEL JENNER: 235cr.

TIMOTHY KOVAR: 76bl; 103tl, 106bl.

© LAMBETH PALACE LIBRARY, LONDON: Plan of the London Vintners' Company Township of Bellaghy, Ulster, 1622 (ms. Carew 634 f.34) (detail) 37cra; FRANK LANE PICTURE AGENCY: Roger Wilmshurst 178bc; © LEEDS CITY ART GALLERY: *The Irish House of Commons*, Francis Wheatley 38cla.

HUGH McKNIGHT PHOTOGRAPHY: 99bl; MANDER AND MITCHESON THEATRE COLLECTION: 22cl; MANSELL COLLECTION: 38bl, 43cra, 79bl, 260bc; ARCHIE MILES: 200br; JOHN MURRAY: 49bl, 94cl, 120c; © MUSEUM OF THE CITY OF NEW YORK: Gift of Mrs Robert M Littlejohn, *The Bay and Harbor of New York 1855*, Samuel B Waugh 40–41.

NATIONAL CONCERT HALL, DUBLIN: Frank Fennell 107bl; © NATIONAL GALLERY OF IRELAND, DUBLIN: *WB Yeats and the Irish Theatre*, Edmund Dulac 20tr, *George Bernard Shaw*, John Collier 20cr, *Carolan the Harper*, Francis Bindon 22tr, *Leixlip Castle*, Irish School 39cla, *The Custom House, Dublin*, James Malton 39br, *Queen Victoria and Prince Albert Opening the 1853 Dublin Great Exhibition*, James Mahoney 41bl, *The Houseless Wanderer*, JH Foley 68tl, *Pierrot*, Juan Gris 68tr, *For the Road*, JB Yeats 68cla, *The Taking of Christ*, Caravaggio 69cra, *The Castle of Bentheim*, Jacob van Ruisdael 69cl, *Judith with the Head of Holofernes*, Andrea Mantegna 69crb, *The Sick Call*, Matthew James Lawless 69bl, *Jonathan Swift, Satirist*, Charles Jerval 80bc, *James Joyce*, Jacques Emile Blanche, *Interior with Members of a Family*, P Hussey 124br, *William Butler Yeats, Poet*, JB Yeats 225tl, *The Last Circuit of Pilgrims at Clonmacnoise*, George Petrie 242tr; © NATIONAL GALLERY, LONDON: *Beach Scene*, Edgar Degas 89br; © NATIONAL LIBRARY OF IRELAND, DUBLIN: 21cla, 21crb, 29b, 32tl, 32clb, 34bl, 36tl, 36clb, 38clb, 40tl, 40cla, 40bl, 41tl, 42clb, 43tl, 43crb, *St. Stephen's Green*, James Malton 50–51, 133tr, 170cra, 236b; © NATIONAL MUSEUM OF IRELAND, DUBLIN: 3, 30tl, 30clb, 30cb 30crb, 30–31, 31c 31clb, 31br, 32cla, 33cb, 33br, 57cr, 64, 65; THE NATIONAL TRUST, NORTHERN IRELAND: *Lord Castlereagh* after Lawrence 274tl, *Hambletonian*, George Stubbs 275tl, 275cra; THE NATIONAL TRUST PHOTOGRAPHIC LIBRARY: Patrick Prendergast 264bl, Matthew Antrobus 265b, Will Webster 269br, John Bethell 276tl, Will Webster 278–9; NATURE PHOTOGRAPHERS: Paul Sterry 178clb, B Burbridge 179bc; NORTHERN IRELAND TOURIST BOARD: 26tr, 250cl, 265tr, 328cl, 329tl; NORTON ASSOCIATES: 72 clb.

KYRAN O'BRIEN 107tr; © THE OFFICE OF PUBLIC WORKS, IRELAND: 164bl, 238cl, 239tl, 239cr, 240br, 242tl; OXFORD SCIENTIFIC FILMS: Frithjof Skibbe 178tl.

MICHAEL PALFRAMAN: 260tl; WALTER PFEIFFER STUDIOS, DUBLIN: 23tr, 23cra, 23c, 23cr, 23crb, 23br; PHOTO FLORA: Andrew N Gagg 178br; PHOTOSTAGE: Donald Cooper 106tr, 107tl; POPPERFOTO: 44cla, 44br, 45tl, Reuter/Crispin Rodwell 45tr.

RANGE PICTURES: 41cra; THE REFORM CLUB, LONDON: 41crb; REPORT/DEREK SPIERS, DUBLIN: 44tl, 44tr, 270bl, 270br; RETNA PICTURES: Chris Taylor 22bl, Jay Blakesberg 22br; RETROGRAPH ARCHIVE, LONDON: © Martin Ranicar-Breese 63br; REX FEATURES: 45ca; Sipa Press 45clb, 45br, 45bl.

SHANNON DEVELOPMENT PHOTO LIBRARY: 330tl; SHANNON-ERNE WATERWAY: 227bc; THE SLIDE FILE, DUBLIN: 14bc, 15t, 15c, 16cla, 16cra, 20cla, 27cra, 27clb, 27bl, 30cla, 46cla, 46bl, 47cb, 48cla, 48cra, 48cb, 48bl, 49cra, 75tr, 75br, 114cla, 121br, 130cl 130br, 138br, 143br, 177br, 203tl, 205tr, 206cb, 206br, 207bc, 216br, 219tr, 222tl, 222b, 224tr, 229b, 232tl, 234tl, 240tl, 242–3, 244cra, 262clb, 329br, 330br; SPORTSFILE, DUBLIN: 27tc; DON SUTTON INTERNATIONAL PHOTO LIBRARY: 282br.

© TATE GALLERY PUBLICATIONS: *Captain Thomas Lee*, Marcus Gheeraedts 36br; TOPHAM PICTURE SOURCE: 39bc, 53bl; © TRINITY COLLEGE, DUBLIN: Ms.58 (Book of Kells) f.129v 4tr, *The Marriage of Princess Aoite and the Earl of Pembroke*, Daniel Maclise 34cla, Ms.57 (Book of Durrow) f.84v 53cr, Ms.57 (Book of Durrow) f.85v 61cr, Ms.58 (Book of Kells) f.129v 62cra, Ms.58 (Book of Kells) f.34r 62cl, Ms.58 (Book of Kells) f.28v 62crb, Ms.58 (Book of Kells) f.200r 62b; TRIP: R Drury 15br, 132c.

© ULSTER MUSEUM, BELFAST: *The Festival of St. Kevin at the Seven Churches, Glendalough*, Joseph Peacock 28, *The Relief of Derry*, William Sadler II 36–7, 37crb, 42cla, 249crb, 270clb.

VIKING SHIP MUSEUM, STRANDENGEN, DENMARK: watercolor by Flemming Bau 33tl.

© WATERFORD CORPORATION: 33bl, 34tl, 34clb, 35bl; © WRITERS MUSEUM, DUBLIN: 20tl.

PETER ZÖLLER: 12, 14tl, 46tc, 46cr, 47cra, 47bl, 192, 208–9, 211bl, 212, 228, 241tr, 334tl.

Front endpaper: all commissioned photography with the exception of PETER ZÖLLER: tl, tc, cb.

Jacket: all commissioned photography with the exception of © TRINITY COLLEGE, DUBLIN: front tl.

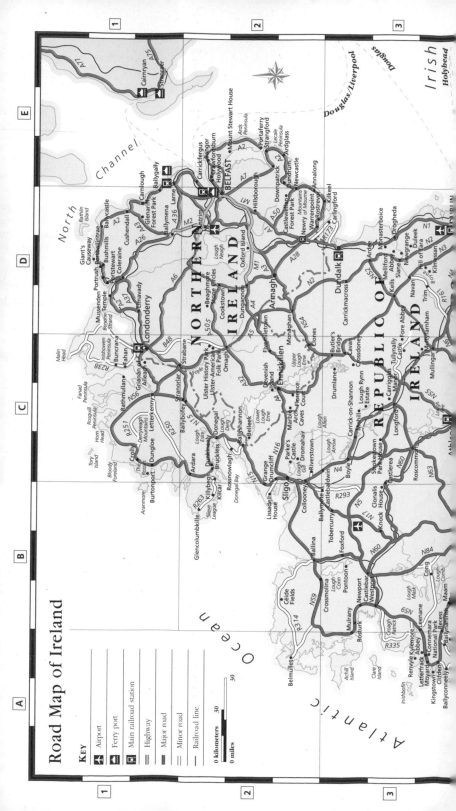

# Road Map of Ireland

## KEY

✈ Airport
⛴ Ferry port
🚉 Main railroad station
▐ Highway
▬ Major road
═ Minor road
— Railroad line

0 kilometers   30
0 miles   30